Funk & Wagnalls New Encyclopedia

VOLUME 2

AMERICAN ENGLISH to ASSINIBOINE

LEON L. BRAM
Vice-President and Editorial Director

NORMA H. DICKEY
Editor-in-Chief

Funk & Wagnalls Corporation

Publishers since 1876

Volumes are published subsequent
to copyright dates to contain
the latest updated information

ISBN 0-8343-0094-x
Library of Congress Catalog
Card Number 72–170933

MANUFACTURED IN THE UNITED STATES OF AMERICA
PRINTED AND BOUND BY R.R. DONNELLEY & SONS COMPANY

aie 10 9 8 7 6 5 4 3 2 1

Funk & Wagnalls New Encyclopedia is liberally provided with **finding devices** that aid in the search for information. The brief descriptions and suggestions that follow are intended to encourage the proper use of these devices so that full use is made of the information resources within these pages.

The **index** in volume 29 should be the starting point in a search for information. If a search is made *without* the use of the index, the following suggestions should be kept in mind:

- If the search is *unsuccessful*, the index should be used to search again. The topic may be discussed in an article that was overlooked. Only after use of the index can a search be considered thorough or completed.

- If the search is initially *successful*, the index should be used to find additional information. A topic may be discussed in several articles; the index can locate the less-obvious ones.

The use and structure of the index is explained in the Guide to the Index, volume 29, pages 6–8.

Cross-references of several types are used frequently within most articles in Funk & Wagnalls New Encyclopedia. Each cross-reference directs the search for information to other articles that contain additional or related information. The types of cross-references and their specific uses are explained in the Guide to Funk & Wagnalls New Encyclopedia, volume 1, pages 60–63, under the subhead, Cross-references.

Bibliography cross-references follow all the major articles in Funk & Wagnalls New Encyclopedia. They direct the search for further information from the articles to appropriate **reading lists** of books and periodicals in the **bibliography** in volume 28. The reading lists may also be used for independent study. A full description of bibliography cross-references and reading lists is found in the Preface and Guide to the Bibliography, volume 28, pages 186–87.

SELECTED ABBREVIATIONS USED IN TEXT*

AC	alternating current
AD	*anno Domini* (Lat., "in the year of the Lord")
alt.	altitude
AM	*ante meridiem* (Lat., "before noon")
AM	amplitude modulation
amu	atomic mass unit(s)
Arab.	Arabic
Arm.	Armenian
A.S.	Anglo-Saxon
ASSR	Autonomous Soviet Socialist Republic
atm.	atmosphere
at.no.	atomic number
at.wt.	atomic weight
b.	born
BC	before Christ
b.p.	boiling point
Btu	British Thermal Unit
bu	bushel(s)
Bulg.	Bulgarian
C	Celsius
c.	*circa* (Lat., "about")
cent.	century
Chin.	Chinese
cm	centimeter(s)
Co.	Company, County
cu	cubic
Czech.	Czechoslovakian
d.	died
Dan.	Danish
DC	direct current
Du.	Dutch
E	east; eastern
ed.	edited, edition, editors
e.g.	*exempli gratia* (Lat., "for example")
Egypt.	Egyptian
Eng.	English
est.	established; estimated
et al.	*et alii* (Lat., "and others")
EV	electron volt(s)
F	Fahrenheit
Finn.	Finnish
fl.	flourished
FM	frequency modulation
Fr.	French
ft	foot, feet
g	gram(s)
gal	gallon(s)
Ger.	German
GeV	billion electron volts
Gr.	Greek
ha	hectare(s)
Heb.	Hebrew
hp	horsepower
hr	hour
Hung.	Hungarian
Hz	hertz or cycle(s) per second
Icel.	Icelandic
i.e.	*id est* (Lat., "that is")
in	inch(es)
inc.	incorporated
Ital.	Italian
Jap.	Japanese
K	Kelvin
kg	kilogram(s)
km	kilometer(s)
kw	kilowatt(s)
kwh	kilowatt hour(s)
Lat.	Latin
lat	latitude
lb	pound(s)
long	longitude
m	meter(s)
mass no.	mass number
MeV	million electron volts
mg	milligram(s)
mi	mile(s)
min	minute(s)
ml	milliliter(s)
mm	millimeter(s)
m.p.	melting point
mph	miles per hour
Mt(s).	Mount, Mountain(s)
N	north; northern
Nor.	Norwegian
O.E.	Old English
O.Fr.	Old French
O.H.G.	Old High German
O.N.	Old Norse
Op.	*Opus* (Lat., "work")
oz	ounce(s)
Pers.	Persian
PM	*post meridiem* (Lat., "after noon")
Pol.	Polish
pop.	population
Port.	Portuguese
q.v.	*quod vide* (Lat., "which see")
r.	reigned
R.	River
repr.	reprinted
rev.	revised
Rom.	Romanian
Rus.	Russian
S	south; southern
sec.	second(s); secant
SFSR	Soviet Federated Socialist Republic
Skt.	Sanskrit
Span.	Spanish
sp.gr.	specific gravity
sq	square
sq km	square kilometer(s)
sq mi	square mile(s)
SSR	Soviet Socialist Republic
St.	Saint, Street
Sum.	Sumerian
Swed.	Swedish
trans.	translated, translation, translator(s)
Turk.	Turkish
Ukr.	Ukrainian
UN	United Nations
U.S.	United States
USSR	Union of Soviet Socialist Republics
v.	versus; verse
Ved.	Vedic
vol.	Volume(s)
W	west; western
yd	yard(s)

* For a more extensive listing, see ABBREVIATIONS AND ACRONYMS. Charts of pertinent abbreviations also accompany the articles DEGREE, ACADEMIC; ELEMENTS, CHEMICAL; MATHEMATICAL SYMBOLS; and WEIGHTS AND MEASURES.

FUNK & WAGNALLS NEW ENCYCLOPEDIA

AMERICAN ENGLISH, English spoken in the U.S. It differs from English spoken elsewhere in the world not so much in particulars as in the total configuration. That is, the dialects of what is termed Standard American English share enough characteristics so that the language as a whole can be distinguished from Received Standard (British) English or, for example, Australian English. *See* ENGLISH LANGUAGE

The differences in pronunciation and cadence between spoken American English and other varieties of the language are easily discernible. In the written form, however, despite minor differences in vocabulary, spelling, and syntax, and apart from context, it is difficult to determine whether a work was written in England, the U.S., or any other part of the English-speaking world.

The American lexicographer Noah Webster was among the first to recognize the growing divergence of American and British usages. His *American Dictionary of the English Language* (1828) marked this difference with its inclusion of many new American words, indigenous meanings attached to old words, changes in pronunciation, and a series of spelling reforms that he devised (*-er* instead of British *-re, -or* to replace *-our, check* instead of *cheque*). Webster went so far as to predict that the American language would one day become a distinct language. Some later commentators, notably H. L. Mencken, compiler of *The American Language* (3 vol., 1936–48), have also argued that it is a separate language, but most authorities today agree that it is a dialect of British English.

PATTERNS OF AMERICAN ENGLISH

In the late 19th and early 20th centuries the study of American English was concerned mainly with identifying Americanisms and giving the etymologies of Americanisms in the vocabulary: words borrowed from Indian languages (*mugwump, caucus*); words retained after having been given up in Great Britain (*bug,* to mean insects in general rather than *bedbug* specifically, as in Great Britain); or words that developed a new significance in the New World (*corn,* to designate what the British call *maize,* rather than *grain* in general). Large numbers of American terms (*elevator, truck, hood* [of an automobile], *windshield, garbage collector, drugstore*) were shown to differ from their British counterparts (respectively: *lift, lorry, bonnet, windscreen, dustman, chemist's*). Such lexical differences between Standard American and British English still exist; but as a result of modern communications, speakers of English everywhere have no trouble in understanding one another. More recently,

If the Edith Cavell Shop were in the U.S. instead of in Norwich, England, its sign would read TO GO *or* TAKEOUT *instead of* TAKE-AWAY. *Similarly,* OAP SPECIALS *would be* SENIOR CITIZEN SPECIALS. © FPG International

linguistic researchers have turned their attention to the study of variation patterns in American English and to the social and historical sources of these patterns.

Regional Dialects. Regionally oriented research before 1940 distinguished three main regional dialects of Standard American English, each of which has several sub-dialects. The Northern (or New England) dialect is spoken in New England and New York State; one of its subdialects is the "New Yorkese" of New York City. The Midland (or General American) dialect is heard along the coast from New Jersey to Delaware, with variants spoken in an area bounded by the Upper Ohio Valley, West Virginia, eastern Kentucky, and eastern Tennessee. The Southern dialect, with its varieties, is spoken from Delaware to South Carolina. From their respective focal points these dialects, according to this theory, have spread and mingled across the rest of the country.

Social/Cultural Dialects. Social/cultural dialects vary both the vocabulary and grammar of Standard American English and are not always intelligible to speakers of the standard language. The most distinctive variety of American English, in terms of vocabulary and grammar, is the social/cultural dialect known as Gullah, actually a contact language, or creole, spoken by blacks in the Georgia-South Carolina low country, but also as far away as southeast Texas. Gullah, combining 17th- and 18th-century Black English and several West African languages, has given to American English such words as *goober* (peanut), *gumbo* (okra), and *voodoo.* It is the dialect used in the novel *Porgy* (1925) by the American writer Du Bose Heyward. "Me beena shum" (I was seeing him/her/it) is barely intelligible to a speaker of Standard American English, and almost all Gullah speakers shift to more standard usage when conversing with outsiders.

Pennsylvania Dutch, another distinguishable dialect, is actually English heavily influenced by literal translations from the original German language of settlers in Pennsylvania. In this dialect such a construction as "He may come back bothsides, ain't?" (He might come back on either side, mightn't he?) is possible. Most Pennsylvania Dutch speakers also readily adapt themselves to standard usage.

Black English. Until the 19th century, most blacks throughout the country spoke a creole similar to Gullah and West Indian English. Change in the direction of Standard American English vocabulary and syntax, particularly in the 20th century, has been rapid but never complete; the Black English of the inner cities characteristically retains such locutions as "He busy" (He is busy) as opposed to "He be busy" (He is busy indefinitely) and "She been said that" to express action markedly in the past (she had said that). In the 1960s Black English became a topic of linguistic controversy in educational circles because of its supposed deficiencies and ultimately was the subject of legislative action under the Bilingual Education Act (1968). Nevertheless, Black English has made its own rich contributions to American English vocabulary, especially through jazz—from the word *jazz* itself, to such terms as *nitty-gritty, uptight,* and *O.K.* The last, now thought to be of African origin, is also the Americanism most widely diffused throughout the world.

DEVELOPMENT OF AMERICAN ENGLISH

English commentators in the 18th century noted the "astounding uniformity" of the language spoken in the American colonies, excepting the language spoken by the slaves. (Subvarieties of English, however, were spoken by American Indians and other non-British groups.) The reason for this uniformity is that the first colonists came not as regional but as social groups, from all parts of England, so that dialect leveling was dominant.

Grammatical Formality. Against this background of uniformity, deviations from Standard American English have frequently met with disapproval from those who promulgate "correct" English. Grammatical formality is the most notable feature of Standard American English, and particular stigma is attached to the use of nonstandard verb forms. Rigidity in grammar and syntax in written Standard American English is greater than in British English in part because large numbers of immigrants acquired English as a second language according to formal rules. Also, social mobility in the U.S. has produced certain anxieties and confusion about "correct" usage as an indication of status. What is considered Standard American English is today spoken for business and professional purposes by people in all parts of the country, many of whom speak very differently in private. In writing, however, many feel constrained to use formal, Latinate locutions even when addressing close friends.

Regional Variations. In earlier times, the dialect of New England, with its British form of pronunciation (*ah* for *a* in path, dance; loss of the *r* sound in barn, park), was considered prestigious, but such pronunciations failed to inspire nationwide emulation. Indeed, no single regional characteristic has ever been able to dominate the language. (One of the reasons that some linguists define Black English as a language rather than a dialect is that its vocabulary, pronunciation, and syntax are similar in all parts of the country, rural and urban.)

Today, the concept of so-called Network Standard, promoted by radio and television, provokes some argument from dialectologists, who champion diversity and richness of speech; but regional variations have by no means been obliterated. The Midland (or General American) distinct *r* sound persists (car), and even educated speakers in the South do not differentiate *pen* from *pin*.

Growth of the American Vocabulary. The uniformity of the English spoken by the British colonists to about 1780 was soon disrupted by non-English influences. First, many American Indian words were taken over directly to describe indigenous flora and fauna (sassafras, raccoon), food (hominy), ceremonies (powwow), and, of course, geographic names (Massachusetts, Susquehanna). Phrasal compounds, translated or adapted from the Indian, were also added to English: warpath, peace pipe, bury the hatchet, fire water. Other borrowings came in time from the Dutch (boss, poppycock, spook), German (liverwurst, noodle, coleslaw, semester), French (levee, chowder, prairie), Spanish (hoosegow, from *juzgado,* "courtroom"; mesa, ranch[o]; tortilla), or Finnish (sauna).

Other modifications in vocabulary came about presumably because of lack of education or because of confusion on the part of explorers and settlers who applied incorrect names to things encountered in the New World—for example, partridge, used indiscriminately for quail, grouse, or other game birds, and buffalo, applied to the American bison.

American English vocabulary has been and still is enriched with jargon (q.v.), terms coming from trades and professions. The social sciences, law, and the academic disciplines in particular are accused of contributing gobbledygook (an Americanism referring to verbal obfuscation). Slang (q.v.), argot, and even certain euphemisms have also been a constant source of language enrichment, although some terms die out before they are admitted to the standard vocabulary. In the 19th century prudishness influenced the language; legs were called "limbs," and pregnant "in the family way." Similarly, in the 20th century, Americans, in their reluctance to confront reality, have coined such euphemisms as "senior citizen" or "golden ager" for old people and "nursing home" for old folks' home and poorhouse.

As might be expected in a nation originating from 13 maritime colonies, a great admixture of nautical expressions has been in the language since early times: freight (used as a verb), slush fund, shove off, hail from. Baseball took over skipper (to mean manager), on deck, and in the hole (originally hold) from the nautical vocabulary and contributed many of its own colorful idiomatic expressions to the general language (for example, get to first base).

Influence on British English. Spread by motion pictures, books, and television, Americanisms—especially American slang—have in large numbers found their way to Great Britain, more and more blurring the distinctions between the two forms of the English language. Although nonstandard phrases, such as "met up with" or "try out" (in the sense of test), may still encounter objections from purists, the very force of their objections shows how influential such words have been on everyday British English speech. J.L.D.

For further information on this topic, see the Bibliography in volume 28, sections 356, 358–63.

AMERICAN EXPEDITIONARY FORCE. *See* WORLD WAR I: *Military Operations.*

AMERICAN FEDERATION OF LABOR AND CONGRESS OF INDUSTRIAL ORGANIZATIONS (AFL-CIO), organization of autonomous trade unions

Lane Kirkland (right), president of the AFL-CIO, and Thomas R. Donahue (left), AFL-CIO secretary-treasurer, greet Frank Hanley, president of the International Union of Operating Engineers. AFL-CIO

Labor leaders and rank-and-file union members gather for the 1991 Solidarity Day march along the Mall in Washington, D.C., to demand action on domestic issues facing the U.S.
Reuters/Bettmann Archive

formed in December 1955 by the merger of the American Federation of Labor and the Congress of Industrial Organizations. Of some 20 million members in all U.S. unions, about 14 million are in the AFL-CIO's 89 affiliated unions. *See* TRADE UNIONS IN THE UNITED STATES.

History. The AFL was founded in Columbus, Ohio, in December 1886, during a period of widespread strikes by workers seeking an 8-hour day. The Federation of Organized Trades and Labor Unions of the United States and Canada, established in 1881 to encourage labor legislation, and several unaffiliated trade unions merged to form the AFL. Its primary objectives were unionization of workers, support of legislation beneficial to labor, reduction of working hours, and improvement of working conditions and wages. The American labor leader Samuel Gompers was elected president, and, under his leadership, the AFL adopted a policy of supporting political candidates considered friendly to labor, regardless of party affiliation.

AFL membership decreased during the 1920s and the early depression years between 1929 and 1933. Later the federation grew rapidly as union organization was encouraged and protected by New Deal (q.v.) legislation. Historically, the AFL had always welcomed groups of differing political and economic philosophies. With the coming of the New Deal in 1933, improved opportunities for trade union growth raised the issue of whether to organize by occupation or industry.

In 1935, under the leadership of John L. Lewis, a Committee for Industrial Organization was created within the AFL. Its purpose was to organize workers rapidly, assigning them to existing or new industrial unions, without regard to jusisdictional lines. A majority of the unions, however, challenged the committee's organizing efforts; within three years, eight unions were expelled from the AFL. In consequence these eight unions formally established the CIO.

Rivalry between the two groups actually resulted in a sharp increase in total union membership. Both organizations cooperated with the government during World War II, and their stature and strength were thereby greatly enhanced.

Merger. At the end of the war American voters elected a more conservative Congress, which acted to limit union privileges; this encouraged interunion cooperation to conserve gains and ward off further attacks. During the Korean War, the AFL and the CIO formed a United Labor Policy Committee to deal with government labor policies. The committee soon became involved in other areas of organizational cooperation.

In November 1952 Dwight D. Eisenhower was elected president of the U.S., the first Republican in the White House in 20 years. The election result sharpened labor's perceived need for united action in facing the government. Shortly thereafter, the deaths of William Green, president of the AFL, and Philip Murray, president of the CIO, removed two of the major participants in the bitter rivalry of the 1930s. These events brought the two organizations closer to a merger.

Early in 1955 a Joint Unity Committee was formed, and a new constitution was drafted. The formal merger of the AFL-CIO took place at a convention held in New York City in December 1955. George Meany, who had succeeded Green as head of the AFL, was elected president of the new organization. When Meany retired in 1979, he was succeeded by Lane Kirkland.

Activities. Under the AFL-CIO constitution, the parent body cannot determine policies of member unions, except to require that affiliates remain in good financial standing, maintain democratic, honest procedures, and outlaw all forms of discrimination. Within these limits, individual unions have full autonomy. The main function of the AFL-CIO is to provide the affiliates with assistance in a broad spectrum of programs in such areas as economic research, workers' education, legislative and political lobbying, civil rights, health services, and industrial safety.

The AFL-CIO maintains a strong interest in the political process. Through its Committee for Political Education, the organization encourages members to register to vote and to go to the polls on election day. Financial contributions to political candidates may not be drawn from regular union funds; separate collections for this purpose are made on a voluntary basis.

The International Department oversees a broad range of relationships with unions in other countries. It provides assistance to unions in the developing nations of the world. It also appoints representatives to international trade unions and intergovernmental bodies.

Membership. For 25 years after the merger, AFL-CIO membership did not fluctuate significantly. Then membership began to decrease yearly; by 1984 there were just over 13 million members, as compared with 16 million in 1955. This condition may be accounted for partly by the loss of some 3 million members in the 1957 expulsion of the Teamsters' Union on grounds of leadership corruption, as well as by the lack of interest in unions among many younger workers. (Membership rose to about 14 million in 1987 after the reinstatement of the Teamsters' Union.) Although the AFL-CIO represented 30 percent of all those employed in 1955, this proportion decreased to less than 19 percent by the mid-1980s. The decline has been attributed to the shift in concentration of employment from the relatively well-organized mass-production industries to the white-collar and service sectors, where union strength, although growing, is still weak.

Problems and Trends. The AFL-CIO has lost strength also because of economic trends such as fluctuations in the value of the U.S. dollar against foreign currencies and its effect on international trade, and the consequent loss of jobs as a result of foreign competition. These issues cannot be dealt with adequately in normal bargaining negotiations. The organization, therefore, has become more active in advocating government policies to deal with international trade and productivity incentives, as well as other issues, in the hope that such policies will contribute to a stable economy.

AFL-CIO president Lane Kirkland has been trying to negotiate the affiliation of unions now outside the federation. He also joined with employers and independent experts to serve on a government-sponsored committee working on issues of wages, prices, employment, and productivity. This effort added a new dimension to labor's historical political role of concentration on electoral activity and on the advocacy of labor legislation. M.W.

For further information on this topic, see the Bibliography in volume 28, sections 220–22.

AMERICAN FEDERATION OF STATE, COUNTY, AND MUNICIPAL EMPLOYEES (AFSCME), the largest union of public workers in the U.S., representing more than 1 million people. The membership includes employees of state, county, and municipal governments, of the federal government, and of universities and nonprofit agencies. Health and hospital workers compose the largest occupational group; white-collar employees account for approximately one-third of the membership.

The AFSCME is organized into about 3000 local unions and 70 district councils, which adopt their own constitutions, elect their own officers, and administer local affairs. The International Union in Washington, D.C., provides legislative, organizational, legal, educational, and public information services. Its executive board determines policy and programs. The union is affiliated with the American Federation of Labor and Congress of Industrial Organizations. The AFSCME, which began as a number of separate locals in Wisconsin in the early 1930s, is now the fastest-growing union in the U.S.

AMERICAN FEDERATION OF TEACHERS (AFT), international organization of teachers and other nonsupervisory educational employees, affiliated with the American Federation of Labor and Congress of Industrial Organizations. The AFT was founded in 1916, and by the late 1980s it had some 665,000 members in more than 2200 locals throughout the U.S. and at American schools abroad. The AFT serves several functions: It works for increased benefits for its members; it helps them to deal with current issues such as school finance reform, in-service training for teachers, and on-the-job stress; and it seeks to influence legislation affecting schools and to secure adequate government funds for education.

An active union, the AFT during its early years fought for academic freedom and full professional rights for teachers. In the 1960s it pioneered collective bargaining for teachers and is now the bargaining agent in most major city school districts. In 1978 the union established a health-care division, the Federation of Nurses and Health Professionals; it now represents some 50,000 nurses and health technicians.

AMERICAN INDIAN LANGUAGES, the indigenous languages of the native peoples of North, Middle, and South America. The precise number of American Indian languages is unknown; estimates are that about 200 distinct languages are still spoken in North America (that is, north of Mexico). Perhaps 300 to 400 more were spoken at the time of first European contact. In Middle America (Mexico and Central America) about 350 languages are known. South America has been the least studied, linguistically. About 450 languages are in use there today; information survives for 120 extinct languages, and another 1500 to 2000 languages are mentioned in documents.

For the number of past and present speakers of these languages, only rough estimates can be given, useful for comparison. It is believed that when Europeans arrived in the Americas, about 1.5 million people spoke Indian languages in North America (down to about 200,000 today), about 5 million in Middle America (up to about 6 million today), and about 10 to 20 million in South America (about 11 to 12 million today).

Major Languages. In present-day North America the indigenous languages with the most speakers are Navajo (about 80,000), Ojibwa (about 40,000), and Inupiaq, or Inuktitut (*see* INUIT). Inupiaq has more than 60,000 speakers and its Greenlandic variety serves as a national language. In Middle America, Nahuatl (Aztec) is spoken by more than 1 million people, the various Mayan languages by about 2 million, and a number of other languages by several hundred thousand each. In South America, Quechua, with more than 8 million speakers, is the most widely used of all American Indian tongues today. Guaraní is the only Indian language to have become a national and literary language spoken by large numbers of non-Indians (half of its 2 million speakers are Paraguayans of European descent). In the Andes, Aymara has about 800,000 speakers, and in Chile, Araucanian has about 200,000. The vast majority of American Indian languages, however, have from a few hundred to a few thousand speakers; many have fewer than 50 or 100 speakers; still many other languages have only 2 or 3 surviving speakers.

Linguistic Borrowings. Indian and European colonial languages have borrowed words from one another; Indian languages have taken words from Dutch (in the Antilles), English, Spanish, Portuguese, Russian (in Alaska), and French (in Canada and Louisiana). In turn, many of the European languages took over Indian place names and terms for plants and animals; examples include Alaska, from the Aleut name for the Alaskan Peninsula; Connecticut, from Mohegan (Algonquian-Ritwan), "long river"; Minnesota, from Dakota, or Sioux, "cloudy water"; Mexico and Guatemala, from Nahuatl; and Nicaragua, from an Aztec dialetc, Pipil. English has many loanwords from American Indian languages, among them kayak (Eskimo); chipmunk, opossum, raccoon, tomahawk, moccasin, squash (Algonquian); abalone (Costanoan); tomato, coyote, chili, chocolate, peyote (Nahuatl); puma, condor, jerky (beef), pampa, llama, alpaca (Quechua); canoe, maize, tobacco, potato (Taino—Arawakan stock; see chart). In Latin America, the Spanish language has influenced and been influenced by Quechua, Guaraní, and Nahuatl, in particular.

CLASSIFICATION

The classification of American Indian languages into families is not without controversy. By the mid-20th century, many scholars classified the North American languages into roughly 60 different language families, recognizing no demonstrable genetic relationships among them. In Middle America they proposed 19 different families, and in South America, perhaps 80 families. Other scholars proposed fewer families, claiming to see genetic relationships among most of the Indian languages. Although it is believed that the original population of the Americas came from Asia via the Bering Strait, the great genetic diversity of American languages suggests that the New World may have been populated by multiple migrations.

A major aim of linguistic work with American Indian languages is their genetic classification—the organization of this vast diversity into manageable family schemes. The immensity of the body of data, coupled with the steady disappearance of language after language, makes the task awesome. In 1891 the American ethnographer, geologist, and linguist John Wesley Powell proposed 58 families for North America, mainly on the basis of superficial resemblances. About the same time, the American linguist Daniel Brinton (1837–99) proposed 80 families for South America. Although methods of classification have since become more rigorous, these two schemes form the basis of all subsequent classifications. In

1929 the American anthropologist Edward Sapir (1884–1939) grouped the families into 6 superstocks, or phyla, in North America and 15 in Middle America. Recently, however, areal studies—investigations of the borrowings of grammatical and other traits from one family to another, within a given geographic area—have shown that many remote relationships proposed earlier must now be reconsidered. The U.S. linguist Joseph Greenberg (1915-) and others have proposed that the native languages of the Americas can be classified into just three families—Eskimo-Aleut, Na-Dene, and Amerind (with 11 branches). The classification presented in the accompanying chart, however, is conservative; in most cases, families have not been assigned to superstocks (the names of rejected superstock groupings are shown in footnotes), nor are Greenberg's families indicated.

LINGUISTIC TRAITS

Given their extreme genetic diversity, it is not surprising that American Indian languages differ greatly from one another in their phonology (sound systems) and grammar. No linguistic trait exists, however, that is the exclusive property of American Indian languages. This diversity is illustrated by the broad range of traits listed below, which show the structural characteristics of American Indian languages.

Phonology. American Indian languages show great variety in their sound systems.

Consonants. Glottalized consonants are produced by closing the vocal cords while articulating the sound under increased pressure. Such sounds are found in North America in the Athabascan, Siouan, and Salishan languages, among others; in Middle America in Mayan and other languages; and in South America in Quechua, Aymara, and others.

Aspirated consonants are produced with a puff of air after the release of the consonant (the *t* in English *tip,* for example). The Siouan, Pomoan, and Yuman families have such sounds in North America, as do Tarascan and the Otomanguean languages in Middle America and Island Carib (Arawakan stock), Quechua, and others in South America.

Retroflexed consonants are produced by curling the tip of the tongue up and back toward the hard palate; examples include certain *d* and *t* sounds heard in the English spoken by natives of India. Pomoan, Yuman, and various California languages have such consonants in North America; they also occur in the Mamean and Kanjobalan branches of Mayan in Middle America and in the Panoan and Tacanan families, Araucanian, and other languages in South America.

Uvular consonants are produced even farther back in the mouth than *k* or *g;* they are also found in Hebrew and Arabic (the stop transliterated as *q*). They occur in the Eskimo-Aleut family, the northern Uto-Aztecan languages, and California Athabascan in North America; in Totonacan and Mayan in Middle America; and in Toba (Opayé-Guaicurú family), Quechua, and Aymara in South America.

The velar nasal consonant is the *ng* sound of English *song*. It occurs in Eskimo, Haida, Yuman, the California Athabascan languages, and the northern Uto-Aztecan languages in North America; in Mayan and Zoque in Middle America; and in Araucanian, Jívaro, and other languages in South America.

Voiceless nasals and glides are sounds similar to whispered *m, n, w,* and *y.* In North America they occur in eastern Pomo dialects and in Tuscarora (Iroquoian); in Middle America in Nahuatl, in the Otomanguean languages, and as final consonants in Quiché Maya and Totonac; and in South America as final consonants in Toba and as nasals in Zamuco.

Voiceless *l* (like a whispered *l*) is found in some Yupik Eskimo, in various California languages, and in the Athabascan, Salishan, and Muskogean families in North America; in Tequistlatec in Middle America; and in Araucanian, Itonama, and others in South America.

Lateral affricates resemble a forcefully aspirated *tl* sound. The Athabascan, Sahaptian, and Wakashan families have such sounds in North America, as do Nahuatl and Totonac in Middle America.

Vowels. Voiceless, or whispered, vowels are found in North America in Zuñi, Hopi, and Keresan (all spoken by Pueblo Indians), in the Plateau Shoshoni languages (Uto-Aztecan), and in Cheyenne (Algonquian-Ritwan); in Middle America in Totonacan and some Otomanguean languages; and in South America in the Ticuna and others.

Nasalized vowels (as in Fr. *bon*) occur in North America in the Athabascan, eastern Algonquian, Iroquoian, Siouan, Muskogean, and Kiowa-Tanoan groups. They are also found in Middle America in the Otomanguean languages and in South America in various languages, notably in the Macro-Gê, Tupian, and Panoan groups.

The vowel *i*, a high, central, unrounded sound, occurs in North America in Comanche (Plateau Shoshoni) and Coast Tsimshian, and in Middle America in the Mixe-Zoquean family, Cholan and Yucatecan Mayan, Otomí (Otomanguean), and others. It is common in South America, occurring in Araucanian, Guaraní, Guaymí (Chibchan), the Panoan and Tucanoan families, and elsewhere.

NORTH AMERICA

Family	Division	Branch or Group	Languages
1. Eskimo-Aleut	Aleut		Aleut—Alaskan islands
	Eskimo	Yupik	Central Alaskan Yupik (17,000?); Pacific Gulf Yupik—Alaska; Siberian Yupik—USSR, Alaska
		Inupiaq	Inupiaq (a chain of dialects; *see* INUIT)—Greenland, arctic Canada, Alaska (64,000?) (national language in Greenland)
2. Haida[1]			Haida—British Columbia, Alaska
3. Athabascan-Eyak[1]	Eyak**		Eyak**—Alaska
	Tlingit		Tlingit—Alaska, western Canada
	Athabascan	Northern	Koyukon—Alaska; Carrier, Chipewyan—central Canada; about 20 other languages
		Pacific*	Hupa* and a few other languages in California and Oregon
		Apachean	Navajo (80,000+)—Arizona, New Mexico; Western Apache—New Mexico; a few others
4. Wakashan	Northern or Kwakiutlan		Kwakiutl, Heiltsuk* or Bella Bella, Kitamat*—British Columbia
	Southern or Nootkan		Nootka, Nitinat**—Vancouver Island (B.C.); Makah—Washington
5. Chimakuan**			*Chamakum*, Quileute**—Washington
6. Kutenai			Kutenai—British Columbia, Idaho, Montana
7. Salishan	Main Body	Coast	CENTRAL SALISH: Comox—Vancouver Island; Squamish—British Columbia; etc.
		Tillamook**	Tillamook**—Oregon
	Tsamosan	Inland*	Upper Chehalis**, Cowlitz**—Washington
		Maritime*	Lower Chehalis**, Quinault**—Washington
	Interior	Northern	Lillooet, Thompson, Shuswap—British Columbia
		Southern	Columbian—Washington; Okanagan or Colville—British Columbia; Kalispel or Flathead or Spokan—Idaho, Montana; Coeur d'Alene—Idaho
			Bella Coola—British Columbia
8. Algonquian-Ritwan[2]	Algonquian	Blackfoot	Blackfoot—Minnesota, Alberta
		Cheyenne	Cheyenne—Wyoming
		Arapaho	Arapaho, Atsina—Great Plains; etc.
		Menomini	Menomini—Great Lakes region
		Ojibwa	Ojibwa-Potawatomi—Michigan, Ontario (41,000)
		Fox	Fox, Sauk—Oklahoma; Kickapoo—Texas, Mexico (Coahuila)
		Shawnee	Shawnee—Oklahoma
		Miami	Miami-Illinois—Oklahoma
		Eastern Algonquian	Cree-Montagnais—eastern Canada (35,000); Micmac—Canadian Maritime provinces; *Narragansett*—New England; Munsee-Delaware**, *Mohegan*, and others—New England
	Wiyot**		Wiyot**—California
	Yurok**		Yurok**—California
9. Iroquoian[3]	Cherokee		Cherokee—Oklahoma, North Carolina (11,000)
	Northern Iroquoian	Tuscarora	Tuscarora-Nottoway*—New York, Ontario
		Lawrentian	*Lawrentian*—Quebec (first Indian language recorded in North America)
		Huron-Wyandot	*Huron-Wyandot*—Ontario, Quebec, Oklahoma
		Five Nations	Seneca, Onondaga—New York, Ontario; Cayuga—Oklahoma, Ontario; Oneida—New York, Wisconsin, Ontario; Mohawk—New York, Ontario
		Others	*Various extinct languages*
10. Caddoan[3]	Caddo		Caddo—Oklahoma
	Wichita	Wichita	Wichita—Oklahoma
		Kitsai	Kitsai—Oklahoma
		Arikara	Arikara—North Dakota; Pawnee—Oklahoma
11. Muskogean[2]		Western	Choctaw-Chickasaw—Alabama, Michigan, Louisiana, Oklahoma
		Eastern	Creek of Muskogee-Seminole Creek—Alabama, Georgia, Oklahoma (10,000?); Hichiti-Mikasuki Seminole—Alabama, Florida; etc.
12. Siouan[3]	Catawba**		Catawba**—North Carolina, South Carolina
	Main Body	*Southeastern*	*Ofo, Biloxi*—Louisiana; *Tutelo*—Mississippi
		Missouri River	Crow—Minnesota; Hidatsa—North Dakota
		Mandan	Mandan—North Dakota
		Mississippi Valley	Omaha, Osage, Ponca, Kansa, Quapaw, Iowa-Oto-Missouri—central Plains; Winnebago—Wisconsin; Dakota or Sioux—north central Plains; Dhegiha—Mississippi Valley
13. Tsimshian[4]			Tsimshian—British Columbia
14. Chinookan*[4]			Chinook*—Oregon, Washington (main basis on Chinook trade jargon); Wishram—Washington; etc.
15. Sahaptian[4]			Sahaptin (Yakima, Umatilla, Wallawalla, etc.)—Oregon, Nez Percé—Idaho
16. Yokutsan*[4]			Yawelmani,* Yawdanchi,* Chukchansi*—California
17. Wintun*[4]			Patwin*; Wintu*, Nomlaki**—California

Numbers of Speakers: Italics = extinct; ? = probably extinct; ** = 10 or fewer speakers; * = 100 or fewer speakers; if more than 10,000 speakers, approximate number given in parentheses.
Former superstock classifications: [1] Na-Dené; [2] Macro-Algonquian; [3] Macro-Siouan; [4] Penutian; [5] Hokan; [6] Aztec-Tanoan.

18. Miwokan-Costanoan*[4]	Miwokan*		Miwok (Lake, Sierra, Bodega, etc.)*—California
	Costanoan		*Costanoan, Mutsun, Rumsen*—California
19. Yuman[5]		Northern	Walapai, Hawasupai, Yavapai—Arizona; Paipai—Baja California
		Central	Mojave—California; Maricopa, Yuma—Arizona
		Delta-California	Cocopa-Diegueño-Tipai**—Arizona, southern California, Baja California
		Kiliwa	Kiliwa**—Baja California
20. Pomoan[5]	*Southeastern*		*Southeastern Pomoan*
	Eastern*	Central	Northern*, Northeastern**, and Southern* Pomoan, etc.; Kashaya*—California
21. Karok*[5]			Karok*—California
22. *Shasta*[5]			*Shasta, Konomihu*—California
23. Palaihnihan**			Atsugewi**, Achomawi**—California
24. *Chumashan*[5]			*Ventureño, Barbareño, Inezeño*—California
25. Washo*[5]			Washo*—California, Nevada
26. Yukian**	Wappo**		Wappo**—California
	Core Yukian**		Yuki**, Coast Yuki**, Hachnom**—California
27. Kiowa-Tanoan[6]	Kiowa		Kiowa—Oklahoma
	Tanoan	Tiwa	Taos, Picuris, Isleta, Sandia, Piro—New Mexican Pueblos
		Tewa	Hopi Tewa, Santa Clara-San Juan—New Mexican Pueblos
		Towa	Towa—New Mexican Pueblos
28. Zuñi[5]			Zuñi—New Mexico (Zuñi Pueblo)
29. Keresan		Western	Acoma, Laguna—New Mexican Pueblos
		Eastern	Cochiti, Santo Domingo, etc.—New Mexican Pueblos
30. Uto-Aztecan[6]	Northern	Numic	WESTERN: Paviotso-Northern Paiute, etc.—Oregon, Nevada, Idaho; Mono*—California. CENTRAL: Shoshoni—Nevada, Utah, Wyoming; Comanche—Texas
		Tübatulabal	Tübatulabal**—California
		Takic	Luiseño, Cahuilla*, Cupeño**, and others—California
		Hopi	Hopi—Arizona (Hopi Pueblos)
	Southern	Pimic	Pima-Papago—Arizona, Mexico (Sonora) (13,000?); etc.
		Taracahitic	Tarahumara, Tubar—Mexico (Chihuahua) (12,000?); Yaqui-Mayo-Cahita—Arizona, Mexico (Sonora) (13,000?); etc.
		Corachol-Aztecan	CORA-HUICHOL: Cora, Huichol—western Mexico. AZTECAN (1 million +): Nahuatl, *Pochutec*—Mexico; Pipil—Central America; *other extinct languages.*

31–59. *Plus the following extinct or nearly extinct single-language and small families; Beothuk*—Newfoundland; *Adai*—Louisiana; Yuchi*[3]—Georgia, Oklahoma; *Timucua*—Florida; *Natchez*[2], *Tunica*[2], *Chitimaca*[2], *Atakapa*[2]—Louisiana; Tonkawa**[3]—Texas; *Takelma*[4], *Siuslaw*[4], *Alsea*[4], *Cayuse*[4] *Molale*[4], Kalapuya**[4], Coos**[4]—Oregon; Klamath-Modoc—Oregon, California; Maiduan**[4], *Chimariko*[5], *Yana*[5], *Esselen*[5], Salinan**[5]—California; *Aranama-Tamique, Karankawa*—Texas; *Coahuilteco*—Texas, northwestern Mexico; *Cotoname, Comecrudo*[5], Solano, *Mamulique*—northwestern Mexico

MIDDLE AMERICA

Family	Division	Branch or Group	Languages
1. Otomanguean	Mixtecan	Trique	Trique—southern Mexico
		Mixtecan	Mixtec—central and southern Mexico (250,000); Cuicatec—southern Mexico (12,000)
	Popolocan	Mazatec	Mazatec—central Mexico (85,000)
		Popolocan	Popoloca—central and southern Mexico (15,000); Chocho—central Mexico
		Ixcatec*	Ixcatec*—central Mexico
	Chiapanec-Mangue		*Chiapanec-Mangue*—southern Mexico, Nicaragua
	Otopamean	Otomian	MAZAHUA SUBGROUP: Mazahua—central Mexico (100,000). OTOMI SUBGROUP: several languages called Otomi (300,000). MATLAZINCAN SUBGROUP: Matlazinca—central Mexico; Ocuilteco—central Mexico.
		Pamean	Pame—central Mexico
		Chichimec	Chichimec—north central Mexico
	Greater Zapotecan	Zapotecan	*Papabuco* and numerous languages called Zapotec—southern Mexico (300,000)
		Chatino	Chatino—southern Mexico (18,000)
	Chinantecan		Several languages called Chinantec—southern Mexico (18,000)
	Amuzgo		Amuzgo—southern Mexico (12,000)
2. Tequistlatecan or Chontalof Oaxaca[5]			Huamelutec or Lowland Chontal, Tequistlatec or Highland Chontal—southern Mexico
3. Seri[5]			Seri—northern Mexico (Sonora)
4. Jicaque or Tol[5]			Two languages, both called Jicaque or Tol—Honduras
5. Tlapanec-Subtiaba[5]			Tiapanec or Yope—central Mexico (50,000); *Subtiaba*—Nicaragua
6. Huave			Huave—southern Mexico
7. Totonacan			Totonac, Tepehua—central and eastern Mexico (130,000 together)
8. Mixe-Zoquean	Mixe		Eastern Mixe—southern Mexico (48,000); *Tapachultec*—southern Mexico; others, some called Popoluca—eastern and southern Mexico
	Zoquean		Various languages, some called Zoque, some called Popoluca—eastern and southern Mexico (30,000)

9. Mayan	Huastecan		Huastec—eastern Mexico (60,000); *Chicomuceltec*—southern Mexico
	Western Mayan	Yucatecan	Yucatec—southern Mexico (350,000); Mopán—Guatemala; etc.
		Greater Cholan	Chol, Chontal—southern Mexico; Chortí—Guatemala (80,000 together)
		Tzeltalan	Tzeltal, Tzotzil—southern Mexico (200,000)
	Greater Kanjobalan	Chujean	Chuj—Guatemala (13,000); Tojolabal—southern Mexico (12,000)
		Kanjobalan	Kanjobal—Guatemala (40,000); Motozintlec—southern Mexico; etc.
	Eastern Mayan	Mamean	Mam (350,000), Ixil (20,000), etc.—Guatemala
		Quichean	Kekchí (300,000), Uspantec—Guatemala. CORE QUICHEAN SUBGROUP: Quiché, Cakchiquel, etc. (860,000?); Pokom (40,000)—all Guatemala
10. Tarascan			Tarascan—central Mexico (50,000)
11. Xincan*			Several extinct or dying languages formerly spoken in a part of Guatemala
12. Misumalpan			Miskito (35,000), Sumu, etc.—Honduras, Nicaragua

13. Uto-Aztecan, including Aztecan (Nahuatl), Cora-Huichol, etc.: see chart for North America.

14.–19. *Plus the following extinct or probably extinct single-language and small families: Cuitlatec, Guaicurian, Maratino, Naolan*—Mexico; *Alagüilac* (possibly a Xincan language)—Guatemala; *Lencan?*—El Salvador, Honduras

SOUTH AMERICA

Family	Division	Branch or Group	Languages
1. Chibchan[7]			Guaymi-Dorasque—Panama (25,000); Cuna or Cueva—Panama, Colombia (21,000); Tunebo—Colombia; Paya—Honduras; Rama**—Nicaragua; *Chibcha*—Colombia (language of the pre-Hispanic Muisca culture); etc.
2. *Atacaman*[7]			Several extinct languages of Chile, Argentina, and Brazil
3. Paezan[7]			Paez (30,000), *Popayán, Moguex-Coconuco?*—all Colombia
4. Barbacoan[7]			Cayapa-Colorado—Ecuador; Coaiquer or Pasto—Colombia
5. Itonama or Machoto[7]			Itonama or Machoto—Bolivia
6. Warao or Guarao[7]			Warao or Guarao—Venezuela (10,000)
7. Yungan[7]			Chipaya-Uru[8]—Bolivia; *Puruhá-Cañari*—Ecuador; *Yunga*—Peru (language of the pre-Hispanic Chimú culture)
8. Chocó[7]			Chocó or Cholo or Emperá—Colombia (20,000); Guanana—Colombia
9. Quechumaran[8]			Several languages called Quechua—Peru, Bolivia, Ecuador, Argentina, Colombia (8 million speakers; language of the Inca empire); Aymara—Bolivia, Peru, Chile, Argentina (800,000); Jaqaru, Cauqui—Peru
10. Catacan[8]			Catacan—Peru, Ecuador
11. Leco-Tallán[8]			Leco—Bolivia; *Tallán*—Ecuador
12. Simacu or Chimacu[8]			Simacu or Chimacu—Peru
13. Yámana or Yaghan[8]			Yámana or Yaghan**—southern Argentina
14. Ona-Tehuelche[8]			Ona-Selknam**, Tehuelche or Chon*—southern Argentina
15. Araucanian or Mapuche[8]			Araucanian or Mapuche—Chile, Argentina (200,000)
16. Alacaluf[8]			Alacaluf—Chile
17. Jívaroan[8]		Jívaro	Jívaro-Aguaruna-Huambisa-Achual—Ecuador, Peru
		Cahuapanan	Cahuapana, Jébero—Peru
		Candoshi-Chirino	Candoshi—Peru; *Chirino*—Colombia
		Cofán	Cofán—Colombia, Ecuador
18. Yaruro[8]			Yaruro—Venezuela
19. Mosetenan[9]			Mosetén, Chimane—Bolivia
20. Panoan[9]			Marinahua—Peru; Chácobo—Bolivia; etc. CENTRAL SUBGROUP: Shipibo (10,000), Cashibo, Capanahua, etc.—all Peru
21. Tacanan[9]			Cavineña, Tacaná—Bolivia; Chama—Peru, Bolivia; etc.
22. Opayé-Guaicuru[9]		Opayé	Opayé—Brazil
		Guaicuruan	Toba (16,500), Guaicurú, Apibón, Mocovi—Argentina
23. Guachí[9]			Guachí—Argentina
24. Matacoan[9]			Mataco-Mataguayo—Bolivia, Argentina, Paraguay; Chorote, etc.—Paraguay
25. Yurumanguí[5]			Yurumanguí—Colombia

26. MACRO-GÊ STOCK:[9]			
Bororoan			Bororó—Brazil; Chiquito, *Otuque?*—Bolivia
Botocudan			*Botocudo*, Araña, Crecmun, etc.—Brazil
Camacanan			*Camacán? Cutashó, Meniá*, Masacará—Brazil
Caingang-Gé	Caingangan		Caingang, Shocleng, *Dorin?*—Brazil; Ivitorocai-Taven—Paraguay
	Gêan	Apinayé	Apinayé, Craho—Brazil
		Cayapó	Cayapó—Brazil (10,000); etc.
		Others	Geicó, etc.—Brazil
Coroadoan			Fulnió; *Mashacalí-Malalí: Purí-Coropó*—Brazil
Others			*Patashó? Otí?*—Brazil
27. Mirandela or Tapuya			Mirandela or Tapuya—Brazil
28. Cariban[9]		Northern	Carib—Brazil, northeast South America; Oyana—Brazil, Surinam; Macushi-Tehueya—Brazil, Guayana; Yabarana—Venezuela; etc.
		Southern	Bacairí, Parirí—Brazil
		Northwestern	Motilón-Mapé-Macoíta—Colombia, Venezuela; Carare—Venezuela; Opón—Colombia
		Others	Cuicurú, Hishcariana, etc.—Brazil
29. Peba-Zápara[7]		Peban	Yagua-Peba, Yameo—Peru
		Záparoan[8]	Shimigae-Andoa-Gae-Iquito, Záparo-Arabela—Peru
		Sabela	Auca, Huarani, etc.—Ecuador
		Omurano?	*Omurano?*—Ecuador
30. Huitotoan[9]		Boran	Bora—Colombia; Ocaina*—Peru; etc.
		Others	Huitoto, Andoque*, *Orejón*—Colombia
31. Nambicuaran			Nambicuara, Sabané—Brazil
32. Carayá-Yavahé-Shambioá[9]			Carayá-Yavahé-Shambioá—Brazil
33. Arawakan[9]	Arawakan	Northern	Island Carib or black Carib—Belize, Guayana, Honduras (30,000); Locono or Arawak—Colombia, French Guiana, Guyana; Goajiro—Colombia, Venezuela (30,000); Resígaro**—Peru, Colombia; *Manao?*—Brazil
		Bolivian	Ignaciano-Mojo-Baure, Trinitario—Bolivia; Ariti—Brazil
		Pre-Andean	Campa—Peru, Brazil, Bolivia (33,000); Machiguenga, etc.—Peru; Ipurina—Brazil
		Others	Saraveca—Brazil, Bolivia; Terena—Brazil, Paraguay; Palicur, Huapishana—Brazil, Guyana; Paresi—Brazil; Baniva-Yavitero—Colombia, Venezuela
	Others		Amuesha, Chamicura—Peru; *Apolista*—Brazil; etc.
34. Arahuá-Curcurá[5]		Arahuán	Arahuá, Paumari-Yamamadí—Brazil; Culina—Brazil, Peru
		Cucurá	*Cucurá?*—Brazil
35. Chapacura-Shirianá[8]		Chapacuran	Chapacura, Huañam—Bolivia, Brazil
		Shiriánán	Waican-Shirianá—Brazil, Venezuela (15,000); Carimé—Brazil
36. Tupian[8]	Tupian		*Tupí*-Guaraní—Paraguay, Brazil, Bolivia (2 million, half of these non-Indian; second national language of Paraguay); Guayayara, Canoeiro, etc.—Brazil; Pauserna—Bolivia; Oyampí—Brazil, French Guiana; etc.
	Cocama		Cocama or Omagua—Peru, Bolivia, Brazil (10,000)
	Others		Mundurucú—Brazil; Sirionó—Bolivia; Guayaquí—Paraguay; etc.
37. Sálivan[8]			Sáliva, Piaroa, Maco**—Venezuela
38. Camsá-Mocoa[8]			Camsá or Mocoa or Coche, etc.—Colombia
39. Tinigua-Guahibo[8]		Tinigua	Tinigua—Colombia
		Guahiboan	Guajibo (20,000), Churuya—Colombia, Venezuela
40. Timotean[8]			Timoté, Cuica—Venezuela
41. Yuracaré[8]			Yuracaré—Bolivia
42. Zamucoan[8]			Ayoré or Zamuco, Chamacoco—Bolivia, Paraguay
43. Tuyuneri[8]			Tuyuneri or Masco—Peru
44. Muniche[8]			Muniche or Paranapura—Peru
45. Yurí-Ticuna[8]			Ticuna—Peru, Brazil (15,000); *Yurí?*—Brazil
46. Tucano-Ahuishira[8]		Tucanoan	Tucano—Colombia (used as regional lingua franca); Cubeo, Desano—Colombia; Siona-Secoya—Colombia, Ecuador
		Coto-Tama	Coto, Tama—Colombia, Peru
			Ahuishira—Peru; etc.
47. Catuquina[8]			Catuquina—Brazil
48. Puinavean[8]			Puinave, Macú—Brazil, Colombia
49. Movima[8]			Movima—Bolivia
50. Majcú or Sope[8]			Majcú or Sope—Brazil

51–68. *Plus the following extinct or nearly extinct single-language and small families: Andaquí*[7]—Colombia; Mura-Matanahui**[7], Trumaí[8], *Carirí-Sapuya?*—Brazil; *Jirajaran?*[7] *Ahuaqué-Calianá?*[8] *Otomaco-Taparita?*[8]—Venezuela; Puelche or Pampa**[8], *Huarpe-Allentiac*[9]—Argentina; *Cholonan*[8], *Colán*[8]—Peru; *Sec or Sechura*[8]—Peru, Ecuador; Esmeralda-Cayuvava*[8]—Ecuador, Bolivia; Lule**[9]—Argentina, Uruguay; *Guató?*[9]—Brazil, Bolivia; *Tarumá?*—Brazil, Paraguay; *Guamo*—Brazil, Venezuela; *Canishana?*[8]—Bolivia

69–86. *Plus the following unclassified languages:* Carapotó, Catahuishi, Natú, Pancararú, Tarairirú, Teremembé, Tushá, Yabuti or Aricapú, *Omahuaca, Shocó? Shucurú*—Brazil; Gamela—central South America; Cauqui, Maina, Huari or Masaca—Colombia; *Aconipa?*—Ecuador; *Sanaviron, Chechehet*—Argentina

Sometimes-cited superstock groupings proposed by the American linguist Joseph Greenberg (1915–): [7] Macro-Chibchan; [8] Andean-Equatorial; [9] Gê-Pano-Carib.

Tonal accent. In tonal or pitch accent, a difference in pitch distinguishes words that would otherwise sound the same. Tonal accent is found in North America in the Athabascan languages; Mohawk and Cherokee (Iroquoian); Crow (Siouan); Cheyenne, Arapaho, Penobscot (Algonquian-Ritwan); and some Pomo dialects. In Middle America it occurs in Yucatec and Uspantec Mayan, the Otomanguean languages, and others, and in South America in Tucano and in the Panoan, Chibchan, and Huitotoan families.

Grammar. American Indian languages display striking differences in grammatical structure. Following are some common grammatical traits.

Word order. Languages are often classified into basic word-order types because word order often correlates with other grammatical characteristics. For example, languages with the basic order subject-verb-object (as in English) also tend to have the orders adjective-noun and preposition-noun. On the other hand, languages having the basic order subject-object-verb tend to place the modifiers after nouns, for example, noun-adjective and noun-postposition.

Although the role of word order may vary in its importance and function from one language to another, the following American Indian languages have distinguishable word orders. The subject-verb-object word order occurs in Totonac and Tarascan in Middle America. The subject-object-verb order is found in Zapotec in Middle America, the Panoan languages in South America, and several California languages. Still other word orders occur: verb-subject-object in Guaraní, verb-object-subject in Quiché Mayan, object-subject-verb in Haida.

Ergative typology. The concept of ergative typology refers to a case system that is different from the nominative-accusative system found in English, German, and most familiar languages. In such familiar languages, the subject of the sentence is in the nominative case—that is, the subject has the same form and function, whether the sentence is transitive (has a direct object) or intransitive (lacks an object). In ergative-absolutive languages, however, the subject of a transitive verb has one form (called the ergative case), but the subject of an intransitive verb has a different form—the same form as the object of a transitive verb (the absolutive case). In North America, ergative-absolutive case distinctions are made in eastern Pomo, Tsimshian, and a few other languages. The system is found in Mayan and Mixe-Zoquean languages in Middle America and in a few languages in South America.

Switch reference. Languages that have switch reference indicate whether a subject or object of a clause is the same as or different from the subject or object of an earlier clause. In English, for example, if someone says "Sam met John coming out of his house," the listener does not know who was coming or whose house was involved, because English lacks switch reference. Algonquian, southern Paiute, Papago, and Yuman have this trait in North America, Jicaque in Middle America, and Ecuadorian Quechua in South America.

Grammatical distinctions. Various grammatical distinctions that are marked (indicated) on a certain word category (such as nouns) in one language may be marked on another category (such as verbs) in another language.

Languages such as Russian and Latin, which distinguish the role of a noun (such as subject, direct object, or indirect object) by case marking are said to have nominal case systems. Eskimo makes this distinction, as do Yuman, Nez Percé (Sahaptian), and various California languages in North America, and the Uto-Aztecan languages in North America and Middle America.

In some languages certain nouns occur only in possessed form. Usually they are kinship terms and names of body parts. This distinction, called inalienable possession, occurs in Eskimo and in the Algonquian, Wakashan, Salishan, Iroquoian, and Siouan language families in North America, in Uto-Aztecan, Mayan, and most other languages in Middle America, and in a few languages in South America.

In languages with dual number, singular (one) is contrasted with dual (two) and with plural (more than two). Dual number is found in Eskimo and in the Athabascan, Siouan, Iroquoian, Muskogean, and Plateau Shoshoni groups in North America, and Araucanian and others in South America. Some languages have dual constructions only with pronouns, as in Tehuelche *ma,* "you" (sing.), *makma,* "you two," and *mešma,* "you" (pl.).

Languages with inclusive/exclusive *we* have different terms for *we,* according to whether the listener is included. In Quechua, for example, *ñuquayku* means "we" in the sense of "he, she, or they and I," and *ñuquančis* means "we" in the sense of "you and I." In North America this distinction occurs in the Plateau Shoshoni, Iroquoian, and some Siouan languages, in Blackfoot and Cheyenne (Algonquian-Ritwan), and other languages. It is found in Middle America in Cholan Mayan and some Otomanguean languages, and in South America in the Cariban family, Quechua, and other languages.

Masculine and feminine gender are distinguished in South America in the Arawakan, Huitotoan, and Tucanoan languages, in North America in Coast Salishan and a few other languages, and—for pronouns only—in Pomo and Iroquoian. Animate and inanimate gender are distinguished in Algonquian, Dakota, Kowa, Comanche, and other languages in North America, and in a few languages in South America.

Numeral classifiers are forms occurring with counted nouns to indicate what kind of object is being counted. They are somewhat akin to English "four loaves of bread." They occur in North America in Menominee and Ojibwa (Algonquian-Ritwan), Wakashan, Salishan, Tlingit, and Tsimshian; in Middle America in Mayan, Tarascan, Nahuatl, and Totonac; and in South America in Auca (Peba-Zápara).

In noun incorporation, some nouns, such as the receiver of an action, are incorporated directly into the verb, as in English *to babysit* or in Nahuatl *ni-tlaškal-čiwa,* "I-tortillas-make." In North America noun incorporation occurs in northern Athabascan, Tsimshian, some Caddoan, the Iroquoian, Uto-Aztecan, and Tanoan families, and other languages; it is found in Nahuatl, Mayan, and Totonac in Middle America and is common in South America.

A verbal directional is an element incorporated into the verb to indicate the direction of the action (usually toward or away from the speaker or hearer). In Mohawk, *tasatáweya't* means "come in," but *ya'satáweya't* means "go in." Verbal directionals are found in North America in the Uto-Aztecan, Algonquian, Athabascan, Iorquoian, Siouan, and other families; in Middle America in Mayan, Uto-Aztecan, Otomanguean, Tarascan, and Totonacan languages; and in South America in Quechua, Itonama, Toba, and Záparo.

Languages with classificatory verb systems use different verbs for nouns representing different shapes or other characteristics (akin to the English use of *to drink* for liquids and *to eat* for solids). Classificatory verbs occur in North America in Muskogean, Siouan, Athabascan, Iroquoian, and other families; in Middle America in Mayan and Tarascan; and in South America in the Chibchan and Tucanoan families and elsewhere.

In many languages, verbal aspect (distinguishing, for example, the duration, repetition, or completion of an event) is relatively more important than verbal tense (the time of the event). Verbal aspect is stressed in Tsimshian and the Salishan, Athabascan, and Iroquoian families in North America, in most Mayan languages in Middle America, and in Jébero (Jívaroan family) and other languages in South America. In many American Indian languages, however, tense is relatively more important than aspect.

Instrumental verb affixes (prefixes, suffixes, infixes) are attached to verbs to indicate the instrument or means by which an action is performed. In Karok, for example, the prefix *pa-* indicates use of the mouth. Thus *páčup* means "to kiss" and *paxut* means "to hold in the mouth." Such prefixes occur in Haida, Tlingit, and other languages in North America, in Uto-Aztecan, Totonac, and other languages in Middle America, and in Jébero in South America.

Social and Cultural Traits. In some Indian languages, distinct forms of speech are used by or for women as opposed to men. Such distinctions occur in North America in Yana, Muskogean, and Atsina, and in South America in several languages, including Island and Black Carib (Arawakan), Cocoma (Tupian), and Tacaná. Ritual languages—special forms of speech for ceremonies—exist within Zuñi, Iroquoian, Mayan, Nahuatl, Quechua, and some other languages. In a few multilingual regions, trade jargons emerged (*see* PIDGIN). These reduced, simplified languages include Chinook jargon, Mobilian, and Delaware trade jargon in North America. A few languages developed forms of whistle speech, in which the melody of the whistling parallels the tones of the language. Whistle languages are used for purposes such as courtship. Such languages occur in Kickapoo (Algonquian-Ritwan) in Mexico near Texas; several Otomanguean languages, Nahuatl dialects, and the Totonacan languages in Middle America; and the Aguaruna (Jívaroan) and the Sirionó (Tupian) in South America.

Writing Systems. The Incas, speakers of Quechua, employed the quipu (a knotted cord used for numerical calculations) as a device for recording information; they also painted some sort of communication on beans and wove iconographic symbols into textiles. All these communicate information, but none approaches true writing. In North America, due to stimulus from—or, in most cases, direct study of—European writing, several groups developed interesting forms of writing. Examples include the syllabaries (writing systems in which each symbol represents the sound of a different syllable) of the Cherokee, Micmac, Cree, and Inuit.

True pre-Columbian writing systems developed only in Middle America. Hieroglyphic writing was used at least by the Aztecs, the Mixtecs, the Zapotec of Oaxaca, the Mixe-Zoque speakers, and the Maya. Most Middle American hieroglyphs are based on morpheme signs; that is, they are logograms, in which the sign represents a whole word. These signs were augmented by the rebus principle (pictorial punning), in which the sign for one word is used to represent another word that sounds the same (for example, in English, using a picture of an eye to represent both *eye* and *I*). In classic Mayan, in addition, phonetic signs were developed that had the syllabic value of a consonant plus a vowel (CV). The typically one-syllable Mayan roots (consisting of a vowel between two consonants) could be "spelled" with two signs (CV-CV), with the last vowel understood to be silent.

The study of American Indian languages has provided rich insights for linguistic theory, language change, the prehistory of the Americas, and the relation of language to culture as well as to modes of thought and perception. Many of these languages will soon become extinct and deserve urgent attention. It is encouraging that, in the 20th century, more and more native speakers have become involved with the formal study of their own languages. L.Ca. & M.M.

For further information on this topic, see the Bibliography in volume 28, section 364.

AMERICAN INDIANS, indigenous peoples of the Americas. The name Indian was first applied to them by Christopher Columbus, who believed mistakenly that the mainland and islands of America were part of the Indies, in Asia.

This article focuses on the Indians of North America, Mesoamerica, and South America. The indigenous population at the time of European contact is estimated, the general physical characteristics of native American peoples are described, and a summary is given of what is known about their arrival and early prehistory in the New World. The major culture areas of North, Central, and South America are discussed, and a survey follows of the traditional ways of life of American Indians. Social and political organization are considered, as well as their food, clothing, and housing, their trade, religion, and warfare, and their crafts, visual arts, music, and dance. Finally, the history of American Indians after European contact and their condition today in North and Latin America are examined.

Member of the Navajo tribe, Monument Valley, Arizona.

Early Population. At the time of first European contact, North and South America may have been peopled by more than 90 million American Indians: about 10 million in America north of present-day Mexico; 30 million in Mexico; 11 million in Central America; 445,000 in the Caribbean islands; 30 million in the South American Andean region; and 9 million in the remainder of South America. These population figures are a rough estimate (some authorities cite much lower figures); exact figures are impossible to ascertain. When colonists began keeping records, the American Indian populations had been drastically reduced by war, famine, forced labor, and epidemics of European diseases.

Physical Traits. American Indians are physically most similar to Asians and appear to have descended from Asian peoples who began migrating across the Bering land bridge during the Pleistocene epoch, or Ice Age, of the Quaternary period (q.v.), some 30,000 years ago. Like other Mongoloid peoples, American Indians tend to have light brown skin, brown eyes, and dark, straight hair. They differ from Asians in their characteristic blood types (*see* RACES, CLASSIFICATION OF). Because many American Indians today have had one or more European-Americans or blacks among their ancestors, numerous people who are legally and culturally American Indian may look fairer or darker than Mongoloids or may have markedly non-Mongoloid facial features.

Over the thousands of years the Indians have lived in the Americas, they have developed into a great number of local populations, each differing from its neighbors. Some populations (such as those on the Great Plains of North America) tend to be tall and heavy in build, whereas others (for example, many in the South American Andes and adjacent lowlands) tend to be short and broad chested; furthermore, every population includes persons who vary from the average. Some physical characteristics of American Indian populations have been influenced by diet or by the environmental conditions of their societies. For example, the short stature of

Guatemalan Indian peasants seems to result at least in part from diets poor in protein; the broad chests and large hearts and lungs of Andean Indians represent an adaptation to the low-oxygen atmosphere of the high mountains they inhabit.

Earliest Migrations. Evidence indicates that the first peoples to migrate into the Americas, coming from northeastern Siberia into Alaska, would have been carrying stone tools and other equipment of types exemplified by Middle Paleolithic and Upper Paleolithic styles. These peoples would have lived in bands of about 100 persons, hunting herd animals such as reindeer and mammoths, and fishing. They would have used skin tents for shelter, and they must have tanned reindeer skins and sewn them into clothing similar to that made by the Inuit (Eskimo)—parkas, trousers, boots, and mittens. These peoples would have been nomadic, moving camp at least several times each year to take advantage of seasonal sources of food. It is likely that they gathered each summer for a few weeks with other bands to celebrate religious ceremonies and to trade, compete in sports, gamble, and visit. At such gatherings, valuable information could be obtained about new sources of food or raw materials (such as stone for tools); sometimes, such news might lead families to move into new territory—eventually into Alaska and then farther south into America.

Evidence for the earliest migrations into the Americas is scarce and not as clear as archaeologists would wish. In the Yukon, bone tools have been discovered that have been radiocarbon dated to about 22,000 BC. Campfire remains in the Valley of Mexico have been dated to 21,000 BC, and a few chips of stone tools have been found near the hearths, indicating the presence of humans at that time. In a cave in the Andes Mountains of Peru, near Ayacucho, archaeologists have found stone tools and butchered game bones that have been dated to 18,000 BC. A cave in Idaho, in the U.S., contains similar evidence—stone tools and butchered bone—dated to 12,500 BC. In none of these sites do distinctive American styles characterize the artifacts (manufactured objects such as tools). Artifacts having the earliest distinctive American styles appeared about 11,000 BC and are known as Clovis stone blades.

MAJOR CULTURE AREAS

To understand how different peoples live and how their societies have developed, anthropologists find it convenient to group societies into culture areas. A culture area is first of all a geographical region; it has characteristic climate, land forms, and biological population—fauna and flora. Humans who live in the region must adapt to its characteristics to obtain the necessities of life: No one can grow grain in the Arctic or hunt seals or whales in the desert, but people can survive in the Arctic by hunting seals, or in the desert by gathering foods such as cactus fruits. Each culture area, then, has certain natural resources as well as the potential for certain technologies. Humans in the culture area use many of its resources and develop technologies—and social organizations—to fit the area's physical potential and its hazards (such as winter cold). Neighboring peoples learn of one another's inventions and begin to use them. Thus, societies within a given culture area resemble one another and differ from those in other regions.

Paiute woman gathering straw to use in weaving baskets.
© Jonathan Wright–Bruce Coleman, Inc.

The Americas may be divided into many culture areas, and each scholar's divisions may differ from those of others. Here, nine areas are used for North America, one for Mesoamerica (Mexico and Central America), and four for South America.

North America. The culture areas of North America are the Southwest, the Eastern Woodlands, the Southeast, the Plains, the California-Intermountain region, the Plateau, the Subarctic, the Northwest Pacific Coast, and the Arctic.

The Southwest. The Southwestern culture area encompasses Arizona, New Mexico, southern Colorado, and adjacent northern Mexico (Sonora and Chihuahua states). It can be subdivided into three sectors: northern (Colorado, northern Arizona, northern New Mexico), with high, pleasant valleys and pine forests; southern (southern Arizona, southern New Mexico, adjacent Mexico), with deserts covered with cactus; and western (the Arizona-California border area), a smaller area with desert terrain cut by the valley of the lower Colorado River.

The first known inhabitants of the Southwest hunted mammoths and other game with Clovis-style spearpoints by about 9500 BC. As the Ice Age ended (about 8000 BC), mammoths became extinct. The people in the Southwest turned to

Arts and crafts of the southwestern area. Left, Tularosa olla, *Pueblo jewelry, and Yokut basket against the background of a Navajo chief's blanket. Right, Hopi kachina dolls.* Courtesy of ACA American Indian Arts, New York; © Heard Museum, photograph by Jeffrey Crespi

hunting bison (buffalo) and spent more time collecting wild plants for food. Climate gradually became warmer and drier, and a way of life—called the Archaic—developed from about 8000 BC to about 300 BC. Archaic peoples hunted mostly deer, small game, and birds, and they harvested fruits, nuts, and the seeds of wild plants, using stone slabs for grinding seeds into flour. About 3000 BC the Southwesterners learned to grow maize (corn), which had been domesticated in Mexico, but for centuries it was only a minor food.

About 300 BC, Mexicans with a culture based on the cultivation of maize, beans, and squash by irrigating fields migrated to southern Arizona. These people, called the Hohokam, lived in towns in adobe-plastered houses built around public plazas. They were the ancestors of the present-day Pima (q.v.) and Papago, who preserve much of the Hohokam way of life.

The peoples of the northern sector, after centuries of trading with the Hohokam, had by AD 700 modified their life into what is called the Anasazi tradition. They grew maize, beans, and squash, and lived in towns of terraced stone or adobe apartment blocks built around central plazas; these blocks had blank walls facing the outside of the town, thereby protecting the people within. During the summer many families lived in small houses at their fields. After 1275 the northern sector suffered severe droughts, and many Anasazi farms and towns were abandoned; those along the Rio Grande, however, grew and expanded their irrigation systems. In 1540 Spanish explorers visited the descendants of the Anasazi, who are called Pueblo Indians (q.v.). After 1598 the Spanish imposed their rule on the Pueblos, but in 1680 the Pueblos organized a rebellion that kept them free until 1692. Since that time, Pueblo towns have been dominated by Spanish, then Mexican, and finally U.S. government. The Pueblos attempted to preserve their culture: They continued their farming and, in some towns, secretly maintained their native governments and religion. Twenty-two Pueblo towns exist today. *See also* ACOMA; CLIFF DWELLER; HOPI; ISLETA; LAGUNA; ZUÑI INDIANS.

In the 1400s, hunters speaking an Athabascan language—related to languages of Alaska and western Canada—appeared in the Southwest, having migrated southward along the western Plains. They raided Pueblo towns for food and (after slave markets were established by the Spanish) for captives to sell; from the Pueblos, they learned to farm, and from the Spanish, to raise sheep and horses. Today these peoples are the Navajo Indians (q.v.) and the several tribes of Apache (q.v.).

The western sector of the Southwest is inhabited by speakers of Yuman languages, including the isolated Havasupai (q.v.), who farm on the floor of the Grand Canyon; and the Mojave Indians (q.v.), who live along the lower Colorado River. The Yuman-speaking peoples inhabit small villages of pole-and-thatch houses near their floodplain fields of maize, beans, and squash.

Eastern Woodlands. The Eastern Woodlands consist of the temperate-climate regions of the eastern U.S. and Canada, from Minnesota and Ontario east to the Atlantic and south to North Carolina. Originally densely forested, this large region was first inhabited by hunters, including

The Weaver, by Gregory Perillo. *Having adopted the loom from the Pueblo Indians and the sheep from Spanish settlers, the Navajo of the Southwest became the master weavers of beautifully colored blankets incorporating traditional tribal designs.*

those who used Clovis spearpoints. About 7000 BC, with the warming climate, an Archaic culture developed. The peoples became increasingly dependent on deer, nuts, and wild grains. By 3000 BC human populations in the Eastern Woodlands had reached cultural peaks that were not again achieved until after AD 1200. The cultivation of squash was learned from Mexicans, and in the Midwest sunflowers, amaranth, marsh elder, and chenopods such as goosefoot were also farmed. All of these were grown for their seeds, which—except for those of the sunflower—were usually ground into flour. Fishing and shellfish gathering increased, and off the coast of Maine the catch even included swordfish. In the western Great Lakes area, copper was surface mined and made into blades and ornaments, and throughout the Eastern Woodlands, beautiful stones were carved into little sculptures.

After 1000 BC the climate became cooler and food resources scarcer, causing a population decline in the Atlantic part of the region. In the Midwest, however, populations organized into wide trading networks and began building large mound-covered tombs for their leaders and for use as centers for religious activities. These peoples, called the Hopewell, raised some maize, but were more dependent on Archaic foods. The Hopewell culture declined by about AD 400.

By 750 a new culture developed in the Midwest. Called the Mississippian culture, it was based on intensive maize agriculture, and its people built large towns with earth platforms supporting temples and rulers' residences. Across the Mississippi River from present-day Saint Louis, Mo., the Mississippians built the city of Cahokia, which may have had a population of 50,000. Cahokia, in addition to hundreds of lesser mounds, had its principal temple erected on a mound 30 m (100 ft) high and about the length and width of a football field (the largest such mound in North America, now part of Cahokia Mounds State Park, Illinois). During this time period, maize agriculture also became important in the Atlantic region, but no cities were built. *See also* MOUND BUILDERS.

European contacts with the Eastern Woodlands date at least from AD 1000, when colonists from Iceland tried to settle Newfoundland. Throughout the 1500s, European fishermen and whalers used the coast of Canada. European settlement of the region began in the 1600s. It was not strongly resisted, partly because terrible epidemics had spread among the Indians from the European fishermen and from Spanish explorers in the Southeast. By this time the Mississippian cities had also disappeared, probably as a consequence of the epidemics.

The historic peoples of the Eastern Woodlands include the Iroquois (q.v.) and a number of Algonquian-speaking peoples, including the Lenape, or Delaware Indians (q.v.), the Micmac, the Narragansett Indians, the Shawnee Indians, the Potawatomi, the Menominee, and the Illinois Indians (qq.v.). Some Eastern Woodlands peoples moved west in the 19th century; others remain throughout the region, usually in their own small communities.

The Southeast. The Southeast culture area is the semitropical region north of the Gulf of Mexico and south of the Middle Atlantic-Midwest region; it extends from the Atlantic coast west to central Texas. Much of this land once consisted of pine forests, which the Indians kept cleared of underbrush by yearly burnings, a form of livestock management that maintained high deer populations for hunting.

The early history of the Southeast is similar to that of adjacent areas. Cultivation of native plants was begun in the Late Archaic period, about 3000 BC, and populations were high. In 1400 BC a town, called Poverty Point by archaeologists, was built near present-day Vicksburg, Miss. Like the Mississippian towns of 2000 years later, Poverty Point had a large public plaza and huge earth mounds that served as temple platforms or covered tombs.

Populations in the Southeast remained high until European contact. Maize agriculture appeared about 500 BC. Towns continued to be built, and crafted items were widely traded. The first European explorer, the Spaniard Hernando de Soto, marched around the Southeast with his army between 1539 and 1542; epidemics introduced by the Spaniards killed thousands.

Southeastern peoples of historic times include the Cherokee, the Choctaw, the Chickasaw, the Creek, and the Seminole (qq.v.), known as the Five Civilized Tribes because they resembled European nations in organization and economy, and because they quickly incorporated desirable European imports (such as fruit trees) into their way of life. Another famous Southeastern people were the Natchez Indians (q.v.), whose elaborate mound-building culture was destroyed by Europeans in the 18th century.

The First Explorers, by Gregory Perillo. *The great lakes and rivers of the Eastern Woodland area served the Indian nations as arteries of transportation (otherwise hampered by the vast forests) and facilitated further exploration of the land.*

The Plains. The North American Plains are the grasslands from central Canada south to Mexico and from the Midwest westward to the Rocky Mountains. Bison hunting was always the principal source of food in this culture area, until the wild bison herds were exterminated in the 1880s. Most of the Plains peoples lived in small nomadic bands that moved as the herds moved, driving them into corrals for slaughter. From 850 onward, along the Missouri River and other rivers of the central Plains, agricultural towns were also built.

Plains Indians customs have become well known as the stereotyped Indian customs—the long feather headdress, the tepee (tipi), the ceremonial pipe, costumes, and dancing. They are the best-known Indians because European-Americans invaded and conquered them during the 19th century, when newspapers, magazines, and photography popularized the frontier.

Among early Plains peoples were the Blackfoot (q.v.), who were bison hunters, and the Mandan and Hidatsa (qq.v.), who were Missouri River agriculturalists. As European colonists took over the Eastern Woodlands, many Midwest peoples moved onto the Plains, among them the Sioux, the Cheyenne, and the Arapaho (qq.v.). Earlier, about 1450, from the valleys west of the Rockies, some Shoshoni and Comanche (qq.v.) had begun moving onto the Plains. After 1630 these peoples took horses from Spanish ranches in New Mexico and traded them throughout the Plains. The culture of Plains Indians of historic times thus included elements from adjacent culture areas.

The California-Intermountain area. The mountain ridges and valleys of Utah, Nevada, and California resemble one another in the pine forests of the mountains and the grasslands and marshes in the valleys. An Archaic way of life—hunting deer and mountain sheep, fishing, netting migratory birds, harvesting pine nuts and wild grains—developed by 8000 BC and persisted with no radical changes until about AD 1850. Villages were simple, with thatched houses, and in the warm months people often did not bother with much clothing; but the technology of getting, processing, and storing food was sophisticated. Basketry was developed into a true art. On the California coast, people fished and hunted sea lions, dolphins, and other sea mammals from boats; the wealth of resources stimulated a well-regulated trade using shell money.

The Paiute, Ute (q.v.), and Shoshoni are the best-known peoples of the Intermountain Great Basin area; the tribes of California include the Klamath, the Modoc, and the Yurok (qq.v.) in the north; the Pomo, Maidu, Miwok, Patwin, and Wintun in the central region; and the "mission tribes" in the south, given names derived from those of the Spanish missions that conquered them—for example, the Diegueño.

The Plateau region. In Idaho, eastern Oregon and Washington, western Montana, and adjacent Canada, mountains are covered with evergreen forests and separated by grassy valleys. As in the Great Basin, an Archaic pattern of life persisted on the Plateau, but it was enriched by annual runs of salmon up the Columbia, Snake, Fraser, and tributary rivers, as well as by harvests of camas and other nutritious tubers and roots in the meadows. People lived in villages made up of sunken round houses in winter and camped in mat houses in summer. They dried quantities of salmon and camas for winter eating, and on the lower Columbia River, at the site of the present-day city of The Dalles, Oreg., the Wishram and Wasco peoples kept a market town where travelers from the Pacific Coast and the Plains could meet, trade, and buy dried food.

Historic Plateau peoples include the Nez Percé, Wallawalla, Yakima Indians (qq.v.), and Umatilla in the Sahaptin language family, the Flathead Indians (q.v.), Spokan, and Okanagon in the Salishan language family, and the Cayuse (q.v.) and Kutenai (with no linguistic relatives).

The Subarctic. The Subarctic region comprises the major part of Canada, stretching from the Atlantic Ocean west to the mountains bordering the Pacific, and from the tundra south to within about 300 km (about 200 mi) of the U.S. border. The eastern half of this region was once heavily glaciated, and its soil and drainage are poor. No agriculture is possible in the Subarctic because summers are extremely short, and so the region's peoples lived by hunting moose and caribou (reindeer) and by fishing. They were nomadic, sheltering themselves in tents or, in the west, sometimes in sunken round houses (as in the Plateau region). To move camp, they used canoes in summer and sleds in winter. Because of the limited food resources, Subarctic populations remained small; even the summer rendezvous at good fishing spots drew only hundreds, compared to the thousands of persons who gathered at seasonal rendezvous in the Great Lakes or Plains regions.

Impact, by Gregory Perillo. *The acquisition of horses from the Spaniards in the 17th century revolutionized the life of the Plains Indians. It made hunting the bison much easier and enabled them to be swifter, more formidable warriors.*

The indigenous peoples of the eastern half of the Subarctic are speakers of Algonquian languages; they include the Cree (q.v.), the Ojibwa (q.v.), or Chippewa, the Montagnais, and the Naskapi. In the western half live speakers of northern Athabascan languages, including the Chipewyan, the Beaver, the Kutchin, the Ingalik, the Kaska, and the Tanana. Many Subarctic Indians, although now settled in villages, still live by trapping, fishing, and hunting.

Northwest Pacific Coast. The west coast of North America, from southern Alaska to northern California, is the Northwest Coast culture area. Bordered on the east by mountains, the habitable land is usually narrow, lying between the sea and the hills. The sea is rich in sea mammals and in fish, including salmon and halibut; on the land are mountain sheep and goats, elk, abundant berries, and edible roots and tubers similar to potatoes. These resources supported a dense population organized into large villages where people lived in wooden houses, often more than 30 m (100 ft) long. Each house contained an extended family, sometimes with slaves, and was managed by a chief. During the winter, villagers staged elaborate costumed religious dramas, and they also hosted people from neighboring villages at ceremonial feasts called potlatches, at which gifts were lavishly given (*see* POTLATCH). Trade was important, and it extended toward northern Asia, where iron for knives was obtained. The Northwest Coast is known for its magnificent wooden carvings.

Northwest Coast culture developed after 3000 BC, when sea levels stabilized and movements of salmon and sea mammals became regular. The basic pattern of life changed little, and over the centuries carving and other crafts gradually attained great sophistication and artistry. Tribes of the Northwest Coast include the Tlingit, Tsimshian, Haida, Kwakiutl, Nootka, Chinook (qq.v.), Salish, Makah, and Tillamook.

The Arctic. The Arctic culture area rings Alaska and northern Canada, along the coasts. Because winters are long and dark, agriculture is impossible; people live by fishing and by hunting seal, caribou, and (in northern Alaska and eastern Canada), whale. Traditional summer houses were tents. Winter houses were round, well-insulated frame structures covered with skins and blocks of sod; in central Canada the winter houses often were made of blocks of ice. Populations were small because resources were so limited.

Wooden Inuit (Eskimo) mask, representing the spirit of a ptarmigan, from the Kuskokwim region of southwestern Alaska. Masks are worn at religious festivals and on other ceremonial occasions. **Brooklyn Museum**

The Arctic was not inhabited until about 2000 BC, after glaciers finally melted in that region. In Alaska the Eskimo—the Inuit (q.v.) and the Yupik, or Yuit—developed ingenious technology to deal with the difficult climate and meager economic resources. About AD 1000 bands of Alaskan Inuit migrated across Canada to Greenland; called the Thule culture, they appear to have absorbed an earlier people in eastern Canada and Greenland (the Dorset culture). Because of this migration, historic Inuit culture and language are similar from Alaska to Greenland. Living in southwestern Alaska (and the eastern end of Siberia) are the Yupik, who are related to the Inuit in culture and ancestry but whose language is slightly different. Distantly related to the Inuit and Yupik are the Aleuts, who since 6000 BC have remained in their homeland on the Aleutian Islands, fishing and hunting sea mammals. Like the Subarctic Indians but unlike most U.S. Indians, the Inuit, Yupik, and Aleut (q.v.) peoples today retain much of their ancient way of life, because their culture areas are remote from American cities and their lands cannot be farmed.

Mesoamerica. Impressive civilizations developed in Mexico and upper Central America after about 1400 BC. Their ultimate origins were in an Archaic hunting-and-gathering way of life that by 7000 BC included cultivation of small quantities of beans,

Northwest Coast, by Gregory Perillo. *Accomplished canoeists, the people of the Pacific Northwest were also superb wood-carvers, who decorated their fishing craft and erected elaborately chiseled totem poles around their dwellings.*

Rising impressively above the Avenue of the Dead, the Pyramid of the Moon in Teotihuacán served the population of the city and the surrounding Valley of Mexico as a religious and ceremonial center. Waugh–Peter Arnold, Inc.

squash, pumpkins, and maize. By 2000 BC Mexicans had come to depend on their planted fields of these crops, plus amaranth, avocado and other fruits, and chili peppers. Towns developed, and by 1400 BC the Olmec Kingdom boasted a capital with palaces, temples, and monuments built on a huge constructed platform about 50 m (about 165 ft) high and nearly 1.6 km (1 mi) long. The Olmecs lived in the jungle of the east coast of Mexico; their trade routes extended hundreds of miles, both to Monte Albán in western Mexico (modern Oaxaca State) and to the Valley of Mexico in the central highlands. As the power of the Olmecs declined (about 400 BC), these latter centers grew, and by AD 200 the greatest city in pre-Columbian Mexico had developed at Teotihuacán in the Valley of Mexico. From 450 to 600 Teotihuacán dominated Mexico, trading with Monte Albán and with the Mayan kingdoms (*see* MAYA) that had arisen in southwestern Mexico and conquering rivals as far south as the Valley of Guatemala. The capital city covered some 20 sq km (some 8 sq mi) with blocks of apartment houses, markets, many small factories, temples on platforms, and palaces covered with murals.

About 800 Teotihuacán suffered attacks that destroyed its power. Later in the same century many Mayan cities were abandoned, perhaps economically ruined when their trade with Teotihuacán ended. Other Mayan cities, mostly in northern Yucatán, were not so affected. By 1000 in central Mexico, a new power—the Toltecs—began building an empire that extended into the Valley of Mexico and into Mayan territory (*see* ITZÁ). The Toltec Empire collapsed in 1168. By 1433 the Valley of Mexico had regained domination over much of Mexico as a result of an alliance of three neighboring kingdoms. This alliance secured the homeland from which one king, Montezuma I (1390?-1464?) of the Aztecs, began territorial conquests. The empire flourished until 1519, when a Spanish soldier, Hernán Cortés, landed in eastern Mexico and advanced with Mexican allies upon the Aztec capital, Tenochtitlán. Internal strife and a smallpox epidemic weakened the Mexicans and helped Cortés conquer them in 1521 (*see* AZTEC).

At the time of these initial Spanish conquests the native peoples of Mexico included those in the domains of the Aztec Empire and of the powerful kingdoms of the Mixtec (q.v.) rulers in modern Puebla State and the Tarascan (q.v.) in Michoacán State, and of the Zapotec in Oaxaca, the Tlaxcalan in Michoacán, the Otomí in Hidalgo, and the Totonac in Veracruz; the subjects of the remnants of the Mayan state of Mayapán in the Yucatán and of a number of smaller undestroyed Mayan states to the south (*see* QUICHÉ); and many independent groups in the frontier regions, such as the Yaqui, Huichol, and Tarahumara in northern Mexico and the Pipil in the south. After the Spanish conquest—which took more than two centuries to reach throughout Mexico—most of the Indian peoples continued to survive as peasants governed by the Spanish-Mexican upper class.

The culture area of Mesoamerica—Mexico, Guatemala, El Salvador, western Honduras, and western Nicaragua—was one of farming villages producing maize, beans, squash, amaranth, turkeys, and other foods, supporting large city markets where traders sold tools, cloth, and luxury goods imported over long land and sea trade routes. In the cities lived manufacturers and their workers, merchants, the wealthy class, and priests and scholars who recorded literary, historical, and scientific works in native-language hieroglyphic texts (astronomy was particularly advanced). Cities were adorned with sculptures and brilliant paintings, often depicting the Mesoamerican symbols of power and knowledge: the eagle, lord of the heavens; the jaguar, lord of the earth; and the rattlesnake, associated with wisdom, peace, and the arts of civilization.

South America. The culture areas of South America extend from lower Central America—eastern Honduras, Nicaragua, and Costa Rica—to the southern tip of South America. Four principal areas can be distinguished: northern South America, including the Caribbean and lower Central America; the central and southern Andes Mountains and adjacent Pacific coast; the Tropical Forest of eastern South America; and the tip and eastern portion of the narrow southern third of the continent, an area supporting only nomadic hunting-and-gathering peoples.

Northern South America and the Caribbean. The culture area of northern South America and the Caribbean includes jungle lowlands, grassy savannah plains, the northern Andes Mountains, some arid sections of western Ecuador, and the islands of the Caribbean. Given its geographical location, the region might seem to link the great civilizations of Mexico and Peru; but because land travel through the jungles and mountains of lower Central America is difficult, pre-Columbian contacts between Peru and Mexico took place mostly by sea, from Ecuador's Gulf of Guayaquil to western Mexican ports. The native peoples of northern South America and the Caribbean lived in small, independent states. Although they traded directly with Mexico and Peru by way of Ecuador, they were bypassed by the empires.

Finds of Clovislike spearpoints indicate the presence of hunters in the area by 9000 BC; other evidence suggests that people were in the northern region by 18,000 BC. An Archaic style of living continued from the time of the extinction of the mastodons and mammoths, in the Clovis period, until about 3000 BC. About this time, village dwellers developed the cultivation of maize in Ecuador, and of manioc (a tropical tuber) in Venezuela, and pottery making flourished. Also after this date, the Caribbean islands began to be settled. By 500 BC, in towns in some areas of northern South America, distinctive local styles had developed in sculpture and metalwork. Population growth and technological progress continued until the Spanish conquered the region; at that time the Chibcha (q.v.) kingdoms of Colombia were famous for their fine gold ornaments. Around the Caribbean, smaller groups such as the Mískito of Nicaragua, the Cuna (q.v.) of Panama, and the Arawak and Carib (qq.v.) peoples of the Caribbean islands farmed and fished around their villages; Caribs also lived along the coast of Venezuela. These peoples, however, lived a simpler life than did the peoples of the northern Andean states.

Central and southern Andes. The lofty chain of the Andes Mountains that stretches down the western half of South America, together with the narrow coastal valleys between the mountains and the Pacific, were the home of the great civilizations of native South America.

In recent years, excavation at the Monte Verde site in southern Chile has yielded unequivocal evidence of human occupation dating back to 11,000 BC. Excavations farther north, in Peru, show that by 7000 BC beans, including the lima bean, were cultivated, as were chili peppers. A few centuries later the domestication of llamas was begun. Guinea pigs were eventually raised for meat; cotton, potatoes, peanuts, and other foods gradually became part of Peruvian agriculture, and about 2000 BC maize was brought from the northern Andes. The peoples of the Pacific coast, from Chile through Peru into Ecuador, also made use of the rich sea life, which included many species of fish, as well as water birds, sea lions, dolphins, and shellfish.

After 2000 BC peoples in villages in several coastal valleys of central Peru organized to build

A ceramic vessel from the Nazca culture (c. 200 BC–AD 600) of Peru. The double spout connected by a handle bar was a frequent feature of Nazca pottery.
Loren McIntyre–Woodfin Camp & Associates

The sophisticated Nazca artisans made ceramics in varied shapes and decorative patterns, ranging from the stylized parrot at left to the geometric design at right. Nazca ware is noted for its fine palette. Loren McIntyre—Woodfin Camp & Associates

impressive temples of stone and adobe on large platforms. After about 900 BC these temples appear to have served a new religion, centered in the mountain town of Chavín de Huántar. This religion had as its symbols the eagle, the jaguar, the snake (probably an anaconda), and the caiman (alligator), which seems to have represented water and the fertility of plants. These symbols are somewhat similar to those of the Mexican Olmec religion, but no definite link between the two cultures is known. After 300 BC Chavín influence—or possibly political power—declined. The Moche Kingdom then appeared on the northern coast of Peru, and the Nazca on the southern coast. In both, large irrigation projects, towns, and temples were constructed, and extensive trade was carried on, including the export of fine ceramics. The Moche depicted their daily life and their myths in paintings and in ceramic sculpture; they showed themselves as fearsome warriors, but they also made molded ceramic sculptures depicting homes with families, cultivated plants, fishermen, and even lovers. They were also expert metalworkers.

By about AD 600 the Moche and Nazca cultures declined, and two new, powerful states appeared in Peru: Huari in the central mountains, and Tiahuanaco in the southern mountains at Lake Titicaca. Tiahuanaco seems to have been a great religious center, reviving symbols from the Chavín. These states lasted only a few centuries; after 1000, coastal states again became important, especially Chimú in the north, with its vast and magnificent adobe-brick capital city of Chanchan. All Peru was eventually conquered by a state that arose in the central mountains at Cuzco; this was the Quechua (q.v.) state, ruled by an emperor known as the Inca (q.v.) Pachacuti Inca Yupanqui (c. 1391–1471) began large-scale expansion of the empire, and by 1525 Inca rule extended from Ecuador to Chile and Argentina. Civil war raged within the empire from 1525 to 1532. At its conclusion, the Spanish adventurer Francisco Pizarro landed in Peru and had little trouble conquering the war-wasted Inca empire.

The central and southern Andes were then populated by farmers who raised a variety of crops. Local products, transported by llama caravans, were exported and traded between the coast, the mountains, and the eastern tropical jungle. The region's kingdoms were governed by administrators aided by soldiers and priests. Prehistoric Peru had the only great civilization known that did not use writing; but the Peruvians did use the abacus for arithmetic calculations, and they kept numerical records for government by means of abacuslike sets of knotted strings called quipus.

The Tropical Forest. The jungle lowlands of eastern South America seem to have been settled after 3000 BC, for archaeologists have not found evidence of any earlier peoples. Population was always relatively sparse, clustered along riverbanks where fish could be obtained and manioc and other crops planted. Various herbs and foods were cultivated, including hallucinogens for use in religious rituals; these were also exported to Peru. Although animals such as tapirs and monkeys were hunted, little game was supported by the jungle forests. No large towns existed—peo-

South American metalwork. Left, a pendant figurine of gold (AD 1500–50), the work of the Tairona tribe of Colombia. Right, a golden disk (AD 800–1500) from Cocle Province of Panama, probably used as a breast ornament. Brooklyn Museum

ple lived in thatch houses in villages. Sometimes the whole village slept in hammocks, which were invented here. Little clothing was worn, because of the damp heat, but cotton cloth was woven, and the people ornamented themselves with painting. Among the many small groups of the Tropical Forest are the Makiritare, the Yanomamo, the Munducuru, the Tupinamba, the Shipibo, and the Cayapó. Speakers of Arawak and Carib languages—linguistic relatives of Caribbean peoples—also live in the northern Tropical Forest. Although Tropical Forest peoples retain much of their traditional way of life, today they suffer from European diseases and from destruction of their lands by ranchers, loggers, miners, and agribusiness corporations.

Southernmost South America. In Uruguay, Argentina, and Chile, farming peoples such as the Mapuche (Araucanians) of Chile still live in villages and cultivate maize, potatoes, and grains. Although they once kept llamas, after the Spanish invasions, they began to raise cattle, sheep, pigs, and chickens, and used horses for herding and for warfare. Farther south, on the Pampas, agriculture was not suitable; people lived by hunting guanacos and rheas and, on the coasts, by fishing and gathering shellfish. In Tierra del Fuego evidence of this hunting-and-gathering life dates from 7000 BC. On the Pampas, hunting was transformed when the horse was obtained from the Spaniards after AD 1555. The Tehuelche pursued guanacos from horseback, and like the North American Plains Indians, once they had horses for transport, they enjoyed larger tepees as well as more clothing and other goods. Farthest south, around the Strait of Magellan, the

Indians of the Panare tribe in the Venezuelan section of the Guiana Highlands rest in their forest camp. The hammock originated among the dwellers of the jungle.
Jacques Jangoux–Peter Arnold, Inc.

Ona, Yahgan, and Alacaluf lacked the game animals of the Pampas; they survived principally on fish and shellfish, but also hunted seals and sea lions. Nomadic peoples, they lived in small wigwams covered with bark or sealskins. In spite of the cold, foggy climate, they wore little clothing. Tierra del Fuegian life seems to have changed little over 9000 years, for no agriculture or herding is possible in the climate. The native peoples suffered greatly from European diseases, and few survive today.

TRADITIONAL WAY OF LIFE

Among the elements of the traditional ways of life of American Indians are their social and political organization, their economic and other activities, and their religions, languages, and art.

Social and Political Organization. Social organization among American Indians, as among peoples throughout the world, is based on the family of a man and a woman and their children. Some American Indian societies emphasize the economic cooperation of husband and wife, others that of adult brothers and sisters. As among other peoples, men's work has been largely separate from women's work. Women usually took responsibility for the care of young children and the home, and for the cultivation of plants, while men frequently hunted, traveled for trade, or worked as laborers.

American Indian societies also resemble societies elsewhere in that their size and complexity are affected by the economic potential of their environment. Accordingly, the smallest societies are found in regions that are poor in food resources. Examples include the Cree and the Athabascan-language peoples of the Canadian Subarctic, the Paiute of the Nevada desert, and the Ona and Yahgan of Tierra del Fuego. Among these peoples, two or three couples and their children often lived together, hunting, fishing, gathering plant foods, and moving camp several times a year to take advantage of seasonal foods in different localities. During the season when food was most available, usually summer, these small groups would gather together, with several hundred persons spending a few weeks in feasting, trading, and visiting. When agriculture is possible, communities have been larger, from one or two hundred to thousands of persons. In most of the present-day U.S., people lived in villages and formed a loosely organized alliance with nearby villages. The alliance and each village were governed by councils; village councils usually consisted of representatives from each family, and the alliance council was made up of representatives from the villages. The council selected a man or, in some areas (especially the North American Southeast), sometimes a woman to act as chief—that is, to preside over the council and act as principal liaison in dealing with other groups. Often the chief was selected from a family that trained its children for leadership. In many areas families in the villages were linked together in clans, or groups believed to be descended from one ancestral couple. Clans usually owned resources such as agricultural plots and fishing stations; they allotted these as needed to member families and protected their members. Similar societies became common in the Tropical Forest area of South America.

In pre-Columbian times in Mesoamerica and the Andes of South America, kingdoms that had hundreds of thousands of subjects and empires with millions of subjects were established. These societies were stratified, with a large lower class of farmers, miners, and craft workers; a middle class of merchants and officials; and an upper class of rulers who maintained armies and a priesthood. In many of these states, children were educated in formal schools; most children were trained to follow their parents' occupations, but talented youth might be selected for more suitable work. Citizens supported the state religion, although in the empires local religious observances were sometimes permitted to coexist with the state religion. War captives and debtors often became slaves. The Inca state in Peru was tightly organized and controlled, moving persons and even whole villages around the empire to meet its needs. In Mesoamerican kingdoms, on the other hand, clanlike local groups were generally allowed limited power.

On first encountering American Indian societies, Europeans frequently did not understand their organization, which differed in various ways from European types of social organization; subsequently, the native organization was modified by the British or Spanish conquerors. In North America, Europeans failed to recognize the respect and power accorded to women of the Iroquois, Creek, and a number of other peoples. Among the Iroquois, for example, women made the final decisions in major areas of government. In California, Europeans who saw the local upper class living in thatch houses and wearing little clothing failed to understand that the region's Indian communities did have different social classes and highly organized ownership of property. Many descriptions of Indian societies were written after European-Indian wars and epidemics of European diseases had severely reduced populations and disrupted the native societies. Other accounts were written with a particular bias, to support an author's

The Falls at Colville, *by Paul Kane. In the summer the Indians of the Plateau region would camp near the great rivers and catch quantities of salmon by spear and weir. Some of the catch was stored for the winter.* Royal Ontario Museum

ideas of how humans ought to live. Thus, many false stereotypes of American Indians and their societies became common.

Food. Since at least 2000 BC, most American Indians have lived by agriculture. Maize was the most common grain, but certain grainlike plants were also popular, notably amaranth in Mesoamerica and quinoa (of the chenopod family) in the Andes. Several varieties of beans and squash were grown alongside maize; many varieties of potato were cultivated in the Andes; and manioc, a tropical tuber, was raised in the Tropical Forest area of South America. All these plants, as well as peanuts, cotton, cacao (chocolate), avocados, and many others, were domesticated and developed as crops by American Indians.

Livestock was less important to American Indians than to peoples on other continents. In the Andes guinea pigs were bred for meat and llamas for transport and meat, and in Mesoamerica turkeys were domesticated. Protein was often obtained from plants, especially beans. Maize-growing peoples obtained calcium by soaking maize in a lime solution as a step in preparing it to eat. Throughout the Americas additional protein was obtained from fish and game animals, especially deer. Outside Mesoamerica and the Andes, in many American Indian communities game ranges were regularly burned to improve pasture, thereby maintaining favorable conditions for deer and, on the Plains, for bison. In Mesoamerica and Peru, land was too valuable to pasture animals; instead, land was cultivated, intensively irrigated, and, in mountain regions, terraced.

Hunting and fishing techniques were highly developed by American Indians, particularly in regions not suited to agriculture. Traps of all kinds were common. Plains Indians relied on corrals hidden under bluffs or in ravines; herds of bison were driven into the corrals, where they were easily slaughtered. Inuit and Subarctic Indians drove caribou into corrals, or they ambushed them in mountain passes or river fords. Guanacos were similarly hunted in the South American Pampas. Fish were usually taken in nets or weir traps, except in the Northwest Pacific Coast area, where tons of salmon could be speared at the river rapids.

Techniques of food preparation have varied according to the type of food and the culture area. In maize-growing regions, tortillas remain common, as does a similar flat bread of manioc flour in the Tropical Forest. Techniques of drying foods, including meats, have always been important. In pre-Hispanic Mesoamerica and the Andes, nobles indulged in elaborate feasts of richly prepared dishes.

Clothing and Adornment. In their traditional clothing American Indians differed from Europeans in that they placed less importance on covering the body completely. The peoples of warm

Indian Encampment on Lake Huron, *an oil painting by Paul Kane, depicts Ojibwa wigwams made of saplings covered with birch bark.* Art Gallery of Ontario, Toronto

climates, in California and the Tropical Forest, for example, often did not bother with clothing except at festivals; then they adorned themselves with flowers and paint, and often with intricate feather headdresses. In Mesoamerica and Peru, men wore a breechcloth and a cloak knotted over one shoulder, and women wore a skirt and a loose blouse; these garments were woven of cotton or, in Peru, sometimes of fine vicuña wool. North American hunting peoples made garments of well-tanned deer, elk, or caribou skin; a common style was a tunic, longer for women than for men, with detachable sleeves and leggings. Northwest Pacific Coast peoples wore rain cloaks of woven cedar fiber. In the Arctic, the Inuit and Aleuts wore parkas, pants, and boots of caribou or, when needed, of waterproof fish skin. Except in Canada and Alaska, where parkas and coats were worn, American Indians in cold weather usually wrapped themselves in robes, cloaks, or ponchos.

Housing and Construction. Modes of shelter, like food, show adaptation to environment. Some houses that appear simple, such as the Inuit *iglu* or the Florida Seminole chikee, are quite sophisticated: The *iglu* (Inuit, "house"), usually made of hide or sod over a wood or whalebone frame, is a dome with a sunken entrance that traps heat indoors but allows ventilation; the chikee, naturally air-conditioned, consists of a thatch roof over an open platform. The tepee (q.v.) of the Plains Indians constitutes efficient housing for people who must move camp to hunt; tepees are easily portable and quickly erected or taken down, and an inner liner hung from midway up the tepee allows ventilation without drafts, so that the enclosed space is comfortable even in winter.

Some peoples in cold climates that were well supplied with wood, such as the Fuegians and the Subarctic Athabascan-language peoples, relied on windbreaks with good fires in front, rather than on tents. Many other peoples, including some Athabascan tribes as well as Inuit, Californians, Intermountain peoples, and early Southwesterners, spent cold weather in dome-shaped houses that were sunk well into the ground for insulation. Plains farming peoples, including the Pawnee (q.v.) and Mandan, built aboveground dome houses insulated with earth applied over pole frames. The Navajo hogan, a round log house banked with earth, is similar.

Mesoamerican and Andean peoples constructed buildings of stone and cement as well as of wood and adobe. Public buildings and the houses of the upper class were usually built on raised-earth platforms, with a large number of rooms arranged around atria and courtyards. In cities and in the Pueblo towns of the Southwest, multistoried apartment blocks were built.

Trade and Transportation. To all American Indians, trade was an important economic activity. The early empire of Teotihuacán in Mexico was founded on the manufacture and export of blades of obsidian, a natural volcanic glass that made the best stone knives. Several centuries later, the Aztecs organized their conquests by sending merchants into other kingdoms to develop trade, act as spies, and help plan conquest if the foreign ruler failed to give favorable terms to Aztec trade. In the Inca Empire excellent highways were built over difficult mountain terrain in order to move quantities of local specialty products in pack trains of llamas. Trade was also conducted by sea along South America and around Mexico and the Caribbean. Much sea trade was carried in large sailing rafts or, in the Caribbean, in canoes made from huge logs. Trade goods in Mesoamerica and the Andes included foodstuffs, manufactured items such as cloth, knives, and pottery, and luxuries such as jewelry, brilliant tropical bird feathers, and chocolate. Both medicinal and hallucinogenic drugs were widely traded. Goods were bought and sold in large open markets in towns and cities.

Outside the kingdoms of Mesoamerica and the Andes, trade was often carried on by traveling parties who were received in each village by its chief, who supervised business as the people gathered around the trader. In many areas, including California and the Eastern Woodlands, small shells or shell beads—called wampum (q.v.) in the Eastern Woodlands—were used as money. Because traders carried their goods on their backs or in canoes, trade goods were usually relatively light, small items. Furs and bright-colored feathers were valued in trade nearly everywhere. In western North America dried salmon, fish oil, and fine baskets were major trade products, and in eastern North America expertly tanned deer hides, copper, catlinite pipe-bowl stone, pearls, and conch shells were widely traded.

Recreation and Entertainment. The games and amusements of American Indians have had much in common with those of peoples elsewhere. Children traditionally played with dolls and with miniature figures and implements, imitating adult activities; in groups they played tag, the one who was "it" often pretending to be a jaguar or similar animal. Youths and adults played games with balls—rubber balls in Mesoamerica and northern South America, hide or fiber balls elsewhere. The Mesoamerican ball game called *tlatchtli* was somewhat similar to basketball in that it was played in a rectangular court and had the goal of knocking a hard ball through a stone hoop high on the court wall; players, however, were not allowed to use their hands, but only body parts such as the hips and knees. In Mesoamerica these ball games often were seen as rituals of cosmic significance. Lacrosse (q.v.) was popular in the eastern region of North America and eventually was adopted by European settlers. In southern South America a game was played that resembled field hockey. Chunkey, a kind of bowling with a stone disk instead of a ball, was a favorite in the Midwest. Hoop-and-pole, in

A train of llamas near Cuzco, Peru. Even as it was in the days of the Inca Empire, the llama is still widely used for transportation in the Andean mountain area.
Ted Gruen–Bruce Coleman, Inc.

The Great Serpent Mound, near Peebles, Ohio, is the crowning achievement of the Adena, an obscure people of almost 3000 years ago. Although not a burial mound, the earthwork was probably associated with funerary rites. Tony Linck–Shostal Associates

which players throw sticks at a rolling hoop, was played throughout most of the Americas.

Guessing games, with the players trying to guess where a token piece is hidden, continue to be popular among North American Indians, but are not common in South America; players usually sing and beat a rhythm, trying to confuse their opponents. In both North and South America games of chance using dice are still played, and the Aztecs of earlier times had a board game similar to the modern game of Parcheesi.

Competitions—in foot racing, wrestling, archery, and, after the Spanish invasions, horse racing—were generally popular, as were variants of snow snake, in which a smooth stick is slid along a course. Minor amusements that are still popular include cat's cradle, in which a symbolic string figure is constructed on the player's fingers, and the use of tops and swings.

Religion and Folklore. American Indian religious beliefs and practices display great diversity. As among other peoples, educated and philosophical persons may hold beliefs that differ from those of most people living in the same community; this was also true in the past.

The Mexican and Andean nations, the peoples of the North American Southwest and Southeast, and some Northwest Coast peoples had full-time religious leaders as well as shrines or temple buildings. Peoples of other areas had part-time priests and generally lacked permanent temples. Part-time priests and shamans (faith healers, who often also used medicinal plants to cure; *see* SHAMAN) learned to conduct ceremonies by apprenticing themselves to older practitioners; in the larger nations priests were trained in schools attached to the temples. In some regions religious leaders formed fraternal orders to train initiates and share knowledge; examples include the Ojibwa of the Eastern Woodlands and the Pawnee of the Plains.

Most American Indians believed that in the universe there exists an Almighty—a spiritual force that is the source of all life; many Indians continue in this belief, because native religions have tended to become fused with Christianity or to persist alongside it. The Almighty of Indian belief is not pictured as a man in the sky; rather, it is believed to be formless and to exist throughout the universe. The sun is viewed as a manifestation of the power of the Almighty, and Europeans often thought Indians were worshiping the sun, when, in fact, they were addressing prayers to the Almighty, of which the sun was a sign and symbol.

In many areas of the Americas, the Almighty was recognized in several aspects: as light and life-power, focused in the sun; as fertility and strength, centered in the earth; as wisdom and the power of earthly rulers, observed in creatures such as the jaguar, the bear, or snakes. In most places in the Americas, religious devotees enhanced their ability to perceive aspects of the Almighty, sometimes by using hallucinogenic plants (*see* PEYOTISM), or sometimes by fasting and singing prayers until they achieved a spiritual vision. In northern and western North America, most boys and many girls were sent out to stay alone, fasting and praying until they thought they saw a spirit that promised to help them achieve the power to succeed in adult life. Shamans among the Inuit, along the Northwest Coast, in South America, and in some other areas went into trances, believing that their souls could then battle evil spirits or search the earth for the wandering souls of sick patients.

Most American Indian peoples have myths in which a time is described when the earth was not as it now appears, and during which it became transformed by the actions of legendary persons, or animals who spoke with humans. Unlike many Europeans, American Indians tend not to consider humans entirely different from animals and plants; instead, they often believe that other beings are like humans and that all are dependent on the life-giving power of the Almighty. Some Indian myths, such as, on the Plains, the Mandan myth of Lone Man, describe a wise leader who teaches the arts of life to the people; others, such as the California-Intermountain myths about Coyote, describe foolishly clever antics.

American Indians generally have shown less interest in an afterlife than have Christians. Indians have traditionally tended to assume that the souls of the dead go to another part of the universe, where they have a pleasant existence carrying on everyday activities. Souls of unhappy or evil persons might stay around their former homes, causing misfortunes. Many Indian peoples celebrated an annual memorial service for deceased relatives; in Latin America this observance later became fused with the Christian All Souls' Day.

Both private prayer and public rituals are common among American Indians. Individuals regularly give thanks to the Almighty; communities gather for symbolic dances, processions, and feasts. The Sun Dance (q.v.) of the Plains Indians is an annual summer assembly at which a thousand or more usually scattered people meet to fast and pray together, praising and beseeching the blessings of the Almighty. The Pueblos of the Southwest, like the Iroquois of the Eastern Woodlands, continue to observe a yearly cycle of festivals: In spring they pray for good crops; in autumn they celebrate the harvests (for an example of a recurring festival, *see* SNAKE DANCE). Various tribes used certain ritual objects (such as the long-stemmed pipe used by priests in North America to blow tobacco-smoke incense) to symbolize the power of the Almighty; when displayed, these objects reminded people to cease quarrels and remember moral obligations.

The folktales (q.v.) of Indians, as well as their myths, frequently express ideas about the nature

Reconstruction of a northwestern village at Hazelton, B.C. The houses are made of split wooden planks, their gables decorated with carvings; in front, the ever present totem poles, bearing heraldic symbols of the people whose home they mark.
S. J. Kraseman–Peter Arnold, Inc.

of humans, other creatures, and the universe. Among the Mexican nations, detailed historical records are maintained; elsewhere, in general, no sharp distinction was drawn between history and legend. Many Indian folktales are fables, pointing out a moral; others are simply exciting or amusing stories. Translations of Indian stories and myths—like descriptions of native religious beliefs and ceremonies—seldom capture the full Indian meaning; a nonnative reader is rarely aware of the background of ideas that native listeners brought to a story or ceremony.

Warfare. The common belief that American Indians were extremely warlike arose because, when Europeans first came into contact with them, the Indians were usually defending their homelands, either against European invaders or against other Indians supported by European invaders. Archaeological evidence of fortifications, occasional destroyed towns, and men killed in battle indicates, however, that Indian wars did take place before the European invasions.

Most American Indians fought in small groups, relying on surprise to give them victory. The large nations of Mexico and Peru sometimes relied on surprise attacks by armies, but their soldiers also fought in disciplined ranks. The Aztecs fought formal battles called "flower wars" with neighboring peoples; the purpose was to capture men for sacrifice (the Aztecs believed that the sun would weaken if it were not fed with human blood). Other Indian peoples, including many in present U.S. territory, conducted war raids to obtain captives, but these captives were used as slaves, rather than as victims for sacrifice. Some Indian battles were fought for revenge. The most common cause of war between Indian groups was probably to defend or enlarge tribal territory.

Before the Spanish colonizations, warfare was conducted on foot or from canoes. Both the Mexican and the Andean nations, as well as smaller Indian groups, employed hand-to-hand combat with clubs, battle-axes, and daggers, as well as close-range combat with javelins hurled with great force from spear-thrower boards (atlatls). Bows and arrows were used in attacks, and fire arrows could be effective against thatched-house villages. When the Spanish brought riding horses to the New World, Indians in both North and South America developed techniques of raiding from horseback.

Languages. About a thousand distinct languages are presently spoken by Indian peoples in North and South America, and hundreds more have become extinct since first European contact. In many areas, among them the Intermountain and Plateau regions of North America, people often spoke not only their native language but also the languages of groups with whom they had frequent contact. In various cases one language served as a lingua franca for a multilingual region; examples include Tucano (western Amazon area) and Quechua (Andean region). Some regions had a traders' language or pidgin (q.v.), a simplified language or mixture of several languages, helpful to traders of different native languages; among these were Chinook Jargon (Pacific Coast, North America), Mobilian (U.S. Southeast), and lingua geral (Brazil). Linguists have grouped many of the Indian languages into roughly 180 families, but many other languages have no known relatives; scholars differ in proposing more distant relationships among families. Grammatical traits, sound systems, and word formation often vary from family to family, but families in a given region often influence one another. *See* AMERICAN INDIAN LANGUAGES.

Crafts and the Arts. Distinctive craft needs and artistic styles characterize each culture area of the Americas. Nearly all the major technologies known in Europe, Asia, and Africa in the 16th century were known also to American Indians before European contact, but these technologies were not always used in the same way. For example, although the Andean nations had superb metallurgists, they made few metal tools (people used stone tools for most tasks); instead they applied their skills to creating magnificent ornaments. In architecture, the Maya built a few true (keystone) arches, but for roofing their buildings, Mayan architects preferred not the true arch but the narrow corbeled vault. *See also* PRE-COLUMBIAN ART AND ARCHITECTURE.

Stonework. The earliest American art known to archaeologists is flint knapping, or the chipping of stone. Between about 9000 and 6000 BC, stone spear and dart points of sharp beauty, such as the Folsom and Eden points, were produced with great skill. Although flint knapping eventually declined somewhat in other culture areas, in Mesoamerica the art of chipping flint and, especially, obsidian continued to be highly prized. In the Late Archaic period, after 3000 BC, the pecking and grinding (rather than chipping) of stone developed into art. In the region that is now the eastern U.S. lovely small sculptures, particularly of birds, were made as weights for spear-thrower boards. Between about 1500 and 400 BC in Mesoamerica, the Olmec made small ornaments of semiprecious stones, as well as fine naturalistic stone sculptures in the round that were close to or larger than life size. Jade was a favorite stone of the Olmec, and it continued to be carved throughout Mesoamerican prehistory. Northwest

The Indians of the California-Intermountain area raised basketry to the level of art. Clockwise, beginning at the left, are baskets woven around the turn of the century by the Pima, Yokut, Apache, Pima, Pomo, and Maidu peoples.
Courtesy of ACA American Indian Arts, New York

Coast Haida carvings in argillite and modern Inuit soapstone carvings are examples of the continuing expression of American Indian art through stone.

In architecture, the pre-Hispanic Andean nations developed stone masonry to a high degree, fitting smoothed stone blocks together so expertly that no mortar was needed for walls that have stood for more than a thousand years. The Mesoamerican peoples also built in stone, and they preferred to cover their buildings in stucco plaster and adorn them with murals.

The ancient Peruvians excelled as weavers, and this miniature shirt from the Tiahuanaco culture (AD 600–1000) bears witness to their skills. Brooklyn Museum

Pottery. The earliest pottery in the Americas was made about 3500 BC. By 2000 BC several known styles of ceramics had emerged, and in the wares of the following centuries everyday cooking pottery can be distinguished from fine serving pieces. Among outstanding styles are the Mayan vessels painted with scenes of royalty and mythology; the molded vessels of the Moche culture of Peru, reproducing objects and scenes from daily life as well as images from mythology; and the pottery of the Pueblos of the U.S. Southwest, painted in geometric or stylized naturalistic designs. *See* POTTERY.

Basketry. Ever since its beginnings as an Archaic-period art in the Americas (by about 8000 BC or perhaps earlier), basketry continued to develop, reaching its finest levels of achievement in western North America. There, baskets became a true art form, prized as objects of wealth when of highest quality. In most parts of the Americas several basketry techniques were known, among them weaving, twining, and coiling; decorative techniques included embroidery and the use of bright feathers, shells, and beads.

Weaving. Throughout the Americas weaving of one kind or another was practiced, but the craft reached its highest development in the Andean nations. In ancient South America twining seems to have been in use earlier than true weaving, and this early technique continued in use in both North and South America for bags, belts, and other items. Almost as widespread as twining was the use of the backstrap loom, in which the tension on the threads is maintained as the weaver leans against a strap attached to the lower ends of the warp threads (the upper ends are attached to a hanging bar). On this simple loom a skilled weaver can make extremely fine, although narrow, textiles. Heddle looms appeared in Peru after about 2000 BC, allowing wider cloth to be woven (a heddle is a mechanism that raises and lowers the warp threads in the pattern required). Peruvian weavers, using cotton as well as llama and vicuña wool, produced some of the finest textiles known, from filmy gauzes to double-faced brocades. Into their fabrics the Indian weavers sometimes wove feathers or ornaments of precious metal, shell, or beads. The Aztec emperor and the Inca wore cloaks completely covered by brilliant feathers of rare birds, or by gold. *See also* NEEDLEWORK.

A woman's wedding dress from Alaska, made of caribou skin, with appliqué decoration. Inuit clothes are a perfect answer to harsh environment. Brooklyn Museum

Metalworking. In North America, in the upper Midwest, copper had been beaten into knives, awls, and other tools in the Late Archaic period (c. 2000 BC), and since that time it had been used for small tools and ornaments. The use of copper in this region, however, was not true metallurgy, because the metal was hammered from pure deposits rather than smelted from ore. The earliest metallurgy in the Americas was practiced in Peru about 900 BC, and this technology spread into Mesoamerica, probably from South America, after about AD 900. Over the intervening centuries a variety of techniques developed, among them alloying, gilding, casting, the lost-wax process, soldering, and filigree work. Iron was never smelted, but bronze came into use after about AD 1000. Thus, copper and, much later, bronze were the metals used when metal tools were made; more effort, however, was put into developing the working of precious metals—gold and silver—than into making tools.

The best-known modern American Indian metalwork is that of Navajo and Hopi silversmiths; their craft began when they adopted Mexican silver-working techniques in the mid-19th century.

Work in other materials. Among hunting peoples leather was used extensively for clothing, tents, shields, and containers (quivers, baby carriers, food storage, sheaths, ritual paraphernalia). In North America leather clothing was often embroidered with dyed porcupine quills. After European trade began, quill embroidery gave way to decoration with glass beads. Indians in eastern North America copied embroidery designs of the French, and they substituted silk threads for quills and moose hair.

Wood carving was a widespread craft among American Indians. The Northwest Coast Indians developed a truly distinctive art style in their wood carvings, with variations from tribe to tribe; the most famous examples of this style are its totem poles, tall logs carved and painted to represent the noted ancestors of a clan and figures from mythology.

Bark was employed in several Indian crafts. In northeastern North America it was used for roofing, canoes, and containers; along the Northwest Coast, shredded cedar bark was woven into rain capes and ornaments; in South America bark was beaten in a felting process into a kind of cloth; and in Mexico bark pulp was made into paper.

Among Southwestern peoples such as the Navajo, Pueblo, and Yumans, pollen, pulverized charcoal and sandstone, and other colored powdery materials are distributed over a ground of sand to create symbolic sand paintings that are used in healing rites and then destroyed (see Music, below). In the 20th century a number of Indian artists in Canada and the U.S. have adopted tempera, watercolor, and oil painting, using both traditional imagery and modern Western styles. The Northwest Coast Indians and the Inuit have also adapted traditional pictorial styles to printmaking.

Music and Dance. In North America six distinctive musical styles or regions have been recognized: Inuit and Northwest Coast; California and nearby Arizona; the Great Basin; Athabascan; Plains and Pueblo; and Eastern Woodland. The music of northern Mexico has much in common with that of western Arizona; farther south, however, in the regions of the Mesoamerican and Andean civilizations, complex musical cultures existed. Little information has been preserved about the music of these civilizations, and whatever remains of the original styles survived the Spanish conquest principally in the form of highly complex and varied blends of native and assimilated Spanish elements. Elsewhere in South America the aboriginal music, like that of North America, was relatively insulated from non-Indian influence; the South American music, however, has been less extensively studied than that of North America.

Instruments and vocal styles. Among the persisting aboriginal styles of the Americas, singing is the dominant form of musical expression, with instrumental music serving primarily as rhythmic accompaniment. Exceptions occur, notably the North American love songs that men play on flutes. The Indians of South America tend to use a softer singing voice than those of North America, whereas a tense vocal production is characteristic east of the Rocky Mountains.

Throughout the Americas the principal instruments have been drums and rattles (shaken in the hand or worn on the body), as well as flutes and whistles. In Mesoamerica and the Andes, greater variety exists; the pre-Hispanic ensembles of the Aztecs are known to have included, besides rattles and drums, double and triple flutes, trumpets played in harmony in pairs, rasps, and the slit-drum (*teponaztli*), a resonant, carved hollowed log struck with a stick. In Panama and the Andes, panpipes continue to be played in harmony. Instruments have often had ritual or religious significance; among some Brazilian tribes, for example, women must not view the men's flutes. In North America the tambourinelike frame drum, and in South America the maraca rattle, were frequently played by shamans.

Inuit and Northwest Coast. The Inuit and the peoples of the Northwest Coast use more complex rhythms than are common elsewhere in North America, and on the Northwest Coast, songs may have more complex musical forms and may use exceptionally small melodic intervals (a semitone or smaller). Northwest Coast dance dramas are lengthy, elaborate productions with magnificent costumes and tricky props, and the songs for these dramas are carefully taught and rehearsed. Inuit dance and costumes are simpler, possibly because their communities are smaller, and the dances often feature men using the forceful movements of harpooning while women sing accompaniment.

California and the Great Basin. The singing of the Indians of California and the Great Basin is produced by a more relaxed throat than that of other North American musical areas. The melodies and texts, however, are like those found elsewhere in North America in that the songs are short (although they may be repeated or combined into series) and the texts are often brief sentences. Such texts tend to refer to myths, events, or emotions, rather than telling stories, and sections of text may alternate with song sections sung to meaningless syllables. Listeners must know the background to appreciate the poetry and meaning of a song. Both social dances and costumed ritual dances are found in the Great Basin and in California, where they are more elaborate. Some California (and western Arizona, particularly Yuman) music is characterized by a rise in pitch in the middle section of a song. Songs of the Great Basin often have a structure consisting of paired phrases.

Athabascan music. The music of the Athabascan peoples—those of northwestern Canada and Alaska as well as the Navajo and Apache of the Southwest—is characterized by melodies that have a wide range and an arc-shaped contour, and by frequent changes in meter; falsetto singing is prized. Costumed ritual dances are unusual except among the Apache, who, like the Navajo, have been influenced by the Pueblos. Much Navajo music belongs to healing rituals designed to restore patients to harmony by seating them in beautiful sand paintings while they listen to poetic songs.

Plains and Pueblo music. The music of the Great Plains is the best known of the North American Indian styles and is the source of the musical styles heard at present-day powwows (social gatherings, often intertribal, featuring Indian dancing). Singing is in a tense, pulsating, forceful style; men's voices are preferred, although a high range and falsetto are valued. Melodic ranges are wide, and the typical melodic contour is terrace shaped—beginning high, and descending as the

Bull Dance of the Mandan Indians *(1832), by George Catlin. The ceremonial dance was performed to secure a good bison hunt, the braves dancing individually, executing symbolic steps.* Smithsonian Institution

song progresses. Plains music is often produced by a group of men sitting around a large double-headed drum, singing in unison and drumming with drumsticks (at powwows, the group itself is called a drum). In Plains dancing, men usually dance solo with bent body (several may dance at once, independently), but there are also ritual dances with symbolic steps and social round dances for couples. The Pueblos add some lower-voiced music; they make more use of chorus, and they perform elaborate costumed ritual dances (often with clowns that entertain between serious dances).

Eastern Woodland styles. Eastern Woodland music resembles Plains music, but it tends to have narrower melodic ranges, and Eastern singing makes use of polyphony (multipart music) as well as forms that are antiphonal (with alternating choruses) and responsorial (with alternating solo and chorus). Dances include men's solos, as well as ritual dances and social round dances. In the Stomp Dance of the Southeast, a snakelike line of dancers follows a leader who calls out in song and is answered by the followers.

Mexico and the Andes. Almost no archaeological evidence exists for prehistoric music in the Americas; all that is known from pre-Hispanic civilizations is a few preserved instruments (such as panpipes and ocarinas in Peru) and painted or carved scenes of musicians and dancers. In Mexico and Peru at the point of European contact, the nobles and the temple personnel maintained professional performers. In Mexico officials organized rituals for each month, with hundreds of richly costumed, carefully rehearsed dancers and musicians. Responsorial singing was practiced; sophisticated scales and chords were apparently used, and compositions seem to have been formally structured, with variety in melody and in combinations of meters. Secular dramas with professional actors were also produced, and bards composed epics. The harps, fiddles, and guitars found in the Indian music of present-day Mexico and Peru were taken from the Spanish.

Other South American areas. Elsewhere in South America, where the indigenous music persisted, it was relatively unaffected by European music. The pentatonic (five-note) scale of the Incas spread to some other regions, but earlier scales of three or four notes also survived. Polyphonic singing developed in some areas, notably in Patagonia. Flutes are still sometimes played in harmony, and the music of some Tropical Forest peoples is often a complex combination of voices, percussion, and flutes.

See also ANTHROPOLOGY; ARCHAEOLOGY. A.B.K.

EUROPEAN CONTACT AND IMPACT

Those first Europeans to step ashore in the New World—whether in San Salvador (West Indies), Roanoke Island (North Carolina), or Chaleur Bay (New Brunswick)—were enthusiastically welcomed by the copper-hued indigenes. The natives regarded their white-complexioned visitors as something of a marvel, not only for their outlandish dress and beards and winged ships but even more for their wonderful technology—steel knives and swords, fire-belching arquebus and cannon, mirrors, hawkbells and earrings, copper and brass kettles, and so on. It was the remarkable paraphernalia that dazzled.

Initial Reaction to Europeans. Nonetheless, the Europeans themselves—Spanish, French, and English alike—were soon recognized by the Indians as very human. Indeed, 16th- and 17th-century Indians very often regarded Europeans as rather despicable specimens. The early records are full of harangues by disenchanted natives on European character flaws. Whites, for instance, were constantly accused of being stingy with their wealth and avaricious in their insatiable desire for beaver furs and deer hides. Likewise, Indians throughout the hemisphere were amazed at European intolerance for native religious beliefs, sexual and marital arrangements, eating habits, and other customs. They would scoff at the Europeans for living out of a book—the Bible—and for not doing their own thinking. Even European architecture came under fire: Indians thought it absurd to build permanent structures of wood and stone, thus precluding movement. Even village- and town-dwelling tribes recognized the need to relocate when local game, fish, and especially firewood gave out.

White people, in short, seemed attuned to another world; they appeared to be oblivious to the rhythms and spirit of nature. Nature to the Europeans—and the Indians detected this—was something of an obstacle, even an enemy. It was also a commodity: A forest was so many board feet of timber, a beaver colony so many pelts, a herd of buffalo so many robes and tongues. Even the Indians themselves were a resource—souls ripe for the Jesuit, Dominican, or Puritan plucking. It was the Europeans' cultural arrogance, coupled with their materialistic view of the land and its animal and plant beings, that the Indians found repellent. Europeans, in sum, were regarded as something mechanical—soulless creatures who wielded diabolically ingenious tools and weapons to accomplish mad ends.

Relations with the Colonial Powers. The Spanish, declared the 19th-century U.S. historian Francis Parkman, "crushed the Indian," the English "scorned and neglected him," but the French "embraced and cherished him." Although poetically appealing, the characterizations are oversimplified.

In truth, no people agonized more over the

A meeting between Portuguese explorers and the natives of Brazil, as depicted in a line engraving (1592) by Theodore de Bry. Granger Collection ethics of conquest than 16th-century Spaniards. Distinguished Spanish jurists and humanists argued at length over the legality of depriving the Indians of their land and coercing them to submit to Spanish authority, over the morality of dragooning Indians to work for Spanish plantation and mine owners—in short, over the justice of Spanish relations with *los indios.*

"We came here to serve God, and also to get rich," announced a member of the conquistador Hernán Cortes's entourage, and that essentially summed up the Spanish outlook. Both programs, the commercial and the religious-humanist, needed the Indians in order to be successful. The conquistadors and other profit-oriented adventurers wanted their land and labor; the priests and friars laid claim to their souls and minds. Ultimately, both programs were destructive to the Indian victims. The first robbed them of their freedom and health and, in many cases, their lives; the second deprived them of their culture.

The situation was considerably more benign in Canada, where French commercial interests centered on the fur trade. Indians were vital suppliers of beaver, otter, muskrat, mink, and other valuable pelts. It would have been ruinous to have mistreated such business partners. It was also unnecessary, as the lure of trade goods was sufficient incentive for the native hunters to transport the pelts to Montréal, Trois-Rivières, and Québec.

Another factor favoring the independence enjoyed by Canadian Indians was the French need for allies in their wars with the British—both to the south, in the thirteen colonies, and to the north, on the shores of Hudson Bay. European powers took the Indian auxiliaries very seriously.

Things were not nearly so congenial in the thirteen English colonies. The French tended to regard the Indians as equals and intermarriage as acceptable, but the English were not so inclined. English scorn for the Indians (Parkman was correct in that respect) no doubt derived in large measure from the tensions and friction generated by land transfers. Unlike the French in Canada, the English settled the Atlantic seaboard of the present-day U.S. on a relatively massive scale, and in the process displaced the Indians. Moreover, the Indians were not nearly as important to the English economy as they were to the French. The result was that the English generally viewed them as an obstacle to progress and a nuisance—except when war with France threatened; at such times Indian support or neutrality was purchased with outlays of gifts and other blandishments.

The Ravages of Disease. The rumor among the Indians in New Spain (the Spanish viceroyalty north of present-day Panama) was that the mere sight and smell of a Spaniard was enough to send an Indian to the grave—a wry bit of humor not far from the truth. In 1492 the Caribbean, Mexico, Central America, and Andean South America were among the most densely populated regions of the hemisphere. Yet, within a span of several generations, each experienced a cataclysmic population decline. The culprit was largely microbial infection: eruptive diseases such as smallpox, pulmonary ailments, and gastrointestinal disorders, all of which had been unknown in the pre-Columbian New World. The American Indian was immunologically unprimed to deal with this most insidious conqueror.

The destruction was especially visible in Latin America, where great masses of susceptible individuals were congregated in cities such as Tenochtitlán and Cuzco, not to mention the innumerable towns and villages dotting the countryside. More than anything else, it was the appalling magnitude of death that prompted a vigorous debate in Spain and New Spain over the morality of conquest.

As the native population in the Caribbean plummeted, Spaniards resorted to slave raids on the mainland of La Florida to bolster the work force. When the time came that this, too, proved inadequate, they took to importing West Africans to work the cane fields and silver mines. The Indians, it seemed, simply could not be kept alive, especially in the West Indies.

Those who did survive were often assigned (commended) en masse, as an entire village or community, to a planter or mine operator to whom they would owe all their services. The encomienda system, as it came to be known, amounted to virtual slavery. This, too, broke the spirit and health of the Indians, making them all the more vulnerable to the Europeans' diseases.

Death from microbial infection was probably not as extensive in the Canadian forest, where most of the natives lived as migratory hunter-gatherers. Village farmers, such as the Huron north of Lake Ontario, did, however, suffer serious depopulation in waves of epidemics—epidemics that may have been occasionally triggered by Jesuit priests and their lay assistants, who had established missions in their midst.

Wars and Enforced Migrations. Without a doubt, Canadian Indians suffered fewer dislocations than did their brethren in Latin or English America. This can be partly explained by the nature of the fur trade, the leading business in Canada well into the 19th century, which militated against settlement; the idea was to maintain the wilderness so that fur-bearing animals would continue to flourish. Furthermore, French settlement in Canada was restricted to a thin line of seigneuries and villages along the banks of the Saint Lawrence and lower Ottawa rivers. The French, in short, were simply not interested in moving the Indians off vast tracts of land, a fact that the latter appreciated. This demographic and commercial legacy continues to be felt in Canada, where numerous Indian groups may be found living in more or less traditional manner, at least for part of the year.

In contrast, English-Indian relations in the 17th and 18th centuries were marked by a series of particularly vicious wars, all of them won by the English, who exercised the moral and military mandate of victory to insist that the vanquished tribesmen submit to English sovereignty and either confine their activities to strictly delimited tracts of land near areas of English settlement or move out beyond the frontier.

Disease was also a grim reaper in the American colonies, where the majority of the Eastern Woodlands people lived as village farmers. Withered by smallpox, hammered in war, and constantly harassed by back-country Scotch-Irish and other settlers, many of the coastal Indian groups gathered together their remnants and sought refuge west of the Appalachians.

Relations with the U.S. One of the problems confronting the young American nation was what to do with the Indian tribes, particularly those in the Old Northwest (today called the Midwest) and South. The Treaty of Paris (1783), which formally ended the American Revolution, had made no mention of the Indians, reflecting Britain's ambiguous jurisdiction over them. The U.S. would have to chart its own course, which it did in Article I, Section 8, of the Constitution: "The Congress shall have Power . . . To regulate Commerce with foreign Nations, and among the several States, and with the Indian Tribes." Here was the organic law from which more than 200 years of federal legislation and programs would derive.

In the closing years of the 18th century, Americans were responding to the siren song of the land companies and streaming across the Alleghenies and the Blue Ridge into the Ohio Valley, Kentucky, and Tennessee—areas where various Indian nations were still intact and strong. Once there, many whites simply squatted on Indian land, with the predictable result: war. A series of battles culminated in 1794 in Gen. Anthony Wayne's victory at Fallen Timbers in northwestern Ohio; it was followed, a year later, by the forced Treaty of Greenville, establishing a defi-

Overwhelmed by Gen. Anthony Wayne's cavalry and bayonet charge, the Indians of the Old Northwest were routed at the Battle of Fallen Timbers on Aug. 20, 1794.
Granger Collection

The Trail of Tears, a painting by Robert Lindneux. The forced march of the Cherokee nation to the West in 1838 took the lives of thousands, who perished from hunger and hardship.
Granger Collection

nite boundary between Indian territory and white settlement.

The Trade and Intercourse Acts. These were difficult years for the fledgling government. Dominated by easterners, who were far removed from the brutality and anxieties of the trans-Appalachian frontier, the Congress was genuinely interested in pursuing a just and humane policy toward the Indians. This was the rationale behind the passage of the Trade and Intercourse Acts, a series of programs at the turn of the century aimed at reducing fraud and other abuses in commerce with the Indians. The Congress sought to extinguish Indian title to land through peaceful negotiation before white settlement.

Fate, however, seemed to have decreed otherwise. Washington policymakers and eastern humanitarians could not control the frontier. To the frontier dwellers in Kentucky or Ohio, the Indians were vermin to be exterminated. Providence, many believed, had ordained that the white should overcome the red, that Anglo-Saxon stock should push west until it could go no farther. The Indians' day had passed; America would now reverberate to the sound of the homesteaders' axes, cattle, and plows—the clatter of progress. It was progress to dispossess the Indians of their land, which had lain idle for millennia. Americans would break the soil and use it.

The Indians were thus regarded as an anachronism—irreclaimable children of the forest by some, particularly those west of the Appalachians, and redeemable savages by many eastern philanthropists and humanitarians. It was the latter group, which included President Thomas Jefferson, that sought to incorporate the Indians into the mainstream of U.S. society by means of an ambitious, largely church-operated educational program. Education would civilize the savage. The goal was to convey the virtues of the independent yeoman farmer to the tribespeople, in the hope that they would emulate them.

The Removal Act. The project was ill-conceived and culturally chauvinistic. By the 1820s even its staunchest defenders were admitting defeat. Many put the blame on the Indians' ingrained degeneracy coupled with the powerful vices of the frontier. Thus, the thing to do was to remove "the noble red man" beyond the Mississippi, west of the line of frontier settlement, to the recently acquired (1803) Louisiana Territory. Beyond the Mississippi, where many naively felt white settlement would never penetrate, the Indians could then travel the road to civilization at their own pace. They would be free of white hostility and pressures to run them off their land, free of the debauchery of the frontier barroom, free to hunt, trap, and farm as they pleased—free to live as they chose.

The Indian Removal Act was passed in May 1830; it empowered the president of the U.S.—Andrew Jackson, at the time—to move eastern Indians west of the Mississippi, to so-called Indian Territory (now essentially Oklahoma). Although it was supposed to be voluntary, removal became mandatory whenever the federal government felt it necessary. The memory of brutal forced marches west, sometimes in the dead of winter, remained vivid for years to come in the minds of many of its victims—those who survived. To many in the North, where support for the removal idea was at best tepid, the whole scheme represented yet another outrage against humanity committed by slaveholding southerners. Removal would be another wedge separating the North from the South.

By midcentury, as it became increasingly clear that U.S. expansion was going to swallow up the trans-Mississippi West as well, the removal concept was further refined into the reservation idea. As wagon trains clattered west along the Oregon, Santa Fe, Mormon, and California trails, invading the Great American Desert (the Plains), Washington officialdom concluded that the vast, unspecified tracts of Indian territory would have to be more sharply defined, as reservations. And when resident Indians sought to thwart that westward expansion, the same Washington officialdom decided that they were to be rounded up by the U.S. Army and glued to these reservations by force—and the dole. That, in essence, was the point of the celebrated Plains Indian Wars, which raged during the last half of the 19th century, ending, poignantly, with the slaughter of Sioux men, women, and children, as well as the U.S. 7th Cavalry, at Wounded Knee (q.v.), S.Dak., shortly after Christmas 1890.

The Allotment Act. By that time, Americans had achieved their manifest destiny: They had settled the continent all the way to the Pacific. The frontier era had ended. Well before that date, however, it had become clear to many that a new policy had to be adopted toward the Indians, whose dwindling numbers made them appear on the brink of extinction. The government would have to act quickly and decisively to rescue them. Congress began moving in this direction in 1871, when it unilaterally decided to abandon the treaty process and simply legislate on the Indians' behalf. Whereas a century before they had

Grim-faced cavalrymen look on as local officials dump the bodies of hundreds of Oglala Sioux into mass graves. The Indians were slaughtered by the 7th U.S. Cavalry at Wounded Knee, S.Dak., on Dec. 29, 1890, in the last major clash between Indians and the U.S. Army. Montana Historical Society

functioned as sovereign nations, American Indians were now wards of the U.S. government.

The new plan to rescue the vanishing Indians called for an aggressive assault on tribalism by the simple expedient of parceling out communally owned reservation land on an individual, or severalty, basis. The plan, called the Dawes Act, or General Allotment Act, went into effect in 1887, with the enthusiastic support of many well-meaning but misguided friends of the Indians: philanthropists, humanitarians, reformers, and social scientists. Hundreds of thousands of acres remaining after the individual 160-acre allotments had been made were then sold at bargain prices to land-hungry or land-speculating whites.

Allotment, designed to absorb the Indians into mainstream America, turned out to be a monumental disaster. In addition to losing their "surplus" tribal land, many Indian families lost their allotted land as well, despite the government's 25-year period of trusteeship. The poorest of the nation's poor—many of them now landless and the majority still resisting assimilation—American Indians reached rock bottom in their population shortly after the turn of the 20th century. Mired thus, the Congress granted these original Americans citizenship in June 1924.

White Stereotypes of Indians. Europeans never did understand the American Indian. Nor do white Americans today. The U.S., as a nation, has never really grasped the complexity and genius of the Indian's thought-world—a mythic place of talking animals, of magic, of dreams and songs and visions, a Corn Mother, a salmon people, and other beings. Instead, all of this was arrogantly dismissed as juvenile and superstitious—in other words, as primitive. The primitive Indian, equipped with a rudimentary technology (the logic of which eluded whites) and a child's mind, is surely the most fundamental and ancient of all white stereotypes of the Indian.

Those who were courageous and wise and selfless were dubbed noble—the noble savage—a contradiction in terms. By the early 19th century, however, noble savages were a vanishing breed, as James Fenimore Cooper reminded readers in *The Last of the Mohicans* (1826). All that was left, it seemed, was the dregs: the disheveled, snake-eyed, beggarly survivor who hung around the frontier outpost—the drunken Indian. By the end of the century even the drunken Indian seemed on the verge of extinction, and there was much sober talk and head-shaking about "Lo, the poor Indian." Far from vanishing, however, the Indian eventually turned up in Hollywood as a breechclothed Plains warrior in a B-grade Western. Finally, in the 1960s, as the Hollywood cliché faded, the Indian emerged as the model ecologist, hero of the ecology and counterculture movement.

Flattering or unflattering, the images are all caricatures. White culture as a whole has yet to discover and appreciate the world of the American Indian. C.Ma.

INDIANS IN CONTEMPORARY SOCIETY

The Native American population in the U.S. has increased steadily in the 20th century; by 1990 the number of Indians, Aleuts, and Inuits (Eskimos) was almost 2 million, or 0.8 percent of the total U.S. population. Slightly more than one-third of these people live on reservations; about half live in urban areas, often near the reservations. The U.S. government holds about 23 million ha (56 million acres) in trust for 314 federally recognized Indian tribes and bands in the form of reservations, pueblos, rancherias, and trust lands. There are 278 Indian reservations in 35 states. The largest reservation is the Navajo (mostly in Arizona), with nearly 6.4 million ha (16 million acres) with more than 140,000 people; the smallest is the state reservation of Golden Hill in Connecticut, with 0.1 ha (0.25 acre) and 6 people. In Alaska the situation is different (see below: Self-determination).

Tribal Sovereignty. The most fundamental distinction that sets Indian tribes apart from other U.S. minority groups is their historic existence as self-governing peoples, whose nationhood preceded that of the U.S. As nations, they signed treaties with colonial authorities and later with the U.S. government, and today, on what remains of their former lands, they continue to function as separate governments within the federal framework.

The U.S. has long acknowledged a special "government-to-government" relationship with the recognized Indian tribes and with the Alaskan Native Villages. Also, the federal government is deemed to have a trust relationship with Indian people, which means that the U.S., in return for vast tracts of Indian lands, assumed contractual and statutory responsibilities to protect remaining Indian lands and to promote the health, welfare, and education of the tribal occupants.

20th Century U.S. Policies. In practice, the federal government, as trustee, has subjected the tribes to bewildering policy switches, often without their consent, as new theories have caught the fancy of Washington officialdom.

The Indian Reorganization Act. The passage of the Indian Reorganization Act (1934) signaled the end of the "Allotment Era," during which it had been hoped that Indians could be coaxed or coerced to abandon their traditional tribal ways and to assimilate into mainstream America. Assimilationists never doubted that Western civilization was superior to tribal cultures; great emphasis was placed on the need to "civilize" and to teach Christianity to the tribes. To this end, young Indian children were sent to distant government- or church-run boarding schools, often thousands of miles from the "detrimental" influences of their home reservations.

With the Indian Reorganization Act, U.S. policy took a dramatic swing and acknowledged the continuing force and value of tribal existence. The "Indian New Deal," ushered in by the reform-minded commissioner of Indian affairs, John Collier (1884–1968), put an end to further allotment of lands. Tribes were encouraged to organize governments under the terms of the Indian Reorganization Act and to adopt constitutions and by-laws, subject to the approval of the U.S. Department of the Interior.

The act further provided for the reacquisition of tribal lands and established preferential hiring of Indians within the U.S. Bureau of Indian Affairs. Tribes were authorized to set up business corporations for economic development, and a credit program was established to back tribal and individual enterprises.

The termination period. Implementation of the Indian Reorganization Act slowed considerably after the U.S. entered World War II in 1941, and in the postwar period a new policy was formulated—that of terminating federal trust responsibility to Indian tribes. Whereas earlier the assimilationists had envisioned a time when tribal entities and reservations would disappear because of inevitable assimilation, the proponents of termination decided the time had come to legislate them out of existence. Arguing that Indians should be treated exactly as all other citizens, Congress resolved in 1953 to work toward the withdrawal of all federal support and responsibility for Indian affairs.

In the next two decades—the termination period—federal services were withdrawn from about 11,500 Indians, and federal trust protection removed from 600,000 ha (1.5 million acres). The land was often sold and the proceeds divided among tribal members. A few years after their termination (1961), the Menominees of Wisconsin, the largest tribe so treated, were almost totally dependent on welfare.

In 1970 President Richard M. Nixon officially repudiated termination as a policy. The need to reevaluate federal Indian policy once again became evident, as Indian activists staged public protests—first with their occupation (1970) of Alcatraz Island in San Francisco Bay, then with their occupation (1972) of the Bureau of Indian Affairs in Washington, D.C., and finally with their 71-day armed siege (1973) at Wounded Knee.

Self-determination. In the 1970s, Indian demands that they be given greater authority over their own lives and reservations led to a new federal policy, encouraging Indian self-determination. Still in effect, this policy in many ways reflects the earlier goals of the Indian Reorganization Act; its most significant feature is the emphasis on tribal administration of federal Indian programs, including health, education, and welfare, law enforcement, and housing.

Displaying renewed self-confidence, Indian tribes have increasingly resorted to federal court actions to test the extent of their jurisdiction on reservations and to assert long-ignored treaty rights to land, water, and off-reservation hunting and fishing. Congressional efforts have also led to the return of many Indian religious sites to tribal possession, including the sacred Blue Lake of the Taos Pueblo.

The Alaska Native Land Claims Settlement Act of 1971 resolved long unsettled claims of that state's Inuit, Indian, and Aleut population, with a cash settlement of $962 million and 16 million ha (40 million acres) of land. The act established 12 Native Regional Corporations and more than 200 Native Village Corporations to manage the land and money. Many observers feared that this act might eventually—as did the Allotment Act of 1887—result in the loss of much land to nonnatives. In 1988 Congress passed amendments to correct flaws in the act, thus diminishing the risk that most corporations and their land will be controlled by nonnatives. The amendments do not address native sovereignty or subsistence rights. Sections of the native community continue to be concerned as to whether the amendments adequately protect long-term control of the land.

Many eastern tribes initiated land claims in the 1970s, based on an obscure law from 1790, and in 1980 Congress agreed to a settlement providing three Maine tribes with 120,000 ha (300,000 acres) and a $27 million trust fund. The U.S. government also established a procedure whereby tribes not recognized as such could petition for review of their nontribal status.

North American Indians Today. Statistics of health, education, unemployment rates, and income levels continue to show Indians as disadvantaged, compared to the general population. In the 1980s, federal government policies have led to budget cuts for social and welfare services on the reservations.

The Indians are now increasing faster than any other group in America, and pride in their tribal

Wilma Mankiller, at left, became the first woman principal chief of the Cherokees in 1985.
© T. Campion–Sygma

heritage has survived government efforts to discourage them; on many reservations tribal languages and religious ceremonies are enjoying renewed vigor. Traditional arts and crafts, such as Pueblo pottery and Navajo weaving, are still pursued, and some contemporary Indian artists, such as Fritz Scholder (1937–) and R. C. Gorman (1933–), have successfully adapted European styles to their paintings and prints of Indian subjects. The strength of the Native American narrative tradition can be felt in the poetry and novels of the Indian writer N. Scott Momaday (1934–), who won a Pulitzer Prize in fiction for his *House Made of Dawn* (1969). Other prestigious contemporary Indian writers include Vine Deloria (1933–), best known for his indictments of U.S. Indian policy, *Custer Died for Your Sins* (1969) and *Behind the Trail of Broken Treaties* (1974); novelists James Welch (1940–) and Leslie Marmon Silko (1948–); and William Least Heat-Moon (1939–), author of the widely popular *Blue Highways: A Journey into America* (1983), an account of his travels in the United States.

Latin American Indians. The Indian population of Latin America is estimated at 26.3 million, of whom 24 million live in Bolivia, Ecuador, Guatemala, Mexico, and Peru. Generally classified as campesinos, or peasants, the vast majority live in extreme poverty in remote rural areas where they eke out subsistence living from the land. Indian campesinos make up 60 percent of the total population of Bolivia and Guatemala. In all of Latin America, only Uruguay has no remaining indigenous population.

Only 1.5 percent of the total Indian population is designated as tribal, mainly in Brazil, Colombia, Panama, Paraguay, and Venezuela. Many of the tribal groups live in the remote jungle environment of the Amazon Basin, where they subsist by hunting, fishing, and gathering manioc and other roots. Current Brazilian expansion into the Amazon, however, threatens the physical and cultural survival of the Amazon tribes, as diseases brought by outsiders decimate the Indian populations, and mineral exploration and highway construction destroy tribal hunting grounds.

The largest unacculturated Brazilian tribe today is the Yanomamo, numbering more than 16,000 people, for whom the Brazilian government plans to create a special park where they may be protected. Anthropologists estimate that they would need at least 6.4 million ha (16 million acres) to continue their traditional life-style.

The total indigenous population of Latin America includes slightly more than 400 different Indian groups, with their own languages or dialects. They live in vast extremes of climate and conditions, like North American Indians, ranging from the Amazon jungle to the heights of the Andes, where one group, on Lake Titicaca, subsists on artificial islands of floating reeds. S.L.C.

For further information on this topic, see the Bibliography in volume 28, sections 117, 643, 645, 665–66, 727, 1105–9, 1119–21.

AMERICAN KENNEL CLUB (AKC), nonprofit organization devoted to maintaining standards for the breeding and showing of dogs. The AKC, founded in 1884, is made up of over 400 clubs throughout the U.S. It recognizes breeds (130 currently), registers individual purebred dogs upon application, establishes rules for dog shows and trials, and generally promotes interest in pedigreed animals.

At its New York City headquarters, the AKC maintains one of the world's most complete reference libraries on dogs and issues several publications, among them the monthly magazine *Pure-Bred Dog—American Kennel Gazette.*

AMERICAN LABOR PARTY (ALP), organized in New York State in 1936. In the presidential elections of 1936, 1940, and 1944 it supported the Democratic party candidate, Franklin D. Roosevelt. The right wing of the party seceded in May 1944 to form the Liberal party, contending that Communists had infiltrated into and seized control of the parent organization. In July 1948, the ALP was part of the coalition that founded the Progressive party, of which it subsequently became a part. It retained its original name, however. The ALP was dissolved in October 1956.

AMERICAN LAW INSTITUTE, organization that seeks "to promote the clarification and simplification of the law and its better adaptation to social needs, to secure the better administration of justice, and to encourage and carry on scholarly and scientific legal work." Founded in 1923, with headquarters in Philadelphia, the institute is managed by a council of 42 judges, lawyers, and law teachers.

The institute published its first *Restatement of the Law,* in 22 volumes, in 1944; this was subsequently revised. In deciding cases, courts increasingly use the law recorded in the *Restatement.* Since 1944 the institute has published a model code of evidence, a uniform commercial code, a model penal code, studies on federal income and on estate and gift taxation, and a study of the division of jurisdiction between state and federal courts.

AMERICAN LEGION, organization of U.S. veterans of World Wars I and II and of the Korean and Vietnam wars, chartered in 1919.

The legion aided in World War II by assisting in war bond drives, blood bank contributions, and civilian defense programs; by upholding government foreign policy; and by supporting army and navy strategy. Similar services were provided during the Korean and Vietnam wars. Exerting considerable political influence, the legion lobbied for veterans' legislation such as the G.I. Bill of Rights, for the construction of government veterans' hospitals, and for pensions and other benefits for veterans and their families.

The peacetime program in general is directed to upholding the U.S. Constitution. To this end, the legion sponsors annual youth-training programs to teach the principles of American self-government and awards medals to encourage scholarship and leadership among elementary and high school students.

Affiliated with the organization is the American Legion Auxiliary for women of veterans' families. National headquarters of the American Legion is in Indianapolis, Ind.

AMERICAN LIBRARY ASSOCIATION (ALA), a nationwide library association founded in Philadelphia in 1876 and comprising mainly librarians, library trustees, and persons and organizations interested in the improvement of library facilities. Among the objectives of the association are promoting professional library training, improving library service, and encouraging the use of books and libraries.

Activities of the ALA include international coordination of library resources, making awards for distinguished service in librarianship, administering prizes for outstanding publications, and publishing books, films, and periodicals relating to the library field. It establishes standards for education for librarianship and accredits graduate library schools. The activities of the ALA are carried on by various divisions, each of which is concerned with a particular phase of library work, for example, the Association for Library Service to Children.

The ALA, with a related organization, the Special Libraries Association, has contributed considerably to the evolution of the modern library movement. Throughout its early years it advocated public access to library collections, circulation of books for home reading, extension of library service to rural areas, and municipal, state, and federal aid to libraries. In 1939 the ALA adopted the Library Bill of Rights (amended in 1961 and 1967), endorsing the right of libraries and readers to freedom of choice in reading materials.

The publications of the ALA include the monthly *American Libraries,* the official bulletin of the association; *The Booklist,* a book and film selection guide; and *Choice,* a book selection guide for college libraries. The ALA currently numbers about 43,000 members worldwide; headquarters is in Chicago.

AMERICAN LITERATURE, literature written in the English language by inhabitants of the U.S.; it includes the literature written by residents of the 13 original colonies.

COLONIAL AND PREREVOLUTIONARY PERIOD

The first American literature is generally considered certain accounts of discoveries and explorations in the New World that frequently display the largeness of vision and vigor of style characteristic of contemporary Elizabethan writers. Such qualities are evident in the work of Capt. John Smith, the first great figure in American letters. His *Generall Historie of Virginia, New-England, and the Summer Isles* (1624) had the enormous vitality of much English prose in the epoch of the King James Bible.

This rich energy diminished as literature, especially in the New England colonies, became preoccupied with theology. A religious explanation for every event was eloquently provided. Among the notable works in this vein are *History of Plimmoth Plantation* (posthumously pub. 1856) by William Bradford, an early governor of Plymouth Colony and *The History of New England* by John Winthrop, earliest governor of the Massachusetts Bay Colony, first published in relatively complete form in 1853. The vast theological work *Magnalia Christi Americana* (1702), subtitled *The Ecclesiastical History of New England From Its First Planting,* by the Puritan clergyman Cotton Mather was, in spite of its awkward style and didacticism, a masterpiece of religious scholarship and thought. Cotton Mather was the author of more than 400 printed works, and his father, Increase, also a clergyman, wrote about 100.

A countervoice was that of Thomas Morton (c. 1590–c. 1647), an English adventurer in America, who in *The New English Canaan* (1637) expounded the point of view of an early rebel against Puritanism.

Modern readers have probably found more of interest in the accounts of Indian wars and of captivities. Notable among the former are narratives such as *A Brief History of the Pequot War* by the English colonist John Mason (1600?–72), edited in 1736 by the historian Thomas Prince (1687–1758). Among the many published reports about colonists captured by Indians, perhaps the most celebrated is the narrative by Mary Rowlandson (1635?–78?).

Much pious verse was written during the early colonial period. The first book printed in the colonies, in fact, was a hymnal, *The Whole Book of Psalmes Faithfully Translated into English Metre* (1640), better known as the *Bay Psalm Book;* this was the work of three New England clergymen, Richard Mather, John Eliot, and Thomas Weld (1595–1661). The most remarkable colonial poets were Anne Bradstreet (*The Tenth Muse Lately Sprung Up in America,* 1650); Edward Taylor, whose exceptionally fine *Poetical Works* was first published in 1939; and the clergyman Michael Wigglesworth, whose once-popular poem *The Day of Doom* (1662) recounts in ballad meter the end of the world from a firmly Calvinist viewpoint.

The literature of the colonies outside New England was generally of a less theological cast. Present-day readers may still be amused by the wit and satire of *A Character of the Province of Maryland* (1666) by George Alsop (b. 1638), an indentured servant; and they will be charmed by *A Brief Description of New York* (1670) by the publicist Daniel Denton (fl. 1670). Other writings of this period may be found in the collection edited by Albert C. Myers, *Narratives of Early Pennsylvania, Delaware, and West Jersey, 1630–1708* (1912).

With the 18th century, interest moved to more secular, practical problems. The work of the Puritan theologian Jonathan Edwards remains significant, however. Popularly associated with his sermon "Sinners in the Hands of an Angry God" (1741), Edwards is distinguished for his clarity of expression in such metaphysical works as *A Faithful Narrative of the Surprising Work of God* (1737) and *Freedom of the Will* (1754).

Two names commonly associated with provincial life illustrate the growing secularism of American writing. The first is William Byrd, a plantation owner; his *History of the Dividing Line* (written 1738, first pub. 1841) has remained a humorous masterpiece, and his even more belatedly published diaries, *Secret Diary* (1941), and *Another Secret Diary* (1942), are comparable to the work of his near contemporary, the English diarist Samuel Pepys. The other, greater name is that of Benjamin Franklin, whose masterly unfinished *Autobiography* has become a classic of world literature. His letters, satires, "bagatelles," almanacs, and scientific writings are the writings of a great citizen of the world.

The earliest known work by a black American writer is "Bar's Fight, August 28, 1746," 28 lines of verse by Lucy Terry (1730–1821). Shortly afterward came the poem "An Evening Thought; Salvation by Christ, with Penitential Cries" (1760) by a slave, Jupiter Hammon (1720?–1800). The African-born poet Phillis Wheatley, the servant of a tailor's wife in Boston before her release from slavery, was the first black American to receive considerable critical acclaim as a writer. Her collection *Poems on Various Subjects: Religious and Moral* (1773, London) is predominantly religious in tone.

THE REVOLUTION AND AFTER

The brilliance of American thought between the

Phillis Wheatley Culver Pictures, Inc.

accession of King George III in 1760 and the creation in 1789 of a federal government is notable in intellectual history.

Revolutionary Period. The writings of the American statesmen of the period deserve to be read, as the monumental *Literary History of the American Revolution* (1897) by the historian Moses Coit Tyler (1835–1900) makes evident. Better known to the modern reader is the famous series of papers known as *The Federalist,* written in 1787–88 by the statesmen John Jay, James Madison, and Alexander Hamilton, whose cogent defense of the new U.S. Constitution still offers one of the most persuasive arguments on behalf of constitutional government.

Although American literature did not achieve full maturity in the 18th century, its scope was widened. The first newspaper, *Publick Occurrences,* appeared in Boston in 1690; its one edition was suppressed by colonial authorities because it did not have a license. Fourteen years later the journalist John Campbell (1653–1728) founded the *Boston News-Letter.* The first magazines appeared in 1741 in Philadelphia, when the printer Andrew Bradford (1686–1742) founded the *American Magazine* and Benjamin Franklin established the *General Magazine and Historical Chronicle.* Toward the end of the century, amid the tumult of the American Revolution, several notable writers emerged, particularly the propagandist Thomas Paine, whose pamphlets *Common Sense* (1776) and the 12 issues of *Crisis* (1776–83) awakened American enthusiasm for independence. Paine, however, lost favor in America when he published in London *The Age of Reason* (1794–96), which argued against Christianity—but also against atheism. An important political satire was the mock epic *M'Fingal* (1775–82) by the lawyer and poet John Trumbull. The most versatile and sensitive poet of the period was Philip Freneau, whose "The House of Night" (1779) was a powerful exercise in Gothic romanticism.

The Interesting Narrative of the Life of Gustavus Vassa, the African (1789, London), regarded as the fullest and most penetrating account of an 18th-century black man's life, was the first published autobiography by a black American. It is attributed to Olaudah Equiano (c. 1750–97), a slave who bought his freedom, settled in England, and afterward became active in the antislavery movement.

Postrevolutionary Period. During the administration of President George Washington one literary center of the new nation was Hartford, Conn., where a group of young writers, including the clergyman Timothy Dwight and the poets John Trumbull and Joel Barlow (1754–1812), became known as the Hartford Wits. They wrote in many forms, including the epic, but only their lighter verse is still read. Of greater later significance was the emergence at this time of the American novel, as exemplified by *The Power of Sympathy* (1789), a sentimental work by the writer William Hill Brown (1765–93), and *Modern Chivalry* (1792–1815) by the poet and novelist Hugh Henry Brackenridge (1748–1816), a realistic and satirical account of frontier manners. The romances of the novelist and journalist Charles Brockden Brown, which were popular in Europe, included *Wieland; or, The Transformation* (1798),

Alexander Hamilton, painting by his contemporary John Trumbull. Courtesty of The New-York Historical Society, New York City

Arthur Mervyn (1799-1800), and *Edgar Huntly* (1799). Strange compounds of Gothic terror and pseudoscience, they point to the work of Edgar Allan Poe and Nathaniel Hawthorne.

THE 19TH CENTURY

The years from 1815 to 1861 have been called the "First National Period." The phrase is useful, for imaginative energies, gathering force after the War of 1812, reached a climax in the 1850s, during which more first-class literary work was produced than in any previous decade. In American history the Civil War was a dividing line between the simpler antebellum days and the more troubled industrial postwar period. Most of the leading prewar writers lived on, but after 1865 they had little new to say.

Early 19th Century. The literary task before the young nation was to prove that it had attained cultural maturity. Proof was sought in opposite ways. Anticipating the position later developed by the essayist Ralph Waldo Emerson and the poet Walt Whitman, some writers argued that a radical political experiment should be matched by a radically new literature. Others, however, especially in Boston, thought that American writers should seek to meet European standards. Although little literature of lasting value was produced in Boston in the opening decades of the epoch, *The North American Review,* long an influential literary quarterly, was founded there in 1815. In New York City, the main center of those who wanted to create a new literature, the first three important creators of an indigenous but still cosmopolitan American literature worked: Washington Irving, William Cullen Bryant, and James Fenimore Cooper.

The writing of Washington Irving retains its charm and deserves to be more widely read. In *A History of New York, by Diedrich Knickerbocker* (1809) he gave New York City its legendary father, travestied conventional histories with consummate skill, and rivaled Franklin in urbanity. In *The Sketch-Book of Geoffrey Crayon, Gent.* (1819-20), particularly in the story of Rip Van Winkle and the legend of Ichabod Crane, Irving further enriched American mythology. Although distinctly American, Irving's writing preserved the style of 18th-century English prose, especially perhaps that of the British writer Oliver Goldsmith, whose biography Irving wrote in 1849. Like Goldsmith, he turned to history, interpreting the Spain of Ferdinand V and Isabella I in *The Alhambra* (1832). With diminished success he wrote about the Far West, as in *A Tour of the Prairies* (1835). His work includes also substantial biographies of Christopher Columbus (1828) and George Washington (5 vol., 1855-59).

William Cullen Bryant, although born in New England, in 1825 went to live in New York City, where his best-known poem, "Thanatopsis" (1817), had already established his fame. In his long career he wrote verse and fiction, books of travel, an important work on the theory of poetry, and faithful translations of Homer. He edited the *New York Evening Post* from 1829 to his death in 1878, defending the abolitionists in the newspaper's pages. Present poetical fashions are exactly contrary to Bryant's stately rhetoric, and he has been somewhat unfairly demoted to a minor place in American literature.

James Fenimore Cooper was the first American author after Franklin to achieve a worldwide reputation. The great Leatherstocking series of novels (*The Pioneers,* 1823; *The Last of the Mohicans,* 1826; *The Prairie,* 1827; *The Pathfinder,* 1840; *The Deerslayer,* 1841) form a prose epic of the conquest of America. Endless forests and lonely waters, hunters, Indians, and hostile Europeans provided a setting for the exploits of the hero, the wilderness scout Natty Bumppo. Cooper's sea novels, of which *The Pilot* (1823) is most often read, were superior to those by his predecessors. Social, political, economic, and religious issues in American life are evident in his work, as in the trilogy known as the *Littlepage Manuscripts* (1845-46). He was a great, if uneven, genius, and Europeans such as the French novelist Honoré de Balzac and, more recently, the English novelist D. H. Lawrence readily acknowledged his power.

Among those who wrote with a greater consciousness of European traditions were the Cambridge poets, so called because of their attachment in one way or another to Harvard College. Henry Wadsworth Longfellow, the best-known member of this cosmopolitan group, appealed to the religious, patriotic, and cultural yearnings of the middle class. He translated works from many European languages (his *The Divine Comedy of Dante Alighieri,* 3 vol., 1865-67, is admirable), wrote exquisite short poems of religious and moral sentiment, and became the foremost American writer of sonnets of the century. In a series of narrative poems on American themes, for example, *Evangeline* (1847), *The Song of Hiawatha* (1855), and *The Courtship of Miles Standish* (1858), Longfellow sought to dignify and elevate life in the New World.

The literary reputation of the physician and writer Oliver Wendell Holmes has faded; nevertheless, in verse and prose, especially in the 12 essays titled *The Autocrat of the Breakfast-Table* (1858), he helped liberate the American mind

The jacket of an 1872 edition of The Last of the Mohicans, *by James Fenimore Cooper, illustrated by Felix Darley, depicts the frontier scout Natty Bumppo and his Indian friend Chingachgook.* Granger Collection

from the tyranny of the Puritan theologians. The poet and critic James Russell Lowell, once regarded as an American counterpart to the German poet Johann Wolfgang von Goethe, is important historically. His lively *Biglow Papers* (first series, 1848; second series, 1867), his great patriotic document known familiarly as "The Harvard Commemoration Ode," and his collection of critical essays, such as *Among My Books* (first series, 1870; second series, 1876), broadened and enriched the national mind. Associated peripherally with the Cambridge group was the poet John Greenleaf Whittier, who wrote the well-known poem "Snow-Bound" (1866) and many religious lyrics, and who vigorously denounced the slave-holders in poems such as "Massachusetts to Virginia" (1843).

During the early and mid-19th century, with the intensification of the slavery issue in the U.S., most of the writing produced by black Americans was concerned with dramatizing the immorality and agony of slavery and refuting the romanticized, antebellum vision of slavery as presented by a host of white Southern writers of the so-called plantation tradition. Outstanding works concerned with the question of slavery are the three autobiographies of the great abolitionist Frederick Douglass, written at different times in his life. The first, *Narrative of the Life of Frederick Douglass, an American Slave,* was published in 1845 just after Douglass had escaped from slavery in Maryland. This was followed by enlarged versions in 1855 (*My Bondage and My Freedom*) and in 1881 (*Life and Times of Frederick Douglass,* final rev. 1882). Another important work is *The Condition, Elevation, Emigration, and Destiny of the Colored People of the United States* (1852), by Martin Robinson Delany (1812–85), who is now considered by some historians as the first major black nationalist.

The historian, novelist, and playwright William Wells Brown (1816–84), who escaped from slavery in 1834, wrote the first novel by a black American, *Clotel; or, The President's Daughter* (1853, London). The theme of *Clotel,* miscegenation, or racial intermarriage, thereafter was dealt with frequently by other 19th-century authors who, like Brown, were torn between their African heritage and a need for roots in the U.S.

Looking back at the 19th century, modern readers generally prefer the writers who sought more radical solutions to cultural problems. Foremost were the essayists Ralph Waldo Emerson and Henry David Thoreau and the novelists Nathaniel Hawthorne and Herman Melville. In his famous address "The American Scholar" (1837) Emerson did more than repudiate a genteel cosmopolitanism; he proclaimed an exhilarating philosophy of idealistic individualism that is evident in the book *Nature* (1836), the "Address at Divinity College" (1838), the *Essays* (first series, 1841; second series, 1844), and *Representative Men* (1850). Although philosophies similar to his had been developed in Germany and in Great Britain, Emerson spoke with an American accent.

Thoreau's writings may have been less broad in range than Emerson's, but *Walden; or, Life in the Woods* (1854) is presently more widely read than anything of Emerson. Thoreau's essay "Civil Disobedience" (1849) has had worldwide political influence, and "Life Without Principle," compounded from passages in Thoreau's journal and published posthumously in 1863, is one of the great statements of the idea that without integrity the individual perishes. Emerson disliked slavery, but Thoreau actively opposed it, and Thoreau's writings are still used to controvert the kind of slavery that reduces human beings to parts of a machine.

The greatness of Hawthorne and of his masterly novel *The Scarlet Letter* (1850) is secure, but critics continue to study and interpret his character and his literary purpose. Many 19th-century readers took him at his own ironic valuation as a dreamy romantic; later knowledge has altered the picture of the dreamer into that of the sardonic commentator on public event and private character. The enigma of evil is central to many stories in the collections *Twice-Told Tales* (first series, 1837; second series, 1842) and *Mosses from an Old Manse* (1846); as it is to the novels *The House of the Seven Gables* (1851), *The Blithedale Romance* (1852), and *The Marble Faun* (1860).

More drastic has been the modern reevaluation of Herman Melville. Known originally as the man who lived among the cannibals, from the adventures recounted in his first novel, *Typee: A Peep at Polynesian Life* (1846), he puzzled his contemporary readers with the romance *Mardi* (1849) and still more with his masterpiece, *Moby-Dick; or, The White Whale* (1851); *Pierre: or the Ambiguities* (1852) was a complete failure. Forgotten in the second half of the 19th century, Melville was discovered again during the 20th. As with Hawthorne, the problem of evil is central to Melville's work, most explicitly so in the short novel *Billy Budd, Foretopman* (not pub. until 1924); but this conception of evil is so shrouded in myth and allegory that critics disagree about its personal significance, in terms of the writer's life and about its broader meaning.

The poet, critic, and short-story writer Edgar Allan Poe was one of the major figures of the first half of the century. Although a southerner, Poe was not preoccupied with the life and history of the South. Poe simultaneously inhabited the world of journalism and a weird and lonely universe of his own imagining, characterized by relentless logic and a haunting sense of anguish. In his criticism Poe was capable of extreme partiality and extreme severity. His poetry profoundly affected the development of French symbolist verse, and his short stories, such as *Tales of the Grotesque and Arabesque* (1840), are among the triumphs of romantic horror. He launched the American detective story with "The Murders in the Rue Morgue" (1841), "The Purloined Letter" (1844), and other tales. His poem "The Raven" (1845) has grown so familiar it has lost some of its appeal, but poems such as "Ulalume" (1847) have kept their inexplicable magic of image and music.

The opposite of Poe in virtually every respect, the poet Walt Whitman, after much unsuccessful writing, produced in 1855 the first version of *Leaves of Grass,* which he continued to expand until 1882. To this volume all else that he wrote—*Drum-Taps* (1865), *Democratic Vistas* (1871), *Specimen Days & Collect* (1882), and

Edgar Allan Poe Granger Collection

much else—is subsidiary. Of his books he wrote, "Who touches this touches a man," and the man was bombastic, affirmative, self-involved, yet mystical and sensitive. Whitman's exuberance dictated the creation of a new, unrestrained verse form. The long, rhythmic lines, the heaping up of details, the affirmation of mystic identity with all that exists were intended to celebrate the spiritual strength in the democracy of "powerful uneducated persons."

The American Civil War and the Later 19th Century. President Abraham Lincoln humorously described Harriet Elizabeth Beecher Stowe, author of the novel *Uncle Tom's Cabin* (1852), as "the little woman who caused this big war." The work, weak perhaps as literature, was powerful as propaganda and expressed the deep antislavery feeling of the North. Lincoln himself can be included in the roster of significant American writers because of the measured succinctness of his occasional prose. Profoundly moved by the tragic conflict of the Civil War, he turned American oratory away from the ornate rhetoric of the statesman Daniel Webster to the inspirational simplicity of his address at Gettysburg (1863) and of his second inaugural address (1865). No other American public figure has quite equaled Lincoln's command of forceful, accurate, and inspiring prose.

After the war, many new writers emerged, especially in fiction. Among the forces that brought about change in American literature at that time were the increasing concentration of publishing houses in a single city, New York; new schemes for the manufacture, sale, and distribution of printed matter; the effectiveness of the public school systems, which created a larger reading public; the wider teaching of English literature and of foreign languages and literatures; and the increasing effectiveness of literary periodicals. The decades following 1870 were the golden age of the American magazine; the single instance of the prestigious and influential *Atlantic Monthly* magazine, founded in 1857, four years before the Civil War, is interesting. James Russell Lowell, its editor, appealed for stories emphasizing what came to be known as local color, and local color dominated the writing of the 1870s and the 1880s.

From the South, fiction by the authors George Washington Cable (*Old Creole Days,* 1879), Joel Chandler Harris (*Uncle Remus, His Songs and Sayings,* 1880), and the painter and writer Francis Hopkinson Smith (1838–1915), author of *Colonel Carter of Cartersville* (1891), presented a sentimental picture of life in the Confederacy. The name of Kate O'Flaherty Chopin (1851–1904), a Louisiana-born author, may be added here or to the late 19th-century realists discussed below. Her last novel, *The Awakening* (1899), realistically depicts Creole life and a woman's struggle for both independence and fulfillment.

Walt Whitman Granger Collection

Best known of a group of able women who wrote of New England life, Sarah Orne Jewett wrote many short stories about Maine people, such as those collected in *The Country of the Pointed Firs* (1896). California was the setting of the stories of Bret Harte, whose *The Luck of Roaring Camp and Other Sketches* (1870) has been called the "father of Western local-color stories."

Local color also appeared in poetry; the works of Joaquin Miller and James Whitcomb Riley, who wrote about the Midwest, are characteristic of this trend.

From 1865 to 1910 poetry largely was in a state of decline. The taste of the period was summed up in the standard collection *An American Anthology, 1787–1899* (1900) by the conservative critic Edmund Clarence Stedman (1833–1908). Of more interest to modern readers are the works of the leading southern poet Sidney Lanier, whose best-known poems are "The Marshes of Glynn" (1879) and "The Revenge of Hamish" (1878); the philosopher George Santayana, who also wrote exquisitely crafted poetry (*Sonnets and Other Verses,* 1894); or Paul Laurence Dunbar, whose *Lyrics of a Lowly Life* (1896) brought him national attention. Emily Dickinson, now recognized as a unique genius and the most important poet of the period, was unknown to her contemporaries. The first collection of her poetry (*Poems,* 1890) was not published until four years after her death and was little read before the 1920s.

Humor. American humor can be studied as a special manifestation of the national literature. It has fluctuated between humor of the people and urbane humor. Humor of the people tends to retain the qualities of popular speech, as in Lowell's *The Biglow Papers.* Even before Lowell, however, the humorists of the southwestern frontier, such as the clergyman and writer Augustus Baldwin Longstreet (1790–1870), author of the sketches *Georgia Scenes* (1835), had followed this lead. In the mid-century and after, popular idiom and spelling were used as humorous devices in lectures and newspaper columns. Representatives of this later phase were the humorists Josh Billings (*Josh Billings, His Sayings,* 1865), Petroleum V. Nasby (*The Nasby Papers,* 1864), and Artemus Ward (*Artemus Ward, His Book,* 1862). Using illiterate speech, these authors not only satirized the eternal human follies but also powerfully influenced public opinion and political events. The genre was continued later by Finley Peter Dunne (*Mr. Dooley's Opinions,* 1901).

Out of this tradition emerged the most powerful literary personality of the postbellum era, Samuel Langhorne Clemens, known to the world as Mark Twain. His first book, *The Celebrated Jumping Frog of Calaveras County and Other Sketches* (1867), retains the characteristics of the oral tale; successes such as *The Innocents Abroad* (1869), *Roughing It* (1872), and *Life on the Mississippi* (1883) waver between journalism and literature; but with the novels *The Adventures of Tom Sawyer* (1876) and *The Adventures of Huckleberry Finn* (1884) Mark Twain transcended his own tradition of satire and created two master pictures of life on and along the Mississippi River. The genius of Twain was that he understood the moral realism of childhood. In this connection both works may be compared and contrasted with *Little Women* (1868–69) by Louisa May Alcott. This still enormously popular novel is one of a series of works by Alcott that show her serious concern with childhood and adolescence. Mark Twain's later fictional works such as "The Man That Corrupted Hadleyburg" (1900), the compelling *The Mysterious Stranger* (1916), and philosophical works such as *What is Man?* (1906) express the pessimism already evident in *The Gilded Age* (1873).

Fiction. Twain's friend and mentor, the novelist and critic William Dean Howells, expressed in theory and practice the philosophy that literary art ought to mirror the facts of human life. His theory was best expounded in *Criticism and Fiction* (1891), and in a succession of novels (*A Modern Instance,* 1882; *The Rise of Silas Lapham,* 1885; *A Hazard of New Fortunes,* 1890) illustrating that the business of literature is with the present and not with the remote and far away. No writer had a more sensitive ear for American conversation.

About Howells were grouped other realists and naturalists, notably the novelists and short-story writers Hamlin Garland (*Main-Travelled Roads,* 1890), Stephen Crane (*The Red Badge of Courage,* 1895), and Frank Norris (*McTeague,* 1899; *The Octopus,* 1901), as well as that singular genius, perhaps better known as a satirist, Ambrose Gwinett Bierce (*In the Midst of Life,* 1898). Their successors in the early years of the next century were novelists such as Jack London (*The Sea Wolf,* 1904); David Graham Phillips (1867–1911), who wrote *Susan Lenox: Her Fall and Rise* (written 1908, pub. 1917); and Upton Sinclair (*The Jungle,* 1906). Towering among these figures was the novelist and journalist Theodore Dreiser, who began as a writer in the naturalist style and ended as a religious mystic. His novel *Sister Carrie* (1900) was withdrawn from sale as immoral; better received were his novels *The Financier* (1912) and *The Titan* (1914), which trace the career of a ruthless businessman. His best-known novel, *An American Tragedy* (1925), is, like Norris's *McTeague,* one of the most representative American novels of naturalism. Dreiser's lack of stylistic distinction was a weakness, but his dedication to truth and his compassionate insights into American society have made his novels endure.

While realists and naturalists argued about the degree to which human actions are determined by forces external to the will, the novelist Henry James concentrated on subjective experience and personal relationships. His great theme, the conflict between European and American values, is explored in novels from *The American* (1877) through *The Portrait of a Lady* (1881) to *The Wings of the Dove* (1902), *The Ambassadors* (1903), and *The Golden Bowl* (1904). As he moved toward ever greater subtlety of insight and precision of statement, he developed a uniquely complex style that has as many detractors as devotees. James was a master of the short

Samuel Clemens, who wrote under the pseudonym Mark Twain.

Harper & Row, Publishers, Inc.

novel, for example, the ghost story *The Turn of the Screw* (1898); his criticism is impressive (an example is *Notes on Novelists,* 1914); and the prefaces to the famous New York edition of his books (1907-16), later gathered into *The Art of the Novel* (1934), were the first full revelation in American literature of the psychology of literary creation. The influence of such a genius was immense, and later novelists as diverse as Edith Wharton (*The House of Mirth,* 1905; *The Age of Innocence,* 1920), Ellen Glasgow (*In This Our Life,* 1941), and Willa Cather (*A Lost Lady,* 1923; *Death Comes for the Archbishop,* 1927) owed something to his great example.

In the late 19th and early 20th centuries, most major black writers came from the black middle class. The sociologist and writer W. E. B. Du Bois, author of the essay collection *Souls of Black Folk* (1903) and the novel *The Quest for the Silver Fleece* (1911), appealed to this successful group, which he called "the talented tenth," to lead the fight for equality for all black Americans. Much of their literature reflects struggle and anger. *The Garies and Their Friends* (1875) by Frank J. Webb (d. 1940) and *Imperium in Imperio* (1899) by a Baptist preacher, Sutton Griggs (1872-1930), are examples of works that vacillate between a cry for militancy and a plea for acceptance. Another member of "the talented tenth," Charles Waddell Chesnutt (1858-1932), who practiced law in Cleveland, wrote about racial dilemmas in a volume of short stories, *The Conjure Woman* (1899), and in a novel, *The Marrow of Tradition* (1901).

19th-Century Nonfiction. Didactic literature made steady progress in many directions. In biographies ranging from that of Horace Greeley (1885) to that of Thomas Jefferson (1874), James Parton (1822-91) laid the foundations of modern biography. Much significant writing was done in the field of history, for example, the work of George Bancroft (*History of the United States,* 10 vol., 1834-74, rev. ed. 1884-87); and the two great "romantic" historians, William Hickling Prescott, whose *History of the Conquest of Mexico* (3 vol.) was published in 1843, and Francis Parkman, whose distinguished studies of the roles of France and England in North America appeared from 1851 to 1892. Stylistically, Parkman was the greatest of these historians, but his preeminence was challenged by the brilliance of Henry Brooks Adams in *History of the United States of America During the Administrations of Thomas Jefferson and James Madison* (9 vol., 1889-91). The analytical approach of the latter in some ways foreshadowed his analysis of medieval culture, *Mont-Saint-Michel and Chartres* (1904), and his enigmatic, skeptical autobiography *The Education of Henry Adams* (1906), in which he tried to balance the claims of medievalism and modernism.

Willa Cather Culver Pictures, Inc.

The treatise *Progress and Poverty* (1897), by the economist Henry George, as well as the novel *Looking Backward, 2000-1887* (1888) by the journalist Edward Bellamy, present disturbing analyses of a laissez-faire industrial philosophy; both works inspired movements toward reform. The social sciences in America came of age with studies such as *Past, Present, and Future* (1848) by the economist Henry Charles Carey (1793-1879), and *Dynamic Sociology* (1883) by the pioneering sociologist Lester Frank Ward (1841-1913). Meanwhile, the literature of science had expanded steadily, reaching its finest expression in the philosopher and psychologist William James's classic *The Principles of Psychology* (1890), a work that had profound influence not only on psychology but on literary expression in the U.S. and abroad. As the 19th century ended, a profound shift in the basis of American thought was taking place, gradually giving way to the pragmatism (q.v.) expounded by James in his *The Will to Believe and Other Essays* (1897).

THE 20TH CENTURY

With the 20th-century communications revolution—the advent of motion pictures, radio, and, later, television—books became a secondary source of amusement and enlightenment. With new modes of transportation, American society became more mobile and homogeneous, and regionalism, the dominant mode of 19th-century literature, all but vanished, except in the work of some southern writers. At the same time, American writers began to exert a major influence on world literature.

Fiction of the 1920s. The reaction against 19th-century romanticism, already being felt at the turn of the century, was given great impetus by the searing experience of World War I. The horrors and brutal reality of the war had a lasting impact on the American imagination. Novels such as William Faulkner's *Soldiers' Pay* (1926) and Ernest Hemingway's *The Sun Also Rises* (1926) and *A Farewell to Arms* (1929) portray war as a symbol of human life, savage and ignoble. The fiction of the 20th century emerged from World War I on a realistic and antiromantic path, and it has seldom strayed significantly since. American writers, especially, became more and more firmly committed to the replacement of sentimentality by new psychological insights. One such writer was Ellen Glasgow, a Virginian, whose novels *Barren Ground* (1925) and *Vein of Iron* (1935) are candid examinations of southern traditions, especially as regards the role of women; they have enjoyed a revival of interest in light of the women's movement of the late 1970s.

The decade after World War I is often referred to as the Jazz Age or the Roaring Twenties. Rapid changes took place in society, as Americans rebelled against the strictures of Puritanism and the Victorian age. Rapid changes occurred also in literature, most notably in fiction. Most influential was the powerful fiction of Sherwood Anderson, including *Winesburg, Ohio* (1919), a collection of psychologically penetrating short stories. F. Scott Fitzgerald, disillusioned but at the same time yearning, turned a satiric eye on upper-class society in such novels as *This Side of Paradise* (1920) and *The Great Gatsby* (1925); critics have called the latter, a commentary on the American dream of the acquisition of wealth and power, a "perfect" novel. Sinclair Lewis, the first American writer to win a Nobel Prize in literature (1930), brilliantly satirized the "get-rich-quick" business culture of the age in the novels *Main Street* (1920) and *Dodsworth* (1929). Thornton Wilder, author of *The Bridge of San Luis Rey* (1927), began a long career during which he produced a series of urbane comments on human existence—plays as well as novels. His successful *Theophilus North* (1973) was published almost half a century after his first novel.

Ernest Hemingway talks with servicemen while stationed at Normandy, France, as a war correspondent in 1944. UPI

It was Gertrude Stein, an American author resident in Paris, who gave the name the "lost generation" to the group of rootless young Americans who flocked to Europe after the war. The group included Anderson, Fitzgerald, and Wilder, but the most prominent, who was to become one of the most important American writers of the century, was Hemingway. In addition to his novels about the war, Hemingway wrote books of short stories during the 1920s, including *In Our Time* (1924) and *Men Without Women* (1927). He epitomized the disillusioned and cynical survivors of the war to end wars, as World War I had been proclaimed. Stein herself was a significant influence on the writers of that generation, not only as a friend but also as a literary stylist in her own right, with her flaunting of tradition and her experiments with language, beginning with the three short novels in *Three Lives* (1908). More influential, however, was the Irish novelist and poet James Joyce. His use of stream-of-consciousness narration, symbols, and consciously poetic prose was reflected in virtually all the important American (and European) fiction written after World War I.

The Harlem Renaissance. From 1920 to 1930 a major outburst of creative activity was notable among black Americans in all fields of art. The focus of this activity was Harlem, in New York City; thus the period is often called the Harlem Renaissance. Black Americans were encouraged to celebrate their heritage, to become "The New Negro," to use a term coined in 1925 by the sociologist and critic Alain LeRoy Locke (1886–1954) in a landmark anthology of black writers by the same title. From the Harlem Renaissance came Jean Toomer (1894–1967), author of *Cane* (1923), a work of short stories, poems, and a short novel;

the Jamaican-born Claude McKay, author of the novels *Home to Harlem* (1928) and *Banjo* (1929); the well-known poet Countee Cullen, author of *Color* (1925) and *The Ballad of the Brown Girl* (1927); and the equally famed poet and short-story writer Langston Hughes, author of *The Weary Blues* (1926) and numerous other volumes of poetry and creator of Jesse B. Simple of the Simple tales. As developed by Hughes, Simple is the symbol of the black American living in the contemporary urban ghetto.

The Depression Years. Ending the glitter and excess of the Jazz Age, the catastrophe of the 1929 stock-market crash ushered in the "angry decade" of the 1930s. Many novels of neonaturalism and social protest were produced, inspired by the rigors of the Great Depression.

During the 1930s, and into the decade 1940–50, the novelists Zora Neale Hurston (1901–60), author of *Their Eyes Were Watching God* (1937), and Arna Bontemps (1902–73), author of *God Sends Sunday* (1931) and *Black Thunder* (1936), dealt realistically with social issues. The works of John Steinbeck, including *Of Mice and Men* (1937) and *The Grapes of Wrath* (1939) exude despair; Steinbeck was to win a Nobel Prize in literature in 1962. Class conflict is the underlying theme of the prolific John O'Hara's most important work, the novel *Appointment in Samarra* (1934). Two monumental trilogies, James Thomas Farrell's *Studs Lonigan* (1932–35) and John Dos Passos's *U.S.A.* (1930–36), are suffused with bitterness and rage. The intense, often poignant, and unstructured novels of Thomas Clayton Wolfe, *Look Homeward, Angel* (1929) and *The Web and the Rock* (1939), express personal torment, as well as a mystical optimism about America. The intricately narrated novels of William Faulkner in this period, *The Sound and the Fury* (1929), *Sanctuary* (1931), and *The Hamlet* (1940), combine dark violence and earthy humor in their vision of the tragically contorted, wounded society of the post–Civil War South. His superb short stories have been issued in *Go Down, Moses* (1942) and *Collected Stories* (1950). Faulkner, who won the Nobel Prize in literature in 1949, was a leader of the group who kept southern regional writing alive through the next three decades.

World War II and After: Fiction. The extensive fictional literature that arose out of World War II lacked the tendency to shock that had energized previous war novels. Authors were, perhaps, able by this time to regard armed conflict with greater philosophical detachment. The most impressive novels of World War II, all hard-edged and all concerned with the adaptation of the individual to restrictive military life, were *From Here to Eternity* (1951) by James Jones, and *The Naked and the Dead* (1948) by Norman Mailer. Two popular novelists began their successful careers with war books: James Michener, with a collection of short stories, *Tales of the South Pacific* (1947); and Irwin Shaw (1913–84), with his novel about the war in Europe, *The Young Lions* (1948). Humor, a persistently recurring strain in American writing, appeared in such novels as *A Bell for Adano* (1944), in which John Hersey dealt with the occupation of an Italian town by U.S. Army forces; and *Mr. Roberts* (1946), a bittersweet story about the U.S. Navy (later dramatized for stage and screen), by Thomas Heggen (1919–49).

Just as the novels of World War II seemed to emphasize individuality, the novels written in the decades following continued that emphasis. Authors, determined to assert their individuality, worked in a wide range of styles and dealt with an even wider range of material. A few uniquely original writers, however, can be distinguished. Vladimir Nabokov, born in Russia, became one of the greatest masters of English prose style. His novels with American settings, such as *Lolita* (1955) and *Pale Fire* (1962), written many years after he became an American citizen, are remarkable examples of tragicomedy. J. D. Salinger's novel of rebellious adolescence, *The Catcher in the Rye,* is both a humorous and a terrifyingly precise observation; written in 1951, it remains enormously popular. So too does Joseph Heller's (1923–) *Catch-22* (1961), about World War II. A statement about authority, it employs a sardonic, wildly imaginative style that has come to be known as black humor. Another very popular novelist in this vein, Kurt Vonnegut, Jr., based one of his several innovative novels, *Slaughterhouse-Five* (1969), on his experiences in a German prison camp during the war. Alternating surrealistically between this setting and a fictional planet, the multilevel narrative brilliantly combines elements of science fiction (q.v.), a genre that became increasingly popular in the decades after World War II.

Among the postwar southern writers who continued the tradition of Faulkner—sometimes referred to as "southern Gothic"—were Carson McCullers (*The Heart Is a Lonely Hunter,* 1946), Truman Capote (*Other Voices, Other Rooms,* 1947), Eudora Welty (*The Ponder Heart,* 1954), and Flannery O'Connor (*The Violent Bear It Away,* (1960). Best known for his Pulitzer Prize-winning novel *All the King's Men* (1946), a powerful characterization of a southern politician, Kentucky-born Robert Penn Warren was also a noted poet, critic, and literary historian.

Two of the major novelists of the later 20th century, John Cheever and John Updike, share a similar concern and approach in their somewhat detached, rueful, or more openly satirical ruminations on upper middle-class suburban life in the Northeast. Cheever's career as a novelist ranges from the relatively benign *The Wapshot Chronicle* (1957), the story of an eccentric family, to the bleak tale of a fratricide, *Falconer* (1977). His last work, the novella *Oh What a Paradise It Seems* (1982), was more hopeful in tone. Updike is perhaps best known for his books begun in 1960 about a man fleeing disillusion. Two in the series, *Rabbit is Rich* (1981) and *Rabbit at Rest* (1991) won Pulitzer prizes. Another fine critic and teacher of writing, Joyce Carol Oates (1938–), remains one of the most prolific of more recent writers. *A Garden of Earthly Delights* (1967) and *Them* (1969) are major examples of her Gothic fiction, a genre she continued in the multigeneration family saga *Bellefleur* (1980). *Mysteries of Winterthurn* (1984) is a re-creation of the traditional Victorian mystery story.

Ethnic and Regional Writing. Concern about their ethnic heritage and role in American society has characterized the work of a large number of black and Jewish writers.

Examining their lives as Jews in urban 20th-century America, sometimes with despair and sometimes with hilarity, several writers created a remarkable body of introspective fiction from the immediate postwar period on. Chief among them were Saul Bellow, author of *The Adventures of Augie March* (1953) and *Herzog* (1964), who received the Nobel Prize in literature in 1976; Bernard Malamud, who wrote *The Assistant* (1957) and several collections of haunting short stories, including *Idiots First* (1963); and Philip Roth, author of *Goodbye, Columbus* (1959), the very popular *Portnoy's Complaint* (1969), and the trilogy *Zuckerman Bound* (1985).

William Faulkner UPI

Against the background of the transition from the Great Depression to involvement in World War II may be set several novels that deal on a personal level with the long-standing American problem of racial prejudice. Richard Wright's *Native Son* (1940) and his autobiographical *Black Boy* (1945) are powerful statements, written in a starkly realistic manner. Passionate indignation about the black experience was voiced again in Ralph Ellison's novel *Invisible Man* (1952) and in James Baldwin's novel *Go Tell It on the Mountain* (1953), as well as in his later essays such as *Nobody Knows My Name* (1961).

The long tradition of American regional writing has continued into the later part of the 20th century. Baltimore is the specific setting of the novels and stories of Anne Tyler (1941–). She was much praised for her *Dinner at the Homesick Restaurant* (1982), the story of the members of a broken home coming to terms with their lives. Alice Walker (1944–), poet and novelist, first won attention for *Meridian* (1976). In the highly acclaimed *The Color Purple* (1982), which won the Pulitzer Prize and was also made into a film, she evokes by the structure of the dialogue the speech of rural southern blacks; and she weaves a multilayered narrative of their lives much in the manner of Faulkner.

Writing from their special vantage point as black women, a number of other talented novelists have re-created the settings and lives with which they are intimately familiar in fiction that speaks, however, to a wide audience. Toni Morrison (1931–) in *The Bluest Eye* (1969) and her *Song of Solomon* (1977) deals largely with the black experience in the south. And Gloria Naylor (1950–), in *The Women of Brewster Place* (1982), a series of short fictions, gives a realistic picture of women's lives in a northern urban housing project.

20th-Century Poetry. The founding by the poet and editor Harriet Monroe (1860–1936) of *Poetry: A Magazine of Verse* (1912) signaled an extraordinary poetic renaissance after a long fallow period. The first phase of the revival was imagism (q.v.), a movement initiated by the poets Amy Lowell (*Men, Women, and Ghosts,* 1916) and Ezra Pound (*Ripostes,* 1912). Imagists set out to revolutionize poetic style, but two other phases of the poetic revival of the early 20th century were more popular: the work of an Illinois group, including the poets Vachel Lindsay, (*The Congo and Other Poems,* 1914), Edgar Lee Masters (*Spoon River Anthology,* 1915), and Carl Sand-

Eudora Welty Richard O. Moore–Harcourt Brace Jovanovich

burg (*Chicago Poems,* 1915); and the work of a New England group, including Edwin Arlington Robinson (*The Town Down the River,* 1910) and Robert Frost (*North of Boston,* 1914). The works of Frost and Sandburg, during their long careers, became especially beloved and were regarded as the authentic expression of an American poetic spirit. Outside these literary groups, but widely popular and influential, was Edna St. Vincent Millay (*The Ballad of the Harp Weaver,* 1922).

The publication of *The Waste Land* (1922) by the American-English poet T. S. Eliot marked a turning point. The tendency to the esoteric in verse forms, language, and symbolism was augmented by Pound's *Cantos* (pub. between 1925 and 1960). Both Eliot and Pound, through their poetry as well as their critical writings, had an immense influence on the course of 20th-century poetry. So did the work of William Carlos Williams, whose 40 volumes of prose and poetry, among them *Paterson* (Books I–V, 1946–58), affected the writing of generations of poets.

Experiments with verse employing complex, often difficult imagery and symbolism were also carried on by Hart Crane, best known for his epic *The Bridge* (1930), Wallace Stevens (*The Man with the Blue Guitar,* 1937), and Marianne Moore (*Collected Poems,* 1951). The highly inventive work of e. e. cummings, from *Is 5* (1926) to *73 Poems* (1963), played with typographical form and aural imagery.

Other poets who established a more direct communication with the reader include Robinson Jeffers, whose eloquent lines, as in *Roan Stallion, Tamar, and Other Poems* (1925), express his reverence for nonhuman forms of life; Randall Jarrell, whose poetry, for example, *Losses* (1948), was formed by grief over World War II; and Archibald MacLeish (*Collected Poems, 1917–1952,* 1952) and Richard Wilbur (*Things of This World,* 1956), who in their lyrical, contemplative verse express humanist concerns. The protest poetry of the Beat Generation (q.v.) certainly communicates directly, with great impact. Far different in tone is the strain of southern black oral narrative tradition that can be detected in some of the work of Gwendolyn Brooks (*Annie Allen,* 1949), Nikki Giovanni (1945– ; *Black Feeling, Black Talk, Black Judgement,* 1970), and Maya Angelou (1928– ; *Just Give Me a Cool Drink of Water 'fore I Die,* 1971). Theodore Roethke managed two styles: free-form for the expression of surrealistic ideas, and a simpler, lyrical form for the expression of more rational modes of thought; both styles are exemplified in his collection *The Far Field* (posthumously pub. 1964).

With Robert Lowell (*Lord Weary's Castle,* 1946), there began what has been termed the "confessional" mode in poetry, explicit references to personal anxieties and disabilities. The verse of Sylvia Plath (*Ariel,* 1965) and Anne Sexton (1928–74; *Live or Die,* 1967, and *The Awful Rowing Toward God,* 1975) is similarly informed by images of personal torment.

A resurgence of poetry manifested itself from the late 1960s on, as a proliferation of literary magazines provided outlets for work and colleges and universities sponsored poetry workshops and offered courses taught by poets in residence. Among the many contemporary poets—encompassing a wide variety of forms and styles—May Swenson (1919–89), Robert Bly (1926–), and Galway

James Baldwin Dial Press

Kinnell (1927–) are noted for their clearly defined imagery, often based on the close observation of nature. In contrast, the use by James Merrill (1926–) of highly personal images, often inspired by the occult, and the notoriously convoluted syntax employed by John Ashbery (1927–) make their verse very difficult to apprehend. Ashbery won a Pulitzer Prize in 1976 for his *Self-Portrait in a Convex Mirror;* Merrill won the 1977 Pulitzer Prize for his *Divine Comedies.* Mona Van Duyn (1921–), the nation's sixth poet laureate (1992) and author of seven volumes of verse, including *Near Changes* (Pulitzer Prize, 1991), is noted for the warmth and intellect, the wit and the emotions of her poetry about parents and children, married life, and love.

20th-Century Nonfiction. A traditional view of American history was presented by the historians Charles Austin Beard and Mary Ritter Beard, in *The Rise of American Civilization* (1927), and by Samuel Eliot Morison (*The Oxford History of the American People,* 1965) and Henry Steele Commager (*The Search for a Usable Past,* 1967). Accounts of specific trends and eras include *Anti-Intellectualism in America* (1963) by Richard Hofstadter (1916–70), a study of the effects of conservatism; and *The Guns of August* (1962), about the beginnings of World War I, and *A Distant Mirror: The Calamitous Fourteenth Century* (1978), by Barbara Tuchman (1912–89).

Much brilliant political reporting and analysis was done in the 1930s. Such books as *Inside Europe* (1936), by the journalist John Gunther (1901–70); *The Life and Death of a Spanish Town* (1937), by the novelist Elliot Harold Paul (1891–1958); and *Not Peace but a Sword* (1939), by the foreign correspondent Vincent Sheean (1899–1975), helped prepare perplexed Americans for World War II. After the war, the novelist John Hersey's landmark report *Hiroshima* (1946; reissued with an update in 1985) described the effects of the first atomic bomb.

Other writers of fiction frequently turned to nonfiction during the postwar period. Truman Capote invented what he called the "nonfiction novel" with *In Cold Blood* (1966), a harrowing account of the murder of a Kansas family. Norman Mailer's *The Armies of the Night* and *Miami and the Siege of Chicago* (both 1968) vividly describe and interpret headline-making contemporary political protest.

Out of the civil rights movements of the 1950s and 1960s came writers whose works reveal the experiences of black Americans. Among these was the dramatist and poet Imamu Amiri Baraka (originally named LeRoi Jones; 1934–), who also probed the situation in his *Home: Social Essays* (1966) and *Raise, Race, Rays, Raze: Essays Since 1965* (1971). Eldridge Cleaver (1935–) contributed significant essays on American society in *Soul on Ice* (1967). More subjective accounts were contributed by several writers. The black nationalist leader Malcolm X (originally named Malcolm Little) wrote his influential *Autobiography of Malcolm X* (1965) with Alex Haley (1921–92), who later became famous as the author of the bestselling *Roots* (1976), a semifictional account of Haley's family history from its African beginnings to the present. Maya Angelou, the poet-novelist and children's author, wrote a powerful memoir of her own growing up in the South, *I Know Why the Caged Bird Sings* (1969).

Other serious concerns addressed by American writers from the 1960s on have been the war in Indochina, the pollution of the environment, and women's rights. The Vietnam War has been the subject of extensive, often highly critical analysis. The lengthier reports include *My Lai 4* (1970), detailing the massacre of Vietnamese civilians by American troops in 1968. For this book, Seymour M. Hersh (1937–) won a Pulitzer Prize, as did Frances Fitzgerald (1940–) for *Fire in the Lake: The Vietnamese and the Americans in Vietnam* (1972). A pioneering work on women's role in society was Betty Friedan's *The Feminine Mystique* (1963), an analysis of the reasons for the failure of women to achieve the goals promised by earlier women's rights efforts.

20th-Century Literary Criticism. Literary criticism in the 20th century began with the neohumanists, who upheld the classical tradition and called for a firmer ethical basis for art. These theories were expounded by such critics as Paul Elmer More (1864–1937; *Shelburne Essays,* 11 vol., 1904–21), William Crary Brownell (1851–1928; *American Prose Masters,* 1909), and the Harvard University professor Irving Babbit (*The New Laokoön,* 1910). The appraisal of American writing as a distinct national literature began in the 1920s, introduced by the English novelist D. H. Lawrence in his groundbreaking *Studies in Classic American Literature* (1923). The American scholar Vernon Louis Parrington provided a sociopolitical interpretation of American literature in his treatise *Main Currents in American Thought* (3 vol., 1927–30). A more popular survey of American letters was contributed by the literary historian Van Wyck Brooks in his multivolume series beginning with *The Flowering of New England, 1815–1865* (1936). Coincident with these studies was the direct assault unleashed by H. L. Mencken in his *American Mercury* reviews, 1924–33, on contemporary tastes and prejudices of what he called the American "boobocracy."

From the professional scholars of literature came, between the late 1930s and 1945, an approach known as the New Criticism. Taking its name from a 1941 essay by John Crowe Ransom, it emphasized close analysis of text and structure rather than consideration of social or biographical contexts. Among the critics expounding these tenets were Cleanth Brooks (1906–), Kenneth Burke (1897–1986), Ransom, Alan Tate, and Robert Penn Warren. Independent of this approach were several notable scholars, including Joseph Wood Krutch, whose essays were collected in *The Modern Temper* (1929) and *The Measure of Man* (1954); and Lionel Trilling, author of one of the most influential of modern critical essays, *The Liberal Imagination* (1950). Also noteworthy were Malcolm Cowley (1898–1989), author of *Exile's Return* (1934); Alfred Kazin (1915–), *On Native Grounds* (1942) and *The Inmost Leaf* (1955); and Leslie Fiedler (1917–), whose *Love and Death in the American Novel* (1960) provided a new interpretation of certain themes and approaches.

Perhaps the best-rounded literary critic and theorist to emerge in 20th-century America was Edmund Wilson. Independent of mind, widely erudite yet never drily pedantic, he remained unaligned with formal academic criticism. His study *Axel's Castle* (1931) indicated a mature, sensitive literary intelligence, and such later critical works as *The Wound and the Bow* (1941) and *The Bit Between My Teeth: A Literary Chronicle of 1950–1965* (1965) confirmed his stature.

In recent years a school of literary criticism has flourished at Yale University. There, Harold Bloom (1930–), author of *The Anxiety of Influence: A Theory of Poetry* (1973), is particularly concerned with the effects of literary influence, while other scholars advocate deconstructuralism (the essential meaningless of all writing), a theory promulgated by a group of contemporary French critics. Harvard University professor Helen Vendler (1933–), considered by some the best contemporary critic of poetry, has won respect for her sensitive analyses such as *Part of Nature, Part of Us: Modern American Poets* (1980) and *The Odes of John Keats* (1983), and for her reviews in various journals.

See biographies of all persons mentioned in this article whose life dates are not given. *See also* BLACKS IN THE AMERICAS; CRITICISM, LITERARY; DRAMA AND DRAMATIC ARTS; NOVEL; POETRY; SHORT STORY.

For further information on this topic, see the Bibliography in volume 28, sections 815–32.

AMERICAN MEDICAL ASSOCIATION (AMA), federation of state and territorial medical associations, founded in 1847 and incorporated in 1897, to promote medical knowledge and protect the welfare of U.S. physicians. Activities of the association include maintaining standards of medical education and ethics, providing scientific information to the profession and health education information to the public, and developing programs to advance the practice of medicine and serve the health needs of the public. The AMA publishes the *Journal of the American Medical Association, The AMA News* (weekly), and nine specialty journals. The association holds semiannual conventions and scientific assemblies. It maintains headquarters in Chicago.

Barbara Tuchman Bert Verhoeff, Duivendrecht, Holland

AMERICAN MUSEUM OF NATURAL HISTORY, an institute located in New York City that houses public exhibitions and scientific research projects. The museum, the largest of its kind in the world, covers several city blocks and contains 22 interconnected buildings used for exhibits, lectures, laboratories, and storage. Combined floor space of the American Museum and the American Museum-Hayden Planetarium totals about 139,350 sq m (1.5 million sq ft), half of which are devoted to public exhibition halls.

Notable exhibits relate to anthropology, archaeology, geology, mineralogy, paleontology, and biology. Outstanding anthropological halls include the Hall of South American Peoples, Hall of Asian Peoples, Hall of Man in Africa, Peoples of the Pacific, Hall of the Eskimo, Hall of Mexico and Central America, and several halls devoted to the North American Indians.

The John Lindsley Hall of Earth History contains exhibits of the structure of the earth and the early history of life. In the mineralogy collections is the famous Star of India, the largest of all known sapphires.

Prehistoric skeletal remains and restorations on view in the paleontological halls include a brontosaur, a dinosaur more than 20 m (more than 66 ft) long, and a tyrannosaur, a giant carnivorous dinosaur.

A number of vivid displays depicting species in their native habitat appear in the Akeley Memorial Hall of African Mammals, the Hall of Oceanic Birds, the Hall of the Biology of Invertebrates, and the Hall of Ocean Life and Biology of Fishes, which contains a 28.7-m (94-ft) replica of the blue whale, the largest such model in the world.

One of the most popular divisions is the American Museum-Hayden Planetarium, which is devoted to astronomical displays and photographs. The building contains a complex optical device that projects representations of the night sky against a dome 22.9 m (75 ft) in diameter.

Besides its public exhibitions, the museum conducts research activities, maintains four field stations, and presents educational programs. It has a library of some 400,000 volumes that is open to the public.

The American Museum of Natural History was founded in 1869 by a group of public-spirited Americans, including Theodore Roosevelt, Sr. (1831–78), the financier John Pierpont Morgan, and the writer and editor Charles Anderson Dana (1819–97). The museum was first housed in a Central Park building known as the Arsenal. After it was moved to its present site in 1877, its resources grew steadily more extensive. Notable additions included the American Museum-Hayden Planetarium (1935) and the Theodore Roosevelt Memorial Building, completed in 1936. The museum is administered by a self-perpetuating board of trustees. It receives financial suppport from New York City.

AMERICAN MUSIC, the folk, popular, and classical music of the U.S.—created by American-born or American-trained composers, or originating in American culture, or written primarily for American audiences.

Colonial Era Through 1820. The colonial roots of American music are English. The first book printed in the English colonies was the *Bay Psalm Book.* Its ninth edition (1698) contained 13 psalm tunes, all of them from Europe; some, including "Old Hundred," are still sung. After 1750 native-born composers in New England established a distinctive religious music. Spread through "singing schools" (informal courses of musical instruction), Yankee hymnody—with its angular melodies and open-fifth chords—was unconventional by European standards. A favorite form was the fuguing tune, a four-part piece that began like a hymn and ended like a round. The most famous of the New England "tunesmiths" was William Billings, whose collection *The New England Psalm Singer* (1770) marked the appearance of the new style. His colleagues included Oliver Holden (1765–1844) and Daniel Read (1757–1836).

Some religious sects, such as the Ephrata Cloisters Community, the Shakers, and the Moravians, also produced original music, which, however, failed to have lasting influence on American musical styles. One Shaker melody, "'Tis a Gift to Be Simple," became famous when it was used by the composer Aaron Copland in his ballet *Appalachian Spring* (1944). The Moravians, who were musically the most prolific and sophisticated of these sects, re-created in their chamber and church music the instrumental music of their Old World German culture. The three string trios written about 1780 by the Moravian composer John Antes (1740–1811) were the first chamber works composed in the colonies.

Political songs, broadsides (one-page song sheets), dance music, and piano music—largely reflecting English models or imported from England—were also published during this era. Among such tunes of English origin are "The Star-Spangled Banner" (1814), with words by the American lawyer and poet Francis Scott Key; "Yankee Doodle" (pub. about 1780); and "America" (1831), with words by the American clergyman and poet Samuel F. Smith (1808–95). The lawyer, author, and politician Francis Hopkinson was one of the first Americans to compose secular music; he is best known for his Seven Songs for the Harpsichord (1788). Professional European-born musicians resided in several of the larger cities; among them were the English-born James Hewitt (1770–1827) in New York City and the German-born Alexander Reinagle (1756–1809), a composer of ballad operas in Philadelphia.

Early 19th Century. After the American Revolution, European taste reasserted itself in church music. The music of the New England tunesmiths was scorned as "unscientific" by such composers as Thomas Hastings (1784–1872) and William Batchelder Bradbury (1816–68). The dominant figure was Lowell Mason (1792–1872), who had a profound influence on 19th-century musical life in America. Besides introducing music into the Boston schools in 1838, Mason composed more than 1200 hymns and compiled five major collections of church music, the most important and most successful being *The Boston Handel and Haydn Society Collection of Church Music*

A round from the frontispiece of The Continental Harmony, *a collection of hymns by William Billings, a Boston singing teacher and church pianist. The script in the center of the circle reads, "This tune is thus disposed to shew that every tune is a Compleat circle, and that what may be deficient in the first barr is supplied in the last."*

(1822). Several of Mason's descendants became performers and teachers of music, as well as builders of pianos and organs; his grandson, Daniel Gregory Mason (1873–1953), was a respected composer of impressionistic and romantic music.

Traditional New England religious music migrated to the South, where a new kind of folk hymnody emerged from the camp meetings of the religious revival movement. Close to modern gospel tunes in their repetitious, catchy refrains, the revival hymns and spirituals include such well-known examples as "Amazing Grace" and "Wayfaring Stranger." Southern folk hymns were typically printed in "shape notes," an easy-to-read system of notation in which the notes had different shapes to represent the seven syllables of the scale. The shape-note collection of greatest and most lasting popularity was *The Sacred Harp* (1844) of Benjamin Franklin White (1800–79) and E. J. King (d. 1844).

American classical music was in its infancy during this period. The most noteworthy classical composer was Bohemian-born Anthony Philip Heinrich (1781–1861), a romantic who wrote several descriptive symphonies and a massive collection of songs and piano pieces, *The Dawning of Music in Kentucky* (1820).

Mid-19th Century Through the American Civil War. The presence of the African in America surfaced in popular music in the blackface minstrel show (q.v.). Its characteristic white, four-man troupe was defined by the Virginia Minstrels in the 1840s, performing on banjo, tambourine, bone castanets, and fiddle. The banjo virtuoso Daniel Decatur Emmett was the outstanding composer of minstrel songs; his best-known work is "Dixie" (1859). By midcentury the first blacks began to perform in minstrel shows.

Genuine Afro-American music was already established in oral tradition at the beginning of the 19th century. The first published collection of it, *Slave Songs of the United States,* appeared in 1867. Among the famous tunes the collection contains are "Michael, Row Your Boat Ashore" and "Roll, Jordan, Roll." After the Civil War, the fund-raising concerts of the Fisk University Jubilee Singers made such spirituals the first Afro-American folk music to reach a national and international audience.

Parlor songs overflowed with sentiment, lavished on the ordinary aspects of domestic life. One example is "The Old Arm Chair" (1840) by the English singer Henry Russell (1812–1900), who barnstormed the U.S. in the 1830s and '40s. Russell's American successors included the

Hutchinson family, who espoused in song such causes as abolition and woman suffrage.

The greatest songwriter of the period, and perhaps of the century, was Stephen Collins Foster, who composed songs for the famous Christy Minstrels, such as "Oh, Susanna" (1848) and "Camptown Races" (1850), and parlor songs, such as "I Dream of Jeanie with the Light Brown Hair" (1854) and "Beautiful Dreamer" (1864). Foster was immortalized by his folklike melodies and his ability to combine Anglo-Irish and Afro-American idioms with those of Italian operatic song. Notable composers after Foster were Henry Clay Work (1832–84), George Root (1820–95), and James Bland (1854–1911).

In classical music, Americans favored pianists, and the first great American keyboard virtuoso, the New Orleans-born Louis Moreau Gottschalk, became an international celebrity. The best of his salon music for piano—such as "La Bamboula" (the name of a dance) and "Le Banjo"—blended an exotic mixture of Afro-Caribbean rhythms, Creole melodies, and romantic pyrotechnics.

The country's first orchestra was the New York Philharmonic Society, founded in 1842. Outstanding symphonic and operatic composers during this period were rare. The most prominent was William Henry Fry (1813–64), who composed *Leonora,* the first opera by an American; it was performed in Philadelphia in 1845. Fry is best remembered, however, for four symphonies written in the 1850s and '60s. George F. Bristow (1825–92) wrote the first opera on an American theme; his *Rip Van Winkle* was performed in New York City in 1855.

Late 19th and Early 20th Centuries. In the decades after the Civil War, classical music came of age in the U.S. Conservatories were founded (Peabody Institute, 1860; Oberlin College, 1865; New England Conservatory, 1867); concert halls were built (Carnegie Hall, 1891); and orchestras were established in more cities, including the Chicago Symphony Orchestra (1891), led by the first American virtuoso conductor, Theodore Thomas (1835–1905).

The music of the German romantics Robert Schumann and Johannes Brahms formed the model for most American composers of the late 19th century, of whom the largest number belonged to a New England-based circle known as the Boston Group. Members of the group included John Knowles Paine (1839–1906); Arthur Foote (1853–1937); George Chadwick (1854–1931), known for his *Symphonic Sketches* (1907) and his opera *Judith* (1901); Horatio Parker, whose cantata *Hora Novissima* (1892) was widely performed; and Amy Cheney Beach

Title page of the first edition of Stephen Foster's "Beautiful Dreamer," composed and published in 1864.
The Granger Collection

(1867–1944), generally referred to as Mrs. H. H. H. Beach, whose *Gaelic* Symphony (1896) was the first symphony written by an American woman.

The most prominent composer of classical music, however, was not part of this New England school. Edward MacDowell sought his own inspiration in the "new German school" represented by the Hungarian composer Franz Liszt and the German composer Richard Wagner. MacDowell's works, written between 1880 and 1902, are mainly for piano. They include 2 piano concertos and 16 collections of character pieces. His single most famous work is "To a Wild Rose," from *Woodland Sketches* (1896).

The next generation reacted against the Germanic cast of MacDowell and of the New England school. Some composers used indigenous folk music; among them, Arthur Farwell (1872–1951) drew on Indian music, and Henry F. Gilbert (1868–1928) utilized Afro-American music. Influences of the French impressionists and of the composers of the Russian School, particularly Aleksandr Scriabin, appeared first in the music of Charles Tomlinson Griffes, in such compositions as *Tone-Image* and *Four Impressions.*

The most original and, indeed, the first truly great American classical composer was Charles Ives, whose use of polytonality and dissonance made him a modernist prophet. In such works as *Three Places in New England* (1903–14), for orchestra, the Second Piano Sonata, *Concord, Mass., 1840–1860* (1920), and the choral work

General Booth Enters into Heaven (1914), Ives combined quotations of gospel, ragtime, and parlor music with complex symphonic and chamber structures.

The most prominent American musician at the end of the century was John Philip Sousa, the leader of a large concert band, and a world-famous figure. Known as the March King, Sousa composed about 140 marches, including "Semper Fidelis" (1888) and "The Stars and Stripes Forever" (1897).

Popular music became big business in the 1890s, especially after Charles K. Harris (1867–1930) wrote "After the Ball" (1892), which sold a million copies. Music publishers clustered in Union Square in New York City, nicknaming it Tin Pan Alley. In the following ten years two Afro-American styles, ragtime (q.v.) and blues (q.v.), demonstrated their commercial potential. Ragtime, which evolved from minstrel songs, was a heavily syncopated music; its greatest composer was Scott Joplin, one of whose piano pieces, "Maple Leaf Rag" (1899), started a national craze. Joplin, who had had some training in classical music, later wrote a ragtime opera, *Treemonisha* (1911). It met with no success, but was revived with great acclaim in 1975. In the first two decades of the 20th century, blues, in the hands of singers such as Bessie Smith and composers such as W. C. Handy, became stabilized as popular rather than folk music.

Edward MacDowell Granger Collection

In the theater, echoes of the Viennese style could be heard on Broadway in the operettas of Victor Herbert. Together with the vaudeville spectaculars of Florenz Zeigfeld, Herbert's operettas were the forerunners of the musical (q.v.), or musical comedy.

World War I to World War II. The 1920s marked the realization of a distinctive American modernist movement in classical music. Its pioneers were Henry Cowell, who introduced the tone cluster; Carl Ruggles; Ruth Crawford-Seeger (1901–53); and Edgard Varèse, whose compositions, not dependent on melody or harmony, had great influence on later 20th-century music. Varèse's percussion piece *Ionisation* (1931) is a landmark.

Often called "the jazz age," the 1920s saw the emergence of a distinct style of music, separate from its roots in ragtime and blues. In the hands of its major composer-performers, Louis Armstrong, Jelly Roll Morton, and Duke Ellington, jazz remained popular through the 1940s. The '20s "roared" with popular song as well, and a number of composers produced small masterpieces within the limits of the 32-bar song form. Among the finest were Jerome Kern, Cole Porter, and Irving Berlin. George Gershwin's style encompassed both popular and classical forms, in such works as the piano concerto *Rhapsody in Blue* (1924), the Concerto in F (1925), and the opera *Porgy and Bess* (1935).

The Great Depression of the 1930s stilled the young champions of "new music." An Americanist trend, a self-conscious search for a musical identity, characterized the classical music of the next two decades. Aaron Copland, the most famous composer of the second quarter of the century, abandoned the acerbic language of his Piano Variations (1930) for an accessible melodic style of clear tonality, permeated by American folk music. His ballet scores *Billy the Kid* (1938), *Rodeo* (1942), and *Appalachian Spring* (1944) are among his best-known works. Kindred composers included William Grant Still (1895–1978) and Roy Harris, who quoted folk music in their symphonies. Virgil Thomson gave a modern treatment to older styles of music, as in his whimsical opera *Four Saints in Three Acts* (1934, with a libretto by Gertrude Stein).

Other composers rose to prominence with music that was international rather than nationalistic. Some, perhaps inspired by the work of the Russian-born composer Igor Stravinsky during the 1920s and '30s, were energized by neoclassi-

Aaron Copland rehearsing the Atlanta Symphony Orchestra in Atlanta Municipal Auditorium.
Photo Researchers, Inc.

cism. Among them was Walter Piston, who often used baroque textures and genres. Piston, like Thomson, Harris, and Copland, had studied composition in Paris, the postwar center of music study, with the influential French teacher Nadia Boulanger. Three notable neoromantics were Howard Hanson, Samuel Barber, and Gian-Carlo Menotti, the latter well known for his Christmas fantasy opera *Amahl and the Night Visitors* (1951).

After World War II more and more American musicians received their training at home at conservatories such as the Juilliard School in New York City and the Eastman School of Music in Rochester, N.Y., and in the music departments of such institutions as Indiana University in Bloomington and Harvard University.

World War II Through the Late 20th Century. In the 1930s and '40s a number of Europe's leading composers fled from fascist oppression to the U.S. Under their influence, international modernism superseded Americanist tendencies in the late 1940s and '50s. The most influential immigrant was the Austrian-born Arnold Schoenberg, whose twelve-tone system triumphed as the major way of organizing new music. Schoenberg's approach was adopted by many Americans, including Wallingford Riegger, Roger Sessions, Copland, and David Diamond. It was expanded theoretically and artistically by Elliott Carter and Milton Babbitt, who developed it into systematic serialism that extended beyond a twelve-tone series of pitches and encompassed other musical elements.

One of the crucial developments of the 1950s was the new medium of electronic music (q.v.), pioneered by Varèse, which allowed composers to achieve unprecedented control over a musical work. The Columbia-Princeton electronic music studio, established in 1952, became a center for such composers as Babbitt, Charles Wuorinen (1938-   ), and Otto Luening (1900-   ).

One of the shaping forces of experimental music was John Cage, in whose aleatoric compositions chance helps determine the outcome of a particular performance. Cage's openness to various aesthetic trends foreshadowed the eclecticism of style from the 1960s on. Most characteristic of these decades was a willingness to utilize all kinds of sound—electronic, acoustic, or environmental—as potential musical material. George Crumb's song cycle *Ancient Voices of Children* (1970), for example, uses a toy piano, a Tibetan prayer stone, and electronically manipulated voices. Other significant eclectic composers are Norman Dello Joio; David Del Tredici (1937-), noted for his *Scenes and Arias from Alice in Wonderland* (1969 ff.); John Corigliano (1938-); and Ellen Taaffe Zwilich (1939-). Zwilich, the first woman to win a Pulitzer Prize for music—for her Symphony No. 1: *Three Movements for Orchestra* (1982)—blends 19th-century harmonic and tonal elements with various features of avant-garde 20th-century classical music.

In the mid-1980s some critics advanced the theory that since about 1968 there had been a swing away from the cool rationality of modern music to more tonal, more immediately accessible forms. The concept of a "new romanticism" was much debated, however. Evidence of the new trend was claimed to exist in such orchestral compositions as *Imago Mundi* (1973) by George Rochberg (1918-), generally a serialist; *Baroque Variations* (1967) by Lukas Foss; and *Windows* (1972) by Jacob Druckman (1928-), a professor of electronic music. Del Tredici's eighth *Alice* piece, "All in the Golden Afternoon" (1983), and the *Chromatic Fantasy* (1979) for narrator and six instruments by Barbara Kolb (1939-) were also cited as examples.

In popular music the postwar period was equally dynamic and expansive. In the 1940s the lyrical-theatrical tradition of the musical was strengthened through the work of Richard Rodgers and Oscar Hammerstein II. The standard was maintained with eloquence and energy in *West Side Story* (1957) by Leonard Bernstein, an acclaimed conductor and composer of classical music. In the 1970s and '80s the music of Stephen Sondheim contributed an urbane sophistication to the form.

The influence of the musical was drastically undercut, however, by the rock-and-roll revolution of the 1950s. The popular "standard" song disappeared, replaced by rhythm and blues and its offspring, rock and roll. Like ragtime, rock music (q.v.) testified to the vitality of Afro-American music. Despite the hegemony of rock in the 1960s, other new styles of popular music surfaced. The folk-music revival, spread by professional urban folksingers such as Pete Seeger, Joan Baez, and Bob Dylan, brought rural blues and ballads to national attention. Country music achieved a national market in the 1970s (*see* COUNTRY AND WESTERN MUSIC).

With the profusion of popular styles and the eclecticism of classical and jazz composers, the boundaries separating these three types of music were often blurred. The modal explorations of John Coltrane and the "free" improvisations of

Leonard Bernstein Christian Steiner

Ellen Taaffe Zwilich Music Associates of America

Ornette Coleman bring the classical concerns of atonality and nonstandard scales into the realm of jazz. Classical and popular elements overlap in the minimalist music of Steve Reich and Philip Glass, composer of the opera *Einstein on the Beach* (1976). Tonally stable melodic patterns are manipulated by repetitions and subtle rhythmic shifts. Favored tone colors are those of percussion instruments of all kinds. The meditative effect praised by some critics of this music has given rise to the label "trance music" and indeed evokes the music of the Far East and Indonesia.

The strength of American music continues to be its openness to new influences and the variety of its ethnic and national styles, which interact and alter one another in ever-new syntheses.

See also AFRO-AMERICAN MUSIC; BAND; FOLK MUSIC; MUSIC, WESTERN; POPULAR MUSIC; SPIRITUAL. For additional information on composers, see biographies of those whose names are not followed by dates. J.Ti.

For further information on this topic, see the Bibliography in volume 28, sections 725, 727, 734–35, 741–42, 745.

AMERICAN NATIONAL THEATRE AND ACADEMY (ANTA), nonprofit theatrical organization chartered and incorporated by the U.S. Congress in 1935 to present theatrical productions and to stimulate public interest in and further the study of the drama. ANTA, headquartered in New York City, was financed through membership dues, gifts, and receipts from its own productions.

Partially as a consequence of World War II, ANTA did not begin to make its presence felt in the American theater until 1946. After the 1950s ANTA carried on a wide range of activities, including presenting theatrical productions, publishing magazines and newsletters, and promoting the study of drama in universities, colleges, and other schools. In the late 1980s, ANTA was inactive while undergoing major reorganization.

AMERICAN PHILOSOPHICAL SOCIETY, oldest existing learned society in the U.S., founded by Benjamin Franklin in 1743 "for the promotion of useful knowledge."

Membership in the society has always been limited to persons distinguished in science, scholarship, and public affairs. In 1988 the society had 600 resident and foreign members. Members represent many fields of learning: biology and medical sciences; mathematics and physical sciences; social sciences; the humanities; and public affairs. Past members included the 15 signers of the Declaration of Independence, 18 members of the Constitutional Convention, and 13 U.S. presidents.

The archives of the society are especially rich in letters and manuscripts dealing with early colonial history and the beginnings of the U.S. government. Such documents include the charter of privileges granted by William Penn to the colonists in 1701; the original manuscript minutes of the provincial council from 1663 to 1716; the minutes of the commission to determine the boundary between Maryland and Pennsylvania, known as Mason and Dixon's Line, of 1760–68; a set of several treaties with the Indians; one of the original copies of the Declaration of Independence in the handwriting of Thomas Jefferson; and the largest collection in existence of the letters and works of Benjamin Franklin.

The library contains bound volumes, manuscripts, pamphlets, and maps. Regular publications of the society are the *Transactions, Proceedings, Memoirs,* and the yearbook. The society distributes much of its income in the form of research grants. Two general meetings are held each year. The headquarters is in Philadelphia.

AMERICAN PSYCHOLOGICAL ASSOCIATION, organization for the promotion of psychology as a science, founded in 1892 at Clark University, Worcester, Mass., and incorporated in 1925. Voting membership in the association is limited to persons holding a Ph.D. degree in psychology. The association publishes an annual directory and some 28 periodicals, including the *Journal of Experimental Psychology, Psychological Abstracts,* and *Psychology Today.* The headquarters of the association is in Washington, D.C.

AMERICAN RED CROSS. *See* RED CROSS.

AMERICAN REVOLUTION (1776–83), conflict between 13 British colonies on the eastern seaboard of North America and their parent country, Great Britain. France intervened at a later stage as an ally of the colonies, and the war resulted in the colonies becoming a separate nation, the United States of America. It is also known as the American War of Independence.

Causes of the Revolution. The end of the Seven Years' War (1756–63), which had its North American beginning in 1754 and was known in America as the French and Indian War, resulted in the final expulsion of France both from the continent of North America and from India. In both cases French power was replaced by that of Great Britain. Britain was thus left victorious in both hemispheres, supreme on the high seas, and secure against invasion. It also possessed an enormous and growing volume of maritime commerce. Britain's king, George III, had recently succeeded to the throne, in 1760. Unlike his Hanoverian predecessors, the third George was determined to establish personal rule by using the substantial resources of the Crown to influence individual members of the Whig majority in the House of Commons. A parliamentary faction known as "the King's Friends" soon became powerful in the home government.

The Stamp Act. Burdened with a considerable war debt, the administration began stricter enforcement of the Navigation Acts restricting colonial trade with other nations. In addition, on the principle that the colonies ought to pay a share of the empire's defense costs, Parliament in 1765 passed the Stamp Act. The revenues derived from this act were intended to pay part of the cost of maintaining a permanent force of British troops to prevent hostilities between the colonists and the Indian tribes of the western frontiers. By this act no official documents, deeds, mortgages, newspapers, or pamphlets could be issued in the colonies unless they bore stamps issued and sold by the British government.

The Stamp Act provoked almost unanimous opposition among the colonists, who regarded it as taxation without representation in Parliament. The act brought to a head the most important of the political issues in dispute between Great Britain and the colonies, namely, whether the legislative authority of Parliament took precedence over that of the various colonial assemblies in America. Since the founding of the colonies the assemblies had passed laws, raised taxes and armies, and carried out most of the other functions of authentic legislative bodies. The colonists insisted that only their own assemblies had the right to make their laws. In addition, they questioned even the right of the king to veto acts of the colonial assemblies.

On these grounds a storm of protest arose against the Stamp Act. In October 1765, delegates from nine colonies met in New York City in the so-called Stamp Act Congress. The delegates petitioned Parliament and the king concerning the grievances of the colonies. To add strength to the formal protest, American merchants banded together and agreed not to buy British goods until the Stamp Act was repealed. The boycott was so effective that commerce between Great Britain and America was brought to a standstill. The following year, yielding not so much to colonial opposition as to the demands of British merchants, Parliament repealed the Stamp Act.

British attempts to coerce Massachusetts. Parliament did not, however, thereby give up the right to legislate for the colonies. In 1767, at the urging of the British minister of finance Charles Townshend, Parliament passed the Townshend Acts, which imposed duties on glass, lead, and tea. Furthermore, in violation of the English Bill of Rights, the Townshend Acts denied trial by jury in revenue cases in America and provided for the issuance of general warrants, called writs of assistance. These warrants permitted the search of warehouses, stores, and even homes at any time for smuggled goods.

Once again the colonists violently protested. Boston declared in town meeting that it would thereafter import no British goods on which the new duties had been placed, and the Massachusetts legislature circulated a letter among the other colonies urging similar boycotts.

The king and his ministers thereupon determined to make an example of Massachusetts and particularly the city of Boston. Two battalions of British infantry were ordered from Halifax, N.S., to Boston to frighten the rebellious inhabitants into submission to royal authority. The troops had to be sent from Halifax, because virtually no British troops were stationed in the 13 colonies except a small garrison at New York City and caretaker detachments of artillerymen in the various harbor forts. The colonies had contributed both men and money to the support of the British in the century-long although intermittent struggle with France, and the colonial soldiers had earned the praises of British commanders. The colonies had maintained no regular forces of their own in peacetime, however; they preferred to rely on militia forces, which were well organized and had a number of experienced officers and men, but were generally neglectful of peacetime training. Small arms (mostly smoothbore muskets) were plentiful, especially in rural areas, where hunting was a favorite avocation as well as a means of providing food. Ammunition, especially the basic element, gunpowder, was not plentiful beyond the modest requirements of country households.

The militia was useful only in support of laws that proceeded from the elected colonial assembly. It did not, however, occur to the king's ministers that colonial militia either would be needed to enforce the king's authority or would have any capability for resisting British regular forces if such an attempt was made. The troops sent to Boston in 1768 did not particularly frighten the populace, however. Originally numbering about 1000, under the command of Maj. Gen. Thomas Gage, these troops were gradually reinforced to about 3500 by the spring of 1770. In March of that year, a riot occurred between Boston citizens, jeering and taunting the soldiers, and the British troops. The troops fired, killing five people. The so-called Boston Massacre aroused great colonial resentment. This anger was soon increased by further parliamentary legislation.

Parliament repealed the Townshend Acts in 1770 but, to assert its right to tax the colonies, retained a small tax on tea. In 1773, to induce the colonists to buy British East India Co. tea, Parliament reduced British taxes so that the company could sell tea in America at a price even lower than that of duty-free, smuggled tea. The colonists, however, refused to buy the lower-priced English tea as a matter of principle. In Philadelphia and New York City they would not permit British ships to unload tea. In Boston, in the so-called Boston Tea Party, a group of citizens disguised as Indians swarmed over British ships in the harbor and dumped the cargoes of tea into the water.

In retaliation, Parliament passed (1774) a series of laws designed to punish the province of Massachusetts. By these laws, known in the colonies as the Intolerable Acts, the port of Boston was declared closed to trade until compensation was made for the destroyed tea; town meetings were forbidden; and certain public buildings were taken over for the use of British troops.

The First Continental Congress. The Intolerable Acts secured for Massachusetts the indignant

The Boston Massacre *(1770), an engraving by Paul Revere.* Amer. Library Color Slide Co.

The Destruction of Tea in Boston Harbor *(1846), a lithograph by Nathaniel Currier.* Bettmann Archive

Engagement at the North Bridge at Concord *by Amos Doolittle, a depiction of the Battle of Concord in 1775, the first armed engagement of the American Revolution.*
The Connecticut Historical Society

sympathy of all the colonies. The Virginia assembly sent out a call for a meeting of representatives from the 13 colonies and Canada to consider joint action against the encroachments of parliamentary power on colonial rights. The meeting, known as the First Continental Congress, took place in Philadelphia in September 1774. The Congress consisted of representatives from all 13 colonies except Georgia.

The Congress did not seek independence from Great Britain but attempted to effect a reconciliation with Britain without giving up any colonial rights. It urged the colonies not to carry on any trade with Britain until the Intolerable Acts were repealed. At the same time the Congress respectfully petitioned King George III to prevent Parliament from violating the rights of the colonists as British subjects, specifying 13 instances in which Parliament had done so. The Congress then adjourned, arranging for a second meeting in May 1775. By that time, however, hostilities had begun between Great Britain and the colonies.

Lexington and Concord. The first armed encounter of the American Revolution took place in Massachusetts, where the British force in Boston numbered some 3500 men. General Gage was aware that the militia members of the outlying towns were being trained and reorganized into active elements known as minutemen, ready for immediate service. Ammunition and military stores were being gathered under direction of a Committee of Safety acting for the provincial assembly. On the night of April 18–19, 1775, Gage sent out about 800 men to seize munitions being gathered at Concord, some 29 km (about 18 mi) from Boston. The move did not escape the vigilance of the Committee of Safety, whose mounted messengers, including a local silversmith named Paul Revere, spurred into the countryside to give the alarm. Early on the morning of April 19, the advance guard of the British force exchanged fire with a party of militia at Lexington; eight Americans were killed, and the British continued marching on to Concord. Lt. Col. Francis Smith (1720?–91), the British commander, found militia companies assembling near the town. Most of the military stores had already been removed, and a British attempt to seize one of the two bridges near the town was forestalled by an American counterattack. More militia companies were appearing. Smith, having sent back for reinforcements, took his time reassembling his men for the return march to Boston. That 800 British regulars should be seriously threatened by colonial militiamen, no matter how many, was impossible for a British officer to conceive. British regulars were trained to encounter other regulars in the mechanical formations and volley firing of the rigid European school of war. They were not, however, prepared to use small-unit tactics to drive off persistent attacks by opponents who were accustomed to the individual use of firearms in the open country against targets such as birds and small animals. The British retreat had become a disorganized flight by the time the troops met a supporting force of 1200 men under

An artist's portrayal of Paul Revere's ride, which warned militiamen in Lexington and Concord, Mass., of the approach of an armed British force.

Sir Hugh Percy (1742–1817). This checked the Americans briefly and enabled the retreat to be continued in somewhat better order. British casualties were 73 killed, 174 wounded, and 26 missing, as against 49 killed, 39 wounded, and 5 missing for the colonists. Militia companies from at least 23 towns took part in this operation, which was nothing less than an uprising in arms of a whole countryside against the British. The American offensive did not end with chasing the invaders back to Boston; militia forces kept coming, closing in on the city, which remained in a stage of siege from April 20, 1775, until the British evacuation on March 17, 1776. Gen. Artemas Ward (1727–1800) of Massachusetts assumed temporary command of the besieging troops, which included units from New Hampshire under Col. John Stark, from Rhode Island under Gen. Nathanael Greene, and from Connecticut under Gen. Israel Putnam. Greene was a self-taught military expert; Stark and Putnam had extensive prior service in the French and Indian War, as did many other officers and men of the New England militia units. Perhaps more important for the time being was the paralyzing effect on General Gage of the rough handling of Smith's units by those same militia companies. He could not explain how they had done it, and he showed that he did not want to repeat the experience—rather than trying to break the siege lines that had closed around him, he waited for the arrival by sea of reinforcements being sent by the royal government.

The Second Continental Congress and the Siege of Boston. The Second Continental Congress met in Philadelphia on May 10, 1775, to face the fact that the New England colonies had taken arms against the king's troops. The delegates realized the consequences of this action. They established the Congress as a central government for "The United Colonies of America," adopted the troops engaged in the siege of Boston as their own "Continental Army," and by unanimous vote appointed George Washington as commander in chief. This was a deserved tribute to the high military reputation Washington had earned as an officer of the Virginia troops in the French and Indian War. That Washington, a Virginian, was being chosen to command an army then entirely composed of New England militia had little weight against the general confidence in his character as a man and his skill and experience as a soldier. The vote was taken on June 15; Washington received his commission on June 20 and without delay set out for Boston to take up his new responsibilities.

Meanwhile, Gage's expected reinforcements had arrived, raising the strength of his garrison to 8000 men. He now felt that his forces were strong enough to occupy the heights overlooking Boston from the north at Charlestown and from the south at Dorchester. The colonists had advance notice of his intention and promptly sent troops to confront him at Charlestown, where they occupied and began to fortify a height known as Breed's Hill. (The original purpose had been to hold nearby Bunker Hill, but the orders were changed; however, the designation Battle of Bunker Hill has been perpetuated as the name of the ensuing engagement.) On the night of June 16–17, 1200 Americans under Col. William Prescott (1726–95) occupied Breed's Hill, overlooking Charlestown and the Boston waterfront, and began digging in. On June 17, Gage sent Maj. Gen. William Howe with about 3000 British infantry to storm the position. The British were confident' that in a conventional battle they could readily defeat the American militia, although they still had to face unexpectedly accurate American musket fire, aimed at individual targets. Two British assaults were beaten off with severe losses. A third attack, more carefully prepared, penetrated the American lines. The Americans, almost out of ammunition and without bayonets, fell back in some disorder to Bunker Hill; later they withdrew from this position as well. The British loss was about 1000 men killed and wounded, the American loss about half that number. Technically, the British had won, but the moral effect on both sides was that of an American victory.

On July 3, 1775, Washington assumed command of the American forces with a total strength varying from 13,000 to 16,000, as men came and went almost at will. Washington devoted his immediate efforts to training and reorganizing his army. He could not press the siege of Boston without heavy artillery. For that he would have to wait until winter, when frozen roads and rivers would enable him to drag overland to Boston the guns that had been captured on May 10, 1775, when Ethan Allen of Vermont and Benedict Arnold of Connecticut had surprised and captured the British fort at Ticonderoga on Lake Champlain.

In August 1775 an American force under Gen. Richard Montgomery, a veteran of 15 years service in the British army, invaded Canada; it took Montréal in November, but the following month it was defeated at Québec, where Montgomery was killed.

During this winter, however, Col. Henry Knox, Washington's chief of artillery, brought 59 heavy guns and mortars from Ticonderoga to Boston. On the night of March 4, 1776, Washington occupied Dorchester Heights, overlooking Boston from the south, and began emplacing his newly arrived artillery there. General Howe, who had succeeded Gage, taken completely by surprise, realized that he must storm those gun-crowned heights if he hoped to hold Boston by sea; rather than do this, on March 17 Howe embarked his troops and more than 1000 Loyalists and sailed for Halifax, N.S.

The British Invasion of the North. Washington was under no illusion that Howe's departure from Boston meant the end of British attempts to reduce the American colonies to submission. George III was not likely to give up at a first rebuff, and already word had come that he was engaged in recruiting mercenary troops from Germany. Howe had withdrawn only to reorganize and receive reinforcements. Washington foresaw that when Howe returned in force, New York City with its spacious harbor and immediate access to the interior by way of the Hudson River was by far the most likely place for the British to begin their invasion.

While the Continental Congress in Philadelphia began to think seriously of declaring the independence of the colonies from Great Britain, Washington in New York was wrestling with the problems of preparing to beat off a British invasion, which this time was sure to be made in great force. On June 29, 1776, General Howe arrived off Sandy Hook with a fleet commanded by his brother, Adm. Richard Howe. In this fleet were transports carrying troops of the strongest expeditionary force Britain had ever sent overseas. When fully assembled, this force would number 30,000 troops including 8000 German mercenaries who came chiefly from Hesse-Kassel and Hesse-Hanau. To face this onset, Washington had less than 20,000 men, of whom nearly half were inexperienced as soldiers.

In the leisurely manner that was typical of all his operations during the remainder of the war, Howe waited nearly two months before attempting a landing in force. While he waited, the Con-

Portrait of George Washington *(1795) by Charles Wilson Peale.* Amer. Library Color Slide Co.

tinental Congress—which was unfrightened by the appearance of such a large British force off its principal seaport—adopted, on July 4, 1776, a Declaration of Independence declaring that the colonies "are and of right ought to be free and independent States." Thereafter the Americans fought no longer as dissatisfied British subjects in rebellion against their king, but as the citizens of a sovereign nation repelling invasion by a foreign power.

Battles around New York. Washington had taken up positions on Long Island and Manhattan Island awaiting Howe's opening move. On Aug. 22, 1776, it came at last, as British troops began landing in Gravesend Bay. During the next five days the American troops were driven back to Brooklyn Heights, where they were defeated in the Battle of Long Island. They were removed in boats across the East River to Manhattan during the night of August 29–30, under Washington's personal supervision and without interference by a greatly superior enemy force. Still moving with great caution, Howe pushed Washington's forces northward; an indecisive combat on Manhattan Island was followed by the Battle of White Plains (October 28), also without a clear victor. In November the two forts Washington had constructed to keep the British fleet from using the Hudson River were taken. Washington retreated southwestward across New Jersey and then (December 8) across the Delaware River into Pennsylvania. Convinced that the Americans were thoroughly beaten and that the Continental Congress would sue for peace, Howe did not pursue Washington, but merely established several outposts in New Jersey and settled down in winter quarters to wait for spring.

Trenton and Princeton. Howe had hardly underestimated the weakness of the American army toward the end of 1776. It consisted of less than 3000 men, badly clothed and equipped and poorly fed. In spite of strenuous efforts on the part of Washington and others to recruit new troops, few citizens cared to join an army that appeared on the point of collapse. It seemed as if total defeat and the end of the new nation were at hand, but by a master stroke of strategy Washington redeemed the situation.

On Christmas night, during a blinding snowstorm, Washington led his troops across the Delaware and with a surprise attack overwhelmed a force of about 900 Hessian soldiers in Trenton. On January 3 Washington struck again, routing three regiments of a force under Gen. Charles Cornwallis, 1st Marquis Cornwallis, in the Battle of Princeton. Washington then took up a strong position on high ground at Morristown in north central New Jersey. The British retreated to New York, leaving the American army in full control of New Jersey.

The Campaign of 1777–78. For the campaigning of 1777 the British colonial ministry, headed by Lord George Germain, prepared a plan by which they hoped to end the rebellion in the colonies before the end of the year. The plan was to cut the colonies in two by separating New England, already blockaded by sea, from the southern colonies. A British army under Gen. John Burgoyne was to land in Canada and move south from Montréal to Albany, N.Y. Another force of British and Indians under Col. Barry St. Leger (1737–89) was to move east from Lake Ontario through the Mohawk Valley and meet Burgoyne's troops at Albany. Finally, Howe was to

Baron von Steuben drilling George Washington's troops at Valley Forge. The Prussian officer was inspector general of the Continental army and also acted as a close adviser to Washington.
Library of Congress

send a force from New York City up the Hudson Valley to join the other two columns at Albany.

The plan was too complicated to be successful in such terrains and with poor communications. St. Leger marched east to Fort Stanwix but was unable to capture it, and he retreated on the approach of a relief force under Benedict Arnold.

Saratoga. Burgoyne, at the head of 7000 men, was at first successful. On July 6 he took Fort Ticonderoga, and by July 29 he had reached the upper Hudson River. While waiting there for additional supplies from Canada, Burgoyne sent a Hessian foraging party east into Vermont; this force was cut to pieces in the Battle of Bennington by New Hampshire militia commanded by Gen. John Stark. The American victory not only cost Burgoyne heavy casualties but stimulated American militia enlistments. Burgoyne proceeded south in September but was defeated in two battles at Saratoga by American militiamen and Continental troops commanded by Maj. Gen. Horatio Gates. On October 17 Burgoyne surrendered his army, reduced to 5000 men, to Gates.

Howe's capture of Philadelphia. Germain's plan calling for Howe to move his forces north up the Hudson to support Burgoyne was not followed. Howe, having received no orders to go north, moved south to attack Philadelphia. Such a move, Howe imagined, would end the war at a blow, and he had urged it on London. He landed (August 25) at the head of Chesapeake Bay and marched on Philadelphia. Washington vainly tried to check him at Brandywine Creek, Pa., and on September 26 Howe entered Philadelphia. Before his advance, the Continental Congress fled to Baltimore. On October 4, Washington attacked Howe again at Germantown, just north of Philadelphia, but was defeated after hard fighting. Washington, with about 11,000 men, then went into winter quarters at Valley Forge. A few months later he was joined there by Baron Friedrich Wilhelm von Steuben, the Prussian general who would later become inspector general of the Continental army and take part in the Battle of Monmouth and the siege of Yorktown.

The French alliance. The year 1777 marked the turning point of the war in favor of the American cause. France, defeated by Great Britain in 1763, had been sending money and supplies secretly to the colonists since the beginning of the Revolution. The American victory at Saratoga and the fight waged by Washington at Germantown convinced the French that the Americans now had a good chance of winning the war. In February 1778, France recognized the independence of the colonies and signed a treaty of commerce and alliance with the new country. Thereafter, French support for the U.S. with arms and money was open rather than clandestine, and Washington's great hope for French naval assistance off the American coast seemed about to be realized. A French fleet commanded by Charles Hector, comte d'Estaing (1729–94) sailed for America in April 1778. Warned by admiralty dispatches, Adm. Richard Howe and Gen. Henry Clinton, who had succeeded Gen. William Howe in command of the British troops at Philadelphia, decided on immediate evacuation of that city. They feared that d'Estaing's superior fleet would interrupt their sea communications with New York. As had been the case during the evacuation of Boston, large numbers of Loyalists in Philadelphia had supposed themselves safe and now had to be carried away as fugitives. These people along with the heavier army equipment were loaded into Lord Howe's ships and reached New York City safely. Clinton evacuated Philadelphia and marched north across New Jersey. He was pursued by Washington, who overtook and attacked him at Monmouth Courthouse on June 28. Washington was not victorious, however, because of the misconduct of Maj. Gen. Charles Lee. Clinton returned to New York City in safety; Lee was court-martialed and suspended from the army for 12 months.

D'Estaing's French fleet with 12 ships of the line (the capital ships of the days of sail) arrived off the mouth of the Delaware on July 8, found the British fleet gone, and reached Sandy Hook on July 14. There the French admiral established contact with Washington's headquarters and planned to attack Lord Howe's inferior force. At the last moment, however, d'Estaing decided not to risk his heavy battleships because of low water on the bar. Instead he decided to drive the British out of Newport, R.I., but was prevented from doing so by Lord Howe's skillful tactics and by a gale that scattered both fleets. D'Estaing then went to Boston to refit and sailed for the West Indies on November 4.

The Changing Character of the War. During 1779, neither the American army nor the British force in New York was strong enough for major operations, but the advantage was the American's. Washington had accomplished his primary object: to prevent the British from reconquering the northern colonies by keeping British forces off balance until a well-trained Continental army could be organized to support the militia. The latter could not fight pitched battles by itself, but it did prevent the British from reconquering much American territory. No British army could sustain itself in an armed and hostile countryside except in close contact with its seaborne supplies. Now, at the beginning of 1779, the Americans were no longer fighting alone against Great Britain. Spain had joined France, and Great Britain faced the prospect of a major European war. The British public was bound to be more concerned with a war in Europe than with happenings far away across the Atlantic. As a consequence, more and more British naval and military forces would be taken away from the war in America. George III, in his bitterness against his rebellious American subjects, would not listen to those of his advisers who counseled abandoning the war. These advisers argued that the military conquest of more than 2 million resolute Americans on the other side of the ocean was an impossible task; that the greatest effort of which Britain was capable had been made with the landing of the army under General Howe at New York in 1776, but that Howe's failure to follow up his early success had wasted time that could not be regained; and that the mismanagement of the campaign of 1777 by Howe and Burgoyne and the hard fighting of the Americans had given time for the European enemies of Great Britain to take advantage of the situation. In 1779 Britain could no longer hope to gain a decisive military victory in America. The ancient maxim that "time is the one military commodity that can be irrevocably lost" had been proven once again.

The British Campaign in the South. The king's ministers, caught between the king's bitterness and the American resistance, began a new strategy. They attempted to expand their hold on the southern colonies. They hoped that even if the north could not be retaken, Britain at least might still retain a foothold in the south. On Dec. 28, 1778, a British seaborne expedition of 3500 men from New York captured Savannah. They then proceeded to regain control of other settlements in Georgia.

Further to the west, meanwhile, an American expedition under George Rogers Clark began the new year by capturing the British Fort at Vincennes (now in the state of Indiana). This success established American power in the entire region north of the Ohio River. Later in the year, Washington sent a strong force under Gen. John Sullivan into the Indian country in western New York to destroy the lands and villages of the Iroquoian Confederacy. By doing this Washington hoped to end the British-instigated Indian raids on border settlements in New York and Pennsylvania. The surprise capture of the British post at Stony Point on the Hudson River by "Mad Anthony" Wayne in July was followed in August by the capture of the British garrison at Paulus Hook on the Jersey shore by Henry Lee. In the south, on the other hand, the tide of war was running against the Americans.

Maj. Gen. Benjamin Lincoln (1733-1810) was sent to Charleston to command the southern campaign. There he joined with the French forces of d'Estaing in a hastily prepared assault on Savannah, on Oct. 9, 1779, which was beaten off by the British with heavy loss. D'Estaing then sailed for France, as his orders from Paris required. Lincoln's army was soon besieged in Charleston by a strong British seaborne force of 8000 men that arrived from New York under the command of Sir Henry Clinton. Lincoln allowed his army to be shut up in the city and was forced to surrender in May 1780. Clinton thereupon returned to New York City, leaving Cornwallis with some 7000 regular and Loyalist troops to complete the conquest of the Carolinas. Although Cornwallis was a better and far more energetic general than Howe, he still had to face the problem of maintaining British troops in a hostile countryside. He routed an American force under Maj. Gen. Horatio Gates at Camden, S.C., on August 16, but partisan warfare was again spreading throughout the Carolinas. Two British columns were overwhelmed in the Battle of Kings Mountain on October 7 and at Cowpens on Jan. 17, 1781. In March, Cornwallis fought a bloody but inconclusive battle at Guilford Courthouse in North Carolina, against Maj. Gen. Nathanael Greene, Gates's able successor in the American southern command. He then withdrew to the sea at Wilmington because his supplies were on ships. Thereafter Cornwallis moved north into Virginia and fortified a position at Yorktown, on the sea-flanked peninsula thrusting into Chesapeake Bay between the York and Gloucester rivers. Greene meanwhile cleared the Carolina backcountry of British forces and shut the remainder up in Charleston. He won no set battles, but he remained in control of the countryside.

In the north, Washington had been greatly encouraged by the arrival (July 1780) in Newport, R.I., of about 6000 French troops under the comte de Rochambeau. The British had taken all their troops out of Newport earlier in the year in order to build up forces for their southern campaign. In September, however, Washington discovered the treachery of Maj. Gen. Benedict Arnold, who had proposed to surrender the key fortress of West Point to the British. Arnold, warned that his plot had been discovered, escaped to a British warship in the Hudson River.

Pressures for peace. More promising news was on the way, however. For two years Washington had patiently been working toward a decisive

The USS Bonhomme Richard *(right) battles the British frigate* Serapis *off the English coast on Sept. 23, 1779. Commanded by John Paul Jones, the* Bonhomme *won one of the most notable naval engagements of the American Revolution.*
U.S. Naval Academy Museum

conclusion of the war. He had been kept well informed of events in Great Britain and France by an intelligence service of which the moving spirit was Benjamin Franklin, the American ambassador in Paris. As a result of these reports Washington reached the conviction that British public opinion was turning definitely against continuing the American war. One more British military disaster such as that of Saratoga would bring irresistible pressure on the king and his ministers to make peace and recognize American independence. Washington knew that British armies could not stay in the interior but always had to return to the seacoast for supplies. He had patiently tried to trap the British army between the American land forces and a superior French fleet off the coast. If this could be done for a sufficient period of time the American forces could compel another British surrender like the one at Saratoga. Franklin had impressed the importance of this idea on the French ministry. Fortunately for the Americans, the British navy had, since the end of the Seven Years' War in 1763, been badly neglected and allowed to fall into virtual decay. Meanwhile, French ministers, such as Duc Étienne François de Choiseul, eager to avenge the loss of the French colonial empire to Great Britain, had labored to build the French navy to the highest level of efficiency both in ships and in training for war.

In September 1779 the fleets and armies of France and Spain attacked the British fortress of Gibraltar. Great Britain could not afford, either strategically or economically, to lose its precious gateway to the Mediterranean. Because Gibraltar could only be reinforced and supplied by sea, its support became the most important responsibility of the British fleet.

The standard British strategic principle in a war with France was to maintain overwhelmingly superior fleets and to blockade the two principal French ports at Brest on the Atlantic and at Toulon on the Mediterranean. If a French fleet got to sea, it was to be relentlessly pursued. In 1781, however, the Royal Navy did not have enough ships of the line to blockade both French ports and at the same time to supply the garrison at Gibraltar, which required continuous fighting to break through the allied fleets off that port. The escape of the French fleet from Toulon in 1778 was one result of British naval weakness. In 1781, when Gibraltar was especially hard pressed, the admiralty had to leave Brest unguarded also, so 26 French ships of the line under Vice Adm. François Joseph Paul de Grasse were able to sail from Brest on March 22, bound for the West Indies. De Grasse had orders to get in touch with Washington about a combined operation.

The French frigate *Concorde* brought this news to Boston on May 6. On July 16 it rejoined de Grasse at Cap-François (now Cap-Haïtien), Haiti, with an American proposal for de Grasse to bring his fleet and as many French troops as could be spared to Chesapeake Bay.

Yorktown. The plan was to combine with Washington's forces in trapping Cornwallis. The *Con-*

corde returned on August 12, with de Grasse's acceptance. With this exchange of messages, and the steady good luck of the *Concorde* in avoiding British blockaders, the decisive operation of the war was set in motion. The troops of Washington and Rochambeau marched south, leaving a containing force to watch Clinton in New York. De Grasse's fleet arrived at the Chesapeake capes on August 30, drove off a British fleet under Adm. Thomas Graves (1725?–1802), and established a tight blockade of Cornwallis's army. A total of 16,000 American and French troops and Virginia militia, under Washington's command, laid siege to Yorktown. Cornwallis made several vain attempts to break through the allied lines, but on Oct. 19, 1781, he was obliged to surrender to Washington.

Treaty of Paris. Yorktown marked the end of serious hostilities, although peace negotiations dragged on until the Treaty of Paris was finally signed on Sept. 3, 1783. Great Britain recognized the independence of the former colonies as the United States of America and acknowledged its boundaries as extending west to the Mississippi, north to Canada (with fishing rights in Newfoundland), and south to the Floridas.

Washington, to whose genius and determination the victory was due, took leave of his officers in New York City on Dec. 4, 1783, surrendered his commission to Congress at Annapolis on December 23, and, in words that were to prove something less than prophetic, took leave "of all the employments of public life." G.F.E.

See also CONTINENTAL CONGRESS; INTOLERABLE ACTS; PARIS, TREATY OF; STAMP ACT; TOWNSHEND ACTS; and separate articles on most of the battles mentioned above. For additional information on historical figures, see biographies of those whose names are not followed by dates.

For further information on this topic, see the Bibliography in volume 28, sections 1139–40, 1149–51.

AMERICAN SAMOA, unincorporated territory of the U.S., formed by a group of seven islands in the S Pacific Ocean, comprising Tutuila, on which a U.S. naval station is located; the Manua group, consisting of Tau, Olosega, and Ofu; Aunuu; Rose Island; and Swains Island. All except Rose Island, which is an uninhabited coral atoll, are mountainous and of volcanic formation. Tutuila is the largest island of the group, covering an area of about 143 sq km (about 55 sq mi) and with a 1990 population, including Aunuu, of 45,043. Pago Pago, on Tutuila (1990 pop. 3519), is the seat of government of American Samoa and has one of the finest harbors in the South Pacific. The total area of American Samoa is 200 sq km (77 sq mi); in early 1990 the population was 46,773.

Population and Education. Samoans are Polynesians, and most are Christians. Foreigners, including Americans, are prohibited by local laws from buying Samoan-owned land. Education is free and compulsory for all children between the ages of 6 and 18. Instruction is provided by about 30 public and 6 private schools, 160 village schools for early education, and a community college. In the consolidated public elementary schools television is used for instruction purposes.

Economy. Agriculture is the principal occupation. The most important crops include taro, coconuts, bananas, oranges, pineapples, papayas, breadfruit, and yams. Industry is limited to the canning of fish for export; grass mats and other handicrafts are also made and exported. Tourism is of increasing importance. The economy, however, remains largely dependent upon grants and appropriations by the U.S. Congress. Regular shipping services connect American Samoa with the mainland U.S., Fiji, Hawaii, Australia, New Zealand, and Japan. The airport at Pago Pago is an important stop for transpacific flights.

Government. The islands are administered by the U.S. Department of the Interior. Under the constitution of 1966, executive authority lies with the governor, who, since 1977, has been elected by popular vote. Samoans are U.S. nationals, and the constitution contains most of the guarantees of the U.S. Bill of Rights. Legislative authority is vested in the Samoan legislature, or Fono, which consists of a senate and house of representatives. The senate has 18 members, who are elected, according to Samoan custom, from the local chiefs, and the house has 20 members, elected by popular vote. The islands are divided into three districts, each having a Samoan governor. Local administrative matters are conducted by village, county, and district councils composed of hereditary chiefs and their advisers. The judicial system includes a high court and five district courts. The secretary of the interior appoints the chief justice and an associate justice, who are assisted by four Samoan associate judges. Medical attention is provided by the government, which operates a general hospital, eight dispensaries, and a tropical disease medical center.

History. According to native tradition the Samoan Islands were the original home of the Polynesian race, from which colonists peopled the other Polynesian islands of the Pacific. Ethnologists, however, now believe that two separate waves of immigrants peopled Samoa, the first group probably originating in southwestern Asia.

The later migration displaced the original Samoans, who then began to colonize the more easterly islands of Polynesia. The islands were discovered in 1722 by Jacob Roggeveen (1659–1729), a Dutch navigator. In 1768 Louis Antoine de Bougainville, a French explorer, named the group the Navigators Islands. During the 19th century Germany, Great Britain, and the U.S. established commercial posts on the islands. In 1878 the U.S. annexed Pago Pago for use as a naval coaling station. In 1888 native disturbances resulting from the selection of a king created a crisis among the three powers. The matter was settled by the Act of Berlin in 1889, which proclaimed the independence and neutrality of the islands and guaranteed the natives full liberty in the election of their king. In 1899, during the course of a native civil war, the U.S. and Great Britain formed an alliance against Germany, and Apia, the site of the German station, was shelled by British and U.S. ships. Agreement, however, was reached in the same year. By the treaty then concluded, Germany received the islands west of long 171° W, U.S. sovereignty was recognized over the islands east of the meridian, and Great Britain received the Solomon Islands and Tonga as compensation. The chiefs of Tutuila and Aunuu ceded these islands to the U.S. in 1900, and the Manua group was ceded in 1904. Swains Island was annexed by the U.S. in 1925 and added to American Samoa. The islands were administered by the U.S. Navy until 1951, when they came under the U.S. Department of the Interior. In December 1991, typhoon Val caused $80 million in damages.

For further information on this topic, see the Bibliography in volume 28, section 1250.

AMERICAN SOCIETY OF COMPOSERS, AUTHORS, AND PUBLISHERS (ASCAP), organization founded under the leadership of the Irish-American composer Victor Herbert in New York City in 1914 to protect its members from copyright infringements and to work for the improvement of copyright laws. ASCAP occupies first place among societies in the U.S. that grant licenses and collect royalties under copyrights assigned to it by its members. It is the American affiliate of the International Confederation of Societies of Composers and Authors, organized in Paris in 1926; in particular, ASCAP cooperates with the section of the international body that deals with nondramatic and musical rights. ASCAP is managed by a board of directors who represent various fields of music.

Royalty earnings from radio and television performances are the chief source of income for ASCAP. A nonprofit organization, ASCAP distributes this income, after deduction of operating expenses, equally between the group of publishers and the group of composers and authors, but not equally among the individual members of each group; the royalties of each member are based on the extent of use of works by that member by the licensees of the society.

Membership includes music publishers, composers, and lyricists. The society's main offices are in New York City.

AMERICAN SOCIETY FOR THE PREVENTION OF CRUELTY TO ANIMALS. *See* PETS.

AMERICAN STAFFORDSHIRE TERRIER, breed of dog, originally developed in England, from a mixture of bulldog and terrier, for the purpose of dogfighting. The breed's name was officially adopted in 1972 to distinguish it from the Staffordshire bullterrier. Before that it was known simply as the Staffordshire terrier, the name under which it was first recognized by the American Kennel Club in 1935. The dog has a broad head, strong jaws with pronounced cheek muscles, a thick neck, forelegs set apart, and a short tail. The short, stiff-haired coat may be any color; the ears are preferably left uncropped. The dog stands 43 to 48 cm (17 to 19 in) high and weighs 15.9 to 22.7 kg (35 to 50 lb).

AMERICAN UNIVERSITY, independent institution of higher learning in Washington, D.C., originally chartered by Congress in 1893 as a Methodist church-related institution. Major academic divisions are the college of arts and sciences (including schools of communication and education); schools of international service and public affairs; Kogod College of Business Administration; and Washington College of Law.

AMERICAN UNIVERSITY IN CAIRO, institution of higher learning in Cairo, Egypt. Founded in 1919, the university is administered by an American board of trustees. Undergraduate and graduate faculties offer courses (in English) in Arabic and English studies and in the social and physical sciences. The university operates centers for adult and continuing education, desert development, and social research, and the Abdul Latif Jameel Center for Middle East Management Studies.

AMERICAN VETERANS COMMITTEE (AVC), organization of U.S. veterans of World War I, World War II, and the Korean and Vietnam wars; it also includes former members of the U.S. Merchant Marine. It was founded in 1943 by a group of servicemen; its first president was Charles Guy Bolte (1920–).

The AVC has campaigned for improvements in civil rights and civil liberties and for equal opportunities for all citizens and has concerned itself with such economic problems as adequate housing and employment and inflation. It has supported assistance for veterans returning to civilian life and adequate medical and financial assistance for disabled veterans. The AVC constitution prohibits its chapters from organizing or endorsing a political party or candidate. The national headquarters is in Washington, D.C.

AMERICAN VETERANS OF WORLD WAR II, KOREA, AND VIETNAM (AMVETS), association of veterans founded in 1944 and chartered by the U.S. Congress in 1947. Anyone who served in the U.S. Armed Forces or any American citizen who served in the armed forces of an Allied nation during World War II or during the Korean and Vietnam wars is eligible for membership, if the recipient of an honorable discharge.

Objectives of the AMVETS include upholding the principles of the U.S. Constitution, promoting peace and goodwill among nations, and perpetuating the friendships of wartime service. Its programs include legislation, education, scholarships, community service, civil defense, traffic safety, hospital work, and rehabilitation. The national headquarters is in Washington, D.C.

AMERICAN WATER SPANIEL. *See* SPANIEL.

AMERICAN YOUTH HOSTELS, INC. *See* HOSTEL.

AMERICA'S CUP RACE, yacht race for a trophy, symbolizing international supremacy in sailing competition. The first contest for the prize, originally the Queen's Cup, was sponsored by the Royal Yacht Squadron of Great Britain in 1851. Members of the New York Yacht Club competed in the race with the 170-ton schooner *America,* which in August 1851 sailed against 14 Royal Yacht Squadron ships in a race around the Isle of Wight. *America* won the prize, a silver cup. In July 1857 the cup was presented to the New York Yacht Club, to be held as a world trophy; thereafter it was known as the America's Cup. The deed of gift stipulated, among other things, that competing yachts must have a load waterline of not less than 65 ft (19.81 m) and must proceed exclusively under sail to the contest area.

From 1870 to 1895, two Canadian and seven British challengers lost to American defenders of the trophy. The craft in the matches of 1870, 1871, and 1876 were schooners; in 1881 all craft were sloops. Thereafter, competitors were all single-mast craft, such as sloops, cutters, or J boats. The British yachtsman Sir Thomas Lipton made five attempts to win the cup between 1899 and 1930.

From 1930 to 1983 the races were held off Newport, R.I., with a hiatus during World War II and after. Postwar challengers were discouraged by the costs of building and maintaining craft with the required load waterline. On the initiative of the New York Yacht Club, the 1857 deed was amended (Dec. 7, 1956) by the New York State Supreme Court to permit a load waterline of not less than 44 ft (13.41 m). Under the court's order, yachts of the 12-m class became eligible. Since 1958 the race has been run over a triangular 39-km (24-mi) course; the yacht coming in best in four of seven heats is the winner. The 1988 contest, held off Fremantle, Australia, was the first in which a catamaran, *Stars & Stripes,* was matched against a traditional single-hull yacht. After the "cat" won, New Zealand contested the victory in court, unsuccessfully. In 1989 guidelines for the International America's Cup Class yachts were established, and ships up to 75 ft (22.86 m) became eligible. The 1992 competition, off San Diego, Calif., was won by the U.S. entry, *America³*.

AMERICA'S CUP CONTESTS

Year	Races	Winning Yacht	Losing Yacht
1870	1	Magic (U.S.)	Cambria (Brit.)
1871	5	Columbia and Sappho (U.S.)	Livonia (Brit.)
1876	2	Madeleine (U.S.)	Countess of Dufferin (Can.)
1881	2	Mischief (U.S.)	Atalanta (Can.)
1885	2	Puritan (U.S.)	Genesta (Brit.)
1886	2	Mayflower (U.S.)	Galatea (Brit.)
1887	2	Volunteer (U.S.)	Thistle (Brit.)
1893	3	Vigilant (U.S.)	Valkyrie II (Brit.)
1895	3	Defender (U.S.)	Valkyrie III (Brit.)
1899	3	Columbia (U.S.)	Shamrock (Brit.)
1901	3	Columbia (U.S.)	Shamrock II (Brit.)
1903	3	Reliance (U.S.)	Shamrock III (Brit.)
1920	5	Resolute (U.S.)	Shamrock IV (Brit.)
1930	4	Enterprise (U.S.)	Shamrock V (Brit.)
1934	6	Rainbow (U.S.)	Endeavor (Brit.)
1937	4	Ranger (U.S.)	Endeavor II (Brit.)
1958	4	Columbia (U.S.)	Sceptre (Brit.)
1962	5	Weatherly (U.S.)	Gretel (Aust.)
1964	4	Constellation (U.S.)	Sovereign (Brit.)
1967	4	Intrepid (U.S.)	Dame Pattie (Aust.)
1970	5	Intrepid (U.S.)	Gretel II (Aust.)
1974	4	Courageous (U.S.)	Southern Cross (Aust.)
1977	4	Courageous (U.S.)	Australia (Aust.)
1980	5	Freedom (U.S.)	Australia (Aust.)
1983	7	Australia II (Aust.)	Liberty (U.S.)
1987	4	Stars & Stripes (U.S.)	Kookaburra III (Aust.)
1988	2	Stars & Stripes (U.S.)	New Zealand (N.Z.)
1992	5	America³ (U.S.)	Il Moro di Venezia (It.)

AMERICIUM, radioactive metallic element, symbol Am, one of the transuranium elements (q.v.) in the actinide series (q.v.) of the periodic table (*see* PERIODIC LAW); at.no. 95, at.wt. (most stable isotope) 243. Americium melts at about 994°C (about 1821°F) and has a sp.gr. of about 14.

Americium is a malleable metal somewhat similar to lead. The fourth transuranic element to be synthesized, it was discovered in 1944–45 by the American physicist Glenn Seaborg and his associates at the University of Chicago. They synthesized the americium isotope of mass number 241 by bombarding plutonium-239 with neutrons. Americium isotopes with mass numbers 237 to 247 have been formed; they are all radioactive, with half-lives of from 0.9 min (americium-232) to about 7400 years (americium-243). Americium-243 is used as target material in nuclear reactors or particle accelerators (q.v.) for the production of even heavier synthetic elements. *See* RADIOACTIVITY.

AMERIGO VESPUCCI. *See* VESPUCCI, AMERIGO.

AMERSFOORT, city, central Netherlands, in Utrecht Province, on the Eem R., near Utrecht. A market town, it is also an important railway junction and industrial center. The principal manufactures include chemicals, tobacco products, silk and woolen goods, and foodstuffs.

Amersfoort was chartered in 1259. The old central part of the town, which still stands, was built with a surrounding wall into which houses and water gates were set. It is one of the best-preserved medieval towns in Europe, with several fine churches and a notable 95-m (312-ft) bell tower. Pop. (1988 est.) 93,500.

AMES, city, Story Co., central Iowa, on the Skunk R., near Des Moines; inc. 1893. Ames is the seat of Iowa State University of Science and Technology (1858), the National Animal Disease Center, and the National Veterinary Services Laboratory. The city's manufactures include water-analysis and -treatment equipment, processed food, and animal feed. Founded 1854, it is named for Oakes Ames (1804–74), a congressman from Massachusetts who supported a railroad project here. The city is a leader in veterinary research. Pop. (1980) 45,775; (1990) 47,198.

AMES, Fisher (1758–1808), American statesman, born in Dedham, Mass., and educated at Harvard College (now Harvard University). He studied classics and ancient history, taught school occasionally, studied law, and was admitted to the bar in 1781. He was a delegate to the 1788 convention in Massachusetts that ratified the U.S. Constitution. A political essayist and orator, he became prominent in the affairs of the Federalist party. Ames was elected to the U.S. House of Representatives in 1789 and subsequently led the legislative fight for many Federalist policies, notably in 1796 for the appropriation to effectuate Jay's Treaty with Great Britain. Although he retired from public life in 1797, after completing his fifth term in Congress, he remained a leader of the Federalist party until his death. His speeches and writings, hostile to the democratic policies of Thomas Jefferson, were published as *Works of Fisher Ames* (2 vol., 1854) and *Speeches of Fisher Ames in Congress, 1789–96* (1871).

AMETHYST, variety of quartz, differing from common quartz and rock crystal chiefly because it is violet to purple in color, which is caused by the presence of compounds of iron or manganese.

Specimen of amethyst, showing the typical six-sided crystal prisms. © Martin Land–Science Photo Laboratories

It is a birthstone for February and is used to make seals and rings. The finest specimens occur in India, Sri Lanka, and Brazil. Amethyst is common in Europe and in many parts of Scotland.

AMHARIC LANGUAGE. *See* SEMITIC LANGUAGES.

AMHERST, town, Hampshire Co., W Massachusetts, in the Pioneer Valley; inc. 1776. Located in a rich farming area, it is an educational center, the seat of Amherst College, the University of Massachusetts, and Hampshire College (1965). Its many old homes include those of the poets Emily Dickinson and Robert Frost. The lexicographer Noah Webster and the sculptor Daniel Chester French also lived here. The town is named for the British soldier Lord Jeffrey Amherst. Pop. (1980) 33,229; (1990) 35,228.

AMHERST, town, seat of Cumberland Co., N Nova Scotia, on the isthmus of Chignecto between Northumberland Strait and Chignecto Bay (an arm of the Bay of Fundy); inc. 1889. Amherst is an industrial center located in an agricultural and coal-mining area. Major manufactures include metal, wood, and plastic products; clothing; chemicals; aircraft parts; processed food; machinery; and electronic equipment. Originally settled as an Acadian community known as Les Planches, the site was resettled by the English in 1759 and named for the British soldier Lord Jeffrey Amherst. Pop. (1986) 9671; (1991) 9742.

AMHERST, Jeffrey Amherst, Baron (1717–97), British soldier, born in Riverhead, Kent. He entered the British army as an ensign in 1731. He served in the War of the Austrian Succession and in the early stages of the Seven Years' War. In 1758 he was promoted to the rank of major general and put in command of an expedition against Louisbourg, N.S., which, after a short siege, surrendered on July 27, 1758.

In September 1758, Amherst became commander in chief of the British forces engaged in the American phase of the war (known as the French and Indian War). He led a successful expedition against Fort Ticonderoga and Crown Point in 1759, and in 1760 he commanded the British forces at Montréal and secured its capture. For his services he was appointed governor-general of British North America, formally acknowledged by Parliament, and made a knight of the Bath. He returned to England in 1763. From 1772 to 1782 and from 1783 to 1793, he was acting commander in chief of the British army. He became a general in 1778, commander in chief in 1793, and a field marshal in 1796.

AMHERST COLLEGE, privately controlled school of higher learning, in Amherst, Mass. The college was opened in 1821 and chartered in 1825; Noah Webster was one of its founders. Amherst offers courses of instruction in the arts and sciences leading to the B.A. degree.

AMIDE, any of a large group of organic compounds containing the radical $CONH_2$ and, usually, a hydrocarbon. Amides are common in nature, one of the most familiar being urea (q.v.), a diamide containing no hydrocarbon. Proteins and peptides consist of amides. An example of a longchain polyamide is nylon (q.v.).

AMIENS, city, N France, capital of Somme Department, on the Somme R., the historical capital of Picardy. The city has been a textile center since the 16th century; other manufactures include machinery, metal goods, chemicals, and perfumes. Of note is the Cathedral of Notre Dame (1220–70), the largest Gothic cathedral in France; it is 143 m (470 ft) long, and its nave is 43 m (140 ft) high. Amiens is the seat of the University of Picardy (1965).

The city was a center of the Ambiani Gauls, from whom its name is derived, and it later was a Roman settlement. For centuries Amiens was a major fortress, guarding Paris from attack from the N. The fortifications are now boulevards, but the old citadel still stands. An Anglo-French truce was agreed to here in 1264, and the Treaty of Amiens, resulting in a brief respite in fighting between Great Britain and France during the Napoleonic Wars, was signed in the city in 1802. During the Franco-Prussian War, the Germans defeated the French at Amiens in November 1870. The city was captured by the Germans in World Wars I and II. Pop. (1982) 136,358.

AMIENS, TREATY OF, peace treaty signed on March 27, 1802, between Great Britain on one side and France, Spain, and the Batavian Republic on the other. This treaty finally ended the War of the Second Coalition, one of the Napoleonic Wars, already partly brought to a close by the Peace of Lunéville in 1801. By the terms of the Treaty of Amiens, Great Britain was to surrender to France and the French allies all British conquests except Ceylon (now Sri Lanka) and Trinidad. France agreed to evacuate Egypt, Naples, and the Papal States. Among the territories Great Britain was to give up were the Cape of Good Hope Colony (to the Batavian Republic) and Malta (to the Order of the Knights of Malta). None of the treaty provisions was fully observed, and hostilities resumed in 1803.

AMIN, Idi (1925–), president of Uganda (1971–79). Born in Koboko of Muslim parents, Amin received a primary education before joining the British colonial army in 1946. He was one of only two native officers in Uganda's military forces when the country became independent in 1962. A supporter of President Milton Obote, he rose quickly through the ranks and was promoted to major general and commander of the armed forces in 1968. Finally, he overthrew Obote in January 1971. As president, Amin followed an erratic, tyrannical, and increasingly bloody course that left the country in shambles. He expelled some 50,000 Asians (1972), nationalized foreign companies, and had up to 300,000 Ugandans killed. The economy collapsed, and in 1979 Amin was overthrown by an invasion force from Tanzania supported by Ugandan rebels.

AMINDIVI ISLANDS. *See* LACCADIVE, MINICOY, AND AMINDIVI ISLANDS.

AMINE. *See* CHEMISTRY, ORGANIC.

AMINO ACIDS, important class of organic compounds that contain both the amino ($—NH_2$) and carboxyl ($—COOH$) groups. Of these acids, 20 serve as the building blocks of proteins (*see* PROTEIN). Known as the standard, or alpha, amino acids, they comprise alanine, arginine, asparagine, aspartic acid, cysteine, glutamic acid, glutamine, glycine, histidine, isoleucine, leucine, lysine, methionine, phenylalanine, proline, serine, threonine, tryptophan, tyrosine, and valine. All 20 are constructed according to a general formula:

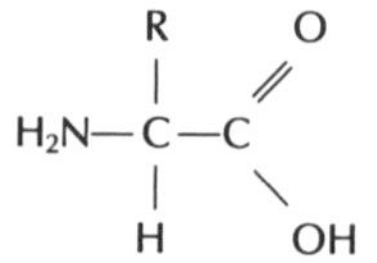

As the formula shows, the amino and carboxyl groups are both attached to a single carbon atom, which is called the alpha carbon atom. Attached to the carbon atom is a variable group

(R); it is in their R groups that the molecules of the 20 standard amino acids differ from one another. In the simplest of the acids, glycine, the R consists of a single hydrogen atom. Other amino acids have more complex R groups that contain carbon as well as hydrogen and may include oxygen, nitrogen, or sulfur, as well.

When a living cell makes protein, the carboxyl group of one amino acid is linked to the amino group of another to form a peptide bond. The carboxyl group of the second amino acid is similarly linked to the amino group of a third, and so on, until a long chain is produced. This chainlike molecule, which may contain from 50 to several hundred amino acid subunits, is called a polypeptide. A protein may be formed of a single polypeptide chain, or it may consist of several such chains held together by weak molecular bonds. Each protein is formed according to a precise set of instructions contained within the nucleic acid (*see* NUCLEIC ACIDS), which is the genetic material of the cell. These instructions determine which of the 20 standard amino acids are to be incorporated into the protein, and in what sequence. The R groups of the amino acid subunits determine the final shape of the protein and its chemical properties; an extraordinary variety of proteins can be produced from the same 20 subunits.

The standard amino acids serve as raw materials for the manufacture of many other cellular products, including hormones (*see* HORMONE) and pigments. In addition, several of these amino acids are key intermediates in cellular metabolism (*see* METABOLISM).

Most plants and microorganisms are able to use inorganic compounds to make all the amino acids they require for normal growth. Animals, however, must obtain some of the standard amino acids from their diet in order to survive; these particular amino acids are called essential. Essential amino acids for humans include lysine, tryptophan, valine, histidine, leucine, isoleucine, phenylalanine, threonine, methionine, and arginine. They are found in adequate amounts in protein-rich foods from animal sources or in carefully chosen combinations of plant proteins.

In addition to the amino acids that form proteins, more than 150 other amino acids have been found in nature, including some that have the carboxyl and amino groups attached to separate carbon atoms. These unusually structured amino acids are most often found in fungi and higher plants. M.L.H.

For further information on this topic, see the Bibliography in volume 28, sections 415, 439, 443–44.

AMIOT, (Jean) Joseph Marie (1718–93), French scholar of Chinese culture, born in Toulon. Amiot (or Amyot) was a Jesuit missionary in China from 1750 until his death. His French-Chinese dictionary (1789) contains vocabularies of Tatar and Manchu. Amiot introduced Chinese literature and customs to Europe.

AMIS, Kingsley (1922–), English novelist, born in London. He was educated at Saint John's College, University of Oxford. His first novel, *Lucky Jim* (1953), was a bitingly satirical story of an unheroic young college instructor. The book influenced a group of British playwrights and novelists who were known as the angry young men because of their rebellious and critical attitude toward postwar British society. *That Uncertain Feeling* (1955) and *Take a Girl Like You* (1960) are later novels in which Amis further explored his disillusionment. Amis also has written poetry, criticism, and short stories. *The Green Man* (1970) is a novel of the supernatural. He also wrote *The Riverside Villas Murder, On Drink* (both 1973), *Jake's Thing* (1979), and the antifeminist *Stanley and the Women* (1984).

AMISH, North American Protestant group of Mennonite origin. The Amish have maintained a distinctive and conservative agricultural way of life despite the influences of modern industrial society.

The name Amish is derived from Jakob Amman (c. 1644–1730), a Swiss Mennonite bishop. He insisted that discipline within the church be maintained by excommunication. This entailed the avoidance (shunning) by the faithful of those excommunicated (under the ban). Conventional social relationships with the excommunicated, such as eating at the same table, buying and selling, and, in the case of a married person, marital relations, were forbidden. Persecuted in Europe, the Amish migrated in the 18th century to Pennsylvania, where their descendants are called Pennsylvania Dutch. They then spread into Ohio, other midwestern states, and Canada. A rural people, their skill in farming is exemplary.

The most conservative are known as Old Order Amish. They dress in a severely plain style, using hooks and eyes instead of buttons. They ride in horse-drawn buggies instead of automobiles, and the adult males are bearded. Religious services are held in homes; foot washing is practiced in connection with the communion service; discipline is enforced by shunning; and marriage with outsiders is condemned. Other Amish groups, such as the Conservative Mennonite Conference and the Beachy Amish Mennonite Churches, are milder in discipline and less set apart from the world. All share the practice of

Their old-fashioned buggies visible at the right, a number of Amish farmers attend a community auction. The conservative Amish lead a primarily rural existence not dependent on modern conveniences. Jane Latta

believer's, or adult, baptism and often refuse to take part in civil affairs—to vote, serve in the military, and so forth. The total membership of all groups is probably not more than 50,000.

The Amish have sometimes come into conflict with the larger society. In particular, they have resisted compulsory education requirements as a threat to their separate way of life. In the case of *Wisconsin* v. *Yoder* (1972), the state sought to require the children of an Amish family to attend school until the age of 16. The parents were willing to allow them to attend through the eighth grade but argued that high school education would make them unfit to carry on the Amish tradition. The U.S. Supreme Court agreed that their right to the free exercise of their religion is protected and that the state's concern for compulsory public education must yield to that consideration.

See also MENNONITES.

For further information on this topic, see the Bibliography in volume 28, sections 106, 110.

***AMISTAD* CASE,** case before the U.S. Supreme Court in 1841 involving the legal status of some black men who had been sold into slavery in Africa and put on the Spanish vessel the *Amistad* to be transported abroad. Two years earlier, the defendant slaves had killed some of the crew and seized control of the vessel on which they were being transported. They then had ordered the crew to steer for Africa. Subsequently, the *Amistad* was seized by a U.S. warship, and the slaves were held as pirates. Martin Van Buren, president of the U.S., wished to surrender the men to the Spanish government, but the Supreme Court held that they were free on the basis of international law prohibiting the slave trade. Charitable donations purchased passage for the men back to Africa.

AMMAN (biblical *Rabbah Ammon;* anc. *Philadelphia*), capital of Jordan and Amman governorate, N Jordan, near Jerusalem. Amman is the commercial, industrial, and administrative center of Jordan. Industries here manufacture textiles, tobacco products, dry batteries, leather products, tiles, and cement and process flour and other food products. The extraction of phosphate and petroleum refining are other important industries. International rail and airline services are in operation.

The city Rabbah Ammon had its origins in the period about 1500 BC, and was important as the chief city of the Ammonites (q.v.). In the 3d century BC the Egyptian king Ptolemy Philadelphus captured it and renamed it Philadelphia, under which name it was known throughout the eras of the Roman and Byzantine empires. Many ruins of this period can be seen in Amman today. In the 1st century AD it was a leading city of the Roman province of Arabia. Lost to the Byzantines at the rise of Islam and subsequently conquered by Arabs in the 7th century, the city fell by about 1300 into decline, again taking its former name, Rabbah Ammon. It was revived in the 20th century. An important Turkish base during World

War I, it was taken from the Turks by the British in September 1918. Amman became the capital of newly independent Jordan in 1946. During the Arab-Israeli War of 1948–49, the city received many Palestinian refugees from the new Jewish state of Israel; their number increased after the Arab-Israeli War of 1967, when Jordan lost control to Israel of areas W of the Jordan R. occupied by Palestinians. In 1970, as a result of political differences between the militant Palestine Liberation Organization (PLO) and the Jordanian government, fighting occurred in Amman, and the city suffered heavy damage. Pop. (1989 est.) 936,300.

AMMANATI, Bartolommeo (1511–92), Italian Mannerist sculptor and architect. Born in Settignano, he studied and worked in Venice and Rome before settling in Florence in 1555. His most important works are in the latter city. Ammanati's masterpiece is the gracefully arched Ponte Santa Trinità (1567–70; bombed 1944, rebuilt 1957) spanning the Arno River. He also built the enlargements of the Palazzo Pitti (1558–70), including the heavily Mannerist three-story courtyard entirely in rusticated (rough) stone. The suave bronze basin figures of his colossal Neptune Fountain (1576, Piazza della Signoria) are admired more than the stiffly posed marble figure of the sea god in its center.

AMMETER. *See* ELECTRIC METERS.

AMMON. *See* AMON.

AMMONIA, colorless, pungent gas, NH_3, highly soluble in water. A saturated aqueous (water) solution of ammonia contains 45 percent ammonia by weight at 0° C (32° F) and 30 percent at ordinary room temperatures. On solution in water, ammonia becomes ammonium hydroxide, NH_4OH, which is strongly basic and similar in chemical behavior to the hydroxides of the alkali metals (*see* ACIDS AND BASES; ALKALIES).

Ammonia was known to the ancients, who derived both the name and the substance from sal ammoniac, which was produced at the Temple of Jupiter Ammon in Libya by the distillation of camel dung. During the Middle Ages in Europe ammonia was obtained by heating the horns and hoofs of oxen and was called spirits of hartshorn. Free ammonia was obtained by the German alchemist Basil Valentine (b. 1414?); its composition was determined by the French chemist Comte Claude Berthollet about 1777.

In the 19th century the principal source of ammonia was the destructive distillation of coal; it was an important by-product of the manufacture of fuel gases (*see* GASES, FUEL). Today most ammonia is produced synthetically from hydrogen and nitrogen (*see* NITROGEN FIXATION). Ammonia is an important refrigerant (*see* REFRIGERATION) and is widely used in the chemical industries, especially in the manufacture of fertilizer, nitric acid, and explosives (qq.v.).

Ammonia melts at −77.7° C (−107.9° F), boils at −33.35° C (−28.03° F), and has a density (q.v.) of 0.68 at its boiling point and 1 atm (760 torrs) of pressure.

AMMONITES, ancient Semitic people who inhabited the region between the Syrian Desert and the Jordan River in present-day Jordan. According to Gen. 19:38, they were the descendants of Benammi, the son of Lot, and close kin to the Moabites. The Ammonite civilization began in the 13th century BC and lasted until the 6th century BC. The chief city of the Ammonites was Rabbah Ammon (now Amman, Jordan). The Israelites were often at war with them. David, king of Judah and Israel, suppressed the Ammonites (see 2 Sam. 12:26–31) and subjected them to forced labor. In 721 BC, after the fall of the kingdom of Israel, the Ammonites settled in the districts east of the Jordan River. The autonomous Ammonite state had ceased to exist by the middle of the 6th century BC. By the 1st century BC, their territory had been incorporated into the Roman Empire, and by the 3d century AD, they had been virtually absorbed by Arab tribes. The language of the Ammonites apparently was related to Hebrew.

AMNESIA, loss or impairment of memory. It may be caused by organic disorders, such as brain injury or cerebral arteriosclerosis, or by functional nervous disorders, such as hysteria. Amnesia may be total, with complete loss of recall; or partial, occurring only immediately before or after a traumatic event; or systematic, relating to a particular type or group of experiences. Amnesia is a symptom rather than a disease, and treatment attempts to determine and remove the basic cause.

AMNESTY, in international law, act of effacing and forgetting past offenses granted by the government to persons who have been guilty of neglect or crime. The term is applied to rebellious acts against the state. Amnesty differs from pardon (q.v.) in that amnesty causes the crime to be forgotten, whereas pardon, given after a conviction, exempts the criminal from further punishment. Amnesty is usually granted to a class of criminals or group of persons who may have committed a crime and is offered in order to restore tranquility in the state.

Some examples of amnesty in U.S. history were those granted by President Andrew Johnson after the American Civil War and those given to certain wartime offenders after World Wars I and II. Amnesty may be conditional upon fulfillment of certain obligations within a specified period. In 1974 President Gerald Ford instituted a program for Vietnam War deserters and draft evaders, requiring them to spend two years doing public service work as the condition for amnesty. Few people took advantage of these terms within the time allowed for the program.

AMNESTY INTERNATIONAL (AI), private, nonprofit, nonpartisan organization founded in 1961 by the British lawyer Peter Benenson (1921–). Dedicated to the release of "prisoners of conscience," to securing fair and prompt trials for political prisoners, and to the abolition of the death penalty, torture, and other cruel, inhumane, or degrading treatment of those in custody, AI has intervened on behalf of some 30,000 prisoners in more than 100 countries. In the late 1980s the organization claimed 700,000 members and supporters in more than 150 nations, including the U.S. AI's International Secretariat is in London, where most of its research is conducted; representatives are frequently dispatched for on-the-spot investigation of human rights abuses. In 1977 AI received the Nobel Peace Prize for "its efforts on behalf of defending human dignity against violence and subjugation."

AMNIOCENTESIS, in medicine, a procedure for withdrawing a sample of the amniotic fluid that envelops the developing human fetus in the uterus. Fetal cells obtained from the fluid are cultured for indications of chromosomal abnormalities, defective enzymes, or deficient growth. It is usually performed during the fourth month of pregnancy in conjunction with genetic counseling of parents with suspected inheritable defects, when the pregnant woman's age might predispose the fetus to genetic abnormalities, or when the woman has been exposed to substances harmful to fetal development.

After injection of a local anesthetic into the abdominal skin, a very fine needle is inserted through the abdomen and the uterine wall into the amnion, the sac that contains the amniotic fluid. About 30 ml (about 1 oz) of fluid is removed by suction for analysis. The procedure has been shown to pose no harm to the fetus or the mother, especially if the placement of the needle is guided by an ultrasonic device.

More than 75 abnormalities and the sex of the fetus can be ascertained by analyzing the fetal cells in amniotic fluid. Perhaps the most common use of the test is to detect Down's syndrome (q.v.). *See also* BIRTH DEFECTS.

For further information on this topic, see the Bibliography in volume 28, section 449.

AMOEBA, a one-celled organism in the phylum Sarcodina, kingdom Protista (q.v.). In older sys-

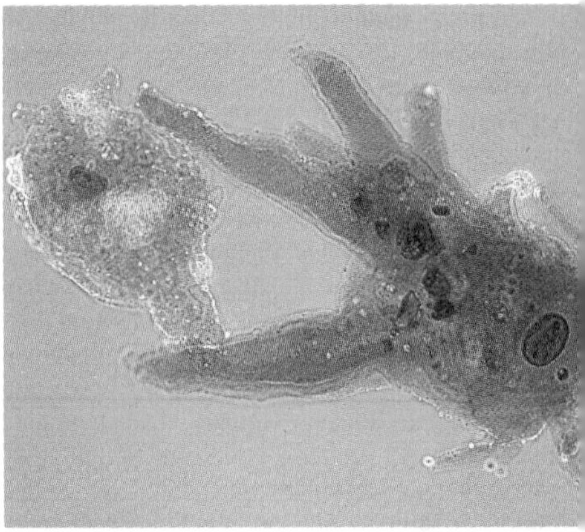

Amoeba, highly enlarged; the average size of this one-celled organism is 0.025 mm (1/1000 in).

tems of classification, the amoebas are classed as animals. The cell is composed of a thin membrane, a semirigid layer of ectoplasm, a granular, jellylike endoplasm, and an oval nucleus. The average size of the organism is 0.025 mm (1/1000 in). Some species of amoeba live on aquatic plants; some in moist ground; others are parasitic in animals.

Amoebas move by extending some cytoplasm outward to form pseudopodia (false feet). Chemical stimuli from smaller organisms, the amoeba's food, also induce the formation of pseudopodia, pairs of which envelop the organism, at the same time forming a cavity, or vacuole. An acid secreted into the cavity breaks down this food into soluble chemical substances that then diffuse from the cavity into the cytoplasm. Undigested food and wastes are excreted through the ectoplasm, which also absorbs oxygen from the surrounding water and eliminates carbon dioxide, a by-product of metabolism, in a form of respiration. Following a period of growth, the amoeba reproduces by splitting into two equal parts.

At least six forms of amoeba are parasitic in humans. Most important of these is *Entamoeba histolytica,* which causes amebiasis and dysentery (qq.v); the diseases often occur in epidemics when raw sewage contaminates water supplies or when soil is fertilized with untreated human wastes.

AMON *or* **AMMON** *or* **AMEN** (Egypt., "hidden"), ancient Egyptian deity, originally a local Theban god of reproductive forces, represented as a ram. Amon, his wife, Mut (Egypt., "the mother"), and his son, the moon god Khon (Egypt., "to traverse the sky"), formed the divine triad of Thebes. Later Amon was identified with the sun god Ra of Heliopolis, and was known as Amon-Ra, "the father of the gods, the fashioner of men, the creator of cattle, the lord of all being." As a universal god he became the god of the Egyptian nation and the empire. The power of his high priest rivaled that of the pharaoh, provoking political problems similar to modern church-state rivalry. The most massive temple ever built was constructed for Amon-Ra at al-Karnak. Amon was worshiped in the ancient Greek colonies of Cyrene, where he was identified with Zeus, and in Rome, where he was associated with Jupiter.

AMORITES, ancient tribe of Canaanites who inhabited the country northeast of the Jordan River as far as Mount Hermon. In the 13th century BC, the Amorites defeated the Moabites, crossed the Jordan, conquered the Hittites, and overran Canaan to the sea. Their power was broken (see Josh. 9–10) by the Hebrews, under their leader Joshua, at Gibeon. The Amorite ancestry of the Hebrews is mentioned in Ezek. 16:3.

The Amorites have been identified with the Amurru, a people who invaded Babylonia in the 21st century BC and two centuries later founded the first dynasty of Babylon.

AMOS, book of the Old Testament noted for its pastoral imagery and poetic language. It is attributed to the prophet Amos, a herdsman. It is one of 12 books known as the Minor Prophets.

Amos held God to be the God of all people rather than the exclusive God of the Jews (1:3, 6, 9, 11, 13; 2:1, 4, 6). God demanded and expected more from the Jews because of their covenant with him. They were not entitled, according to Amos (2:6–3:2, 9:7), to God's special favor; rather, they bore responsibility for showing exemplary obedience to his law. Amos was especially concerned with the oppression of the poor by the rich and with immoral religious practices. He stressed the personal responsibility of each individual before God and prophesied that Israel would be destroyed if the people did not turn from their corrupt ways.

In addition, Amos condemned the observance of ritual unaccompanied by true righteousness in all human and divine interrelations, and he prophesied a "day of the Lord" (5:18, 20), when the Jews would be called upon to account for their sins before God. In the last few verses (9:9–15), Amos foresaw the eventual redemption, peace, and prosperity of the people of Israel. These verses may have been a later addition.

AMOY, conventional name of Xiamen or Hsiamen, city, S China, in Fujian (Fukien) Province, on Amoy Island, a port at the mouth of the Jiulong (Chiu-lung) R. Strategically situated near Quemoy and Taiwan, it is a fishing and manufacturing center. Products include ships, processed food, and chemicals.

Portuguese traders arrived here in the 1540s; they were followed by British merchants in the 17th century and by French and Dutch traders in the 18th century. The port was closed to foreigners in the 1750s and was not reopened until 1842, when it became one of the first treaty ports. Amoy was an important tea-exporting center in the late 19th century, and a large foreign population lived on the island of Gulang Xu (Ku-lang Hsü), in the harbor here. It was also a gateway for commerce with Taiwan. Japanese forces occupied the port during 1938–45. The city was developed as an industrial center, with improved rail and road links with inland China, after trade with Taiwan ended in 1949. Pop. (1988 est.) 579,500.

AMPERE, basic unit of electric current, symbol A or amp, named for the 19th-century French physicist André Marie Ampère. The ampere was first defined as a flow of 1 coulomb of electricity per second, and later in terms of the current required to produce a certain amount of force between two wires. It is now defined as the current needed to deposit a specified amount of material on an electrode during electrolysis. *See* ELECTRICAL UNITS; INTERNATIONAL SYSTEM OF UNITS.

AMPÈRE, André Marie (1775–1836), French scientist, known for his important contributions to the study of electrodynamics. Ampère, the son of a Lyon city official, was born in Polémieux-au-Mont-d'Or, near Lyon. The ampere, the unit of electric current, is named after him. His electrodynamic theory and his views on the relationship of electricity and magnetism were published in his *Recueil d'observations électrodynamiques* (Collection of Observations on Electrodynamics, 1822) and in his *Théorie des phénomènes électrodynamiques* (Theory of Electrodynamic Phenomena, 1826). Ampère invented the astatic needle, which made possible the modern astatic galvanometer (*see* ELECTRIC METERS). He was the first to show that two parallel conductors carrying currents traveling in the same direction attract each other and, if traveling in opposite directions, repel each other.

AMPHETAMINE. *See* DRUG DEPENDENCE; STIMULANT.

AMPHIBIAN, any member of the vertebrate (q.v.) class lying between fishes and reptiles on the evolutionary scale. The class includes frogs, toads, and salamanders, which occur throughout the world, and other creatures called caecilians, which are limited to tropical regions. Most amphibians live on land and lay their eggs in water. Amphibians were the first true land vertebrates, emerging from the oceans in the early Devonian period, which was almost 400 million years ago.

The three living orders of amphibians are the Caudata, or tailed amphibians, which comprise the salamanders (including newts) and sirens; Anura or Salientia, or tailless amphibians, which include frogs and toads; and the Apoda, or caecilians, wormlike amphibians that are limbless and blind. About 2500 species exist, most of which live in warm and moist countries. A few species live in the Temperate Zone, some frogs penetrating far north but not as far as the polar regions. Two subclasses now extinct are the Labyrinthodontia and Lepospondyli.

General Structure. The skin of amphibians is smooth and moist, except for the caecilians, which have small scales in the outer folds of the body. The skin is frequently supplied with blood, which aids respiration. The numerous skin glands secrete a fluid that is often irritating and poisonous. The inner skin contains color cells that in some cases, by contraction or expansion, cause skin color changes, such as in the tree frog. The outer skin is continually being renewed, is sometimes shed in large patches, and may be eaten by the amphibian.

The skeletal, muscular, digestive, nervous, and other systems of the typical amphibian body are similar to those of higher animals. Consequently, biology students study the frog to gain basic knowledge of these systems.

The brain is remarkable in that the cerebellum is reduced to a mere band. The teeth and tongue vary in form and are sometimes absent. In many frogs the food-snatching tongue is fixed in front and free behind, and in the males of the Anura the lining of the mouth is often pushed outward into resonating vocal sacs. The adult heart consists of a muscular ventricle and two auricles, but during the gill-breathing larval stage the circulation resembles that of fishes. Body temperature, which is dependent on environmental temperatures, varies considerably and is much lower than that of birds and mammals. Male and female often differ in size and color. The male may be distinguished in some cases by the presence of vocal sacs, swollen thumbs, and skin frills. Some amphibians, such as the Mexican axolotl, *Siredon mexicanum,* become sexually mature in the larval stage.

Habits. Most amphibians are much more at home in water than on land, but sometimes adaptation to terrestrial life is complete. Even the majority of the lung-breathing forms, however, remain in the vicinity of water.

In both mating and feeding, amphibians are especially active at night. The food of the adults consists mostly of insects, slugs, and worms, but the larval forms are often vegetarian. Because they rely on external sources of warmth, amphibians hibernate through the winter in cool regions. They have a considerable power of regenerating lost parts. *See* AXOLOTL; FROG; HELLBENDER; NEWT; SALAMANDER; SIREN; TOAD; TREE FROG. J.A.O.

For further information on this topic, see the Bibliography in volume 28, section 470.

AMPHIBIOUS WARFARE, method of combat in which an attack is launched from the sea by naval and landing forces, embarked in ships or craft involving a landing on a hostile shore. In armed services such as those of the U.S., with large naval components, primary responsibility for these operations is assigned to a marine corps. Amphibious assaults employ special vessels and vehicles able to land large numbers of troops and equipment; air envelopment using helicopters is an important recent addition to the land, sea, and air strike forces.

The first amphibious assault was probably made during the Persian Wars; at the Battle of Marathon in 490 BC, the Persians established beachheads in their attempt to invade Greece. The Romans under Julius Caesar used merchant vessels to carry infantry and cavalry in an expedition against the British Isles in 55 BC.

The invention of naval guns made it possible to subdue opposing shore forces more efficiently; at the same time, shore-based heavy guns increased the hazard of bringing vessels within range of protected coasts and harbors. In the years when short-range guns and wooden ships predominated, regular naval vessels were augmented by merchant ships carrying troops, horses, and supplies to form an amphibious force.

The first modern amphibious operation using rifled long-range naval guns and steel vessels took place in 1915–16 at Gallipoli in World War I (*see* GALLIPOLI CAMPAIGN), when British, French, Australian, and New Zealand naval and military forces attempted to take the Straits of Bosporus. Turkish forces supplied by their German allies withstood the disastrously uncoordinated attack, however, and the campaign failed. Through these and other operations before World War II, the armed forces of many countries recognized the need for coordinated planning, for practice landings (to ensure precise timing), and for developing a specialized amphibious doctrine.

Current needs for rapid movement of forces in the face of an increasingly high-technology-threat environment have led to the development of high-speed vessels with capacities beyond those used in World War II and to more versatile landing craft. Amphibious assault ships, capable

An ancient Roman amphitheater at Pompeii, Italy.
Shostal/Superstock

of launching helicopters and discharging loaded landing craft from a flooded well deck are now in operation. New amphibious hovercraft ensure rapid movement to and across the beach, where massed forces are particularly vulnerable to conventional air or surface attack. E.C.C.

For further information on this topic, see the Bibliography in volume 28, section 284.

AMPHICTYONIC LEAGUE, league of ancient Greek tribes, which was formed to protect the temple of Demeter at Anthela (now Anthíli), near Thermopylae. Protection was later extended to the temple of Apollo at Delphi. Originally a religious organization, the league eventually became the political instrument of its strongest members. The 12 members of the league met semiannually, alternately at Delphi and at Thermopylae. Each tribe represented had two votes but could send additional delegates. The league fought three sacred wars; the first (595-585 BC) was fought against the Phocian city of Crisa (near modern Khrisón). During the second and third sacred wars (355-346 BC and 339-338 BC), King Philip II of Macedonia used his position in the league to dominate the affairs of Greece.

AMPHION. *See* NIOBE.

AMPHIOXUS. *See* LANCELET.

AMPHIPOD. *See* CRUSTACEAN.

AMPHITHEATER, in architecture, spacious open-air building generally oval in form. It was originally constructed of wood, and later of stone, and was used by the Romans for gladiatorial combats, fights of wild beasts, and other spectacles. The exhibition area was encircled by seats. The first amphitheater was constructed in 59 BC by the Roman pontifex maximus Gaius Scribonius Curio (125?-53 BC). The first partial stone amphitheater was built in 30 BC by Augustus, before he became first emperor of Rome. This amphitheater remained the only one in Rome not entirely of wood until the erection of the Colosseum by the Roman emperor Vespasian, whose son and successor, Titus, dedicated the edifice in AD 80. The upper part of the Colosseum itself, however, was originally of wood; it was replaced by stone after 223. The example of Rome was followed by all the cities of any importance throughout the Roman Empire. According to a 4th-century document the Colosseum at Rome seated 87,000 persons; modern scholars, however, believe that only about 50,000 persons could be seated. The colosseums of Pozzuoli, Capua, Verona, and Tarragona (all in Italy) are about the same size. *See also* CIRCUS MAXIMUS.

AMPHITRITE, in Greek mythology, sea goddess, daughter of Nereus or of Oceanus, and wife of Poseidon. In sculpture, she often appears sitting next to Poseidon in a chariot drawn by Tritons.

AMPHITRYON, in Greek mythology, prince of Tiryns. He married Alcmene, daughter of King Electryon of Mycenae. During his absence on a military expedition, the god Zeus visited Alcmene disguised as Amphitryon. Alcmene gave birth to twin sons: Hercules, the son of Zeus, and Iphicles, the son of Amphitryon.

AMPLIFIER, device for increasing the amplitude, or power, of an electric signal. It is used to amplify the weak electric current drawn from the antenna of a radio-receiving set, the weak output of a photoelectric cell (electric eye), the diminished current in a long-distance telephone circuit, the electrical signal representing sound in a public address system, and for many other purposes. One commonly used amplification device is the transistor. Other forms of amplifying devices are various types of thermionic vacuum tubes such as the triode, pentode, klystron, and magnetron (*see* ELECTRONICS; VACUUM TUBES).

Typically, small variations in the input voltage produce corresponding, but much larger, variations in output voltage. The ratio of these voltage changes is called the amplification factor. When the amplification factor exceeds a certain amount in a thermionic tube, the output signal no longer matches the input signal; it is distorted. This condition is alleviated by operating the amplifier at less than the maximum amplification factor. When greater amplification is required than is possible with one stage of amplification (that is, one transistor or one vacuum tube and its associated circuits), a multistage amplifier is used. The output of one stage is used as the input of another. Amplification in photoelectric circuits may be increased by the use of highly sensitive phototubes known as photomultipliers (*see* PHOTOELECTRIC CELL).

Transistors have largely replaced electron tubes in most common devices. These solid-state semiconductive elements exhibit a high amplification factor, operate without distortion over a wide frequency range, and can be made extremely small. Using integrated-circuit techniques, thousands of transistor amplifiers can be placed on very small wafers of silicon.

The pulse response of an amplifier determines its ability to reproduce a square-wave input pulse (a type of regular electric signal) quickly and accurately; square-wave inputs are fed to an amplifier for timing or counting purposes. Pulse response is important in digital-computer circuits, pulse-code modulation, and radar and nuclear instrumentation, that is, wherever high-frequency square-wave pulses are processed. In a radiation counter, for example, the frequency with which radiation particles impinge upon a sensitive element such as a semiconductor junction diode is a measure of the particle intensity or concentration. The resulting diode output may be a series of pulses, which are then amplified and fed to a transducer so that they may be seen.

Amplifiers with low noise characteristics are critical to communications satellites. Microwave (extremely high frequency) electromagnetic signals are amplified by maser devices (microwave amplification by the stimulated emission of radiation). Instead of amplifying electric current, the maser directly amplifies electromagnetic signals (*see* LASER; MASER).

Amplifiers are frequently classified by the type of electrical elements in the circuit. Inductance-coupled amplifiers are connected chiefly by coils and transformers; capacitance-coupled by condensers; and impedance-coupled by resistors. Direct-coupled amplifiers are connected directly, without such electrical components, and are used for alternating currents of very low frequency such as those that occur in many analog computers. The other types are used for a wide range of frequencies. Audio-frequency amplifiers operate at 0 to about 100,000 cycles per second (hertz), or 100 kilohertz (kHz). Intermediate-range amplifiers deal with frequencies from 400 kHz up to 5 million Hz, and so on.

For further information on this topic, see the Bibliography in volume 28, sections 543, 547, 549.

AMPLITUDE MODULATION. *See* RADIO: *Modulation*

AMPUTATION, removal, usually by surgery, of an external part of the body, most often a limb or part of it. Amputation may be required when an arm or leg has been severely crushed or, in diabetic persons, following death of an extremity due to impaired blood circulation. Limb tissue may also die from infection (*see* GANGRENE), frostbite, burns, or arteriosclerosis (*see* ARTERY). Removal of a limb may also be required to prevent the growth of a bone cancer called osteosarcoma, a malignancy that usually occurs in children. Some amputees continue to feel painful sensations from the area of the former limb, a condition called phantom-limb pain.

In recent years surgeons have developed the ability to reattach severed limbs, fingers, toes, ears, and hands. The technique is called microsurgery because the surgeon reconnects the severed nerves, tendons, and blood vessels with the aid of a microscope.

See also PROSTHETICS.

AMRAVATI, town, central India, in Maharashtra State, near Nagpur. It is a major trade center of the Berar region and the terminus of a rail spur in an important cotton-growing and grain-producing area. Cotton ginning and oilseed milling are important industries. Amravati is the site of a college of arts. The town was formerly called Amraoti. Pop. (1981 prelim.) 261,387.

AMRITSAR, city, N India, in Punjab State, near Lahore, Pakistan. The city, surrounded by a fertile region where grain, sugarcane, and cotton are produced, is an important trade, transportation, and manufacturing center with extensive textile and chemical industries. Amritsar was founded in 1574 by Ram Das (1534?–81), a guru, or teacher, of the Sikh religion. In the city is the principal shrine of Sikhism, the Golden Temple, surrounded by the sacred Amrita Saras (Pool of Immortality), in which Sikhs bathe to become spiritually purified. Amritsar was a center of Indian resistance to British rule; in 1919 nearly 400 demonstrators were killed when British troops fired upon a political gathering. The city was a center of protest against the 1947 partition of Punjab between India and Pakistan. Amritsar was again an arena of conflict in June 1984, when the Indian government, in an effort to check terrorism by Sikhs demanding greater autonomy for the Punjab, sent troops to occupy the Golden Temple, claiming the terrorists had been using it as their headquarters; hundreds were killed in the confrontation. Pop. (1981 prelim.) 589,229.

AMSTERDAM, seaport, constitutional capital, and principal city, W Netherlands, in North Holland Province, on the IJ (an arm of the IJsselmeer), near The Hague. The real seat of national government, however, is in The Hague. Amsterdam is divided by canals into about 90 islands joined by about 400 bridges. Almost the entire city rests on a foundation of piles driven through peat and sand to a firm substratum of clay.

Commerce. Amsterdam is one of the most important commercial centers in Europe. The city is a major port linked to the North Sea and other European countries by a network of railways and canals, notably the North Sea Canal, which is navigable by oceangoing vessels. Among leading industries in the city are shipbuilding, sugar refining, publishing, and the manufacture of heavy machinery, paper products, textiles and clothing, porcelain and glass, aircraft, automobiles, and chemicals. The city is also famous as a center for polishing and cutting diamonds and as the chief financial center of the Netherlands. A major European stock exchange is located in Amsterdam, as are the Bank of the Netherlands and several insurance firms.

Cultural Life. Amsterdam has been an important center of European cultural life since the 17th century. The city is the site of the National Academy of Art, the Royal Netherlands Academy of Sciences, and the University of Amsterdam (1632). Its Rijksmuseum contains one of the largest collections of Dutch and Flemish paintings in the world, and its Stedelijk Museum has an extensive collection of modern works. Amsterdam is also noted as the home of the renowned painter Rembrandt; his home is now a museum. The city has numerous examples of 16th- and 17th-century architecture, as well as two historic churches: Oude Kerk (Old Church), built about 1300, and Nieuwe Kerk (New Church), built in the 15th century. The royal palace, originally built in the 17th century as the town hall, stands on a large square in the center of the city.

History. Amsterdam, chartered as a city in 1300, became a member of the Hanseatic League in 1369. In the 17th century, after the successful

Canals border many of the picturesque streets of Amsterdam, the constitutional capital of the Netherlands.

conclusion of the Dutch wars for independence from Spain, Amsterdam became the chief commercial center of N Europe. The city held this position until the late 18th century, when trade declined as a result of the silting of the Zuider Zee and the British blockade before and during the Napoleonic Wars. In 1810 Napoleon incorporated the Netherlands into the French Empire, but after his downfall the Netherlands regained its independence and Amsterdam was made the official capital of the country. In the latter part of the 19th century, commercial activities revived with the opening of the North Sea and North Holland canals. During World War II, Amsterdam was occupied by the German army for five years. The people suffered great hardship and the port was badly damaged, but it has since been rebuilt and improved. Pop. (1988 est.) 691,700.

For further information on this topic, see the Bibliography in volume 28, section 993.

AMSTERDAM, city, Montgomery Co., E New York, on the Mohawk R.; inc. as a city 1885. It is a manufacturing and shipping center in an agricultural area; products include toys, plastics, clothing, and novelty items. Settled in 1783 by the Dutch, the community was called Veedersburg until 1804, when it was renamed for Amsterdam, Netherlands. Pop. (1980) 21,872; (1990) 20,714.

AMSTERDAM, UNIVERSITY OF, institution of higher learning, in Amsterdam, Netherlands. The university is under the jurisdiction of the ministry of education and is supported almost entirely by the national government. The University of Amsterdam was founded in 1632 as the Athenaeum Illustre; in 1877 it became a municipal university and in 1961 an autonomous institution. The university has faculties of theology, law, medicine, dentistry, mathematics and information science, physics and astronomy, chemistry, biology, arts, economics, political and social science, psychology, education, philosophy, and geography and archaeology. Depending on the field of study, the *kandidaat* examination is taken after two to four years of study and the *doctoraal* examination after an additional two to three years of study. The longer courses of study for the *kandidaat* and *doctoraal* examinations are generally equivalent to curricula in the U.S. leading to the degrees of bachelor and master. The degree of *Doctoraat* is awarded subsequently upon completion of a thesis.

AMU DARYA (anc. *Oxus*), large river, W Central Asia, originating in the lofty Pamir Plateau. The course it follows is NW between Tajikistan and Afghanistan, then NW between Turkmenistan and Uzbekistan, and then N through the Karakalpak autonomous region into the Aral Sea. The river is about 2495 km (about 1550 mi) long and is navigable for light draft vessels for nearly half its length. The chief importance of the river is as a water supply for irrigation.

AMULET, any object worn as a charm. An amulet is most often a stone, or piece of metal, with either an inscription or figures engraved on it. Usually suspended from the neck, it is worn as a guard against sickness or witchcraft. The ancient Egyptians wore amulets, sometimes in the form of necklaces. Among the Greeks, such a protective charm was called *phylaktērion.* The amulets of the Jews, slips of parchment on which passages of the Law were written, were evidently worn as badges of piety by the Pharisaic school, but were also regarded as protection from evil spirits and from other harm. The use of amulets was inherited by the Christian church, the usual inscription on them being *ichthys* (the Greek word for "fish"), because it contained the initials of the Greek words for Jesus Christ, Son of God, Savior. Among Gnostic sects, abraxas stones, gems with the Greek word *abraxas* engraved on them, were often used. Amulets became so common among Christians that, in the 4th century, the clergy were forbidden to make or sell them on pain of deprivation of holy orders; in 721 the wearing of amulets was solemnly condemned by the church. With the spread of Arabian astronomy, the astrological amulet, or talisman, became increasingly popular. Throughout the Middle East today, the practice of wearing amulets is almost universal.

AMUNDSEN, Roald (1872–1928), Norwegian polar explorer, born in Borge, and educated at the University of Christiania (now the University of

Ancient Egyptian amulets, such as this one (dated about 305–30 BC), had religious as well as representational significance. John Parnell–Brooklyn Museum

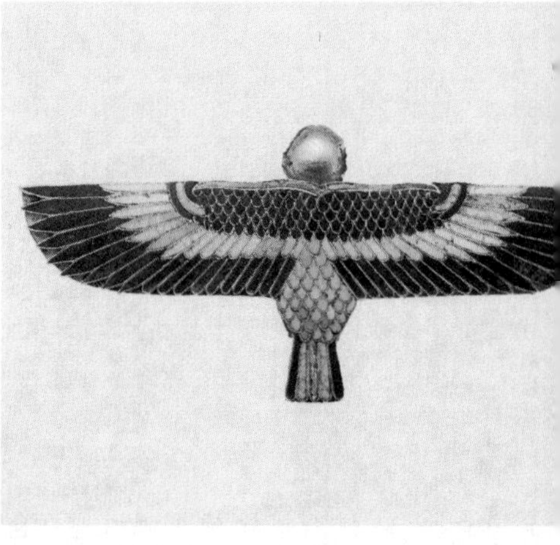

Oslo). He entered the Norwegian navy in 1894 and spent the following nine years studying science. From 1903 to 1906 he led his first important expedition in the small sloop *Gjöa.* During this voyage he sailed successfully through the Northwest Passage from the Atlantic to the Pacific Ocean and determined the position of the north magnetic pole. His next expedition (1910–12) sailed in a larger ship, the *Fram,* and gained fame as one of the most successful undertakings in the history of Antarctic exploration. With his companions, he lived in Antarctica for over a year, conducting explorations and scientific investigations. On Dec. 14, 1911, he reached the South Pole, becoming the first person known to have accomplished this feat. He had favorable weather conditions during the voyage, but his success was due primarily to his knowledge of polar conditions, his attention to minute details, and his ability to endure great physical stress.

Amundsen's plans for an expedition into the north polar regions were interrupted by the outbreak of World War I; in 1918, however, he sailed from Norway in an attempt to drift eastward across the North Pole with the ice currents of the Arctic Ocean. The ocean currents proved too variable to permit an actual crossing of the pole, and he was forced to follow a more southerly route through the Northeast Passage along the northern coast of Europe and Asia. The voyage ended in 1920, when he arrived in Nome, Alaska. In 1922 another attempt to reach the pole by both ship and airplane was unsuccessful, and in 1924 Amundsen came to the U.S. to raise funds for further expeditions. In May 1926 he finally succeeded in crossing the North Pole during a flight of more than 70 hours from Spitsbergen (Svalbard), Norway, to Teller, Alaska; he was accompanied by the American explorer Lincoln Ellsworth and the Italian explorer and engineer Umberto Nobile (1885–1978). This flight was made in the dirigible *Norge,* designed and built by Nobile with the support of the Italian government. Nobile and Amundsen subsequently quarreled, each claiming that the credit for the flight belonged to his respective country. In 1928, however, when Nobile's airship *Italia* was wrecked during a polar flight, Amundsen, who had retired, volunteered to search for him. Nobile was eventually rescued, but Amundsen was last heard from June 28, 1928, a few hours after he and five others had left Tromsø, Norway, by airplane. The remains of his airplane were found near Tromsø on August 31.

For most of his life Amundsen was a well-known lecturer and magazine writer. His books include *North West Passage* (1908), *The South Pole* (1912), *The North East Passage* (1918–20), *Our Polar Flight* (with Lincoln Ellsworth, 1925), *First Crossing of the Polar Sea* (with Lincoln Ellsworth, 1927), and *My Life as an Explorer* (1927).

Roald Amundsen, first person to reach the South Pole (Dec. 14, 1911).

AMUR, river, E Asia, formed by the junction of the Shilka and Argun rivers. From this junction the Amur flows generally E between Russia and Manchuria, China, as far as the city of Khabarovsk. It then flows NE and empties into Tatar Strait near the city of Nikolayevsk-na-Amure. The Amur is one of the great rivers of the world. Including the chief headstreams, it has a length of about 4345 km (about 2700 mi). The length of the Amur, exclusive of headstreams, is about 2865 km (about 1780 mi). The Amur is navigable throughout its entire course, and the Shilka is navigable to Sretensk, Russia. The Amur is closed to navigation for about six months in winter. Among the major tributaries are the Zeya, Sungari, Ussuri, and Bureya rivers. Important Chinese towns on the Amur R., known in Chinese as Heilong Jiang (Heilung Chiang), include Aihui (Heihe) and Tongjiang (Tungchiang). Besides Khaborovsk and Nikolayevsk-na-Amure, the principal Russian cities on the river are Blagoveshchensk and Komsomolsk.

AMYOTROPHIC LATERAL SCLEROSIS (ALS), disease in which degeneration of motor neurons of the spinal cord and brain stem results in progressive muscular atrophy leading to total paralysis. Symptoms commonly first appear in middle to late adulthood; death usually ensues within two to five years. It is also called motor neuron disease and Lou Gehrig's disease (*see* GEHRIG, LOU). The cause is unknown, and there is no cure.

ANABAPTISTS, name applied to certain religious sects that arose in Europe, particularly in Germany, the Netherlands, and Switzerland, during the Reformation. The name means "one who baptizes again"; it refers to the Anabaptists' practice of adult baptism, even of persons who had been baptized in infancy. Orthodox reformers, such as Huldreich Zwingli of Zürich and Martin Luther, and their followers often used the name Anabaptist as an opprobrious designation for any radical or unorthodox Protestant sect.

Doctrines and Practices. Like Lutherans and Calvinists, the Anabaptists believed in the paramount importance of personal faith in God, as opposed to ritualism, and to the right of independent personal judgment. The Anabaptists differed from Lutherans and Calvinists, however, in that they advocated, among other practices, nonviolence and opposition to state churches. They based their movement on voluntary congregations of converts (those who had undergone believer's baptism). The state church was organized hierarchically, based on the geographic parish, in which the members are all those born and resident in the parish. Some Anabaptists wished to establish communal and egalitarian Christian communities and opposed participation in civil government and the taking of oaths. The ultimate form of church discipline, the ban, was excommunication and ostracism of unrepentant sinners.

History. In the early 1520s, several religious leaders began to preach against church and social practices in Switzerland, Germany, and Austria. Among them were the Zürich-born Konrad Grebel (c. 1498–1526), the Bavarian Hans Denck (c. 1495–1527), and the German Balthasar Hubmaier (1485–1528). Somewhat younger than Zwingli and Luther, they were caught up in the wars of the peasants and of the empire under the Habsburgs (*see* HABSBURG). Known as the Brethren or the Swiss Brethren, they believed the Bible negated the practice of infant baptism and the celebration of the Mass. Instead, Anabaptists insisted on believer's baptism and a memorial Lord's Supper (*see* BAPTISM; BAPTISTS; EUCHARIST). Because they rejected the hierarchy of the church and the authority of civil bodies in religious matters, they were accused of sedition and heresy, persecuted, and often martyred.

Also characterized as Anabaptists were more radical Protestants, such as Jakob Hutter (fl. 1526–36), a communalist and founder of the Hutterian Brethren (q.v.), and Thomas Münzer. Another, Jan Beuckelzoon (c. 1509–36), or John of Leiden, established himself as king of the so-called New Zion in Münster, Westphalia, in 1534. His rule, under which polygamy was sanctioned and goods were held in common, ended after a year's siege. Beuckelzoon was executed in 1536.

Anabaptist groups continued to arise in Europe under different names. One of the most important was the group known as the Mennonites (q.v.), led by the Dutch reformer Menno Simons.

Anabaptism appealed most strongly to the poor and to uneducated peasants and artisans. Anabaptists in Europe were widely persecuted largely because two influential segments of society—the aristocracy and the Orthodox Reformation leaders—were united against their egalitarianism and their opposition to state churches. *See also* REFORMATION.

Reassessment of the Anabaptist movement has characterized much recent historical study. The movement is now seen as an important stream in the Reformation, especially its sacramental view of life, and incidents such as that in Münster are recognized as departures from Anabaptist spirituality.

For further information on this topic, see the Bibliography in volume 28, section 106.

ANABASIS. *See* XENOPHON.

ANABLEPS, any of three species of fish, *Anableps,* constituting the "four-eyed" fish family Anablepidae, order Cyprinodontiformes, found in rivers from Mexico to northern South America. The fish, about 20 cm (about 8 in) long, swim at the surface with their protruding eyes extending halfway above the waterline. Each eye is divided horizontally by a membrane into two corneas and retinas; thus, the fish can see above and below the water at the same time. A large external scale forces the phallic organ of some males to move only to the left and of others to move only to the right. The females' genital opening is similarly affected; a left-directed male can mate only with a right-directed female, and vice versa. The female produces one to five live offspring.

ANACONDA, city, seat of Deer Lodge Co., SW Montana; inc. 1833. Originally called Copperopolis, the community was renamed Anaconda in 1888 for the Anaconda Copper Mining Co., which had established a copper-smelting plant on nearby Warm Spring Creek in 1883. The city's economy grew to depend heavily on the great ore-smelting operations, which were ended in the early 1980s. Nearby recreational areas include Deerlodge National Forest, Georgetown Lake, Pintlar Wilderness Area, and Lost Creek State Park. Pop. (1980) 12,518; (1990) 10,278.

ANACONDA, common name for a large South American snake, *Eunectes murinus,* of the family Boidae (*see* BOA). The upper front of the head is covered with shieldlike plates, which are replaced farther back by scales. The minute vertical nostrils at the end of the snout can be entirely closed while the snake is swimming. The anaconda is the largest serpent of the western hemisphere. A large adult may be 6 m (19 ft) long and weigh 107 kg (235 lb).

The anaconda is oviparous, that is, the female produces eggs that develop and hatch outside the body. It is found in the rivers of the Guianas and Brazil. The anaconda kills by constriction.

ANACREON (c. 572–488 BC), Greek lyric poet, born in Teos, Asia Minor (now Siğacik, Turkey). He spent most of his life in Sámos, Athens, and Thessalía. Anacreon was known for his satires and short poems on love and wine, which have given the name *anacreontic* to a similar type of poetry. Only a few fragments of his poems have been preserved. They are marked by urbanity, simplicity, and a delicate and airy quality.

ANAEROBE, an organism that can live without oxygen. Anaerobes have metabolisms (*see* METABOLISM) that derive energy from oxygen-lacking nutrients, usually through fermentation (q.v.) but sometimes—as at deep-sea hydrothermal vents (*see* MARINE LIFE)—through reactions using inorganic chemicals. All anaerobes are simple organisms, such as yeast and bacteria; those that actually die in the presence of oxygen are called obligate anaerobes, while the rest of them are called facultative anaerobes.

ANAGRAM (Gr. *ana,* "up," "back," or "anew"; *graphein,* "to write"), transposition of the letters of a word or phrase to form a new word or phrase. The medieval philosophic doctrine of cabalism attached great importance to anagrams, asserting some relation between them and the character or destiny of the persons from whose names they were formed. A famous example is the anagram formed from the name Florence Nightingale: "Flit on, cheering angel." *See also* CROSSWORD PUZZLE.

ANAHEIM, city, Orange Co., SW California, near Los Angeles; inc. 1876. A tourist and convention center, it is the site of the world-famous Disneyland amusement park and the large Anaheim Convention Center. Anaheim Stadium, home of professional sports teams, also is here. Manufactures include electronic equipment, batteries, printed materials, and processed food. Anaheim was founded (1859) by German settlers as a grape-growing community. Most vines were killed by disease in the 1880s, but productive citrus groves later were developed in the region. The city's name is derived from the nearby Santa Ana R. and from *heim,* German for "home." Pop. (1980) 221,847; (1990) 266,406.

ANÁHUAC (Aztec, "country by the waters"), once thought to have been the name of an ancient Indian kingdom in Mexico, and formerly applied to the section of New Spain that became independent of Mexico in 1821. The name now refers to either the whole central plateau of Mexico or the valley in which Mexico City is located. The height of the Mexican plateau varies from about 1800 to 2400 m (about 6000 to 8000 ft) above sea level; the great volcano of Popocatépetl rises from it. The plateau, which comprises three-fifths of Mexico, is bounded on the E and W by two cordillera mountain chains, the Sierra Madre Oriental and Sierra Madre Occidental.

ANALGESIC, class of drugs that relieve pain without causing loss of consciousness. The drugs range from the narcotic opium derivatives morphine and codeine (*see* OPIUM) to a wide range of nonnarcotics such as aspirin (q.v.), acetaminophen (q.v.; Tylenol), zomepirac (Zomax), and ibuprofen (q.v.; Advil), the last entering the nonprescription category in the U.S. in 1984. External analgesics include such drugs as hydrocortisone. Anesthetics in low doses, or local anesthetics such as benzocaine, are also analgesic in function. *See* ANESTHESIA.

Narcotics affect the central nervous system, are addictive, and are used only for severe pain; but synthetic opiates such as propoxyphene (Darvon), pentazocine (Talwin), and butorphanol (Stadol) are used with greater safety. The nonnarcotics act by inhibiting the synthesis of prostaglandins (q.v.) in the body. Aspirin is a good anti-inflammatory but can irritate the stomach, whereas milder acetaminophen is less effective against inflammation. Ibuprofen is both mild and anti-inflammatory, but some doctors suggest it could aggravate high blood pressure and damage the kidneys. With the discovery of natural opiate receptors in the brain, and of hormones such as endorphins and encephalins that link to them, much research has been devoted to ways in which these systems could be manipulated to ease pain.

ANALOG COMPUTER. *See* COMPUTER.

ANALOG-TO-DIGITAL CONVERTER *or* **ADC,** an electronic device for converting data from analog to digital form for use in electronic equipment such as digital computers (*see* COMPUTER), digital audio and video recorders, and communication equipment. Analog or continuously varying electrical waveforms are applied to the device and are sampled at a fixed rate. Sample values are then expressed as a digital number, using a binary numbering system consisting only of 0's and 1's. The resulting digital codes can be used in various types of communications systems.

ANALOGY, a relationship of similarity or likeness between two or more entities. For example, an analogy, or similarity, between the human heart and a mechanical pump has been argued.

In logic, analogy is the name of an inductive form of argument which asserts that if two or more entities are similar in one or more respects, then a probability exists that they will be similar in other respects.

In theology, theorists have held that knowledge of God's nature can be partially gained from knowledge of his creation through the analogical use of language. From the knowledge that human beings are good, goodness is also predicated of God. When God and human beings are both referred to as good, however, the term *goodness* is not being used univocally—that is, the term is not being used in exactly the same sense. Neither is the term *good* being used equivocally when predicated of God and human beings. That is, the term is not being used in altogether different senses. Thus, it is argued, the term is being used analogically. Although the creature is not precisely like the creator, the creature is, in some sense, like (analogous to) the creator. Thus, ascribing goodness to God on the basis of what it means to ascribe goodness to human beings does result in knowledge, however limited, of the nature of God.

Historically, analogies have been used for a variety of purposes. Literary analogies have been used to paint vivid word pictures. Scientific analogies have been used for explanatory purposes. In philosophy, Plato illustrated his ideas by the use of well-developed analogies. R.M.B.

ANALYTICAL CHEMISTRY, one of the major branches of modern chemistry (q.v.). It is subdivided into two main areas, qualitative and quantitative analysis. The former involves the determination of unknown constituents of a substance, and the latter concerns the determination of the relative amounts of such constituents. *See* CHEMICAL ANALYSIS.

ANALYTIC GEOMETRY. *See* GEOMETRY.

ANALYTIC AND LINGUISTIC PHILOSOPHY, 20th-century philosophical movement, dominant in Great Britain and the U.S. since World War II, that aims to clarify language and analyze the concepts expressed in it. The movement has been given a variety of designations, including "linguistic analysis," "logical empiricism," "logical positivism," "Cambridge analysis," and "Oxford philosophy." The last two labels are derived from the universities in England where this philosophical method has been particularly influential. Although no specific doctrines or tenets are accepted by the movement as a whole, analytic and linguistic philosophers agree that the proper activity of philosophy is clarifying language, or, as some prefer, clarifying concepts. The aim of this activity is to settle philosophical disputes and resolve philosophical problems, which, it is argued, originate in linguistic confusion.

Approaches. A considerable diversity of views exists among analytic and linguistic philosophers regarding the nature of conceptual or linguistic analysis. Some have been primarily concerned with clarifying the meaning of specific words or phrases as an essential step in making philosophical assertions clear and unambiguous. Others have been more concerned with determining the general conditions that must be met for any linguistic utterance to be meaningful; their intent is to establish a criterion that will distinguish between meaningful and nonsensical sentences. Still other analysts have been interested in creating formal, symbolic languages that are mathematical in nature. Their claim is that philosophical problems can be more effectively dealt with once they are formulated in a rigorous logical language.

By contrast, many philosophers associated with the movement have focused on the analysis of ordinary, or natural, language. Difficulties arise when concepts such as time and freedom, for example, are considered apart from their normal linguistic context. Attention to language as it is ordinarily used is the key, it is argued, to resolving many philosophical puzzles.

Early History. Linguistic analysis as a method of philosophy is as old as the Greeks. Several of the dialogues of Plato, for example, are specifically concerned with clarifying terms and concepts. Nevertheless, this style of philosophizing has received dramatically renewed emphasis in the 20th century. Influenced by the earlier British empirical tradition of John Locke, George Berkeley, David Hume, and John Stuart Mill and by the writings of the German mathematician and philosopher Gottlob Frege, the 20th-century English philosophers G. E. Moore and Bertrand Russell became the founders of this contemporary analytic and linguistic trend. As students together at the University of Cambridge, Moore and Russell rejected Hegelian idealism, particularly as it was reflected in the work of the English metaphysician F. H. Bradley, who held that nothing is completely real except the Absolute. In their opposition to idealism and in their commitment to careful attention to language, they set the mood and style of philosophizing for much of the 20th century English-speaking world.

For Moore, philosophy was first and foremost analysis. The philosophical task involves clarifying puzzling propositions or concepts by indicating less puzzling propositions or concepts to which the originals are held to be logically equivalent. Once this task has been completed, the truth or falsity of problematic philosophical assertions can be determined more adequately. Moore was noted for his careful analyses of such puzzling philosophical claims as "time is unreal," analyses that then aided in determining the truth of such assertions.

Russell, strongly influenced by the precision of mathematics, was concerned with developing an ideal logical language that would accurately reflect the nature of the world. Complex propositions, Russell maintained, can be resolved into their simplest components, which he called atomic propositions. These propositions refer to atomic facts, the ultimate constituents of the universe. The metaphysical view based on this logical analysis of language and the insistence that meaningful propositions must correspond to facts constitute what Russell called logical atomism. His interest in the structure of language also led him to distinguish between the grammatical form of a proposition and its logical form. The statements "John is good" and "John is tall" have the same grammatical form but different logical forms. Failure to recognize this would lead one to treat the property "goodness" as if it were a characteristic of John in the same way that the property "tallness" is a characteristic of John. Such failure results in philosophical confusion.

Wittgenstein and the Logical Positivists. Russell's work in mathematics attracted to Cambridge the Austrian philosopher Ludwig Wittgenstein, who became a central figure in the analytic and linguistic movement. In his first major work, *Tractatus Logico-Philosophicus* (1921; trans. 1922), in which he first presented his theory of language, Wittgenstein argued that "all philosophy is a 'critique of language' " and that "philosophy aims at the logical clarification of thoughts." The results of Wittgenstein's analysis resembled Russell's logical atomism. The world, he argued, is ultimately composed of simple facts, which it is the purpose of language to picture. To be meaningful, statements about the world must be reducible to linguistic utterances that have a structure similar to the simple facts pictured. In this early Wittgensteinian analysis, only propositions that picture facts—the propositions of science—are considered factually meaningful. Metaphysical, theological, and ethical sentences were judged to be factually meaningless.

Influenced by Russell, Wittgenstein, Ernst Mach, and others, a group of philosophers and mathematicians in Vienna in the 1920s initiated the movement known as logical positivism (*see* POSITIVISM). Led by Moritz Schlick (1882–1936) and Rudolf Carnap, the Vienna Circle initiated one of the most important chapters in the history of analytic and linguistic philosophy. According to the positivists, the task of philosophy is the clarification of meaning, not the discovery of new facts (the job of the scientists) or the construction of comprehensive accounts of reality (the misguided pursuit of traditional metaphysics).

The positivists divided all meaningful assertions into two classes: analytic propositions and empirically verifiable ones. Analytic propositions, which include the propositions of logic and mathematics, are statements the truth or falsity of which depend altogether on the meanings of the terms constituting the statement. An example would be the proposition "two plus two equals four." The second class of meaningful propositions includes all statements about the world that can be verified, at least in principle, by sense experience. Indeed, the meaning of such propositions is identified with the empirical method of their verification. This verifiability theory of meaning, the positivists concluded, would demonstrate that scientific statements are legitimate factual claims and that metaphysical, religious, and ethical sentences are factually empty. The ideas of logical positivism were made popular in England by the publication of A. J. Ayer's *Language, Truth and Logic* in 1936.

The positivists' verifiability theory of meaning came under intense criticism by philosophers such as the Austrian-born British philosopher Karl Popper. Eventually this narrow theory of meaning yielded to a broader understanding of the nature of language. Again, an influential figure was Wittgenstein. Repudiating many of his earlier conclusions in the *Tractatus,* he initiated a new line of thought culminating in his posthumously published *Philosophical Investigations* (1953; trans. 1953). In this work, Wittgenstein argued that once attention is directed to the way language is actually used in ordinary discourse, the variety and flexibility of language become clear. Propositions do much more than simply picture facts.

This recognition led to Wittgenstein's influential concept of language games. The scientist, the poet, and the theologian, for example, are involved in different language games. Moreover, the meaning of a proposition must be understood in its context, that is, in terms of the rules of the language game of which that proposition is a part. Philosophy, concluded Wittgenstein, is an attempt to resolve problems that arise as the result of linguistic confusion, and the key to the resolution of such problems is ordinary language analysis and the proper use of language.

Recent Developments. Additional contributions within the analytic and linguistic movement include the work of the British philosophers Gilbert Ryle, John Austin, and P. F. Strawson and the American philosopher W. V. Quine. According to Ryle, the task of philosophy is to restate "systematically misleading expressions" in forms that are logically more accurate. He was particularly concerned with statements the grammatical form of which suggests the existence of nonexistent objects. For example, Ryle is best known for his analysis of mentalistic language, language that misleadingly suggests that the mind is an entity in the same way as the body.

Austin maintained that one of the most fruitful starting points for philosophical inquiry is attention to the extremely fine distinctions drawn in ordinary language. His analysis of language eventually led to a general theory of speech acts, that is, to a description of the variety of activities that an individual may be performing when something is uttered.

Strawson is known for his analysis of the relationship between formal logic and ordinary language. The complexity of the latter, he argued, is inadequately represented by formal logic. A variety of analytic tools, therefore, is needed in addition to logic in analyzing ordinary language.

Quine discussed the relationship between language and ontology. He argued that language systems tend to commit their users to the existence of certain things. For Quine, the justification for speaking one way rather than another is a thoroughly pragmatic one.

The commitment to language analysis as a way of pursuing philosophy has continued as a significant contemporary dimension in philosophy. A division also continues to exist between those who prefer to work with the precision and rigor of symbolic logical systems and those who prefer to analyze ordinary language. Although few contemporary philosophers maintain that all philosophical problems are linguistic, the view continues to be widely held that attention to the logical structure of language and to how language is used in everyday discourse can often aid in resolving philosophical problems.

For additional information on individual philosophers, see biographies of those whose names are not followed by dates. R.M.B.

For further information on this topic, see the Bibliography in volume 28, section 35.

ANAN BEN DAVID (fl. 8th cent.), Jewish religious leader in Persia (now Iran). Anan ben David was the founder of the antirabbinic sect of Karaites and author of *The Book of Precepts* (c. 770). His theological doctrine, called Karaism, or Ananism, developed in the course of a struggle for leadership of the Jewish communities in Persia. Karaism teaches that the Old Testament is the sole source of religious authority in Judaism and thereby rejects the law based on tradition and compiled in the Talmud. The doctrine especially criticizes the rabbinic teachings concerning the Sabbath, the calendar, and marriage. Anan ben David was imprisoned for political reasons; after his release he emigrated from Baghdad to Palestine and made Jerusalem the center of his movement. From Jerusalem the sect expanded across Egypt and Syria to southern Russia.

ANARCHISM, political theory that is opposed to all forms of government. Anarchists believe that the highest attainment of humanity is the freedom of individuals to express themselves, unhindered by any form of repression or control from without. They hold that the perfection of humanity will not be attained until all government is abolished and each individual is left absolutely free. One limitation on such freedom, however, is the ban against injuring other human beings. From this limitation arises another: If any human being attempts to injure others, all well-meaning individuals have the right to organize against him or her, and the orderly class may repress the criminal class, although only by voluntary cooperation and not under any governmental organization.

The 19th-century French writer Pierre Joseph Proudhon is generally regarded as the father of the system of so-called philosophic anarchism. According to Proudhon and his followers, anarchism would exclude authority from society, setting up extreme individualism. Philosophic anarchists, however, repudiate violent methods and hope for a gradual evolution of society toward anarchic organization. Those anarchists who reject Proudhon's theories maintain that the entire trend of human development is toward achievement by cooperation and that social cooperation can never be wholly voluntary.

Another school of anarchism, relying on organized action and even deeds of terror to achieve its purposes, grew out of the socialist movement and appeared toward the end of the 19th century. At the congress of the International Workingmen's Association, or the First International, held at Basel, Switzerland, in 1869, the anarchists, led by the Russian revolutionist Mikhail Bakunin, were outvoted by the socialists; in 1872 the anarchists were expelled from the International. Since that time socialism and anarchism have diverged sharply, although both are basically anticapitalist. Philosophic anarchists continue to differ from socialists in their emphasis on freedom from control, especially from state control. Many anarchists participated in the trade union movement, usually as members of unions with a syndicalist program (*see* SYNDICALISM). Others accepted the terrorist policy and practiced assassination.

Although most anarchists have not advocated terrorism, the popular view has unjustly identified all anarchism with violence. Assassinations such as those of Humbert I, king of Italy; William McKinley, president of the U.S.; George I, king of Greece; and the president of France, Marie François Sadi Carnot—all committed by anarchists—have given support to the popular opinion of anarchy. Some crimes that were blamed on anarchists, including a bomb thrown during the Haymarket Square Riot in Chicago (1886) and the payroll murder at South Braintree, Mass. (*see* SACCO-VANZETTI CASE), were almost certainly not committed by anarchists. Persons who profess or advocate anarchism are denied admission to the U.S. by a federal law enacted in 1902.

Modern anarchists include the Russian follower of Bakunin, Prince Pyotr Alekseyevich Kropotkin, who called himself an anarchistic Communist, and the Americans Alexander Berkman (1870–1936) and Emma Goldman. Anarchism declined steadily as a political philosophy and as an organized movement during the second quarter of the 20th century.

ANASTASIUS I (430?–518), Byzantine emperor (491–518), born in Dyrrhachium (now Durrës, Albania). As a palace official in Constantinople, the capital of the Byzantine Empire, he was known for his ability and integrity. Anastasius was proclaimed emperor on the death of Zeno in 491; later that same year, he married Zeno's widow. Anastasius's reign was troubled by a revolt of the Isaurians (whom he had removed from power), a war with Persia (502–05), and invasions of Huns, Slavs, and Bulgars. To protect the capital and its vicinity, Anastasius built (512) a wall that still bears his name about 56 km (about 35 mi) west of Constantinople. Unpopular with many because he favored the Monophysitic doctrine, he was praised by others for suppressing licentious dances and gladiatorial combats with wild beasts. When he died, the empire was intact. He left a substantial treasury and a well-disciplined army.

ANASTASIUS II (d. 721), Byzantine emperor (713–15). During his reign, he organized a formidable navy, which he dispatched to Rhodes, and he also tried to reorganize the army. His troops mutinied, however, and proclaimed as emperor Theodosius III (r. 715–17), a tax official of humble birth. Theodosius captured Constantinople about six months later, but Anastasius escaped to Thessalonica (now Thessaloníki, Greece) and became a monk. In 720 Anastasius led a revolt against Leo III (c. 680–741), who had overthrown Theodosius. Anastasius was subsequently captured and killed.

ANATOLIAN LANGUAGES, ancient languages of Asia Minor, forming a subfamily of the Indo-European language family. They include Hittite (the most important), Luwian, Palaic, Lycian, and Lydian. *See* HITTITE LANGUAGE; INDO-EUROPEAN LANGUAGES.

ANATOMY (Gr. *anatomē*, "dissection"), branch of natural science dealing with the structural organization of living things. It is an old science, having its beginnings in prehistoric times. For centuries anatomical knowledge consisted largely of observations of dissected plants and animals. The proper understanding of structure, however, implies a knowledge of function in the living organism. Anatomy is therefore almost inseparable from physiology (q.v.), which is sometimes called functional anatomy. As one of the basic life sciences, anatomy is closely related to medicine and to other branches of biology.

It is convenient to subdivide the study of anatomy in several different ways. One classification is based on the type of organisms studied, the major subdivisions being plant anatomy (*see* PLANT) and animal anatomy. Animal anatomy is further subdivided into human anatomy (see below) and comparative anatomy, which seeks out similarities and differences among animal types (*see* ANIMAL). Anatomy can also be subdivided into biological processes, for example, developmental anatomy, the study of embryos, and pathological anatomy, the study of diseased organs. Other subdivisions, such as surgical anatomy and anatomical art, are based on the relationship of anatomy to other branches of activity under the general heading of applied anatomy. Still another way to subdivide anatomy is by the techniques employed, for example, microanatomy, which concerns itself with observations made with the help of the microscope (see the section on the history of anatomy).

HUMAN ANATOMY

The human body operates through systems that are summarized below. This encyclopedia contains separate articles on all of the mentioned systems and organs, to which the reader is referred for more comprehensive discussions. References to articles discussing the senses and perception are listed in SENSE ORGANS.

Musculoskeletal System. The human skeleton consists of more than 200 bones bound together by tough and relatively inelastic connective tissues called ligaments. The different parts of the

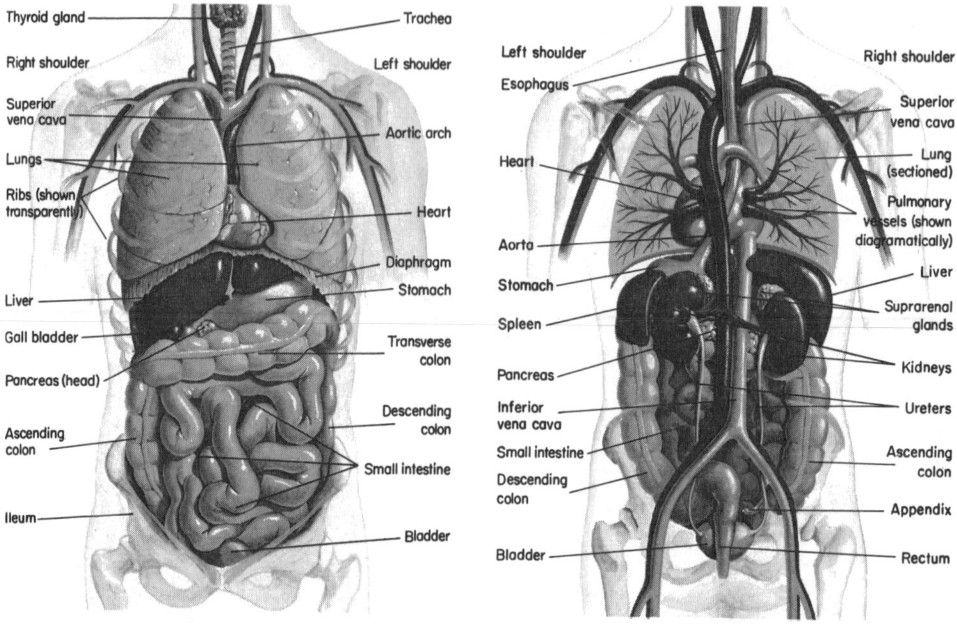

The structural organization of the human body and the placement of the organs; front view left, back view right.

body vary greatly in their degree of movement. Thus, the arm at the shoulder is freely movable, whereas the knee joint is definitely limited to a hingelike action. The movements of individual vertebrae are extremely limited; the bones composing the skull are immovable. Movements of the bones of the skeleton are effected by contractions of the skeletal muscles, to which the bones are attached by tendons. These muscular contractions are controlled by the nervous system. *See* MUSCLE; SKELETON.

Nervous System. The nervous system has two divisions: the somatic, which allows voluntary control over skeletal muscle, and the autonomic, which is involuntary and controls cardiac and smooth muscle and glands. The autonomic nervous system has two divisions: the sympathetic and the parasympathetic. Many, but not all, of the muscles and glands that distribute nerve impulses to the larger interior organs possess a double nerve supply; in such cases the two divisions may exert opposing effects. Thus, the sympathetic system increases heartbeat, and the parasympathetic system decreases heartbeat. The two nervous systems are not always antagonistic, however. For example, both nerve supplies to the salivary glands excite the cells of secretion. Furthermore, a single division of the autonomic nervous system may both excite and inhibit a single effector, as in the sympathetic supply to the blood vessels of skeletal muscle. Finally, the sweat glands, the muscles that cause involuntary erection or bristling of the hair, the smooth muscle of the spleen, and the blood vessels of the skin and skeletal muscle are actuated only by the sympathetic division.

Voluntary movement of head, limbs, and body is caused by nerve impulses arising in the motor area of the cortex of the brain and carried by cranial nerves or by those that emerge from the spinal cord to reach skeletal muscles. The reaction involves both excitation of nerve cells stimulating the muscles involved and inhibition of the cells that stimulate opposing muscles. A nerve impulse is an electrical change within a nerve cell or fiber; measured in millivolts, it lasts a few milliseconds and can be recorded by electrodes.

Movement may occur also in direct response to an outside stimulus; thus, a tap on the knee causes a jerk, and a light shone into the eye makes the pupil contract. These involuntary responses are called reflexes. Various nerve terminals called receptors constantly send impulses into the central nervous system. These are of three classes: exteroceptors, which are sensitive to pain, temperature, touch, and pressure; interoceptors, which react to changes in the internal environment; and proprioceptors, which respond to variations in movement, position, and tension. These impulses terminate in special areas of the brain, as do those of special receptors concerned with sight, hearing, smell, and taste.

Muscular contractions do not always cause actual movement. A small fraction of the total number of fibers in most muscles are usually contracting. This serves to maintain the posture of a limb and enables the limb to resist passive elongation or stretch. This slight continuous contraction is called muscle tone.

Circulatory System. In passing through the system, blood pumped by the heart follows a winding course through the right chambers of the heart, through the lungs, where it picks up oxygen, and back into the left chambers of the heart. From these it is pumped into the main artery, the aorta, which branches into increasingly smaller arteries until it passes through the smallest, known as arterioles. Beyond the arterioles, the blood passes through a vast amount of tiny, thin-walled structures called capillaries. Here, the blood gives up its oxygen and its nutrients to the tissues and absorbs from them carbon dioxide and other waste products of metabolism. The blood completes its circuit by passing through small veins that join to form increasingly larger vessels until it reaches the largest veins, the inferior and superior venae cavae, which return it to the right side of the heart. Blood is propelled mainly by contractions of the heart; contractions of skeletal muscle also contribute to circulation. Valves in the heart and in the veins ensure its flow in one direction.

Immune System. The body defends itself against foreign proteins and infectious microorganisms by means of a complex dual system that depends on recognizing a portion of the surface pattern of the invader. The two parts of the system are termed cellular immunity, in which lymphocytes are the effective agent, and humoral immunity, based on the action of antibody molecules.

When lymphocytes recognize a foreign molecular pattern (termed an antigen), some release antibodies in great numbers; others store the memory of the pattern for future release of anti-

Lymph, formed from blood plasma, carries food to and poisons away from body cells through thin-walled vessels. It returns to the circulatory system through the thoracic duct. The nodes aid in filtering out poisons.

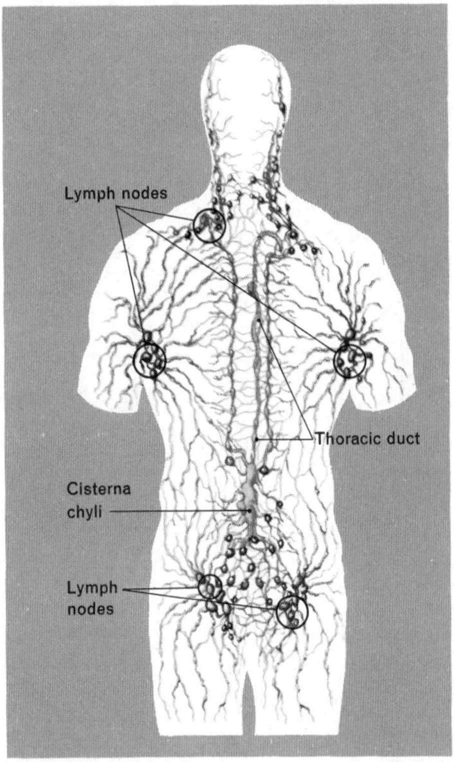

The brain and spinal cord (the central nervous system) and the nerves extending out from them (peripheral system) mainly control conscious activities and sensations. The autonomic system controls involuntary functions.

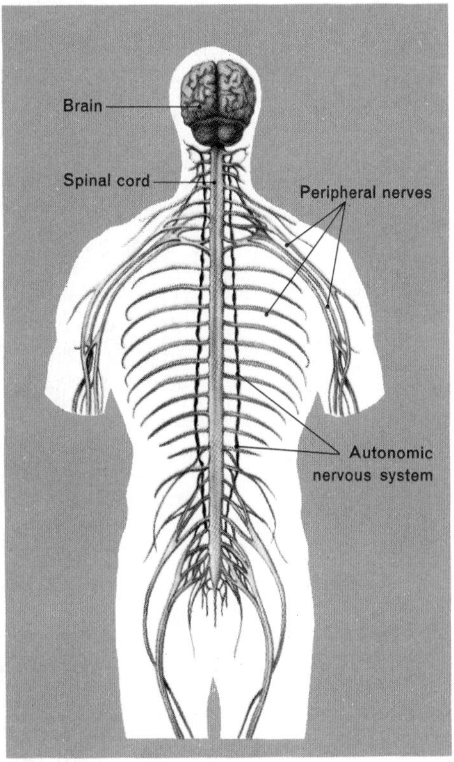

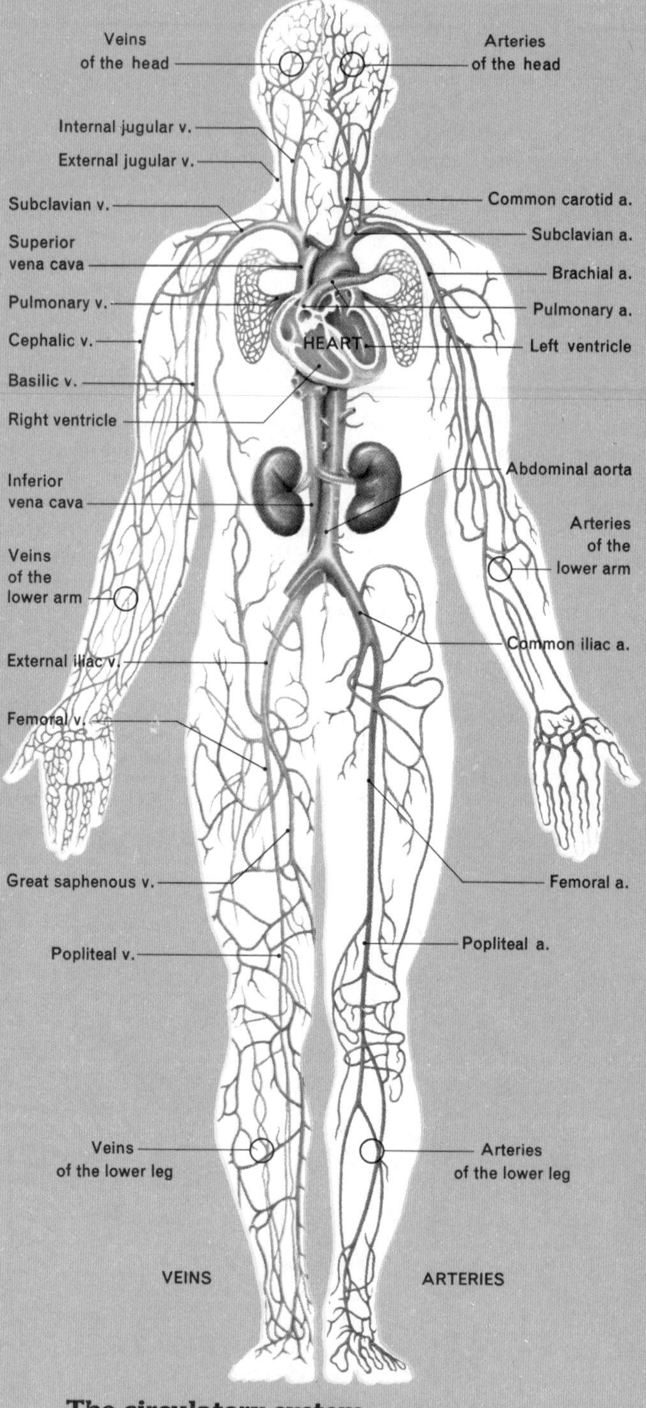

The circulatory system

This system carries the blood through the body and is composed of many sizes of flexible tubes. The diagram shows veins (blue) on one side and arteries (red) on the other side. Of course, the body has arteries and veins on both sides.

bodies should the molecule reappear. Antibodies attach themselves to the antigen and in that way mark them for destruction by other substances in the body's defense arsenal. These are primarily complement, a complex of enzymes that make holes in foreign cells, and phagocytes, cells that engulf and digest foreign matter. They are drawn to the area by chemical substances released by activated lymphocytes.

Lymphocytes, which resemble blood plasma in composition, are manufactured in the bone marrow and multiply in the thymus and spleen. They circulate in the bloodstream, penetrating the walls of the blood capillaries to reach the cells of the tissues. From there they migrate to an independent network of capillaries that is comparable to and almost as extensive as that of the blood's circulatory system. The capillaries join to form larger and larger vessels that eventually link up with the bloodstream through the jugular and subclavian veins; valves in the lymphatic vessels ensure flow in one direction. Nodes at various points in the lymphatic network act as stations for the collection and manufacture of lymphocytes; they may become enlarged during an infectious disease. In anatomy, the network of lymphatic vessels and the lymph nodes are together called the lymphatic system; its function as the vehicle of the immune system was not recognized until the 1960s.

Respiratory System. Respiration is carried on by the expansion and contraction of the lungs; the process and the rate at which it proceeds are controlled by a nervous center in the brain.

In the lungs, oxygen enters tiny capillaries, where it combines with hemoglobin in the red blood cells and is carried to the tissues. Simultaneously, carbon dioxide, which entered the blood in its passages through the tissues, passes through capillaries into the air contained within the lungs. Inhaling draws into the lungs air that is higher in oxygen and lower in carbon dioxide; exhaling forces from the lungs air that is high in carbon dioxide and low in oxygen. Changes in the size and gross capacity of the chest are controlled by contractions of the diaphragm and of the muscles between the ribs.

Digestive and Excretory Systems. The energy required for maintenance and proper functioning of the human body is supplied by food. After it is broken into fragments by chewing (*see* TEETH) and mixed with saliva, digestion begins. The food passes down the gullet into the stomach, where the process is continued by the gastric and intestinal juices. Thereafter, the mixture of food and secretions, called chyme, is pushed down the alimentary canal by peristalsis, rhythmic contractions of the smooth muscle of the gastrointestinal system. The contractions are initiated by the parasympathetic nervous system; such muscular activity can be inhibited by the sympathetic nervous system. Absorption of nutrients from chyme occurs mainly in the small intestine; unabsorbed food and secretions and waste substances from the liver pass to the large intestines and are expelled as feces. Water and water-soluble substances pass in the blood to the kidneys, where all the constituents of the blood plasma except protein pass through the thin membranes of the blood capillaries into the kidney tubules. The remaining water, salts, and waste products pass down the kidney tubes, which return most of the water and salts to the body and secrete other salts and waste products from the blood. Urine, the fluid that remains, is stored in the urinary bladder until it is expelled.

The Endocrine System. In addition to the integrative action of the nervous system, control of various body functions is exerted by the endocrine glands. An important part of this system, the pituitary, lies at the base of the brain. This master gland secretes a variety of hormones, including the following: (1) a hormone that stimulates the thyroid gland and controls its secretion of thyroxine, which dictates the rate at which all cells utilize oxygen; (2) a hormone that controls the secretion in the adrenal gland of hormones that influence the metabolism of carbohydrates, sodium, and potassium and control the rate at which substances are exchanged between blood and tissue fluid; (3) substances that control the secretion in the ovaries of estrogen and progesterone and the creation in the testicles of testosterone; (4) the somatotropic, or growth, hormone, which controls the rate of development of the skeleton and large interior organs through its effect on the metabolism of proteins and carbohydrates; and (5) an insulin inhibitor—a lack of insulin causes diabetes mellitus.

The posterior lobe of the pituitary secretes vasopressin, which acts on the kidney to control the volume of urine; a lack of vasopressin causes diabetes insipidus, which results in the passing of large volumes of urine. The posterior lobe also elaborates oxytocin, which causes contraction of smooth muscle in the intestines and small arteries and is used to bring about contractions of the uterus in childbirth. Other glands in the endocrine system are the pancreas, which secretes insulin, and the parathyroid, which secretes a hormone that regulates the quantity of calcium and phosphorus in the blood.

The Reproductive System. Reproduction is accomplished by the union of male sperm and the

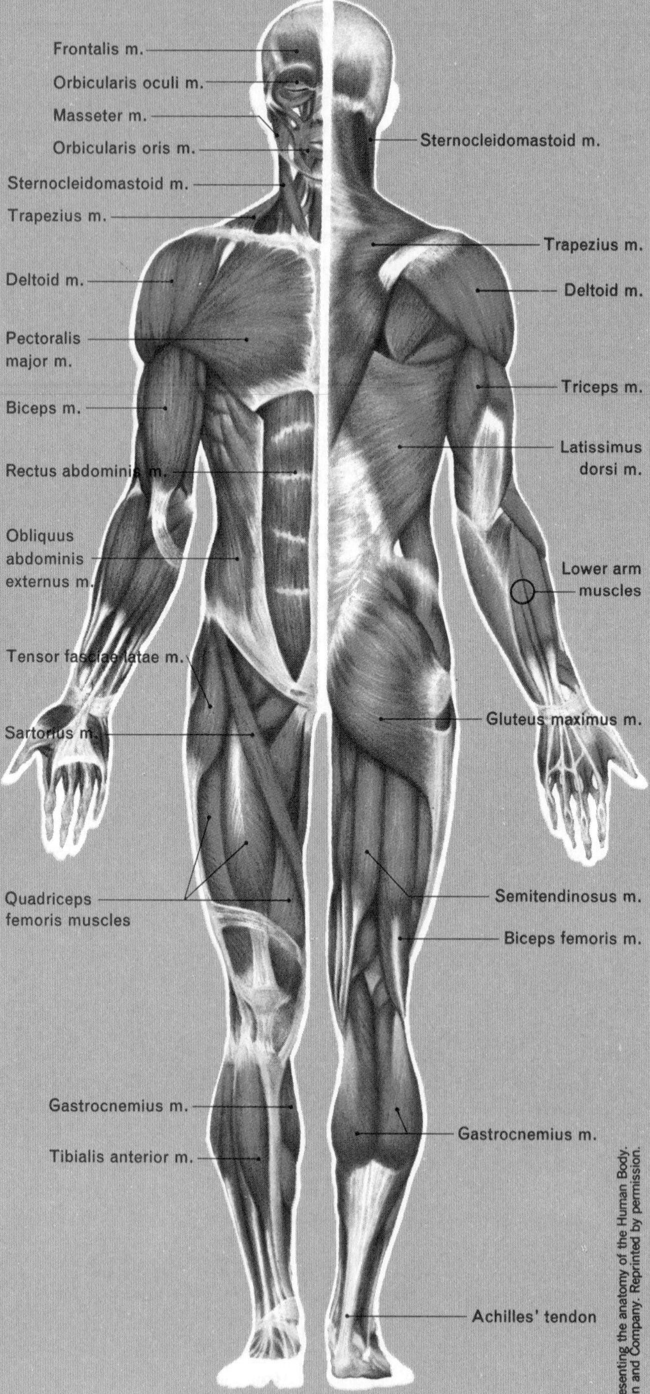

The muscular system

There are more than 650 muscles that surround the internal organs and skeleton of the body. The left half of the diagram shows the outside muscles of the front of the body. The right half shows the outside muscles of the back.

female ovum. In coitus, the male organ ejaculates more than 250 million sperm into the vagina, from which some make their way to the uterus. Ovulation, the release of an egg into the uterus, occurs approximately every 28 days; during the same period the uterus is prepared for the implantation of a fertilized ovum by the action of estrogens. If a male cell fails to unite with a female cell, other hormones cause the uterine wall to slough off during menstruation. From puberty to menopause, the process of ovulation, and preparation, and menstruation is repeated monthly except for periods of pregnancy. The duration of pregnancy is about 280 days. After childbirth, prolactin, a hormone secreted by the pituitary, activates the production of milk.

Skin. The skin is an organ of double-layered tissue stretched over the surface of the body and protecting it from drying or losing fluid, from harmful external substances, and from extremes of temperature. The inner layer, called the dermis, contains sweat glands, blood vessels, nerve endings (sense receptors), and the bases of hair and nails. The outer layer, the epidermis, is only a few cells thick; it contains pigments, pores, and ducts, and its surface is made of dead cells that it sheds from the body. (Hair and nails are adaptations arising from the dead cells.) The sweat glands excrete waste and cool the body through evaporation of fluid droplets; the blood vessels of the dermis supplement temperature regulation by contracting to preserve body heat and expanding to dissipate it. Separate kinds of receptors convey pressure, temperature, and pain. Fat cells in the dermis insulate the body, and oil glands lubricate the epidermis.

HISTORY OF ANATOMY

The oldest known systematic study of anatomy is contained in an Egyptian papyrus dating from about 1600 BC. The treatise reveals knowledge of the larger viscera but little concept of their functions. About the same degree of knowledge is reflected in the writings of the Greek physician Hippocrates in the 5th century BC. In the 4th century BC Aristotle greatly increased anatomical knowledge of animals. The first real progress in the science of human anatomy was made in the following century by the Greek physicians Herophilus and Erasistratus, who dissected human cadavers and were the first to distinguish many functions, including those of the nervous and muscular systems. Little further progress was made by the ancient Romans or by the Arabs. The Renaissance first influenced the science of anatomy in the latter half of the 16th century.

Modern anatomy began with the publication in 1543 of the work of the Belgian anatomist Andreas Vesalius. Before the publication of this classical work anatomists had been so bound by tradition that the writings of authorities of more than 100 years earlier, such as the Greek physician Galen, who had been restricted to the dissection of animals, were accepted in lieu of actual observation. Vesalius and other Renaissance anatomists, however, based their descriptions on their own observations of human corpses, thus setting the pattern for subsequent study in anatomy.

Morphology. For many years anatomists (even those of the modern era) were concerned mainly with the accumulation of a vast amount of information known as descriptive morphology. Descriptive morphology has been supplemented, and to a certain extent supplanted, by the development of experimental morphology, which attempts to identify the hereditary and environmental determinants in morphology and their relationships by controlled-environment and grafting experiments on embryos. Ideally, anatomical investigation consists of a combination of descriptive and experimental approaches. Present-day anatomy involves scrutiny of the structure of organisms at many levels of observation. For example, the anatomist studies the cells and tissues of organisms with the unaided eye, with simple and compound lenses, with various kinds of microscopes, and by chemical methods of analysis.

Microscopic Anatomy. The 17th-century invention of the compound microscope led to the development of microscopic anatomy, which is divided into histology, the study of tissues, and cytology, the study of cells. Under the leadership of the Italian anatomist Marcello Malpighi, the study of the microscopic structure of animals and plants flourished during the 17th century. Many great anatomists of the period were reluctant to accept microscopic anatomy as part of their science. By contrast, modern anatomy is studied usually with the aim of correlating the structure of organisms as seen by the naked eye with their structure as revealed by more refined methods of observation.

Pathological anatomy was established as a branch of the science by the Italian physician Giovanni Morgagni, and in the late 18th century comparative anatomy was systematized by the French naturalist Georges Cuvier.

In the late 18th and early 19th centuries restrictive legislation limiting the use of unclaimed human bodies for the study of anatomy and surgery gave rise in England and the U.S. to an era of body snatching. The scandals arising from this practice forced the repeal of the English restric-

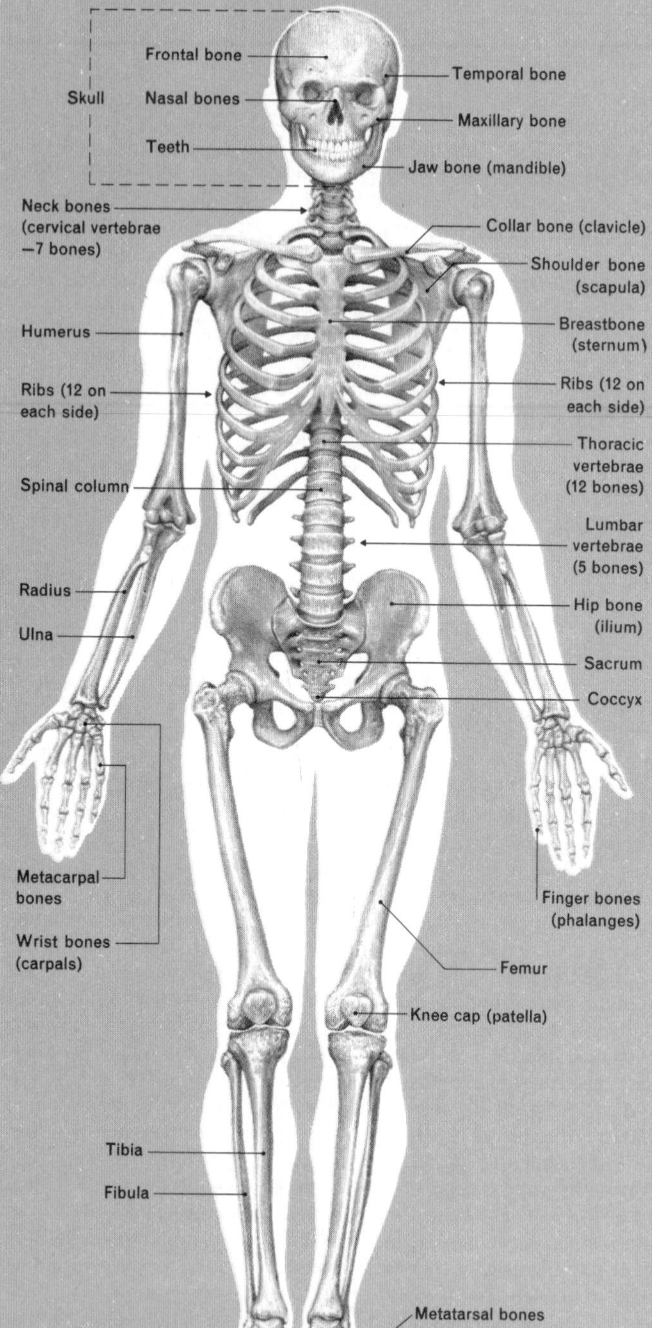

The skeletal system

The skeletal system consists of 206 bones that make up the strong framework that supports the softer organs of the body and provides a firm attachment for the muscles. Most of the bones are labeled on the diagram.

tions in 1832 and the enactment of more advanced legislation.

Microscopic anatomy developed rapidly in the 19th century. During the second half of the century many basic facts about the fine structure of organisms were discovered, largely as a result of greatly improved optical microscopes and of new methods that made cells and tissues easy to study with this instrument. The method of microtomy, the cutting of tissue into thin, practically transparent slices, was perfected. Microtomy was rendered incomparably more valuable by the application to the tissue slices of various types of dyes and stains that make it much easier to see various parts of the cell.

Knowledge of microscopic anatomy was greatly expanded during the 20th century as a result of the development of microscopes that provided much greater resolution and magnification than had conventional instruments, thus revealing formerly unclear or invisible detail; and expanded laboratory techniques helped facilitate observation. The ultraviolet microscope allows the observer to see more because the wavelengths of its probing rays are shorter than those of visible light (the resolving power of a microscope is inversely proportional to the wavelength of the light used). It also is used to emphasize particular details through selective absorption of certain ultraviolet wavelengths. The electron microscope gives even greater magnification and resolution. These tools have opened up formerly unexplored fields of anatomical investigation. Other modern microscopes have made visible unstained and living materials that would be invisible under the conventional microscope. Two examples are the phase-contrast microscope and the interference microscope. Through utilization of ordinary light beams, both these instruments differentiate parts of living, unstained cells.

The discovery of X rays by the German physicist Wilhelm Roentgen enabled anatomists to study tissues and organ systems in living animals. The first X-ray photograph, taken in 1896, was of a human hand. Today's techniques permit three-dimensional X-ray photographs of the soft tissues of the viscera after ingestion of special opaque fluids, and of "slices" of the body with computer-aided X-ray beams. (*see* RADIOLOGY). The latter is called computerized tomography, or CT scanning. Other noninvasive techniques that have been developed include the use of ultrasonic waves for imaging soft tissues and the application of nuclear magnetic resonance (q.v.) systems to research and diagnosis.

Another 20th-century technique of anatomical investigation is tissue culture, which involves the cultivation of cells and tissues of complex organisms outside the body. The technique permits the isolation of living units so that the investigator can directly observe the processes of growth, multiplication, and differentiation of cells. Tissue culture thus has added a new dimension to anatomical science.

Histochemistry and Cytochemistry. The closely related techniques of histochemistry and cytochemistry are concerned with the investigation of chemical activities of tissues and cells. For example, the presence of certain colors within cells indicates that particular chemical reactions have occurred. In addition, the density of the color reaction may serve as an index of the intensity of the reaction. Histochemical methods have been particularly successful in the study of enzymes, catalytic substances that control and direct many of the cell's activities. Much knowledge of enzymes was gained in studies carried out after removal of the enzymes from their cells of origin, but not until the advent of histochemistry could the anatomist see through the microscope which cells carry specific enzymes or gauge how active these enzymes are in different cells under various conditions.

An important technique of histochemistry involves the use of radioactive isotopes of various chemical elements that are present in cells and tissues (*see* ISOTOPE; RADIOIMMUNOASSAY; ISOTOPIC TRACER). Elements or compounds "tagged" or "labeled" with radioactive isotopes are administered to living materials, permitting the investigator to trace the pathways taken by these substances through the various tissues. The degree of concentration and dilution of elements within specific cellular constituents may be estimated by measuring the radiations emanating from these tissues. The technique of labeling compounds with radioactive isotopes makes it possible to study the distribution and concentration of isotopes in tissue slices similar to those studied routinely under the microscope. This study, called autoradiography, is accomplished by bringing the radioactive tissue slices into contact with photographic films and emulsions that are sensitive to radiation.

Another technique of localizing chemical compounds within tissue slices is microincineration: the heating of microscopic sections to the point at which the organic materials present are destroyed and only the mineral skeleton remains. The remaining minerals can then be identified by special chemical and microscopic procedures. Thus, microincineration provides still another way of locating specific chemical elements within particular cell or tissue components.

Another development in the field of histochemistry is microspectrophotometry, a precise method of color analysis. In this process the colors within a tissue slice are analyzed with a spectrophotometer, an instrument that measures the intensity of each color as a function of wavelength. Microspectrophotometry can be used to estimate the characteristics of unstained cells and tissues by measuring their absorption of particular wavelengths. Another application permits precise judgments to be made concerning the nature and intensity of color reactions. These judgments provide, in turn, accurate information about the location and intensity of chemical reactions in the components of living organisms.

See PHYSIOLOGY. For further information on individual anatomists, see biographies of those whose names are not followed by dates.

For further information on this topic, see the Bibliography in volume 28, sections 438–39, 493–95.

ANATOSAURUS, also *Trachodon,* genus of large, plant-eating, ornithischian (bird-hipped) dinosaurs (*see* DINOSAUR) of the suborder Ornithopoda. This duck-billed dinosaur of western North America—its name means "duck lizard" (Lat. *anatos,* "duck"; *sauros,* "lizard")—lived during the Late Cretaceous period and survived up to the end of the Mesozoic era, about 65 million years ago. Adults measured 9 m (30 ft) long, stood over 4 m (13 ft) tall, and weighed more than 3 metric tons. The front of *Anatosaurus*'s duckbill-covered beak was toothless, but its cheeks contained several rows of closely packed teeth that numbered in the hundreds. *Anatosaurus* was bipedal but probably assumed a four-legged stance while grazing.

ANAXAGORAS (500?–428 BC), Greek philosopher who introduced the notion of *nous* (Gr., "mind" or "reason") into the philosophy of origins; previous philosophers had studied the elements (earth, air, fire, water) as ultimate reality.

Born in Clazomenae (near modern İzmir, Turkey), Anaxagoras was the first philosopher to settle (c. 480) in Athens, later a flourishing center of philosophy. His pupils included the Greek statesman Pericles, the Greek dramatist Euripides, and probably Socrates. Anaxagoras had taught in Athens for about 30 years when he was imprisoned for impiety for suggesting that the sun is a hot stone and the moon made of earth. Later he went to Ionia (in Asia Minor) and settled at Lampsacus, a colony of Miletus, where he died.

Anaxagoras explained his philosophy in *Peri Physeos* (On Nature), but only fragments of the books have survived. He held that all matter had existed originally as atoms, or molecules; that these atoms, infinitely numerous and infinitesimally small, had existed from all eternity; and that order was first produced out of this infinite chaos of minute atoms through the influence and operation of an eternal intelligence (*nous*). He also believed that all bodies are simply aggregations of atoms, for example, that a bar of gold, iron, or copper is composed of inconceivably minute particles of the same material.

Anaxagoras marks a great turning point in the history of Greek philosophy: His doctrine of the *nous* was adopted by Aristotle, and his doctrine of atoms prepared the way for the atomic theory of the philosopher Democritus.

ANAXIMANDER (c. 611–c. 547 BC), Greek philosopher, mathematician, and astronomer, born in Miletus in what is now Turkey. He was a disciple and friend of the Greek philosopher Thales. Anaximander is said to have discovered the obliquity of the ecliptic, that is, the angle at which the plane of the ecliptic is inclined to the celestial equator. He is credited with introducing the sundial into Greece and with inventing cartography. Anaximander's outstanding contribution was his authorship of the earliest prose work concerning the cosmos and the origins of life. He conceived of the universe as a number of concentric cylinders, of which the outermost is the sun, the middle is the moon, and the innermost is the stars. Within these cylinders is the earth, unsupported and drum-shaped. Anaximander postulated the origin of the universe as the result of the separation of opposites from the primordial material. Hot moved outward, separating from cold, and then dry from wet. Further, Anaximander held that all things eventually return to the element from which they originated.

ANAXIMENES (c. 570–500 BC), Greek philosopher of nature, the last member of the Ionian school founded by the philosopher Thales. Born at Miletus, Ionia, in Asia Minor, he held that air is the primary element to which everything else can be reduced. To explain how solid objects are formed from air, he introduced the notions of condensation and rarefaction. These processes, he claimed, make air, in itself invisible, visible as water, fire, and solid matter. He thought that air becomes warmer and turns to fire when it is rarefied and that it becomes colder and turns solid when it is condensed. His importance lies not in his cosmology but in his attempt to discover the ultimate nature of reality.

ANCESTOR WORSHIP, reverence granted to deceased relatives who are believed to have become powerful spiritual beings or, less frequently, to have attained the status of gods. It is based on the belief that ancestors are active members of society, still interested in the affairs of their living relatives.

The cult of ancestors is common, although not universal. It has been extensively documented in West African societies (the Bantu and the Shona), in Polynesia and Melanesia (the Dobu and the Manus), among several Indo-European peoples (the ancient Scandinavians and Germans), and especially in China and Japan. In general, ancestors are believed to wield great authority, having special powers to influence the course of events or to control the well-being of their living relatives. Protection of the family is one of their main concerns. They are considered intermediaries between the supreme god, or the gods, and the people, and can communicate with the living through dreams and by possession. The attitude toward them is one of mixed fear and reverence. If neglected, the ancestors may cause disease and other misfortunes. Propitiation, supplication, prayer, and sacrifice are various ways in which the living can communicate with their ancestors.

Ancestor worship is a strong indication of the value placed on the household and of the strong ties that exist between the past and the present. The beliefs and practices connected with the cult help to integrate the family, to sanction the traditional political structure, and to encourage respect for living elders. Some scholars have also interpreted it as a source of individual well-being and of social harmony and stability. J.A.Sa.

ANCHISES. *See* AENEAS.

ANCHOR, device used to attach a floating vessel to the water bottom for the purpose of holding the vessel in place. Anchors are connected to the vessel by ropes, cables, or chains. Primitive anchors held a vessel only by their enormous weight and friction along the sea bottom. The structure of modern anchors enables them to dig into the underwater surface and powerfully grip the seabed against the drift of the vessel. The common anchor consists of a shaft with a movable crosspiece called the stock at its top end and two curved arms ending in spadelike points called flukes at its bottom end. Modern anchors usually are made of forged steel and may weigh thousands of pounds. Large ships usually carry several heavy anchors. Among the many anchor designs are the stockless anchor, mushroom anchor, grapnel anchor, Danforth anchor, plow anchor, and sea anchor.

ANCHORAGE, municipality, S Alaska, a seaport on Knik Arm of Cook Inlet; inc. 1920. Anchorage is the largest city in the state and serves as the transportation and commercial center for much of central and W Alaska. It is connected to the Alaska Highway by Glenn Highway and is served by Anchorage International Airport, which is a major international hub for air freight. The city's economy is largely associated with Alaska's petroleum, natural-gas, and fishing industries. In addition, tourism is a growing part of the economy, and two nearby U.S. military bases built during World War II, Fort Richardson and Elmendorf Air Force Base, are important local employers. The Museum of Art and History, a sports arena, a convention center, and the Alaska Center for the Perfoming Arts were built during the 1980s. Alaska Pacific University (1959) and the Anchorage campus of the University of Alaska system are here.

The community was established in 1914–15 as the main supply base for the Alaska Railroad and grew rapidly during World War II, when it became the headquarters for the U.S. Alaska Defense Command. An earthquake in 1964 caused extensive damage to the city. Pop. (1980) 173,017; (1990) 226,338.

ANCHOVY, name applied to any of several small schooling fishes of the family Engraulidae. Related to the herring (q.v.) in the order Clupeiformes, it is a bony fish that reaches a length of about 20 cm (about 8 in) but is generally much smaller. It is common in the offshore open waters of tropical climates and is especially abundant off Peru and Chile. One of the world's most important commercial fishes, it is used in animal meal, oil, and fertilizer. Some species are filleted, salted, packed in oil, and sold as a delicacy.

ANCONA, city, central Italy, capital of Ancona Province and of Marche Region, a seaport on the Adriatic Sea. It is a busy commercial and fishing port. Other industries include shipbuilding, petroleum refining, and the manufacture of sugar, sailcloth, paper, chemicals, machinery, and musical instruments.

Ancona was founded about 390 BC by Greek merchants from Syracuse. The city later became a Roman colony. It was used as a Roman naval station during the Illyrian War in 178 BC, and it was captured by Julius Caesar after he crossed the Rubicon in 49 BC. Trajan later enlarged the harbor, and it became an important Roman trade port and naval base.

With the fall of Rome in AD 476, Ancona became part of the Byzantine Empire. It was overrun in about 493 by Goths. In the 6th century Ancona became one of the five cities of the Pentapolis, part of the Byzantine province of Ravenna, which was conquered about 752 by the Lombards. Destroyed in 848 by the Saracens, Ancona was rebuilt in 876, coming under the rule of the Holy Roman emperors. Recognized as a papal possession in the early 13th century, it became a semi-independent republic under papal rule. In 1532 it became part of the Papal States.

During the French Revolution and the Napoleonic Wars, Ancona was captured (1797) by the French, recaptured (1799) for the papacy by the Austrians, captured (1801) again by the French, absorbed (1808) into the kingdom of Italy, and finally returned to the papacy. The revolts of 1831 and 1849 against papal rule were crushed by Austrian troops. In 1860 Ancona was captured by the Italian nationalist forces and became a part of Italy. The city was badly damaged in World War II. Pop. (1988 est.) 104,300.

ANCUS MARCIUS (fl. 7th cent. BC), legendary fourth king of Rome (641?–616 BC). According to ancient historians, he tried to restore in Rome the almost forgotten worship of the gods. He was forced to engage in wars with aggressive neighboring Latin tribes and with the Etruscans. Ancus Marcius is believed to have established the class of plebeians from among his Latin prisoners settled on the Aventine Hill and to have built the port of Ostia. From the evidence of a prison for public criminals, built in his day, some historians have concluded that he made a distinction between public and private crimes.

ANCYRA. *See* ANKARA.

ANDALUSIA, autonomous region, S Spain, comprising the provinces of Almería, Cádiz, Córdoba, Granada, Huelva, Jaén, Málaga, and Seville. It is bounded on the N by the Sierra Morena; on the E by the provinces of Albacete and Murcia and the Mediterranean Sea; on the S by the Mediterranean Sea, Gibraltar, and the Atlantic Ocean; on the W by Portugal. The capital is the city of Seville. The most important river is the Guadalquivir, which flows into the Atlantic Ocean N of Cádiz. S of the valley of the Guadalquivir are the Sierra Nevada mountains. The highest peak is Mulhacén (3478 m/11,411 ft). Most of Andalusia is fertile. The climate on the Mediterranean coast is subtropical, on the Atlantic coast, temperate. In the highlands, a lower temperature prevails, and snow is not unusual. The warm climate of the valleys and plains allows the cultivation of oranges, olives, and sugarcane; wheat, corn, and other grains flourish. Mineral deposits in the mountainous areas include lead, silver, copper, mercury, and coal.

Andalusia was probably the biblical Tarshish (from Tartessus, an ancient kingdom on the SW coast of the Iberian Peninsula). The Carthaginians settled here in the 5th century BC. The district was conquered by the Romans, who called it Baetica (from Boetis, the Roman name of the Guadalquivir River). Under the Roman Empire the region was very prosperous. The country was overrun by the Vandals early in the 5th century. From the Vandals the region took the name Vandalusia, which, in later centuries, was corrupted into Andalusia. The Vandals were succeeded by the Visigoths, who ruled until the Arab invasion of 711, after which Andalusia became the center

The town of Ronda, with its Roman ruins and Moorish fortifications, is one of Andalusia's most colorful tourist attractions. © 1990 Masahiro Sano–The Stock Market

of the Saracen and Moorish civilization. The cities of Granada, Córdoba, Seville, and Jaén were seats of Islamic culture, industry, and commerce. Students from all parts of Europe attended the great Muslim universities. Andalusia, established as a Moorish emirate in 756, later developed into the caliphate of Córdoba (*see* CÓRDOBA). Lower Andalusia, corresponding to the lower reaches of the Guadalquivir, was taken from the Moors in 1212. The Upper Andalusia survived as the kingdom of Granada (*see* GRANADA) until 1492, when it was conquered by the sovereigns of Castile and Aragón, Ferdinand V and Isabella. From 1516 the history of Andalusia merges with that of the united kingdom of Spain. Area, 87,268 sq km (33,694 sq mi). Pop. (1986) 6,875,628.

ANDAMAN ISLANDS, island group, E India, between the Bay of Bengal and the Andaman Sea, forming the N part of the Andaman and Nicobar Islands, a union territory of India. The three principal islands are North Andaman, Middle Andaman, and South Andaman. To the E is a cluster of small islands known collectively as Ritchies Archipelago; to the S is Little Andaman. Port Blair, the administrative capital, has a fine harbor, and ships from the mainland call there regularly. The Andamans are generally hilly and are heavily forested. Timber, coconuts, hemp, tea, coffee, and rubber are the principal products. Most of the inhabitants are Indian; the aborigines, numbering now only in the hundreds, are primitive Negritos. Area of the Andamans, 6475 sq km (2500 sq mi). Pop. of Andaman and Nicobar Islands (1981) 188,254. *See also* NICOBAR ISLANDS.

ANDAMAN SEA, NE arm of the Indian Ocean, bounded on the W by the Andaman and Nicobar Islands; on the N by Burma; on the E by Burma, Thailand, and Malaysia; and on the S by Sumatra. It is linked to the South China Sea by the Strait of Malacca. The Andaman Sea receives the Irrawaddy, Sittang, and Salween rivers. Area, about 798,000 sq km (about 308,000 sq mi).

ANDERLECHT, city, central Belgium, part of metropolitan Brussels, in Brabant Province, on the Charleroi Canal. Manufactures include textiles, chemicals, leather, paper, glass, and food products. It is the site of the 15th-century Gothic church of Saint Pierre, with an 11th-century crypt, and of the residence (1517–21) of Dutch humanist Desiderius Erasmus. Pop. (1989 est.) 89,600.

ANDERSEN, Hans Christian (1805–75), Danish author of fairy tales. He was born in Odense; his childhood was one of poverty and neglect, and when he was 14 years of age he ran away to Copenhagen. There he became an apprentice at the Royal Theater and attracted patrons who provided for his education. Although Andersen

An organ grinder begins his day on the streets of Córdoba, a historic provincial capital city in central Andalusia.
© Glaubach–Photo Researchers, Inc.

had poetry and prose published and plays produced from 1822 on, his real success did not begin until his first novel, *The Improvisatore, or Life in Italy* (1835; trans. 1845), was well received by the critics, and a collection of four of his fairy tales was published. He traveled through Europe, Asia, and Africa and wrote many plays, novels, and travel books. His more than 150 stories for children established him as one of the great authors of the world. Among his famous tales of fantasy are "The Ugly Duckling," "The Emperor's New Clothes," "The Snow Queen," "The Red Shoes," and "The Little Mermaid." His stories have been translated into more than 80 languages and have been the source of plays, ballets, films, and works of sculpture and painting.

ANDERSON, city, seat of Madison Co., central Indiana, on the White R., in a grain-, soybean-, and livestock-raising area; platted 1823, inc. as a city 1865. Its many manufactures include motor-vehicle parts, machinery, shipping containers, and food products. Anderson University (1917) is here, and Mounds State Park, containing large Indian earthen mounds, is nearby. The city is named for a Delaware Indian leader, known as Capt. Anderson, who lived in the area. Pop. (1980) 64,695; (1990) 59,459.

ANDERSON, city, seat of Anderson Co., NW South Carolina, in the foothills of the Blue Ridge Mts.; inc. 1882. Manufactures include textiles, electrical machinery, and fiberglass products. A junior college is here, and Hartwell Reservoir is nearby. The community, founded in 1826 as the county seat, is named for Gen. Robert Anderson (1741–1813), a hero of the American Revolution. Pop. (1980) 27,965; (1990) 26,184.

ANDERSON, Carl David (1905–91), American physicist and Nobel laureate. Anderson was born in New York City and educated at the California Institute of Technology, where he attained full professorial rank in 1939. In 1932 he discovered the positron, or positive electron, one of the fundamental subatomic particles. For this achievement he was awarded, with Victor Franz Hess, the 1936 Nobel Prize in physics. In 1936 Anderson also confirmed experimentally the existence of the elementary nuclear particle called the meson, which had been predicted in 1935 by the Japanese physicist Yukawa Hideki.

ANDERSON, Dame Judith, professional name of FRANCES MARGARET ANDERSON-ANDERSON (1898–1992), American actor, born in Adelaide, Australia. She made her professional acting debut in 1915 in Sydney. Three years later she moved to the U.S. and became a leading Broadway performer. Anderson was especially noted for her performances in roles requiring sustained dramatic intensity. In plays adapted from ancient Greek legends by the American poet Robinson Jeffers, she created two of her most memorable roles: *Medea* (1947) and *The Tower Beyond Tragedy* (1950). Among her earlier stage successes were *Strange Interlude* (1928) and *Mourning Becomes Electra* (1932), both by the American playwright Eugene O'Neill. In 1936 she played Queen Gertrude in Shakespeare's *Hamlet* opposite the English actor Sir John Gielgud.

On the motion picture screen she appeared as Mrs. Danvers in *Rebecca* (1940) and as Big Mama in *Cat on a Hot Tin Roof* (1958). She also repeated a number of her stage successes on television. In 1960 she was made a Dame Commander of the Order of the British Empire.

ANDERSON, Marian (1902–), American contralto, born in Philadelphia, and trained there, in Chicago, and in Europe. In 1925 she won a competition for an appearance with the New York Philharmonic. Her reputation was established through a concert tour of Europe in 1933. Her 1955 debut at the Metropolitan Opera House, New York City, as Ulrica in Verdi's *A Masked Ball* was the first appearance of a black singer with the Metropolitan. In 1958 she was an alternate delegate from the U.S. to the UN. Anderson, who retired from singing in 1965, was awarded the Presidential Medal of Freedom in 1963 and a Congressional gold medal in 1978. Her autobiography is *My Lord, What a Morning* (1956).

For further information on this person, see the section Biographies in the Bibliography in volume 28.

ANDERSON, Maxwell (1888–1959), American playwright, born in Atlantic, Pa., and educated at the University of North Dakota and Stanford University. He was a schoolteacher and journalist until 1924, when his play *What Price Glory?* was successfully produced in New York City. Written in collaboration with Laurence Stallings (1894–1968), *What Price Glory?* is a colorful drama of World War I. Anderson, noted for the wide-ranging dramatic style of his 30 produced plays, wrote several historical dramas in blank verse, including *Elizabeth the Queen* (1930), *Mary of Scotland* (1933), and *Anne of the Thousand Days* (1947). He also wrote *Saturday's Children* (1927) and *The Bad Seed* (1954), as well as the librettos for several musicals, including *Knickerbocker Holiday* (1938) and *Lost in the Stars* (1949). Anderson was awarded the Pulitzer Prize in drama for *Both Your Houses* (1933). His verse play *Winterset* (1935), inspired by the 1920s murder trial of two anarchists, known as the Sacco-Vanzetti case (q.v.), is considered a classic.

ANDERSON, Robert (1805–71), American army officer, born near Louisville, Ky. He graduated from the U.S. Military Academy in 1825 and became second lieutenant in the U.S. Army (artillery). Outstanding in his career was his defense of Fort Sumter in the harbor of Charleston, S.C., April 12–13, 1861, against bombardment by Confederate forces, the first action of the American Civil War. He was forced to surrender the fort on April 14. In 1863 Anderson retired with the rank of brigadier general, and two years later he was brevetted major general.

ANDERSON, Sherwood (1876–1941), American author, born in Camden, Ohio. He left school at the age of 14 and worked at various jobs until

Marian Anderson in 1958.

1898. He served in Cuba during the Spanish-American War. After the war he went to Chicago, where he began to write novels and poetry. His work won praise from Theodore Dreiser, Carl Sandburg, and Ben Hecht.

Anderson's talent was not widely recognized until the publication of the collection of short stories *Winesburg, Ohio* (1919), which deals with the instinctive, if inarticulate, struggle of ordinary people to assert their individuality in the face of standardization imposed by the machine age. Noted for his poetic realism, psychological insight, and sense of the tragic, Anderson helped also to establish a simple, consciously naive short-story style. Among his other works are several novels, short stories, and essays. His autobiographies are *Tar, a Midwest Childhood* (1926) and *Sherwood Anderson's Memoirs* (1942).

ANDERSONVILLE PRISON, military stockade of the Confederate army during the American Civil War, near Andersonville, Ga., used to confine captured Union army enlisted men. A total of 49,485 prisoners were detained at Andersonville between February 1864 and April 1865. As many as 30,000 men were confined there at one time. More than 13,700 prisoners died in confinement. The prison burial ground is now a national cemetery, and the prison site and surrounding area were designated a national historic site in 1970.

Constant exposure to the elements, together with inadequate food, impure water, congestion, and filth, led inevitably to epidemics of scurvy and dysentery. As a result, the two Confederate medical officers appointed to investigate the prison in 1864 recommended that the majority of the prisoners be transferred elsewhere, and many prisoners were removed that fall to Millen, Ga., and to Florence, S.C. A year later the superintendent of the prison, Maj. Henry Wirz (1822–65), was tried by a U.S. military court, convicted of murder, and hanged.

The action of the Pulitzer Prize-winning novel *Andersonville* (1955), by the American writer MacKinlay Kantor (1904–77), is set in the prison.

ANDES, mountain chain of South America, one of the greatest mountain systems of the world, extending almost parallel with the Pacific coast from Cape Horn nearly to Panama. The chain, about 7240 km (about 4500 mi) long, has an average breadth of 241 km (150 mi) and an average height of about 3660 m (about 12,000 ft). From their narrow S end in Chile, the Andes spread into several parallel ranges in N Argentina, Bolivia, Peru, and Colombia. In Venezuela the chain divides into three distinct ranges. Along its entire length the chain rises abruptly from the Pacific coast. In the Amazon Valley area and in Argentina, the land rises toward the mountains, while the mountains rise steeply everywhere.

Uplift and folding of the sedimentary rocks that comprise the Andes began during the Cretaceous period (q.v.), when the Pacific crustal plate began to subduct the South American plate (*see* PLATE TECTONICS). Tectonic forces generated by this collision still trigger volcanic eruptions and earthquakes and have lifted parts of the Andes over 1500 m (5000 ft) during the past 20 million years.

The passes through the Andes, N of Patagonia, are all at a great height and are narrow, steep, and dangerous. The pass from Arequipa to Puno, in Peru, is 4468 m (14,660 ft) high; the one from Lima to Tarma and Cerro de Pasco, also in Peru, is 4804 m (15,760 ft) high; and the Uspallata Pass, between Mendoza, Argentina, and Santiago, Chile, is 3900 m (12,795 ft) high. Railroads have been built through a number of these passes. They include the railroad uniting Mollendo with Puno on Lake Titicaca; the Central Railroad in Peru, which links Lima and La Oroya and is considered the most remarkable railroad construction in the world; and the Transandine Railroad.

The Andes contain many volcanoes, notably Tungurahua (5033 m/16,512 ft), Cotopaxi (5897 m/19,347 ft), and Chimborazo (6267 m/20,561 ft), in Ecuador; Nevado del Tolima (5215 m/17,110 ft), in Colombia; and Llullaillaco (6723 m/22,057 ft), on the border of Argentina and Chile. Other peaks are Ancohuma (6550 m/21,489 ft), in Bolivia; Huascarán (6768 m/22,205 ft), in Peru; and Aconcagua (6959 m/22,831 ft), in Argentina, the highest mountain in the western hemisphere. Within the range are lofty plateaus, such as the plateau of Quito (about 3050 m/about 10,000 ft) and that of Lake Titicaca (3960 m/13,000 ft). The snow line lies at an elevation of about 1220 m (about 4000 ft) at the S extremity of Patagonia; it ranges from an elevation of about 4570 m (about 15,000 ft) to about 5490 m (about 18,000 ft) near the equator.

The timberline ranges from an average elevation of 3500 m (11,500 ft) at the equator to about 910 m (about 3000 ft) in Tierra del Fuego, Argentina. Potatoes grow at elevations of 3050 m (10,000 ft) and above, and oats ripen on the plateau of Lake Titicaca at an elevation of nearly 3960 m (13,000 ft). The mineral riches of the Andes, which have not been fully exploited, include gold, silver, copper, platinum, mercury, lead, iron ore, petroleum, and sulfur.

The rivers flowing toward the Pacific are short and small in volume because the rainfall on the W slopes of the mountains is limited. The streams to the E are long and supplied with an abundance of water brought by the trade winds and precipitated as the winds approach the mountains. The Andes of Colombia are drained N to the Caribbean Sea by the Magdalena, Cauca, and Atrato rivers, and E to the same body of water by the Orinoco R. and to the Atlantic by the Negro and Japura rivers, which are tributaries of the Amazon R.

For further information on this topic, see the Bibliography in volume 28, section 867.

ANDESITE, a dark, fine-grained volcanic rock, the extrusive equivalent of diorite (q.v). Intermediate in composition between basalt and rhyolite (qq.v.), andesite consists mostly of plagioclase feldspar and lesser amounts of biotite or hornblende. The rock occurs as lava flows and dikes in regions where the plates of the earth's crust collide with one another—in the Aleutian islands, the Andes and Cascades mountains, Japan, and Siberia. In other areas of volcanic activity, basalt predominates. *See also* PLATE TECTONICS.

ANDHRA DYNASTY, also called Satavahana (c. 230 BC–AD 230), Indian ruling house originating in what is now the state of Andhra Pradesh. The dynasty may have begun as a family of high officials of the Mauryan Empire, gradually becoming independent as the empire declined. From the 2d century BC to the 2d century AD, the Andhras ruled over much of southern and central India, conquering the Sungas of Magadha in 27 BC and vying with the Sakas for control of the Deccan.

The greatest ruler of the dynasty was probably Satakarni I (fl. 1st cent. AD), who extended his kingdom over the northwestern Deccan, establishing his capital at modern Paithan in Maharashtra State. Although subsequently forced out of the area by the Sakas, the Andhras surged back in the 2d century AD under Gautamiputra Satakarni (d. about AD 128), a great champion of Hinduism. The last great king of the dynasty was Yajna Sri Satakarni (fl. late 2d cent.), who once more asserted Andhra authority over the Sakas. The dynasty declined during the 3d century, when the kingdom broke up into smaller units.

ANDONG. *See* DANDONG.

ANDORRA, also Valleys of Andorra, semiautonomous coprincipality of Europe, situated in the E Pyrenees Mts., bordered on the N and E by France, and on the S and W by Spain. The country has an area of 453 sq km (175 sq mi) and its population (1986 census) was 45,877. The overall population density in 1986 was about 101 persons per sq km (about 262 per sq mi). The capital is Andorra la Vella (pop., 1986, 15,600). For the location of Andorra, see the map of Spain.

Andorra is a region of narrow valleys and mountain peaks that reach heights of more than 2700 m (about 8860 ft). The principal stream is the Valira R. The land has iron and lead deposits and marble quarries; forests of pine and birch are found on the mountains, and in low-lying areas are pastureland where sheep are grazed. Andorra has no railroad or airport but possesses an excellent road system. The native-born inhabitants of Andorra (only about one-fourth of the entire population) are Catalan in ancestry and language; Spanish, and to a lesser extent, French, immigrants make up the majority of the remainder. The main religion is Roman Catholicism.

Andorra's economy was formerly based on pastoral farming and the processing of tobacco and

Andorra la Vella, the small capital city of Andorra, is in the Gran Valira Valley of the Pyrenees Mountains.
© Everett C. Johnson–Leo de Wys

timber. Tourism has boomed since the 1950s and now dominates the principality's economic life. Tourists are drawn by the winter ski facilities, the cool summer climate, and the availability of duty-free goods. Immigration and investment have been encouraged by low tax rates.

Andorra is governed by a general council of 28 members, headed by a first and second syndic; it appoints the executive council, which is headed by a president. Nominal authority over Andorra is exercised jointly by the president of France and the Spanish bishop of Urgel, who are acknowledged as coprinces. Each is represented by a deputy, an Andorran resident, whose duties are judicial in nature. France controls Andorran foreign relations. Andorra has no currency of its own; both French and Spanish currency are used.

Andorra is traditionally held to have been declared a free state by Charlemagne in the 9th century AD. In 1278 it came under the joint suzerainty of the Catalan bishop of Urgel and of the count of Foix of France; through the latter, French rights passed successively to the kings and chiefs of state of France. Andorra pays a nominal biennial tribute to France and to the bishop of Urgel. In 1970 women received the right to vote.

ANDOVER, town, Essex Co., NE Massachusetts, on the Merrimack and Shawsheen rivers; inc. 1646. Manufactures include electronic equipment, analytical instruments, and rubber products. Andover is the site of Phillips Academy (1778), one of the country's oldest private preparatory schools, which in 1973 merged with Abbot Academy, formerly for girls (1829). The notable Addison Gallery of American Art is located on the grounds of Phillips Academy. Textile mills were established in Andover in the late 18th century, and by the 1840s the town had become a nationally important producer of woolen goods. Before the American Civil War, Andover was a center of the antislavery movement and was the home of the author Harriet Beecher Stowe. The town is named for Andover, England. Pop. (1980) 26,370; (1990) 29,151.

ANDRÁSSY, Gyula, Count (1823–90), Hungarian statesman, born in Kassa, then part of the Austrian Empire (now Košice, Czechoslovakia). He became a member of the Hungarian diet (legislature) in 1847. An ardent nationalist, Andrássy participated in the 1848 revolution against Austria. At the surrender of the rebels, Andrássy was serving as envoy to Turkey. He was condemned to death and remained in exile until 1857, when he obtained amnesty and returned home. He was returned to the diet in 1861 and became vice-president of the legislative body in 1865.

Upon the formation of Austria-Hungary as a dual monarchy in 1867, Andrássy became Hungarian prime minister. His primary influence was in foreign affairs, maintaining neutrality in the Franco-Prussian War of 1870–71. From 1871 until his resignation in 1879 Andrássy was minister of foreign affairs of the Austro-Hungarian Empire. In that capacity he helped to lay the groundwork of the Triple Alliance. He also served as plenipotentiary from Austria-Hungary to the Congress of Berlin in 1878, at which his plan for the occupation of Bosnia and Hercegovina was approved.

ANDRÁSSY, Gyula, Count (1860–1929), Hungarian diplomat and statesman, son of Count Gyula Andrássy, born in Budapest. At the age of 24 he entered the Austrian Reichstag, and after holding various offices, he became minister of the interior (1906–9). Subsequently he represented Austria in an effort to prevent the Balkan War (1912). In 1915, during World War I, he urged that Austria-Hungary make peace with the Allies. As Austro-Hungarian foreign minister in 1918, in a note to U.S. President Woodrow Wilson, he offered to arrange a separate peace. The offer failed, however, and Andrássy retired from office. He was imprisoned in 1921 for an attempt to place Charles I, the former emperor of Austria, on the Hungarian throne.

ANDRÉ, John (1751–80), British soldier, born in London, of Swiss-French parentage. He joined the British army in 1771 and was sent to Canada in 1774. His advancement was rapid, and in 1778 he was appointed adjutant general of the British forces in America and aide to the British general Sir Henry Clinton. His great personal charm and wit and his artistic and literary abilities were partly responsible for his rapid advancement in the army. In 1780, when the American general Benedict Arnold began negotiations with Clinton for the betrayal of West Point, André acted for Clinton. Following his secret meeting with Arnold, André, disguised as a civilian, set out for the British lines on horseback with the plans of West Point in his boots. Near Tarrytown he was captured and taken to the headquarters of Gen. George Washington at Tappan, N.Y., where a military court sentenced him to death. He was hanged at Tappan, Oct. 2, 1780. André kept a journal of British military movements in America from 1777 to 1778; discovered in England in 1902, it was published as *André's Journal*.

ANDREA DA PONTADERA. *See* PISANO, ANDREA.

ANDREA DEL CASTAGNO (c. 1421–57), Florentine painter of the early Renaissance. Originally named Andrea di Bartolo di Bargilla, he was born in Castagno, near Florence. Except for a brief period in Venice about 1442, Andrea worked in

Florence chiefly on frescoes for the church and for the Medici and other rich families. Particularly outstanding are the *Last Supper* and a series on the Passion of Christ painted for the convent of S. Apollonia (1445–50). The influence of the Florentine painter Masaccio is seen in Andrea's broad, solid figures and the emotional intensity expressed in both posture and face. The architectural backgrounds, including columns, stairs, and windows, display Andrea's skill in the then new science of perspective.

Andrea's later work shows the increasing influence of the graceful sculpture of Donatello. This group includes *Famous Men and Women,* a series of nine works for the Villa Carducci at Legnaia (c. 1450, S. Apollonia) and the equestrian fresco *Niccolò da Tolentino,* a portrait of the military leader (1456, Florence Cathedral).

ANDREA DEL SARTO (1486–1530), Florentine painter of the High Renaissance, who made his reputation with a series of frescoes on the life of John the Baptist.

Originally named Andrea Domenico d'Agnolo, Andrea was born on July 16, 1486. He studied painting under Piero di Cosimo and from about 1508 to about 1512 collaborated with Franciabigio (1482–1525). At about the same time, he was employed by the Servites, a religious brotherhood, to execute fresco decorations in their Church of the Sant' Annunziata at Florence. By 1510 he completed five scenes depicting events in the life of Filippo Benizzi (1233–85), founder of the Servite order. These works were widely acclaimed as examples of faultless painting in drawing, color, and light and shade. Many commissions followed, including the frescoes of St. John in the cloister of the Scalzi in Florence.

Madonna of the Harpies *(1517) by Andrea del Sarto.*
Scala/Art Resource

Andrea's reputation became international, and in 1518 he was summoned to the court of Francis I of France, who entrusted him with money to purchase works of art in Italy. He returned to Florence in 1519, used the money for his own purposes, and remained in Florence, completing the fresco series in the cloister of the Scalzi. In 1525 he painted in the cloister of the Servite church the *Madonna del Sacco,* which is generally considered his masterpiece. He executed his last major work in fresco, the *Last Supper* (1527) in the refectory of the convent of San Salvi near Florence. He died on Sept. 29, 1530.

Andrea also painted numerous easel paintings, including portraits, such as those of his wife and of himself in the Pitti Palace, Florence; and religious subjects, such as the *Madonna of the Harpies* (1517, Uffizi Gallery, Florence). Included among his other noted works are *Pietà* (1524, Pitti Palace) and *Assumption* (1530, Pitti Palace). The architect and painter Giorgio Vasari was one of his pupils.

ANDREW, Saint, one of the twelve apostles of Jesus Christ and the brother of Simon (later the apostle Peter). A Galilean fisherman of Bethsaida, he was originally a disciple of John the Baptist. In the Gospel of John (see 1:35–42), Andrew was the first called of Jesus' disciples. According to tradition, Andrew was crucified at Patmos, in Achaia, on an X-shaped cross, the form of which became known as St. Andrew's Cross (*see* CROSS). He is the patron saint of Scotland and Russia. His feast day is November 30.

ANDREWES, Lancelot (1555–1626), English churchman and scholar, who influenced the development of a distinctively Anglican theology. Born in London, he was educated at Pembroke College, University of Cambridge, where he was elected fellow in 1575. In 1580 he was ordained a deacon. In 1589 he was appointed, successively, vicar of Saint Giles Church, Cripplegate, and master of Pembroke College. Queen Elizabeth I later appointed him one of her chaplains and dean of Westminster. In 1605 Andrewes was consecrated bishop of Chichester. One of the most learned men of his time, he was appointed (1607) with nine other theologians to translate the first 12 books of the Old Testament for the Authorized, or King James, Version of the Bible. He was an outstanding theologian of the High Church movement in the Church of England, writing from a uniquely Anglican point of view about the church, the sacraments, and episcopacy. Andrewes was transferred to the see of Ely in 1609; the same year he was appointed a privy councilor for England. He became bishop of Winchester in 1619 and was dean of the chapels royal from that year until his death.

ANDREWS, Roy Chapman (1884–1960), American naturalist and explorer, born in Beloit, Wis. In 1906 he joined the staff of the American Museum of Natural History in New York City, becoming its director in 1935. He led paleontological expeditions to Tibet, China, Burma, Outer Mongolia, and the Gobi Desert. Among Chapman's discoveries were dinosaur eggs and remains of the baluchitherium, the largest land mammal. His writings include *Quest of the Snow Leopard* (1955).

ANDREYEV, Leonid Nikolayevich (1871–1919), Russian writer, born in Orël, and educated in law at the universities of Moscow and Saint Petersburg. Finding his law practice unremunerative, he became a reporter for a Moscow newspaper. In about 1900, when his early short stories were enthusiastically reviewed by the writer Maksim Gorki, Andreyev's literary career really began. From that time until his death he was one of the most prolific writers in Russia, producing many short stories, sketches, and dramas. English translations of his fiction include *The Red Laugh* (1905), *The Seven Who Were Hanged* (1909), and *The Little Angel and Other Stories* (1916). His plays include *The Life of Man* (1906), *Anathema* (1909), *The Sabine Women* (1912), and *He Who Gets Slapped* (1915).

ANDRIĆ, Ivo (1892–1975), Yugoslav novelist, short-story writer, and Nobel laureate, born in Doc, near Travnik, Bosnia (then part of Austria-Hungary). He was educated at the universities in Zagreb, Kraków, Vienna, and Graz. Before World War I he was a member of a revolutionary nationalistic movement in Bosnia and Hercegovina. Because of his political activities, Andrić was interned by the Austrian government during World War I. Under the newly formed kingdom of the Serbs, Croats, and Slovenes (later the kingdom of Yugoslavia), Andrić held a number of diplomatic posts, including that of ambassador to Germany. He resigned his ambassadorship in 1941 and spent World War II in Belgrade. The material for his works was drawn from the history and life of his native Bosnia. Andrić wrote in the Serbo-Croatian language, and of his works translated into English the best known are: *The Bridge on the Drina* (1945; trans. 1959), *The Woman from Sarajevo* (1945; trans. 1965), and *The Vizier's Elephant* (1948; trans. 1962). He received the Nobel Prize for literature in 1961.

ANDROGEN, term embracing any of the male sex hormones, substances that induce and maintain secondary sex characteristics in males. The principal androgens are testosterone and androsterone. They are found in the male testes and adrenal glands, in which they are produced; in the blood, in which they circulate; and in the urine, in which they are excreted. Androgens function principally, beginning at puberty, in the stimulation of such secondary sex characteristics as development of the genital organs and maturation of sperm, growth of body hair, and changes in the larynx that lower the voice. They also account for the growth of muscle mass and bone tissue in the developing male. For a discussion of the related female sex hormones, *see* ESTROGEN.

ANDROMACHE, in Greek mythology, wife of Hector, the Trojan hero. Her husband was slain by the Greek warrior Achilles shortly before Troy was captured by the Greeks in the Trojan War. Andromache's only son was hurled from the battlements of the city, and she was given to Neoptolemus, son of Achilles, as a prize of war. She bore Neoptolemus three sons, and after he was slain at Delphi, she married Helenus, brother of Hector and king of Epirus.

ANDROMEDA, in Greek mythology, princess of Ethiopia. Her mother, Cassiopeia, angered the god Poseidon by boasting that she herself was more beautiful than the sea nymphs, the Nereids. As punishment, Poseidon sent a horrible sea monster to ravage the land. The Ethiopians learned from an oracle that they would be freed of the monster only if they offered Andromeda as a sacrifice. The maiden was chained to a rock on the seashore, but was rescued by the hero Perseus, who slew the monster and claimed the hand of Andromeda as his reward.

ANDROMEDA, in astronomy, large constellation of the northern hemisphere situated just south of the constellation Cassiopeia and west of the constellation Perseus. Andromeda contains no stars of the first magnitude but is noted as the area of sky containing the Andromeda Galaxy, a member of the local group to which our own Milky Way (q.v.) belongs. At a distance of 2.2 million light-years, the Andromeda Galaxy is both the nearest spiral galaxy and the most distant object that can be seen with the naked eye. Before its nature was determined by means of powerful telescopes, it was erroneously believed to be a nebula, or cloud of interstellar matter. Through telescopes it is seen to have two small companion galaxies of elliptical form.

ANDRONICUS, Livius. *See* LIVIUS ANDRONICUS, LUCIUS.

The Andromeda Galaxy, about 2.2 million light-years distant from the earth, can be seen with the naked eye. © Science Source–Photo Researchers, Inc.

ANDRONICUS I COMNENUS (1118–85), Byzantine emperor (1183–85). Much of his life was spent in exile. After the death of his cousin Emperor Manuel I Comnenus and the accession of Manuel's young son, Alexius II Comnenus (1169–83), Andronicus returned to Constantinople. In 1182 he became regent for the emperor, then about 14 years old; the following year he had Alexius killed and became emperor himself. After two years, a revolt was led by Isaac II Angelus (c. 1135–1204). Andronicus I was deposed and tortured to death; he was the last ruler of the house of Comnenus.

ANDROPOV. *See* RYBINSK.

ANDROPOV, Yuri Vladirmirovich (1914–84), Soviet political leader. Andropov was born near Stavropol and became an official of the Young Communist League (Komsomol) in the late 1930s. Beginning about 1944, he rose as a leader of the Communist party in Karelo-Finnish SSR (now Karelian autonomous region). In 1951 Andropov became a party official in Moscow, and he subsequently was a diplomat in Hungary, serving as Soviet ambassador during the revolt there against Communist rule in 1956. He returned to Moscow in 1957 and from 1967 to early 1982 was chairman of the State Security Committee (*see* KGB), the Soviet secret police. Shortly after the death of Leonid Brezhnev in late 1982, Andropov succeeded him as the Communist party's general secretary. He assumed the posts of head of the defense council and president in 1983. He died of kidney failure on Feb. 9, 1984.

ANDROS, island, Bahama Islands, in the Atlantic Ocean. The largest of the Bahamas, Andros is actually an archipelago about 160 km (100 mi) long, traversed by several narrow channels. It has a large freshwater lake and the only river in the Bahamas, Goose R. The island is heavily forested, and timber is the major export. Area, 4144 sq km (1600 sq mi); pop. (1980 prelim.) 8397.

ÁNDROS, island, SE Greece, in Cyclades Prefecture, in the Aegean Sea. The northernmost island in the Cyclades (Kikládhes) island group, it is wooded and mountainous. Industries here produce wine and citrus fruit. The chief settlement is Ándros (pop. est. 2032), on the E coast. Originally inhabited by Ionians, Ándros revolted against Athens about 411 BC, after being forced to accept Athenian settlers, and established an independent state. It became part of Pergamum (centered in Asia Minor) in 200 BC and was annexed by Rome in 133 BC. Venice controlled the island from AD 1207 to 1566, when it passed to the Ottoman Turks. It became part of Greece in 1829. Area, 376 sq km (145 sq mi); pop. (1981) 9020.

ANDROS, Sir Edmund (1637–1714), English governor in colonial America. Appointed by James, duke of York and brother of King Charles II, Andros was governor of New York from 1674 to 1681. When his patron became king as James II, the colonies and regions of New England were united as a single province, the Dominion of New England, and Andros was made its governor (1686). Jealous of its independence, Connecticut refused to recognize his authority. According to tradition, when he appeared in Hartford to demand the surrender of the colony's charter, the colonists hid it in an oak tree, known thereafter as the Charter Oak. Nevertheless, Andros continued to rule Connecticut, and in 1688 New York and New Jersey were put under his jurisdiction.

In April 1689, when word reached Boston that King James had been deposed, Andros was arrested and sent to England for trial, but he was released almost immediately. Returning to America as governor of Virginia in 1692, he once again came into conflict with the colonists and was recalled in 1698. He also served as governor of Maryland in 1693–94 and of the island of Guernsey in 1704–6.

ANDROSCOGGIN, river, northeast U.S., in New England. It rises in Umbagog Lake, on the boundary between New Hampshire and Maine, and flows S through New Hampshire to Gorham. Turning E, it flows into Maine, crosses the state in a generally SE direction, and empties into the estuary of the Kennebec R. at Bath. About 282 km (about 175 mi) long, it is the source of extensive waterpower.

ANEIRIN (fl. early 6th cent.), Welsh bard, the son of a chief of the Gododdin tribe, born in Scotland. He wrote the *Book of Aneirin,* containing a long poem called *Y Gododdin,* which concerns the ill-fated expedition of the Britons to recapture the fortress at Catraeth from the Saxons in 603. Mistakenly called an epic, it is a series of odes to the heroism of various participants in the siege, which Aneirin probably witnessed. The work shows great technical skill, served as a model for later Welsh poets, and exerted great influence on early romantic poetry.

ANEMIA (Gr., "bloodlessness"), a blood condition involving an abnormal reduction in the number of red blood cells (erythrocytes) or in their hemoglobin (q.v.) content. These cells are the means by which oxygen is carried to the various parts of the body. People who are anemic develop symptoms owing to the inadequate delivery of oxygen to their body tissues. There are three primary causes of anemia: (1) reduced production of red blood cells, which may result from deficiency in nutrients or hormones, or from bodily disorders, or from disease or other conditions; (2) excessive destruction of red blood cells, often a hereditary problem; and (3) excessive blood loss.

The most common type of anemia is iron-deficiency anemia, which occurs when the body's need for iron increases, as during certain periods of childhood and in pregnancy, or when there is insufficient iron in the diet. Pernicious anemia, a chronic ailment that mostly affects people over 40, is a result of vitamin deficiency. The most common symptoms of anemia are pallor, shortness of breath, low vitality, dizziness, and digestive disorders. Sickle-cell anemia (q.v.) is the result of a hereditary defect in the synthesis of hemoglobin.

Past treatment of the disease has included removal of the spleen, repeated transfusions of blood, and a diet featuring beef or calf's liver. Transfusions are still used in cases of acute blood loss; iron supplements for iron-deficiency anemia and injections of vitamin B_{12} for pernicious anemia are often effective. Synthetically manufactured erythropoietin (normally produced by the human kidney) is now used to stimulate the production and growth of red blood cells. Other therapy focuses on curing the underlying causes of the nutritional or hormonal deficiency.

See also BLOOD: *Blood Diseases.*

ANEMOMETER (Gr. *anemos,* "wind"; *metron,* "measure"), an instrument that measures wind speed. The most common kind of anemometer consists of three or four cups attached to short rods that are connected at right angles to a vertical shaft. As the wind blows, it pushes the cups, which turn the shaft. The number of turns per minute is translated into wind speed by a system of gears similar to the speedometer of an automobile. Wind velocity is also measured by the pressure of the air blowing into a Pitot tube (an **L**-shaped tube, one end open toward the flow of air and the other end connected to a pressure-measuring device), and electrically by the cooling effect of the wind on a heated wire, which causes the electric resistance of the wire to change.

ANEMONE, genus of plants comprising about 120 species belonging to the family Ranunculaceae (*see* BUTTERCUP), distributed chiefly in the North Temperate Zone. About 25 species occur in North America. The plants of this genus are perennial herbs and are sometimes called windflowers because many species grow in windward places. Most flower early in the spring. One species, *Anemone quinquefolia,* the American wood anemone, is found in eastern North America. It has white flowers tinged with pink or crimson and blossoms in April or May. The plant is similar to the European wood anemone, *A. nemorosa.* Another species, *A. pulsatilla* or *Pulsatilla vulgaris,* the pasqueflower, is found in chalky pastures in some parts of England and also blossoms in April or May. The American pasqueflower, *A. patens,* resembling the European species, is the state flower of South Dakota. The poppy anemone, *A. coronaria,* is a widely cultivated American species and is a favorite in gardens. Red and blue flowers have been introduced. The Japanese anemone, *A. japonica,* is an autumn-blooming species that is also extensively cultivated.

ANEMONE, SEA. *See* SEA ANEMONE.

ANESTHESIA, loss of sensation, especially the sensation of touch. It may be general (affecting the entire body and usually accompanied by loss of consciousness) or local (affecting limited areas of the body). The condition may be the result of damage to nerves or nerve centers by disease or injury, or it may be intentionally induced by the administration of drugs for the prevention or relief of pain.

History of Anesthetics. Of the few anesthetic agents known to the ancients, opium (q.v.) and hemp (*see* CANNABIS) were the most important. Both were taken by ingestion or by burning the drug and inhaling the smoke. Nitrous oxide (*see* NITROGEN), discovered by the British chemist Sir Humphry Davy about 1800, was first used as an anesthetic in 1844 by the American dentist Horace Wells (1815–48). In 1842 the American surgeon Crawford Long successfully used ethyl ether (q.v.) as a general anesthetic during surgery. He failed to publish his findings, however, and credit for the discovery of the anesthetic properties of ether was given to the American dentist William Morton, who in 1846 publicly demonstrated its use during a tooth extraction. In 1847 the British physician Sir James Simpson (1811–70) discovered the anesthetic properties of chloroform (q.v.). Many other general anesthetics have since been discovered. Ether and chloroform have been largely abandoned because of their dangerous side effects and flammability. Some anesthetics act by depressing the central nervous system (barbiturates, halothane), whereas others induce amnesia and dissociation (nitrous oxide, enflurane).

General Anesthesia. Surgical anesthesia (complete general anesthesia, characterized by muscular paralysis sufficient to permit surgical manipulation) is produced by the so-called inhalation anesthetics: gases or volatile liquids such as cyclopropane, nitrous oxide, halothane, and enflurane. The anesthetic, usually mixed with oxygen, is either inhaled or administered into the windpipe through a tube.

Modern anesthesia almost always involves a combination of agents. Before administering the inhalation anesthetic, the anesthesiologist may give an intravenous agent such as a short-acting barbiturate (q.v.), for example, pentobarbital or sodium pentothal (more properly called thiopental sodium or thiopentone), or an anti-anxiety drug, such as diazepam, to induce

First public demonstration of the use of ether as an anesthetic, at Massachusetts General Hospital in Boston on Oct. 16, 1846. Harvard Medical School

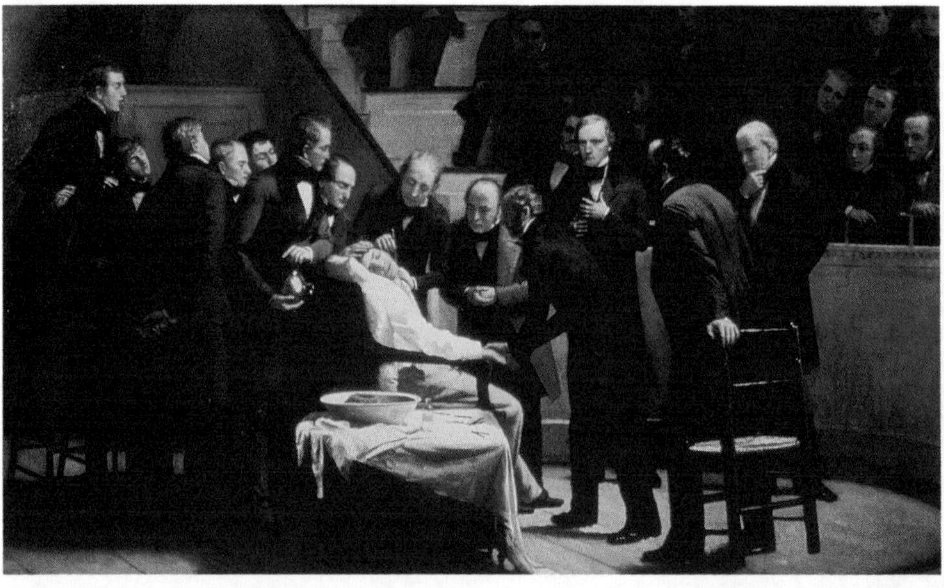

unconsciousness. A narcotic analgesic, such as meperidine or fentanyl, may be used in addition. To allow use of smaller amounts of the inhalation anesthetic, special muscle-paralyzing drugs are given. These include tubocurarine, gallamine, and succinylcholine. The combination of a narcotic, a barbiturate, a muscle-paralyzing drug, and nitrous oxide is called balanced anesthesia. Because muscular activity is prevented in all these procedures, the anesthesiologist must induce breathing in the patient mechanically.

Surgical anesthesia must continue throughout the operation, but prolonged anesthetization can kill, paralyzing first the respiratory system and then the heart. The correct level is maintained by continuous administration of the anesthetic, increasing or decreasing the dosage.

Thiopental sodium in small doses is sometimes used in psychiatry because it allows patients to talk uninhibitedly. This quality has also given the drug some value in law enforcement as a "truth serum." *See also* SCOPOLAMINE.

Local Anesthesia. Some surgical procedures do not require total muscular relaxation and can be performed using local anesthetics, which temporarily block nerve conduction without damaging nerve fibers. Local anesthesia is produced by injecting into the tissues to be affected a solution of a natural alkaloid such as cocaine, the oldest of all local anesthetics, or a synthetic agent such as procaine (q.v.), widely known under the trade name Novocaine, or lidocaine (Xylocaine).

Block anesthesia, a much more extensive local anesthesia, is produced by injecting the agent into a nerve trunk, next to a nerve, or all around the operative field, thereby deadening the entire area. The best-known block anesthesia is probably the spinal block, produced by injecting an anesthetic into the spinal canal.

A mild local anesthesia, useful in many minor dental and medical procedures, can be produced by numbing the tissues with cold either by applying ice or by spraying with a volatile liquid such as ethyl chloride.

See also ACUPUNCTURE; HYPNOSIS; NARCOTICS.

For further information on this topic, see the Bibliography in volume 28, section 488.

ANEURIN. *See* ANEIRIN.

ANEURYSM. *See* ARTERY; STROKE.

ANGARA, river, Russian Federation, in S Siberia, rising near the SW end of Lake Baykal. The river flows N past the city of Irkutsk to Kezhma and then turns W to join the Yenisey R. near Yeniseysk. The Angara is about 1850 km (about 1150 mi) long, varies in width from about 485 to 2740 m (about 1600 to 9000 ft), and is navigable for most of its length. Several large hydroelectric stations are on the river providing power to the Irkutsk industrial area.

ANGEL (Gr. *aggelos,* "messenger"), heavenly spirit believed to be a messenger, or intermediary, between God, or the gods, and humankind. All religions are concerned with the relationship human beings have or may have with the supernatural realm. In ancient Greek religion, in Judaism and Christianity, and in Islam this relationship is thought to involve angels—divine messengers sent to humans to instruct, inform, or command them. An angel can function also as a protective guardian, as a heavenly warrior, and even as a cosmic power. Moreover, the line between a good angel and a bad angel, or demon, is sometimes unclear. Hence, angels can be broadly described as personified powers mediating between the divine and the human.

Even in its devotion to monotheism, the worship of one God, ancient Israel was able to embrace the image of a council of gods by turning all but one of them into angels who serve the one God, much as earthly courtiers serve one king. This acceptance of a belief in angels was a development made relatively easy because both lesser gods and angels could be called "sons of God." In traditional Israelite thought, angels were assumed to have the form of human males, thus sometimes being mistaken for men.

After the period of Israel's Babylonian exile (597–538 BC), Jewish thought about angels was considerably altered and enriched. Drawing on Mesopotamian art, artists and writers began to provide wings even for the anthropomorphic angels, and an interest developed in the angels' garments, names, and relative ranks. In addition to the Mesopotamian influence, the Persian dualistic tradition (*see* ZOROASTRIANISM) added another dimension to the Jewish conception of angels by positing hostile and destructive angels who are rebellious against God. The Jewish Qumran sect, or Essenes (q.v.), for example, saw the world as a battleground, the scene of a struggle between the Spirit of Truth and the Spirit of Wickedness, the latter an angelic power opposed to God called Belial (*see* DEVIL).

Later developments in both Judaism and Christianity show a remarkable growth of angelic folklore, not least as the result of continuing the ancient practice of absorbing the gods of polytheistic religions by turning them into angels. Although belief in angels is amply attested in the Bible, many theologians nevertheless suggest that the concept was adopted by biblical writers both as a literary device to personify the divine presence and as a means of demoting the gods of polytheistic religions. J.L.Ma.

ANGEL DUST. *See* PHENCYCLIDINE.

ANGELES, city, Pampanga Province, on the island of Luzon, N Philippines. It is located on a major railroad line in a rice- and sugarcane-growing region. Its chief industries are sugar refining and food processing. Pop. (1980 prelim.) 185,995.

ANGEL FALLS, waterfall, SE Venezuela, on the Rio Churún. It is the highest uninterrupted cataract in the world, dropping 979 m (3212 ft) from the mesa of Auyántepuí in the rain-forest–covered Guiana Highlands. The waterfall was discovered in 1935 by the American aviator and adventurer James C. Angel (1899–1956), after whom it is named.

Queen angelfish, Holocanthus ciliaris, *photographed in the Florida Keys.* © James T. Spencer–Photo Researchers, Inc.

ANGELFISH, name used for several different fishes, including the true angelfishes (family Pomacanthidae) and the butterfly fishes (family Chaetodontidae) in the order Perciformes (*see* PERCH). Angelfishes differ from butterfly fishes in having a spine near the lower edge of the gill cover. These laterally compressed fishes are among the most beautiful of the tropical reef fishes. Most species are only a few centimeters long, but some grow to 61 cm (24 in). In many species the juveniles and adults are colored differently; the young French angelfish, *Pomacanthus paru,* of tropical Atlantic waters is black with bright yellow bands; the adult is mainly black. The well-known queen angelfish, *Holocanthus ciliaris,* is also differently colored as a juvenile. Most angelfishes feed on small invertebrates. Certain species of the family Cichlidae are often called freshwater angelfish and are popular as aquarium fishes, especially *Pterophyllum scalare* (*see* CICHLID). In the U.S. a spadefish, *Chaetodipterus faber,* is sometimes incorrectly called an angelfish.

ANGELICO, Fra (c. 1400–55), Italian painter of the early Renaissance, who combined the life of a devout friar with that of an accomplished painter. He was called Angelico (Ital., "angelic") and Beato (Ital., "blessed") because the paintings he did were of calm, religious subjects and because of his extraordinary personal piety.

In Fiesole. Originally named Guido di Pietro, Angelico was born in Vicchio, Tuscany. He entered a Dominican convent in Fiesole in 1418 and about 1425 became a friar using the name Giovanni da Fiesole. Although his teacher is unknown, he apparently began his career as an illuminator of missals and other religious books. He began to paint altarpieces and other panels; among his important early works are the *Madonna of the Star* (c. 1428–33, San Marco, Florence) and *Christ in Glory Surrounded by Saints and Angels* (National Gallery, London), which depicts more than 250 distinct figures. Among other works of that period are two of the *Coronation of the Virgin* (San Marco and Louvre, Paris) and a *Deposition and Last Judgment* (San Marco). His mature style is first seen in the *Madonna of the Linen Weavers* (1433, San Marco), which features a border with 12 music-making angels.

In Florence and Rome. In 1436 the Dominicans of Fiesole moved to the convent of San Marco in Florence, recently rebuilt by Michelozzo. Angelico, sometimes aided by assistants, painted many frescoes for the cloister, chapter house, and entrances to the 20 cells on the upper corridors. The most impressive of these are the *Crucifixion, Christ as a Pilgrim,* and *Transfiguration.* His altarpiece for San Marco (c. 1439) is the first representation of the *Sacred Conversation* among the Madonna, angels, and saints.

In 1445 Angelico was summoned to Rome by Pope Eugenius IV to paint frescoes for the now destroyed Chapel of the Sacrament in the Vatican. In 1447, with his pupil Benozzo Gozzoli, he painted frescoes for the cathedral in Orvieto. His last important works, frescoes for the chapel of Pope Nicholas in the Vatican, are *Scenes from the Lives of Saints Stephen and Lawrence* (1447–49); they were probably painted from his designs by assistants. From 1449 to 1452 Angelico was prior of his convent in Fiesole. He died in the Dominican convent in Rome on March 18, 1455.

Angelico combined the influence of the elegantly decorative Gothic style of Gentile da Fabriano with the more realistic style of such Renaissance masters as the painter Masaccio and the sculptors Donatello and Ghiberti, all of whom worked in Florence. Angelico was also aware of Leon Battista Alberti's theories of perspective. Angelico's representation of devout facial expressions and his use of color to heighten emotion are particularly effective. His skill in cre-

The Annunciation *(c. 1440–50) is one of the many frescoes executed by the early Renaissance painter Fra Angelico for the monastery of San Marco, Florence, Italy.*
Editorial Photocolor Archives

ating monumental figures, representing motion, and suggesting deep space through the use of linear perspective, especially in the Roman frescoes, mark him as one of the foremost painters of the Renaissance.

ANGELL, Sir Norman (1872?-1967), English author and economist. Originally named Ralph Norman Angell Lane, he was educated at the Lycée de Saint-Omer, France, and the University of Geneva. His studies and his experience as a prospector, rancher, journalist, and editor made him an economist of vision and reputation. According to his principal doctrine, as expressed in *The Great Illusion* (1910) and *The Great Illusion, 1933* (1933), modern nations are so closely related economically and socially that they are logically committed to cooperation with one another, rather than to economic competition, which inevitably leads to war. From 1929 to 1931 Angell served as a member of Parliament. He was knighted in 1931 and was awarded the Nobel Peace Prize in 1933 for his writings and lectures advocating peace. Later works include *The Money Game* (1936), *America's Dilemma* (1940), and the autobiography *After All* (1951).

ANGELSEA. *See* ANGLESEY.

ANGELUS, in the Roman Catholic church, devotion commemorating the incarnation of Jesus Christ. It consists of several short prescribed verses, three recitations of the "Hail Mary," and a brief concluding prayer. Traditionally accompanied by the ringing of the Angelus bell, it is said three times daily, usually at 6 AM, noon, and 6 PM. The devotion takes its name from the first word of the Latin version. It is the subject of a famous painting, *The Angelus* by the French artist Jean François Millet; the canvas depicts farmers pausing in their field chores to pray.

ANGERS, city, W France, capital of Maine-et-Loire Department, on the Maine R. The city is a market center for the fruit, vegetables, and flowers grown in the surrounding countryside. Manufactures include electronic equipment, machinery, textiles, and processed food. A state university and a Roman Catholic university are in the city.

Angers, the capital of the historic province of Anjou, is considered one of the most beautiful cities in France. Foremost among its many notable structures is the magnificent twin-spired Cathedral of Saint Maurice (12th–13th cent.). Also significant are the Hospital of Saint Jean, built in the 12th century by Henry II of England and now housing a museum; the massive Castle of Angers (early 13th cent.), with its moat and soaring towers; and the Logis Pincé, a beautifully preserved Renaissance mansion. Pop. (1982) 141,143.

ANGEVIN. *See* ANJOU.

ANGINA PECTORIS, symptom of reduced oxygen supply to the heart muscle, usually caused by narrowing or obstruction of the coronary artery. It is marked by a viselike squeezing sensation beneath the breastbone. Pain may radiate from the front of the chest, often into the arm. The attacks usually last several minutes. They may be caused by emotional stress but are more likely to result from physical activities that require an increased supply of blood to the heart. The disease occurs most commonly in middle-aged and older persons, particularly those who suffer from arteriosclerosis. Relief is obtained by rest and relaxation. Patients can be treated with drugs that relax and dilate blood vessels, and surgery can be performed to improve coronary circulation. The attacks themselves cause no damage. *See* HEART.

ANGIOSPERM (Lat. *angi-*, "enclosed"; Gr. *sperma*, "seed"), common name for the division or phylum Magnoliophyta, comprising flowering plants, the dominant form of plant life. Members of the division are the source of most of the food on which humans and other mammals rely and of many raw materials and natural products. Included in the Magnoliophyta are most shrubs and herbs, most familiar trees except pines and other conifers, and specialized plants such as succulents, parasites, and aquatic types. Although about 230,000 species are known, many remain obscure. Flowering plants occupy almost every ecological situation and dominate most natural landscapes. About two-thirds occur in the Tropics, where they are rapidly being exterminated by human activities. Only about 1000 species are of major economic importance, and the bulk of the world's food supply is derived from only 15. Many hundreds more could be useful if properly investigated and developed.

Description. The characteristic feature of angiosperms is the flower (q.v.), the function of which is the reproduction of the plant through the development of seeds. Flowers are highly modified shoots made up of four fundamental parts arranged in separate series, or whorls, on specialized stem tips. The outer series consists of the sepals, which are modified leaves or bracts that are usually green. The next inner series, the petals, are also modified leaves, but they are usually finer textured and more conspicuously colored. The third series consists of the stamens, the pollen-producing male portion of the flower. The innermost series is the carpels, female structures that produce the seeds. Carpels are often fused into a structure called the pistil.

The seeds of angiosperms develop in an ovary, a part of the carpel that surrounds and protects the egg-containing ovules. Seeds develop from the ovules after pollination and fertilization of the eggs. Ovules and seeds are not exclusive to angiosperms. The "naked-seed" plants (*see* GYMNOSPERM), which include the conifers, cycads, and ginkgo, have ovules that lie exposed on the surface of specialized, scalelike leaves arranged into cones. The development of seeds from ovules enclosed in an ovary, which enlarges into a fruit (q.v.) as the fertilized seeds grow, is a feature unique to the angiosperms.

Evolution. The unique angiosperm flower probably evolved from a now extinct gymnosperm group that had insect-pollinated cones combining male and female reproductive parts. Living gymnosperms are mostly wind pollinated, but among certain fossil and extant groups evidence of insect pollination exists. Although insects facilitate pollination, they also eat ovules, and it is believed that the development of the ovule-enclosing carpel of the angiosperm was an adaptation to protect the ovules and developing seeds from insect predation. The carpel also provided protection from other harmful environmental influences, such as dryness, and it allowed reduction in the size of the ovule, refinement of the process of pollination, and the development of other parts of the flower, all of which improved the chances of successful reproduction.

Classification. Angiosperms are divided into two classes, the Magnoliopsida and Liliopsida, popularly termed dicots and monocots (qq.v.), representing separate evolutionary lines that must have diverged early in the history of the group. The direct predecessors of angiosperms are thought to have been woody gymnosperms; certain woody groups of dicots (*see* MAGNOLIA) are thought to be primitive angiosperms. Monocots are more advanced than dicots, and they evolved from a primitive dicot group (*see* WATER LILY).

M.R.C. & P.H.R.

For further information on this topic, see the Bibliography in volume 28, section 451.

ANGKOR, capital city of Cambodia from the 9th to the 15th century. Its ruins are one of the world's great architectural monuments. Located near Siemreab in northwestern Cambodia, Angkor was founded early in the 9th century and became the country's capital under King Yasovarman I (r. 889–900), who called it Yasodharapura. The original city was built around the Phnom

Bakeng, a temple on a hill symbolizing the mountain that stands in the center of the world according to Hindu cosmology. Successive kings enlarged the city, building other temples devoted to various Hindu deities and large reservoirs used for irrigation, which also symbolized the ocean surrounding the holy central mountain. The greatest of the Angkor temple complexes is Angkor Wat, constructed under King Suryavarman II (r. 1113–50) to celebrate the king as the incarnation of the god Vishnu. An immense rectangle, measuring about 850 by 1000 m (about 2800 by 3300 ft), Angkor Wat contains concentric walled courtyards surrounding a central structure with five graceful lotus-shaped towers. Its galleries are decorated with sculptures depicting legends of Vishnu. King Jayavarman VII (c. 1130–1219) built the Angkor Thom complex, which contains the Bayon, a Buddhist temple embellished with huge stone heads of the king.

In the 13th century Angkor covered about 100 sq km (about 39 sq mi) and was one of the largest cities in the world. Shortly thereafter, it began to decline. Threatened by attacks from the neighboring Thais, the Cambodians left Angkor about 1430, moving their capital south for greater security. Angkor Wat survived for a time as a Buddhist pilgrimage center, but the rest of the city was covered by the jungle until French archaeologists began to excavate it in the 1860s. A six-to-eight-year restoration project was begun in 1987.

ANGLE, a measure of the rotation of a line segment about a fixed point. Angles are usually expressed in degrees or in minutes and seconds of a degree; one complete rotation is 360°. (Positive rotation is conventionally counterclockwise, negative rotation clockwise.) Angles are also expressed in radians, 2 π radians being equal to 360°. *See* DEGREE; GEOMETRY; TRIGONOMETRY.

For further information on this topic, see the Bibliography in volume 28, sections 372–73.

ANGLER, common name for any of several saltwater fishes of the order Lophiiformes, having appendages resembling fishing rods or lures with which they entice their prey. The name is particularly applied to species of the genus *Lophius,* found along the coasts of Europe and North America from the British Isles and Nova Scotia to Barbados. About 1.5 m (about 5 ft) long, they live on the ocean floor, creeping along on modified pectoral fins in search of food. With a huge mouth and distensible stomach, an angler can swallow other fish as large as itself. In the U.S. the angler is also known as the goosefish and is often marketed under the name monkfish.

ANGLES (Lat. *Angli*), Germanic tribe that occupied the region still called Angeln in what is now the state of Schleswig-Holstein, Germany. Together with the Saxons and Jutes, they invaded Britain during the 5th century AD. With their kindred ethnic groups, they formed the people who came to be known as the English. The name England is derived from them.

ANGLESEY *or* **ANGELSEA,** former county, NW Wales; Llangefni was the county town. It comprised the island of Anglesey, which is separated from the Welsh mainland by Menai Strait, and the small nearby Holy Island, both in the Irish Sea. Anglesey was settled by the Celts by about 100 BC and became known as a center of Druidism. The Romans conquered (AD 61–78) the island and suppressed the religion. Anglesey was subsequently invaded by Vikings, Saxons, and Normans and fell to Edward I, king of England, in the 13th century. In 1974 Anglesey became part of the new county of Gwynedd (q.v.).

ANGLICAN CHURCH. *See* CHURCH OF ENGLAND.

ANGLICAN CHURCH OF CANADA, autonomous member of the Anglican Communion in Canada. It is nationwide, with four ecclesiastical provinces—Canada, Ontario, Rupert's Land, and British Columbia—each with its own metropolitan or archbishop, provincial synod, and executive council. The tenets of the church are those of Anglicans generally. The church dates from the beginning of the 18th century, although Anglicans came to Canada with the first explorers. It has been self-governing since 1893 and self-supporting since 1941. The see of the primate of the church is in Toronto. Recent figures list 952,489 members in 3212 churches.

ANGLICAN COMMUNION, worldwide fellowship of national and regional churches in communion with the Church of England and the archbishop of Canterbury. With about 385 dioceses throughout the world, the total membership of the churches, including the Episcopal church in the U.S., is approximately 73 million. Intended to promote mutual understanding and cooperation in common tasks, the Communion unites churches that share a common heritage and subscribe to the Lambeth Quadrilateral of 1884. The Quadrilateral, a statement of the doctrines considered essential from the Anglican standpoint, upholds the catholic and apostolic faith and order of the Christian church as found in Scripture, the sacraments of baptism and the Eucharist, the Apostles' Creed and Nicene Creed (qq.v.), and episcopal government (*see* BISHOP). All the churches use the Book of Common Prayer (q.v.), reformed and adapted to the needs of the times and of particular locales.

Although the Anglican Communion has existed since the 16th and 17th centuries, when the

Church of England established foreign missions, its effective function as a communion of independent churches began in 1867. In that year, the first Lambeth Conference, an assembly of the bishops of the whole Anglican Communion under the presidency of the archbishop of Canterbury, was held at Lambeth Palace, London. A conference has met there about every ten years since then to deal with doctrinal, disciplinary, and ecumenical matters, as well as missionary responsibilities. Much of the agenda has concerned the unity of the church. In 1948, the Lambeth Conference heralded the birth of the Church of South India, which united certain Anglican dioceses with non-Anglican churches in that area. The Lambeth Conference of 1968 established the Anglican Consultative Council under the presidency of the archbishop of Canterbury. The council, composed of 60 representatives from every part of the Anglican Communion who meet every two to three years, is intended to supply guidance on policy matters of importance to the Communion, to forward ecumenical relations, and to provide cooperation in missionary work. Regional councils are also active in South America, East Asia, the South Pacific, and North America, with more to be established. These councils were created to promote better communication among the churches of a given area and to advance cooperative planning efforts. J.E.B.

For further information on this topic, see the Bibliography in volume 28, section 92.

ANGLO-EGYPTIAN SUDAN. *See* SUDAN, REPUBLIC OF THE.

ANGLO-NORMAN LITERATURE. *See* NORMAN FRENCH LANGUAGE AND LITERATURE.

ANGLO-SAXON ART, art produced in England by invading Germanic peoples from the 7th century to the Norman conquest in 1066. This included small monastic churches, freestanding stone crosses, metalwork, and illuminated manuscripts in the Hiberno-Saxon and Winchester styles. Anglo-Saxon decoration combined Celtic interlaced ornament, Germanic interlaced animal forms, and bright, flat color. *See also* CELTS; ILLUMINATED MANUSCRIPTS; IRISH ART; METALWORK.

ANGLO-SAXON CHRONICLE, common designation of several texts in Old English that record the history of England from the beginning of the Christian era to the middle of the 12th century. The *Anglo-Saxon Chronicle* is the primary source for English history from the 10th to the 12th century, including the language and literature of that period. It is the earliest known history of a European people recorded in the language of that people by successive generations of scribes.

Those parts of the *Chronicle* originating before the reign of Alfred, king of Wessex (r. 871–99), were based, in part, on earlier Latin sources. Such sections of the *Chronicle* are less important historically and less abundant than the sections dating from his reign. King Alfred may have ordered the collation of the earlier records and begun the systematic registration of events that characterizes later sections of the *Chronicle*, especially those dealing with his own reign and with the two and a half centuries that followed it. No proof of this exists, however.

The *Anglo-Saxon Chronicle* is the first important prose work in English literature. Although it contains chiefly unadorned annals, it has some vivid descriptive passages and notable poems. One of the best, the ballad account of the Battle of Brunanburh in 937, was translated by the British poet Alfred Tennyson into modern verse. There are seven known versions of the *Chronicle*. They deal in part with the same material but differ in the historical periods covered and in the emphasis given to the various events.

ANGLO-SAXON LANGUAGE. *See* ENGLISH LANGUAGE.

ANGLO-SAXON LITERATURE. *See* ENGLISH LITERATURE.

ANGOLA, formerly PORTUGUESE WEST AFRICA, officially People's Republic of Angola, independent state, SW Africa, bounded on the N and E by the Republic of Zaire, on the E by Zambia, on the S by Namibia, and on the W by the Atlantic Ocean. A small enclave, Cabinda, is located some 30 km (19 mi) to the N and is bounded on the N by the Republic of the Congo, on the E and S by Zaire, and on the W by the Atlantic Ocean. Angola has a coastline of more than 1650 km (1025 mi) and a total area of 1,246,700 sq km (481,354 sq mi).

LAND AND RESOURCES

Angola is the seventh largest country in Africa, comprising an area more than twice as large as France and the Low Countries combined.

Physiographic Regions. The country can be divided into three major regions. They are, from W to E, the coastal plain, a transition zone, and a vast inland plateau. The low-lying coastal plain varies from about 50 to 150 km (about 30 to 90 mi) in width. The transition zone, which consists of a series of terraces or escarpments, is about 150 km (about 90 mi) wide in the N, but diminishes to about 30 km (19 mi) in the center and S. To the E of this zone is the vast Angolan plateau, which covers approximately two-thirds of the country and has an average elevation of 1000 to 1520 m (3300 to 5000 ft). Higher elevations are reached in the mountains of the central section, which culminate in Mt. Moco (2620 m/8597 ft), the country's highest point.

Rivers and Lakes. Most of the country's rivers rise in the central mountains. Of the many rivers that drain to the Atlantic Ocean, the Cuanza and Cunene are the most important. Other major streams include the Cuango (Kwango) R., which drains N to the Congo R. system, and the Kwando (Cuando) and Cubango rivers, both of which drain generally SE to the Okavango Swamp. Angola has no sizable lakes.

Climate. Angola has a tropical climate, with a dry season that lasts from September to April. The cool Benguela Current offshore moderates the temperatures of the coastal region and reduces the precipitation, especially in the S. Annual rainfall at Luanda is 338 mm (13 in) and only 51 mm (2 in) at Namibe, which is surrounded by the Moçâmedes Desert. In the cooler central plateau, rainfall decreases from 1500 mm (about 60 in) in the N to 750 mm (about 30 in) in the S.

Vegetation and Animal Life. Vegetation varies with the climate. Thick tropical rain forests are found in the N and in the Cabinda exclave. To the S the rain forests give way to savanna, lands of mixed trees and grasses, which in turn grade into grasslands on the S and E. Palm trees are found on much of the coast, and sparse desert vegetation grows S of Namibe. Wildlife is as diverse as the vegetation and includes many of the larger African mammals, such as elephant, rhinoceros, giraffe, hippopotamus, zebra, antelope, lion, and gorilla. Also found are crocodile and a diversity of birdlife and insects.

Mineral Resources. Angola is rich in mineral resources, and further geological exploration is likely to add to the list of known mineral reserves. Among the most notable resources are petroleum, diamonds, iron ore, manganese, copper, uranium, phosphates, and salt.

POPULATION

The population of Angola is made up of more than 90 ethnic groups. Despite this diversity, the four most important groups represent about three-fourths of the total population. These are the Mbundu in central and S Angola, the Bakongo, or Kongo, in the NW, the Kimbundu in the N and center, and the Chokwe-Lunda in the E. Prior to independence in 1975, Angola had a community of about 400,000 Portuguese; more than 90% of these have since departed for Portugal.

Population Characteristics. The total population of Angola, including Cabinda, is 9,739,000 (1989 est.). The overall population density is only about 8 persons per sq km (about 20 per sq mi). Distribution, however, is uneven, with about 70% of the population concentrated in the N and along the coast. The natural rate of population increase was about 3% annually in the late 1980s. The population is overwhelmingly rural; only about one-third of the people live in urban areas.

Principal Cities. The capital and chief city is Luanda, with a population of 1,200,000 (1988 est.). Other major cities are (1983 est.) Huambo (203,000), Benguela (155,000), the port of Lobito (150,000), and Lubango (105,000).

Language and Religion. Portuguese is the official language. More than 90% of the population speaks Bantu languages, the most important of which are Kimbundu, Umbundu, and Kikongo. Before independence an estimated 2.2 million Roman Catholics lived in the country, including most of the 400,000 Portuguese, as well as a smaller number of Protestants. By the late 1980s about 53% of the population was Christian, and the remainder adhered to traditional religions.

Education. In principle, education is free and compulsory for children between the ages of 7 and 15. Each year in the mid-1980s approximately 930,000 pupils were enrolled in primary schools, 157,000 were enrolled in secondary schools, and 4500 were enrolled at the country's one university, the University Agostinho Neto (1976) in Luanda. The government has pledged a campaign to reduce drastically the illiteracy rate, but is hampered by the lack of teachers. Education was not well served under colonial rule; only about 20 to 30% of the adult population is literate.

GOVERNMENT

Angola is governed under a constitution promulgated in 1975 and subsequently amended. Actual power has been wielded by the Popular Liberation Movement of Angola-Labor Party (Movimento Popular de Libertação de Angola-Partido de Trabalho, or MPLA-PT). In May 1991 the MPLA-PT government agreed to allow multi-party elections by the end of 1992.

Executive. The MPLA-PT's Central Committee, the government's major policymaking body, elects a chairman, who serves as the republic's president upon official appointment by the National People's Assembly.

Legislature and Judiciary. The constitution provides for the election of a National People's Assembly, which is nominally the supreme organ of the state. The assembly has 289 full and 29 alternate members, indirectly elected by universal suffrage to 3-year terms.

Local Government. Angola is divided into 18 provinces, which are further divided into councils and communes. Each level of local government has a direct representative of the MPLA-PT.

Political Parties. The country's dominant political party originated in 1956 as the Popular Liberation

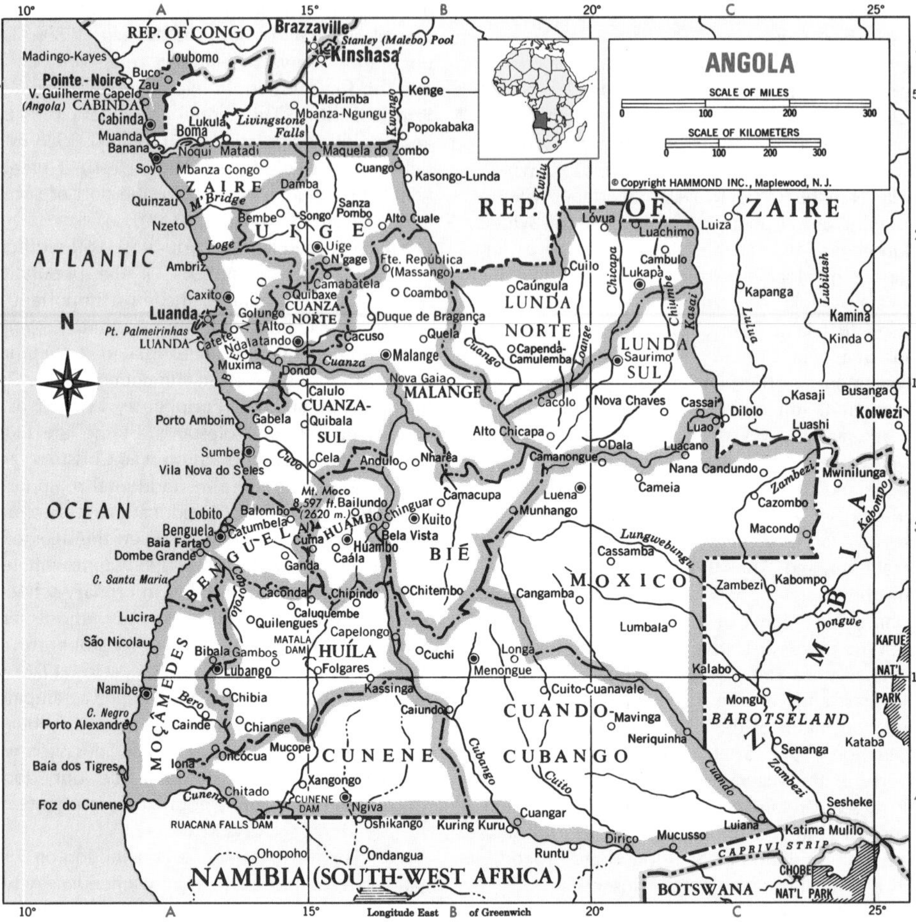

Movement of Angola (MPLA). In 1977 it was reorganized as a Marxist-Leninist party and renamed the Popular Liberation Movement of Angola-Labor Party (MPLA-PT); in April 1991 it formally renounced its Marxist orientation. The U.S.-backed National Union for the Total Independence of Angola (União Nacional para a Independência Total de Angola, or UNITA), founded in 1966, has waged a guerrilla struggle against the MPLA-PT government.

ECONOMY

Angola's economy has suffered severe setbacks since independence. The shortage of skilled workers created by the departure of the Portuguese, and the devastating effects of the civil war (1975–76) along with continuing guerrilla activity, halted economic growth. Production of nearly all goods except crude petroleum either remained stagnant or declined. An upsurge of guerrilla activity in the 1980s severely disrupted agricultural production.

National Output and Labor. In the late 1980s Angola had an annual gross domestic product (GDP) of $4.7 billion; the annual GDP per capita was about $600. The total labor force in the mid-1980s was estimated at 3.7 million, of which more than 70% were engaged in agriculture.

Agriculture. Arable land constitutes only about 2.8% of Angola's total area. Less than one-sixth of this land is under permanent cultivation. The leading export crop, coffee, is grown in the N part of the country; annual output in the late 1980s was about 15,000 metric tons. The leading subsistence crop is cassava, or manioc (2 million metric tons). Other major crops include sugarcane (330,000 metric tons), bananas (280,000), and corn (270,000). Also important are vegetables, cotton, palm products, and sisal. Livestock raising, mostly in the S, remains a subsistence activity and suffers from the presence of the tsetse fly.

Forestry and Fishing. The rich rain forests of Cabinda and the NW furnished about 5.1 million

INDEX TO MAP OF ANGOLA

Districts

Bengo	A 2
Benguela	A 3
Bié	B 3
Cabinda	A 2
Cuando Cubango	B 4
Cuanza-Norte	A 2
Cuanza-Sul	B 3
Cunene	B 4
Huíla	B 3
Huambo	B 3
Luanda	A 2
Lunda Norte	B 2
Lunda Sul	C 2
Malange	B 3
Moçâmedes	A 4
Moxico	C 3
Uige	A 2
Zaire	A 2

Cities and Towns

Alto Chicapa	B 3
Alto Cuale	B 2
Ambriz	A 2
Andulo	B 3
Baía dos Tigres	A 4
Baia Farta	A 3
Bailundo	B 3
Balombo	A 3
Bela Vista	B 3
Bembe	A 2
Benguela	A 3
Bibala	A 3
Buco-Zau	A 1
Caála	B 3
Cabinda	A 2
Cacolo	B 3
Caconda	A 3
Cacuso	B 2
Cainde	A 4
Caiundo	B 4
Calulo	B 3
Caluquembe	A 3
Camabatela	B 2
Camacupa	B 3
Camanongue	B 3
Cambulo	C 2
Cameia	C 3
Cangamba	B 3
Capelongo	B 3
Capenda-Camulemba	B 2
Cassai	C 3
Cassamba	C 3
Catete	B 5
Catumbela	A 3
Caúngula	B 2
Caxito	A 2
Cazombo	C 3
Cela	B 3
Chiange	A 4
Chibia	A 4
Chinguar	B 3
Chipindo	B 3
Chitado	A 4
Chitembo	B 3
Coambo	B 2
Cuangar	B 4
Cuango	B 2
Cuchi	B 3
Cuilo	B 2
Cuito-Cuanavale	B 4
Cuma	B 3
Dala	C 3
Damba	A 2
Dirico	C 4
Dombe Grande	A 3
Dondo	A 2
Duque de Bragança	B 2
Folgares	B 3
Forte República	B 2
Foz do Cunene	A 4
Gabela	A 3
Gambos	A 3
Ganda	A 3
Golungo Alto	A 2
Huambo	C 6
Iona	A 4
Kassinga	B 4
Kuito	B 3
Lobito	A 3
Lóvua	C 2
Longa	B 3
Luacano	C 3
Luachimo	C 2
Luanda (cap.)	A 2
Luao	C 3
Lubango	A 3
Lucira	A 3
Luena	B 3
Luiana	C 4
Lukapa	C 2
Lumbala	C 3
Macondo	C 3
Malange	B 2
Maquela do Zombo	C 5
Massango (Forte República)	B 2
Mavinga	C 4
Mbanza Congo	A 2
Menongue	B 3
Mucope	A 4
Mucusso	C 4
Munhango	B 3
Muxima	A 2
Namibe	A 4
Nana Candundo	C 3
Ndalatando	A 2
Neriquinha	C 4
Ngage	B 2
Ngiva	B 4
Nharêa	C 6
Nóqui	A 2
Nova Chaves	C 3
Nova Gaia	B 2
Nzeto	A 2
Oncócua	A 4
Porto Alexandre	A 4
Porto Amboim	A 3
Quela	B 2
Quibala	B 3
Quibaxe	A 2
Quilengues	A 3
Quinzau	A 2
Sanza Pombo	B 2
São Nicolau	A 3
Saurimo	C 2
Songo	B 2
Soyo	A 2
Sumbe	A 3
Uíge	B 2
Vila Guilherme Capelo	A 2
Vila Nova do Seles	A 3
Xangongo	B 4

Other Features

Bero (river)	A 4
Chicapa (river)	C 2
Chiumbe (river)	C 2
Coporolo (river)	A 3
Cuando (river)	B 2
Cuango (river)	B 2
Cuanza (river)	B 2
Cubango (river)	B 4
Cuito (river)	B 4
Cunene (river)	A 4
Cunene (dam)	A 4
Cuvo (river)	B 6
Kasai (river)	C 2
Kwilu (river)	B 2
Loange (river	B 2
Loge (river)	A 2
Lungwebungu (river)	C 3
Matala (dam)	A 3
M'Bridge (river)	A 2
Moco (mt.)	B 3
Negro (cape)	A 4
Palmeirinhas (point)	A 2
Ruacana Falls (dam)	A 4
Santa Maria (cape)	A 3
Zambezi (river)	C 3

cu m (about 180 million cu ft) a year of roundwood for fuel and industrial purposes in the late 1980s. Because of the cool Benguela Current, the waters off the coast of Angola are particularly rich in marine life. Fishing has thus been a traditionally important activity; in the late 1980s the total yearly catch was approximately 81,000 metric tons, primarily mackerel and sardines. Namibe and Lobito are the principal fishing ports.

Mining. Petroleum accounts for some 90% of national exports by value. Most production is from the offshore fields of Cabinda, which were first worked in the 1960s. The total annual output of crude petroleum in the mid-1980s was 11.4 million metric tons. Diamonds remain the second most important mineral; annual output in the late 1980s was 240,000 carats. Iron ore, formerly the third most important mineral, has not been produced commercially since 1975 because the mines were destroyed during the civil war. Production of salt and natural gas has continued, despite the disruption of the war.

Manufacturing. The development of the industrial sector has been limited. The principal manufactured products are beverages and processed foods, such as refined sugar, fishmeal, flour, and beer. Other products include textiles, cement, glass, and chemicals. Petroleum refineries are located in Cabinda and at Luanda.

Energy. Angola has great hydroelectric potential in the numerous streams that descend from the central plateau. Hydroelectric plants have been constructed on the Cuanza, Cunene, Dande, and Catumbela rivers. The total production of electric energy in the late 1980s was 1.8 billion kwh, of which some 75% was generated from hydroelectric plants. At present Angola's power production exceeds its needs.

Transportation. Angola's road system consists of about 73,900 km (about 45,900 mi) of roads, of which 51% are paved. The road network is inadequate for so large an area and is supplemented by a relatively well-developed internal air service, provided by the country's national airline. Total railroad trackage is about 2800 km (about 1740 mi). The principal line, the Benguela Railroad, links mineral-rich Zambia and Shaba province of Zaire with the Atlantic port of Lobito. Because of guerrilla activity, it was closed to international traffic from 1975 to 1980 and has since operated sporadically. The country's chief ports are the cities of Lobito, Luanda, and Namibe.

Currency and Banking. The basic unit of currency is the kwanza (30.04 kwanzas equal U.S.$1; 1990), which in 1977 replaced the Angolan escudo. The National Bank of Angola is the central bank and bank of issue and functions as the state treasury. All commercial and foreign banks were nationalized in 1975.

Foreign Trade. In the late 1980s yearly imports totaled $1.4 billion and annual exports $2 billion. The chief imports were textiles, foodstuffs, heavy machinery, and iron and steel. Petroleum accounted for some 90% of the exports, which have traditionally included coffee, diamonds, sisal, fish, and palm oil. Since independence, Portugal has been replaced as Angola's leading trading partner by the U.S., the former Soviet republics, Cuba, and Brazil.

HISTORY

About all that is known of the early history of Angola is that the Stone Age hunters and gatherers of the region were replaced by metalworking Bantu as early as the 7th century AD. The country was on the migration routes of peoples from the north and east, which resulted in considerable admixture of populations. Thus, the culture of the Lunda, on the Kasai River in the east, affected the Chokwe to the extent that they are now known as the Lunda-Chokwe; similarly, the Kongo, at the time of their migration into northern Angola, put their stamp on the preexisting local chiefdoms.

Advent of Europeans. When the Portuguese arrived in 1483, seeking the legendary kingdom of Prester John (q.v.), as well as precious metals, they found the realm of the Kongo well established. The ruler of the state proved friendly to the newcomers, and in 1491 a Portuguese delegation of traders and missionaries bearing gifts was sent to the court of Manikongo ("king") Nzinga Nkuwu (r. about 1482–1505), who converted to Christianity. So did the succeeding manikongo, Afonso I (r. 1505–43), who also accepted Portuguese guidance in the administration of his realm. The Portuguese, however, were more interested in profit from a booming trade in slaves than in either missionary work or spreading European civilization. The slave traffic, greedily aided by local chiefs, gradually undermined the authority of the manikongo, and 25 years after Afonso's death the state succumbed to the onslaught of the Jaga, a belligerent horde of nomads from the east.

Native Resistance. The Portuguese, meanwhile, had extended their reach southward to the area around and south of present Luanda, over which they soon claimed colonial authority; it was the title of the local ruler, ngola, that became the name of the country. Portugual appointed royal governors who tried to impose their will on the population, but foreign rule was stubbornly resisted. Prolonged warfare ensued, while slave raids helped to keep the country in continuous turmoil. In addition, the Jaga overran the area after they had devastated the Kongo, and in the middle of the 17th century, Luanda, founded by the Portuguese in 1575, was temporarily taken by the Dutch. Practically no white settlement was attempted during this time, owing to the much greater profits to be made in the slave trade; by 1845 there were still only 1800 Europeans in all of Angola. The slave trade went on almost uninterrupted throughout the 19th century. By that time an estimated 3 million people had been exported.

Portugal did not gain full control over the country's interior until the early 20th century. After that it was governed under the so-called *regime do indigenato,* an invidious system of economic exploitation, educational neglect, and political repression that remained in force until 1961. In 1951 Angola's official status was changed from colony to overseas province; soon after, a policy of accelerated white settlement was adopted—the last futile attempt of the colonial power to stave off the inevitable. During the 1950s a nationalist movement grew rapidly, and in 1961 a guerrilla war against the Portuguese was initiated.

War and Independence. The nationalists, however, were split into three rival groups: the National Front for the Liberation of Angola (Frente Nacional de Libertação de Angola, or FNLA), the Popular Liberation Movement of Angola (Movimento Popular de Libertação de Angola, or MPLA), and the National Union for the Total Independence of Angola (União Nacional para a

On the day of Angola's liberation from Portugal, Agostinho Neto, the first leader of the independent government, proclaims the constitution of the new state.
Jean Pierre Laffont–Sygma

Independência Total de Angola, or UNITA). All three had armed forces in the field, but none made much headway until the revolution in Portugal in April 1974. After that, the whole Portuguese colonial empire began to fall apart. By January 1975 the new Lisbon regime was ready to set a date for the transfer of power, and on Nov. 11, 1975, Angola was declared independent.

At that time two governments claimed to represent the new nation, one formed by the MPLA in Luanda, the other by UNITA in Huambo. The ensuing civil war assumed international overtones as the MPLA, armed by the Soviet Union, also received the aid of Cuban troops, while the Western powers and South Africa aided UNITA. By early 1976 the MPLA had definitely gained the upper hand, and its government, with MPLA leader Agostinho Neto as president, was gradually recognized throughout the world.

When Neto died in 1979, leadership of the country was assumed by José Eduardo dos Santos (1942–). In the mid-1980s up to 50,000 Cuban troops remained in Angola, supporting the central government against UNITA guerrillas. UNITA received military assistance through both the U.S. Central Intelligence Agency and from South African forces, which often forayed deep into Angola in pursuit of Namibian insurgents. In August 1988, negotiators for Angola, South Africa, and Cuba declared a cease-fire in Angola, as part of a comprehensive peace plan that included independence for Namibia. In May 1991 the last Cuban troops were withdrawn from Angola, and Dos Santos signed a cease-fire with UNITA that called for multiparty elections by the end of 1992.

For further information on this topic, see the Bibliography in volume 28, sections 970, 1029.

ANGORA. *See* ANKARA.

ANGOSTURA. *See* CIUDAD BOLÍVAR.

ANGOULÊME, Louis Antoine de Bourbon, Duc d' (1775–1844), eldest son of Charles X of France. He was appointed lieutenant-general of the kingdom by his uncle, Louis XVIII, but he failed to overcome the forces of Napoleon—when the latter returned from exile in Elba in 1815—because the royal troops deserted. In 1823 Angoulême led the French invasion of Spain to restore absolutism in that country in the name of the Holy Alliance. In 1799 he married his cousin Marie Thérèse Charlotte (1778–1851), the only daughter of Louis XVI of France and Marie Antoinette. When the July Revolution broke out in 1830, Angoulême and his wife were exiled, living out their lives in Austria.

ÅNGSTRÖM, Anders Jonas (1814–74), Swedish astronomer and physicist. Ångström was born in Lögdö, Medelpad, and educated at the University of Uppsala. After graduating, he taught physics there from 1839 until his death. From 1867 he was secretary of the Royal Society of Sciences in Uppsala. Ångström was a pioneer in the study of spectra. This work led to his discovery, in 1862, of the existence of hydrogen in the atmosphere of the sun. A unit of measurement of wavelength, the angstrom, is named in his honor.

ANGUS, also Forfarshire, former county, E Scotland; Forfar was the county town. Pictish and Roman remains are found in the area, which later was held successively by the Angles and the Danes. Flemish immigrants established a wool and linen industry here in the 12th century. Subsequently Angus—and especially the city of Dundee—developed as a major center of Scottish textile manufacture. Glamis Castle, home of the Scottish king Macbeth, is near Forfar. In 1975 Angus was made part of the newly created Tayside Region (*see* TAYSIDE).

ANGUS. *See* CATTLE.

ANHINGA, genus of aquatic birds, of the family Anhingidae, order Pelecaniformes. Anhingas are related to and somewhat similar to the cormorant, but have straight rather than hooked bills, and a very long, thin neck with a trigger-like mechanism that aids in the underwater spearing of fish. Their tails are long and narrow, with a peculiar transverse ribbing. Anhingas live near freshwater swamps, lakes, and rivers of warm regions around the world. The American species, *Anhinga anhinga*, is widely distributed in the tropics and ranges north to the Gulf states and the Carolinas. Adult males are glossy black, with silvery-white streaks and spots on the back and wings. Females and young have buffy heads, necks, and breasts. The Old World species, *A. melanogaster*, known as the darter, is found in Africa, Asia, and Australia. It resembles the American species, but males have a pale stripe the length of the neck. Both species are excellent swimmers, often swimming with just the head and neck above water, thus their other name, snakebird. They also frequently soar on motionless wings.

ANHUI, also Anhwei, province, E China. It comprises the broad alluvial lowland of the flood-prone Huai R. in the N, the intensively cultivated alluvial lowlands along the Yangtze in the S, and a rugged, hilly area in the extreme S. Chief crops are wheat and cotton in the N, rice and silk in the Yangtze lowlands, and tea in the S upland areas. Fish culture is important. Rich iron-ore deposits support a large iron- and steel-manufacturing complex at Ma'anshan (Ma-an-shan). Coal and copper are mined. Major cities include the capital, Hefei (Hofei), Huainan (Huai-nan),

Bengbu (Pangpu), Anqing (An-ch'ing), and Wuhu (Wu-hu).

Once part of the ancient S state of Ch'u, the region that is now Anhui was absorbed into China during the Ch'in dynasty (221 BC–206 BC). It was made a separate province in 1667. The Huang He (Yellow R.) flowed through Anhui until it changed course to the N in 1851; it was diverted here in 1938 by the Nationalist government in an attempt to halt the Japanese invasion, an act that resulted in a tremendous loss of lives. Area, about 130,000 sq km (about 50,200 sq mi); pop. (1982) 49,660,000.

ANIAKCHAK NATIONAL MONUMENT, SW Alaska, proclaimed 1978, established 1980. Located on the Alaska Peninsula, the monument has as its main feature Aniakchak Crater (1303 m/4275 ft), a volcano in the Aleutian Range. Its crater (78 sq km/30 sq mi), one of the world's largest volcanic craters, contains a lake, a river, and a volcano that erupted in 1931 and 1933. Area, 554.2 sq km (214 sq mi).

ANILINE, also phenylamine, colorless liquid, $C_6H_5NH_2$, slightly soluble in water and soluble in organic solvents. It was first prepared in 1826 as one of the products obtained by heating indigo to a high temperature. The word *aniline* is derived from the specific name, *anil,* of the indigo plant, which in turn is derived from the Sanskrit word *nila* ("blue" or "indigo").

In 1856 the British chemist Sir William Perkin, while attempting to synthesize quinine, treated impure aniline with potassium dichromate and obtained a violet substance that could be used as a dye. Perkin named this material mauve and set up a factory to manufacture it. The enterprise was highly successful, and in a short time other synthetic dyestuffs, prepared from aniline or from other derivatives of coal tar, were competing with natural dyes.

Aniline is most readily prepared for commercial use by the reduction of nitrobenzene by iron and hydrochloric acid. It is also prepared commercially by the action of ammonia under high pressure on chlorobenzene in the presence of a catalyst. The raw material in both cases is made from benzene. The commercial product is known as aniline oil. Its principal use is as a dye intermediate, that is, a raw material for the manufacture of synthetic dyes. It also has important uses in making drugs (for example, sulfanilamide), explosives, and many other synthetic chemicals.

Aniline melts at −6.2° C (20.8° F) and boils at 184.3° C (363.8° F).

ANIMAL, any member of the kingdom Animalia, which comprises all multicellular organisms that obtain energy by ingesting food and that have cells organized into tissues. Unlike plants, which manufacture nutrients from inorganic substances by means of photosynthesis, or fungi, which feed by absorbing organic matter in which they are usually embedded, animals actively acquire their food and digest it internally. Associated with this mode of nutrition are many of the additional features that readily distinguish most animals from other life forms. Specialized tissue systems permit animals to move about freely in search of food or, for those that are fixed in place during most of their lives (sessile animals), to draw the food toward themselves. The well-developed nervous systems and complex sense organs that have evolved in most animals enable them to monitor the environment and, in association with specialized movements, to respond rapidly and flexibly to changing stimuli.

Almost all animal species, in contrast with plants, have a limited growth pattern and reach a characteristically well-defined shape and size at maturity. Reproduction (q.v.) is predominantly sexual, with the embryo passing through a blastula phase (*see* EMBRYOLOGY).

The conspicuous differences between plants and animals first led to a formal division of all life into two kingdoms, Plantae and Animalia. When the world of microorganisms was later investigated, some were seen to be clearly plantlike, with walled cells and chlorophyll-containing bodies that conducted photosynthesis, whereas others resembled animals in that they moved about (by means of flagella or pseudopodia) and digested food. The latter type, protozoa (q.v.),

This young bear (Mammalia) and its catch, a salmon (Osteichthyes) exemplify two major classes of Chordata.
Tom Bledsoe–Photo Researchers, Inc.

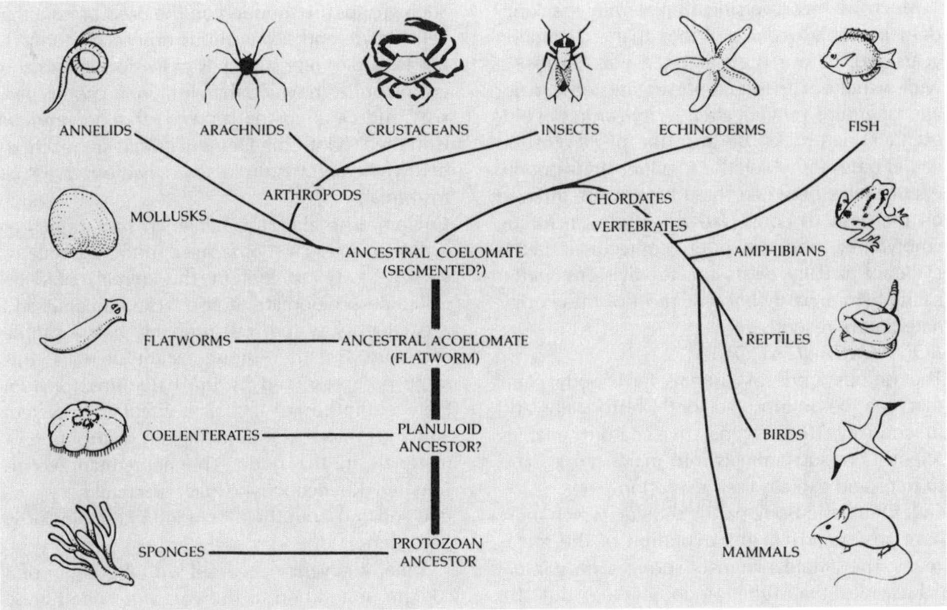

This evolutionary tree shows the ancestry of today's divisions of the animal kingdom.
From Helena Curtis, *Biology:* Third Edition, Worth Publishers, Inc., New York, 1979.

was categorized as a subkingdom of Animalia. Difficulties arose, however, with many forms that showed mixed characteristics and with groups in which some organisms were plantlike but had close relatives that were animallike (*see* FLAGELLATES). Eventually, classification schemes with several kingdoms were proposed, in which the definitions of Plantae and Animalia became more restricted. What constitutes an animal, therefore, depends on the scheme followed.

In the five-kingdom system used in this encyclopedia (*see* CLASSIFICATION), animals are limited to organisms with differentiated tissues, and the protozoan groups are assigned to the kingdom Protista (q.v.). The separation of the protozoa from the higher animals is not entirely satisfactory, however, because classification systems should reflect evolutionary relationships, and multicellular forms are believed to have evolved from protozoan ancestors more than once. Moreover, some protozoans form colonies that are difficult to distinguish from simple multicellular animals. The problem in deciding on the limits of the Animalia is a reflection of the natural world, in which boundaries are blurred and evolution leaves intermediates between major groups in its path. W.J.B.

ORIGINS AND RELATIONSHIPS

The multicellular animals (metazoa), as stated, evidently arose from animallike, unicellular creatures (protozoa). Precise relationships are unclear because of the poor fossil record and the extinction of intermediate forms, but several evolutionary routes are possible. For example, certain animallike flagellates occur as colonies and could readily have evolved into more elaborate organisms. In addition, the embryonic stages of some animals display a sequence of changes that provides a reasonable evolutionary model: a unicellular stage, followed by an undifferentiated colonylike stage, a hollow ball of cells (blastula), and then a gut (gastrula stage). Other theories suggest different transitional forms, such as a protozoan with many nuclei in one cell.

Since its uncertain beginnings, the animal kingdom has diversified into several major lineages or branches, which in turn have subdivided into phyla, classes, and smaller groups. The old notion that a single series of organisms has progressed from lower to higher forms, in a so-called chain of life, has long since been rejected. The course of evolution is more comparable to a tree or bush, with many branches undergoing diversification or adaptive radiation (*see* ADAPTATION), and with some progressive evolution occurring throughout the kingdom. Thus, insects, cephalopods, and vertebrates followed different evolutionary routes, but all of them can be described as "higher" animals. *See* CEPHALOPOD; INSECT; VERTEBRATE.

Much of the diversification within the kingdom probably occurred more than 600 million years ago, before the Cambrian era, because a wide variety of fossils, representing most major animal groups (phyla), already appear in the oldest Cambrian rocks. Because the phyla arose in earlier times for which the fossil record is poorer, relationships between them have to be inferred on the basis of conservative features, including embryology, and are often conjectural. Better evidence usually exists for subdivisions within each phylum, partly because most of these originated more recently.

BODY ORGANIZATION

The various kinds of animals have body plans that can be interpreted both historically and functionally. Thus, comparative anatomy enables scientists to sort animals into major groups and to trace and explain their evolution.

Gut. One basic body part is the gut, which must have arisen early in the evolution of the metazoans. The simplest animals, sponges, have internal cavities that function in feeding, but the openings are not comparable to a mouth or anus. Furthermore, they have tissues but no real organs or nerves, and they lack symmetry. The more complex jellyfish and their allies, more active animals that generally feed with tentacles, have a gut with a mouth but no anus. A nervous system is present, but no brain or head. A jellyfish body also has no bilateral symmetry—that is, no left or right side—as have the bodies of more advanced animals, including humans. Instead, the animals exhibit radial symmetry, or symmetry around a central axis.

Symmetry. Symmetry thus provides a basis for further dividing most animals into two grades: Radiata and Bilateria. The tissues of the Radiata have only two major layers, whereas the Bilateria have three. This came about through the addition of a middle layer (mesoderm) between the outer layer (ectoderm) and inner layer (endoderm). (In the embryological development of animals in general, the ectoderm gives rise to the skin and nervous system, the endoderm to the lining of the gut and some of its derivatives, and the mesoderm to the remaining structures, such as muscles.) Bilateral symmetry is also an evolutionary development linked with an increasing capability of active locomotion, although such locomotion has often been lost in later lines of evolution. Movement in one direction is facilitated by the development of a head, with brain and sense organs at the leading end.

Protostomia and Deuterostomia. Within the Bilateria, a number of phyla that differ as adults have been linked on the basis of early embryology. Such groups are founded on the basis of how the cells divide and how various organs are formed. For example, one such basic division is into the Protostomia, in which the embryonic mouth persists, and Deuterostomia, in which a new mouth is formed. (Until the Deuterostomia are reached, below, the animals discussed henceforth are Protostomia.)

Coelom. The ancestral bilaterian had a gut but no other body cavity; because of the absence of such a cavity, or coelom, the animal could be called an acoelomate. It also lacked an anus and a circulatory system but probably had a simple excretory system. Among extant animals, this stage is represented by the flatworms (phylum Platyhelminthes). Lack of a circulatory system and anus makes for an inefficient distribution of materials in the body. The nemertean worms (phylum Rhynchocoela) have a circulatory system and anus, but their locomotion remains slow and clumsy.

A major advance occurred with the origin of a coelom in addition to the gut. This added body cavity allowed for the movement of internal organs. In some animals it may also double as a circulatory system and as a skeleton, if its contents are under pressure. Two basic types exist. A true coelom is a cavity within the mesoderm, covered with a layer of tissue called an epithelium. A pseudocoelom, however, lacks such a covering. A number of phyla of mainly wormlike animals have this latter kind of body cavity and hence are called pseudocoelomates. Such animals generally are of modest size and have poor locomotion. They lack a circulatory system and are simple in various other respects. Nevertheless, they are quite successful in some habitats. The remaining organisms have a true coelom and are called eucoelomates.

Manner of Coelom Formation. Eucoelomates can be subdivided (but not rigorously) on the basis of how the coelom forms in embryology. The Schizocoela form a coelom by splitting the mesoderm, whereas the Enterocoela form it as an outgrowth of the gut. Transitional between these two are the lophophorates, or Tentaculata. Members of this small group have a crown of tentacles, or a lophophore, used in feeding, and are modified to a sedentary way of life.

The true Schizocoela are related to the annelid worms (phylum Annelida). Metamerism, or segmentation (a serial repetition of groups of body parts), arose in this group, an arrangement that is thought to have allowed better locomotion. The arthropods (phylum Arthropoda) retain segmentation but add a hard external skeleton (exoskeleton) that improves locomotion and provides

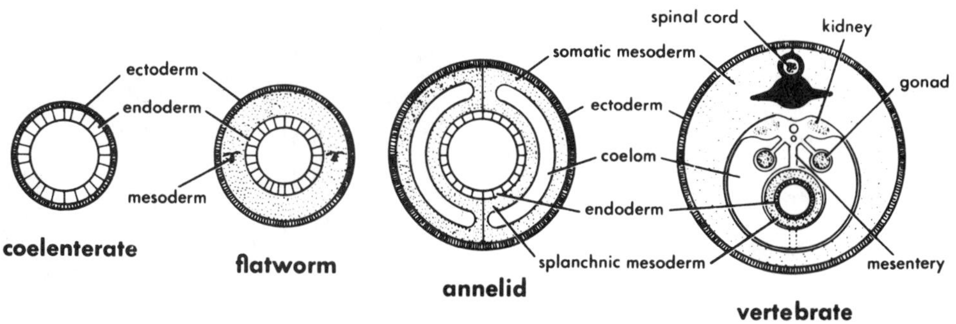

Diagrammatic cross sections of different body types.

support and protection. The mollusks (phylum Mollusca) have reduced coeloms and little indication of segmentation, but they have a characteristic shell and soft body.

Deuterostomia. The Deuterostomia comprise the enterocoels—echinoderms, arrowworms, hemichordates, and chordates—the rest of the animal kingdom. These phyla are united mainly by developmental characteristics and may be related to the lophophorates, some of which also have an enterocoelous manner of forming the coelom. In addition, no segmentation exists of the sort found in annelids. Another important link of the deuterostomes to the lophophorates is the presence, in some members of both groups, of three pairs of coelomic cavities and three corresponding body regions. Adult deuterostomes have become quite modified. Thus, arrowworms are equipped for floating and swimming; echinoderms have lost their bilateral symmetry and reverted to radial symmetry (often with five rays, as in most starfish); the wormlike hemichordates have a very simple structure; and such advanced features as a complex brain and the capability for rapid locomotion evolved within the chordate lineage.

What follows is a brief summary of the phyla, which are grouped into some of the larger assemblages discussed above. Further information is given in separate articles under the common name of the phyla or superphyla. The number of known animal species, about 1 million, is approximate and does not include fossil species.

THE PARAZOA

Only one phylum exists in this most primitive division of the animal kingdom.

Phylum Porifera (sponges). Sponges are simple, multicellular animals with tissues but no distinct organs. Most are marine, but a few occur in fresh water. They live attached to a substrate and feed by drawing water into the body through pores, then extracting food particles with flagellated cells. Most of the activities of the body are carried out by cells acting independently or in small groups. Sponges have no nervous system but do react to stimuli. A skeleton that consists of fibers, minerals, or both is usually present. 4800 species.

THE MESOZOA

This group consists of two minor phyla of simple, parasitic worms of uncertain relationships: Orthonectida and Dicyemida. Mesozoa, which means "middle animals," suggests that they are living fossils, but they may be degenerate forms of unknown ancestors. 50 species.

THE RADIATES

Animals with radial symmetry (except when secondarily modified), radiates have a body with two cell layers: endoderm and ectoderm.

Phylum Coelenterata (true jellyfish and hydroids, corals, and sea anemones). The phylum is also called Cnidaria, especially when extended to include the Ctenophora (see below). The stages of a coelenterate's life history include an attached polyp (as in sea anemones), a free-swimming medusa (as in jellyfish), or both. Prey is taken with stinging capsules, generally located on the tentacles. The animals are marine, except for a few freshwater forms such as *Hydra.* 3 classes and 5300 species.

Phylum Ctenophora (comb jellies). These marine animals resemble true jellyfish but have no polyp stage, and they swim using bands of hairlike cells resembling combs. Prey is usually taken with sticky tentacles. 80 species.

THE ACOELOMATE BILATERIA

The two major phyla consist of small to moderate-sized worms with bilateral symmetry and no coelom.

Phylum Platyhelminthes (flatworms). These worms have no anus or circulatory system and are structurally simple, although the generally hermaphroditic reproductive system is often quite intricate. Their flat shape is necessary because the tissues must be near the surface to facilitate gas and nutrient exchange with the environment. The free-living class Turbellaria is abundant in the sea and fresh water and rare on land. Two classes are parasitic: Trematoda (flukes) and Cestoda (tapeworms). An obscure marine group, Gnathostomulida, is sometimes put here and sometimes made a separate phylum. 13,000 species.

Phylum Nemertina, or Rhynchocoela (ribbon worms). Elongate worms with a circulatory system and an anus, ribbon worms are common in the sea and rare on land. Prey is taken with an extensible proboscis. 800 species.

THE PSEUDOCOELOMATES

The body cavity of these usually small to microscopic, worm-shaped animals is a pseudocoelom, and they lack a circulatory system. Most pseudocoelomates are often grouped into a single phylum, Aschelminthes (q.v.), with several classes. Alternatively, as here, each class is a phylum, and Aschelminthes is a superphylum. This leaves one wormlike group (Acanthocephala) and one group of "moss animals" (Endoprocta) outside the aschelminths proper.

Phylum Nematoda (roundworms). These elongate worms have a firm covering called a cuticle and a body supported by fluid under pressure. They generally feed by sucking fluid or taking in small particles or soft materials. Abundant but inconspicuous, they live in soil and marine and freshwater sediments. Some, as parasites, cause serious diseases. 10,000 species.

Phylum Gastrotricha. These are tiny (less than 1 mm/0.04 in long), short-bodied, marine and freshwater worms. 170 species.

Phylum Nematomorpha. Worms of this minor group resemble roundworms. They are parasitic in arthropods when young and briefly free-living and aquatic as adults. 230 species.

Phylum Acanthocephala (spiny-headed worms). Parasitic as adults in the guts of vertebrates, and as juveniles in the tissues of various animals, these worms lack a gut and have a spiny attachment organ on the head. They superficially resemble tapeworms. 500 species.

Phylum Kinorhyncha. These tiny (less than 1 mm/0.04 in), short-bodied marine worms have spiny bodies and a spiny proboscis. 100 species.

Phylum Rotifera (wheel animalcules). Rotifers are so named because of the wheel-shaped organ on the head, used in feeding and swimming. Often microscopic, these animals are abundant in fresh water. 1500 species.

A sea anemone, Epiactis prolifera, *of the phylum Coelenterata, brooding young in a groove around its body.*
R.N. Mariscal–Bruce Coleman, Inc.

Phylum Priapulida. These free-living marine worms have spiny heads. 8 species.

Phylum Endoprocta (moss animal). Very small, stalked, marine or freshwater animals, endoprocts feed with tentacles. 75 species.

Phylum Loricifera. This phylum, established in 1983, consists of marine sediment dwellers only 0.5 mm (0.02 in) long. Free-swimming larvae and sedentary adults have mouth cones that can be retracted into a spiny head, itself retractable.

EUCOELOMATES: THE TENTACULATA

These coelomate animals have a short body and a crown of tentacles called a lophophore.

Phylum Phoronida. Phoronids have a U-shaped gut because the lower part of the body is greatly elongated. They live in tubes, with the lophophore and anus at the open end. Adults are about 1 to 10 cm (about 0.4 to 4 in) long, and all phoronids are marine. 18 species.

Phylum Ectoprocta, or Bryozoa (moss animal). The ectoprocts, polyzoans, or true bryozoans are small, colonial animals that resemble simplified phoronids. Almost all inhabit a hardened covering and are primarily marine. 3500 species.

Phylum Brachiopoda (lampshells). These animals superficially resemble clams but have upper and lower shells rather than left and right ones. All are marine. 230 species.

EUCOELOMATES: THE TROCHOZOA

The following phyla frequently possess a juvenile stage called a trochophore larva. They all may be derived from an annelidlike ancestor, judging from their widespread metamerism (segmentation) and the frequent occurrence of paired nerve cords ventral to the gut.

Phylum Annelida. Annelids have a well-developed coelom, a soft body, and (as a rule) well-developed metamerism. Bristlelike structures (setae) used in crawling are often present. The group includes earthworms (class Oligochaeta), leeches (class Hirudinea), and the less familiar bristle worms (class Polychaeta). Some animals of uncertain position, here treated as classes of annelids, are sometimes made separate phyla: Echiura and Pogonophora (beardworms). Two minor groups within the polychaetes, Archiannelida and Myzostomida, are often considered independent classes. 8700 species.

Phylum Sipuncula (peanut worms). These moderate-sized (about 3 cm/1.2 in) marine worms have a saclike body and a long proboscis. They may be simplified annelids. 250 species.

Phylum Mollusca. The second largest animal phylum, including snails and clams, mollusks typically have a hard shell and a soft body. Few traces of metamerism are observed, and the coelom is small; the main body cavity is part of the circulatory system. Some forms, such as octopuses and squid, attain considerable size. The seven mollusk classes are Aplacophora, Polyplacophora (chitons), Monoplacophora, Gastropoda (snails and slugs), Bivalvia (clams and allies), Cephalopoda (octopuses, squid, and allies), and Scaphopoda (tusk shells). 50,000 species.

Phylum Arthropoda. The body of an arthropod is covered with a hard, jointed skeleton. This is the largest animal phylum, partly because so many kinds of insects exist. Arthropods are abundant and successful in almost all habitats. The body remains segmented, and the coelom has been reduced. Three small, transitional groups are sometimes included in the Arthropoda and sometimes made independent phyla: Onychophora, Tardigrada, and Pentastomida. The classes of higher arthropods can be grouped into assemblages. Those with jaws (mandibulates) include the Crustacea (lobsters, crabs, and allies), the allied Myriapoda (centipedes and millipedes), and Insecta (insects). Arthropods with mouthparts called chelicerae include the Pycnogonida (sea spiders), Merostomata (horseshoe crabs), and Arachnida (spiders and their allies). 838,000 species.

EUCOELOMATES: THE DEUTEROSTOMIA

This large group includes all the remaining animals. The group's name indicates that the mouth is produced secondarily, as a new formation, in embryological development.

Phylum Chaetognatha (arrowworms). These animals are small, active, exclusively marine swimmers of uncertain relationship. 50 species.

Phylum Echinodermata. Echinoderms derive their name from their spiny skins. The group includes starfish and sea cucumbers. They are slow moving and rely mainly on small processes called tube feet for locomotion. All are marine. The five extant classes are as follows: Crinoidea (feather

This giant land snail, Achatina fulica, *belongs to the phylum Mollusca; other mollusks include the clam, the oyster, and the octopus.* O.S.F.–Bruce Coleman, Inc.

The victor, a green lynx spider (class Arachnida), and the vanquished, a wasp (class Insecta); both belong to the huge phylum Arthropoda. J. H. Robinson–Photo Researchers, Inc.

stars), Asteroidea (sea stars), Ophiuroidea (brittle stars), Echinoidea (sea urchins), and Holothuroidea (sea cucumbers). 6000 species.

Phylum Hemichordata (acorn worms). These simple, wormlike marine animals have a few characteristics linking them to chordates. Among these are traces of what may be a notochord (see discussion under Phylum Chordata) and a dorsal nerve cord, as well as a system of gill slits. The larval body of the worms, however, indicates a link to the echinoderms. 230 species.

Phylum Chordata. Chordates include vertebrates (animals with backbones) and some related invertebrates. At some time in their lives, all possess a stiff rod, called a notochord, that lies above the gut. In vertebrates, a series of bones (vertebrae) replaces the notochord.

Two subphyla of invertebrate chordates exist. The Tunicata (tunicates, or sea squirts) become highly modified as adults and attach to a substrate, feeding with gill slits. Only the free-swimming larvae retain a notochord. All are marine, and about 1300 species exist. The Cephalochordata (lancelets) resemble very simple fish. They live in the sea and extract food from the water with their gill slits. About 25 species exist.

The remaining Chordata belong to the subclass Vertebrata and have a backbone. Half of the 42,000 species are fish. Thus, although the group is very successful, it is outnumbered by arthropods and mollusks. Seven classes are generally recognized. The old class Pisces (fish) has long since been broken down into three classes: Agnatha (jawless fish such as lampreys), Chondrichthyes (cartilaginous fish such as sharks and rays), and Osteichthyes (bony fish). The class Amphibia contains such semiaquatic forms as salamanders, toads, and frogs. The class Reptilia is better adapted to life on land; it includes turtles, lizards, and crocodilians. The class Aves (birds) is noteworthy not only for flight but also for warm blood and an insulating layer of feathers. The class Mammalia is characterized by the possession of hair and of mammary glands that secrete milk. This group also is warm-blooded.

ANIMALS IN THE ECOSYSTEM

Animals have diversified so as to occupy many ecological niches (*see* ECOLOGY). Herbivores form a basic link in the food chain, or food web. They are eaten by carnivores, which in turn are eaten by other carnivores. Many animals are parasites or scavengers or feed on sediments. Every animal has adaptations, such as sense organs and teeth, that enable it to find and utilize food.

Some use a wide variety of foods; others specialize. Features such as camouflage and protective shells enable them to cope with predators.

Animals compete with one another for scarce resources, including food and a place to live. The interactions between predator and prey have involved a coevolution of these different parts of the ecosystem—that is, the evolution of prey is affected by the evolution of predators. Parasites, which are harmful but usually do not kill their hosts, must be able to overcome defensive adaptations. On the other hand, mutualists have cooperative arrangements with other organisms. Plants and animals can also cooperate, in the sense that food is provided by plants, and various animals effect pollination or seed distribution.

A great variety of strategies enable animals to survive and reproduce. When food in an ecosystem is abundant, the animals involved generally tend to reproduce in quantity. When intense competition for food is involved, however, the animals have to develop a more effective use of resources and tend to care for the young for a prolonged period. Where the ecosystem is stable, as in the Tropics, competition leads to complex life cycles and intricate adaptations, both structural and behavioral. *See* ANIMAL BEHAVIOR.

Animals often move from place to place. This enables them to locate food, avoid predators, and reproduce effectively. Through migration (*see* ANIMAL MIGRATION), birds and other animals can feed and reproduce where food is seasonally abundant. The movement of animals is limited only by the food supply, the terrain, and their individual capabilities for locomotion, and each local area and habitat has tended to evolve its own distinctive fauna. *See* ANIMAL DISTRIBUTION.

M.T.G.

ANIMALS IN THE HUMAN COMMUNITY

Ever since true humans appeared on earth, they have lived in close association with other animals. Throughout most of that time, humans existed as hunter-gatherers who depended on wild animals for food and clothing. They also found a source of aesthetic pleasure and spiritual strength in the animal life about them. Evidence of this exists in the remarkable paintings of Paleolithic people in the caves of southern France. The religious practices of North American Indians involved the veneration of certain animals, such as the bear, wolf, and eagle, in an attempt to acquire the power, wisdom, courage, and speed that these animals supposedly possessed.

Human societies have continued to exhibit traces of these relationships. The aesthetic appeal of animals is expressed in the mosaics and frescoes of ancient Greece, Rome, and Egypt; in the paintings of the Renaissance masters; and in countless works of more recent artists. Mystical feelings toward animals are reflected in myths and folktales, moralistic fables involving animals, and anthropomorphic animal stories for children, as well as the adoption of animal names for cars, sports teams, and so on.

This five-rayed starfish, Mediaster aequalis, *is a member of the phylum Echinodermata, which also includes sea urchins, sea cucumbers, sand dollars, and sea lilies.*
R. N. Mariscal-Bruce Coleman, Inc.

Despite highly developed technology and agriculture and the domestication of many species, modern humans still depend on wild stocks of a variety of other animals, such as fish and shellfish, for food. Unmanaged commercial exploitation, however, has greatly reduced this resource and has driven some species to the edge of extinction (*see* ENDANGERED SPECIES; ENVIRONMENT). In addition, wild animals provide recreation in the form of sport hunting and sportfishing, birdwatching, and visits to zoos and wildlife refuges.

As humans advanced from a hunting to an agricultural existence, relationships between humans and animals changed. Animals that preyed on livestock or that destroyed crops were reduced or exterminated, and the alteration of the landscape eliminated habitats for many other species. As humans became more concentrated in cities, however, animals such as rats multiplied and became important carriers of disease.

Humans domesticated some animals for food, clothing, power, and companionship. How this came about is a matter of speculation. Through protection and selective breeding, humans changed early domesticated forms into highly productive dairy and beef cattle, sheep, swine, and poultry. Also contributing to human welfare are the dogs, cats, white rats and mice, guinea

The phylum Chordata, which contains all the vertebrate animals, includes such varied forms as this roadrunner (class Aves) and the snake (class Reptilia) it has captured.
Anthony Mercieca–Photo Researchers, Inc.

pigs, and rhesus monkeys that medical research has used to gain an understanding of human physiology and to develop drugs and procedures to combat human illnesses.

As humans continue to spread across the earth, however, they encroach on or pollute the environments of many animals, reducing remaining habitats to smaller and smaller areas. Unless this trend is reversed, much of the world's animal life faces extinction. R.L.S.

For further information on this topic, see the Bibliography in volume 28, sections 438, 460–82, 594–95.

ANIMAL BEHAVIOR. The behavior of animals has fascinated inquiring minds since at least the time of Plato and Aristotle. Particularly intriguing has been the ability of simple creatures to perform complicated tasks—weave a web, build a nest, sing a song, find a home, or capture food—at just the right time with little or no instruction. Such behavior can be viewed from two quite different perspectives, discussed below: Either animals learn everything they do (from "nurture"), or they know what to do instinctively (from "nature"). Neither extreme has proven to be correct.

NURTURE: THE BEHAVIORISTS

Until recently the dominant U.S. school in behavioral theory has been behaviorism (q.v.), whose best-known figures are J. B. Watson and B. F. Skinner. Strict behaviorists hold that all behavior, even breathing and the circulation of blood, according to Watson, is learned; they believe that animals are, in effect, born as blank slates upon which chance and experience are to write their messages. Through conditioning, they believe, an animal's behavior is formed. Behaviorists recognize two sorts of conditioning: classical and operant.

In the late 19th century the Russian physiologist Ivan Pavlov discovered classical conditioning while studying digestion. He found that dogs automatically salivate at the sight of food—an unconditioned response to an unconditioned stimulus, to use his terminology. If Pavlov always rang a bell when he offered food, the dogs began slowly to associate this irrelevant (conditioned) stimulus with the food. Eventually the sound of the bell alone could elicit salivation. Hence, the dogs had learned to associate a certain cue with food. Behaviorists see salivation as a simple reflex behavior, something like the knee-jerk reflex doctors trigger when they tap a patient's knee with a hammer.

The other category, operant conditioning, works on the principle of punishment or reward. In operant conditioning a rat, for example, is taught to press a bar for food by first being rewarded for facing the correct end of the cage, next being rewarded only when it stands next to the bar, then only when it touches the bar with its body, and so on, until the behavior is shaped to suit the task. Behaviorists believe that this sort of trial-and-error learning, combined with the associative learning of Pavlov, can serve to link any number of reflexes and simple responses into complex chains that depend on whatever cues nature provides. To an extreme behaviorist, then, animals must learn all the behavioral patterns that they need to know.

NATURE: THE ETHOLOGISTS

In contrast, ethology—a discipline that developed in Europe but that now dominates U.S. studies as well—holds that much of what animals know is innate (instinctive). A particular species of digger wasp, for example, finds and captures only honeybees. With no previous experience a female wasp will excavate an elaborate burrow, find a bee, paralyze it with a careful and precise sting to the neck, navigate back to her inconspicuous home, and, when the larder has been stocked with the correct number of bees, lay an egg on one of them and seal the chamber. The female wasp's entire behavior is designed so that she can function in a single specialized way. Ethologists believe that this entire behavioral sequence has been programmed into the wasp by its genes at birth and that, in varying degrees, such patterns of innate guidance may be seen throughout the animal world. Extreme ethologists have even held that all novel behaviors result from maturation—flying in birds, for example, which requires no learning but is delayed until the chick is strong enough—or imprinting, a kind of automatic memorization discussed below.

The three Nobel Prize-winning founders of ethology—Konrad Lorenz of Austria, Nikolaas Tinbergen of the Netherlands, and Karl von Frisch of West Germany—uncovered four basic strategies by which genetic programming helps direct the lives of animals: sign stimuli (frequently called releasers), motor programs, drive, and programmed learning (including imprinting).

Sign Stimuli (Releasers). Sign stimuli are crude, sketchy cues that enable animals to recognize important objects or individuals when they encounter them for the first time. Baby herring gulls, for example, must know from the outset to whom they should direct their begging calls and pecks in order to be fed. An adult returning to the nest with food holds its bill downward and swings it back and forth in front of the chicks. The baby gulls peck at the red spot on the tip of the bill, causing the parent to regurgitate a meal. The young chick's recognition of a parent is based entirely on the sign stimulus of the bill's vertical line and red spot moving horizontally. A wooden model of the bill works as well as the real parent; a knitting needle with a spot is more effective than either in getting the chicks to respond.

Sign stimuli need not be visual. The begging call that a chick produces is a releaser for its parents' feeding behavior. The special scent, or pheromone (q.v.), emitted by female moths is a sign stimulus that attracts males. Tactile (touch) and even electrical sign stimuli are also known.

The most widespread uses of sign stimuli in the animal world are in communication, hunting, and predator avoidance. The young of most species of snake-hunting birds, for instance, innately recognize and avoid deadly coral snakes; young fowl and ducklings are born able to recognize and flee from the silhouette of hawks. Similar sign stimuli are often used in food gathering. The bee-hunting wasp recognizes honeybees by

Herring gull and chicks on a beach. The drably colored young remain under the parents' protection until they molt their immature down and develop flight feathers.
David Overcash–Bruce Coleman, Inc.

For owls, high-frequency rustling sounds are a sign stimulus for a foraging mouse, and release a silent, gliding attack in total darkness down from the owl's listening post.
Ronald Austing–Bruce Coleman, Inc.

means of a series of releasers: The odor of the bee attracts the wasp upwind; the sight of any small, dark object guides it to the attack; and, finally, the odor of the object as the wasp prepares to sting determines whether the attack will be completed.

This use of a series of releasers, one after the other, greatly increases the specificity of what are individually crude and schematic cues; it is a strategy frequently employed in communication. Most animal species are solitary except when courting and rearing young. To avoid confusion, the signals that identify the sex and species of an animal's potential mate must be clear and unambiguous. For example, a minnowlike fish called the stickleback uses a system of interlocking releasers to orchestrate its mating. When its breeding season arrives, the underside of each male turns bright red. This color attracts females but also provokes attacks by other males; red objects of almost any description will trigger male stickleback aggression. A female responds to the male's red signal with a curious approach posture that displays her swollen belly full of eggs. This incites the male to perform a zigzag dance that leads the female to the tunnellike nest he has built. The female struggles into the nest, whereupon the male touches her tail with his nose and quivers. The resulting vibration causes the female to release her eggs for the male to fertilize. If the male fails to perform the last part of the ballet, the female will not lay her eggs; vibrating the female with a pencil, however, which she can plainly see is not a male stickleback, works perfectly well, al-

A male wolf spider presents a gift of food to a female. Many species conduct elaborate courtship rituals involving mutual approach and retreat. The giving and receiving of food usually marks the culmination of these rituals and signals the female's acceptance of the male.
Hans Pfletschinger–Peter Arnold, Inc.

though the male in this case, not having gone through the last stage of the ritual, refuses to fertilize the eggs and eats them instead.

Motor Programs. A second major discovery by ethologists is that many complex behaviors come prepackaged as motor programs—self-contained circuits able to direct the coordinated movements of many different muscles to accomplish a task. The dancing of sticklebacks, the stinging action of wasps, and the pecking of gull chicks are all motor programs.

The first motor program analyzed in much detail was the egg-rolling response of geese. When a goose sees an egg outside its nest, it stares at the egg, stretches its neck until its bill is just on the other side of the egg, and then gently rolls the egg back into the nest. At first glance this seems a thoughtful and intelligent piece of behavior, but it is a mechanical motor program; almost any smooth, rounded object (the sign stimulus) will release the response. Furthermore, removal of the egg once the program has begun does not stop the goose from finishing its neck extension and delicately rolling the nonexistent object into the nest. Such a response is one of a special group of motor programs known as fixed-action patterns. Programs of this class are wholly innate, although they are frequently wired so that some of the movements are adjusted automatically to compensate for unpredictable contingencies, such as the roughness and slope of the ground the goose must nudge the egg across. Apparently, the possible complexity of such programs is almost unlimited; birds' nests and the familiar beautiful webs of orb-weaving spiders are examples.

Another class of motor programs is learned. In the human species, walking, swimming, bicycle riding, and shoe tying, for example, begin as laborious efforts requiring full, conscious attention. After a time, however, these activities become so automatic that, like innate motor programs, they can be performed unconsciously and without normal feedback. This need for feedback in only the early stages of learning is widespread. Both songbirds and humans, for example, must hear themselves as they begin to vocalize, but once song or speech is mastered, deafness has little effect. The necessary motor programs have been wired into the system.

Drive. The third general principle of ethology is drive. Animals know when to migrate, when (and how) to court one another, when to feed their young, and so on. In most animals these abilities are behavioral units that are switched on or off as appropriate. Geese, for example, will only roll eggs from about a week before egg laying until a week after the young have hatched. At other times eggs have no meaning to them. The switching on and off of these programs often involves complex inborn releasers and timers. In birds, preparations for spring migration, as well as the development of sexual dimorphisms, territorial defense, and courtship behavior, are all triggered by the lengthening period of daylight. This alters hormone levels in the blood, thereby trig-

A male fox snarls at a more powerful rival intruding on its territory. By such gestures of aggression and submission, animals define their individual territories, thus distributing the population and ensuring that each animal has adequate hunting territory.

Roger Payne uses a receiver monitoring the signals of underwater hydrophones to record the sounds of whales offshore on a calm night in Argentina.
Des & Jen Barilett–Bruce Coleman, Inc.

gering each of these dramatic but essential changes in behavior.

In general, however, no good explanation exists for the way in which motivation is continually modulated over short periods in an animal's life. A cat will stalk small animals or toys even though it is well supplied with food; deprived of all stimuli, its threshold (the quality of stimulus required to elicit a behavior) will drop sufficiently so that thoroughly bored cats will stalk, chase, capture, and disembowel entirely imaginary targets. This unaccountable release of what appears to be pent-up motivation is known as vacuum activity—a behavior that will occur even in the absence of a proper stimulus.

One simple mechanism by which animals alter their levels of responsiveness (and which may ultimately help explain motivation) is known as habituation. Habituation is essentially a central behavioral boredom; repeated presentation of the same stimulus causes the normal response to wane. A chemical present on the tentacles of its archenemy, the starfish, triggers a sea slug's frantic escape behavior. After several encounters in rapid succession, however, the threshold for the escape response begins to rise and the sea slug refuses to flee the overworked threat. Simple muscle fatigue is not involved, and stimulation of some other form—a flash of light, for instance—instantly restores the normal threshold (a phenomenon known as sensitization). Hence, nervous systems are prewired to "learn" to ignore the normal background levels of stimuli and to focus instead on changes from the accustomed level.

Programmed Learning. The fourth contribution ethology has made to the study of animal behavior is the concept of programmed learning. Ethologists have shown that many animals are wired to learn particular things in specific ways at preordained times in their lives.

Imprinting. One famous example of programmed learning is imprinting. The young of certain species—ducks, for example—must be able to follow their parents almost from birth. Each young animal, even if it is preprogrammed to recognize its own species, must quickly learn to distinguish its own particular parents from all other adults. Evolution has accomplished this essential bit of memorization in ducks by wiring ducklings to follow the first moving object they see that produces the species-specific exodus call. The call acts as an acoustic sign stimulus that directs the response of following. It is the physical act of following, however, that triggers the learning process; chicks passively transported behind a calling parent do not imprint at all. (In fact, presenting obstacles so that a chick has to work harder to follow its parent actually speeds the imprinting process.) As long as the substitute parent makes the right sounds and moves, ducklings can be imprinted on a motley collection of objects, including rubber balls, shoe boxes, and human beings.

This parental-imprinting phase is generally early and brief, often ending 36 hours after birth. Another round of imprinting usually takes place later; it serves to define the species image the animal will use to select an appropriate mate when it matures. Ethologists suspect that genetic programming cannot specify much visual detail; otherwise, selective advantage would probably require chicks to come prewired with a mental picture of their own species. As the world has become increasingly crowded with species, the role of sign stimuli in some animals has shifted from that of identifying each animal's species uniquely to that of simply directing the learning necessary to distinguish an animal's own kind from many similar creatures. This strategy works because, at the early age involved, most animals' ranges of contact are so limited that a mistake in identifying what to imprint on is highly unlikely.

Characteristics of programmed learning. Imprinting, therefore, has four basic qualities that distinguish it from ordinary learning: (1) A specific time, or critical period, exists when the learning must take place; (2) a specific context exists, usually defined by the presence of a sign stimulus; (3) the learning is often constrained in such a way that an animal remembers only a specific cue such as odor and ignores other conspicuous characteristics; and (4) no reward is necessary to ensure that the animal remembers. These qualities are now becoming evident in many kinds of learning, and the value of such innately directed learning is beginning to be understood: In a world full of stimuli, it enables an animal to know what to learn and what to ignore. As though for the sake of economy, animals need pick up only the least amount of information that will suffice in a situation. For example, ducklings of one species seem able to learn the voices of their parents, whereas those of another recall only what their parents look like. When poisoned, rats remember only the taste and odor of the dangerous food, whereas quail recall only its color. This phenomenon, known as rapid food-avoidance conditioning, is so strongly wired into many species that a single exposure to a toxic substance is usually sufficient to train an animal for life. The same sorts of biases are observed in nearly every species. Pigeons, for instance, readily learn to peck when food is the reward, but not to hop on a treadle for a meal; on the other hand, it is virtually impossible to teach a bird to peck to avoid danger, but they learn treadle hopping in dangerous situations easily. Such biases make sense in the context of an animal's natural history; pigeons, for example, normally obtain food with the beak rather than the feet, and react to danger with their feet (and wings).

Perhaps the example of complex programmed learning understood in most complete detail is song learning in birds. Some species, such as doves, are born wired to produce their species-specific coos, and no amount of exposure to the songs of other species or the absence of their own has any effect. The same is true for the repertoire of 20 or so simple calls that virtually all birds use to communicate messages such as hunger or danger. The elaborate songs of songbirds, however, are often heavily influenced by learning. A bird reared in isolation, for example, sings a very simple outline of the sort of song that develops naturally in the wild. Yet song learning shows all the characteristics of imprinting. Usually a critical period exists during which the birds learn while they are young. Exactly what is learned—what a songbird chooses to copy from the world of sound around it—is restricted to the songs of its own species. Hence, a white-crowned sparrow, when subjected to a medley of songs of various species, will unerringly pick

Blue tits are often cited as an example of a species capable of insight learning, based on their ability to learn how to open milk bottles to get at the cream just under the cap. In fact, blue tits in the wild search for food by peeling bark, and house-reared tits spontaneously peel the wallpaper from their owners' walls. Hence, the behavior seen here is an automatic part of the birds' repertoire.

R. Thompson—Bruce Coleman, Inc.

out its own and commit it to memory. The recognition of the specific song is based on acoustic sign stimuli.

Despite its obvious constraints, song learning permits considerable latitude: Any song will do as long as it has a few essential features. Because the memorization is not quite perfect and admits some flexibility, the songs of many birds have developed regional dialects and serve as vehicles for a kind of "cultural" behavior.

A far more dramatic example of programmed cultural learning in birds is seen in the transmission of knowledge about predators. Most birds are subject to two sorts of danger: They may be attacked directly by birds of prey, or their helpless young may be eaten by nest predators. When they see birds of prey, birds regularly give a specific, whistlelike alarm call that signals the need to hide. A staccato mobbing call, on the other hand, is given for nest predators and serves as a call to arms, inciting all the nesting birds in the vicinity to harass the potential predator and drive it away. Both calls are sign stimuli. Birds are born knowing little about which species are safe and which are dangerous; they learn this by observing the objects of the calls they hear. So totally automatic is the formation of this list of enemies that caged birds can even be tricked into mobbing milk bottles (and will pass the practice on from generation to generation) if they hear a mobbing call while being shown a bottle. This variation on imprinting appears to be the mechanism by which many mammals (primates included) gain and pass on critical cultural information about both food and danger. The fairly recent realization of the power of programmed learning in animal behavior has reduced the apparent role that simple copying and trial-and-error learning play in modifying behavior.

The importance of maternal care and affection in the development of normal primate behavior has been established by various experiments. Animals reared in isolation become unable to relate properly to other members of their species. Hans Bittner

COMPLEX BEHAVIOR PATTERNS

Evolution, working on the four general mechanisms described by ethology, has generated a nearly endless list of behavioral wonders by which animals seem almost perfectly adapted to their world. Prime examples are the honeybee's systems of navigation, communication, and social organization. Bees rely primarily on the sun as a reference point for navigation, keeping track of their flight direction with respect to the sun and factoring out the effects of the winds that may be blowing them off course. The sun is a difficult landmark for navigation because of its apparent motion from east to west, but bees are born knowing how to compensate for that. When a cloud obscures the sun, bees use the patterns of ultraviolet polarized light in the sky to determine the sun's location. When an overcast obscures both sun and sky, bees automatically switch to a third navigational system based on their mental map of the landmarks in their home range.

Study of the honeybee's navigational system has revealed much about the mechanisms used by higher animals. Homing pigeons, for instance, are now known to use the sun as their compass; they compensate for its apparent movement, see both ultraviolet and polarized light, and employ a backup compass for cloudy days. The secondary compass for pigeons is magnetic. Pigeons surpass bees in having a map sense as well as a compass as part of their navigational system. A pigeon taken hundreds of kilometers from its loft in total darkness will nevertheless depart almost directly for home when it is released. The nature of this map sense remains one of ethology's most intriguing mysteries.

Honeybees also exhibit excellent communication abilities. A foraging bee returning from a good source of food will perform a "waggle dance" on the vertical sheets of honeycomb. The dance specifies to other bees the distance and direction of the food. The dance takes the form of a flattened figure 8; during the crucial part of the maneuver (the two parts of the figure 8 that cross) the forager vibrates her body. The angle of this part of the run specifies the direction of the food: If this part of the dance points up, the source is in the direction of the sun, whereas if it is aimed, for example, 70° left of vertical, the food is 70° left of the sun. The number of waggling motions specifies the distance to the food.

The complexity of this dance language has paved the way for studies of higher animals. Some species are now known to have a variety of signals to smooth the operations of social living. Vervet monkeys, for example, have the usual set of gestures and sounds to express emotional states and social needs, but they also have a four-word predator vocabulary: A specific call alerts the troop to airborne predators, one to four-legged predators such as leopards, another to snakes, and one to other primates. Each type of alarm elicits a different behavior. Leopard alarms send the vervets into trees and to the top branches, whereas the airborne predator call causes them to drop like stones into the interior of the tree. The calls and general categories they represent seem innate, but the young learn by observation which species of each predator class is dangerous. An infant vervet may deliver an aerial alarm to a vulture, a stork, or even a falling leaf, but eventually comes to ignore everything airborne except the martial eagle.

THE QUESTION OF ALTRUISM

One fascinating aspect of some animal societies is the selfless way one animal seems to render its services to others. In the beehive, for instance, workers labor unceasingly in the hive for three weeks after they emerge and then forage outside for food until they wear out two or three weeks later. Yet the workers leave no offspring. How could natural selection favor such self-sacrifice? This question presents itself in almost every social species.

The apparent altruism is sometimes actually part of a mutual-aid system in which favors are given because they will almost certainly be repaid. One chimpanzee will groom another, removing parasites from areas the receiver could not reach, because later the roles will be exchanged. Such a system, however, requires that animals be able to recognize one another as individuals, and hence be able to reject those who would accept favors without paying them back.

A second kind of altruism is exemplified by the behavior of male sage grouse, which congregate into displaying groups known as leks. Females come to these assemblies to mate, but only a handful of males in the central spots actually sire the next generation. The dozens of other males advertise their virtues vigorously but succeed only in attracting additional females to the favored few in the center. Natural selection has not gone wrong here, however; males move further inward every year, through this celibate and demanding apprenticeship, until they reach the center of the lek.

Weaver ants are a social species of Hymenoptera with a strong genetic incentive to cooperate. Here workers construct a communal nest by cementing together several adjacent leaves. John Alcock

The altruism of honeybees has an entirely genetic explanation. Through a quirk of hymenopteran genetics, males have only one set of chromosomes. Animals normally have two sets, passing on only one when they mate; hence, they share half their genes with any offspring and the offspring have half their genes in common with one another. Because male Hymenoptera have a single set of chromosomes, however, all the daughters have those genes in common. Added to the genes they happen to share that came from their mother, the queen, most workers are three-fourths related to one another—more related than they would be to their own offspring. Genes that favor a "selfless" sterility that assists in rearing the next generation of sisters, then, should spread faster in the population than those programming the more conventional every-female-for-herself strategy.

This system, known as kin selection, is widespread. All it requires is that an animal perform services of little cost to itself but of great benefit to relations. Bees are the ultimate example of altruism because of the extra genetic benefit that their system confers, but kin selection works almost as well in a variety of genetically conventional animals. The male lions that cooperate in taking over another male's pride, for example, are usually brothers, whereas the females in a pride that hunt as a group and share food are a complex collection of sisters, daughters, and aunts. Even human societies may not be immune to the programming of kin selection. Anthropologists consistently report that simple cultures are organized along lines of kinship. Such observations, combined with the recent discovery that human language learning is in part a kind of imprinting—that consonants are innately recognized sign stimuli, for instance—suggest that human behavior may be more of a piece with animal behavior than was hitherto imagined. *See* SOCIOBIOLOGY. J.L.Go. and C.G.G.

For further information on this topic, see the Bibliography in volume 28, section 462.

ANIMAL COMMUNICATION. *See* ANIMAL BEHAVIOR.

ANIMAL DISEASES. *See* DISEASES OF ANIMALS; DOG, DOMESTIC; VETERINARY MEDICINE.

ANIMAL DISTRIBUTION, the geographic distribution of animal life on the earth, the study of which is called zoogeography. Animals vary widely in their tolerance of environmental conditions. Some can survive in several types of habitat, whereas others perish when removed from their natural surroundings. No animals other than humans can create sufficient artificial changes to enable them to exist in a totally strange environment without evolving through many generations of adaptation (q.v.). The specific interactions of animals with their environment are the subject matter of ecology (q.v.). The zoogeographer studies the distribution of animal life, using ecological principles to explain the patterns of that distribution.

Animal environments can be roughly classified as either water or land habitats. Winged creatures are classified according to the land or water bases to which they ultimately return. Distribution of aquatic animals is subdivided into saltwater and freshwater habitats.

Saltwater Animals. Many species of whales and predatory fish have been observed in all saltwater seas. Most aquatic animals, however, are limited to relatively definite climatic areas. In general, animals do not leave their climatic zone, and in a zone that is divided by landmasses the animals are prevented from passing to other bodies of water in the same zone.

The environmental conditions in deep waters are markedly different at each level of depth. The water temperature decreases and pressure increases with increasing depth. Feeding conditions, which depend on the number and types of plants and animals present, also vary greatly with depth. The depth of the ocean floor is much more variable than is the elevation of land. Consequently, the few widely distributed saltwater forms are those that live at or near the surface. An aquatic animal that can live only at depths of 6000 to 7500 m (20,000 to 25,000 ft) cannot cross a ridge in the ocean floor if the crest of the ridge is only 3000 m (10,000 ft) below the surface.

Assuming relative uniformity of temperature, pressure, and feeding conditions, saltwater habitats may be divided into three zones: littoral, pelagic, and abyssal. The littoral zone includes the coastal regions of oceans and seas, from the shoreline seaward to a depth of about 180 m (about 600 ft). The animal population includes the crowded life of the shore region, such as corals, mussels, higher arthropods, and fish. The pelagic zone includes the surface waters of the open sea to the same depth as the littoral zone. Many pelagic forms, such as jellyfish and true fish equipped with air bladders, are adapted for floating, but most of the inhabitants of this zone are swimming forms. The abyssal zone is the deep, unilluminated region of the ocean. This region contains almost no plant life, but the abyssal inhabitants, such as crabs, feed on dead organisms that sink from the surface. Unique in this setting are the hydrothermal vent (q.v.) communities of plants and animals, where the food chain is based on sulfur-digesting bacteria.

Freshwater Animals. The composition of freshwater communities is much more dependent on climate than is that of saltwater communities. The oceans of the world cover vast areas and to a great extent flow into each other; bodies of fresh water do not. Consequently, dissemination of freshwater species is much more limited than is that of saltwater species. Variation in chemical composition is greater for inland waters than for ocean waters because minerals dissolved in fresh water cannot dissipate over broad areas to the extent that oceanic minerals can. Within these limits, however, two large subdivisions of inland fresh waters exist: flowing waters and standing waters. Flowing waters are usually connected with the sea, and the many oceanic species that enter the rivers form an important part of the animal population. Swiftness of currents in flowing water requires that animals be strong swimmers (such as salmon), bottom dwellers (such as crayfish), or forms that can attach themselves to rocks, water plants, or debris (such as leeches). Standing waters have little movement, so slow-swimming and sedentary forms are abundant in such areas. Basins of standing water collect organic debris to a much greater extent than does flowing water, making possible plant populations large enough to furnish an abundant food supply for the animal population.

Land Animals. Like aquatic animals, land animals are limited in distribution by environmental conditions, of which the most restrictive is the separation of landmasses by water, high mountain ranges, and extensive desert areas. An isolated island may have fauna strikingly different from the fauna of a nearby continent. On the island of Madagascar, for example, no large mammals are found, but several families of primates are wholly or partly confined to the island, and more than 100 species of native birds occur nowhere else.

The land area of the world is divided into six zoogeographic regions, each having a different fauna: (1) the Palaearctic region, including Europe, Asia north of the Himalaya, and the northern coasts and deserts of Africa; (2) the Oriental region, including India, Burma, Thailand, Indonesia, and the Philippines; (3) the Ethiopian region, including Africa south of the Sahara; (4) the Australian region, including Australia, New Zealand, New Guinea, and the islands of Oceania; (5) the Nearctic region, including Greenland and all of North America north of Mexico City; and (6) the Neotropical region, including southern Mexico, the West Indies, Central America, and all of South America. Within these boundaries animals are grouped according to the particular habitat that they occupy, such as plains, deserts, or forests. The habitat of a land animal is determined by such variables as the type of food available and the amount of protection from predatory animals that the habitat affords.

ANIMAL HUSBANDRY, the breeding, feeding, and management of animals for the production of food, fiber, work, and pleasure. Modern methods concentrate on one type of animal in large, efficient farming units that generate animal products at the highest rate of return for investment. Intensive husbandry conditions include large numbers of animals in small lots, enriched feed, growth stimulation by various means, and vaccination against disease. Most of the world's domestic animals, however, are raised in small units under less efficient conditions and at lower rates of return.

Animals furnish about 28 percent of the world's total value of agricultural products. They supply a much higher proportion of human food in the developed countries than elsewhere. In the U.S. animal products account for as much as 53 percent of the total agricultural income.

Traditional husbandry practices are closely associated with the degree of control needed over the animals that are kept and with the uses to which they are put. Most domesticated animals have multiple uses; for example, animals kept primarily for work also supply milk, meat, and clothing materials. The animals and their uses, however, are closely associated with the culture and experience of the people who care for them (*see* AGRICULTURE: *History*). In some regions of the world cattle are not considered for use in the production of food. Studies have shown that the work power, fertilizer, milk, and the fuel from dung that the cattle provide in these regions are more efficient animal products than meat. Analysis of other cultural practices has often revealed unexpected efficiency of use fitted to local circumstances.

Environmental influences such as climate also play an important role in the domestication and use of animals. Water buffalo are used as draft animals in southern Asia where they are adapted to the high temperature and humidity; whereas horses, which thrive in moderate climates, were the principal draft animals in the temperate regions until they were replaced by tractors. Cattle from India that are acclimatized to hot and humid conditions are prevalent in the southern U.S. because they are better adapted to the climate of the region than European cattle.

Draft Animals. Domesticated animals used primarily for work, transport, and leisure are widely distributed. They include the horse, mule, donkey, ox, buffalo, camel, llama, alpaca, yak, reindeer, and dog.

Modern horses are thought to have descended from one or more of three subspecies of *Equus caballus*—tarpan, Przewalski's horse, and the European forest horse. They are still used for draft in many countries of the world. They are also used for controlling other types of animals, for carrying packs, and for riding for leisure and sport. The world population is estimated at more than 60 million; approximately half are in North and South America and half in Asia and Europe. The 12 million or so mules in the world are fairly evenly divided among Africa, North and Central America, and South America. Of the more than 40 million donkeys, about half are in Asia and one-fourth in Africa. Camels, llamas, and alpacas (family Camelidae) are used as beasts of burden. Of about 17 million camels in the world, approximately three-fourths are found in Africa and the rest in Asia. The llama and alpaca are mostly limited to small areas in South America. Practically all water buffalo are found in Asia. They are used primarily as draft animals but have potential for the production of milk and meat. Oxen are also important draft animals in Asia and in some parts of southeastern Europe. Dogs are used as pack animals in Alaska and Siberia and are also used to control sheep and other animal herds.

Sheep and Goats. Sheep are used for wool, meat (mutton and lamb), and to a small extent for milk. With goats they form the subfamily Caprinae of the family Bovidae. Sheep are commonly divided into three types based on the characteristics of their wool: fine, medium, and coarse. Perhaps the first animals to be used in husbandry, they were domesticated in southwestern Asia about 11,000 years ago. About one billion are now widely distributed throughout the world, with the largest populations in Africa, South America, Asia, Europe, and Oceania. Commercial sheep farming is usually conducted on large tracts of land, divided into operational units containing 1000 or more animals per unit. Sheep are also raised as a secondary enterprise on many small farms. They are well adapted to semiarid regions and to land that is too steep or rough for the cultivation of crops.

Goats were first domesticated in the same region as sheep, and for the same uses, but about 1500 years later. They are about two-fifths as numerous as sheep and show a similar distribution.

Swine. Recent evidence suggests that swine were domesticated about 9000 years ago in several world regions simultaneously. Worldwide population is estimated to be more than 700 million. Approximately half are raised in Asia, primarily in China. Europe, the former USSR, and South America also have large numbers. Unlike most domestic animals, pigs are omnivorous and compete directly with humans for many foods. They are good scavengers, however, and are highly efficient in converting cereal grains into protein and fat. In the U.S. they are concentrated in the Midwest, where pig husbandry is based on the conversion of corn and soybean meal into meat under intensive conditions.

Cattle. Modern cattle (genus *Bos,* family Bovidae) are usually divided into three types: beef, dairy, and dual purpose, an intermediate type used for both milk and meat. It is believed that cattle were domesticated about 8500 years ago in southeastern Europe, with Southeast Asia a probable second center of domestication. World cattle population is more than one billion, with half concentrated in South America, Europe, countries of the former USSR, the U.S., and India. Most beef cattle are raised on large rangelands, but following weaning, the young animals to be used for meat may be fattened in feedlots. Dairy cattle are managed in relatively large herds under intensive conditions near centers of dense population. Cheese, dried milk, and other specialized products, however, usually come from small farms with cattle set out to pasture.

Poultry. Poultry (order Galliformes) includes chickens, ducks, geese, guinea fowl, pea fowl, pigeons, swans, and turkeys. Each of these domesticated groups is descended from a closely related wild bird and was probably first developed in the areas where the wild bird was indigenous. World numbers are estimated at more than 6 billion chickens, with somewhat more than 100 million ducks and somewhat less than 100 million turkeys. Estimates for other types are not available. Chickens are numerous in most regions of the world. Most of the ducks are produced in Europe and Asia and most of the turkeys in the U.S. In the developed countries, production units for meat and eggs are large and intensive, with individual birds housed singly in cages or housed together in large numbers. Under these conditions, one operator can care for large numbers of birds with high labor efficiency and good control of disease and the environmental factors affecting production.

Other Animals. Other domesticated animals of importance include, in the cattle family, the yak (*Bos grunniens*) in Tibet, the mithan (*Bos gauras*) in India, and the banteng (*Bos javanicus*) in Southeast Asia. The reindeer (*Rangifor tarandus*) is important in the northern regions of Europe and northern Asia.

Although a few specialized farms have raised various animals (primarily mink and foxes) for their pelts, most furs are obtained from wild populations by hunting and trapping. In North America, muskrats and raccoons provide slightly more than half the total revenue. The former USSR was also a leading fur nation. *See* FUR INDUSTRY.

Current Trends. The major concern of animal husbandry today is the extent to which production can be maintained as the human population increases. The goal of research has been to increase the efficiency of the production of animal products by genetic selection and genetic engineering. For example, scientists have increased the size of sheep by inserting growth-hormone genes into embryos, and the same method can be applied to cattle and other animals.

Research is also being directed toward the development of animal strains in areas deficient in protein. Thus in South America the capybara is being exploited by Venezuela for its meat; it is taken from the wild in large numbers to lands devoted to cattle raising. In Peru, the government is encouraging the raising of guinea pigs for their food value, and elsewhere in Latin America research is being conducted into the farming of the iguana lizard.

Intensive methods for producing animal products include confinement of poultry in small cages, swine in small pens, and sheep and cattle in small lots. Confinement leads to savings in labor, feed, and other production costs. Confinement in individual pens may also afford savings from improved disease control and better protection from predators. Such practices have come under attack as cruel to the animals, and protective legislation has been advocated. Livestock and poultry farmers, on the other hand, claim that the animals are probably not under much stress because disturbed animals show sharp decreases in productive capacity.

Also at issue are special additives including hormones, antibiotics, vitamins, and other substances used to increase growth or productivity. In the U.S. most of these substances are under the control of the Food and Drug Administration. The general guidelines are that any supplement must be proved safe and effective in the amounts used. The two most controversial growth additives are the hormone diethylstilbestrol (DES) and antibiotics. Diethylstilbestrol is now banned because in high doses it was found to be capable of causing cancer. Scientists who advocate the banning of antibiotics argue that resistant strains of bacteria in animals might transfer their resistance to bacteria that infect humans. The first proven instance of this occurred in 1984, when an outbreak of human salmonella infections in four midwestern states was traced to drug-resistant salmonella bacteria from calves in South Dakota that had been fed chlortetracycline.

Eventually the physiological limits of all domestic animals may prevent further increases in yield. If the human population continues to expand and food supplies become scarcer, the proportion of food that can be used to feed animals will then decrease, and animal products will be in shorter supply and more expensive.

See CATTLE; DAIRY FARMING; FOOD PROCESSING AND PRESERVATION; FOOD SUPPLY, WORLD; MEAT-PACKING INDUSTRY; POULTRY FARMING. *See also* separate articles on the animals mentioned.

P.T.C.

For further information on this topic, see the Bibliography in volume 28, sections 460–61, 594–95.

ANIMAL MIGRATION, seasonal or periodic mass movement of animals away from and back to their natural breeding areas. Migration usually occurs preceding and following breeding seasons. During a breeding season, migratory animals are subjected to seasonal changes in environment and undergo physiological and anatomical changes. In its strictest sense, the term migration is not applicable to the nomadic wanderings of many animal groups constantly threatened with overpopulation, or to the change in habitat of many larval animals during various stages of metamorphosis. Thus, the periodic mass movements of the lemming and the locust (qq.v.) are not considered truly migratory.

Migratory Routes. The best-known examples of true migration are annual bird movements, in which swarms of birds native to the Temperate and Arctic zones seek warmer regions late in the summer and in the autumn and return to their original nesting sites in the spring. A spectacular example is the Arctic tern, which breeds within 8° of the North Pole and winters in the Antarctic.

Such seasonal migrations also occur among some mammals, especially those that live a partially or entirely aquatic life. The Greenland seal, *Pagophilus groenlandicus,* makes long journeys from Greenland to Spitsbergen and Jan Mayen islands, where the young are born; and the fur seal, *Callorhinus ursinus,* native to many Arctic areas, always converges at a rookery in the Pribilof Islands during the breeding season. Many northern bats travel to warmer winter habitats; in northern North America, bats that inhabit hollow trees migrate southward as far as Bermuda to pass the winter. Numerous ruminants undertake migrations at the beginning of the cold season: The wapiti of Yellowstone Park migrate to the valleys of the Rocky Mountains, and caribou move from the tundra to the coniferous forests.

Many fish migrate from open sea to warmer coastal waters and from the north to warmer southern regions during the winter months. Salmon ascend from the ocean upstream through various rivers to spawn, and most eels pass down from the rivers and enter the sea for the same purpose. Some marine invertebrates, such as the sea urchin and the starfish, migrate from deep to shallow water during spring and early summer to spawn.

Navigation Theories. Many theories have been advanced to explain the origin of migrations and the physiological mechanisms that guide animals in migratory journeys, but no single theory has been judged wholly satisfactory by zoologists. The seasonal movements of birds and most other migrating animals are actuated by a combination

Flock of Canada geese, Branta canadensis, *on the wing in the Klamath National Wildlife Reserve, California.* © Tim Davis–Photo Researchers, Inc.

of external and internal stimuli that release a physiological migratory "trigger." Once an animal has begun a migratory journey, however, many factors may act to maintain it on a proper path.

Navigation by the sun and stars seems to be involved in the migration of birds, and fish may be guided through the sea by minute traces of chemical odors from their ancestral rivers. According to current research, birds may possess a sensitivity to the magnetic field of the earth and to the effect of its rotation about an axis. The combination of these two forces, being unique for various parts of the world, could thus supposedly direct a bird to the location desired. Traces of iron in the brain tissue of birds indicate a possible mechanism for this sensitivity to the magnetic field. Other theories involve the use by animals of topographic landmarks during flight, and some redundancy of navigational information may be involved. None of these theories fully explains the usually unerring maiden migrations of animals, unless it is supposed that much of the phenomenon is hereditary and that animals instinctively pursue ancient paths.

See ANIMAL BEHAVIOR; BIOLOGICAL CLOCKS.

W.Be.

For further information on this topic, see the Bibliography in volume 28, section 462.

ANIMAL PSYCHOLOGY. *See* ANIMAL BEHAVIOR.

ANIMATION. *See* MOTION PICTURE: *Animation.*

ANIMISM (from Lat. *anima*, "breath" or "soul"), belief in spiritual beings. Among biologists and psychologists, animism refers to the view that the human mind is a nonmaterial entity that nevertheless interacts with the body via the brain and nervous system. As a philosophical theory, animism, usually called panpsychism, is the doctrine that all objects in the world have an inner or psychological being. The 18th-century German physician and chemist Georg Ernst Stahl coined the word *animism* to describe his theory that the soul is the vital principle responsible for organic development. Since the late 19th century, however, the term has been mainly associated with anthropology and the British anthropologist Sir Edward Burnett Tylor, who described the origin of religion and primitive beliefs in terms of animism.

In *Primitive Culture* (1871) Tylor defined animism as the general belief in spiritual beings and considered it "a minimum definition of religion." He asserted that all religions, from the simplest to the most complex, involve some form of animism. According to Tylor, primitive peoples, defined as those without written traditions, believe that spirits or souls are the cause of life in human beings; they picture souls as phantoms, resembling vapors or shadows, which can transmigrate from person to person, from the dead to the living, and from and into plants, animals, and lifeless objects. In deriving his theory, Tylor assumed that an animistic philosophy developed in an attempt to explain the causes of sleep, dreams, trances, and death; the difference between a living body and a dead one; and the nature of the images that one sees in dreams and trances.

Tylor's theories were criticized by the British anthropologist Robert R. Marett (1866–1943), who claimed that primitives could not have been so intellectual and that religion must have had a more emotional, intuitional origin. He rejected Tylor's theory that *all* objects were regarded as being alive. Marett thought that primitive peoples must have recognized some lifeless objects and probably regarded only those objects that had unusual qualities or behaved in some seemingly unpredictable or mysterious way as being alive. He held, moreover, that the ancient concept of aliveness was not sophisticated enough to include the notion of a soul or spirit residing in the object. Primitive peoples treated the objects they considered animate as if these things had life, feeling, and a will of their own, but did not make a distinction between the body of an object and a soul that could enter or leave it. Marett called this view "animatism" or "preanimism," and he claimed that animism had to arise out of animatism, which may even continue to exist alongside more highly developed animistic beliefs.

Related to animism are ancestor worship (q.v.) and some forms of nature worship.

ANION. *See* ION.

ANISE, common name for an annual plant, *Pimpinella anisum,* of the family Apiaceae, or Umbelliferae (*see* PARSLEY). Native to Egypt, it is also cultivated in Syria, Malta, Spain, and Germany. The seed of the plant, aniseed, is used as a condiment, in the preparation of the liqueur anisette, and in medicine as a stimulant and to relieve flatulence. Aniseed has an aromatic, agreeable smell and a warm, sweetish taste. Both smell and taste are due to its oil, called oil of anise, which contains anethole. Anethole and its derivatives are used in perfumes and flavorings.

Chinese anise, *Illicium vernum,* is a small evergreen tree native to China. It is also known as star anise from the starlike form of its fruit, the badian, which consists of 6 to 12 hard, woody, one-seeded carpels. The qualities of the fruit, seed, and oil closely resemble those of the common anise, and the oil is used for the same purposes.

ANJOU, series of royal dynasties descended from the medieval rulers of Anjou in northwestern France. The original Anjou, or Angevin, line consisted of the counts of Anjou from the time of the founder, Fulk I the Red (888–938). In 1154, Henry, count of Anjou, became Henry II, king of England, the first of the Angevin, or Plantagenet (q.v.), line of English kings. Although Anjou passed out of English hands in 1204, the Plantagenet house of the Angevins continued to reign in England in a direct line of descent until the death of Richard II, king of England until 1399.

A second Angevin dynasty was founded by Charles, count of Anjou, who became king of Naples and Sicily as Charles I in 1266. He lost Sicily to the Spanish in 1282, but his descendants continued to rule in Naples until 1442.

Anise, Pimpinella anisum — Spice Trade Assn.

A third dynasty was established when Charles Robert of the Neapolitan branch became king of Hungary as Charles I in 1308. His line died in 1395.

ANJOU, former province of France, now included in the departments of Maine-et-Loire, Indre-et-Loire, Mayenne, and Sarthe. Its capital was Angers. The ancient inhabitants were the Andecavi, a Gallic tribe that long resisted the Romans. Beginning in the 9th century, Anjou was governed by a dynasty of counts who were among the most powerful feudal lords in France. In the second half of the 12th century, the province was subject to the kings of England; it was conquered by Philip II Augustus of France in 1204. In 1246 Louis IX granted Anjou to his brother Charles I, king of the Two Sicilies and count of Provence. Anjou was a duchy from 1297 to 1328, when it became a possession of the French crown. It again became a duchy in 1360. King Louis XI annexed the duchy to the royal dominions in 1480. In the 17th century Anjou became a province; it retained that status until the French Revolution.

ANJOU, town, Île-de-Montréal Co., S Québec Province, Canada; inc. 1956. It is a residential and industrial suburb of Montréal. Manufactures include steel items, furniture, and building materials. The town's main growth began in the late 1950s. Pop. (1981) 37,346; (1986) 36,916.

ANKARA, formerly ANGORA, city, capital of Turkey and of Ankara Province, in central Turkey. It is principally a residential city and government seat, but a number of small industries produce carpets, leather goods, wine, farm implements, and cement. Ankara is an important market and processing center for mohair and for the fine fruits and wheat grown in the surrounding region. Ankara is a city of contrasts. The old quarter, built around the ruins of an ancient citadel, has narrow, winding streets and crowded buildings. The new city, laid out in 1928, is spacious and well planned, with broad boulevards, libraries, museums, embassies, government buildings, and fashionable shops and hotels. The Museum of Anatolian Civilizations, containing a notable collection of Hittite artifacts, is here.

Ankara has been a trading center since ancient times. Hittites occupied the site about 2000 BC. They were succeeded by the Phrygians about 1000 BC. Alexander the Great subdued the city in 333 BC; after his death, conquering Gaulish tribes (Galatians) made it their capital. Known as Ancyra, it came under Roman rule in 189 BC, and in 25 BC it became capital of the province of Galatia Prima. Later a major city of the Byzantine Empire, it was successively occupied by Persians, Arabs, Seljuk Turks, and Latin Crusaders. The city, renamed Angora by the Seljuks, fell to the Ottoman Turks in 1360, was occupied briefly by Mongols in 1402, but reverted to the Ottoman Empire the following year. In 1923, after the establishment of the republic of Turkey, Angora succeeded İstanbul as the capital. The name was changed to Ankara in 1930. Some ruins from its long history survive. Pop. (1985) 2,251,533.

ANKYLOSAURUS, genus of plant-eating dinosaurs (*see* DINOSAUR) found worldwide in the later Cretaceous period, which ended about 65 million years ago. The heavily armored Ankylosaurs were medium-sized ornithischian (bird-hipped) dinosaurs ranging from 4.5 to 6 m (15 to 20 ft) long. They moved on all fours and, depending on the species, their broad, low bodies were covered with a mosaic of bony plates, with a spiked, clublike tail. Some species had erect plates and spines along the back, like the earlier stegosaurs, to whom they were closely related. The slow-moving ankylosaurs probably resembled armadillos, and their fossils usually occur in once swampy regions.

AN LU-SHAN (703–57), Chinese general of Turkic-Persian origin, who led a revolt against the T'ang emperor Ming Huang (685–762); the revolt marked the beginning of the T'ang dynasty's decline. An Lu-shan, a protégé of the emperor's concubine Yang Kuei-fei (718?–56), was military commander on China's northeast frontier. In 755 he seized the city of Luoyang (Lo-yang) and the imperial capital, Siking (now Xi'an, or Sian), forcing Ming Huang to seek refuge in Sichuan (Szechwan). The general was killed by his own son in 757. The rebellion was finally ended in 763, but the T'ang dynasty, although it lasted until 906, never regained its former strength.

ANN, CAPE. *See* CAPE ANN.

ANNABA, formerly BÔNE, city, NE Algeria, capital of Annaba Department, a seaport on the Mediterranean Sea, near the mouth of the Seybouse R. The picturesque old sector with narrow streets and bazaars remains, and examples of modern French architecture stand alongside original native buildings. Under government impetus, industry has flourished since the end of World War II. Industrial establishments include aluminum and chemical works and motor and railway shops. Annaba is the principal harbor of E Algeria and is a chief exporter of minerals on the Mediterranean. Mineral exports include iron, phosphate, and zinc. Other exports are cork (from the wooded Edough plateau, at the foot of which the city lies), grain, wool, and hides. A railroad connects Annaba with the Algerian cities of Algiers, Constantine, and Biskra and with important cities in Tunisia and Morocco. On the site of Annaba once stood Aphrodisium, port of the ancient city of Hippo Regius, ruins of which still stand. The city was a favorite residence of the Numidian kings; later, as the episcopal see of St. Augustine, who died here in 430, it was a center of early Christianity. The French occupied the city in 1832. Annaba was captured by the Allies during World War II and used by them as an army base. Pop. (1983 est.) 348,300.

ANNA COMNENA (1083–1148?), Byzantine princess and historian, daughter of Emperor Alexius I Comnenus, born in Constantinople. In 1118, after her father's death, she conspired against her brother, Emperor John II Comnenus, in an attempt to have the succession changed in favor of her husband, the Byzantine soldier and historian Nicephorus Bryennius (1062–1137). The plot failed, and she retired to a convent, where she wrote the *Alexiad,* a notable historic work in 15 books (completed in 1148). Although it unduly glorifies her father and his family, the *Alexiad* is considered a valuable historic source. It has been translated into English.

ANNA IVANOVNA (1693–1740), empress of Russia (1730–40). She was a niece of Emperor Peter I. In 1730 the Supreme Council of Russia, an advisory body of Russian nobles, elected her empress but established conditions that considerably reduced her power as a sovereign. After coming to power she disposed of the council by exiling or executing its members. Anna intervened in the War of the Polish Succession and, in alliance with Austria, warred against the Turks (1736–39). Her regime was dominated by her German favorites, especially the unpopular Ernst Johann Biron.

ANNAM, region of Indochina, comprising most of central Vietnam between Cochin China and Tonkin. It adjoins Cambodia and Laos on the west and the South China Sea on the east. The principal city is Hue. Other important cities are Binh Dinh, Da Nang, Quang Tri, and Vinh.

Some confusion exists about the use of the term Annam. It is the ancient Chinese name (Annan, "pacified south") for Vietnam, but the French used it to designate both central Vietnam and the precolonial Annamite Empire, which encompassed most of present-day Vietnam.

Late in the 2d century BC the northern part of the region was conquered by the Chinese. It remained under Chinese control until AD 939, when it was liberated by revolution. During the next few centuries the Cham, a people of Malayo-Polynesian stock who lived in the central and southern parts of the region, were driven southward by the Annamese. The Chinese reconquered the region about 1407 but were expelled again in 1428. Annam then became an independent monarchy embracing most of Indochina.

The French began their penetration in 1787, when they concluded a treaty with the ruler of Cochin China, then an independent principality. With some French assistance, Cochin China subjugated all Annam by 1802. Under continued pressure, however, part of Cochin China was ceded to the French in 1862, and five years later they annexed the remainder. In 1884 the French established a protectorate over the Annamite Empire, although it remained under the nominal rule of native monarchs until World War II.

See also COCHIN CHINA; TONKIN; VIETNAM.

ANNAPOLIS, city, capital of Maryland and seat of Anne Arundel Co., on the S bank of the Severn R., near its mouth on Chesapeake Bay, in the central part of the state; inc. as a city 1796. A port of entry and a commercial and distribution center for the surrounding agricultural area, the city relies economically on government activity, the production of radar electronic equipment and underwater military devices, and communications research and development. The U.S. Naval Academy and Saint John's College (1784) are here. A notable landmark in Annapolis is the State House (1772–80), the oldest U.S. State Capitol in con-

The U.S. Naval Academy is on the Severn River in Annapolis, Md. Just beyond the Academy buildings, center, is the dome of the Maryland State House, 1772–80.

tinuous legislative use. Here the Continental Congress met; Gen. George Washington resigned from the Continental army in 1783; the Treaty of Paris ending the American War of Independence was ratified in 1784; and the Annapolis Convention of 1786 took place. Also of interest are the Old Treasury (1735), the oldest public building still standing in Maryland, and Saint Anne's Church (1858–59), built on the site of an Anglican church of the 1690s.

Originally settled by Puritans from Virginia in 1649 as the town of Providence, Annapolis later became known as Town of Proctor's, Town at the Severn, and Anne Arundel Town. In 1694 the community became the provincial capital of Maryland and was renamed Annapolis in honor of Princess (later Queen) Anne of England. From Nov. 26, 1783, to June 3, 1784, Annapolis served as the capital of the U.S. Pop. (1980) 31,740; (1990) 33,187.

ANNAPOLIS ROYAL, town, seat of Annapolis Co., SW Nova Scotia, at the mouth of the Annapolis R., in an arm of the Bay of Fundy; inc. 1892. It is a commercial center and a summer resort. The oldest permanent European settlement in Canada, Annapolis Royal was founded in 1605 as Port Royal at a nearby site by the French explorers Samuel de Champlain and Pierre du Guast, sieur de Monts. The community was moved to its present location in 1635 and subsequently was fought over by the French and British. The British gained definitive control in 1710, when the settlement was renamed in honor of Queen Anne. Annapolis Royal then served as the capital of Nova Scotia until the founding of Halifax in 1749. A reconstruction of the 1605 Port Royal settlement is included in Port Royal Habitation National Historic Park, and remnants of early fortifications at Annapolis Royal are in Fort Anne National Historic Site. Pop. (1981) 622; (1986) 631.

ANNAPURNA, massif of the Himalayan mountain system, N central Nepal, one of the highest massifs in the world. The massif is 56 km (35 mi) long, culminating in two peaks, Annapurna 1 (8078 m/26,504 ft above sea level) and Annapurna 2 (7937 m/26,041 ft). The summit of Annapurna 1 was reached for the first time on June 3, 1950, by an expedition under the leadership of the French mountaineer Maurice Herzog (1919–).

ANN ARBOR, city, seat of Washtenaw Co., SE Michigan, on the Huron R., in a farm area; inc. 1851. It is a major research, educational, and medical center, seat of the huge University of Michigan, Concordia College (1962), and a community college. The Gerald R. Ford Library (dedicated 1981), housing papers of President Ford, is

Annapurna 1, in north central Nepal.
© Steve Kaufman–Peter Arnold, Inc.

on the grounds of the university. Computer software, electronic equipment, and specific instruments are developed and manufactured here. The name of the city may have been derived from a grape arbor that was owned by the wife of an early settler—hence Ann's Arbor or Ann Arbor. Pop. (1980) 107,316; (1990) 109,592.

ANNE (1665–1714), queen of Great Britain and Ireland (1702–14), the last British sovereign of the house of Stuart. Born in London on Feb. 6, 1665, she was the second daughter of King James II. Her mother was James's first wife, Anne Hyde (1637–71). In 1683 she was married to Prince George of Denmark (1653–1708). Although her father converted to Roman Catholicism in 1672, Anne remained Protestant and acquiesced in James's overthrow by the anti–Roman Catholic Glorious Revolution of 1688, which brought her sister Mary and Mary's husband, William of Orange, to the throne. Becoming queen on William's death in 1702, Anne restored to favor John Churchill, who had been disgraced by her predecessor, making him duke of Marlborough and captain-general of the army. Marlborough won a series of victories over the French in the War of the Spanish Succession (1701–14, known in America as Queen Anne's War), and he and his wife, Sarah (1660–1744), had great influence over the queen in the early years of her reign.

Devoted to the Church of England, Anne was inclined to favor the pro-church Tory faction rather than its Whig opponents, but, influenced by the Marlboroughs and Lord Treasurer Sidney Godolphin, earl of Godolphin (1645–1712), she at first excluded the Tories from office. Later, however, her friendship with the Marlboroughs cooled, and in 1710 she took advantage of popular dissatisfaction with the Whigs to remove Godolphin; Marlborough was dismissed the following year. During Queen Anne's reign the kingdoms of England and Scotland were united (1707). She died in London on Aug. 1, 1714, and, having no surviving children, was succeeded by her German cousin, George, elector of Hannover, as King George I of Great Britain.

ANNEALING, process of heat treatment by which glass and certain metals and alloys are rendered less brittle and more resistant to fracture. Annealing minimizes internal defects in the atomic structure of the material and leaves it free from internal stresses that might otherwise be present because of prior processing steps.

Ferrous metals and glass are annealed by heating them to high temperatures and cooling them slowly; copper and silver, however, are best annealed by heating and cooling quickly, then immersing in water. Large masses of metal or glass are cooled within the heating furnace; sheets are usually annealed in a continuous-process furnace. They are carried on a moving table through a long chamber in which the temperature is carefully graded from initial heat just below the softening point to that of room temperature at the end. Annealing time, especially of glass, varies widely according to the thickness of the individual piece; window glass, for example, requires several hours; plate glass, several days; and glass mirrors for reflecting telescopes, several months. Annealing is required as an intermediate step in metal-forming processes such as wire drawing or brass stamping in order to restore the ductility of the metal lost because of work hardening during the forming operation. *See also* TEMPERING.

ANNE OF AUSTRIA (1601–66), queen of France, daughter of Philip III, king of Spain, born in Madrid. In 1615 she married Louis XIII of France. The marriage was unhappy, and from 1620 until the death of Louis in 1643, the couple lived in virtual separation. The king's chief minister, Cardinal Richelieu, doubted Anne's loyalty to France because of her Spanish origin. He accused her of complicity in several treasonable conspiracies against Louis, but her guilt was never proved. After Louis died, Anne assumed the regency for her five-year-old son, King Louis XIV, but entrusted the government to the prime minister, Jules Mazarin. Together, they upheld the authority of the Crown during the civil wars of the Fronde (1648–53). In 1661, when Louis XIV assumed power, Anne retired to a convent. Queen Anne is the central figure of Alexandre Dumas's *Three Musketeers.*

ANNE OF CLEVES. *See* HENRY VIII.

ANNELID, common name for vermiform invertebrate (q.v.) animals with well-developed segmentation. About 9000 species constitute the phylum Annelida. The three major classes are the bristle worms (Polychaeta, about 5300 species), which are mainly marine and often luminescent; the Oligochaeta (about 3100 species), which are mostly freshwater or inhabit the soil, such as the earthworm (q.v.); and the leeches (Hirudinea, about 300 species; *see* LEECH), which are mainly freshwater but also marine or terrestrial.

Characteristics. Although annelids are diverse in form, the polychaetes ("many setae"), which generally are considered the ancestral stock, can exemplify their structure. The elongate body is rounded in cross section, with a mouth (sometimes jawed) at one end and an anus at the other, and it exhibits bilateral symmetry. The body is made up of several similar units, or segments, separated externally by furrows and internally by partitions (septa). The segments generally bear lobes (parapodia) with bristles (setae) that are used in locomotion. The fluid-filled body cavity (coelom) provides a kind of structural support, so that the body is flexible. The gut is a straight tube and the nervous system fairly simple, with sense organs poorly developed. The head may bear eyes, feelers, or tentacles; a few polychaetes have highly developed eyes. Polychaetes grow by adding segments at the posterior end.

Oligochaetes ("few setae") have fewer setae and no parapodia. The body is streamlined and well adapted to burrowing, and the head does not have eyes or feelers. Leeches are flattened and can swim or crawl by looping movements; they usually lack setae.

Polychaetes generally have separate sexes and reproduce by releasing sperm and eggs into the water. By contrast, the basic pattern in earthworms and leeches is hermaphroditism, with cross-fertilization occurring internally. These animals produce cocoons, and some leeches care for the young.

Ecology and Evolution. Some polychaetes are active predators. Others have taken to a sedentary way of life and extract particles from the water or take up deposits from the bottom. Earthworms feed mainly by passing soil through their bodies to extract nutrients, enriching and aerating the soil and thus playing an essential role in soil ecology. Most leeches suck the blood of other animals and are still used medically for bloodletting,

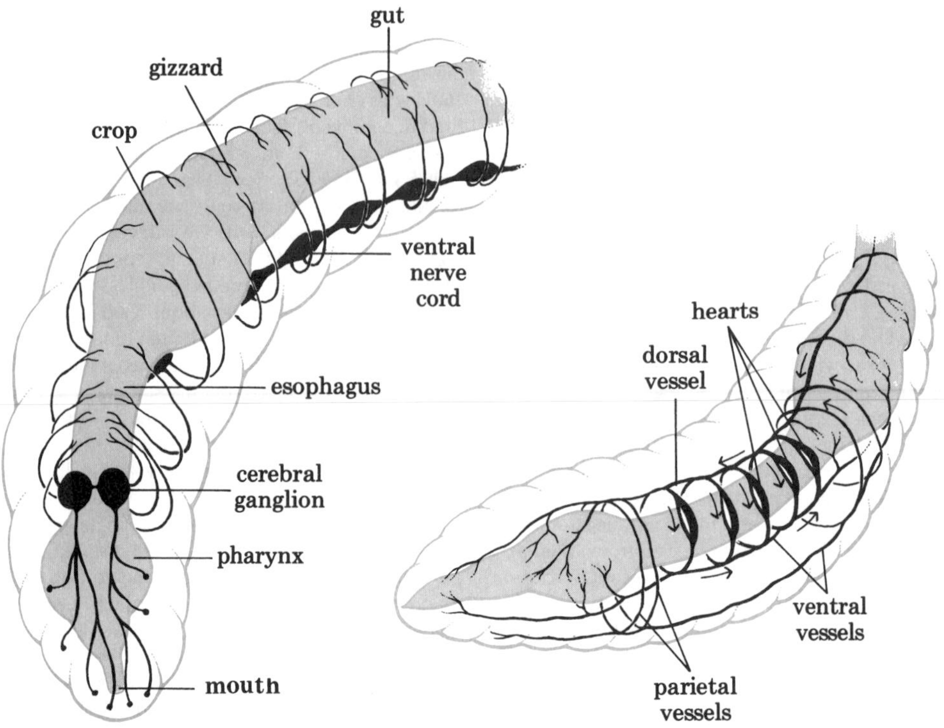

This diagram of the anterior segments of the earthworm, a typical annelid, shows its nervous system as well as its five pairs of hearts and the blood vessels surrounding the digestive tract. From Helena Curtis: *Biology*, Third Edition, Worth Publishers, Inc., New York, 1979

and an extract prepared from their blood is used as an anticoagulant; some leeches are predators.

Fossil annelids are rare because their soft bodies do not preserve well. Existing fossils date from more than 500 million years ago. They may be descended from the flatworms and are thought to have given rise to the arthropods (*see* ARTHROPOD). Some aberrant marine annelids are often placed in separate classes, such as the Archiannelida, which lack parapodia; others may even be in separate phyla, such as the Myzostomaria, which are parasites of echinoderms, and the Echiuroidea, which are unsegmented. M.T.G.

For further information on this topic, see the Bibliography in volume 28, section 464.

ANNIHILATION, in particle physics, the mutual destruction of elementary particles (q.v.) by their antiparticles (*see* ANTIMATTER), with the release of energy in the form of gamma rays or very short-lived particles. An example is the annihilation of an electron when it collides with its positively charged antiparticle, a positron. Annihilation of heavier particles, as in the collision of a neutron and an antineutron, is a more complex type of phenomenon.

ANNISTON, city, seat of Calhoun Co., NE Alabama, in an iron-mining region of the Appalachian foothills; inc. as a city 1879. Primary and fabricated metals, textiles, clothing, lumber, and processed food, as well as stone, clay, and glass items, are produced here. Cultural institutions here include the Anniston Museum of Natural History. Fort McClellan (1912), headquarters of the U.S. Military Chemical Corps and the Military Police Corps, adjoins the city. The Anniston Army Depot, an ordnance and reclamation depot, is nearby. A planned community, Anniston was founded by an iron company in 1872 and is named for Annie Taylor, wife of an early resident. Pop. (1980) 29,523; (1990) 26,623.

ANNUITY, annual allowance, payment, or income derived from funds especially designated for the purpose. Annuities may also be any payments made at fixed intervals. An annuity often represents only the interest derived from a principal fund, but it may also include periodic payments of principal. In many cases the fund is established pursuant to the provisions of a will or a trust agreement. Annuities frequently are funded by the earnings of life insurance policies. Recipients may be paid from the proceeds of funds that were established for their benefit on the deaths of other life insurance policyholders, or they may have policies of their own. Other forms of annuity are social security and unemployment insurance. *See* LIFE INSURANCE.

ANNULMENT OF MARRIAGE, in law, the determination by a court that a supposed marriage was never legally valid. Annulment, also called nullity of marriage, is distinguished from divorce, which is the action of a court in terminating a valid marriage.

Marriages subject to annulment proceedings are classified as "void" or "voidable." A void marriage is one that is deemed invalid in all respects. Examples of void marriages include those involving incest or bigamy.

A voidable marriage occurs when some defect exists in the contractual agreement in which all marriages originate. Examples are marriages of the underaged or the insane or a marriage procured by fraudulent means. Sexual impotency existing at the time of marriage also gives grounds for annulment. A voidable marriage may be annulled only in a lawsuit brought by the aggrieved party directly against the guilty party. In practice, voidable marriages are valid until annulled, and any children are legitimate.

ANNUNCIATION, in the New Testament, the announcement to Mary by the angel Gabriel that she would be the mother of Jesus (see Luke 1:26–38). The Feast of the Annunciation is observed on March 25. The scene between Gabriel and Mary has often been depicted in paintings, notably by the Italian masters Leonardo da Vinci and Sandro Botticelli and the German painter Matthias Grünewald.

ANNUNZIO, Gabriele D'. *See* D'ANNUNZIO, GABRIELE.

ANODE. *See* ELECTRODE.

ANOINTING OF THE SICK, in the Roman Catholic and Orthodox churches, a sacrament of spiritual comfort for the seriously ill or aged, formerly called extreme unction. The rite consists of biblical readings, prayers, and the anointing by a priest of the five senses (eyes, ears, nose, lips, and hands) of the sick person with oil normally blessed by a bishop on Maundy Thursday. In cases of emergency, the forehead alone is anointed. The rite may be celebrated either individually or in a group service. The effects are believed to include not only spiritual healing but also the restoration of bodily health, if God so wills.

The early church practice of anointing the sick was based on two New Testament texts (Mark 6:13; James 5:14–16). After the 8th century, the anointing came to be associated almost exclusively with rites for the dying. The term *extreme unction,* or *last anointing,* was introduced at that time. The 12th-century Italian theologian Peter Lombard listed the rite among the seven sacraments; that listing was recognized as official by the Council of Trent (1543–63).

Since the time of the Reformation, Protestants have generally rejected the sacramental nature of the rite, and some even the practice itself. The Anglican Communion makes provision for an anointing of the sick, but many Anglicans consider it a rite instituted by the church rather than a sacrament established by Christ.

ANOMALON, in nuclear physics, an unusual form of atomic nuclear matter that has been theorized to exist. Evidence for anomalons arose during experiments in which solid targets were bombarded by high-energy atomic nuclei. Some nuclear fragments produced by the bombardments appeared to react more quickly with other nuclei in the target than is normal. Fragments exhibiting such behavior were called anomalons by physicists who proposed that they represented unusual states of nuclear matter. If they do exist, they could perhaps even represent nuclei in which protons and neutrons have been reduced to their constituent quarks and gluons (*see* GLUON; QUARK). Although anomalons have been observed by scientists in the U.S., their existence still remains a subject of controversy.

ANOREXIA NERVOSA, in medicine, a condition characterized by intense fear of gaining weight or becoming obese, as well as a distorted body image, leading to an excessive weight loss from restricting food intake and excessive exercise. Anorexia nervosa is not associated with any preexisting physical illness. It is found chiefly in adolescents, especially young women. Between 5 and 18 percent of known anorexia nervosa victims die of starvation, and the condition may also lead to abnormalities in the menstrual cycle (*see* MENSTRUATION) and increased susceptibility to infection. Persons with the condition may also exhibit the practice, known as bulimia (q.v.), of ingesting large quantities of food and then voiding it through self-induced vomiting in order to remain thin. Repeated vomiting depletes the body of fluids and of the element potassium, and the disturbance can adversely affect heart function.

No generally recognized therapy for anorexia nervosa exists. It is often associated with depression (q.v.) and low self-esteem, and patients may benefit from treatment with antidepressant drugs. Psychotherapy, including family therapy, often helps, and about half of the cases resolve themselves without relapses. The behavioral problem may lead to actual chemical disorders in the body, however, that aggravate the condition.

Because many persons with anorexia nervosa never seek medical treatment, the exact prevalence of the condition is unknown. Studies indicate that it may develop in as many as 1 percent of the young women in the U.S. F.A.J.

ANOUILH, Jean (1910–87), French playwright, born in Bordeaux. During the German occupation of France in World War II, he wrote *Antigone* (1942; trans. 1946), an adaptation of the Greek legend of the daughter of Oedipus. His early plays are essentially pessimistic in tone, with suicide a frequent theme. His later plays are less sardonic and reflect a highly developed skill in dramatic construction and dialogue. Among his plays are *L'invitation au château* (1947), which was presented in New York City in 1950 as *Ring 'Round the Moon; The Waltz of the Toreadors* (1951; trans. 1956), which was selected the best foreign play of 1956–57 by the New York Drama Critics' Circle and produced as a film in 1962; *The Lark* (1953; trans. 1955); *Becket* (1960), produced as a film in 1964; *Dear Antoine or The Love that Failed* (1969; trans. 1971); and *Ornifle* (1970; trans. 1970).

ANSELM, Saint (c. 1033–1109), theologian, philosopher, and church leader, who proposed an argument for God's existence that is still being debated.

Anselm was born of a well-to-do family at Aosta, in northern Italy; in 1060 he joined the Benedictine monastery at Bec, in Normandy, where the English prelate Lanfranc was prior. Some time later, after Lanfranc was called to England to become archbishop of Canterbury, Anselm was elected abbot of Bec. During these years he acquired a reputation for learning and piety, and his monks urged him to write out the meditations that were the basis of his instructions to them. Thus, he composed the *Monologium* (Soliloquy, 1077) in which—reflecting the influence of St. Augustine—he spoke of God as the highest being and investigated God's attributes. Encouraged by its reception, in 1078 he continued his project of faith seeking understanding, completing the *Proslogium* (Discourse), the second chapter of which presents the original statement of what in the 18th century became known as the ontological argument.

Anselm argued that even those who doubt the existence of God would have to have some understanding of what they were doubting: Namely, they would understand God to be a being than which nothing greater can be thought. Given that it is greater to exist outside the mind rather than just in the mind, a doubter who denied God's existence would be making a contradiction because he or she would be saying that it is possible to think of something greater than a being than which nothing greater can be thought. Hence, by definition God exists necessarily.

The basic criticism of Anselm's argument is that one cannot infer the extramental existence of anything by analyzing its definition. In Anselm's own time a fellow monk, Gaunilo of Marmoutier, challenged his argument, as did the later philosophers Thomas Aquinas and Immanuel Kant. Nonetheless, René Descartes, Baruch Spinoza, Gottfried Leibniz, and some contemporary philosophers have offered similar arguments.

In 1093 Anselm was called to succeed Lanfranc as the archbishop of Canterbury. As archbishop, Anselm entered into a time of great strife with King William II, the successor of William the Conqueror, over the church's independence of the king's control (*see* INVESTITURE CONTROVERSY). In and out of England, in exile in Italy, Anselm led a life of conflict with the secular powers. Despite these power struggles, he continued his theological speculations, writing *Cur Deus Homo* (Why God Became Man), a study of the incarnation and crucifixion of Christ as a way of atoning for sin (*see* ATONEMENT).

In 1100, when Henry I succeeded to the English throne, Anselm returned to Canterbury. Controversy with the king continued over investiture, with another period of exile for Anselm. Anselm returned to Canterbury in 1106, where he died on April 21, 1109. He was canonized in 1163 and declared a Doctor of the Church in 1720. His feast day is April 21. D.J.F.

ANSHAN, also An-shan, city, NE China, in Liaoning Province, near Shenyang (Mukden), one of China's leading industrial centers. The integrated iron and steel complex here, one of the world's largest, processes iron ore mined in the region; other important manufactures of the city include chemicals and machinery.

Anshan was founded in 1387 and was fortified in the 16th century. After suffering extensive damage during the Boxer Rebellion (1900) and the Russo-Japanese War (1904–5), the city was rebuilt with broad avenues. Modern industrialization, begun in 1918, accelerated after the Japanese occupied (1931) NE China. Anshan was severely damaged again during the Sino-Japanese War (1937–45), and it was looted of industrial equipment by Soviet forces toward the end of World War II. The city was reconstructed in the 1950s with technologically advanced industrial facilities. Pop. (1987 est., greater city) 1,270,000.

ANSKI, Shloime, pseudonym of SOLOMON SEINWIL RAPOPORT (1863–1920), Russian writer. He became best known for his works in Yiddish. An authority on Jewish folklore, he wove folk materials into his otherwise realistic stories, of which the best known is *Between Two Worlds, or The Dybbuk* (1916; trans. 1926). He adapted it to the stage, and the play has been used as the basis for operas. His poem *Die Shvueh* (The Oath) was set to music and became the theme song of Russia's Jewish Socialist party.

ANSON, Cap, real name ADRIAN CONSTANTINE ANSON (1851–1922), American professional baseball player, born in Marshalltown, Iowa. From 1876 to 1878 he played various infield and outfield positions for the Chicago club of the National League. From 1879 to 1897 Anson managed the team, and under his guidance the Chicago club won five pennants. Known especially as a hitter, he was the National League batting champion four times. He had a lifetime batting average of .339. He was posthumously elected to the Baseball Hall of Fame in 1939.

ANSON, George, Baron Anson (1697–1762), British naval officer, born in Shugborough, Staffordshire. He joined the British navy in 1712. In 1740, during the war with Spain known as the War of Jenkins's Ear, he sailed to the Pacific Ocean with seven vessels and preyed on Spanish colonies and commerce. He returned with only one ship in 1744, but brought back a fortune in Spanish treasure, having circumnavigated the globe in three years and nine months. Anson was made rear admiral in 1744. In 1747, after he had defeated the French off Cape Finisterre during the War of the Austrian Succession, he was created a peer. In 1761 Anson was made admiral of the fleet.

ANT, common name for social insects of the family Formicidae, in the order Hymenoptera (q.v.), which also includes the bees and the wasps. Unlike bees and wasps, some species of which are solitary, all ants are social, living in organized colonies. True ants are to be distinguished from the so-called white ants, or termites, constituting the separate order Isoptera (*see* TERMITE).

In most ant species, males remain winged throughout life, and females are winged until after mating. Certain wingless females, called workers, are usually infertile. The fertilized female becomes the queen of the colony, with the main function of laying eggs. The males die after mating, and the workers gather food, care for the young, and defend the colony. The nests of many species of ants commonly consist of chambers and galleries excavated under stones or logs or underground; some species construct their nests in mounds of earth and vegetable matter or in decayed trees.

The ant family contains more than 4500 described species, widely distributed in temperate and tropical countries. The ant body consists of head, thorax, and abdomen, with the abdomen articulated to the thorax by means of an abdominal pedicel, or stalk.

Development. The four life stages of an ant are egg, larva, pupa, and adult. The minute white or yellowish eggs laid by the queen hatch in two to six weeks and develop into white larvae, or grubs. After feeding a few weeks to several months larvae become pupae, commonly but incorrectly called ant eggs. In some species the pupae are naked, and in others they are covered with cocoons spun from a substance that they secrete at the end of the larval stage. After the pupal stage, during which no food is taken, the adults appear. During development the immature ants are fed, cleaned, and attended by the adult workers. As in all insects with a complete metamorphosis, the ant has attained its full size when it leaves the pupa stage. Left to themselves, males generally die after fertilizing the queens in the nuptial flight, and queens and workers may live for several years. Queens of some species of the genus *Formica* are known to live longer than 15 years.

Food. Ants are generally omnivorous; some species, however, eat only certain specialized foods. Most ants build some sort of nest and store food there. A few species have developed highly specialized agricultural or pastoral habits. *Pogonomyrmex barbatus* of the central U.S. and Mexico frequents fields of grass, harvesting and storing the grass seeds. Some species of the widely distributed harvester ants, which gather grain for food, have developed specialized workers, sometimes called soldiers, with enlarged jaws, and these soldiers do virtually nothing but crack the seeds for the other ants to eat. Ants of the genus *Atta* of the southeastern U.S. and tropical America cultivate inside their nests a species of fungus that is used as food by the colony. The tropical American species are called the leaf-cutting ants, as the workers cut off pieces of leaves, which are carried back to the nest and used to fertilize the fungus gardens.

Many ants eat a sweet fluid, called honeydew, that is excreted by aphids. Some species actually keep and protect the aphids and care for their eggs. Honeypot ants of the genus *Myrmecocystus* of the southwestern U.S. store honeydew, utilizing certain workers as living containers for the fluid. These workers are fed enormous quantities of honeydew; their bodies become so greatly distended that they are unable to crawl about. They remain motionless in the nest, disgorging droplets of food as required.

Many ants practice trophallaxis, an associa-

Army ants, Eciton burchelli, *on the march in the Costa Rican rain forest.*
© Gary Retherford–Photo Researchers, Inc.

tion which involves complex forms of reciprocal feeding and the exchange of chemical stimulation. While feeding the larvae, the worker ants obtain from the surface of the larvae's bodies a salivary secretion that the workers eat avidly. The attraction of such metabolic products for the workers is considered to be the basis for the care of the young and for the organization and unity in the insect colony.

Activities. Colonies of ants usually establish one dwelling or nest. A few types, notably the army and driver ants of the subfamily Dorylinae, are nomadic with nesting phases. The nest of the doryline ants is an open mass formed by the clustered bodies of up to a few million workers hanging from the underside of a raised log or other surface and enclosing the queen and brood. The activities of ant communities are characterized by a certain degree of division of labor, which in some cases involves a permanent functional differentiation among members of the colony. In certain harvester ants, for example, only the large-headed workers crack seeds. More frequently, however, the division of labor is a relative matter, as in most species of carpenter ants of the genus *Campanotus.* The largest workers of these species predominate in defense, the intermediate-sized ones in foraging, and the smallest in brood-tending, but all castes are capable of all types of activity. In many species of campanotine and myrmecine ants, individual workers may be temporarily specialized for foraging or brood-tending.

Like social insects in general, ants may be termed industrious, although colony activity varies from a high degree of intensity at certain times of the day (usually early morning and late afternoon, or early evening in nocturnal ants) to lethargy at other times, as through midday or in the early hours before dawn. Activity in Temperate Zone ants also varies seasonally, from a high level in midsummer to dormancy in winter. Lasting individual differences are present within the worker population of certain species; some are characteristically energetic while others are sluggish.

Some ants, especially those in the genus *Formica,* are capable of learning to find their way through fairly complex mazes, and they normally utilize this ability in establishing individual foraging routes from the nest. The learning capacity of ants is rigidly limited, however, and in contrast to mammalian learning is stereotyped and restricted. The complexities of ant organization that seem so remarkable to humans are actually a series of simple cues and responses (*see* ANIMAL BEHAVIOR).

In foraging from the nest, some ants, including the army and the driver ants, operate in definite columns following chemical trails; others vary in the individual use of cues, for example, the direction and plane of polarization of light. Many ants function only through subterranean galleries, many are strictly arboreal, but commonly the species range both above and below the surface of the earth. Communication among ants is highly efficient and is conducted mainly through tactual and chemical means, although some species exhibit vibratory and even auditory processes. Typically a "finder" ant arouses the colony, and excited nestmates may be influenced in their direction of progress from the nest by one means or another, according to species. For example, in the diminutive reddish-yellow Pharaoh ant, *Monomorium pharaonis,* common in kitchens, the excited finder in returning to the nest incidentally releases a track of chemical secretion that directs others to the food. Usually the excitement of the finder is greater when larger concentrations of food are discovered, and thus correspondingly greater numbers of nestmates are stimulated to forage.

The nests of many ants are inhabited by various beetles and other insects called myrmecophiles, or ant lovers, which are continuous residents; such insects range from definite parasites to somewhat beneficial types. Many ants live as temporary or permanent social parasites in the colonies of other ant species. The Amazon ant, *Polyergus breviceps,* carries out forays against other ants and brings back to the home nest some of the unconsumed brood to serve as slaves when they are mature. These slave ants perform the work of the Amazon colony, including excavation and brood-tending. Other slave-making ants include the sanguinary ant, *F. sanguinea.*

Ant Pests. In the U.S., one of the most harmful pests among the ants is the black imported fire ant, *Solenopsis richteri,* a small stinging ant of the subfamily Myrmicinae that was introduced accidentally from South America, presumably at Mobile, Ala. The large mound communities of this pest disrupt mechanized farming and damage crops. The tiny black ant, *M. minimum,* and its close relative, the sugar ant, infest households in the U.S. In the northern states the carpenter ant, *C. pennsylvannicus,* is another common intruder around dwellings. Ants of this species usually gnaw out the galleries and chambers of their nests in wood initially infested by beetles. Also common in the north is the pavement ant, *Tetramorium çaespitum,* native to the Near East but now cosmopolitan. The bulldog ant, which is indigenous to Australia, has large workers more than 2.5 cm (1 in) in length. These ants have a formidable sting and often build mounds of considerable height.

Most widely known of the American army ants is the tropical species *Eciton burchelli,* the workers of which include the major, or soldier, type. The major has huge hook-shaped mandibles and a potent sting. Each day colonies of this species organize a swarm raid that may have a front almost 14 m (more than 45 ft) wide and that advances at a rate of about 30 cm (12 in) a minute. These ants capture, tear, and carry back to their bivouac any insect or other arthropod, such as roaches and tarantulas, that cannot escape them. At times, nestling birds, cornered snakes, or other small animals are killed by stinging. Driver ants in the African genus *Dorylus* carry out comparable swarm raids, which usually begin in the early evening. Many arthropods and other prey are captured and torn up. Small forest mammals or domestic stock that are cornered in pens and unable to escape the ants are sometimes included in the kill.

The economic significance of ants is difficult to judge. Thus the carpenter ants, which must be considered destructive to wood, actually may contribute to forest economy by hastening the breakdown and recycling of timber previously infested by other insects. Also, the many ants that gather seeds are destructive to agriculture when they become excessively numerous around grain fields or storage centers, but normally their presence may favor good production by opposing the increase of injurious parasitic beetles. Ants such as aphid-tending species of *Lasius* are frequent pests around lawns and gardens; however, the great benefit of these and other ants in aerating and mixing the soil must also be considered. Further, important contributions to forest economy in tropical and subtropical areas may be made by the predatory driver or army ants; they

Leaf-cutting ant, Atta cephalotes, *in Costa Rica.*
© Gary Retherford–Photo Researchers, Inc.

are highly effective exterminators of other, more damaging, insects and are not always unwelcome in human dwellings. T.C.S.

For further information on this topic, see the Bibliography in volume 28, section 466.

ANTA. *See* AMERICAN NATIONAL THEATRE AND ACADEMY.

ANTACIDS, drugs that diminish abnormal acidity in the digestive tract or in the various secretions of other organs. Those that unite directly with free acid in the stomach are known as direct antacids. These include ammonium carbonate, magnesia, potassium bicarbonate, limewater, and chalk. So-called remote antacids, such as the acetates, citrates, and tartrates of the alkalies, act by being changed into carbonates, thus increasing the alkalinity of the blood. Some drugs, such as the carbonates or bicarbonates of sodium, potassium, calcium, magnesium, and lithium, act as both direct and remote antacids.

ANTAKYA. *See* ANTIOCH.

ANTALCIDAS (fl. 4th cent. BC), Greek naval commander and statesman, born in Sparta. In 387 BC he concluded successful negotiations with the Persian king Artaxerxes II (r. 404–358? BC) for aid to Sparta in its war against Athens. In return, Persia received Spartan recognition of Persian supremacy over the Greek cities in Asia Minor. He then commanded the Spartan fleet in battles near the Hellespont (modern Dardanelles) in which the Athenians were driven from the Aegean Sea, and in 386 BC he imposed a peace, known as the Peace of Antalcidas, upon Athens.

ANTANANARIVO, formerly TANANARIVE, city, capital of Madagascar and of Antananarivo Province. It is situated in the central part of the island of Madagascar, on the slopes of a rocky ridge that rises to about 1435 m (about 4700 ft). The city is the chief economic, cultural, and administrative center of the country. It is the trade center for a rice-growing region, and industries here manufacture processed food, tobacco products, textiles, and leather goods. The city has an international airport and has rail links with Toamasina (Tamatave), a seaport on the Indian Ocean. The University of Madagascar (1961), including a museum of art and archaeology, and an astronomical observatory are in Antananarivo.

The city was founded as a fortress in the early 17th century by the Merina rulers, who made it their chief residence in the 1790s; their large palace still overlooks the city from the top of the ridge. The community grew in importance as the Merina dynasty, notably Radama I (c. 1793–1828), gained control of most of the island in the 19th century. The French captured the city in 1895, and subsequently it became the capital of the French dependency of Madagascar. It continued as capital when the country achieved independence in 1960. The city was known as Tananarive until 1977. Pop. (1986 est.) 703,000.

ANTARCTICA, fifth largest of the earth's seven continents, located almost entirely S of lat 66°30′ S (the Antarctic Circle), and surrounding the South Pole. It is mostly circular in shape with a long arm—the Antarctic Peninsula—reaching out toward South America, and with two large indentations, the Ross and the Weddell seas and their ice shelves. Its total area is about 14.2 million sq km (about 5.5 million sq mi) in summer. During the winter Antarctica doubles in size because of the large amount of sea ice that forms at its periphery. The true boundary of Antarctica is not the coastline of the continent itself but the Antarctic Convergence, which is a sharply defined zone in the S extremities of the Atlantic, Indian, and Pacific oceans between about lat 48° S and lat 60° S. At this point the colder waters flowing N from Antarctica mix with warmer waters moving S. The Antarctic Convergence marks a definite physical difference in the oceans. For these reasons, the water surrounding the Antarctic continent is considered an ocean in itself, often known as the Antarctic, or Southern, Ocean.

Antarctica has no native population. Its residents are scientific and support staffs who usually stay no more than a year at a time. The first person born in Antarctica was Emilio Palma, on Jan. 7, 1978, the son of the commander of Argentina's Esperanza Base.

Antarctica is more than 95% ice covered and contains about 90% of the world's fresh water. Because of its thick ice cover, it is the highest of all continents, with an average elevation of more than 1600 m (about 5250 ft). The highest point on the continent is Vinson Massif (5140 m/16,864 ft); the lowest point appears to be the Bentley Subglacial Trench (2499 m/8200 ft below sea level) in West Antarctica. This trench is covered with more than 3000 m (more than 9840 ft) of ice and snow. Lower points may exist under the ice, but they have not yet been discovered.

Seven nations have announced territorial claims to parts of Antarctica. Since the Antarctic Treaty of 1961 these claims have been held aside in the interests of international cooperation in scientific research. Neither the U.S. nor the USSR made a claim to Antarctica, and the claims to Antarctica made by Norway, France, Australia, New Zealand, Chile, Great Britain, and Argentina are not recognized.

THE NATURAL ENVIRONMENT

Antarctica exists today in an ice age. Future economic development of the ice-covered landmass

The Ellsworth Mts., between the West Antarctica ice plateau and the Ronne and Filchner ice shelves, are the highest mountains in Antarctica, exceeding 4572 m (15,000 ft). U.S. Navy

is highly unlikely. Resource exploitation on the continental shelf is possible, but certainly not for many years to come. Currently, the marine life—whale and krill, for example—in the oceans surrounding Antarctica is being developed economically.

Geologic History. Antarctica was a central part of the former supercontinent Gondwanaland. As Gondwanaland broke apart during the late Mesozoic and early Cenozoic eras (some 100 million years ago) to form the continents of the southern hemisphere, Antarctica drifted from the Tropical Zone to its present polar position.

Physiographic Regions. Antarctica consists essentially of two geologic areas. The larger of these, East Antarctica, which is located mostly in the eastern hemisphere, is probably a Precambrian shield covered by thousands of meters of ice. West Antarctica, lying mostly within the western hemisphere, appears to be a continuation of the Andes of South America; glaciologists and geologists speculate that West Antarctica would become an island archipelago if the ice cover were removed.

The two areas of Antarctica are separated by the Transantarctic Mts., an uplift zone of mountains that extends across the entire continent, although portions are buried under the ice cover. Within these mountains are found many coal deposits and fossil remains related to the earlier tropical climate of Antarctica.

In East Antarctica the geologically stable Precambrian shield is generally covered by sedimentary or igneous deposits. The geologic structure of West Antarctica is less well known, but at least two active volcanoes are found in the area, the higher of which is Mt. Erebus (3794 m/12,448 ft). Antarctic soils are classified as dry polar desert soils, and their occurrence is limited to the several deglaciated (ice-free) valleys or oases and to parts of the N Antarctic Peninsula.

Drainage and Water Resources. The ice cover of Antarctica is continuously moving. Great ice rivers drain the interior of the continent and form the ice shelves. Coastal valleys drain parts of the mainland into the sea. Large tabular icebergs are formed as the edges of the ice shelves and glaciers calve off into the sea. Ice also extends over vast areas of the sea in the form of permanent floating ice shelves; the largest of these formations, the Ross Ice Shelf, is the size of the state of Texas.

The snow and ice of Antarctica are the purest in the world. The general isolation of Antarctica

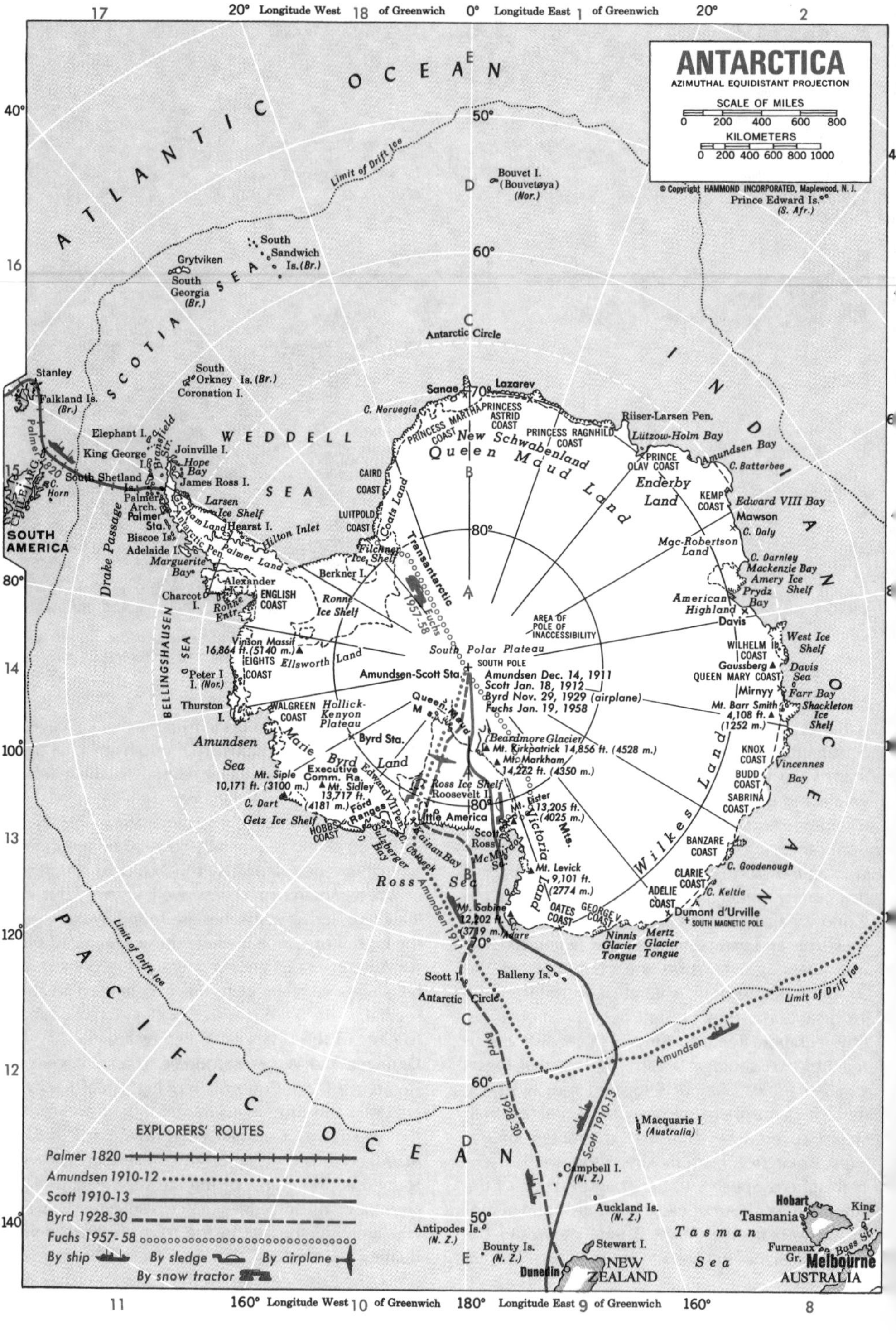
ANTARCTICA
AZIMUTHAL EQUIDISTANT PROJECTION
SCALE OF MILES
0 200 400 600 800
KILOMETERS
0 200 400 600 800 1000
© Copyright HAMMOND INCORPORATED, Maplewood, N. J.
20° Longitude West 18 of Greenwich 0° Longitude East 1 of Greenwich 20°
160° Longitude West 10 of Greenwich 180° Longitude East 9 of Greenwich 160°
ATLANTIC OCEAN
INDIAN OCEAN
PACIFIC OCEAN
SCOTIA SEA
WEDDELL SEA
BELLINGSHAUSEN SEA
Limit of Drift Ice
Antarctic Circle
Bouvet I. (Bouvetøya) (Nor.)
Prince Edward Is. (S. Afr.)
South Sandwich Is. (Br.)
Grytviken
South Georgia (Br.)
South Orkney Is. (Br.)
Coronation I.
Stanley
Falkland Is. (Br.)
Elephant I.
King George I.
South Shetland Is.
Joinville I.
Hope Bay
James Ross I.
Bransfield Str.
C. Horn
SOUTH AMERICA
Drake Passage
Palmer Arch.
Palmer Sta.
Biscoe Is.
Adelaide I.
Marguerite Bay
Larsen Ice Shelf
Hearst I.
Hilton Inlet
Graham Land
Antarctic Pen.
Palmer Land
Alexander I.
Charcot I.
ENGLISH COAST
Ronne Entr.
Berkner I.
Ronne Ice Shelf
Filchner Ice Shelf
Coats Land
CAIRD COAST
LUITPOLD COAST
C. Norvegia
Sanae
Lazarev
PRINCESS MARTHA COAST
PRINCESS ASTRID COAST
PRINCESS RAGNHILD COAST
New Schwabenland
Queen Maud Land
Riiser-Larsen Pen.
Lützow-Holm Bay
Amundsen Bay
PRINCE OLAV COAST
C. Batterbee
Enderby Land
KEMP COAST
Edward VIII Bay
Mawson
C. Daly
Mac-Robertson Land
C. Darnley
Mackenzie Bay
Amery Ice Shelf
Prydz Bay
American Highland
Davis
West Ice Shelf
WILHELM II COAST
Gaussberg
Davis Sea
QUEEN MARY COAST
Mirnyy
Farr Bay
Shackleton Ice Shelf
Mt. Barr Smith 4,108 ft. (1252 m.)
KNOX COAST
Vincennes Bay
BUDD COAST
SABRINA COAST
Wilkes Land
BANZARE COAST
C. Goodenough
CLARIE COAST
C. Keltie
ADELIE COAST
Dumont d'Urville
SOUTH MAGNETIC POLE
Mertz Glacier Tongue
Ninnis Glacier Tongue
GEORGE V COAST
OATES COAST
Transantarctic Mts.
AREA OF POLE OF INACCESSIBILITY
South Polar Plateau
SOUTH POLE
Amundsen-Scott Sta.
Amundsen Dec. 14, 1911
Scott Jan. 18, 1912
Byrd Nov. 29, 1929 (airplane)
Fuchs Jan. 19, 1958
Vinson Massif 16,864 ft. (5140 m.)
EIGHTS COAST
Ellsworth Land
Peter I I. (Nor.)
Thurston I.
WALGREEN COAST
Hollick-Kenyon Plateau
Queen Maud Mts.
Beardmore Glacier
Mt. Kirkpatrick 14,856 ft. (4528 m.)
Mt. Markham 14,272 ft. (4350 m.)
Marie Byrd Land
Byrd Sta.
Amundsen Sea
Mt. Siple 10,171 ft. (3100 m.)
Executive Comm. Ra.
Mt. Sidley 13,717 ft. (4181 m.)
C. Dart
Getz Ice Shelf
HOBBS COAST
Ford Ranges
Edward VII Pen.
Sulzberger Bay
Ross Ice Shelf
Roosevelt I.
Little America
Kainan Bay
Colbeck
Scott
Ross I.
McMurdo Sd.
Mt. Lister 13,205 ft. (4025 m.)
Victoria Land
Mt. Levick 9,101 ft. (2774 m.)
Ross Sea
Mt. Sabine 12,202 ft. (3719 m.)
C. Adare
Scott I.
Balleny Is.
Macquarie I. (Australia)
Campbell I. (N. Z.)
Auckland Is. (N. Z.)
Antipodes Is. (N. Z.)
Bounty Is. (N. Z.)
Stewart I.
Dunedin
NEW ZEALAND
Tasman Sea
Hobart
Tasmania
King I.
Furneaux Gr.
Bass Str.
Melbourne
AUSTRALIA
Palmer 1820
Amundsen 1911
Amundsen
Byrd 1928-30
Scott 1910-13
Fuchs 1957-58
EXPLORERS' ROUTES
Palmer 1820
Amundsen 1910-12
Scott 1910-13
Byrd 1928-30
Fuchs 1957-58
By ship
By sledge
By airplane
By snow tractor

INDEX TO MAP OF ANTARCTICA

from the remainder of the world has allowed it to avoid the industrial pollution common to the other continents. This ice and snow are readily available to be converted into water for human use. Most scientific stations use snow melters to heat the ice and convert it to water for station use.

Climate. Antarctica is the coldest continent. The lowest temperature ever recorded anywhere on earth, −88.3° C (−126.9° F), was on Aug. 24, 1960, at the Soviet Union's Vostok Station. The continent is also characterized by heavy winds. In the interior, winds as high as 320 km/hr (200 mph) have been recorded. These winds flow downslope from the interior toward the coast and, combined with the low temperatures, create dangerous wind-chill conditions.

Three basic climatic regions can be distinguished in Antarctica. The interior is characterized by extreme cold and light snowfall; the coastal areas are characterized by somewhat milder temperatures and much higher precipitation rates; and the Antarctic Peninsula is characterized by a warmer and wetter climate, with above-freezing temperatures common.

Antarctica can be classified as a true desert; in the interior the average annual precipitation (in water) is only about 50 mm (about 2 in). Raging blizzards often occur, however, when winds pick up previously deposited snow and move it from place to place. Annual precipitation is much heavier along the coast, amounting to about 380 mm (about 15 in) in water. Here, heavy snowfalls occur when cyclonic storms pick up moisture from the surrounding seas; this moisture freezes and is deposited as snow over the coastal areas. Along the Antarctic Peninsula, especially the N end, rain is as common as snow.

The interior of Antarctica has almost continuous daylight during the austral summer and darkness during the austral winter. In coastal areas, which are farther N, long periods of sunshine occur during the summer, but sunrises and sunsets occur during much of the rest of the year.

Vegetation. The few plants that survive in Antarctica are restricted to the small ice-free areas. The continent has no trees, and vegetation is limited to about 350 species, mostly lichens, mosses, and algae. Lush beds of such vegetation exist in parts of the Antarctic Peninsula, and lichens have been discovered growing on isolated mountains within 475 km (295 mi) of the South Pole. Three species of flowering plants are also found on the Antarctic Peninsula.

Animal Life. No land-based vertebrate animals inhabit Antarctica. Invertebrates, especially mites and ticks, which can tolerate the lower temperatures, exist in the Antarctic Peninsula but are still considered rare. The surrounding ocean, however, abounds in living creatures. Large numbers

Adélie penguins, Pygoscelis adeliae, *on an ice floe in Antarctica.*

of whales feed on the rich marine life, especially krill, a tiny, shrimplike animal. Six species of seals (including the crabeater, elephant, and leopard) and about 12 species of birds live and breed in the Antarctic. The most prominent inhabitant of the Antarctic is the penguin, with a population numbering in the millions. A flightless bird, it lives in the pack ice and the oceans around Antarctica and breeds on the land or ice surfaces along the coast. Most typical are the Adélie and emperor penguins.

Mineral Resources. Antarctica is thought to have large deposits of valuable mineral resources. Coal in commercially attractive deposits has been found, but no other minerals are known to exist in potentially useful amounts. Large deposits of oil and natural gas are believed to exist in Antarctica's continental shelf.

EXPLORATION

Antarctica was not discovered until the early 19th century, largely because of its remoteness from the other continents. The ancient Greeks first theorized the existence of Antarctica when they realized that the southern hemisphere must have large continents to balance those in the northern hemisphere. The British explorer Capt. James Cook was the first explorer to cross the Antarctic Circle in the 1770s, but even though he circumnavigated Antarctica, he never sighted the continent. From deposits of rock in icebergs at sea, Cook realized that a southern continent existed, but it was not the lush, populated place some had expected.

Early Exploration. From 1819 to 1821 a Russian expedition under the naval officer and explorer Fabian von Bellingshausen circumnavigated Antarctica and discovered some offshore islands. Probably the first parties to sight the continent were that of the American sealer Nathaniel Palmer (1799–1877) and that of the British naval officers William Smith and Edward Branfield (c. 1795–1852), each of which sailed near the tip of the Antarctic Peninsula in 1820. The first known landing was made on Feb. 7, 1821, by another American sealer, Capt. John Davis. In 1823 the British whaler James Weddell (1787–1834) discovered the sea that bears his name and penetrated to the southernmost point that any ship had then reached.

Not until the 1840s, however, was Antarctica's continentality established. Three separate national expeditions—a French expedition under

Jules Dumont d'Urville, a British expedition under Sir James Ross, and an American expedition under Capt. Charles Wilkes—sailed along enough coastline to realize that the ice-covered land they saw was truly a continental landmass.

From the late 19th century until World War I, numerous expeditions visited Antarctica. With the encouragement of the International Geographical Congress, expeditions were sent out by several different nations, including Belgium, commanded by Adrien de Gerlache (1866–1934); Britain, commanded by Robert Scott and Carsten Borchgrevink (1864–1934); and Germany, commanded by Erich von Drygalski (1865–1949). Gerlache took his expedition, the first truly scientific Antarctic expedition, to the Pacific Ocean side of the Antarctic Peninsula, became caught in the ice, and spent the winter of 1897–98 there. The Borchgrevink expedition landed men at Cape Adare in 1899 and became the first group to spend the winter on land. The Scott expedition (1901–4) used Ross Island in McMurdo Sound as a base and explored the Ross Ice Shelf and Victoria Land. Drygalski, who was a geophysicist, led an expedition (1901–3) to the Indian Ocean coast of Antarctica. Both Scott and Drygalski carried captive balloons and used them for aerial observation of the surface of Antarctica. Also in the Antarctic at this time were privately sponsored expeditions from Sweden under Otto Nordenskjöld, from Scotland under William Bruce (1867–1921), and from France under Jean Charcot (1867–1936).

Attaining the South Pole. The search for the South Pole was the dominant theme in the next series of Antarctic expeditions. From 1907 to 1909 Sir Ernest Shackleton led a British expedition to within 156 km (97 mi) of the South Pole before turning back because of exhausted supplies.

A second British expedition went into the field in 1910 under Robert Scott, as did a Norwegian expedition under Roald Amundsen. Using dogs to haul their sledges, Amundsen and a party of four reached the South Pole on Dec. 14, 1911. Scott's party of five reached the pole on Jan. 18, 1912, after hauling their sledges by hand over the roughest part of their route. All of Scott's party died on the return journey after the Norwegians successfully returned to their base. Shackleton returned to Antarctica in 1914 to attempt a crossing of the continent, but his ship, *Endurance*, became trapped in the ice and was crushed. Shackleton and his men made their way across ice floes to Elephant Island and were finally rescued in August of 1916.

Aerial Exploration. In the 1920s aviation came to Antarctica. The Australian Sir George Wilkins and the American C. B. Eielson became the first to fly an airplane over the continent when they explored the Antarctic Peninsula from the air in 1928. The American explorer Richard E. Byrd established a large camp—Little America—on the Ross Ice Shelf in early 1929 and in November flew to the South Pole. Byrd returned to Antarctica in 1934 with another expedition. Both expeditions included a scientific research staff.

Other aviation expeditions included those of Lincoln Ellsworth, an American, who flew across the continent in 1935; the Norwegians, who conducted extensive exploration along the coastlines; the Germans, who sent an aviation expedition in 1938–1939; and the American U.S. Antarctic Service Expedition in 1939–41.

Following World War II, the U.S. sent the largest expedition ever to Antarctica. More than 4000 men participated in Operation Highjump with some 13 ships and more than 20 airplanes. Much of the coast was photographed by air for the preparation of maps.

Recent Activities. Long-term systematic exploration and scientific investigation of Antarctica began with the International Geophysical Year (IGY)—July 1, 1957 to December 31, 1958. Twelve nations established more than 60 scientific stations in Antarctica during the IGY and visited most parts of the continent. When the IGY came to a close, the 12 nations decided to continue their research during a year of International Geophysical Cooperation. Representatives of the 12 nations met in Washington, D.C., in 1959 to draft and sign the Antarctic Treaty, which dedicated the entire continent to peaceful scientific investigation; it came into effect in 1961, suspending all territorial claims. In 1991, 24 nations approved a protocol to the treaty that would ban oil and other mineral exploration for at least 50 years.

For additional information on individual explorers, see biographies of most of those whose names are not followed by dates.

SCIENTIFIC RESEARCH

Significant scientific research has been accomplished in Antarctica, including studies of glaciology, meteorology, geomagnetism, international weather control, seismology, and ionospheric physics. The nutrient-rich oceans that surround Antarctica are an important focus of research. Biologists have discovered that fish in Antarctic waters have an antifreeze component to their blood that allows them to live in subzero temperatures. Studies conducted on the life cycles of penguins, seals, and krill (a potential world food source) have provided much new information on the ecology of these species. Internationally-conducted studies have resulted in an improved understanding of krill reproduction and allowed scientists to improve their predictions of safe limits for krill harvesting.

Geologists have now visited most exposed rock areas of the continent, increasing knowledge of the basic geologic structure and history of Antarctica. Glacial geologists studying the remains of past glaciers have discovered that Antarctica once contained much more ice than it now does. Fossil finds in Antarctica have included such achievements as the 1982 discovery of the first mammal remains found there and in 1986 of the first dinosaur fossil. Such fossils have by now provided a nearly complete sequential record of the breakup of the ancient supercontinent Gondwanaland. Volcanologists have extensively studied Mt. Siple and the active volcano Mt. Erebus. Geologists have collected thousands of meteorites (including a few rare moon fragments), which are especially valued for having been preserved in ice with little weathering or other deterioration.

The ice cover itself has long been the subject of intense study. Glaciologists from several countries have employed modern methods of investigation such as radio glaciology to obtain information on the landscape under the ice cover and to discover large lakes between the earth and the bottom of the ice. Satellites have been utilized to plot the slow movement of the ice surface. Ice cores drilled from Antarctica, including a complete core to the bottom of the Ross Ice Shelf and one through the ice of West Antarctica at Byrd Station, enabled French, Russian, and American scientists to trace changes in the continent's climate over a period of tens of thousands of years. French scientists have put radio transmitters on icebergs to plot their movement, and Australian and Saudi Arabian officials have considered the possibility of towing icebergs to arid regions for fresh water.

Continuous weather records by meterologists have been taken for some 25 years and are providing an understanding of Antarctica's function in world climate. One such contribution has been the discovery, first noted by British scientists in 1985, that a so-called ozone hole develops each Antarctic spring in the stratosphere high above the continent and then more or less disappears by the end of the season. The meaning of this reduction in the ozone layer (q.v.) in the vicinity of the South Pole continues to be studied. It may be partly a natural phenomenon, but evidence indicates that the ozone loss is also related to the problem of the release of fluorocarbons into the atmosphere.

Physicians have made discoveries about the behavior of viruses in a cold isolated environment. Psychological and sleep studies are frequently conducted during the winter, when Antarctica is isolated from the outside world. P.J.A.

For further information on this topic, see the Bibliography in volume 28, sections 1252, 1255.

ANTARCTIC CIRCLE, parallel of latitude on the surface of the earth at 66°30′ S. It marks the N limit of the area in which the sun does not rise on the summer solstice (about June 21) or set on the winter solstice (about December 21). Periods of continuous night or day increase from one day at the Antarctic Circle to six months at the South Pole (*see* SOLSTICE).

ANTARCTIC PENINSULA, northernmost tip of Antarctica, explored (1820) by the American Nathaniel Palmer (1799–1877). Directly S of South America, the peninsula is flanked on the E by Weddell Sea and on the W by Bellingshausen Sea. It was originally called Palmer Peninsula by the Americans and Graham Land by the British, who claimed the peninsula as part of the Falkland Islands Dependencies. Since 1964 the peninsula has been called the Antarctic Peninsula. The N part of the peninsula is called Graham Land; the S part, Palmer Land.

ANTARES, also Alpha Scorpii, first-magnitude variable binary star in the constellation Scorpio. One of the reddest bright stars, Antares is classed as a supergiant, having a diameter of about 482,800,000 km (about 300,000,000 mi), more than 300 times that of the sun. It is approximately 400 light-years from the earth.

ANTEATER, any of three genera of insect-eating mammals of the Central and South American family Myrmecophagidae, of the order Edentata. Anteaters have a long head with a long, tubular mouth and long tongue, but no teeth. Each genus contains a single species. The giant anteater, *Myrmecophaga tridactyla,* weighing up to 23 kg (50 lb), is the largest. It lives in forests and on open plains and is mainly diurnal. The coarse coat is gray, with a white-bordered black stripe on each shoulder, and the tail is long and bushy. The front claws, used to tear open termite hills and for defense, are so long that they are tucked under, and the animal walks on its knuckles. The long tongue flicks rapidly in and out of the small mouth opening, scooping up termites or other insects on its sticky surface.

Cyclopes didactylus, known as the pygmy anteater, is the smallest of the family (about the size of a squirrel) and is covered with golden-brown fur. Its jaws curve to form a short tube, and it eats only termites. Completely arboreal, it has a prehensile tail. *Tamandua tetradactyla,* the lesser anteater, is the size of a large domestic cat and

Giant anteater, Myrmecophaga tridactyla, *in Mato Grosso, Brazil.*
© François Gohier–Photo Researchers, Inc.

has short, coarse, tan to blackish hair, usually with a black band around body and neck. It also lives in trees but frequently comes down to the ground. Both the pygmy and the lesser anteater are nocturnal and walk on the sides of their front feet because of their claws.

All three species are characterized by solitary habits and a low reproductive rate. The female carries the single young on her back during its growth; in the case of the giant anteater, this can last almost one year. Other, unrelated mammals called anteaters are the aardvark, echidna, pangolin (qq.v.), and numbat, or banded anteater, a marsupial.

ANTELOPE, common name applied to a large group of hollow-horned ruminants of the family Bovidae (q.v.), which also includes cattle, goats, and sheep. The group comprises about 150 species, of which most are found in Africa and the remainder in Asia. No true antelope is native to the Americas. The closest relative in the U.S. is the Rocky Mountain goat (q.v.), known as a goat antelope because it has structural characteristics of both the goat and the antelope.

Antelope range in size from the tiny royal antelope, which stands about 25 cm (about 10 in) high at the shoulder, to the giant eland (q.v.), sometimes about 2 m (about 6 ft) in height and weighing up to about 680 kg (about 1500 lb). The corkscrew horns of a large African antelope, the kudu (q.v.), grow up to about 1.5 m (about 5 ft) in length. Unlike the deer, which they resemble in body and in habits, antelope have unbranched, hollow horns that are never shed. Antelope are generally swift, and some species are the fastest of the quadrupeds, attaining speeds of 97 km/hr (60 mph). Antelope are often brilliantly colored and may live in open plains, marshes, deserts, or forests, according to the species. Some are solitary, but many species travel in herds.

The term *antelope* does not designate a sharply defined group; members of the group are included in all the five subfamilies of Bovidae: the Bovinae, the Cephalophinae, the Hippotraginae, the Antilopinae, and the Caprinae. Antelope of the subfamily Bovinae are the oxlike giant eland; the kudu; the broad-horned, elusive bongo; the East African dik-dik, smallest of the antelope; the shy four-horned antelope; the marshbuck, or sitatunga; the nyala; and the nilgai, or blue bull, which is revered in India for its color. The subfamily Cephalophinae contains the numerous small duikers (*see* DUIKER). When frightened, they dive through the bushes and then stand on their hindlegs to look around.

The subfamily Hippotraginae contains the waterbuck (q.v.), which takes to the water when pursued; the water-loving lechwe; the kob, which has lyre-shaped horns; the straight-horned gemsbok (q.v.); the large, glossy sable antelope; the oryx and the addax (q.v.) of the southern Sahara; the blesbok (q.v.), with green-tinged, yellow-tipped horns; the ungainly, long-faced hartebeest (q.v.); and the buffalo-headed gnu (q.v.).

The subfamily Antilopinae contains the small antelopes: the surefooted klipspringer (Afrik., "rock jumper"), the spike-horned grysbok, the suni, and the tiny royal antelope, which, despite its small size, can leap about 3 m (about 9 ft). In addition, the subfamily contains the black buck of India, the graceful impala (qq.v.), and the numerous gazelles (*see* GAZELLE), such as the springbok and the gerenuk, or Waller's gazelle,

The impala, Aepyceros melampus, *is one of the most common African antelope, ranging from Kenya to South Africa. Males have distinctive lyre-shaped horns.*
L. Nielsen–Peter Arnold, Inc.

which stands on its long hindlegs to eat the leaves of trees.

The subfamily Caprinae contains the Siberian saiga, an antelope with a very large nose and with horns that the Chinese grind and use as medicine. Also of the subfamily are the goat antelopes, such as the chamois (q.v.) of the European mountains, the American Rocky Mountain goat, and the large, golden takin of the high Himalaya.

ANTENNA, in electronics, device used to propagate radio or electromagnetic waves or to capture radio waves. Antennas are necessary to transmit and receive radio, television, microwave telephone, and radar signals. Most antennas for radio and television consist of metal wires or rods connected to the transmitter or receiver. When an antenna is used for transmission (propagation) of radio waves, electric currents are made to oscillate along the wires or rods by the transmitter. Energy from this oscillating charge is emitted into space as electromagnetic (radio) waves. When an antenna is used for reception, these waves induce a weak electric current in the antenna wire or rod. This current is amplified by the radio receiver. An antenna can generally be used for reception and transmission on the same wavelength if transmission power is not too great.

The dimensions of an antenna usually depend on the wavelength, or frequency, of the radio wave for which the antenna is designed. Frequency is the number of electromagnetic oscillations per second. The length of a radio wave is equal to the speed of light (300 million m/sec) divided by the frequency. Thus, low-frequency waves have long wavelengths (hundreds of meters); high frequency waves have short wavelengths (centimeters). The length of an antenna must be such that it resonates electrically at the desired wavelength, just as the length of an organ pipe determines its pitch. The basic antenna length must be at least half the wavelength of the radio waves it is designed to transmit or receive. It can also be an integral multiple of the one-half wavelength, that is, 1, 1.5, 2, 2.5, etc., wavelengths. Those with such dimensions are called resonant antennas. A resonant antenna is an efficient propagator and receptor of electromagnetic energy at its design wavelength. The half-wavelength dimensional rule applies to all antennas except wire loop antennas. Small loop antennas used in transistor radios are resonant at the long, 300-m wavelengths of the broadcast

(AM) band because they contain a core of magnetic material called ferrite. Ferrite loop antennas are used in ultracompact transistor radios.

Electric energy is fed to an antenna by means of a transmission line, or coaxial cable, with two conductors. If one conductor is connected to a grounding cable and the other to the end of a horizontal wire antenna, the antenna is said to be an end-fed long wire. If the antenna is split in the middle, with each side connected to one conductor of the transmission line, the antenna is called a dipole, the simplest and most fundamental antenna. The familiar "rabbit-ear" television antenna is a dipole.

A dipole transmits or receives most of its energy at right angles to the wire; little energy is transferred along the length of the wire. Such directivity is one of the most important electric qualities of an antenna. It allows transmission or reception to be beamed in a particular direction, to the exclusion of signals in other directions.

A second fundamental quality of an antenna is its gain, or sensitivity. Gain and directivity can be controlled by carefully spacing numerous dipole elements to make a single antenna array.

A third characteristic of antennas is their bandwidth, or resonance to signals covering a band of wavelengths. Ordinary home radio antennas must have broad bandwidths in order to receive stations of different wavelengths. Helical antennas used for space communications have very narrow bandwidths and high gain.

Vertically positioned antennas include the Marconi, or ground plane, antenna. It is usually a quarter-wave vertical rod, or whip, representing one-half of a vertical dipole, with the ground acting as the other half. Such whip antennas are widely used in high frequency mobile communications. The metal body of the automobile acts as the other half of the dipole. Long wave vertical antenna types include the half-wave used by broadcast (AM) band transmitting stations. The antenna is the entire transmitting tower. Large horizontal rhombic antennas give good directivity at long wavelengths; they are used for international radio communications.

Radio telescopes and radar systems operate at wavelengths shorter than 30 cm, called microwaves. Microwaves behave much like light waves, and microwave antennas are similar to spotlights. The microwave source can be a small dipole or the opening of a special tubing called a wave guide. Microwave energy is reflected from a metallic paraboloid that shapes it into a narrow beam. Many sophisticated radar antennas have been developed. Some of these can change their beam direction electrically, without motion.

ANTHEIL, George (1900–59), American composer, born in Trenton, N.J., and trained at the Sternberg Conservatory in Philadelphia and privately under the Swiss-American composer Ernest Bloch. In 1921 Antheil went to Europe, becoming prominent in the musical avant-garde of France. On his return to the U.S. in 1933 he became associated with motion picture companies as composer and associate producer. His works include *Ballet mécanique* (1925), the score of which includes airplane propellers and electric bells, and the operas *Transatlantic* (1930) and *Volpone* (1953). He also wrote sonatas, quartets, and symphonies. His autobiography, *Bad Boy of Music*, appeared in 1945.

ANTHELMINTIC DRUGS, medicinal drugs used to rid humans or other host animals of infestations by parasitic worms such as tapeworms, roundworms, pinworms, trichinae, flukes, whipworms, schistosomes, and filariae. These drugs are also known as vermifuges. They act by attacking the worms' neuromuscular or respiratory systems, interfering with their metabolism, or making them more susceptible to attack by the host's macrophages. Anthelmintics include mebandazole, pyrantel, diethylcarbamazine, and niclosamide, among several others. The drugs are generally more effective against gastrointestinal infestations than muscular infestations.

ANTHEM, English-language choral composition with a nonliturgical religious text, one of the principal forms of Protestant church music. It developed in 16th-century England as an Anglican counterpart to the motet, sung in Latin during Roman Catholic services. A "full anthem" is for unaccompanied chorus throughout; an example is "Sing Joyfully," by the English composer William Byrd. A "verse anthem" alternates soloist and choir and often has instrumental accompaniment; an example is "This Is the Record of John," for tenor, chorus, and viols, by the English composer Orlando Gibbons. The term *anthem* sometimes refers to secular ceremonial hymns.

ANTHOCYANINS. *See* PIGMENT.

ANTHOLOGY (Gr., "flower gathering"), book consisting of a series of literary selections, usually from various authors and usually of literary value. Such collections have been compiled since antiquity, the first important Greek anthology being that compiled by the philosopher and poet Meleager of Gadara (c. 140–70 BC), about 90 BC. He included in it poems by himself and 46 earlier Greek poets. This collection was added to by four successive editors; in its most extended form, as edited by the 18th-century French scholar Philippe Brunck (1729–1803), it is known as the *Anthologia Graeca* and is still a standard source of Greek poetry. In 1573, during the Renaissance, the French classicist Joseph Justus Scaliger edited, in imitation of the Greek anthology, an anthology of ancient Latin poems. The Arabic, Persian, and Turkish literatures are rich in anthologies. Tatar, Indian, and Chinese anthologies also have been compiled.

The first anthology of English poetry to be published was *Tottel's Miscellany* (1557), compiled by the English publisher Richard Tottel (1525?-94). Significant in the history of anthologies is the *Golden Treasury of English Songs and Lyrics* (1861), compiled by the English poet and critic Francis Turner Palgrave (1824-97), which reflects the tastes and attitudes of the Victorian era. A notable series of English anthologies of world verse and prose has been published throughout the 20th century, beginning with *The Oxford Book of English Verse* (1900; 1939). This was brought up to date by *The New Oxford Book of English Verse 1250-1950* (1972). Others in the series are *The Oxford Book of American Verse* (1950), edited by the American scholar and critic F. O. Matthiessen (1902-50), and *The Oxford Book of French-Canadian Short Stories* (1983).

Anthologies of other literary genres include such works as the multivolume Best American Plays series, and *Documents of American History* (1934; 9th ed., 1974), edited by the American historian Henry Steele Commager, which reprints examples of significant legislation and speeches.

ANTHONY, Saint (251?-c. 350), Egyptian hermit, first Christian monk. As a wealthy young man of 20 he was impressed by the Christian teaching found in Matt. 19:21: "Go, sell what you possess and give to the poor, and you will have treasure in heaven." He dispersed his inheritance and went to live as an ascetic. His "temptations" as a solitary hermit have become a subject for art; his visions attracted followers, and he devoted several years to the instruction of these disciples in monastic life. He did not, however, compile the rule that governed the community thus formed. This was written after Anthony's death by St. Athanasius, Anthony's biographer and personal friend. Anthony left his retreat on various occasions. In about 311 he aided the Christians in Alexandria persecuted by the Emperor Maximin (d. 313), and in 350 he joined Athanasius in the fight against Arianism. St. Anthony's type of asceticism, based on eremitism or solitude, is one of the two strains in monasticism; the other is typified by the communal rule of St. Benedict of Nursia. His feast day is January 17.

ANTHONY, Mark. *See* ANTONY, MARK.

ANTHONY, Susan B(rownell) (1820-1906), outstanding American reformer, who led the struggle to gain the vote for women. She devoted 50 years to overcoming the nation's resistance to woman suffrage (q.v.), but died before the 19th Amendment was adopted (Aug. 26, 1920).

Early Life. Anthony was born on Feb. 15, 1820, in the village of Adams, Mass., the second of eight children. In 1827 her family moved to Battenville, N.Y., and in 1845 settled permanently in Rochester, N.Y. Encouraged by her father, a onetime schoolteacher, Anthony began teaching school when she was 15 years old and continued until the age of 30.

A liberal Quaker and dedicated radical reformer, Anthony opposed the use of liquor and advocated the immediate end of slavery. From 1848 to 1853 she took part in the temperance movement and from 1856 to 1861 worked for the American Anti-Slavery Society, organizing meetings and frequently giving lectures. In 1863, during the American Civil War, she founded the Women's Loyal League to fight for emancipation of the slaves. After the end of Reconstruction she protested the violence inflicted on blacks and was one of the few to urge full participation of blacks in the woman suffrage movement.

Fight for Women's Rights. Anthony's work for women's rights began in 1851, when she met Elizabeth Cady Stanton. From 1854 to 1860 the two concentrated on reforming New York State laws discriminating against women. Anthony or-

Susan B. Anthony Chicago Historical Society

ganized women all over the state to campaign for legal reforms. She would often deliver speeches written by Stanton, who was occupied with her young children.

Anthony and Stanton became convinced that women would not gain their rights or be effective in promoting reforms until they had the vote, and nationwide suffrage became their goal after the Civil War. In 1869 they organized the National Woman Suffrage Association to work for a constitutional amendment giving women that right. Although the newly freed slaves were granted the vote by the 15th Amendment, women of all races continued to be excluded. From 1868 to 1870 Anthony and Stanton published a newspaper, *Revolution,* focused on injustices suffered by women. To dramatize her fight, Anthony defiantly registered and cast a ballot in the 1872 presidential election and, when arrested and convicted, refused to pay the $100 fine. She went to Europe in 1883, met women's rights activists there, and in 1888 helped form the International Council of Women, representing 48 countries. At the age of 80 she resigned as president of the National American Woman Suffrage Association, but she continued to be a regular speaker at its conventions until her death in Rochester, N.Y., on March 13, 1906.

Evaluation. Anthony always acknowledged Stanton as the founder of the women's rights movement. Her own achievement lay in her inspiration and perseverance in bringing together vast numbers of people of both sexes around the single goal of the vote. On July 2, 1979, the U.S. Mint honored her work by issuing the Susan B. Anthony dollar coin. P.G.H.

For further information on this person, see the section Biographies in the Bibliography in volume 28.

ANTHONY OF PADUA, Saint (1195–1231), Franciscan monk, born in Lisbon. He became an Augustinian monk at the age of 15 and ten years later joined the Franciscan order, becoming a provincial, or administrator of a group of monasteries, for that order in 1227. He taught theology in the large cities of Italy and France and preached in those areas, especially in the vicinity of Padua, Italy. In 1230 he resigned his provincialship to devote more time to preaching. The year after his death he was canonized by Pope Gregory IX; in 1946 he was named Doctor of the Church. Anthony is the patron saint of Padua and of Portugal and the saint invoked for the finding of lost articles. His feast day is June 13.

ANTHRACITE (Gr. *anthrax,* "coal"), hard coal with the highest fixed-carbon content and the lowest amount of volatile material of all types of coal (q.v.). It contains approximately 87.1% carbon, 9.3% ash, and 3.6% volatile matter. Anthracite is glossy black, with a crystal structure and conchoidal, or shell-like, fracture. It is used mostly as a fuel and as a source of industrial carbon (*see* ENERGY SUPPLY, WORLD). Although harder to ignite than other coals, anthracite releases a great deal of energy when burned and gives off little smoke and soot. Anthracite was formed primarily at the end of the Carboniferous period by a series of movements of the earth that generated heat and pressure that transformed the carbonaceous material then present in the earth.

In the U.S., 97% of anthracite is found in eastern Pennsylvania, where these coal beds constitute an area of about 1243 sq km (about 480 sq mi), primarily around Wilkes-Barre, Scranton, Hazleton, and Pottsville. The world's leading producers are, in order, China, the former USSR, North Korea, South Korea, Spain, and Germany.

ANTHRACNOSE. *See* DISEASES OF PLANTS.

ANTHRAX, contagious disease of warm-blooded animals, including humans, caused by the bacterium *Bacillus anthracis.* One of the oldest known diseases, it was once epidemic and still appears in many world areas, but only sporadically in the western and southern U.S. It was the first disease for which the causative organism was isolated, by C. J. Davaine (1812–82) in 1863, for which a pure culture was obtained, by Robert Koch in 1876, and for which an effective vaccine was developed, by Louis Pasteur in 1881.

Animals acquire the disease from drinking water draining from contaminated soil, in which the organism may live for years; from eating infected carcasses and feedstuffs; and from the bites of bloodsucking insects. The disease, sometimes manifested by staggering, bloody discharge, convulsions, and suffocation, may be fatal almost immediately in acute cases and within three to five days in subacute cases. Death is caused by toxemia. Preseasonal inoculations and antibiotics are effective.

In humans, the disease appears in both external and internal forms, with a death rate of about 20 percent. The external or cutaneous form is contracted through cuts or abrasions in the skin by those who handle infected hides and carcasses and may be self-limiting, but often disseminates into the bloodstream, with fever and prostration. It is characterized by malignant pustules on exposed skin areas. The internal type is acquired by inhaling anthrax spores, as from animal hair and wool, which invade the lungs and sometimes the intestinal tract to cause hemorrhage. It is speculated that an intestinal variety may be caused by consuming contaminated meat or milk. Workers exposed to animal products, especially wool, are protected by vaccination. Penicillin and tetracyclines are effective in treatment except in rapidly progressing cases.

ANTHROPOLOGY, study of human beings from a biological, social, and humanistic perspective. The field is generally divided into two major areas: Physical anthropology deals with the biological evolution and the physiological adaptations of humans; sociocultural anthropology concerns the ways in which people live in society—that is, the ways in which their language, culture, and customs develop.

Anthropology is fundamentally cross-cultural. Most early anthropological research studied non-European peoples and cultures, but a great deal of recent research has focused on modern settings. Anthropologists are firmly devoted to fieldwork, emphasizing firsthand experience and immersion in people's lives and activities.

HISTORY

From ancient times, travelers, historians, and scholars have studied and written about cultures that were exotic or different from the ways of life that they knew. The Greek historian Herodotus traveled widely among different cultural groups, observing and analyzing their ways of life. As do modern anthropologists, he interviewed "key informants," and he was acutely aware of the significance of differences among cultures in such aspects as family organization and religious practices. Much later the Roman historian Tacitus, in his book *Germania* (about AD 98), described the character, manners, and geographical distribution of the German tribes.

In the Middle Ages a few individuals traveled in many lands and recorded what they saw and heard. The most famous was the Italian adventurer Marco Polo, who chronicled his travels (1271–95) through China and other parts of Asia, providing a wide range of information about the peoples and customs of the Far East.

During the Age of Discovery, which began in the 15th century, new fields of knowledge were explored. The discovery of the diverse peoples and cultures of the New World, Africa, South Asia, and the South Seas introduced revolutionary ideas about human cultural and biological history. In the 18th century scholars of the French Enlightenment, such as A. R. J. Turgot and the Marquis de Condorcet, began theorizing about long-term evolution and the development of human civilization from its earliest stage. These anthropological-philosophical views clashed with the biblical account of creation and with the theological dogma that the simpler cultures and peoples were remnants of groups that had fallen from God's grace and degenerated to a "primitive" condition.

During the 19th century the discoveries of a Neanderthal fossil in Germany (1856) and the remains of Java Man (in the 1890s) gave impressive evidence of an extremely long process of human evolution. Other archaeological finds—such as masses of ancient stone tools found near Paris by the Abbé Boucher de Perthes—testified to a long, slow development of human prehistory, perhaps lasting hundreds of thousands of years.

Anthropology emerged as a distinct field of study in the mid-19th century. In North America the founder of the discipline was Lewis Henry Morgan, who did major research on the Iroquoian Confederacy. Morgan later set out a general theory of cultural evolution as a gradual progression from "savagery" to "barbarism" (marked by simple domestication of animals and plants) to "civilization" (begun with the invention of the alphabet). In Europe the founding figure was the British scholar Edward B. Tylor, who elaborated a theory of human evolution with special concentration on the origins of religion. Tylor, Morgan, and their contemporaries emphasized the rationality of human cultures and theorized that everywhere human culture evolves into more complex and developed forms. Also in the mid-19th century major foundations for scientific archaeology were developed, especially by the Danish archaeologists at the Museum of Northern Antiquities in Copenhagen. From systematic excavations they discovered the sequential development of tools from Stone Age to Bronze Age to Iron Age.

Applied anthropology began in the 19th century with such organizations as the Aborigines Protection Society (1837) and the Ethnological Society of Paris (1838). These societies worked to arouse the European conscience against such cruelties as the vast inhumanity of the slave trade and the slaughter of aboriginal peoples in Australia and the Americas.

PHYSICAL ANTHROPOLOGY

Physical anthropology, a major area of study and experimentation, is primarily concerned with human evolution, human biology, and the study of other primates.

Evolution of Humans. One branch of physical anthropology is now widely known because of the work of a family of paleoanthropologists: Louis S. B. Leakey, who was Anglo-Kenyan; his wife, Mary, who was British; and their son, Richard, Kenyan. Their discovery during the 1960s of a series of fossils in Olduvai Gorge in East Africa led to major revisions in the understanding of human biological evolution. Fossil remains un-

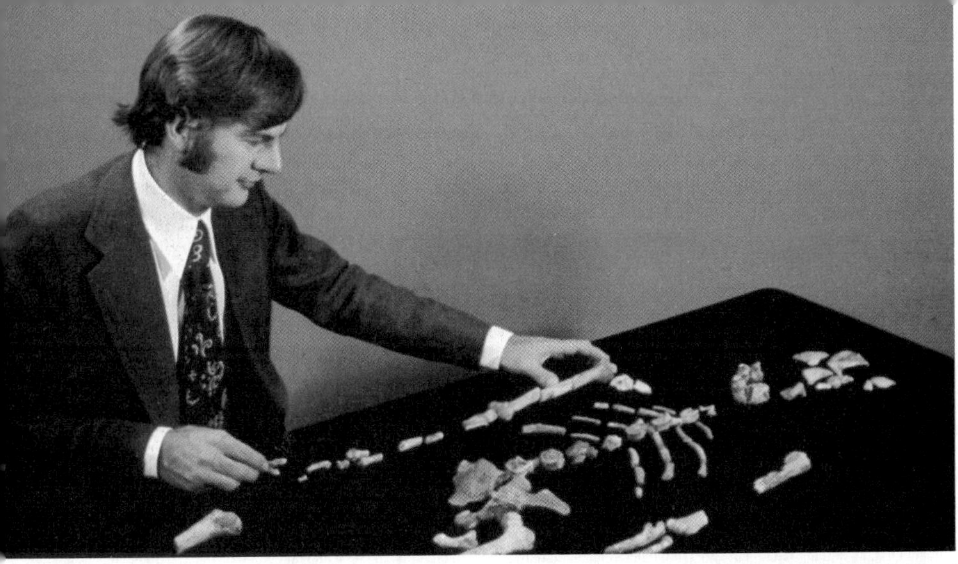

American anthropologist Donald C. Johanson displays the female skeleton, believed to be about 3.7 million years old, that he found in Ethiopia in 1974. Such discoveries help to trace the genealogy of the human species. Cleveland Museum of Natural History

earthed in the late 1970s and '80s have provided further evidence that in the period from 1 to 3 million years ago the genus *Homo* ("true human") coexisted in East Africa with other advanced man-ape forms known as australopithecines. Both of these hominids appear to be descendants of an Ethiopian fossil, *Australopithecus afarensis,* 3 to 3.7 million years old (the famous "Lucy," a skeleton found in 1974). These ancient ancestors of humans had the legs and body for walking bipedally, which freed the hands for manipulating objects. A recently discovered set of remains from the Olduvai Gorge, uncovered by researchers from the University of California, adds further weight to the view that human evolutionary progression was quite uneven. This new fossil, approximately 1.8 million years old, includes arm and leg bones that give evidence of relatively advanced upright, bipedal locomotion, but small brain size and indications of marked differences in stature between males and females, not much different from "Lucy."

Crude stone artifacts found with some *Homo* fossils in the East African sites demonstrate toolmaking and tool-using capabilities going back nearly 3 million years. This technical ability contributed to the apparent evolutionary success—hence the name *Homo habilis* ("handy human"). Compared with the vegetarian australopithecines, the *Homo habilis* ancestors of modern human beings appear to have been developing toward considerable meat eating, judging from the conformation of the teeth and evidence of tool use.

As the number and variety of hominid fossil discoveries have accumulated, it seems that Africa, rather than Asia, is the probable center of earliest human evolution. The newest *Homo habilis* fossil discoveries suggest a creature (female) only about 91 cm (about 3 ft) tall. The usual brain size of the adult form was about 750 cc (about 46 cu in). The remains of a larger *Homo* species, however, with a brain size averaging more than 900 cc (more than 55 cu in), have been discovered in East Africa, dating from about 1.5 million years ago. This larger protohuman, now usually referred to as *Homo erectus,* spread from Africa to Europe and Asia perhaps a million years ago, with an increasingly diversified toolmaking inventory.

The best known remains of *Homo erectus* are the famous Java Man, formerly known as *Pithecanthropus,* and the equally well-known Peking Man, a collection of skeletal materials found at Zhoukoudian (Chou-k'ou-tien) near Peking, originally labeled *Sinanthropus pekinensis.* Both are much younger than the East African *Homo habilis* materials and date from about 750,000 to 300,000 years ago. The Peking fossils are especially interesting because the brain size is even larger than that of the Java materials, averaging more than 1050 cc (more than 64 cu in), and the skull and other bone materials are slightly more "modern." *Homo erectus* fossils have also been found in Europe and Africa, with many stone tools and other evidence of a simple hunting-gathering culture. At Zhoukoudian the archaeologists found the oldest evidence of human use of fire, as well as indications of cannibalism.

The famed Neanderthal specimens and dozens of similar fossils are believed by some anthropologists to be a direct part of human ancestry;

others believe they were a side branch of *Homo sapiens* that died out tens of thousands of years ago. From 100,000 to 35,000 years ago Neanderthals were a numerous hunting-gathering people in much of Europe and the Middle East. They were robustly built, with heavy brow ridges and an average brain size of about 1500 cc (about 92 cu in), greater than that of most modern *Homo sapiens sapiens*. Some fossils have been found that appear to be intermediate between Neanderthal and *Homo sapiens sapiens*. Such remains may be evidence of "intermarriage" between Neanderthal peoples and the direct ancestors of humans; or they may simply reflect a wide range of variation in a single *Homo sapiens* population. Since the last phases of the Ice Ages, about 20,000 to 10,000 years ago, large numbers of skeletal remains resembling modern humans have been found in Europe and Africa and elsewhere.

The Americas have produced no human skeletal materials older than about 15,000 years, and the few specimens that are several thousand years old are all *Homo sapiens sapiens*. It seems clear that biological evolution leading to modern humanity took place in the Old World. *See also* HUMAN EVOLUTION.

Human Biology. Another major branch of physical anthropology is the study of contemporary peoples and their biological features. Much early study and debate centered on the identification, number, and characteristics of "principal races." As refined techniques were developed for measuring skin and eye color, hair texture, blood type, head shape, and other dimensions, the classification of races became more and more complicated (*see* RACES, CLASSIFICATION OF). Modern theorists hold that any ideas of "pure races" or ancestral archetypes are misleading and mistaken. All humans living today are *Homo sapiens sapiens* and are descended from the same general, complex ancestry. Genetic features have always varied geographically, but in every region genetic inheritance results in "ranges of variation" and intermediate types or combinations. Thus, categorization of people by supposed race is more a social and political than a biological statement. "Oriental," "black," "Hispanic," and "white" are socially defined groupings involving much mixing of genetic qualities with cultural characteristics.

Biological anthropologists later shifted their attention to the complex patterns of human genetics. They have studied the interplay of genetic adaptations with physiological and cultural (nongenetic) adaptations in illness, malnutrition, and environmental stresses such as high altitudes and hot climates. Medical and nutritional anthropologists combine biological-genetic perspectives with cultural and social data in studying illnesses such as hypertension and diabetes and in investigating growth and development under varying circumstances of nutrition and health.

One recent Nobel Prize winner, the American physician Daniel Carleton Gajdusek (1923–), gained particular attention for his discovery that the mysterious wasting sickness called kuru, found only among an isolated people in highland New Guinea, was caused by a slow virus (which he isolated and identified) that was communicated through cannibalistic practices. Some biological anthropologists have traced the genetic patterns and other features of such diseases as sickle-cell anemia, thalassemia, and diabetes.

Study of the Primates. Since humans are primates, with biological cousins among the apes and monkeys, the study of the behaviors, population dynamics, dietary habits, and other qualities of baboons, chimpanzees, gorillas, and similar primates is an important comparative dimension of anthropology. British anthropologist Jane van Lawick-Goodall and her colleagues have spent years observing the free-ranging chimpanzees in a national park in Tanzania. They discovered that chimpanzees are capable of using simple tools—notably small sticks to "fish" for termites and ants—and can throw stones and sticks effectively. In a famous experiment chimpanzees were observed using heavy sticks in "beating up" a stuffed leopard. They communicate with each other both vocally and physically. Studies of communications patterns and of group life among monkeys and apes provide insights for understanding the remote past of human evolution.

SOCIOCULTURAL ANTHROPOLOGY

A large portion of anthropological research focuses on fieldwork among different cultures around the world. Between about 1900 and 1950 such studies were aimed at recording the variety of human ways of life before the simpler, non-Western cultures were completely engulfed by modernization and Europeanization. Research describing the food production, social organization, religion, clothing and material culture, language, and other aspects of different cultures is referred to as ethnography. The comparative analysis of these ethnographic descriptions, seeking broader generalizations about cultural patterns, dynamics, and worldwide principles, is the study of ethnology (q.v.).

In the second half of the 20th century ethnology (now usually referred to as cultural anthropology) became more and more interwoven with social anthropology, developed by British and French scholars. For a brief period it was hotly

A mock battle in front of the spirit house of the Arapesh tribe, Ilahita Village, New Guinea, is part of a ceremony that initiates boys into manhood.
Malcolm Kirk–Peter Arnold, Inc.

debated whether anthropology should be concerned with the study of social systems or, following the American style, the comparative analysis of cultures. It was soon realized, however, that research in ways of life and behaviors is practically always a combination—hence the present-day label of sociocultural anthropology.

Kinship and Social Organization. One important discovery of 19th-century anthropologists was that kinship relationships form the core and principal substance of social relations in all premodern societies. In many nonindustrial societies, the most important social groups are clans, lineages, and other kinship organizations. When membership in such kinship "corporations" (for instance, the Roman gens) is assigned to persons through the male line only, the system is called patrilineal descent. Before the growth of commerce and large-scale urbanization, many European peoples were organized economically and politically into patrilineal kin groups.

Matrilineal societies, with kin group membership traced through females, are less common. Herodotus was the first scholar to describe such a social system, which he found among the Lycians of Asia Minor. Several well-known American Indian groups have matrilineal kinship systems, including the Iroquois, Cherokee, Creek, Crow, Navajo, and some Pueblo communities in Arizona and New Mexico.

Bilateral kinship organization, in which kinship relations are traced through both maternal and paternal sides of the family, is prevalent both in the simplest hunting-gathering societies (such as the !Kung peoples of the Kalahari Desert in southern Africa and the Inuit, or Eskimo) and in complex societies. Modern North Americans have bilateral kinship systems. (Contemporary Western bilateral kinship, however, is adapted to a social system largely dominated by nonkinship organizations and relationships.) A study of kinship organization in 860 preindustrial societies showed that about 50 percent had patrilineal systems; some 35 percent, bilateral; and 15 percent, matrilineal.

In kinship-based societies, the members of a lineage, clan, or other kin group are usually descendants of a common ancestor. Similarly, groups of lineages may often consider themselves descendants of a common ancestor (such as "the children of Abraham"). This concept allows large numbers of people to be united for warfare or ritual activities, making them distinct from their neighbors and enemies. For example, among some Central Asian "hordes" that for centuries attacked Europe with their swift cavalry, the complex military organization was based on patrilineal kinship.

Voluntary Associations. Some nonindustrial, small-scale cultural groups also have important social groupings not based on kinship. The Plains Indians were famed for their "military societies"—groups of men who fought and celebrated together, and who also assumed some "police" duties in the communally organized buffalo hunts. The Zuñi, Hopi, and other Indian communities of Arizona and New Mexico still have religious fraternities that provide for a richly elaborate ceremonial life. In some West African cultural groups, secret societies exercise social control and recreational responsibilities.

Practically all ethnic and national groups develop special modes of organizations when they migrate into new surroundings. The familiar Sons of Norway, Italian-American clubs, and other ethnic organizations of North America are matched by similar voluntary associations of migrant groups in African and Asian cities.

The Evolution of Political-Social Systems. The simplest human societies are hunting-gathering groups such as the Inuit, Kalahari San, Congo Pygmies, and Australian aborigines. Among these peoples small numbers of families are grouped together into bands—that is, nomadic groups of perhaps 30 to 100 persons, related by kinship and associated with a particular territory.

The few remaining hunting-gathering bands (in remote parts of Africa, India, and the Philippines) are important because they exemplify, in a general way, the state of social organization and culture of 99 percent of all human experience. Their kin relations, religious ideas, methods of health care, and cultural characteristics illustrate the cultural roots of modern humanity.

More complex social and economic systems were not possible until especially favorable food sources allowed early humans to settle in permanent, year-round communities. Then came the crucial breakthrough—although only a moderate change at first—as people learned to domesticate plants and animals for food, transportation, clothing, and other uses.

The Neolithic transition—that is, the beginnings of domestication of food resources—occurred independently in the Middle East and in East Asia about 12,000 years ago, according to the latest archaeological evidence. With greater population concentrations and permanent living sites, social-political organizations developed that linked together numbers of local groups. The new social systems, often encompassing several thousand people in multicommunity tribes, were united by religious ceremonies, food exchanges, and cultural features.

Although small-scale tribes often had no real "central government," increases in populations and food sources led to the need for, and the possibility of, political centralization. Chiefdoms are the small-scale social systems in which food products and political tribute flow to a central leader, or chief, who in turn redistributes the food and tribute to the community members.

The Rise of Nation-States. The origins of nation-states have been much argued. In the prebiblical Middle East, for example, the first city-states developed when population increases led to expanding food needs, followed by the development of irrigation projects to satisfy these needs. This, in turn, led to the growth of military systems to protect these resources. In other instances, location on crucial trade routes—for example, Timbuktu on the Saharan salt-trade route—favored military and administrative centralization.

Ethnological and archaeological studies support the view that states or kingdoms came into existence somewhat differently in different historical and ecological situations; once started, however, kingdoms nearly everywhere displayed certain patterns of growth. Fledgling kingdoms seldom "stand still"; the tendency to engulf neighboring regions—to exploit them economically and to "pacify" potential invaders—is widespread. In the "first civilizations"—in the Middle East, Egypt, northern India, Southeast Asia, China, Mexico, and Peru—military fortifications soon appeared, usually accompanied by temples and other examples of religious ritual that marked the growth of priesthoods. Social stratification, with a small military-religious elite and a large subservient population of peasants and workers, was an inevitable consequence.

Evolution of Religious Systems. The belief systems of simple hunting-gathering bands can be complex with regard to the supernatural world, the "forces of nature," and the behaviors of spirits and gods. Some small-scale societies, however, such as the !Kung peoples of the Kalahari, seem to possess unelaborate ideas about the supernatural, the causes of things, and the hereafter. The Siriono of eastern Bolivia, for example, are reported to be totally vague about where people go after they die.

Small-scale, relatively egalitarian hunting-gathering groups usually lack the extra resources to support full-time religious specialists. All human groups, however, large and small (including modern North American cultural groups), have shamans—men or women thought to have direct contact with supernatural beings and forces, from which they derive power to affect such problems as illness. The shaman (q.v.) is often the only person with a specialized religious role in small-scale societies.

In the lower middle range of cultures—for example, small societies practicing cultivation—communal religious systems involve the people in complex ritual performances, often with a rotation of priestly responsibilities. Where kinship groups are the main elements of social solidarity, religious observances are often centered around family and lineage.

The rise of centralized social systems with social stratification has almost always been accompanied by the development of ecclesiastical religious systems with full-time priests, complex rituals for the entire populace, and increased tendencies to both moral and political rule making. These complex religious systems seldom eliminated either the practices of individualized shamanism (especially for healing of sickness) or the family-centered religious observances that reflect kinship solidarity.

Archaeological evidence from the earliest city-kingdoms testifies to the frequently close partnerships between the ecclesiastical leaders and the leaders of commerce and statecraft, thus emphasizing the conservative aspect of religion. On the other hand, movements of radical social reform have usually been religious, and both in simpler societies and in more complex "civilizations," new religious systems arise regularly whenever some portion of the society experiences severe frustration and hardship. Thus, religion may at times serve the status quo; but some religions are forces of radical change.

Development of Culture. The rather simple schemes of cultural evolution proposed in the 19th century have been debated, elaborated, and modified as new archaeological and ethnological data have come to light. Some leading anthropologists early in the 20th century, such as the German-American Franz Boas and the American Alfred Kroeber, took a strong antievolutionist point of view. They argued that cultural and social processes have been so diverse throughout the world that no general stages or trends could be discerned. That point of view has now been largely discarded.

Two fundamentally different explanations of cultural evolution have been elaborated. The 19th-century evolutionists held that broadly similar processes of cultural growth and elaboration occur in different societies because of a fundamental psychic unity of all humankind. Thus, the parallels in the rise of social stratification and ruling elites, for example, are seen as caused by human mental qualities.

The contrary view, held by increasing numbers of anthropologists, puts primary emphasis on the material conditions of life—the energy sources, technologies, and production systems of human groups. Environmental influences are also stressed, because the growth of complex cultural systems has been especially favored by certain geographical and climatic features. For example, the prehistoric Middle East was rich in varieties of game animals (wild pigs, sheep, goats) and

A family of the Panare Indian tribe of the Guiana Highlands, Venezuela, at camp in the forest. The woman melts wax over a fire for the making of torches.
Jacques Jangoux–Peter Arnold, Inc.

Anthropologist at work among Guatemalan Indians. The work of the anthropologist consists of observing and taking notes on native customs, handicrafts, and practices.
Yoram Kahana–Peter Arnold, Inc.

wild plants that proved especially amenable to domestication.

Most theorists would now agree that material influences—including available energy, technology, and the organization of production (and reproduction)—are major components in cultural evolution and social processes. Still, the force of ideas also looms large; some widely cited examples of the power of ideas are the spread of Islam, the struggle between Communist and non-Communist ideologies, and the influence of commercial advertising.

A comprehensive theoretical approach gradually emerged in anthropology during the 1970s. Usually called ecological theory, this approach requires a holistic, multivariable research strategy. In the spectrum from materialist to mentalist viewpoints, it can be adjusted to various intermediate positions. The American anthropologist Margaret Mead, for example, studied the development of the individual personality under varying social and economic conditions. In general, when the focus is on larger time frames (such as hundreds or thousands of years), the emphasis shifts toward materialistic determinism. Research centered on shorter time spans, including cultural features of modern society, can emphasize symbols and ideas (such as ethnic identity and religious revivalism) and still remain within the ecological framework.

METHODS AND APPLICATIONS

The research methods of anthropologists are as varied as the topics they study.

Archaeological Research. For archaeological anthropologists it is fundamental to establish chronological patterns—the time sequences of past human activities that have left physical remains to be excavated. Of modern methods of dating archaeological remains, the radio-carbon technique is perhaps the most widely used. The basis of this method is that living plants and animals contain fixed ratios of a radioactive form of carbon, known as carbon-14. Carbon-14 deteriorates at a constant rate, leaving ordinary carbon. Measuring the traces of radiocarbon in pieces of charcoal, remains of plants, cotton fibers, wood, and so forth permits fairly accurate assessment of age in materials that are as much as 60,000 to 70,000 years old.

The ages of ancient fossil remains in East Africa, dating from several million years ago, have been established by another powerful radiological tool, the potassium-argon method. Radioactive potassium (potassium-40) breaks down extremely slowly, yielding argon-40.

Time sequences of archaeological remains are still read primarily through meticulous attention to stratigraphy—the time-ordered deposition of soil, organic materials, and remains of human activity. Such deposits gradually build up and cover each preceding phase in any human living site. The techniques used in establishing stratigraphic sequences include soil analysis, geological assessment, and study of animal and plant remains, as well as the detective work of piecing together the remains of floors, storage pits, and other constructions.

Sociocultural Research. In sociocultural anthropology, research rests on the fundamental idea of participant observation in a community or social system. The anthropologist first becomes immersed in the life of the community and, through daily contacts and observations, establishes rapport with the people. This first phase of field research can take weeks, even months, particularly if one must learn the local language. The early ethnographers obtained their data mainly from extensive interviewing of a few key informants—persons who were "experts" about the local culture and social system. These data were cross-checked among several informants and pieced together with the fieldworker's own direct observations.

Research in complex and changing cultural systems, however, requires additional methodological tools. Structured interviews (with samples of people) are now routinely used to obtain focused information about food use, health behavior, economic resources, labor migrations, recreation, and other topics. Meticulous recording of transactions in the marketplace, hours of work, catches of fish and game, and crop yields are used in analyzing economic behavior. Complex psychological tests are employed when the focus turns to questions of personality. Data from church archives, native texts, government reports, and other written sources are also analyzed.

As field data have become more complex and sophisticated, requiring routine management of thousands or even hundreds of thousands of bits of information, archaeologists have turned to computers to map out time sequences, spatial relationships, and other patterns. Trends of cultural change, relationships of economic activities to social interactions, multiethnic interactions, and other complicated patterns are tested with complex statistical methods.

Such technical, quantified research methods have not replaced traditional field-research styles. Rather, detailed interviews of key informants, as well as complex qualitative analysis of symbol systems, ceremonies, and other cultural features, are still essential parts of eclectic, holistic methodology.

CURRENT TRENDS

Anthropology in the 1980s is increasingly an applied science, as researchers concentrate on social issues in areas such as health care, education, environmental protection, and urban development. Many anthropologists are now employed by government agencies, research corporations, Indian tribal governments, and health-care facilities, and much fieldwork is carried out in complex cultural sciences—school systems, citywide health systems, large-scale agricultural development programs, and multicommunity rural regions.

The shift to the study of complex, multicultural systems and the increase in quantified research methods have led to the need for team research. Early research typically involved a lone fieldworker, isolated for months in some remote village; now, however, many field projects consist of several persons, including statistical consultants, both biological and social scientists, and student assistants.

Another significant trend is to work more closely with community people—ethnic organizations, tribal governments, neighborhood health clinics, migrant labor organizations, women's groups, and other special-interest groups—whose activities require up-to-date quantitative and descriptive data. Linguists have worked with Indian organizations and other ethnic groups to help develop bilingual, bicultural school materials.

Anthropologists have traditionally developed social attachments to their research communities as a matter of practical methodology. Those social relationships, in the 1980s, have often become partnerships in which the people in the communities that are studied directly experience at least some benefits of the projects. In turn, these pragmatic applications of anthropological methods lead to new directions in social and biocultural theory.

See also AMERICAN INDIANS. For additional information on individual anthropologists, see biographies of those whose names are not followed by dates. P.J.P.

For further information on this topic, see the Bibliography in volume 28, sections 137–40.

ANTHROPOMORPHISM, attribution of human form or qualities to that which is not human. Specifically, anthropomorphism is the depiction of God in a human image, with human bodily form and emotions, such as jealousy, wrath, or love. Whereas mythology is exclusively concerned with anthropomorphic gods, more sophisticated religious thought holds that it is inappropriate to regard an omnipotent, omnipresent God as human. In order to speak of God, however, metaphorical language must be employed. In philosophy and theology, seemingly anthropomorphic concepts and language are used because it is impossible to think of God without attributing to him some human traits. In the Bible, for example, God is endowed with physical characteristics and human emotions, but at the same time he is understood to be transcendent. In art and literature, anthropomorphism is the depiction of natural objects, such as animals or plants, as talking, reasoning, sentient, humanlike beings.

ANTIAIRCRAFT WEAPONS, ordnance and missiles used defensively to destroy approaching enemy aircraft and missiles.

Before World War II, antiaircraft weapons consisted of standard infantry rapid-fire automatic rifles and .30-caliber and .50-caliber machine guns on mountings designed specially to direct fire against air targets. During World War II special 20-mm, 37-mm, 40-mm, 90-mm, 3-in., and 5-in. antiaircraft guns were developed for use against high-flying aircraft. In order to increase firepower, the U.S. Navy mounted two 20-mm antiaircraft guns, then two 5-in. guns, and later two 40-mm guns and four 40-mm guns on single carriages for simultaneous aiming and firing of all guns on the mount. The U.S. Army used four .50-caliber machine guns on a single carriage, thereby quadrupling the fire output. "Quad 50s" and "twin 40s" were commonly used against both air and ground targets during the Korean and Vietnam wars.

Antiaircraft fire was extremely effective because of the invention during World War II of the proximity fuze, a tiny radar set located in the nose of a shell that detonated the charge when the explosion of the shell could be expected to be most effective against the target.

Antiaircraft gunners in World War II aimed at sight. In order to increase the accuracy of fire, automatic aiming and range-finding systems were developed, culminating after the war in radar-directed systems that aimed and fired the guns automatically. By the 1960s these fire-direction systems had evolved into computer-controlled systems that could digest a great volume of information quickly and could automatically set in motion the appropriate countermeasures.

The development of rocket-propelled missiles after World War II introduced an entirely new dimension in antiaircraft defense. A great many surface-to-air missiles were developed that were capable of intercepting aircraft and ballistic missiles approaching their targets at supersonic speeds. Defending missiles were guided by infrared homing devices attracted by the heat given off by the targets, or by radar receivers in the missile that guided it electronically.

The U.S. Army began developing antiaircraft missiles in 1945. The first missile deployed was the Nike Ajax in 1953, followed shortly by the Nike Hercules; both were designed to provide long-range defense against enemy aircraft and missiles. Later, the Hawk missile was developed to provide shorter-range, tactical air defense. A successor to the Nike Hercules and Hawk systems, the Patriot missile is a mobile, medium- to long-range air defense weapon. Patriot missiles based in Israel and Saudi Arabia intercepted Scud missiles launched from Iraq during the Persian Gulf War (q.v.).

For close-in air defense, automatic weapons and short-range missiles have been developed. The U.S. Army uses the 20-mm Vulcan automatic gun in conjunction with Chaparrals—heat-seeking missiles—for short-range air defense. In the 1970s the U.S. and the Soviet Union developed missiles for use against supersonic aircraft; the U.S. Army's Redeye was a heat-seeking missile that could be launched by one person. In the 1980s the Redeye was replaced by the Stinger missile. M.B.

ANTIBIOTIC (Gr. *anti,* "against"; *bios,* "life"), chemical substance produced by one organism that is destructive to another. This process traditionally has been called antibiosis and is the opposite of symbiosis (q.v.). More specifically, an antibiotic is a type of chemotherapeutic agent, that is, it has a toxic effect on certain types of disease-producing microorganisms without acting dangerously on the patient. Some chemotherapeutic agents differ from antibiotics only in that they are not secreted by microorganisms, as are antibiotics, but rather are made synthetically in a chemical laboratory. Examples are quinine (q.v.), used against malaria; arsphenamine, used against syphilis; the sulfa drugs (q.v.), used against a wide variety of diseases, notably pneumonia; and the quinolones, used against hospital-derived infections (zoonoses). A few antibiotics, among them penicillin (q.v.) and chloramphenicol, have now been produced synthetically also.

History. The first observation of what would now be called an antibiotic effect was made in the 19th century by the French chemist Louis Pas-

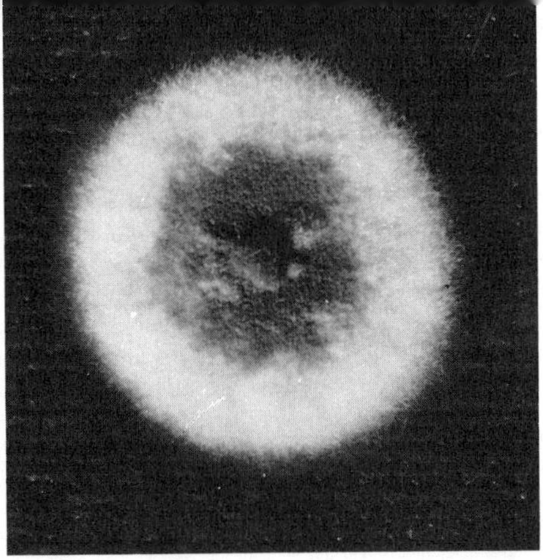

Mold growth of Penicillium chrysogenium, *of which a mutant form now produces most of the world's commercial penicillin.* Chas. Pfizer & Co., Inc.

teur, who discovered that certain saprophytic bacteria can kill anthrax germs. About 1900 the German bacteriologist Rudolf von Emmerich (1852–1914) isolated a substance called pyocyanase, which can kill the germs of cholera and diphtheria in the test tube. It was not useful, however, in curing disease. In the 1920s the British bacteriologist Sir Alexander Fleming, who later discovered penicillin, found a substance called lysozyme in many of the secretions of the body, such as tears and sweat, and in certain other plant and animal substances. Lysozyme has strong antimicrobial activity, but mainly against harmless bacteria.

Penicillin, the archetype of antibiotics, was discovered by accident in 1928 by Fleming, who showed its effectiveness in laboratory cultures against many disease-producing bacteria, such as those that cause gonorrhea and certain types of meningitis and bacteremia (blood poisoning); however, he performed no experiments on animals or humans. Penicillin was first used on humans by the British scientists Sir Howard Florey and Ernst Chain during the 1940–41 winter.

The first antibiotic to be used in the treatment of human diseases was tyrothricin (one of the purified forms of which was called gramicidin), isolated from certain soil bacteria by the American bacteriologist René Dubos in 1939. This substance is too toxic for general use, but it is employed in the external treatment of certain infections. Other antibiotics produced by actinomycetes (filamentous and branching bacteria) occurring in soil have proved more successful. One of these, streptomycin (q.v.), discovered in 1944 by the American microbiologist Selman Waksman and his associates, is effective against many diseases, including several in which penicillin is useless, especially tuberculosis.

Present Use. Since then, such antibiotics as chloramphenicol, the tetracyclines, erythromycin, neomycin, nystatin, amphotericin, cephalosporins, and kanamycin have been developed and may be used in the treatment of infections caused by some bacteria, fungi, viruses, rickettsia, and other microorganisms. In clinical treatment of infections, the causative organism must be identified and the antibiotics to which it is sensitive must be determined in order to select an antibiotic with the greatest probability of killing the infecting organism.

Recent Developments. Strains of bacteria have arisen that are resistant to commonly used antibiotics; for example, gonorrhea-causing bacteria that high doses of penicillin are not able to destroy may transfer this resistance to other bacteria by exchange of genetic structures called plasmids (*see* CONJUGATION). Some bacteria have become simultaneously resistant to two or more antibiotics by this mechanism. New antibiotics that circumvent this problem, such as the quinolones, are being developed. The cephalosporins, for instance, kill many of the same organisms that penicillin does, but they also kill strains of those bacteria that have become resistant to penicillin. Often the resistant organisms arise in hospitals, where antibiotics are used most often, especially to prevent infections from surgery.

Another problem in hospitals is that many old and very ill persons develop infections from organisms that are not pathogenic in healthy persons, such as the common intestinal bacterium *Escherichia coli.* New antibiotics have been synthesized to combat these organisms. Fungus infections (q.v.) have also become more common with the increasing use of chemotherapeutic agents to fight cancer, and more effective antifungal drugs are being sought.

The search for new antibiotics continues in general, as researchers examine soil molds for

The mold growth Streptomyces fradiae, *which is used in the production of the antibiotic neomycin.* Chas. Pfizer & Co., Inc.

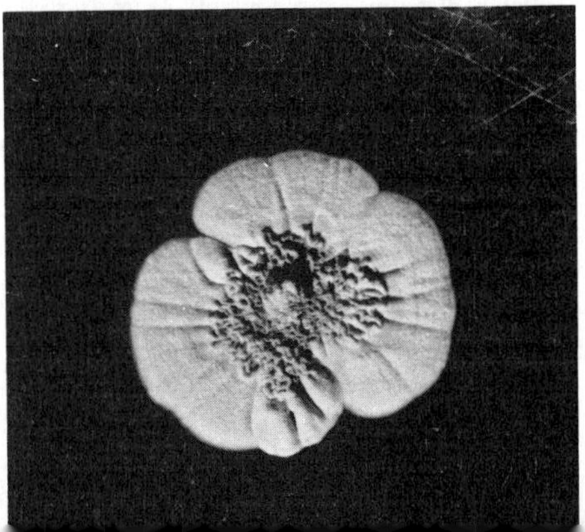

possible agents. Among those found in the 1980s, for example, are the monobactams, which may also prove useful against hospital infections. Antibiotics are found in other sources as well, such as the family of magainins discovered (in the late 1980s) in frogs; although untested in humans as yet, they hold broad possibilities.

Antibiotics have also been used effectively to foster growth in animals. Concern has arisen, however, that this widespread use of antibiotics in animal feed can foster the emergence of antibiotic-resistant organisms that may then be transmitted to human beings. An instance of one such transfer was documented in the U.S. in 1984.

S.A.W.

For further information on this topic, see the Bibliography in volume 28, section 503.

ANTIBODY, any of perhaps a million kinds of normally occurring protein molecules that are produced in the body of cells called lymphocytes and that act primarily as a defense against invasion by foreign substances. An important component of the immune system (q.v.), antibodies are found in the blood of all vertebrates, in the fraction of the blood called gamma globulin.

The synthesis, or manufacture, of antibodies is initiated when a foreign substance, referred to as an antigen (q.v.), enters the body. Lymphocyte cells respond to the foreign substance by making an antibody with a molecular arrangement that fits the shape of molecules on the surface of the substance so that the antibody combines with it. Common antigens are the protein components of bacteria and viruses. These antigens may enter the body during infection or may be deliberately introduced by vaccination (*see* IMMUNIZATION) in order to stimulate the production of antibodies. The binding of antibodies to the surfaces of bacteria, viruses, or toxins (*see* TOXIN) can neutralize and eliminate these harmful substances in any or all of three ways: (1) by directly inactivating them, (2) by enabling other blood cells to engulf and destroy them (*see* PHAGOCYTOSIS), and/or (3) by weakening their surfaces and rendering them vulnerable to destruction by other blood proteins (collectively called complement). Animals do not have antibodies to substances to which they have not been exposed, but one animal is able to produce enough different kinds of antibodies to fit the molecular arrangement of any foreign substance it is likely to encounter.

In diseases such as multiple sclerosis and systemic lupus erythematosus, the body mistakenly makes antibodies against normal tissue components (*see* AUTOIMMUNE DISEASES). Sometimes viruses may disturb the immune mechanism.

The five known classes of antibody are distinguished by the letters M, G, E, A, and D; all are preceded by the abbreviation Ig for immunoglobulin, another name for antibody. IgM is the first antibody made by newborns and the first made during an infection. IgG is the predominant antibody in serum; it is made on the second exposure to an antigen. IgE is associated with allergy (q.v.). IgA is found in saliva and mother's milk. The role of IgD is not known.

A high concentration of one type of antibody is found in the blood of persons with a form of malignant tumor called multiple myeloma. In the 1970s scientists learned how to fuse these myeloma cells with lymphocytes from tissues that had been exposed to an antigen. The resulting hybrid cells ("hybridomas") were able to produce large amounts of antibody of one specific arrangement ("clones"), called monoclonal antibodies. By selecting the appropriate hybridoma, scientists can obtain pure antibody that combines with any chosen foreign substance. The use of monoclonal antibodies has become a valuable tool in biology and medicine because pure lines of antibody can combine with and therefore mark, or identify, the component substances of cells and tissues. Under investigation is the use of monoclonal antibodies for immunization, for typing tissue used in transplants (as blood is now typed in transfusions), and for targeting drugs to specific sites in the body.

For further information on this topic, see the Bibliography in volume 28, sections 443, 448.

ANTICHRIST, opponent or antagonist of Christ; also, a false Christ. In the Bible, the word is used only in the Epistles of St. John, but the concept of an opponent of the Messiah appears in the Old Testament. Its earliest form is probably that of the warrior King Gog, in the Book of Ezekiel. The term *Antichrist* was variously applied by the early Christians to any opponent or enemy of Christ, whether a person or power, or to a false claimant of the characteristics and attributes of Christ. The "false Christs" were predicted by Jesus to precede the coming of the Son of man (see Matt. 24). Opposition to Christ's teaching on the part of the anti-Messiah was also prophesied (see 1 John 2:18). The development of this conception of active hostility is apparent in the Epistles of St. Paul, who bore the brunt of Jewish opposition (see 1 Thess. 2:15). The "man of sin," as Paul saw him, was a Jew, because he would regard the temple at Jerusalem as the seat of God's worship (see 2 Thess. 2:3, 4).

In the Book of Revelation, Antichrist is identified with paganism. Different interpreters have at various times identified the Antichrist with the Roman emperors Nero, Diocletian, Julian, and

Caligula; with the Samaritan sorcerer Simon Magus (see Acts 8:9–24); and with Muhammad, the founder of Islam. At the time of the Reformation, Protestants quite generally held the pope to be the Antichrist, and Roman Catholics regarded Martin Luther similarly. In the controversy between the Roman church and the Greek church, the name was applied, by those who opposed them, to popes and Byzantine emperors.

ANTICOSTI ISLAND (Fr. *Île d'Anticosti*), island of SE Québec Province, Canada, in the Gulf of Saint Lawrence, at the mouth of the Saint Lawrence R. The low-lying, heavily forested island is about 220 km (about 137 mi) long and has an area of 7941 sq km (3066 sq mi). From 1926 to 1974 it was owned by a private pulp and paper corporation, and pulpwood cutting remains the principal industry of the island. The first European to visit Anticosti Island was the French explorer Jacques Cartier, in 1534. Pop. (1981) 275; (1986) 335.

ANTIDOTE, drug or other remedy that counteracts the effects of a poison. It may neutralize the poison chemically, as bicarbonate taken as an antidote for acid; it may render the poison insoluble and therefore harmless, as Epsom salt as an antidote for lead; it may absorb the poison, as charcoal as an antidote for alkaloids; it may coat the stomach, as olive oil as an antidote for ammonia poisoning; or it may produce a physiological effect opposite that of the poison, as strong coffee as an antidote for morphine. *See* POISON.

ANTIETAM, BATTLE OF, important battle of the American Civil War. About 50,000 Confederate troops led by Gen. Robert E. Lee attempted an invasion of the North. They were intercepted on Sept. 17, 1862, near Sharpsburg, Md., by a Union army of 70,000 men under the command of Gen. George Brinton McClellan. In the ensuing action, the Union army suffered approximately 12,000 casualties, including 2108 killed; at least 2700 Confederate soldiers were killed, and about 10,000 were wounded or missing. Lee's army retreated across the Potomac River the following day, making the outcome technically a Union victory. The name of the battle is derived from Antietam Creek, near the battle area; the area was designated a national battlefield site in 1890. Antietam National Cemetery is in the vicinity.

For further information on this topic, see the Bibliography in volume 28, section 1155.

ANTIFREEZE, chemical substance added to a liquid to lower its freezing point. It prevents the freezing of the coolants used in airplane, automobile, and tractor engines, in refrigeration liquids, and in snow-melting and deicing agents.

The ideal antifreeze should be chemically stable, be miscible in the coolant, have low viscosity and electrical conductivity and a high boiling point, be noncorrosive, and have good heat-transfer properties. The most widely used antifreeze materials in automotive engines today are methyl alcohol, ethyl alcohol, and ethylene glycol; most of them contain a phosphate, nitrate, or other anticorrosive agent.

ANTIGEN, any substance that evokes the production of antibody (q.v.) when introduced into the body of an animal. Antigens can enter the body through the respiratory tract, digestive tract, skin, or blood vessels. The most common antigens are proteins such as those found in bacteria and viruses. *See also* ALLERGY.

ANTIGONE, in Greek mythology, daughter of Oedipus, king of Thebes, and Queen Jocasta. Antigone accompanied her father into exile but returned to Thebes after his death. In a dispute over the throne her brothers, Eteocles and Polynices, killed each other. The new king, Creon, gave Eteocles an honorable burial but ordered that the body of Polynices, whom he regarded as a traitor, remain where it had fallen. Antigone, believing divine law must take precedence over earthly decrees, buried her brother. Creon condemned her to be buried alive. She hanged herself in the tomb, and her grief-stricken lover, Haemon, Creon's son, killed himself. Antigone was the subject of plays by the ancient Greek playwright Sophocles and the 20th-century French playwright Jean Anouilh.

ANTIGONUS II (c. 80–37 BC), king of Judea (40–37 BC), the son of Aristobulus II, of the Hasmonaean dynasty. His father had disputed the royal power with his brother King Hyrcanus II until the Roman general Pompey the Great intervened, captured (63 BC) Jerusalem, and made Hyrcanus high priest. Pompey later (60 BC) took Aristobulus and his sons to Rome as prisoners. After being released, Antigonus, with Parthian aid, drove the Roman governor of Judea, Herod the Great, from Jerusalem in 40 BC and reigned as the last Hasmonaean king until 37 BC. In that year, the Romans, under the Roman orator and general Mark Antony, beheaded him and set Herod on the throne.

ANTIGONUS I, called Monophthalmos ("one-eyed") or Cyclops (382–301 BC), king of Macedonia (306–301 BC). A general of Alexander the Great, Antigonus secured a large part of Asia Minor after the breakup (323 BC) of Alexander's empire. In the ensuing wars with the other successors, or *diadochi,* to the empire, he claimed at various times Syria, Persia, and Greece, as well as Macedonia, and, aided by his son Demetrius I, he also attacked Egypt. Antigonus almost realized the ambition of all Hellenistic monarchs to become the sole successor to Alexander's empire, but Lysimachus (c. 355–c. 281 BC), king of Thrace, and Seleucus I, king of Babylonia, in alliance with other generals, finally defeated and killed him at the Battle of Ipsus, in Phrygia. Demetrius retained Macedonia and the dependent Greek cities for the Antigonid dynasty.

ANTIGONUS II, called Antigonus Gonatus (319?–239 BC), king of Macedonia (283–239 BC). The son of Demetrius I Poliorcetes, Antigonus did not gain full control of Macedonia until 276 BC. During most of his reign, he was at war with other Hellenistic princes, especially Ptolemy II of Egypt, over whom he won naval victories in 258 and 246 BC. He was a patron of learning and the arts.

ANTIGONUS III, called Doson (c. 263–221 BC), king of Macedonia (227–221 BC), the nephew of Antigonus II. He was a usurper of the throne, having deposed the young son of King Demetrius II after Demetrius's death. Antigonus allied himself with the Achaean League against the Spartans, who refused to recognize Macedonian authority over Greece, and defeated them in the Battle of Sellasia (222 BC). He then abolished the monarchy of Sparta and restored ephorian (by five magistrates) rule.

ANTIGUA, also Antigua Guatemala, town, S Guatemala, capital of Sacatepéquez Department, near Guatemala City. Antigua is situated in a narrow valley at the foot of the dormant volcano Agua (about 3752 m/12,310 ft). It is the market town for the surrounding highlands in which fine grades of coffee beans are grown. Wheat, sugarcane, and fruits and vegetables are other important crops. Founded in 1527, Antigua was for more than 200 years the seat of the military governor of the Spanish colony of Guatemala, a large region that included almost all of present-day Central America. The town was almost completely destroyed in 1773 by an earthquake. A number of well-preserved Spanish colonial buildings survive, however, and make the town a tourist attraction. Pop. (1983 est.) 26,631.

ANTIGUA AND BARBUDA, independent island state, West Indies, in the E Caribbean Sea. It consists of three of the Leeward Islands—Antigua and two smaller islands, Barbuda to the N and Redonda, an uninhabited rocky islet, to the SW. The total area is 443 sq km (171 sq mi), and the country had a population (1989 est.) of 78,400. Antigua is a generally low-lying island but rises to 405 m (1330 ft) atop Boggy Peak. Barbuda is a flat coral island with fine beaches. The climate is tropical, but the islands are subject to drought. The country's economy is largely dependent on tourism; also important are the raising of cotton, fruits, and sugarcane. Fishing is important in Barbuda. Manufactures include refined petroleum, rum, clothing, furniture, and electrical equipment. The unit of currency is the East Caribbean dollar of 100 cents (2.69 East Caribbean dollars equal U.S. $1; 1990). Saint John's (pop., 1982 est., 30,000), the capital and principal port, is located on the NW coast of Antigua. The country's people are mostly of African descent.

Christopher Columbus was the first European to land on the island he named Antigua in 1493. Inhabited by Carib Indians, the island was not successfully colonized until 1632, when the British established a settlement. Barbuda was colonized by settlers from Antigua in 1661. From 1958 to 1962 Antigua (which included the dependencies of Barbuda and Redonda) was a member of the Federation of the West Indies. In 1967 it became an internally self-governing state in association with Great Britain. On Nov. 1, 1981, it became the independent state of Antigua and Barbuda. Executive power is nominally invested in a governor-general, who represents the British crown. Actual executive power belongs to a prime minister, who is a member of the parliament.

ANTIHISTAMINE, any drug that blocks the action of histamine (q.v.). Antihistamines are used primarily to control symptoms of allergic conditions such as hay fever. They alleviate runny nose and sneezing and, to a lesser extent, minimize conjunctivitis (q.v.) and breathing difficulties. Antihistamines can also alleviate itching and rash caused by food allergy. Chemically, antihistamines comprise several classes, and a person who does not obtain relief from one type may benefit from another. Side effects of these drugs can include drowsiness, loss of concentration, and dizziness. People taking antihistamines should not drink alcoholic beverages or perform tasks requiring mental alertness, such as driving. Although antihistamines are included in many over-the-counter cold remedies, their usefulness in such preparations is questionable. Antihistamines may relieve symptoms of allergy accompanying a cold, or they may have an anticholinergic effect that dries cold secretions, but they do not have any influence on viral infections, which are the cause of colds (*see* COLD, COMMON). Moreover, the drying effect may be undesirable, especially for persons with bronchial infection, glaucoma, or urinary tract difficulties.

ANTI-LEBANON *or* **ANTI-LIBAN** (Gr. *Antilibanus;* Arab. *Jabal ash-Sharqi,* "Eastern Mt."), mountain range, SW Syria and E Lebanon, about 145 km (about 90 mi) long. The crest of the range forms much of the border between Syria and Lebanon. The range extends from the plain around the Syrian city of Homs in the N to Mt.

Hermon in the S. The Anti-Lebanon is separated from the Lebanon range to the W by a fertile valley, the ancient Coele-Syria (now Bekaa), which lies in both Lebanon and Syria. A railway and road connects Damascus, Syria, to Beirut, Lebanon. Some geographers refer to the two ranges together as the Lebanons. The Anti-Lebanon has few trees and in the N is barren and rocky. The highest peaks are Mt. Hermon (2814 m/9232 ft), which is the source of the Jordan R., and Tal at Musa (about 2669 m/8755 ft). East of the Anti-Lebanon range is the Helbun Valley, the site of the city of Helbon of the Old Testament.

ANTILLES, term applied to the whole of the West Indies (q.v.) except the Bahama Islands. The Greater Antilles include Cuba, Jamaica, Haiti, the Dominican Republic, and Puerto Rico. The Lesser Antilles, extending in an arc from Puerto Rico to the NE coast of South America, include the Virgin Islands, Windward Islands, Leeward Islands, S group of the Netherlands Antilles, and, usually, Barbados and Trinidad and Tobago.

ANTI-MASONIC PARTY, American political organization founded in 1827-28, chiefly as a result of the mysterious disappearance of William Morgan (1774?-1826?) of Batavia, N.Y., a Freemason, who was planning to publish a book revealing the secrets of the order. Morgan, an itinerant worker, was arrested in 1826 and charged with stealing and indebtedness, apparently as a pretext for seizing him. Convicted and jailed, he was reportedly kidnapped shortly afterward. Although his actual fate was never learned, it was widely believed that he had been abducted and murdered by Masons. This incident touched off a wave of anti-Masonic sentiment.

Opponents of Freemasonry, including sections of the press, churches, and antislavery elements, joined in the condemnation of the order. Thurlow Weed (1797-1882), publisher of the *Rochester* (N.Y.) *Telegraph* and later of the *Anti-Masonic Enquirer,* led the press attack on Freemasonry and endorsed anti-Masonic candidates for New York State offices in the election of 1827. When 15 of these candidates were elected to the state Assembly, an Anti-Masonic party was formed and in 1828 held its first state convention. National conventions were held in Philadelphia in 1830 and in Baltimore in 1831. At the latter, William Wirt (1722-1834), who had served as U.S. attorney general under Presidents James Monroe and John Quincy Adams, was nominated for president in opposition to Andrew Jackson, who supported Masonry. Wirt himself was a Freemason. The convention required a three-fourths majority to nominate, thereby setting a precedent for the two-thirds rule used by the Democrats in subsequent national conventions for more than 100 years. In the 1832 elections, however, the Anti-Masonic party carried only the state of Vermont. It did win a considerable number of seats in the 23d Congress (1833-35). The party survived until about 1834, when several prominent leaders founded the Whig party or shifted to the Democratic party.

ANTIMATTER, matter composed of elementary particles (q.v.) that are, in a special sense, mirror images of the particles that make up ordinary matter as it is known on earth. Antiparticles have the same mass as their corresponding particles but have opposite electric charges or other properties related to electromagnetism. For example, the antimatter electron, or positron, is positively charged but is identical in all other respects to the electron. The antimatter equivalent of the chargeless neutron, on the other hand, differs in having a magnetic moment of opposite sign (magnetic moment is another electromagnetic property). In all of the other parameters involved in the dynamical properties of elementary particles, such as mass, spin, and partial decay, antiparticles are identical with their corresponding particles.

The existence of antiparticles was first proposed by the British physicist Paul Adrien Maurice Dirac, arising from his attempt to apply the techniques of relativistic mechanics (*see* RELATIVITY) to quantum theory. In 1928 he developed the concept of a positively charged electron; its actual existence was established experimentally in 1932. The existence of other antiparticles was presumed but not confirmed until 1955, when antiprotons and antineutrons were observed in particle accelerators (q.v.). Since then, the full range of antiparticles has been observed or indicated.

A profound problem for particle physics and for cosmology (q.v.) in general is the apparent scarcity of antiparticles in the universe. Their nonexistence, except momentarily, on earth is understandable, because particles and antiparticles are mutually annihilated with a great release of energy when they meet. Distant galaxies could possibly be made of antimatter, but no direct method of confirmation exists. Most of what is known about the far universe arrives in the form of photons, which are identical with their antiparticles and thus reveal little about the nature of their sources. The prevailing opinion, however, is that the universe consists overwhelmingly of "ordinary" matter, and explanations for this have been proposed by recent cosmological theory (*see* INFLATIONARY THEORY).

For further information on this topic, see the Bibliography in volume 28, sections 389-90.

ANTI-MONOPOLY PARTY, American political party organized in Chicago in May 1884. At its founding convention, the party nominated the American general and politician Benjamin Franklin Butler for the presidency and adopted a platform calling for a new law to regulate interstate commerce, a direct popular vote for U.S. senators, a graduated income tax, the establishment of labor unions throughout the country, the repeal of all tariffs, and the prohibition of governmental grants of land to corporations. In the presidential election of 1884, the Anti-Monopoly party united with the Greenback-Labor party, and Butler received about 175,000 votes. Both parties passed out of existence soon afterward and were succeeded in the 1890s by the Populist party.

Benjamin Franklin Butler, nominated for the presidency of the U.S. by the Anti-Monopoly party in 1884. The cartoon is by the noted contemporary political satirist Thomas Nast. **Granger Collection**

ANTIMONY, metalloid element, symbol Sb, in group 15 (or Va) of the periodic table (*see* PERIODIC LAW); at.no. 51, at.wt. 121.75. Antimony melts at about 630°C (about 1166°F), boils at about 1750°C (about 3182°F), and has a sp.gr. of 6.7.

Antimony's compounds were known in ancient times, and the element was probably discovered by the German alchemist Basil Valentine (b. 1414?) about 1450. It was certainly known by about 1600, but was confused with other elements, such as bismuth, tin, and lead. Antimony generally shows the properties of a metal, but sometimes shows those of a nonmetal. It exists in several allotropic forms (distinctly different physical forms), the most common of which is metallic in appearance.

Antimony ranks about 64th in natural abundance among the elements in crustal rock. It occasionally occurs as a free element, usually associated with silver, arsenic, or bismuth. It crystallizes in the hexagonal system (*see* CRYSTAL), but crystals are rarely found. It has a hardness (q.v.) of 3. The principal ore of antimony is stibnite (q.v.), a sulfide of antimony, which is mined in China, France, Italy, Japan, Mexico, and, on a small scale, in the western U.S. Considerable amounts of antimony are produced as a by-product in the refining of ores of copper and lead.

Liquid antimony has the exceptional property, when cooling, of expanding as it solidifies (water is one of the few other substances with this same property). It will thus fill in the crevices of a mold and yield castings of exceptionally sharp outlines. For this reason, it is used in making type metal; it is also a constituent of many other alloys, such as Britannia metal, pewter, Babbitt metal (q.v.), and antimonial lead.

Among important compounds of antimony are tartar emetic, a double tartrate of antimony and potassium used as a medicinal agent; red antimony sulfide, used on safety matches and in vulcanizing rubber; glass of antimony, a mixture of antimony sulfide and oxide, used as a yellow pigment in glass and porcelain; and butter of antimony, antimony trichloride, used for bronzing steel, as a mordant in dyeing, and as a caustic in medicine.

ANTINOMIANISM (Gr. *anti,* "against"; *nomos,* "law"), doctrine that faith in Christ frees the Christian from obligation to observe the moral law as set forth in the Old Testament. The insistence in the Epistles of St. Paul upon the inadequacy of the law to save, and upon salvation by faith without "works of the law" or "deeds of righteousness" (see Rom. 3:20, 28; Eph. 2:9; 2 Tim. 2:9; Titus 3:5) could easily be interpreted as a claim of freedom from all obligation to obey the moral law. Thus, righteous persons might well hold such a doctrine and behave in an exemplary way, not from compulsion but from a devotion higher than the law. Gross and vicious persons, however, might well interpret the exemption from obligation as positive permission to disregard the moral law in determining their conduct. Such concepts had evidently begun in the apostles' own day, as appears from the arguments and warnings in the epistles of the New Testament (see Rom. 6, 8; 1 Pet. 3:5). The term was first used during the Reformation by Martin Luther to describe the opinions of the German preacher Johann Agricola (1494–1566). The Antinomian Controversy of this time, in which Luther took a very active part, terminated in 1540 in a retraction by Agricola. Views more extreme than his were afterward advocated by some of the English nonconformists and by the Anabaptists.

ANTIOCH, city, Contra Costa Co., W California, on the San Joaquin R., near the mouth of the Sacramento R.; inc. 1872. It is a rapidly growing residential and industrial area. Manufactures in the city include paper products, steel, and chemicals. The city is named for the biblical Antioch. Pop. (1980) 43,559; (1990) 62,195.

ANTIOCH *or* **ANTAKYA,** city, S Turkey, capital of Hatay Province, on the Orontes R., near the Mediterranean Sea. The modern city is a trade and processing center for the adjacent agricultural plain. Citrus fruit and grapes are grown in abundance; other important crops are olives, melons, wheat, and cotton. Manufactured products include soap, silk and leather goods, and metal handicrafts.

It was the ancient capital of the Seleucid dynasty in Syria and of a province of the Roman Empire. The city was founded in 301 BC by Seleucus I, one of the generals and successors of Alexander the Great. Strategically located at the crossroads of important caravan routes, it soon became a center of commerce and one of the leading cities of the world, famous for a magnificence of architecture rivaled only by Rome and Alexandria. When Syria was conquered by Rome in 64 BC, Antioch became the eastern capital of the Roman Empire. The Romans added to the architectural splendors of the city, building temples, palaces, and theaters, extending aqueducts, and paving main streets with marble.

Antioch was the center of Christendom outside Palestine. The apostles preached there before starting out on their missionary journeys, and in Antioch the term Christian, designating converts of St. Paul, first came into use. In AD 260 Antioch fell to the Persians. Over the next 13 centuries it was conquered by Arabs, Byzantines, Seljuk Turks, Frankish Crusaders, and Egyptians. The devastations of war and persistent earthquakes, including one in 526 that reportedly killed 250,000 people, reduced the once great city to relative unimportance.

Antioch, known as Antakya in modern history, was captured by the Turks in 1516, and it remained a part of the Ottoman Empire until shortly after World War I, when it was conveyed to Syria under a French mandate. The province of Hatay, of which Antakya is the capital, became autonomous in 1938, and the following year it was ceded to Turkey.

Although little of the ancient city remains, portions of the high walls that girded the city and of catacombs and aqueducts still stand. An archaeological museum houses a superbly preserved collection of mosaics dating from the 2d and 3d centuries. Nearby is Saint Peter's Grotto, in which the apostle preached; a church was built in the cave by Crusaders in the 12th and 13th centuries. Pop. (1985) 107,821.

ANTIOCH UNIVERSITY, privately controlled institution of higher learning comprising Antioch College, in Yellow Springs, Ohio; the School for Adult and Experiential Learning, also in Yellow Springs; Antioch New England Graduate School, in Keene, N.H.; and campuses in Los Angeles and Santa Barbara, Calif., and Seattle, Wash. Antioch College was opened in 1852 by the educator Horace Mann, who became its first president. In 1921 the curriculum was revised to combine academic study with practical, off-campus experience in private and government employment in the U.S. and abroad. Antioch became a university in 1977.

ANTIOCHUS I, called Soter ("the preserver") (324–262 or 261 BC), king of Syria (280–262 or 261 BC). The second of the Seleucids, he was the son of Seleucus I, one of the generals and successors of Alexander the Great. In 275 BC Antiochus won a victory over the Galatians in Asia Minor but lost considerable territory to Ptolemy II. He was killed in battle during a war (263–261 BC) against Eumenes I (r. 263–241 BC), ruler of Pergamum in Asia Minor.

ANTIOCHUS II, called Theos ("the divine") (c. 287–246 BC), king of Syria (261–246 BC), son and successor of Antiochus I. The citizens of Miletus, in Asia Minor, called him Theos after he freed them from the tyrant Timarchus (fl. 3d cent. BC) in 258 BC. Having fought a long and costly war (260–255 BC) against Ptolemy II, king of Egypt, Antiochus won back most of the territories his father had lost, only to be defeated in 250 BC by his own satrap, or provincial governor, Diodotus I (r. about 256–235 BC), who seized the Syrian province of Bactria. Subsequently, Antiochus also lost the province of Parthia to the Parthian dynasty of the Arsacids.

ANTIOCHUS III, called The Great (242–187 BC), king of Syria (223–187 BC), the son of Seleucus II and brother of Seleucus III, whom he succeeded. He was the most distinguished of the Seleucids. Having made vassal states out of Parthia and Bactria, he warred successfully against the Egyptian king Ptolemy V and in 198 BC obtained possession of all of Palestine and Lebanon. He later became involved in a conflict with the Romans, who defeated him at Thermopylae in 191 BC and at Magnesia (now Manisa, Turkey) in 190 BC. As the price of peace, he was forced to surrender all his dominions west of the Taurus Mountains and to pay costly tribute. Antiochus, who early in his reign had restored the Seleucid Empire, finally forfeited its influence in the eastern Mediterranean by his failure to recognize the rising power of Rome.

ANTIOCHUS IV, called Epiphanes ("the illustrious") (c. 215-164 BC), king of Syria (175-164 BC), son of Antiochus III. From 171 to 168 BC, he was involved in a war aginst Egypt, defeating two Egyptian kings, Ptolemy VI and Ptolemy VII. He captured Jerusalem, prohibited Judaism, and tried to establish the worship of Greek gods. Under the leadership of the Jewish priest Mattathias (died c. 166 BC) and his sons, the Maccabees, the Jews revolted (167-160 BC) and drove Antiochus from Jerusalem. Later he won victories over the Armenians and Persians.

ANTIPATER (398?-319 BC), Macedonian general, lieutenant of Alexander the Great. When Alexander went off to conquer the Persian Empire in 334 BC, he left Antipater in sole charge of affairs in Macedonia. Antipater discharged the duties of his office with great ability, suppressing insurrections in Thrace and Sparta and supporting Alexander with fresh troops from home. In the partition of Alexander's domain after his death in 323 BC, the government of Macedonia was again assigned to Antipater, and he was soon after called upon to defend himself in the Lamian War against an alliance of Greek states attempting to regain their independence from Macedonia. He at first met with reverses, but, with the assistance of his son-in-law Craterus, he brought the Greeks into subjection in 322 BC.

The Lamian War was followed by a war against the Macedonian general Perdiccas (b. 365 BC), which Antipater also won. After the murder of Perdiccas in 321 BC, Antipater was appointed to the supreme regency of Macedonia and to the guardianship of the children of Alexander. He made a new division of the kingdom but died a short time later, leaving the regency to his colleague Polysperchon (d. after 303 BC) and a subordinate position to his son, Cassander (350?-297 BC), who later became king of Macedonia.

ANTIPOPE, pontiff elected in opposition to one canonically chosen. *See* PAPACY; POPE.

ANTIPROTON. *See* ELEMENTARY PARTICLES; PROTON.

ANTIQUITIES. *See* ARCHAEOLOGY.

ANTISANA, volcano of the Andes Mts., N Ecuador, near Quito. The mountain, 5704 m (18,714 ft) high, was explored by the British mountain climber and writer Edward Whymper in 1880. Signs of volcanic activity last appeared in 1803. On the N slopes are two villages.

ANTI-SEMITISM, political, social, and economic agitation and activities directed against Jews. The term is now used to denote anti-Judaic acts or sentiments based on any grounds, including religious ones. The adjective Semitic originally was applied to all descendants of Shem, the eldest son of the biblical patriarch Noah; in later usage, it refers to a group of peoples of southwestern Asia, including both Jews and Arabs. The word anti-Semitism was coined about 1879 to denote hostility only toward Jews. This hostility is supposedly justified by a theory, first developed in Germany in the middle of the 19th century, that peoples of so-called Aryan stock are superior in physique and character to those of Semitic stock. Although the theory was rejected by all responsible ethnologists, widely read books incorporating anti-Semitic doctrines were written by such men as the French diplomat and social philosopher Comte Joseph Arthur de Gobineau and the German philosopher and economist Karl Dühring. The theory of racial superiority was used to justify the civil and religious persecution of Jews that had existed throughout history.

Many explanations of the phenomenon of anti-Semitism have been advanced. The theory most widely accepted among social scientists views anti-Semitism as being nurtured by periods of social instability and crisis, such as those existing in Germany in the 1880s and in the era preceding World War II. Passions and frustrations engendered during such periods are theoretically deflected onto scapegoats, for example, an available, isolated minority, such as the Jews.

Historical Roots of Anti-Semitism. Although the term anti-Semitism is less than a century old, anti-Jewish agitation has existed for several thousand years. In the ancient Roman Empire, for example, the devotion of Jews to their religion and special forms of worship was used as a pretext for political discrimination against them, and very few Jews were admitted to Roman citizenship. With the rise and eventual domination of Christianity throughout the Western world, discrimination against Jews on religious grounds became universal, and systematic and social anti-Judaism made its appearance. Jews were massacred in great numbers, especially during the Crusades, segregated in ghettos, required to wear identifying marks or garments, and economically crippled by the imposition of restrictions on the business activities open to them. In the 18th and 19th centuries, which saw the French Revolution and the Age of Enlightenment, increasing separation of church and state, and the rise of modern nation-states, Jews experienced less religious and economic persecution and were gradually integrated into the economic and political order.

"Ten Thousand Jews Massacred in One Day by the Inhabitants of Damascus," an engraving from The Whole and Genuine & Complete Works of Flavius Josephus, *American edition edited by G. H. Maynard and published in 1795. Josephus was a Jewish historian and general who took part in the Jewish uprising against the Romans in 66–67.*

In Germany, the process of Jewish emancipation was completed with the formation of the German Empire in 1871. Although legal reforms put an end to discrimination on religious grounds, hostility, falsely based on racism, grew. Racist theories that had been formulated during the preceding decades provided the basis for a new grouping of anti-Semitic political parties after the Franco-German War and the economic crash of 1873. The German political scene was marked by the presence of at least one openly anti-Semitic party until 1933, when anti-Semitism became the official policy of the government under National Socialism (Nazism).

The pattern of German anti-Semitism was followed in other parts of western and central Europe. In Austria, for example, a Christian Socialist party advocated more or less anti-Semitic programs. In France, anti-Semitism became an issue in the larger problem of the separation of church and state. Clerical and royalist factions generally adopted anti-Semitic principles based on the racist theories formulated in Germany and fostered in part by the publication of numerous anti-Semitic publications, notably the newspaper *La Libre Parole,* started in 1892 by the French anti-Semitic journalist and author Edouard Drumont (1844–1917). Anti-Semitism in France culminated in the Dreyfus affair (q.v.) between 1894 and 1906. With the liberation of Alfred Dreyfus (1859–1935), a Jewish officer in the French army who was imprisoned for alleged treason, anti-Semitism almost disappeared as a political issue in France.

Persecution in Eastern Europe: The Pogroms. Opposition to the Jews took a different course in Eastern Europe. Medieval traditions isolating the Jews as an alien economic and social class solely for reasons of religion were never broken. The Jewish emancipation characteristic of Western Europe did not occur. Disabilities imposed on Jews since the Middle Ages became increasingly severe. In Russia, measures were adopted to prevent Jews from owning land and to limit the number of Jews admitted to institutions of higher education to 3 to 10 percent of the total enrollment in those institutions.

The persecution of Jews in Eastern Europe was climaxed by a series of organized massacres, known as pogroms, that began in 1881. Some of the worst outbreaks occurred in 1906 as an aftermath of the unsuccessful 1905 Revolution in Russia. Involving about 600 villages and cities, the pogroms resulted in the slaughter of thousands of Jews and the looting and destruction of their property. Historians agree that the pogroms were the product of a deliberate government policy aimed at diverting the discontent of Russian workers and peasants into religious bigotry. They were fomented by a new type of mass propaganda, including a notorious forgery known as the *Protocols of the Elders of Zion,* which purported to reveal details of an international Jewish conspiracy to dominate the world. First published in book form in Russia in 1905 and circulated continuously thereafter, it contained material clearly traceable to fictional accounts not even concerned with Jews. Such deliberate distortions were used during the pogrom after the 1917 Revolution, which claimed hundreds of thousands of victims.

Origins of Anti-Semitism in the U.S. Russian anti-Semitic propaganda was also circulated in the U.S., where prejudice against Jews previously had assumed such forms as covert social discrimination. In the U.S., the upsurge of anti-Jewish feeling was part of a general wave of resentment of minority groups, including also Roman Catholics and blacks, that swept the country after World

Polish women and children wait to be led away by storm troopers during the Nazi destruction of Warsaw in 1943. This photograph was introduced at the Nuremberg trials as evidence of Nazi terrorism in the Polish capital. UPI

War I. Another element in U.S. anti-Semitism in the 1920s was its identification of Jews with political radicalism. A notable event was the temporary embracing of anti-Semitism by the American automobile manufacturer Henry Ford, who reprinted the discredited *Protocols of the Elders of Zion* in his newspaper the *Dearborn Independent*. Condemned widely, he later apologized for this action. The immigration legislation enacted in the U.S. in 1921 and 1924 was interpreted widely as being at least partly anti-Jewish in intent because it strictly limited the immigration quotas of eastern European nations with large Jewish populations, nations from which 2.5 million Jews had immigrated to the U.S. by 1920.

Organized Anti-Semitism as a Political Tool. During the interwar period, anti-Semitic sentiments persisted and even increased throughout the U.S., in discrimination against Jews in employment, in access to residential and resort areas, and in tightened quotas on Jewish enrollment and teaching positions in colleges and universities. At the same time economic, social, violent and systematic anti-Semitism was developing in central Europe. In Germany during the 1930s and '40s, anti-Semitism reached a zenith under the Nazi regime led by the arch–anti-Semite Adolf Hitler.

The content of Nazi propaganda was varied, consisting basically of racist doctrine but also including elements of religious hatred and, paradoxically, the identification of Jews with both capitalist and Communist elements in Germany and elsewhere. Moreover, the virulent anti-Semitic campaign within Germany was supplemented by movements in Europe and the U.S. organized by Nazi agents and their sympathizers.

More important than this psychological campaign, however, was the physical persecution of the Jewish community. Shortly after the National Socialists came to power in 1933, special legislation was enacted that excluded Jews from the protection of German law. The property of Jews was legally expropriated, and concentration camps were set up in which Jews were summarily executed or condemned to slave labor. Sporadic and local massacres culminated in a nationwide pogrom in 1938, officially organized by the National Socialist party. After the outbreak of World War II, the tempo of anti-Semitic activities increased appallingly. Throughout Europe, puppet, dependent, or military governments of such areas as France, Italy, Poland, and the Ukraine were forced by Germany to adopt anti-Semitic programs. Within Germany, Hitler announced a "final solution of the Jewish problem": the merciless slaughter of the Jewish community, a type of crime now recognized under international law as genocide. By the end of the war, about 6 million Jews, including two-thirds of the Jewish population of Europe, had been exterminated by massacre, systematic execution, and starvation.

After the war the strong reaction against the revealed horrors of the Nazi death camps resulted in the framing of the Universal Declaration of Human Rights, adopted by the UN General Assembly in 1948. At the international war crimes trials (q.v.), which opened in Nuremberg, Germany, in 1945, many Nazi officials were prosecuted for administering the racial laws of the party and implementing the extermination of Jews and other persons in the concentration camps. The government of the Federal Republic of Germany (FRG) continued such prosecutions through the 1950s and '60s and made some restitutions for property, pensions, and estates taken from Jews. Although the official position of the FRG is strongly against anti-Semitism, outbreaks of violence and hostility have occurred sporadically against Jews in postwar Germany. In the other Western democracies, the example of Nazi extremism brought anti-Semitism to a low ebb in postwar years. Nonetheless, strains of such prejudice manifested themselves in small but militant reactionary and racist parties in Great Britain, France, and other countries of Europe and the Americas.

Anti-Semitism After World War II. Outbreaks of acts of vandalism such as defacing or setting fire to synagogues occur periodically. Beginning in the late 1960s and continuing into the 1990s, a new phase of anti-Semitism, involving the antagonism of some black Americans toward Jews, emerged in a series of urban encounters. Small groups of neo-Nazis and white supremacists have also been responsible for anti-Semitic propaganda and violence against individual Jews. The general trends of Christian religious policy have reflected a reaction against the Nazi experience and a desire to eliminate the religious bases of prejudice. During the postwar period, cooperation between Christian and Jewish organizations increased, and at the Second Vatican Council (1962–65) the Roman Catholic church formally repudiated the charge that all Jews are responsible for the death of Christ and condemned genocide and racism as un-Christian.

In Latin America, the chosen refuge of many members of the Nazi party after World War II, occasional anti-Semitic incidents have occurred. Some of the most serious demonstrations were triggered by the Israeli seizure of a Nazi war criminal, Adolf Eichmann, in Argentina in 1960. Eichmann subsequently was tried in Jerusalem for crimes against the Jews and was hanged.

In the Middle East, a region populated by Semitic peoples, a new form of anti-Jewishness was generated as a result of the establishment of the state of Israel in 1948. This homeland for Jews encroached on land also claimed by Arabs and aroused fierce opposition from members of the Arab League. Numerous border clashes occurred between Israel and its Arab neighbors during the following years, escalating into full-scale hostilities in 1948–49, 1956, 1967, 1973, and 1982. The Palestine Liberation Organization, established in May 1964, conducted guerrilla activities against Israel both within its borders and in other nations. The economic sanctions that were imposed by the Arab League nations against various governments and businesses cooperative with Israel became a significant issue after the 1973 war.

In the USSR, the imperial Russian legacy of anti-Semitism apparently survived into the postwar period. As a religion, Judaism was unacceptable to orthodox Soviet Communism, and so was Zionism, whether religious or secular. In the years after World War II, unofficial reports indicated that Soviet Jews were being subjected to social and professional discrimination. According to one report, more than 400,000 White Russian and Ukrainian Jews were forcibly deported to labor camps in Siberia in 1949. In 1953 fifteen doctors, most of them Jewish, were arrested and charged with murdering important Soviet officials on orders from the American Joint Distribution Committee, a Zionist organization. The charges were soon withdrawn, but the Soviet campaign against Jewish culture was intensified, resulting in the suppression of the Jewish press, the liquidation of leading Yiddish writers, and the curtailment of educational opportunities for Jewish youths. Emigration of Jews was made almost impossible; those applying for permission met with severe discrimination. Although somewhat alleviated by the end of the 1970s, these policies led to formation in the U.S. of organizations to protest the plight of Jews in Communist countries. The political upheavals in the USSR and Eastern Europe at the end of the 1980s made it much easier for Jews to emigrate, but the upsurge of nationalism that accompanied the decline of Communism was linked with a rise in anti-Semitic agitation. REV. BY N.N.G.

For further information on this topic, see the Bibliography in volume 28, sections 56, 129, 162-63, 247, 874, 915–16, 958.

ANTISEPTICS, physical or chemical agents that prevent putrefaction, infection, and analogous changes in food and living tissue by destroying or arresting the development of microorganisms. Since ancient times food has been preserved by the use of antiseptic agents such as heat in cooking; niter, salt, and vinegar in corning and pickling; and wood smoke (containing creosote, chemically similar to carbolic acid) in the smoking of meats. In modern times the principal antiseptic agents used in the preservation of food are heat and cold in such processes as canning, pasteurization, and refrigeration. Irradiation is being investigated as a means of preserving food.

The practice of using antiseptics in the care and treatment of wounds was begun by the English surgeon Joseph Lister in 1868. Basing his work on the findings of the German physiologist Theodor Schwann and the French biochemist Louis Pasteur, Lister disinfected surgical and accidental wounds with a solution of carbolic acid, and in five years reduced the death rate from major amputations from 45 percent to about 12 percent. Many other antiseptics have come into use, among which the most important are bichloride of mercury, iodine, boric acid, alcohol, the hypochlorites, mercurochrome, and Merthiolate. Chlorine is used in the sterilization of water, especially in public water systems (*see* WATER SUPPLY AND WATERWORKS) and swimming pools.

ANTI-SLAVERY SOCIETY, AMERICAN. *See* AMERICAN ANTI-SLAVERY SOCIETY.

ANTISTHENES (444?–after 371 BC), Greek philosopher, founder of the school of philosophy called Cynicism. He was born in Athens and became a disciple of Socrates. Antisthenes taught in the gymnasium known as the Cynosarges outside Athens, and his followers were called Cynics. Antisthenes regarded happiness as attainable only through virtue. He denounced art and literature, condemned luxury and comfort, and extolled hard work. His most famous pupil was the Greek Cynic philosopher Diogenes.

ANTITOXIN, antibody produced in the bloodstream of an animal or human being in response to the presence of a bacterial toxin, or poison. The antitoxin neutralizes the effect of the toxin. In 1890, the German physician Emil Adolph von Behring was the first to demonstrate that animals immune to diphtheria have substances in their blood serum that neutralize the toxin produced by the diphtheria bacterium. Serum antitoxins were first prepared and used in the treatment of diphtheria by the French bacteriologist Pierre Paul Émile Roux (1853–1933) in 1894. Today, similar antitoxins are used to combat the toxins produced by tetanus and botulism. Antitoxins for use in human beings are produced in animals such as horses and cattle. The animal is injected with increasingly higher doses of the toxin and its defense processes respond by producing antitoxin. Some of the animal's blood is then removed and processed for use in human beings. An animal may be used to produce antitoxin for many years without apparent damage to itself.

ANTITRUST LEGISLATION. *See* TRUSTS.

ANTIUM, city of ancient Latium, built on a rocky promontory, near Rome. The city was subdued by the Romans in 341 BC. Antium was the birthplace of two Roman emperors, Caligula and Nero. Near the shore are ruins of Roman villas. Various artworks, including the sculpture *Borghese Gladiator,* have been found here. The contemporary town of Anzio is on the site of Antium.

Larva of the ant lion, Myrmeleon.
© Hans Pfletschinger–Peter Arnold, Inc.

ANT LION, common name for insects of the family Myrmeleontidae, order Neuroptera. More than 50 North American species are known, some of which are common in the southern U.S. The larva of the ant lion is about 2.5 cm (about 1 in) long and has large, powerful jaws. It digs a funnel-shaped pitfall in fine, loose sand and lies in wait at the bottom for its prey, which consists of ants and other insects that tumble into the pitfall. It pupates in a sand-covered cocoon during the spring; the adult, which in some ways resembles a dragonfly, emerges from the cocoon in June.

ANTOFAGASTA, city, N Chile, capital of Antofagasta Province. Settled in 1870, it grew rapidly with the mining of rich deposits of nitrates from the adjacent Atacama Desert. Copper and nitrates are the main exports; other metals, such as silver, lead, zinc, and tungsten, are also mined. The city has the only protected harbor on the Pacific coastline of N Chile. It is a shipping center for domestic goods and for the products of neighboring landlocked countries, to which it is linked by rail and highway. Pop. (1987 est.) 204,600.

ANTOINE, André (1858–1943), French actor and theatrical producer, born in Limoges. In 1887, with the support of the French writer Émile Zola, he founded the Théâtre Libre in Paris to produce naturalistic plays, in opposition to the vogue for so-called well-made plays. He produced works by such French dramatists as Zola, Eugène Brieux, and François de Curel (1854–1928). Antoine managed the Odéon in Paris from 1906 to 1913. After World War I he became a drama critic.

ANTONELLI, Giacomo (1806–76), Italian statesman, born in Sonnino. In 1845 he became finance minister of the Papal States. Pope Pius IX made him a cardinal in 1847. In the following year, when the revolutionary activity in Italy made constitutional government advisable, Antonelli became premier of the Papal States. When the insurrection of 1848 compelled the pope to flee, Antonelli accompanied him to Gaeta, Italy. He returned with the pope under French protection in 1850 and became secretary of state, a position he held until his death. His administration was marked by opposition to the restoration of constitutional government in the Papal States and to Italian nationalist aspirations.

ANTONELLO DA MESSINA (1430?–79), Sicilian painter and one of the first Italian masters to use the Flemish technique of painting in oils.

Antonello was born in Messina. His early career is largely conjectural, but he is now believed to have studied and worked in Naples, where a number of works by Flemish artists—notably Jan van Eyck—were known to be at the time and where oil painting was practiced. Antonello journeyed to Venice in 1475–76 and so impressed the Venetians with his virtuosity that he was given a state stipend. Among his known works from this period are a *Crucifixion* (1475, Musée Royal des Beaux-Arts, Brussels) and the *San Cassiano Altarpiece* (1475–76, Kunsthistorisches Museum, Vienna); the latter is famous for its superb handling of perspective, its glowing colors, and an elegance of detail that rivals Flemish art. Antonello returned to Messina in 1476 and there completed his *Annunciation* (c. 1476, Galleria Nazionale, Palermo), his last painting before his death. Among his most notable works are *Portrait of a Young Man* (1474, Dahlem Museum, Berlin), *Ecce Homo* (1474, Metropolitan Museum, New York City), and *Il Condottiere* or *Portrait of a Man* (1475, Louvre, Paris).

ANTONESCU, Ion (1882–1946), Romanian general, born in Piteşti, and educated in French military schools. During the 1930s, he became a sympathizer with the native Romanian Fascist party known as the Iron Guard. On Sept. 5, 1940, Antonescu was appointed premier by King Carol II. Assuming dictatorial powers, he forced the abdication of Carol on September 6 and subsequently set up a regime closely modeled on that of Nazi Germany. He led Romania into participation with Germany in the invasion of the USSR in June 1941 and, in December 1941, plunged the country more fully into World War II with declarations of war against the U.S. and Great Britain. In August 1944, after the penetration of Soviet forces into Romania, Antonescu was deposed, arrested, and executed as a war criminal.

ANTONINUS PIUS, full name TITUS AURELIUS FULVUS ANTONINUS (86–161), Roman emperor (138–161), born in Lanuvium (now Lanuvio, Italy), of a distinguished Roman family. He was consul in 120, and, after a period as governor of the province of Asia he became one of the chief advisers of Emperor Hadrian. In 138 Hadrian adopted Antoninus and named him his successor; he became emperor when Hadrian died later the same year. Antoninus acquired the name Pius ("dutiful" or "conscientious"), probably because of his insistence that divine honors be accorded his predecessor.

As emperor, Antoninus reigned in times of unusual peace and prosperity. In the first decade of his reign, however, a rebellion in Britain forced him to build (140–42) a wall between the Forth and Clyde rivers as a defense against invasions from Scotland. The Antonine Column, in the Piazza Colonna in Rome, was built in his honor by the Roman emperor and Stoic philosopher Marcus Aurelius, his son-in-law and successor.

ANTONIONI, Michelangelo (1912–), Italian film director and screenwriter, born in Ferrara, and educated at the University of Bologna. He began his career as a film critic, writer of screenplays, and maker of documentary films (1945–49). His first feature film was *Cronaca di un Amore* (Story of a Love, 1950). His later films include *L'Avventura* (1959); *La Notte* (1960); *Eclipse* (1962); *Red Desert* (1964), his first color film; *Blow-Up* (1966), his first English-language film; *Zabriskie Point* (1969), filmed in the U.S.; and *The Passenger* (1975). Antonioni has written or coauthored the screenplays of most of his films, which deal in highly personal terms with the themes of alienation, boredom, and loveless eroticism.

ANTONIUS, Marcus. *See* ANTONY, MARK.

ANTONY, Mark, in Latin, Marcus Antonius (83?–30 BC), Roman statesman and general, who defeated the assassins of Julius Caesar and, with Gaius Octavius and Marcus Aemilius Lepidus, formed the Second Triumvirate, which ultimately secured the end of the Roman Republic.

Antony was born in Rome and educated for a short time in Greece. From 58 to 56 BC he served as a leader of cavalry in Roman campaigns in Palestine and Egypt, and from 54 to 50 BC he served in Gaul under Julius Caesar. Subsequently, with Caesar's aid, he attained the offices of quaestor, augur, and tribune of the people. At the outbreak of the civil war between Caesar and the Roman soldier and statesman Pompey the Great, Antony was appointed Caesar's commander in chief in Italy. He commanded the left wing of Caesar's army at the Battle of Pharsalus in 48 BC, and in 44 BC he shared the consulship with Caesar.

After the assassination of Caesar in 44 BC, Antony's skillful oratory, immortalized by Shakespeare in the play *Julius Caesar*, turned the Roman people against the conspirators, leaving Antony for a time with almost absolute power in Rome. A rival soon appeared, however, in the person of Gaius Octavius, later the Roman emperor Augustus, who was grandnephew of Caesar and Caesar's designated heir. A struggle for power broke out when Antony, Octavius, and a third contender for the throne, the Roman general Marcus Aemilius Lepidus, formed the Second Triumvirate and agreed to divide the Roman Empire among themselves.

In 42 BC, at Philippi, the triumvirate crushed the forces led by two assassins of Caesar, the Roman statesmen Marcus Junius Brutus and Gaius Cassius Longinus, who sought to restore the Roman Republic. Later in the same year, Antony summoned the Egyptian queen Cleopatra to attend him in the city of Tarsus, in Cilicia (now in Turkey), and explain her refusal to aid the triumvirate in the civil war. Instead of punishing Cleopatra, however, Antony fell in love with her and returned with her to Egypt in 41 BC. In 40 BC he attended meetings of the triumvirate in Italy, at which a new division of the Roman world was arranged, with Antony receiving the eastern portion, from the Adriatic Sea to the Euphrates River; in the same year he attempted to cement his relations with Octavius by marrying the latter's sister Octavia. Nevertheless, Antony soon returned to Egypt and resumed his life with Cleopatra. Octavius made use of this fact to excite the indignation of the Roman people against Antony. When, in 36 BC, Antony was defeated in a military expedition against the Parthians, popular disapproval of his conduct deepened in Rome, and a new civil war became inevitable. In 31 BC the forces of Antony and Cleopatra were decisively defeated by those of Octavius in a naval engagement near Actium. The couple returned to Egypt, deserted by the Egyptian fleet and by most of Antony's own army. In the following year, besieged by the troops of Octavius in Alexandria and deceived by a false report of Cleopatra's suicide, Antony killed himself by falling on his sword.

ANTRIM, former county, Ulster Province, NE Northern Ireland; Belfast was the county town. Antrim includes a hilly region on the N and E and a fertile lowland area near Lough Neagh on the SW. Located on the N coast is the remarkable Giant's Causeway, a cluster of thousands of hexagonal basaltic columns. County Antrim ceased to exist as an administrative unit in 1973.

ANTSIRANANA, formerly DIÉGO-SUAREZ, town, N Madagascar, capital of Antsiranana Province, on an inlet of the Indian Ocean. The town, which possesses one of the finest harbors in the world, is a naval base and fueling station and the third largest port of the country. Cattle, corn, coffee, vanilla, pepper, sugar, peanuts, and cloves are exported. Important industries of the area are shipbuilding, meat processing, tuna fishing, salt extraction, and the manufacture of oxygen. The bay was the site of a French pirate colony, Libertalia, at the end of the 17th century; the modern town was founded in the 1800s. From 1885 to 1895 it was the capital of the French colony of Diégo-Suarez. The town is also called Antsirane or Antsirana. Pop. (1986 est.) 53,000.

ANTWERP, city, N Belgium, administrative center of Antwerp Province, on the Scheldt R., near the North Sea and Brussels. It is the chief port and second largest city of Belgium. It is connected with the industrial regions of SE Belgium by the Albert Canal, which links it with Liège; it also has an active trade to and from the Ruhr district in Germany. Grain and unrefined metals are major imports; exports include machinery, textiles, and other manufactured products. Antwerp is especially noted for such industries as diamond cutting, shipbuilding, automobile assembly, and the manufacture of metal goods, electronic equipment, chemicals, and dyes.

Among the outstanding features of Antwerp is its system of boulevards, which replaced the defense walls that formerly encircled the city. Perhaps the most interesting edifice in Antwerp is the Gothic Cathedral of Notre Dame (14th and 15th cent.), which is surmounted by a spire 121.9 m (400 ft) high. The cathedral contains several paintings by the Flemish artist Rubens, who spent most of his life in Antwerp. Other points of interest in the city include the town hall and the Gothic Church of Saint Paul, both completed in the 16th century, and the many guild houses dating from the Middle Ages that still line the marketplace. The city has a museum of fine arts with paintings by several of the Flemish masters and botanical and zoological gardens.

A view of Antwerp Harbor, one of the finest in Europe.
Manley Photo–Shostal/Superstock

Antwerp became a port of commercial importance in the 15th century, when the first European stock exchange was founded here. The city rapidly became one of the foremost trading and manufacturing centers of Europe. During the early 16th century, the diamond industry was expanded by the arrival of Jewish craftsmen expelled from Portugal. The city was also a vigorous cultural center, renowned particularly for the Antwerp school of painting. Antwerp rapidly declined after 1576, when mutinous Spanish troops sacked the city. This attack was followed by another in 1584, and the city was forced to surrender to the Spanish in 1585. In 1648 Antwerp suffered a further blow under the provisions of the Peace of Westphalia, which closed the Scheldt R. to navigation; it was reopened in 1795 by the French.

The development of the modern city of Antwerp started in 1863, when the Belgians redeemed their navigation rights by a cash payment. During World War I, Antwerp was occupied by the Germans from October 1914 until the end of the war. During World War II, German troops again occupied the city and held it until September 1944. Antwerp then became an Allied supply base and was heavily bombed. Pop. (1988 est., greater city) 476,000.

For further information on this topic, see the Bibliography in volume 28, section 994.

ANUBIS, in Egyptian mythology, god of the dead. He was considered the inventor of embalming, the guardian of tombs, and a judge of the dead. The Egyptians believed that at the judgment he weighed the heart of the dead against the feather of truth. In art he is represented as jackal-headed. Anubis was sometimes identified with Hermes in Greek mythology.

ANURADHAPURA, city, N Sri Lanka, capital of North-Central Province. Founded in 437 BC, the city was the capital of a Sinhalese kingdom until the 8th century, when it was abandoned temporarily. Today the city is noted for extensive Buddhist ruins, including a rock-hewn temple, the Brazen Palace (2d cent.), and several stupas and statues. Many pilgrimages are made each year to the sacred bo tree, believed to have sprung from a branch of the tree under which the Buddha attained Enlightenment. The branch was supposedly brought from India to Sri Lanka about the middle of the 3d century BC, the time that marks the coming of Buddhism to the island. Pop. (1981) 35,981.

ANUSKIEWICZ, Richard (1930–), American painter and printmaker of op art, whose geometric works seem to pulsate with black-and-white shapes or the interaction of violent color. Born in Erie, Pa., Anuskiewicz studied at the Cleveland Art Institute and at Yale University with Josef Albers, who was experimenting with squares of color. Among Anuskiewicz's paintings is *Convexity II* (1966, Sidney Janis Gallery, New York City). Later he produced three-dimensional painted cubes.

ANVARI, full name AUADUDDIN ALI ANVARI (c. 1126–90), Persian poet, born in Khurasan, and educated at the collegiate institute in Tun (now Firdaus, Iran). His panegyric in honor of the Seljuk sultan Sanjar, or Sinjar (1117–57), ruler of Khurasan, won him royal favor, and he continued to enjoy the patronage of two of Sanjar's successors as well. Anvari (or Anwari) prophesied that a certain combination of the stars in October 1185 would be accompanied by a frightful storm and dire disasters. The prophecy failed, and as a result he suffered virtual banishment.

Anvari's poems, collected in the *Divan,* are masterpieces of artistic form. In his verse he combines the skill of a romantic eulogist with the subtle force of a keen satirist. His elegy *Tears of Khurasan,* translated into English in 1789, is considered one of the most beautiful poems in Persian literature.

ANXIETY, fearful anticipation of impending danger, the source of which is unknown or unrecognized. The central feature of anxiety is intense mental discomfort, a feeling that one will not be able to master future events. The person tends to focus only on the present and on pursuing one task at a time. Physical symptoms include muscle tension, sweaty palms, upset stomach, shortness of breath, feelings of faintness, and a pounding heart. Indeed, until the late 19th century extreme anxiety was routinely mistaken for cardiac or respiratory disorders. At that time Sigmund Freud identified anxiety neurosis as a distinct diagnosis. He believed that anxiety arises when instinctual aggressive or sexual drives threaten to lead a person to behave unacceptably, and that it acts as a signal that triggers defensive action to repress or redirect these drives. When the unconscious defensive maneuvers are unsuccessful, a neurotic anxiety reaction occurs.

Learning theorists see anxiety differently. Some believe that anxiety is learned when innate fears occur together with previously neutral objects or events; for example, an infant often startled by a loud noise while playing with a toy may become anxious just at the sight of the toy. Others stress the importance of imitative behavior and the development of particular thought patterns.

Psychiatrists recognize several conditions in which anxiety is the main disturbance, including panic disorder and generalized anxiety disorder. Panic attacks occur intermittently, whereas generalized anxiety is more chronic. In phobias and obsessive-compulsive disorders, fear is experienced when an individual tries to master other symptoms (*see* MENTAL DISORDERS; PHOBIA).

Anxiety disorders are the most common mental disorders in the U.S., affecting 2 to 4 percent of the population. Evidence suggests that such disorders run in families. Drugs, psychotherapy, behavior modification, and relaxation training, alone or in combination, are used in treating anxiety.

ANYANG, also An-yang, city, N China, in Henan (Honan) Province, in a coal-mining and cotton-growing region. Principal manufactures include cotton textiles and processed food. It is located on the site of Yin, the capital of the Shang (Yin) dynasty (c. 1766 BC–c. 1027 BC). Archaeological work, begun here in 1928, has uncovered the remains of a 16th-century-BC royal palace, several royal tombs, and a collection of oracle bones chronicling early Chinese history. Pop. (1987 est.) 363,200.

ANZAC, acronym used to designate the Australasian troops engaged in the Gallipoli campaign (q.v.) and on other fronts during the two world wars. The word was formed from the initial letters of the words Australian-New Zealand Army Corps.

AOMORI, city and seaport, Japan, capital of Aomori Prefecture, N Honshu Island, on Aomori Bay. Although the city was severely bombed during World War II, today the rebuilt port and new transportation facilities make it the main export center of N Honshu. The chief exports of the area are rice, tobacco, textiles, and machinery. Pop. (1988 est.) 292,300.

AORTA, principal artery of the body. In humans the aorta rises from the left ventricle of the heart, arches back and downward over the root of the left lung, passes through the diaphragm into the abdomen, and divides into the right and left iliac arteries at about the level of the fourth lumbar vertebra. Originating at the heart, the aorta gives rise to the coronary arteries supplying the heart muscle with blood; from the arch arise the innominate, subclavian, and carotid arteries, which supply the head and arms. The descending part of the aorta gives rise, in the thorax, to the intercostal arteries that ramify in the body wall. In the abdomen it gives off the coeliac artery, which divides into the gastric, hepatic, and splenic arteries; the mesenteric arteries to the intestines; the renal arteries to the kidneys; and small branches to the body wall and to reproductive organs.

AOSTA (anc. *Augusta Praetoria),* city, NW Italy, capital of Aosta Province and Valle d'Aosta Region, on the Dora Baltea R., and near the junction of roads through the Great and Little Saint Bernard passes over the Alps. Aosta is a year-round tourist center and also has factories producing iron and steel, chemicals, and textiles. Founded by Emperor Augustus about 24 BC as a Roman military outpost, Aosta has many ruins, some dating from the 1st century AD. Pop. (1988 est.) 36,700.

AOUDAD, the wild horned sheep of North Africa, *Ammotragus lervia,* of the subfamily Caprinae, in the order Artiodactyla. They are also known as Barbary sheep. Seven subspecies are found from Morocco to Tunisia and southward into the mountains of the northern Sahara.

The sandy color of the aoudad provides natural camouflage against the sand and rock of the habitat. About 1 m (about 3 ft) high at the shoulder, the animal is one of the larger inhabitants of the Atlas Mountains. It has massive horns up to 76 cm (30 in) long, terminating in points, and a thick mane hanging from the chest and forelegs. The aoudad gets water from sparse vegetation and dew. The females and their young gather in small herds that the rams join during mating season. During long periods of drought the herds suffer severe losses. They are widely hunted for meat and hides.

APACHE, North American Indians of six culturally related groups descended from Athabascan-speaking peoples. The tribal groups are the Kiowa Apache, who lived between the northern border of New Mexico and the Platte River; the Lipan of eastern New Mexico and western Texas; the Jicarilla of southern New Mexico; the Mescalero of central New Mexico; the Chiricahua of the mountain range of the same name in southwestern Arizona; and the Western Apache of central Arizona.

History. Early Apache inhabitants of the southwestern U.S. were a nomadic people; some groups roamed as far south as Mexico. They were primarily buffalo (*see* BISON) hunters, but practiced limited farming. For centuries fierce warriors, adept in desert survival, they carried out raids on those who encroached on their territory.

The first intruders were the Spanish, who penetrated Apache territory in the late 1500s. The Spanish drive northward disrupted ancient Apache trade connections with neighboring tribes. When New Mexico became a Spanish colony in 1598, hostilities increased between Spaniards and Apaches. An influx of Comanche Indians into traditional Apache territory in the early 1700s drove the Lipan and other Apaches to move south of their main food source, the buffalo. These Apaches began raiding for food.

Apache raids on settlers accompanied the American westward movement and the U.S. acquisition of New Mexico in 1848. The Indians and the U.S. military authorities engaged in fierce wars until all Apache tribes were eventually placed on reservations. Most of the tribes were subdued by 1868, except for the Chiricahua, who continued their attacks until 1872, when their chief, Cochise, signed a treaty with the U.S. government and moved with his band to an Apache reservation in Arizona. The last band of Apache raiders, led by the chief Geronimo, was hunted down in 1886 to be confined in Florida.

Apache Culture. In traditional Apache culture, women gathered food, wood, and water, while men went out to hunt and raid. Most family units lived in wickiups—dome-shaped brush huts erected by the women—or in buffalo-hide tepees. Western Apache tribes were matrilineal; others apparently traced their descent through both parents. Polygamy was practiced when economic circumstances permitted; marriage could be terminated easily by either party. Religion was a fundamental part of Apache life. Among the best-known supernatural beings were the *ga'ns,* protective mountain spirits represented in religious rites such as the girls' puberty ceremony, still performed by Western Apaches.

Today Apaches number about 15,000, with many living on Indian reservations in Arizona and New Mexico. Farming, cattle herding, and tourist-related businesses are important economically; nevertheless, unemployment is high. Present-day culture is a mixture of traditional Apache beliefs, such as witchcraft, and contemporary U.S. elements.

See also AMERICAN INDIANS.

For further information on this topic, see the Bibliography in volume 28, sections 364, 1105–8.

APALACHICOLA, navigable river 145 km (90 mi) long, formed by the junction of the Chattahoochee and Flint rivers, in the extreme SW corner of Georgia. It flows through NW Florida and empties into Apalachicola Bay, a large arm of the Gulf of Mexico. The bay is set off from the gulf by a chain of islands that forms a part of the Gulf Intracoastal Waterway.

APARTHEID. *See* SOUTH AFRICA, REPUBLIC OF.

APATITE (Gr. *apate,* "deception"), mineral so named because it resembles various other minerals for which it might be mistaken. It consists chiefly of phosphate of lime. Apatite is a distinct mineral of composition $Ca_5(PO_4)_3F$ in which some or all of the fluorine may be replaced by chlorine (chlorapatite). The mineral crystallizes in the hexagonal system (*see* CRYSTAL) and has a hardness (q.v.) of 5 and a sp.gr. of 3.2. When pure, apatite is colorless and transparent, but it may exhibit various degrees of color and opacity. These mineral phosphates of lime were often used in the preparation of fertilizers, but they have been replaced by phosphate rock.

APATOSAURUS. *See* BRONTOSAUR.

APE, any member of the primate families Hylobatidae (the lesser apes), which includes the gibbons (*Hylobates*), and Pongidae (the great apes), which includes the orangutan (*Pongo*), the chimpanzees (*Pan*), and gorilla (*Gorilla*). They belong to the superfamily Cercopithecoidea, the Old World monkeys and apes. Apes, or anthropoids, are distinguished from other primates by their complex brains and hence intelligence, their large size, and their lack of tails. They are mainly vegetarian but, except for the gorilla, occasionally eat small animals.

The gibbons, of Southeast Asia, show great skill in brachiation; that is, they swing and leap rapidly through trees on their long arms, using their hands as hooks. On the ground, they often balance themselves with their arms and walk upright. The more advanced orangutan, in Sumatra and Borneo, is also arboreal but slower moving and much larger. The social unit of the orangutan consists of one or two females with young; the solitary males join them only for mating.

Orangutans, Pongo pygmaeus, *mother and child, in Borneo.* © Bios–Peter Arnold, Inc.

The chimpanzee and the massive gorilla—the largest of all primates—are found in Africa. Both also climb trees, especially to nest at night, but are more terrestrial than Asian apes. The chimpanzee lives in fairly large, loosely knit groups in which smaller units form and reform; the gorilla lives in family units.

The orangutan, chimpanzee, and gorilla, collectively known as the great apes, can walk upright but commonly travel on all fours, with knuckles of the hands touching the ground. They have the greatest intelligence of animals other than humans and can use simple tools.

See CHIMPANZEE; GIBBON; GORILLA; ORANGUTAN; PRIMATE. G.H.B.

For further information on this topic, see the Bibliography in volume 28, section 482.

APELDOORN, city, central Netherlands, in Gelderland Province, near Arnhem. The natural beauty of the region attracts many tourists; a national recreation area, Het Veluwe, adjoins Apeldoorn. On the outskirts of the city is Het Loo, formerly the royal summer palace and now a national museum containing a large art collection. Apeldoorn is a growing industrial center; among its industries are copper founding, papermaking, and textile, ink, and soap manufacturing. Pop. (1988 est.) 146,300.

APELLES (fl. 352–308 BC), Greek painter, one of the most celebrated artists of the ancient world. Born in Colophon on the Ionian coast, he studied in Sicyon (now Sikion) under Pamphilus of Amphipolis. Apelles' works, characterized by a unique grace, are known only from literary descriptions, but they inspired Renaissance artists. The works include portraits of Philip of Macedon, his son Alexander the Great, and Alexander's generals, as well as mythological and allegorical scenes, such as *Venus Anadyomene* and *Calumny,* in which Ignorance, Suspicion, Envy, and other qualities are personified. According to a well-known anecdote, a cobbler detected a fault in the shoe of a figure painted by Apelles, who quickly rectified it. When the cobbler criticized the legs, however, Apelles exclaimed *"Ne supra crepidam sutor judicaret,"* advice immortalized as "Let the cobbler stick to his last."

APENNINES, mountain chain, Italy, extending from the Ligurian Alps in the NW through the length of the Italian Peninsula to the Strait of Messina and into Sicily. The chain is a branch of the Alpine system and consists of eight ranges, including the Lucanian, Tuscan, Umbrian, and Calabrian. The chain, generally uniform in appearance, is about 1290 km (about 800 mi) long and up to 129 km (80 mi) wide. Although the highest peaks include Mt. Corno (2914 m/9560 ft) and Mt. Amaro 2795 m (9170 ft), the average elevation is about 1220 m (about 4000 ft) above sea level. Two active volcanoes, Mt. Vesuvius (1227 m/4190 ft) near Naples and Mt. Etna (3369 m/11,053 ft) in Sicily, are part of the system.

The E side of the chain is the source of streams that are generally short and small; the only important river is the Ofanto R. in SE Italy. The W slopes give rise to several important rivers (Arno, Tiber, Volturno, Garigliano) and have some hydroelectric stations. The central and N divisions of the chain contain valuable deposits of iron ore, copper, tin, mercury, lignite, and borax. The famous quarries of Carrara marble are located in the NW part of the system.

Over the centuries the middle and lower slopes of the Apennines were cleared of forests, but a process of reforestation is now slowly progressing. Above the timberline, vegetation consists mainly of shrubs and grasses that are sometimes used for pastureland. The hills and plateau areas support extensive olive groves, vineyards, orchard and nut trees, and pastures.

APERTURE, in optics (q.v.), the opening of a lens (q.v.) through which light can enter. In photography (q.v.), the relative ăperture, or *f* number, is the ratio of the lens's focal length to the diameter of the effective aperture—that is, the diameter of the widest ray of light that can enter the lens.

APERTURE SYNTHESIS, in radio astronomy (q.v.), the combination of smaller radio telescopes to form, in effect, one very large telescope. An example is the Very Large Array (q.v.).

APHASIA (Gr. *a,* "not"; *phanai,* "to speak"), term introduced by the French physician Armand Trousseau (1801–67) to denote inability to express thought by means of speech, as a consequence of certain brain disorders. The meaning has since been extended to cover loss of the faculty of interchanging thought and even a temporary but complete loss of memory.

Motor aphasia involves a loss of memory of the coordinated movements necessary for the formation of symbols. This usually includes gestures, speech, and writing. (The inability to write is commonly termed *agraphia.*) Victims of this disorder are unable to name any object shown to them, although they know what it is. Neither can they reply to any question although they may understand it. In sensory aphasia, a loss of memory of the meaning of symbols occurs. This may affect the recollection of spoken language.

APHID, common name for insects of the superfamily Aphioidea, in the suborder Homoptera (q.v.) of the order Hemiptera. Aphids, also popularly called plant lice or green flies, are found worldwide as parasites on the roots, leaves, and stems of plants, to which they frequently do great damage. The mouthparts of aphids are adapted for piercing and sucking plants and consist of four long, sharp stylets within a proboscis, or sheath. Two projecting cornicles, or horn-shaped tubes, at the posterior end of the body emit a waxy secretion. The legs are long and slender but are not adapted for rapid movement; aphids rarely wander far, except during the spring and autumn migratory flights of the females. In autumn the females lay fertilized eggs that survive the winter in crevices and hatch in the spring, producing wingless females that reproduce parthenogenically (without fertilization from males). After several generations, winged females are produced; they then migrate to other plants and continue asexual reproduction of wingless females. Toward the end of summer winged males are produced, which fertilize the winter eggs.

The presence of aphids is readily detected by marks, wrinkles, or abnormalities on the infested plant. Aphids emit from their anus a sweet glutinous substance called honeydew, which is eagerly sought by ants and other insects; ants may hide aphids and protect them from predators (*see* ANT; LACEWING). Aphids that feed on such plants as turnip, cabbage, potato, bean, apple, pear, and larch have been the cause of widespread damage, often as a result of carrying plant viruses. Birds, spiders, syrphus-fly larvae, and ladybird beetles destroy great numbers of aphids, as do many internal parasites.

See also DISEASES OF PLANTS; PEST CONTROL.

APHRODITE, in Greek mythology, the goddess of love and beauty and the counterpart of the Roman Venus. In Homer's *Iliad* she is said to be the daughter of Zeus and Dione, one of his consorts, but in later legends she is described as having sprung from the foam of the sea and her name may be translated "foam-risen." In Homeric legend Aphrodite is the wife of the lame and ugly god of fire, Hephaestus. Among her lovers was Ares, god of war, who in later mythology became her husband. She was the rival of Persephone, queen of the underworld, for the love of the beautiful Greek youth Adonis.

Perhaps the most famous legend about Aphrodite concerns the cause of the Trojan War. Eris, the goddess of discord, the only goddess not invited to the wedding of King Peleus and the sea nymph Thetis, resentfully tossed into the banquet hall a golden apple, marked "for the fairest." When Zeus refused to judge between the three goddesses who claimed the apple, Hera, Athena, and Aphrodite, they asked Paris, prince of Troy, to make the award. Each offered him a bribe: Hera, that he would be a powerful ruler; Athena, that he would achieve great military fame; and Aphrodite, that he should have the fairest woman in the world. Paris selected Aphrodite as the fairest and chose as his prize Helen of Troy, the wife of the Greek king Menelaus. Paris's abduction of Helen led to the Trojan War.

Probably Oriental in origin, Aphrodite was identified in early Greek religious beliefs with the Phoenician Astarte and was known as Aphrodite Urania, queen of the heavens, and as Aphrodite Pandemos, goddess of the people.

APIA, city, capital of Western Samoa, on the N shore of Upolu Island, in the South Pacific Ocean. It is the country's chief port and economic center; exports include copra, bananas, cacao, and coffee. An international airport is located near Apia, at Faleolo. The island is also linked by boat with Pago Pago in American Samoa. Vailima, the former home of the Scottish writer Robert Louis Stevenson, and Stevenson's gravesite are notable landmarks.

Apia was a small village until European missionaries and traders arrived in the 1830s. It subsequently grew quickly as a European-style port for the Pacific island trade. From 1899 to 1914 it was the capital of the German dependency of Western Samoa. After the defeat of Germany in World War I, New Zealand administered the dependency from Apia, first under a League of Nations mandate (1921–46) and then as a UN Trust Territory (1946–62). Apia continued as the capital when Western Samoa achieved independence in 1962. Pop. (1981) 33,170.

APIS, sacred bull of the ancient Egyptians. It was known to them as Hapi and was regarded as the incarnation of Osiris or of Ptah. A court was set apart for Apis in the temple of Ptah at Memphis. It was believed that when Apis died, a new Apis appeared and had to be searched out; he would be recognizable by certain sacred marks upon his body, such as his color (mainly black) and a knot under his tongue. Apis is sometimes represented as a man with the head of a bull.

APNEA, cessation of breathing. Periods of apnea in which breathing ceases for a few seconds before resuming may occur during sleep. When apnea alternates with periods of rapid, heavy breathing (hyperapnea), such cycles are called Cheyne-Stokes respiration; they may be due to lack of oxygen in the brain, accumulation of acid in the blood, or heart failure. Apnea may be associated with such harmful conditions as irregularities in heartbeat, high blood pressure, and decreased contractile force of the heart muscle. It has also been linked to some cases of sudden infant death syndrome (SIDS) (q.v.).

Sleep apnea may be due to obstruction of the airway (obstructive sleep apnea), to some abnormality in the part of the brain that controls respiration (central sleep apnea), or to both (mixed sleep apnea). Obesity may be a contributing factor; people who suffer from sleep apnea are often advised to reduce, and also to avoid sedative or hypnotic drugs. Researchers can sometimes trace the cause to damage in areas of the brain involved with respiratory control. M.A.

APO, MOUNT, active volcano, S Philippines, on SE Mindanao Island, W of Davao. Of its three volcanic peaks the highest reaches an elevation of 2954 m (9692 ft) and is the highest point in the Philippines. The heavily forested slopes of the mountain and the surrounding area are included in Mt. Apo National Park (1936).

APOCALYPSE. *See* REVELATION (Bible).

APOCALYPTIC WRITINGS, Jewish and Christian writings, most of them composed between about 200 BC and AD 100, distinguished basically by a belief in two opposing cosmic powers and in two distinct ages (eons) of the world. Typically, the authors of apocalyptic literature believe that the present age of the world is irredeemably evil, ruled by a Satan figure personifying evil. These authors reveal, however, that the evil age is soon to be ended, destroyed by God, who is good. The following age, the kingdom of God, will be ruled by God, will be perfect, and will last forever; and only the good, formerly oppressed, will enjoy it.

Because most apocalyptic literature was written at a time when both Jews and early Christians were experiencing exile or persecution, a major secondary characteristic of such literature is the frequent presentation of the authors' beliefs through visions and dreams. In this manner, and by the use of elaborate animal and number symbolism, the authors' beliefs would be revealed only to persons able to perceive the meaning of their visions and symbolism. Unbelievers would find their writings obscure, if not altogether unintelligible.

Several other frequently occurring important secondary characteristics of apocalyptic literature are pseudonymity, the ascribing of an apocalyptic work to some earlier revered figure (for example, a prophet or a saint); contending hierarchies of angels and demons; a faith in God, who will fulfill the promises of the Bible; a belief in a heavenly city and a heavenly paradise reserved for the just in the age to come; and a belief in a messiah.

Certain books of the Bible or portions of them have been termed apocalyptic by various scholars. The best known and most appropriately so termed among canonical books are Daniel and Revelation. Of the apocryphal works, the best known are Enoch and 2 Esdras. N.N.G.

APOCRYPHA (Gr. *apokryphos,* "hidden"), word coined by the 5th-century biblical scholar St. Jerome for the biblical books received by the church of his time as part of the Greek version of the Old Testament (*see* SEPTUAGINT), but that were not included in the Hebrew Bible. In the Authorized, or King James, Version, the books are either printed as an appendix or are omitted altogether; they are not considered canonical by Protestants.

The Septuagint was received by the Christian church from Hellenistic Judaism. The books included in the Septuagint that were excluded by the non-Hellenistic Jews from their canon were Judith, the Wisdom of Solomon, Tobit, Sirach (Ecclesiasticus), Baruch, and the two books of Maccabees. Of these, Judith and Tobit are best described as edifying historical fiction, and Baruch, as an appendage to the Book of Jeremiah, written in the person of Jeremiah's secretary. Wisdom and Sirach are testimonies to the wisdom tradition of Israel otherwise represented in the books of Proverbs, Job, and Ecclesiastes. The books of Maccabees are historical works in the tradition of the books of Samuel, Kings, and Chronicles. Also generally included with the Apocrypha are the two books of Esdras, additions to the Book of Esther (Esther 10:4–10), the Song of the Three Young Men (Dan. 3:24–90), Susanna (Dan. 13), Bel and the Dragon (Dan. 14), and the Prayer of Manasseh.

Roman Catholic and Orthodox Christians still follow the Septuagint and include in the canon of the Bible all the Apocrypha, except the two books of Esdras and the Prayer of Manasseh. They generally refer to the Protestant Apocrypha as deuterocanonical books (q.v.), however, and reserve the term Apocrypha for those books entirely outside the biblical canon, which Protestants call the pseudepigrapha (q.v.).

With the growth of a historical perspective in biblical studies during the 19th century, the value of the Apocrypha as historical sources came to be generally recognized. Derived from the period 300 BC to New Testament times, the Apocrypha shed valuable light on the period between the end of the Old Testament narrative and the opening of the New Testament. They are also important sources of information on the development of belief in immortality, the resurrection, and other questions of eschatology, as well as the increasing impact of Hellenistic ideas on Judaism.

See also BIBLE. B.V.

APOCRYPHAL NEW TESTAMENT (Gr. *apokryphos,* "hidden"), title that refers to more than 100 books written by Christian authors between the 2d and 4th centuries. The books have two characteristics in common: (1) In general form they resemble New Testament writings, many of them falling into the literary categories of gospel, acts, letter, and apocalypse; (2) they belong neither to the New Testament canon nor to the writings of the recognized Fathers of the Church (q.v.).

Some of the documents were written for initiates in groups such as the Gnostics (*see* GNOSTICISM); for those groups, who claimed knowledge derived from a secret tradition, the works were genuinely apocryphal, that is, "books kept hidden." Others were written for open and general use in the churches of which their authors were members; they simply failed to become accepted as part of the orthodox canon of the Bible. Some of the writings, such as the Gospel According to the Hebrews, may have held a place of importance in the common life of Jewish Christians. Others were read in Gnostic circles, such as the Letter of Eugnostos found in the Nag Hammadi texts, a collection of Gnostic treatises discovered in 1945–46. Still others, such as the Infancy Story of Thomas and the Acts of Pilate, addressed the curiosity of common people in the church at large by filling in tantalizing gaps in the biblical writing with highly fanciful details about the unknown aspects of Jesus' life.

Roman Catholics and Protestants use the term Apocrypha (q.v.) differently when referring to biblical literature; both, however, refer to the same books when they speak of the Apocryphal New Testament. J.L.Ma.

APOGEE. *See* ORBIT.

APOLLINAIRE, Guillaume, pseudonym of GUILLAUME APOLLINAIRE DE KOSTROWITSKY (1880–1918), French poet and novelist, born in Rome, and educated at the Lycée Saint-Charles in Monaco. He was editor of the periodical *Les Soirées de Paris* (1913–18). In his attempt to synthesize poetry and the visual arts, Apollinaire had significant influence on both French poetry and the development of modern art. *The Cubist Painters* (1913; trans. 1949) is a landmark document; other prose works include his symbolic novel, based on his experiences as a soldier in World War I, *The Poet Assassinated* (1916; trans. 1923) and the drama *Les mamelles de Tirésias* (written 1903; pub. 1918). Referring to the latter in the introduction as "surrealist," Apollinaire is credited with the first use of this term. His poetry includes *Alcools* (1913; trans. 1964), considered his masterpiece, and *Caligrammes* (1918).

APOLLINARIANISM, heretical doctrine taught by Apollinaris the Younger (c. 310–c. 390), bishop of Laodicea in Syria. A controversial theologian, he maintained that the Logos, or divine nature in Christ, took the place of the rational human soul or mind of Christ and that the body of Christ was a spiritualized and glorified form of humanity. This doctrine was condemned as a heresy by Roman councils (377 and 381) and also by the Council of Constantinople (381). In spite of its repeated condemnation, Apollinarianism persisted into the 5th century. At that time its remaining adherents merged with the Monophysites, who held that Christ had a divine will but no human will.

APOLLO, in Greek mythology, son of the god Zeus and Leto, daughter of a Titan. He was also called Delian from Delos, the island of his birth, and Pythian, from his killing of Python, the fabled serpent that guarded a shrine on the mountains of Parnassus. In Homeric legend Apollo was primarily a god of prophecy. His most important oracle was at Delphi, the site of his victory over the Python. He sometimes gave the gift of prophecy to mortals whom he loved, such as the Trojan princess Cassandra.

Apollo was a gifted musician, who delighted the gods with his performance on the lyre. He was also a master archer and a fleet-footed athlete, credited with having been the first victor in the Olympic games. His twin sister, Artemis, was the guardian of young women, and Apollo was the special protector of young men. He was also the god of agriculture and cattle and of light and truth. He taught humans the art of healing.

Some tales depict Apollo as pitiless and cruel. According to Homer's *Illiad,* Apollo answered the prayers of the priest Chryses to obtain the release of his daughter from the Greek general Agamemnon by shooting fiery, pestilence-carrying arrows into the Greek army. He also abducted and ravished the young Athenian princess Creusa and abandoned her and the child born to them. Perhaps because of his beauty and perfect physique, Apollo was represented in ancient art more frequently than any other deity.

APOLLODORUS (fl. 5th cent. BC), Athenian painter known as Skiagraphos (the "Shadow Painter"). By skillful use of light and shade he improved perspective and the modeling of figures in order to heighten the illusion of three-dimensional space. His innovations were further developed by Zeuxis. None of Apollodorus' works has survived.

APOLLONIUS OF PERGA, called the Great Geometer (fl. 3d cent. BC), Greek mathematician, born in Perga, Pamphylia (now Turkey). He wrote on arithmetical calculation and on statistics and laid the foundation for the geometry of position with his *Treatise on Conic Sections.* This work contained eight books, four of which are extant.

APOLLONIUS OF RHODES (295?–215 BC), Greek poet, born in Alexandria, Egypt. Unlike his teacher, Callimachus, who favored the short poem in the artificial and learned style, Apollonius preferred the lengthy poem in the simple style of Homer. The epic poem *Argonautica,* based on the legend of the Argonauts, is Apollonius's most important and only extant work. Vergil drew much material for the *Aeneid* from the *Argonautica.*

APOLLO PROGRAM, part of the U.S. space program. *See* SPACE EXPLORATION.

APOPLEXY. *See* STROKE.

APOSTASY, the total abandonment of Christianity by a baptized person. In the early church it was considered one of the unpardonable sins, the other two being murder and fornication. Apostasy is to be distinguished from laxity in the practice of religion and from heresy, the formal denial of one or more doctrines of the Christian faith. In Roman Catholic canon law, the term also refers to the abandonment of the religious state by a monk or nun who has taken perpetual vows and leaves the religious life without the appropriate dispensation.

APOSTLE (Gr. *apostolos,* "one sent forth"), messenger, especially one of the 12 disciples whom Jesus Christ sent forth to preach the gospel and to act in his name. Jesus may have selected 12 apostles because of the 12 tribes in Israel, thus signifying that the Christian community is God's Israel (see Gal. 6:16), which inherits the privileges of ancient Israel. The Twelve were Peter, Andrew, James the Great, John, Philip, Bartholomew, Thomas, Matthew, James the Less, Thaddaeus, Simon the Canaanite, and Judas Iscariot. Matthias was chosen in place of Judas (see Acts 1:26). In the early church the title *apostle* was extended to others who spread the Christian message, such as Paul, Barnabas, and Timothy.

The founder of the Christian church in a country is usually spoken of as the apostle of that country; thus, Gregory of Armenia is the apostle of Armenia. Other apostles so identified include St. Boniface, of Germany; St. Augustine, of England; St. Patrick, of Ireland; St. Columba, of Scotland; St. Cuthbert, of Northumbria; and St. Denis, of France.

APOSTLE ISLANDS, island group, N Wisconsin, in Lake Superior. The group includes about 20 picturesque wooded islands, the largest being

Madeline Island, which contains the chief settlement, La Pointe. They support a varied wildlife and are popular with tourists and hunters. The islands, along with a section of the adjacent mainland Bayfield Peninsula, make up Apostle Islands National Lakeshore (*see* NATIONAL PARK SERVICE, table).

APOSTLES' CREED, a brief summary statement of Christian belief traditionally attributed to the 12 apostles. Like most Christian creeds, it contains three paragraphs, one for each person of the Trinity (q.v.). The first paragraph begins, "I believe in God the Father Almighty"; the second, "I believe in Jesus Christ"; the third, "I believe in the Holy Spirit." These three assertions correspond to the three questions that were addressed to candidates for baptism in the early church.

Until the 15th century, it was believed that the Apostles' Creed was written by the apostles, each in turn having contributed a clause. It is now known that the creed was not of apostolic origin, but the title itself suggests that each clause of the creed can be traced to New Testament references and that the creed originated very early.

Today it is widely agreed that the Apostles' Creed developed as the baptismal confession of faith. A similar, but not identical, confession appears in the baptismal liturgy contained in *The Apostolic Tradition of Hippolytus* (c. 215). Similar but variant versions are also found in the writings of the early Fathers of the Church (q.v.), such as Irenaeus and Tertullian, in which they are called "rules of faith." A form identical with what is now called the Apostles' Creed did not emerge until the early 8th century, in the writings of St. Pirminius.

The Apostles' Creed continues to be used as the baptismal profession of faith in most Western churches; Orthodox churches prefer to use the later Nicene Creed (q.v.). In Roman Catholic practice, the Apostles' Creed is also recited in the Daily Office, before the first and after the last service each day. In most Protestant churches, it is used periodically at Sunday worship. Anglicans and Lutherans use it regularly in Morning and Evening Prayer (Matins and Evensong). C.P.P.

APOSTOLIC CONSTITUTIONS, collection of eight books containing ecclesiastical directives supposedly composed by the 12 apostles and transmitted by them to Clement I of Rome. The books contain comprehensive rules for the Christian life. The first six books are similar in content to a 3d-century work known as the *Didascalia Apostolorum.* Part of the seventh book contains material based on the Teaching of the Twelve Apostles, or Didache, written in the 2d century. The eighth book includes the 85 canons, considered the most valuable part of the Constitutions. All eight books were probably compiled and edited by one author, sometimes referred to as Pseudo-Clement, probably of Syrian origin, and with tendencies toward Arianism (q.v.). Historians estimate the date of composition as between AD 340 and 400.

APOSTOLIC FATHERS, term applied to certain disciples and successors of the 12 apostles. In a more restricted sense, the term is applied to a group of Greek-language writers who were among the martyrs and major figures of the 1st and 2d centuries in the Christian church. Although not considered worthy of inclusion in the Bible, their writings may be ranked as a continuation of the writings of the apostles themselves and are considered a valuable source of early church history. Generally accepted as apostolic fathers are Clement I of Rome, St. Ignatius of Antioch, and St. Polycarp. Opinion is divided on whether St. Barnabas (fl. about 130 AD) and Hermas (fl. 140 AD) are apostolic fathers. Among the writings also associated with the apostolic fathers is the Teaching of the Twelve Apostles, or Didache (q.v.); opinion also differs on the authorship of this work.

APOSTOLIC SUCCESSION, in Christian theology, the doctrine asserting that the apostles designated their successors as bishops through prayer and the laying on of hands, and that bishops have in turn designated their successors in the same way ever since.

The doctrine addresses the problem of identifying the continuity of Christian faith and life amid the discontinuous and changing circumstances of history. The idea that church ministers were successors of the apostles, who were in turn successors of Christ, can be traced to St. Clement I before the end of the 1st century. The doctrine, however, was not formalized until the conflict with Gnosticism (q.v.) during the 2d, 3d, and 4th centuries, when the Gnostics claimed a secret tradition traceable to the apostles. Church authorities then began to look to the succession of bishop to bishop as the guarantee of orthodox teaching.

Apostolic succession as the outward and visible sign of inward faithfulness to the Christian message is considered essential to ecclesiastical life by the Orthodox and Roman Catholic churches; and it is held in some form by Anglican and some Lutheran churches. Most Protestant churches, however, emphasize other links with the continuity of Christian faith, such as Scripture and creeds (q.v.). C.P.P.

APPALACHIAN MOUNTAINS *or* **APPALACHIANS,** great mountain system of E North America, nearly parallel with the Atlantic coast, and extending from the province of Québec in Canada to N Alabama. The system is about 2400 km (about 1500 mi) long and varies from about 160 to more than 480 km (about 100 to more than 300 mi) in width. Its altitude varies between about 460 and nearly 2130 m (about 1500 and nearly 7000 ft). The three divisions of the system—N, central, S—vary considerably in geologic age, having been raised by a series of crustal plate collisions that began during the Ordovician period and climaxed in the Permian (*see* PLATE TECTONICS). The N division—including the Green Mountains and the White Mountains (qq.v.), the highlands of Maine, the Shickshock Mts., and the Notre Dame Mts. of Québec—terminates in the hills of Newfoundland. The chief ranges of the central section are the Catskill Mountains, Allegheny Mountains or Alleghenies, and Blue Ridge or Blue Ridge Mountains (qq.v.). The Blue Ridge range is the principal uplift of the Appalachians. This range rises from the Piedmont Plateau to heights far greater than the Alleghenies attain. Beginning prominently in South Mt. in Pennsylvania, it stretches SW in greater and greater heights, through Virginia and W North Carolina, where it divides, the N branch continuing W to Georgia as the Great Smoky Mountains (q.v.). This range, a broad mass of mountains on the border between North Carolina and Tennessee, contains peaks higher than those of the White Mts. of New Hampshire. The culminating group of the Blue Ridge is known as the Black Mountains (q.v.). The highest peak of the Appalachians, Mt. Mitchell (2037 m/6684 ft), and many peaks above 1829 m (6000 ft) in height are situated in this group. The principal range of the S Appalachians, which extend S into Alabama from the New R. valley in Virginia and West Virginia, is the Cumberland Plateau and Cumberland Mountains (q.v.). Elevations in this range average about 610 m (about 2000 ft).

The Appalachian Mts. are heavily forested and contain deposits of iron ore, anthracite, bituminous coal, zinc, slate, limestone, asbestos, mica, granite, and emery. Along the W slope from SW New York through W Pennsylvania, into West Virginia, Kentucky, and Tennessee, lie coalfields.

Numerous rivers make their way through the Appalachians. Among the more important are the Connecticut, Hudson, Delaware, Schuylkill, Susquehanna, Potomac, James, and Rappahannock (flowing E or SE) and the Cumberland, Kanawha, Allegheny, Monongahela, Tennessee, and others (flowing toward the W).

For further information on this topic, see the Bibliography in volume 28, section 867.

APPALACHIAN TRAIL, footpath for outdoor enthusiasts, extending about 3250 km (about 2020 mi) from Maine to Georgia, primarily along the crest of the Appalachian Mts. It is the longest marked, continuous footpath in the world, and at some points is more than 1829 m (6000 ft) high. Wooden signposts and white markings painted on rocks and trees are placed at intervals.

Proposals for a wilderness path were first made in 1921, and in the following year construction of the trail was begun near Bear Mountain, N.Y. By 1937 the footpath, then extending from Mt. Katahdin, in central Maine, to Mt. Oglethorpe, in Georgia, was ready for use. After 1937 the trail was extended as far as Springer Mt., NE of Mt. Oglethorpe. In 1968 the trail became part of the National Park System as one of the initial two units of the National Trail System; it was officially renamed the Appalachian National Scenic Trail.

APPEAL, in law, request to a higher court to reverse the decision made by a lower court. The party who won the decision in the lower court is called the appellee; the party appealing the decision is called the appellant. Except in unusual cases, the appellate court may only review questions relating to law and may not disturb the factual determinations of the lower court. The right of appeal is derived from English law, in which an appeal was obtained by a writ of error. Most states of the U.S., however, use the notice of appeal to initiate appellate action. If an appeal is not undertaken within a limited period usually prescribed by statute, the original decision becomes final and binding on the parties.

The right of appeal provides the opportunity to have an involved legal question given more deliberate and careful study than is possible in the lower courts. Whereas the decision of a lower court is usually rendered by a single judge, in an appellate court several judges hear the case and bring their views to bear on the same problem. The decision is usually available in printed form and indicates the basis for the court's conclusions. These judgments are often cited as precedents in future cases. For detailed information on appeals, *see* COURTS; COURTS OF APPEALS; COURTS IN THE UNITED STATES.

APPENDICITIS, acute inflammation of the vermiform (wormlike) appendix, a blind tube projecting from the cecum, or rounded end, of the large intestine. The appendix, located in the lower right side of the abdomen, is a vestigial organ with no function in humans. If the appendix wall ruptures, infection may spread to the abdominal cavity, causing peritonitis (q.v.). Symptoms of appendicitis include pain and cramps in the area between the right hip bone and the navel, fever, nausea and vomiting, constipation, and diarrhea. The usual treatment is surgical removal of the appendix (appendectomy). Although the frequency of appendicitis is high among children, the ailment can affect persons of any age.

APPIA, Adolphe (1862–1928), Swiss artist, stage designer, and theorist, who pioneered modern staging and lighting techniques. His first publication, *La Mise en scène du drame Wagnérien* (The Staging of the Wagnerian Drama, 1895), set forth his innovative theories in precise staging and lighting plans for the major operas of the German composer Richard Wagner. In *Music and the Art of the Theatre* (1899; trans. 1962) Appia grouped his principles in two major categories—scenery and lighting. Scenery must be three dimensional and multileveled. Lighting must unify the stage picture, enhance the music, and underline the action; thus, it must be mobile, able to change and shift with the mood and action. Appia's final work, *L'oeuvre d'art vivant* (The Living Work of Art, 1921), summarizes all his theories and experience; he reiterated that the designer-director's prime concerns are the actors, their movements, and their words. He illustrated all his works with evocative sketches.

APPIAN WAY, (anc. *Via Appia*), road of ancient Italy. The oldest and most celebrated highway of the Roman Republic, it was built in 312 BC by the Roman censor Appius Claudius Caecus. It led southward from the Servian Wall in Rome to Capua, passing through Appii Forum and Terracina, and was later extended to Brundisium (now Brindisi). The main route to Greece, the Appian Way was more than 560 km (more than 350 mi) long. It was well constructed, although the present pavement of large hexagonal blocks, principally lava, laid on a firm foundation and strengthened by cement, is probably not the original bed. From Rome to Terracina the course is nearly straight, despite the steep grades of the Alban Hills and the swamps of the Pontine Marshes. Near Rome the road was lined with tombs, of which the ruins of many can still be seen. Parts of the road are still in use.

APPIUS CLAUDIUS. *See* CLAUDIUS.

APPLE, common name for any tree of the genus *Malus,* of the family Rosaceae (*see* ROSE), and for the pome fruit of the tree. The tree, a decidu-

A section of the Appian Way, famous Roman military road, which is still usable after 2000 years.
Manley Photo–Shostal/Superstock

ous plant, grows mainly in the temperate areas of the world. The fruit is a firm, fleshy structure derived from the receptacle of the flower. Apple leaves are broadly oval in shape and are somewhat woolly on the undersides. The flowers in bloom have a rounded appearance. Some apple blossoms are as white as the pear bloom, but the majority of apple blossoms have stripes or tints of rose. A few apple species bloom with bright red flowers. Apple wood is hard, durable, and very fine-grained. Formerly it was prized in cabinetmaking, but uncertainty of supply and other factors have greatly restricted its use.

The physical characteristics of the fruit are subject to considerable variation. The skin color may range from green to a deep, blackish red. Shapes, also, are diverse and include oblate and oblong fruits and fruits of a size hardly larger than a cherry or as big as a medium-sized grapefruit.

Varieties. Apple trees have been cultivated for their fruit for many centuries. Early apple growers selected superior strains from wild seedlings and propagated them by grafting. Currently, many apple varieties are developed by controlled crossing of desirable parents. Beneficial mutation in standard varieties is also a source for new varieties. It is generally thought that modern apple varieties resulted from natural cross-pollination involving several species, because modern varieties are heterozygous, that is, they do not reproduce true to type.

Apple trees are best adapted to areas in which the average temperature approaches or reaches freezing during at least two months. The exact chilling requirement varies somewhat with each variety. The trees withstand temperatures down to −40° C (−40° F).

Culture. Apple growing is a highly specialized business and the trend is toward larger orchards, especially because costly mechanical sprayers have been used to control diseases and insects. Leading diseases of apples are apple scabs, mildew, and fire blight. Insect pests include the codling moth, the apple maggot, the red-banded leaf roller, aphids, leaf hoppers, mites, San José scale, and oyster-shell scale. Rodents, particularly pine and meadow mice and rabbits, cause severe damage to trees unless proper control measures are employed.

Several horticultural methods are used in apple culture. One system is based on clean culture, with winter cover crops sown throughout the orchard; another method utilizes permanent sod and sod mulch. If a permanent grass or sod system is used, additional fertilizer is needed to compensate for organic nutrients absorbed by the grass. If clean culture is practiced, no additional cultivating is advisable after the first week in August, in order to permit the trees to harden off, that is, to become adapted to the lower temperatures of fall and winter.

Apple trees are vegetatively propagated by grafting or budding. By these methods a scion (bud of the desired variety) is inserted into the base of the stem or trunk of a seedling tree known as the stock. Sometimes the stock itself is a vegetatively propagated tree. Most trees are propagated, however, on seedling rootstocks. Several size-controlling rootstocks are available. Uniform heights facilitate spraying and harvesting. Extremely dwarfed rootstocks are popular where space is limited.

Most apple varieties require cross-pollination in order to bear satisfactorily. Certain varieties, known as triploids, are of no value as pollinators because of their genetic makeup. Two diploid pollinating varieties must be present to pollinate each other as well as the triploid variety.

Production. Commercial production in the U.S. is limited to about four favored areas: the northwestern states, the Shenandoah-Cumberland region, the northeastern states, and the north-central states. The northwestern area is noted for high yields but uses extensive artificial irrigation.

Of the several thousand varieties of apples, relatively few have commercial importance. Delicious, with its color mutations, is the most widely grown variety in the U.S. It is particularly well adapted to the Northwest but is grown commercially in all apple areas. McIntosh is the leading apple in the Northeast. In the Shenandoah-Cumberland area the most important orchard varieties are York Imperial, Delicious, and Stayman Winesap. Varieties adapted best to the north-central area are McIntosh, Jonathan, Rome Beauty, Wealthy, and Cortland. Eastern Canadian apple growers cultivate nearly the same varieties as those grown in the Northeast. British Columbia is best suited to the varieties grown in the Northwest; McIntosh, however, is a favorite among British Columbian orchardists.

World production of apples was 41 million metric tons annually in the mid-1980s, led by the USSR, China, and the U.S. The leading apple-producing countries in Europe are France, Germany, and Italy; most of the crop is processed as either cider or brandy. Apple production in the U.S. in the mid-1980s was about 9 percent of the world total. Washington is the most important apple-producing state of the U.S. Next ranking in descending order are New York, Michigan, California, Pennsylvania, and Virginia.

Consumption. Apples are eaten in the fresh state; serve as the chief ingredient of such desserts as

Apple trees at the height of their springtime blossom. Insert: *The delicate apple blossom at left foreshadows the ripe, red apple at right.*

baked apples; apple pie and apple strudel; and are processed into dried apples, canned sauce, slices, jelly, and pasteurized juice, cider, and vinegar. Applejack is a common American name for apple brandy. France is the leading producer of apple brandies.

History. The native home of the apple is not definitely known, but the tree originated probably between the Caspian and the Black seas. Charred remains of apples have been found in the prehistoric lake dwellings of Switzerland. Apples were a favorite fruit of the ancient Greeks and Romans.

The apple was introduced to America by early settlers, who brought apple seeds with them. Records of the Massachusetts Bay Co. indicate that apples were grown in New England as early as 1630. Seeds were carried westward by missionaries, traders, and Indians. One man alone, John Chapman (Johnny Appleseed), was responsible for extensive plantings of apple trees in the Middle West.

For further information on this topic, see the Bibliography in volume 28, sections 592–93.

APPLESEED, Johnny, real name JOHN CHAPMAN (c. 1774–1847), American pioneer, born in Leominster, Mass. He settled in the Ohio River valley sometime after 1800 and spent his life planting nurseries of apple seedlings over hundreds of square kilometers during his travels in what are now Ohio, Indiana, and Illinois. As Johnny Appleseed he is celebrated in frontier legends as a symbol of westward-moving American civilization, and he figures in American literature in such works as "In Praise of Johnny Appleseed" (1923), by the American poet Vachel Lindsay.

APPLETON, city, seat of Outagamie Co., and also in Calumet and Winnebago counties, E Wisconsin, on the Fox R., near Lake Winnebago; settled 1835, inc. as a city 1857. Paper and paper products are manufactured in Appleton, as well as machinery, motor vehicles, and farm equipment. Lawrence University (1847), Fox Valley Technical College (1967), and a junior college are all located here. In 1882 Appleton became one of the world's first cities to have water-generated electricity; a replica of the original hydroelectric plant and Hearthstone, a hydroelectric house, are local attractions. The city is named for Samuel Appleton (1766–1853), the father-in-law of the founder of Lawrence University. Pop. (1980) 59,032; (1990) 65,695.

APPLETON, Sir Edward Victor (1892–1965), British physicist and Nobel laureate. Appleton was born in Bradford, Yorkshire, England, and educated at Saint John's College, University of Cambridge. He was a captain in the Signal Corps during World War I. From 1918 to 1939 he taught physics at Cambridge and at the University of London. He was secretary of the Department of Scientific and Industrial Research of the British government from 1939 until 1949. This position gave him overall charge of British research during World War II and brought him into close cooperation with American scientists, particularly in connection with the development of radar. For this work, he was given the U.S. Medal of Merit. In 1947 he received the Nobel Prize in physics for his discovery of the Appleton layer, or F layer, of the ionosphere, from which high-frequency radio waves are reflected.

APPOMATTOX COURT HOUSE NATIONAL HISTORICAL PARK, central Virginia, authorized as Appomattox Battlefield Site 1930 and as a national monument 1935, redesignated as a national historical park 1954. The park contains the restored village of Appomattox Court House, where the Confederate general Robert E. Lee surrendered to the Union general Ulysses S. Grant on April 9, 1865, marking the end of the American Civil War. The park also includes the field headquarters of both Lee and Grant, as well as McLean House, in which the surrender papers were signed. Area, 5.4 sq km (2.1 sq mi).

APPRENTICESHIP, system of learning the skills of a craft or trade from experts in the field by working with them for a set period of time. The apprenticeship system was used extensively by the craft guilds in the Middle Ages. It continued to be important in learning a trade until the Industrial Revolution in the 18th century, after which it was largely replaced by the factory system. Revived in the 20th century, it is used in the U.S. by industries that require highly skilled workers. The terms of modern apprenticeships are specified in a contract and are regulated by trade unions and laws. The National Apprenticeship Act passed in 1937 led to the establishment of the Bureau of Apprenticeship and Training in the U.S. Department of Labor, which works with employers, labor groups, and schools to promote apprenticeship programs.

APPROPRIATION, legislative action authorizing the expenditure of public funds for some designated purpose. Through the power to allocate funds, a legislature can influence the course of government. By relying on this "power of the purse," for example, the British Parliament was gradually able to wrest control of the government from the monarch.

This historical struggle is reflected in the U.S. Constitution, which provides that "no money shall be drawn from the Treasury, but in consequence of appropriations made by law." State constitutions contain similar provisions. Although legislatures retain control over appropriations, executive officials are generally granted substantial discretion over expenditure of funds. The result in many cases has been sharp clashes between the legislative and executive branches, producing additional restrictions and limitations by the legislative body.

The U.S. Congress relies on a two-step appropriation process: authorization of programs as recommended by substantive (legislative) committees, followed by the financing of those programs through measures reported by the funding (appropriations) committees. For example, in each house the Armed Services Committees authorize defense programs; the Appropriations Committees have jurisdiction over the amounts of money to be allotted. Congress has adopted rules to keep the authorization and appropriation steps distinct and sequential, but numerous exceptions exist.

The Congressional Budget and Impoundment Control Act of 1974 created a House budget committee and a Senate budget committee, introducing some competition with the already established authorization and appropriations committees. The act also prohibited two "back-door" spending techniques previously used by authorization committees to circumvent the control of the appropriations committees: contract authority and borrowing authority. Contract authority had allowed agencies to enter into financial obligations in advance of an appropriation; once this legal liability had been made, the appropriations committees had to supply whatever funds were necessary. Borrowing authority had permitted agencies to borrow from the public or from the U.S. Treasury rather than requesting an appropriation from Congress. By the terms of the 1974 statute, agencies must seek an appropriation first before obligating funds.

See also BUDGET; CONGRESS OF THE UNITED STATES; PRESIDENT OF THE UNITED STATES. L.F.

APRAKSIN, Fyodor Matveyevich (1671–1728), Russian admiral. At the age of ten, he entered the service of Czar Fyodor III (1661–82) of Russia as a page; two years later, he became a page to Peter the Great, with whom he subsequently maintained a close friendship. Apraksin rose steadily in rank and favor and after 1700 was the most powerful and influential person in Peter's court. He became chief admiral of the Russian navy, which he strengthened considerably during his lifetime, and in 1709 he was appointed president of the admiralty during the Great Northern War (1700–21) between Russia and Sweden. Largely as a result of his victories, Russia obtained Estonia and other Baltic provinces of Sweden under the terms of the Treaty of Nystadt (1721), which ended the war. Subsequently, Russia became the leading naval power in the Baltic Sea.

APRICOT, common name for a tree, *Prunus armeniaca,* of the family Rosaceae (*see* ROSE), native to eastern Asia, and for its fruit. The tree is small, with heart-shaped leaves on long stalks. Solitary white flowers appear before the leaves, and the fruit, which resembles the peach, is roundish, downy, yellow, and sometimes ruddy on one side, with yellow flesh. More than 20 kinds are distinguished. Some favorites are Moorpark, of English origin, with a large, round, orange-red freestone, ripening in the middle of the season; Newcastle, of California origin, with a medium-size, round, orange-yellow freestone; and Royal, of French origin, with a large, oblate, yellow-red freestone, ready early in the season. The fruit, somewhat smaller than a peach, is known for its delicate flavor. It is marketed fresh, as well as dried and packed. Large quantities are canned or pulped for jam making. California and Oregon are the leading producers in the U.S. It is also a significant crop in British Columbia (Canada), Australia, Italy, the south of France, and Israel.

APRIL, fourth month of the Gregorian calendar year. It has 30 days. The Romans gave this month the name Aprilis, derived from *aperire* ("to open"), probably because it is the season when buds begin to open; it was called Eostre (Easter) month by the Anglo-Saxons. Playing tricks on the first day of April is a custom among European peoples. In France the victim of such practical jokes is called an April fish; in Scotland, a gowk or cuckoo; and in English-speaking countries, an April fool.

APSE, recess in a building, generally a semicircular or polygonal projection from the exterior of a church, roofed with a vault. The word *apse* is derived from Latin *apsis,* meaning "arch" or "vault." The apse was originally a niche in a Roman temple to hold a statue of a god. Later it was the portion of a rectangular, aisled basilica that contained the presiding official's chair. Carried over into Early Christian church architecture, which adapted the basilica form, it customarily occupied the east end of the church, where the altar stood. The apse continued in Romanesque and Gothic churches at the east end of the nave and sometimes at the ends of the transepts as well.

APSIS. *See* ORBIT.

APTERYX. *See* KIWI.

APULEIUS, Lucius (c. 125–200), Roman philosopher and writer, born in Madaros, Numidia (present-day Algeria). His father was a wealthy magistrate. Apuleius (Appuleius) studied in Carthage at a noted school of literature. He then went to Athens, were he studied philosophy. Apuleius traveled extensively and went to Rome in about 150 to practice law. About 155 he married a wealthy but plain middle-aged woman whose relatives accused him of having employed magic to gain her affections. His defense, later published as the *Apologia* and still extant, was an eloquent and successful vindication of his conduct. He thereafter devoted himself to literature and oratory. His popularity was so great that Carthage and other cities erected statues to him.

The novel *Metamorphoses* or *Golden Ass* is his most outstanding work. The principal character, Lucian, is accidentally transformed by magic into an ass. He recovers his human form by eating roses in the hands of a priest of the Egyptian goddess Isis. The *Metamorphoses,* often regarded as a satire on the vices of the age, extensively influenced the works of later writers, such as Henry Fielding, Tobias Smollett, and Giovanni Boccaccio. Apuleius had the exceptional gift of accurate and vivid observation of details, and his stories are extremely realistic.

APULIA (Ital. *Puglia*), region, SE Italy. It is on the Gulf of Taranto, an arm of the Ionian Sea, and on the Adriatic Sea, opposite Albania. The southernmost part of Apulia forms the topographical heel of the Italian boot. The region, which consists of the five provinces of Bari, Brindisi, Foggia, Lecce, and Taranto, is primarily a plain. It also contains hills that are part of the plateaus of the E Apennines. The Testa del Gargano, a peninsula in NE Apulia, rises to about 1000 m (about 3280 ft); it has a steep rocky coast spotted by inlets where the Adriatic towns of Rodi, Peschici, and Viesti are nested. Facing the peninsula are the Tremiti Islands, with grottoes, castles, and monasteries. To the S of the Gargano is the Tavoliere, a vast grain-growing plain extending to the Ofanto R.; farther S are hills and the plains of Bari and of the Salento Peninsula, where olives, almonds, and grapes are cultivated. The coastline of Apulia is lined with fishing villages and resorts. Among the many major attractions are Castellana Caves, the marine grotto of Polignano, and the 13th-century stone-turreted fortress of the Castel del Monte in Andria. The industry that exists in Apulia, such as winemaking and olive-oil refining, is linked to the agriculture of the region. The raising of sheep and livestock is also important. The region has little water, but the Apulian Aqueduct conducts water into the region from the Sele R. through the Apennines via a tunnel. Major cities are Bari (the capital), Foggia, Lecce, Margherita di Savoia, and Taranto.

The original inhabitants of Apulia probably came from Illyria. Their pottery indicates that they were exposed to Greek influence about the 8th century BC. Captured by Rome in the 4th century BC, Apulia was the site of a victory by the Carthaginian general Hannibal during the Second Punic War in 216 BC. Apulia was subject to a series of invasions before it was made a duchy by the Normans in the 11th century. In the 13th century Holy Roman Emperor Frederick II joined Apulia to the kingdom of Sicily. Europeans embarked from Apulian ports during the Crusades. Apulia was part of the kingdom of Naples before becoming part of the kingdom of Italy in 1861.

Area, about 19,347 sq km (about 7470 sq mi); pop. (1988 est.) 4,043,000.

APURE, river, W central Venezuela, formed by the junction of the Sarare and Uribante rivers. The Apure flows generally E across a region of level plains and empties into the Orinoco R. after a course of approximately 676 km (approximately 420 mi). It is navigable by river steamer for about 480 km (about 300 mi).

APURÍMAC, river, S central Peru. It rises in Lake Villafro, in the Andes Mts., and after a N course of about 805 km (about 500 mi), unites with the Urubamba R. to form the Ucayali R., a headstream of the Amazon R. In the lower reaches the river is known as the Tambo or the Ene.

AQABA, GULF OF, NE arm of the Red Sea, SW Asia, separating the Sinai and Arabian peninsulas. It is a narrow body of water, up to about 24 km (about 15 mi) wide and about 160 km (about 100 mi) long, occupying a portion of the great geological fault known as the Rift Valley. The gulf is linked to the Red Sea on the S by the Straits of Tiran; at its head in the N are the port of Aqaba, Jordan, and the port of Elat, Israel.

AQABAH, AL-, also al-Aqaba, (anc. *Elath;* later *Aelana*), city, SW Jordan, seaport at the head of the Gulf of Aqaba, an arm of the Red Sea. In antiquity the town, then called Elath, the principal city of the Edomite peoples, was a major commercial center. As Aelana, it became important as a Roman garrison. Today al-Aqabah is the only seaport of Jordan; its exports include phosphates and shells. Because of its strategic location, the port has figured in various Arab-Israeli confrontations; it was occupied by Israel from November 1956 until January 1957. Pop. (1989 est.) 41,900.

AQUAMARINE (Lat. *aqua,* "water"; *marina,* "sea"), gemstone, a variety of the mineral beryl that is blue, blue-green, or green. The blue variety is the most valuable. Greenish stones can sometimes be changed to the highly prized blue shade by heating them in an electric furnace to 450° C (842° F). Aquamarine is found in Brazil, Siberia, Burma, and parts of the U.S. Other blue stones are sometimes sold under this name; in particular, blue synthetic spinel is sometimes sold as synthetic aquamarine.

The largest aquamarine in the world, a sea-green stone weighing about 23 kg (about 50 lb), was found in 1946 in the state of Espírito Santo, Brazil, and brought to the U.S. in 1947 for cutting.

AQUA REGIA (Lat., "royal water"), mixture of concentrated hydrochloric and nitric acids, containing 82 percent by volume of the former to 18 percent of the latter. Aqua regia is sometimes diluted with water, the slightly diluted mixture being almost as efficacious as the concentrated. Aqua regia was used by the alchemists (*see* ALCHEMY) and its name is derived from its ability to dissolve the noble metals, particularly gold, which are inert to either of the acids used separately. It is still occasionally used in the chemical laboratory for dissolving gold and platinum. Aqua regia is a powerful solvent primarily because of the presence of a strong oxidizing agent (the mixture contains free chlorine) and the presence of chloride ions, which form stable complex ions with gold and platinum.

AQUARIUM, water-filled tank, usually with glass sides, in which aquatic plants and animals, particularly fish, are kept. The term is applied to single tanks for home use in which fish are kept for their decorative effect and interesting habits and to public institutions with tanks that are used for exhibition and also for scientific study of aquatic life.

Home aquariums are often made to simulate a natural environment. Aquatic plants supply the oxygen needed by the fish, but often an aerating device is used to furnish additional oxygen. Goldfish (q.v.) enjoy cool water, but the popular tropical fish (q.v.) must have water at a constant temperature of 22° C (72° F) or more. The water may be kept pure and free of algae for long periods by sufficient aeration and by keeping mollusks in the aquarium. A layer of sand or gravel at the bottom of the tank will hold the roots of such important aquatic plants as tape grass, *Vallisneria spiralis,* and aid in the removal of debris.

The first scientific and popular aquarium was erected in the London Zoological Gardens in 1853; it was closed shortly afterward, and a new one was not erected until 1924. Other large European aquariums were built in Plymouth, England; Paris and Nice, France; Naples; and Berlin; all but the last survived World War II.

Among famous public aquariums in the U.S. are the Steinhart Aquarium in San Francisco, the Shedd Aquarium in Chicago, the New England Aquarium in Boston, and the New York Aquarium in Coney Island, Brooklyn, at which the Osborne Laboratories of Marine Sciences are located. The National Aquarium opened in 1981 in Baltimore, Md. It features a series of aquatic habitats starting with simulated mountain streams at the top of the building, followed in descending order by lowland streams and estuaries that finally reach the sea. The Monterey Bay Aquarium, which opened in 1984 at the edge of Monterey Bay in California, features a re-creation of a Pacific Coast kelp forest.

Marineland, which opened in 1938 near Saint Augustine, Fla., the Miami (Fla.) Seaquarium, and

Marineland of the Pacific, outside Los Angeles, represent new trends in public aquarium architecture. These aquariums are called seaquariums or oceanariums because they usually are located on the ocean and feature very large outdoor tanks or areas having ramps and portholes so that visitors can see such large exhibits as sharks and dolphins from above and below the surface of the water.

For further information on this topic, see the Bibliography in volume 28, section 601.

AQUARIUS (Lat., "the water bearer"), constellation, and also the 11th sign of the zodiac, located between Capricornus and Pisces. The constellation contains no stars brighter than the third magnitude. The name was probably chosen because from January 21 to February 20, when the sun is in Aquarius, the weather in southern Europe is generally rainy.

AQUATINT, method of etching metal plates to reproduce tones rather than lines, and also the resulting print. It achieves wash effects like those of watercolor. Aquatint is usually combined with linear etching techniques such as drypoint. *See also* PRINTS AND PRINTMAKING.

AQUEDUCT, artificial channel built to transport water. The aqueduct may take the form of an open or enclosed canal, a tunnel, or a pipeline; an aqueduct bridge is a structure that bears a canal over a valley or a river.

The Pont du Gard extends across the Gard River near Remoulins in southern France. Close to 274 m (about 900 ft) long and 48.8 m (about 160 ft) high, it is one of the most beautiful of many surviving Roman aqueducts. The water channel rests on three tiers of arches, the lowest of which is still used as a road bridge. The conduit once carried water to Nîmes and is more than 40 km (more than 25 mi) long, with most of it underground.
Walter S. Clark–Photo Researchers

Aerial view of a section of the San Luis unit of the vast Central Valley water project in southern California. Water is taken from the San Luis Canal (bottom) into an intake channel (center). Carried to a pumping plant, the water is lifted more than 55 m (more than 180 ft) to the Pleasant Valley Canal, which carries it 19 m (12 mi) to irrigate farmlands. J. C. Dahilig–U.S. Bureau of Reclamation

Underground aqueducts were in use in ancient Mesopotamia, but the aqueducts that supplied water to ancient Rome are the most famous. The first to be built, Aqua Appia, was an underground aqueduct about 16 km (about 10 mi) long. It was built during the administration of Appius Claudius Caecus, for whom the Appian Way is named, around 310 BC. The Aqua Marcian in Rome, about 90 km (about 56 mi) long and built by the praetor Marcius in 144 BC, was the first Roman aqueduct to carry water above ground, the bridged section being about 16 km (about 10 mi) long. Nine aqueducts were built in all, providing Rome with some 143,845 cu m (38 million gal) of water each day. Parts of several are still in use, supplying water to fountains in Rome. In addition the Romans built aqueducts in all parts of their empire, many of which are still standing.

In modern times, several extensive aqueducts have been built in Europe. The Marseille aqueduct, completed in 1847, is 97 km (60 mi) long. The aqueduct supplying water to Glasgow, Scotland, is 56 km (35 mi) long; the second Kaiser Franz Joseph aqueduct, in Vienna, is 232 km (144 mi) long; that supplying Manchester, England, is 154 km (96 mi) long; and the aqueduct supplying Liverpool is 109 km (68 mi) long.

In the U.S., extensive aqueduct systems supply water to Boston; Baltimore, Md.; Washington, D.C.; Saint Louis, Mo.; New York City; and Los Angeles, among other cities. The system of aqueducts supplying water to New York City is more than 322 km (200 mi) long, most of it underground. The main aqueducts under New York are between 61 and 183 m (200 and 600 ft) below sea level. The Delaware aqueduct (q.v.), which normally carries 3,028,320 cu m (800 million gal) of water daily from the Catskill Mountains to New York, is 137 km (85 mi) long, the longest continuous tunnel in the world.

The most extensive aqueduct system in the world is that which supplies water to southern California, including the cities of Los Angeles and San Diego. One major source of water is the Colorado River. Water is drawn from Parker Dam on the Colorado River and carried 389 km (242 mi) over the San Bernardino Mountains to the terminal at Lake Mathews, Calif. The Colorado River aqueduct has a capacity of more than 3,785,411 cu m (1 billion gal) per day. To further increase the water available to southern California, the State Water Project, an aqueduct system of canals, pipelines, and tunnels totaling 1100 km (684 mi) is under construction, of which 859 km (534 mi) has been completed. The system is based on a unique concept taking into account possible earthquake damage; some of the largest hydraulic pumps and turbines ever installed were used, for instance, to avoid direct tunneling across the Tehachapi Mountains. The water is pumped up part of the mountain and then comes down the other side, driving turbines to generate most of the electricity needed to drive the pumps. The first portion of the system, the aqueduct carrying water 715 km (444 mi) from the Sacramento River delta in northern California to Parris Reservoir south of Los Angeles, was begun in 1966 and completed in 1972. The remaining sections of the system total 385 km (240 mi) in length. Upon completion, the State Water Project will supply more than 6,624,470 cu m (1.75 billion gal) of water per day to southern California.

In addition, the city of Los Angeles has a separate source of water, the Los Angeles aqueduct, which draws water from the Owens River in the Sierra Nevada. The aqueduct is 544 km (338 mi) long and is designed to supply about 15,141,644 cu m (about 4 billion gal) of water a day.

AQUILA, called Aquila of Pontus (fl. about 130), translator of the Old Testament into Greek, born in Sinope, Pontus (now Sinop, Turkey). His translation of the Old Testament was so literal that Jews of his time preferred it to the Septuagint version, as did the Judaistic sect of Christians called Elionites. The remaining fragments of the version may be found in the Hexapla of the Alexandrian theologian Origen.

AQUILA, (Lat., "the eagle"), constellation of the Northern Hemisphere, prominent in summer months. The Milky Way passes through Aquila, and its brightest star is the first-magnitude Altair.

AQUILEIA (anc. *Aquileia;* medieval *Aglar*), town, NE Italy, in Friuli-Venezia Giulia Region, at the head of the Adriatic Sea, near Trieste. Aquileia is a fishing village; it is connected by a causeway to the island of Grado, a bathing resort. Founded as a Roman colony in 181 BC, it became a great center of trade between N and S Europe, earning the name Second Rome. The city was destroyed in 452 by Attila; rebuilt, Aquileia became the seat of a Christian patriarchate in the 6th century. It flourished until occupied by the neighboring city of Venice in 1420. The community was held by the Austrians from the early 16th century until 1918, when it passed to Italy. Pop. (1990 est.) 3450.

AQUINAS, Saint Thomas, sometimes called the Angelic Doctor and the Prince of Scholastics (1225–74), Italian philosopher and theologian, whose works have made him the most important figure in Scholastic philosophy and one of the most prominent Roman Catholic theologians.

Aquinas was born of a noble family in Roccasecca, near Aquino, and was educated at the Benedictine monastery of Monte Cassino and at the University of Naples. He joined the Dominican order while still an undergraduate in 1243, the year of his father's death. His mother, opposed to Thomas's affiliation with a mendicant order, confined him to the family castle for more than a year in a vain attempt to make him abandon his chosen course. She released him in 1245, and Aquinas then journeyed to Paris to continue his studies. He studied under the German Scholastic philosopher Albertus Magnus, following him to Cologne in 1248. Because Aquinas was heavyset and taciturn, his fellow novices called him Dumb Ox, but Albertus Magnus is said to have predicted that "this ox will one day fill the world with his bellowing."

Early Years. Aquinas was ordained a priest about 1250, and he began to teach at the University of Paris in 1252. His first writings, primarily summaries and amplifications of his lectures, appeared two years later. His first major work was *Scripta Super Libros Sententiarum* (Writings on the Books of the Sentences, 1256?), which consisted of commentaries on an influential work concerning the sacraments of the church by the Italian theologian Peter Lombard. In 1256 Aquinas was awarded a doctorate in theology and appointed professor of philosophy at the University of Paris. Pope Alexander IV (r. 1254–61) summoned him to Rome in 1259, where he acted as adviser and lecturer to the papal court. Returning to Paris in 1268, Aquinas became involved in a controversy with the French philosopher Siger de Brabant (1240?–81?) and other followers of the Islamic philosopher Averroës.

Study of Aristotle and the Averroists. To understand the crucial importance of this controversy for Western thought, it is necessary to consider the context in which it occurred. Before the time of Aquinas, Western thought had been dominated by the philosophy of St. Augustine, the Western church's great Father and Doctor of the 4th and 5th centuries, who taught that in the search for truth people must depend upon sense experience. Early in the 13th century the major works of Aristotle were made available in a Latin translation, accompanied by the commentaries of Averroës and other Islamic scholars. The vigor, clarity, and authority of Aristotle's teachings restored confidence in empirical knowledge and gave rise to a school of philosophers known as Averroists. Under the leadership of Siger de Brabant, the Averroists asserted that philosophy was independent of revelation.

Averroism threatened the integrity and supremacy of Roman Catholic doctrine and filled orthodox thinkers with alarm. To ignore Aristotle, as interpreted by the Averroists, was impossible; to condemn his teachings was ineffectual. He had to be reckoned with. Albertus Magnus and other scholars had attempted to deal with Averroism, but with little success. Aquinas succeeded brilliantly.

Reconciling the Augustinian emphasis upon the human spiritual principle with the Averroist claim of autonomy for knowledge derived from the senses, Aquinas insisted that the truths of faith and those of sense experience, as presented by Aristotle, are fully compatible and complementary. Some truths, such as that of the mystery of the incarnation, can be known only through revelation, and others, such as that of the composition of material things, only through experience; still others, such as that of the existence of God, are known through both equally. All knowledge, Aquinas held, originates in sensation, but sense data can be made intelligible only by the action of the intellect, which elevates thought toward the apprehension of such immaterial realities as the human soul, the angels, and God. To reach understanding of the highest truths, those with which religion is concerned, the aid of revelation is needed. Aquinas's moderate realism placed the universals firmly in the mind, in opposition to extreme realism, which posited their independence of human thought. He admitted a foundation for universals in existing things, however, in opposition to nominalism and conceptualism.

Later Years. Aquinas first suggested his mature position in the treatise *De Unitate Intellectus Contra Averroistas* (1270; trans. *The Trinity and the Unicity of the Intellect,* 1946). This work turned the tide against his opponents, who were condemned by the church.

Aquinas left Paris in 1272 and proceeded to Naples, where he organized a new Dominican school. In March 1274, while traveling to the Council of Lyon, to which he had been commissioned by Pope Gregory X (c. 1210–76), Aquinas fell ill. He died on March 7 at the Cistercian monastery of Fossanova.

Aquinas was canonized by Pope John XXII in 1323 and proclaimed a Doctor of the Church by Pope Pius V in 1567.

Assessment. More successfully than any other theologian or philosopher, Aquinas organized the knowledge of his time in the service of his faith. In his effort to reconcile faith with intellect, he created a philosophical synthesis of the works and teachings of Aristotle and other classic sages; of Augustine and other church fathers; of Averroës, Avicenna, and other Islamic scholars; of Jewish thinkers such as Maimonides and Solomon ben Yehuda ibn Gabirol; and of his predecessors in the Scholastic tradition. This synthesis he brought into line with the Bible and Roman Catholic doctrine.

Aquinas's accomplishment was immense; his work marks one of the few great culminations in the history of philosophy. After Aquinas, Western philosophers could choose only between humbly following him and striking off in some altogether different direction. In the centuries immediately following his death, the dominant tendency, even among Roman Catholic thinkers, was to adopt the second alternative. Interest in Thomist philosophy began to revive, however, toward the end of the 19th century. In the encyclical *Aeterni Patris* (Of the Eternal Father, 1879), Pope Leo XIII recommended that St. Thomas's philosophy be made the basis of instruction in all Roman Catholic schools. Pope Pius XII, in the encyclical *Humani Generis* (Of the Human Race, 1950), affirmed that the Thomist philosophy is the surest guide to Roman Catholic doctrine and discouraged all departures from it. Thomism remains a leading school of contemporary thought. Among the thinkers, Roman Catholic and non-Roman Catholic alike, who have operated within the Thomist framework have been the French philosophers Jacques Maritain and Étienne Gilson.

St. Thomas was an extremely prolific author, and about 80 works are ascribed to him. The two most important are *Summa Contra Gentiles* (1261–64; trans. *On the Truth of the Catholic Faith,* 1956), a closely reasoned treatise intended to persuade intellectual Muslims of the truth of Christianity; and *Summa Theologica* (Summary Treatise of Theology, 1265–73), in three parts (on God, the moral life of man, and Christ), of which the last was left unfinished. *Summa Theologica* has been republished frequently in Latin and vernacular editions.

For further information on this person, see the section Biographies in the Bibliography in volume 28.

AQUINO, Corazon (1933–), *and* **Benigno Simeon Aquino, Jr.** (1932–83), Philippine political figures who were husband and wife.

Corazon (Cory), born Corazon Cojuanco, was educated in Manila and at Roman Catholic convent schools in the U.S. She graduated from Mount St. Vincent College in New York City and studied law at Far Eastern University in Manila. She married Benigno (Ninoy) in 1954.

Benigno entered politics at the age of 22. He

was subsequently the youngest mayor, governor, and senator to serve in the Philippines. He was a leading member of the opposition Liberal party when President Ferdinand Marcos declared martial law in 1972. Imprisoned from 1972 until 1980, Aquino was allowed to move his family to the U.S., where he underwent heart surgery and later served as a research fellow at Harvard University and the Massachusetts Institute of Technology. In 1983 he flew back to Manila to work in the legislative election. Despite high security, he was assassinated as he deplaned on Aug. 21.

Corazon went to the Philippines for her husband's funeral and stayed to work in the legislative election campaign. The opposition won one-third of the seats in 1984. Marcos called presidential elections for February 1986, and she became the opposition candidate for president. Marcos, declaring himself victor in the February 7 election, was inaugurated on February 25. An army revolt and demonstrations on her behalf led to Corazon's inauguration on the same day. Unrest prevailed, and Marcos accepted asylum in the U.S., while Corazon formed a provisional government. She implemented a new constitution and held legislative elections in 1987, but opposition within the military, a continuing Communist insurgency, and severe economic problems plagued her throughout her presidency. She declined to run for a second term in 1992.

AQUITAINE (Lat. *Aquitania*), traditional name for southwestern France, first used by Julius Caesar in the 1st century BC. Under the Romans, the province of Aquitania extended almost as far north as the Loire River. Novempopulana (Gascony), the portion south of the Gironde, was made a separate province in the late 3d century. The remainder became a separate kingdom in the Frankish period. The title duke of Aquitaine was held by the counts of Poitiers from the 10th to the 12th century. The last duke was William X (1099–1137). When his daughter, Eleanor of Aquitaine, married the heir to the throne of England in 1152, the area became an English possession and remained so until the 15th century, when it was annexed by France at the end of the Hundred Years' War. From the 13th century until the French Revolution, Aquitaine was usually known as Guyenne. The name Aquitaine was revived in the 1960s to designate the economic region comprising the French departments of Pyrénées-Atlantiques, Landes, Gironde, Dordogne, and Lot-et-Garonne.

ARABIA, great desert peninsula, extreme SW Asia, bounded on the N by Jordan and Iraq, on the E by the Persian Gulf and the Gulf of Oman, on the S by the Arabian Sea and the Gulf of Aden, and on the W by the Red Sea. With an area of about 3 million sq km (about 1,160,000 sq mi) and a population (1989 est.) of about 32 million, it is one of the most sparsely inhabited areas of the world. It comprises the independent states of Saudi Arabia (which occupies nearly three-quarters of the peninsula), Yemen, Oman, United Arab

Vessels in the important port of Dubayy (Dubai), capital of the oil-rich state of Dubayy, one of the seven United Arab Emirates on the eastern Arabian Peninsula of the Persian Gulf. Mathias Oppersdorff

Emirates, Qatar, Kuwait, and the island state of Bahrain.

LAND AND RESOURCES

The peninsula is essentially a vast plateau, rimmed on the W and S by mountains and sloping gently E to the Persian Gulf. It contains some of the largest sandy desert areas in the world, notably the Rub al-Khali (Empty Quarter) in the S and an-Nafud in the N. The climate is extremely arid, few places receiving more than 178 mm (7 in) of rain a year, and no permanent streams exist. Summer temperatures reach as high as 54.4° C (130° F) in some areas. Various minerals, including gold, silver, sulfur, and salt, are produced. The region, however, owes its modern economic life to the vast reserves of petroleum and natural gas, found largely in the area around the Persian Gulf. Major cities include Riyadh, Mecca, Aden, Sana, Abu Dhabi, and Kuwait.

HISTORY

Until comparatively recent times knowledge of Arabia was limited to that provided by ancient Greek and Roman writers and by a few Arab geographers; a large part of this material was unreliable. Ignorance of Arabia persisted because much of the peninsula was forbidden territory to non-Muslims. In the 20th century, however, archaeological exploration has added considerably to the knowledge of the area.

The earliest known events in Arabian history are migrations from the peninsula into neighboring areas. About 3500 BC, Semitic-speaking peoples of Arabian origin migrated into the valley of the Tigris and Euphrates rivers in Mesopotamia, supplanted the Sumerians, and became the Assyro-Babylonians. Another group of Semites left Arabia about 2500 BC and settled along the eastern shore of the Mediterranean Sea; some of these migrants became the Amorites and Canaanites of later times.

Ancient Kingdoms. The better watered, higher portions of southwest Arabia supported three early kingdoms. The first, the Minaean, was centered in the interior of what is now Northern Yemen, but probably embraced most of southern Arabia. Although dating is difficult, it is generally believed that the Minaean Kingdom existed from 1200 to 650 BC. The second kingdom, the Sabaean, was founded about 930 BC and lasted until about 115 BC; it probably supplanted the Minaean Kingdom and occupied

In the United Arab Emirates a Bedouin boy poses with his falcon and camel. Falconry is a traditional sport with many desert Arabs. Mathias Oppersdorff

Royal national guardsmen of Saudi Arabia line up with their mounts. Note the weapons and costumes of the guardsmen. Saudi Arabia is the birthplace of Muhammad and the religion of Islam.
Mathias Oppersdorff

substantially the same territory. The Sabaean capital and chief city, Marib, probably flourished as did no other city of ancient Arabia, partly because it was a focal point of caravan routes between seaports of the Mediterranean and the frankincense-growing region of the Hadhramaut and partly because a large nearby dam provided water for irrigation. The Sabaean Kingdom was widely referred to as Saba, and it has been suggested that the queen of Sheba mentioned in the Bible, who visited King Solomon of Israel in Jerusalem in the 10th century BC, was Sabaean. The Himyarites followed the Sabaeans as the leaders in southern Arabia; the Himyarite Kingdom lasted from about 115 BC to about AD 525. In 24 BC the Roman emperor Augustus sent the prefect of Egypt, Aelius Gallus, against the Himyarites, but his army of 10,000, which was unsuccessful, returned to Egypt. The Himyarites prospered in the frankincense, myrrh, and spice trade until the Romans began to open the sea routes through the Red Sea.

From Nabataeans to Persians. Several states are known to have existed in northern Arabia in the pre-Christian and early Christian era. Earliest among these was the Nabataean Kingdom, which for a brief period (about 9 BC to AD 40) extended as far north as Damascus. The ruins of Petra, the Nabataean capital city, attest to a high degree of culture. The Nabataean form of writing developed into the Arabic script used in the Koran, the holy book of Islam. Rome gained control of the Nabataean Kingdom in AD 106 and established most of it as the Roman province of Arabia Petraea, which lasted little longer than a century. Other north Arabian states were established by other invading peoples.

In the 4th century the Abyssinians, who had adopted Christianity of the Monophysite type (*see* MONOPHYSITISM), spread into Arabia, conquering a large part of it. Judaism, too, was introduced into the region. Both religions were established and to a considerable degree supplanted the existing religious beliefs, which were based mainly on astrology and occultism. Late in the following century, Persia, under the Sassanid kings, assumed control of a substantial part of Arabia, particularly of the region occupied by present-day Yemen.

Islam and the Caliphate. The rise of Islam was the most significant event in the history of Arabia. Muhammad was born in Mecca about 570 and died in Medina in 632. Mecca became the spiritual center of the new religion. From 632 to 661 Medina was the political center of a united Muslim state under the caliphs (vice-regents)

An oil-drilling rig in Kuwait. Petroleum is the chief natural resource of Arabia, and Kuwait is one of the principal producers in the world.

Elgeland–Black Star

Airport terminal at the international airport in Riyadh, Saudi Arabia. The cosmopolitan metropolis is the nation's capital. **FPG–Sedat Pakay**

who followed Muhammad. Arabian armies conquered Syria, Egypt, and Sassanid Persia. After Egypt fell (642), the tide of Muslim conquest swept west over the whole of northern Africa and then over the Spanish Peninsula. During this period of conquest the Koran was completed and canonized. Upon the removal of the caliphate to Damascus in 658, Arabia became less important. The shift (751) of the center of Islam to Baghdad resulted in a further decline.

From the 8th to the early 10th century Arabia was merely a province under the Abbasid caliphs of Baghdad. Then the rule of Baghdad was successfully contested by the Qarmatians, a new Muslim sect, who controlled all of Arabia for a time during the 10th century. Toward the end of the 10th century the Qarmatians lost their power to various Bedouin tribes, and Arabia, again completely disunited, was divided among numerous petty governments. From 1075 to 1094, however, Arabia acknowledged the spiritual leadership of the Abbasid caliph at Baghdad. In 1258 the Mongols conquered Baghdad, and from that time on Baghdad had no influence over Arabia. In 1269 Mecca and al-Hijaz (the Hejaz) region came under the control of emirs (Muslim princes) from Egypt. When the Turks conquered Egypt in 1517, they took control of al-Hijaz and thereafter exerted considerable power in the rest of Arabia.

The Wahhabis. The history of Arabia from about 1750 to the present time is to a great extent the history of the Wahhabis. Under the founder of this religious sect, the stern reformer Muhammad ibn Abd al-Wahhab (1703–92), not only was a great religious revival initiated in Arabia, but Arabian national spirit was aroused against Turkish domination. The Wahhabis took Mecca from the Turks in 1802 and Medina in 1804. In this period the Wahhabi empire extended to the boundaries of modern Yemen and Oman. Under the leadership of the viceroy of Egypt, however, the Turks regained the two cities in 1812.

The conflict between the Turks and the Wahhabis endured until the end of World War I; in the last quarter of the 19th century there was also considerable warfare between various Wahhabi factions. By 1906 the Wahhabis had come under the leadership of the resourceful and intelligent Abdul Aziz ibn Saud, sultan of Najd, and under his direction the Wahhabi state expanded greatly. In World War I Ibn Saud cooperated with Great Britain in fighting Turkey. Final Turkish defeat resulted in its expulsion from al-Hijaz, Asir, and Yemen. Six years of civil war followed between adherents of Ibn Saud and followers of various other Arabian princes and chieftains. In 1924–25 Ibn Saud conquered al-Hijaz, becoming its king in 1926. In 1927 he proclaimed himself king of al-Hijaz and of Najd and its dependencies, and in 1932 he gave his two dominions the name of Saudi Arabia. His annexation of the principality of Asir to al-Hijaz in 1933 caused a war (March–May 1934) between Ibn Saud and the imam of Yemen. The treaty signed by the two countries on May 20, 1934, provided that Asir and the inland region of Najran were to remain within Saudi Arabia.

For the subsequent history of Arabia and of its various political divisions and for other information on these states, *see* BAHRAIN; KUWAIT; OMAN; QATAR; SAUDI ARABIA; UNITED ARAB EMIRATES; YEMEN, REPUBLIC OF.

For further information on this topic, see the Bibliography in volume 28, sections 857, 876, 1047–49.

ARABIAN ART AND ARCHITECTURE. *See* ISLAMIC ART AND ARCHITECTURE.

ARABIAN DESERT *or* **EASTERN DESERT,** arid region, E Egypt, lying between the Mediterranean Sea on the N, the Red Sea and the Gulf of Suez on the E, the Nubian Desert (along lat 22° N) on the S, and the Nile R. on the W. The W edge of the desert is demarcated by cliffs that rise steeply from the Nile Valley. To the E the terrain, mostly a rugged plateau, slopes upward to a range of jagged volcanic mountains bordering the Red Sea. Elevations in the range, which descends abruptly to the sea, exceed 2135 m (7000 ft). Aridity makes human habitation difficult, but a few small agricultural villages subsist in little basins in the plateau and mountains. Deposits of turquoise, phosphate rock, nitrates, petroleum, salt, and building stone are here, but are of limited economic significance.

The name Arabian Desert is also applied popularly to the Rub al-Khali, also called the Great Sandy Desert, of the Arabian Peninsula, one of the hottest and most sparsely inhabited sand dune deserts of the world.

ARABIAN NIGHTS, also *A Thousand and One Nights,* collection of Oriental stories, fairy tales, anecdotes, and fables, gathered from all parts of the East. Most of the stories are of unknown origin, having survived orally in Indian and Arabian folklore. The several early collections differ in story content, but each is characterized by the use of a frame story, a narrative device that gives the collection continuity. A Persian collection of nearly 200 stories, compiled between 988 and 1011, is probably the nucleus of the modern collection numbering 264 tales, first translated by the French Orientalist Antoine Galland (1646–1715) between 1704 and 1715.

In the frame story, Scheherazade, legendary queen of Samarkand, relates one of these tales to her husband Schariar each night to keep him from killing her. By terminating each story before the climax and thereby retaining his interest, she wins a delay of execution for 1000 nights. The king finally relents and grants her a pardon on the thousand and first night. Among the more popular of the *Arabian Nights* stories are "Aladdin," "Sinbad the Sailor," and "Ali Baba." In addition to their value as entertainment, the stories have been extremely valuable to scholars as source material for the study of early Oriental life and habits. The book has been translated into many languages. The best-known English translations are those by Edward William Lane (1801–76) in 1840 and by Sir Richard Francis Burton between 1885 and 1888.

ARABIAN SEA, portion of the Indian Ocean between the Arabian Peninsula on the W and the subcontinent of India on the E. Bounded on the N by Iran and Pakistan, it merges with the main body of the Indian Ocean in the S. Among the principal arms of the Arabian Sea are the Gulf of Aden, which links it with the Red Sea, and the Gulf of Oman, which links it with the Persian Gulf. The maximum width of the sea is about 2400 km (about 1500 mi); the maximum known depth is 5030 m (16,500 ft). The cities of Karachi, Pakistan, and Bombay, India, are the chief ports.

ARABIC LANGUAGE, the language of written communication and of most formal, oral communication for speakers of Arabic dialects from Morocco to Iraq. Among Muslims, Arabic is considered sacred since it is the language through which the Koran is believed to have been revealed. With the rise of Islam as a dominant religion after AD 622, Arabic became the most widespread of the living Semitic languages. Classified as South Central Semitic, Arabic is related to Hebrew, spoken in Israel, and Amharic, spoken in Ethiopia, as well as to the ancient Semitic languages. The earliest written inscriptions in Arabic are found in the Arabian Peninsula and date from the early 4th century AD. Today, Arabic is a unifying bond among Arabs, and it is the liturgical language of Muslims in Turkey, Iran, Afghanistan, Pakistan, Indonesia, parts of Sub-Saharan Africa, Kazakhstan, Kyrgyzstan, Tajikistan, Turkmenistan, and Uzbekistan.

Spoken Arabic. The term Arabic refers to the standard form of the language used in all writing and heard on television and radio as well as in mosques. The diverse colloquial dialects of Arabic are interrelated but vary considerably among speakers from different parts of the Middle East.

These dialects differ from standard Arabic and from one another in pronunciation, vocabulary, and grammar and are usually labeled according to major geographic areas, such as North African, Egyptian, and Gulf. Within these broad classifications, the daily speech of urban, rural, and nomadic speakers is distinctively different. Illiterate speakers from widely separated parts of the Arab world may not understand one another, although each is speaking a version of Arabic.

The sound system of Arabic has 28 consonants, including all the Semitic guttural sounds produced far back in the mouth and throat. Each of the three vowels in standard Arabic occurs in a long and short form, creating the long and short syllables so important to the meter of Arabic poetry. Although the dialects retain the long vowels, they have lost many of the short-vowel contrasts.

Arabic Grammar. All Arabic word formation is based on an abstraction, namely, the root, usually consisting of three consonants. These root sounds join with various vowel patterns to form simple nouns and verbs to which affixes can be attached for more complicated derivations. For example, the borrowed term *bank* is considered to have the consonantal root b-n-k; *film* is formed from f-l-m (*see also* SEMITIC LANGUAGES).

Arabic has a very regular system of conjugating verbs and altering their stems to indicate variations on the basic meaning. This system is so regular that dictionaries of Arabic can refer to verbs by a number system (I–X). From the root k-s-r, the form I verb is *kasar,* "he broke"; form II is *kassar,* "he smashed to bits"; and form VII is *inkasar,* "it was broken up."

Nouns and adjectives are less regular in formation, and have many different plural patterns. The so-called broken plurals are formed by altering the internal syllable shape of the singular noun. For example, for the borrowed words *bank* and *film,* the plurals are, respectively, *bunuk* for banks and *aflam* for films.

Normal sentence word order in standard Arabic is verb-subject-object. In poetry and in some prose styles, this word order can be altered; when that happens, subject and object can be distinguished by their case endings, that is, by suffixes that indicate the grammatical function of nouns. These suffixes are only spelled out fully in school textbooks and in the Koran to ensure an absolutely correct reading. In all other Arabic texts, these case endings (usually short vowels) are omitted, as are all internal short-vowel markings. The Arabic script does not include letters for these vowels; instead, they are small marks set above and below the consonantal script.

Arabic Script. The Arabic script, which is derived from that of Aramaic, is written from right to left. It is based on 18 distinct shapes that vary according to their connection to preceding or following letters. Using a combination of dots above and below 8 of these shapes, the full complement of 28 consonants and the 3 long vowels can be fully spelled out. The Arabic alphabet has been adopted by non-Semitic languages such as Modern Persian, or Farsi, Urdu, Malay, and some West African languages such as Hausa, for example. The use of verses from the Koran in Arabic script for decoration has led to the development over 1400 years of many different calligraphic styles. Calligraphy (q.v.) is a high art form in the Arab world.

The long history of Arabic includes periods of high development in literature. The Arabic of medieval writing is termed Classical Arabic. Modern standard Arabic is a descendant of Classical Arabic; frequently, however, the stylistic influence of French and English is evident. In the 20th century, in particular, much scientific, medical, and technical vocabulary has been borrowed from French and English. *See* ARABIC LITERATURE. C.G.K.

For further information on this topic, see the Bibliography in volume 28, section 350.

ARABIC LITERATURE, the literature of Arabic-speaking peoples, and one of the chief vehicles of Islamic civilization. It originated among the Arabs in Arabia but eventually was produced and appreciated from Spain to China.

Although classical Arabic literature was dominated by religious and scholarly considerations, its intrinsic literary and artistic value is great. The poems are forceful, dynamic, realistic, and vivid, in tune with the poets' harsh environment; and the richness of the Arabic language imparts variety and color to obligatory, almost stereotyped, motifs. Arabic prose too is vivid in style. To the ancient Arab, language was the chief medium of art, and both poetry and prose were meant to be heard. To this day, poetry and oratory can rouse passion and enthusiasm in an Arab crowd.

Medieval Period. The most outstanding example of Arabic literature is the Koran, which Muslims consider revealed by God to his Prophet, Muhammad, in the Arabian Desert in the 7th century, and which they revere the world over. It is the Islamic counterpart of the Jewish Torah or the Christian Gospels. Its literary style, regarded as inimitable by Muslims, is derived from that of the pre-Islamic Arab soothsayers whose utterances were in the form of brief phrases having rhyme and rhythm but no meter. In its earliest suras, or chapters, the Koran expresses religious concepts with a beauty and passion that can be fully appreciated only in the original Arabic text.

The Koran, although the greatest, is not the earliest example of Arabic literary creativity. Hundreds of odes and poems composed about a century before the Prophet's time still exist, some available in European translation. This poetry deals with the life of the Bedouins, their loves, travels through the desert, fights, rivalries, ambitions, and hatreds. The poets praise their tribes, the shieks, and often themselves. They bitterly taunt their enemies, provoking them to fight back with the sword or with equally cutting satire. The most distinguished poets were al-Asha (c. 570–629), Amr ibn-Kulthum (d. 600), and Imru-al-Qays (d. 540?). The last two had their finest odes included among the seven prize poems called the *Muallaqat* (Suspended, the poems allegedly having been suspended inside the great mosque at Mecca). Among other famous collections of pre-Islamic poetry are the *Hamasa* (Fortitude) of abu-Tammam (807–45?); the *Mufaddaliyat,* named for its compiler, al-Mufaddal (fl. 760–84); and the *Kitab al-Aghani* (The Book of Songs).

In the courtly atmosphere of Mecca after Muhammad's death, Umar ibn Abi Rabia (c. 643–719) composed love poems disapproved of by the pious. Poetry continued to flourish under the Ommiad dynasty (Arab. *Umayyad,* 661–750) but tended to become artificial, perpetuating forms that represented a vanishing type of life. The outstanding poets of that period were al-Farazdaq (c. 641–c. 728) and Jarir (c. 650–c. 729), whose long poetic feud with each other was famous. The 10th-century poet al-Mutanabbi (915–65) is considered the last of the great Arab poets. During the succeeding centuries didactic poets, including Abul-Ala al-Maarri (973–1057), dealt with philosophical and political problems.

Arabic prose, like poetry, flourished from early times. The oldest surviving works deal with pre-Islamic *Aiyam al-Arab,* stories commemorating tribal warfare. They too were written down long after the Prophet's death. Following the spread of Islam, research into the history of the Prophet and of the Islamic conquests dominated Arab and Muslim literature. The Arab historian Ibn-Ishaq (c. 704–67) wrote a biography of the Prophet. Another Arabian commentator, al-Tabari (839–923), produced the *Annals,* an account of the world from the creation to AD 914 and the most comprehensive history of early Islam. The search for norms in the conduct of religious, personal, and legal affairs inaugurated the literature of *Hadith* (Traditions) and *Fiqh* (Canon Law). Commentaries on these matters and voluminous biographical dictionaries on the authorities from which laws and customs were derived form the major part of medieval Arabic literature.

In such centers of Islamic life as Basra, Kufah, and Baghdad, as well as in the non-Arab lands of Iran and Spain, academies were founded for the study of philology, theology, law, and philosophy. Islamic philosophical thought had been stimulated by the study of the ancient Greek philosophers, whose works had been translated by Arab, Syrian, and Hebrew scholars into their respective languages. Neoplatonic philosophy too found its way into Arabic thought, most impressively in the writings of al-Farabi (c. 878–c. 950). One of the most outstanding works, *The Ideal City,* deals with a theory of statecraft presented in Neoplatonic terms. In contrast to this work, which idealizes the state as an emanation from the All-One (God) with the Prophet as its ideal leader, other works on statecraft, such as *Principles of Government* by al-Mawardi (974?–1058), deal with practical political and legal problems of the Muslim state. Conflicting ideas on the essence of God and on free will and the eternal nature of the Koran stimulated philosophical discussion and created dissenting schools of thought. In the 12th and 13th centuries Islamic Sufism, or mysticism, found literary expression in the poetry of Ibn al-Farid (1181–1235) and Ibn al-Arabi (1165–1240) and in the *Writings of the Brethren of Purity.* Some of the greatest medieval philosophers wrote in Arabic; their work was studied in the West and greatly influenced the development of Scholasticism. The most outstanding among these Arab philosophers were Averroës (Ibn Rushd), Avicenna (Ibn Sina), and al-Ghazali (qq.v.).

Side by side with the works of the learned, a folk literature developed. It consisted of the narratives recited by storytellers in the bazaars of the old Near East and formed an oral tradition still vital in that part of the world. Heroes of antiquity and the famous 8th-century caliph Harun ar-Rashid became the center of romantic and imaginative tales in the *Romance of Antar* and the well-known *Arabian Nights.* Because these romances were entertainment for the masses, they spurned classical style and language and were therefore considered unworthy of notice by the learned. More to the taste of the scholar and the well-born were the celebrated *Maqamat* (Assemblies) of the poet al-Hamadhani (969–1008) and the *Maqamat* of the writer al-Hariri (1054–1122), which were meant to instruct as well as to amuse. Every line of al-Hariri's work was judged by the grammarian al-Zamakhshari (1074?–1143) to deserve "being written in gold."

After the brilliant intellectual life of the Middle

Ages a long period of stagnation followed. For some six centuries scholarly activity was almost exclusively devoted to commentaries on the works of the earlier masters; to digests of their historical, theological, and legal studies; and to anthologies of earlier books. These works accept tradition without reservation or critical analysis.

Modern Period. Only toward the end of the 19th century, and largely under the influence of the West, did a revival of Arabic literature begin. Egypt had long been the intellectual center, but other Arabic-speaking countries soon began to contribute their share. Scholarly, literary, and political topics are popular subjects for discussion by contemporary Arab writers, and creative writings appear in all forms. One of the most acclaimed writers in Arabic is the Egyptian novelist, playwright, and screenwriter Naguib Mahfouz (1911–), winner of the Nobel Prize for literature in 1988; notable among his novels is the *Cairo Trilogy* (1956–57). The novel is also represented by *Zainab,* an outstanding work by M. Hussain Heikal (1888–1956); poetry, by Shauqi (1868–1932) and A. Z. Abushady (1892–1955); the short story, by Mahmud Taimur (1894–); and the literary and philosophical essay, by Taha Hussein (1889–1973). Among the modern writers, Hussein most consciously uses the rich cadences of Classical Arabic. Other modern writers, under Western influence, have begun to curb the traditional tendency toward florid language. The social life of the Egyptian countryside is vividly and wittily depicted in the *Diary of a Country Judge* by Tawfiq al-Hakim (1898–1976), and modern political and socioreligious problems have been freely and critically discussed by the Coptic writer Salama Musa (1886–1958) and many others. Qasim Emin (1865–1908), in his sociological study *The Liberation of Women,* opened the way to the emancipation of Muslim women. Ahmad Amin (1886–1954) wrote a widely acclaimed *History of Islam.*

Western scholarship merged with Arabic intellectual endeavor at the American University of Beirut, long maintained for the training of intellectual leaders in the Arab world. Arab immigration to the New World produced an outstanding poet, Kahlil Gibran (1883–1931), whose mystical poetry, such as *The Prophet,* is widely read. I.Li.

For further information on this topic, see the Bibliography in volume 28, sections 131, 857.

ARABIC MUSIC. *See* ISLAMIC MUSIC.

ARAB LEAGUE, formal name the League of Arab States, voluntary association of independent countries whose peoples are mainly Arabic-speaking. Its stated purposes are to strengthen ties among the member states, coordinate their policies, and promote their common interests.

Membership. The league was founded in Cairo in 1945 by Egypt, Iraq, Lebanon, Saudi Arabia, Syria, Transjordan (now Jordan), and Yemen. Countries that later joined, listed alphabetically, are the following: Algeria (1962), Bahrain (1971), Djibouti (1977), Kuwait (1961), Libya (1953), Mauritania (1973), Morocco (1958), Oman (1971), Qatar (1971), Somalia (1974), Southern Yemen (1967), the Sudan (1956), Tunisia (1958), and the United Arab Emirates (1971); the Palestine Liberation Organization was also admitted in 1976. Egypt's membership was suspended in 1979, after it signed a peace treaty with Israel, and the league's headquarters was then moved from Cairo to Tunis. The league voted in 1987 to allow its members to restore diplomatic ties with Egypt, and in 1990 the league decided by a narrow majority to move its headquarters back to Cairo.

Structure. The supreme organ of the Arab League is its council, made up of all the member states, each of which has one vote. Unanimous council decisions are binding on all members, majority decisions only on those that have accepted them. Sixteen committees are attached to the council. A secretary-general, appointed by a two-thirds majority of the council, is in charge of the administration and financial offices, called the secretariat. It is, in turn, divided into several departments. Numerous specialized agencies are connected with the league, including the Arab League Educational, Cultural, and Scientific Organization; the Arab Labor Organization; and the Arab Postal Union.

History. The Egyptian government first proposed the Arab League in 1943. Many Arabs wanted to be united into one country, but Egypt and some other Arab states desired closer cooperation without the loss of self-rule resulting from a total union. The original charter of the league created a regional organization of sovereign states that was neither a union nor a federation. The league hoped to win the independence of all Arabs still under alien rule and to prevent the Jewish minority in Palestine (then British-governed) from creating a Jewish state. The league's reputation suffered from its failure to block the establishment of Israel in 1948. The members, however, eventually formed a joint defense council, an economic council, and a permanent military command. Discord among its members has often weakened the league politically, but it has managed to settle some Arab disputes and to limit conflicts such as the Lebanese civil wars of 1958 and 1975–76. The league has been more effective in activities fostering economic, social, and cultural cooperation among Arab states. A.E.G.

ARABS, name given to the ancient and present-day inhabitants of the Arabian Peninsula and often applied to the peoples closely allied to them in ancestry, language, religion, and culture. Presently more than 200 million Arabs are living mainly in 21 countries; they constitute the overwhelming majority of the population in Saudi Arabia, Syria, Yemen, Jordan, Lebanon, Iraq, Egypt, and the nations of North Africa. The Arabic language is the main symbol of cultural unity among these people, but the religion of Islam provides another common bond for the majority of Arabs. Language and religion are united in the Koran (q.v.), the sacred scripture of Islam.

History. Arabia was the site of a flourishing civilization long before the Christian era (*see* ARABIA: *Ancient Kingdoms*). In the centuries following the death (AD 632) of the prophet Muhammad, Arab influence spread throughout the Middle East, to parts of Europe, particularly Sicily and Spain, to sub-Saharan Africa, to the subcontinent of India, and to Madagascar and the Malay Archipelago. The cultural and scientific contributions of the Arabs to Western civilization during the Middle Ages was highly significant, especially in astronomy, mathematics, medicine, and philosophy.

Modern Arabs. During the past two centuries of rapid world change, hundreds of years of cultural unity have been disrupted, and the Arabs, led by the people of Egypt and Morocco, have moved more and more into separate national traditions. In some countries, such as Iran, Afghanistan, and Indonesia, minority communities of Arabs retain only language, religion, and histories of their migrations to their present locations.

Religion. The Islamic religion, which originated in the western Arabian Peninsula in the 7th century, predominates in most Arab nations. Forms of both major divisions of Islam—the Sunni and the various Shiite sects—can be found in the Arab countries. Almost everywhere nationalism, which emerged in the late 19th century, is an important force that sometimes uses the Islamic religious tradition as an ideological tool to justify the power of the ruling class.

Urbanization. Dozens of large cities and hundreds of towns reflect the pronounced urban character of the Arab world; in most of the countries about 40 percent of the people are urban dwellers. All Arab nations suffer from conspicuous economic inequalities, especially the concentration of wealth and power in a ruling elite. Most are also undergoing severe urbanization stresses as the failing rural economies drive poverty-stricken landless peasants to the cities. The growth of modern cities through rural migration has caused serious problems in these urban centers, including unemployment, housing shortages, and the proliferation of vast slums.

Rural populations. Most Arab countries have substantial agricultural, village-based populations. The land, the family, and religion are still the main influences on attitudes and behavior. The traditional prosperous village cultures were altered and largely destroyed during the late 18th and 19th centuries by European penetration and colonization. In most countries today, peasant farming on a subsistence level is pervasive.

Nomadic Arabs. Unitl the mid-19th century, vast semidesert areas in North Africa and the Arabian Peninsula were exploited by nomadic tribes. The camel-breeding Bedouins (q.v.) were well known as warriors and controllers of the caravan routes. Other tribes specialized in sheep and goat husbandry. In Sudan, the Somali Republic, and Djibouti, pastoral economies operating on subsistence levels remain the only means of survival for many poverty-stricken Arab groups.

See also ARABIC LANGUAGE; ARABIC LITERATURE; CALIPHATE; ISLAM; ISLAMIC ART AND ARCHITECTURE.

For further information on this topic, see the Bibliography in volume 28, sections 131, 365, 857, 876, 1042–43, 1047–49, 1060, 1062, 1064.

ARACAJU, city and river port, E Brazil, capital of Sergipe State, on the Cotinguiba R., near the Atlantic Ocean. Linked to the interior by a railroad, the city has industries producing textiles, tanned goods, soap, and lime. Timber, coffee, cotton, hides and skins, sugar, rice, coconuts and oil, and salt are exported. A normal school is located in Aracaju. The city was founded in 1855. Pop. (1980, greater city) 293,485.

ARACHNE, in Greek mythology, a young girl who was so skilled in weaving that she dared to challenge the goddess Athena, a patron of the arts and crafts, to a contest. While Athena wove a tapestry depicting the gods and goddesses in all their splendor, Arachne wove one illustrating their romances. Furious over the perfection of the girl's work, Athena tore it to shreds, and Arachne hanged herself in grief. Out of pity Athena loosened the rope, turning it into a cobweb, and transformed Arachne into a spider.

ARACHNID, term for the scorpion, spider, daddy longlegs, mite, tick (qq.v.), and other invertebrate (q.v.) animals that constitute the class Arachnida in the phylum Arthropoda (*see* ARTHROPOD), which also includes crustaceans and insects. Arachnids are usually carnivorous and terrestrial; fossils suggest that they were among the first animals to invade the land, perhaps in the early Devonian period, nearly 400 million years ago. About 60,000 species now exist, in 11

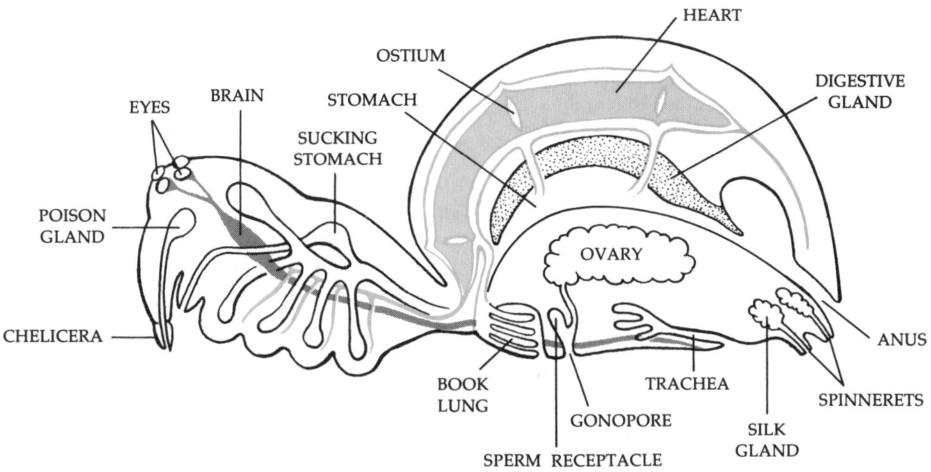

Structure of a typical arachnid, the spider, shows the body's division into two main parts. The so-called book lungs are a series of leaflike plates.
From Helena Curtis: *Biology*, Third Edition, Worth Publishers, Inc., New York, 1979

orders: Acari or Acarina (mites and ticks), Amblypygi (tailless whip scorpions), Araneae (spiders), Opiliones (daddy longlegs), Palpigradi (palpigrades), Pseudoscorpiones (false scorpions), Ricinulei (ricinuleids), Schizomida (micro-whip scorpions), Scorpionida (true scorpions), Solpugida (sunspiders), and Uropygi (whip scorpions).

Characteristics. The arachnid body is divided into two parts. The anterior part (prosoma) has sense organs, mouthparts, and limbs, but no antennae. The first pair of appendages (chelicerae) may form pincers or poison fangs, and the second (pedipalps) may serve as pincers, feelers, or legs. The other pairs, generally four, are used for walking. The posterior body, or abdomen (opisthosoma), bears the genital opening, the respiratory organs—book lungs and trachea—and other structures. Food is partly or wholly broken down by secreted fluids.

Behavior and Importance. Arachnids generally hunt or lie in wait for small animals such as insects. They have simple eyes and various prey-subduing structures, such as the segmented, stinging tail of scorpions and the abdominal spinnerets with which spiders construct elaborate insect traps. Mites, however, have poor locomotor ability and suck the juices of animals and plants; ticks are parasitic bloodsuckers of animals. Most arachnids are solitary except at the time of mating, when they display complex behavior patterns. Sexes are separate, and females may guard eggs or young, which are often born live.

Arachnids are generally beneficial as they eat insect pests, and few spider and scorpion species are dangerously poisonous. Mites and ticks infest humans, domestic animals, and plants, thereby spreading diseases. M.T.G.

For further information on this topic, see the Bibliography in volume 28, sections 464, 466.

ARAD, city, W Romania, in Banat Region, on the Mureş R., near the Hungarian border. Industries include locomotive, machine-tool, and textile manufacturing, flour milling, and distilling. Founded in the 11th century, it was under Turkish, Austrian, and Hungarian rule until 1920, when it passed to Romania. Pop. (1986 est.) 187,700.

ARAFAT, Yasir (1929–), Palestinian commando leader and politician, head of the Palestine Liberation Organization (q.v.; PLO). Born in Jerusalem, he fled after the establishment of Israel in 1948, later studied engineering in Cairo, and also trained as a *fedayeen* (commando). In 1956 he founded the commando group Al Fatah, and for the next few years, while working with a construction firm in Kuwait, repeatedly led *fedayeen* raids deep into Israeli territory. In 1964, he linked Al Fatah with similar groups in the PLO, which he has headed since 1968. After the Arab League recognized the PLO as the sole representative of Palestinian Arabs in 1974, Arafat worked to win the organization international recognition. Also, he made a strong effort to shed his terrorist image for that of the moderate statesman. In 1988 he proclaimed an independent Palestinian state, addressed a special session of the UN General Assembly in Geneva, and recognized Israel's right to exist, thus meeting a pivotal U.S. condition for substantive dialogue with the PLO. His support for Iraq during the Persian Gulf War (q.v.) eroded his international standing, especially with most Arab governments in the Gulf.

ARAFURA SEA, shallow arm of the W Pacific Ocean, between N Australia and islands of E Indonesia. It is bordered by the Banda Sea on the N and by the Timor Sea on the W; the Torres Strait, on the E, connects it with the Coral Sea. The Gulf of Carpentaria is a large SE arm of the Arafura Sea. During the Pleistocene epoch, the present sea floor probably was above sea level, forming a land bridge between Australia and SE Asia. Surveys in the 1960s and '70s indicated that large-scale mineral deposits now underlie the sea.

ARAGO, Dominique François Jean (1786–1853), French astronomer and physicist, who discovered the phenomenon of the production of magnetism by rotation and proved the relationship between the aurora and variations in terrestrial magnetism. Arago was born in Estagel and educated at the École Polytechnique in Paris. At the age of 23, he was elected a member of the Paris Academy of Sciences and was appointed professor of analytical geometry and geodesy at the École Polytechnique. His later studies were in astronomy, magnetism, and light polarization.

ARAGÓN, autonomous region and former kingdom, NE Spain, bordering on the Pyrenees Mountains. The region is now composed of the provinces of Huesca, Saragossa, and Teruel; its capital is the city of Saragossa.

After the Romans defeated the Carthaginians during the Punic Wars, Aragón became a part of the Roman province of Hispania Tarraconensis. The Visigoths conquered the region late in the 5th century, the Moors in the 8th century. Subsequently the region was incorporated with the kingdom of Navarre. In 1035 Ramiro I (d. 1063), a son of the Navarrese ruler Sancho III (970–1035), established Aragón as an independent kingdom. Navarre was annexed in 1076, and during the next 100 years additional territory was added by successful wars against the Moors. In 1137 Aragón was united with Catalonia and Barcelona. Aragón grew into a leading Mediterranean naval power around the port of Barcelona. Aragón gained possession of the Balearic Islands, Sicily, Sardinia, and Naples during the next two centuries; in 1238 Valencia was captured from the Moors. The marriage of Ferdinand II of Aragón (later Ferdinand V of Castile) to Isabella I of Castile united those two regions. Formal merger of the two kingdoms took place on the accession of Charles I in 1516, but Aragón retained its own administration and representative institutions until the end of the 17th century. Area, 47,669 sq km (18,405 sq mi). Pop. (1986) 1,214,729.

ARAGON, Louis (1897–1982), French novelist, poet, and essayist, who was a leader of the movements in French literature known as Dada and surrealism. He was born in Paris. During the early years of his career he wrote a number of experimental works, including the collection of poems *Feu de joie* (Bonfire, 1920) and the long essay *Traité du style* (Treatise on Style, 1928). In 1930 he embraced communism and the related aesthetic doctrine of socialist realism. Thereafter he was one of the most active French Communist propagandists. During World War II he was a leading figure in the French Resistance, and after the war he edited a Communist newspaper.

Aragon's novels, realistic pictures of modern France, include *The Bells of Basel* (1934; trans. 1936), *Residential Quarter* (1936; trans. 1938), *Aurélien* (1945; trans. 1946), and *Holy Week* (1958; trans. 1961). His lyric postsurrealistic poetry includes *The Red Front* (1931; trans. 1933), *Heartbreak* (1941; trans. 1943), and *The Eyes of Elsa* (1942; trans. 1944).

ARAGONITE, calcium carbonate mineral, $CaCO_3$, in its orthorhombic form (*see* CRYSTAL). Aragonite is harder and less common or stable than calcite (q.v.), into which it may change over geologic time. It occurs with iron ore and other deposits, around hot springs, and in stalactites and is also secreted by invertebrates as mother-of-pearl and pearl. Its crystals are long, brittle, usually whitish, and transparent to translucent. It has a hardness (q.v.) of 3.5–4 and a sp.gr. of 2.9–3.

ARAGUAIA, also Araguaya, river, Brazil, rising on the Mato Grosso plateau and flowing NE until, after a course of about 1770 km (about 1100 mi), it joins the Tocantins R. In the lower course it branches around Bananal Island. In the upper course it forms the boundary line between the states of Goiás and Mato Grosso. Falls and rapids hinder use of the river as a trade route.

ARAK, city, W Iran, situated about 1829 m (about 6000 ft) above sea level. Transportation facilities include several railroads and highways. Arak is the center of an agricultural area yielding grains and fruits, and it is noted for the manufacture of fine rugs and carpets. Founded in 1808, the city was formerly known as Sultanabad; it received its present name around 1930. Pop. (1986) 265,349.

ARAKS. *See* ARAS.

ARAL SEA, lake or inland sea, Central Asia, in SW Kazakhstan and NW Uzbekistan, near the Caspian Sea. Formerly the fourth largest lake in the world, it has no outlet. The tributary streams are the Syrdarya and Amu Darya, which have been heavily tapped for irrigation in recent decades; as a result, the Aral's volume has dropped more than 60 percent since 1960. The fishing industry has also dropped off, and the waters are no longer transparent and filled with sturgeon, carp, and herring. The shores are barren and uninhabited. The sea contains numerous islands, of which Kokaral is the largest, hence its Kirgiz name Aral-Denghis (Island Sea). Area, 41,383 sq km (15,978 sq mi).

ARAM (Heb., "highland," in contrast to the lowland of Canaan), ancient country northeast of Palestine, between the Lebanon Mountains and the Euphrates River, roughly corresponding to present-day Syria. The Aramaeans, a Semitic people, moved to this region some time in the late 2d millennium. Their language was the Aramaic language (q.v.).

ARAMAIC LANGUAGE, Semitic language closely related to Hebrew. Originally the language of the Aramaeans (*see* ARAM), it was used, in many dialectical forms, in Mesopotamia and Syria before 1000 BC and later became the lingua franca of the Middle East (*see* ASSYRO-BABYLONIAN LANGUAGE). Aramaic survived the fall of Nineveh (612 BC) and Babylon (539 BC) and remained the official language of the Persian Empire (539–337 BC). Ancient inscriptions in Aramaic have been found over a vast area extending from Egypt to China.

Before the Christian era, Aramaic had become the language of the Jews in Palestine. Jesus preached in Aramaic, and parts of the Old Testament and much of the rabbinical literature were written in that language. Christian Aramaic, usually called Syriac, also developed an extensive literature, especially from the 4th to 7th centuries.

The influence and diffusion of Aramaic began to decline in favor of Arabic at the time of the Arab conquest in the 7th century AD. Aramaic survives today in Eastern and Western dialects, mostly as the language of Christians living in a few scattered communities in Syria, Lebanon, Turkey, Iraq, and Iran.

See also ALPHABET; SEMITIC LANGUAGES.

ARANDA, Pedro Pablo Abarca de Bolea, Conde de (1718–98), Spanish statesman, born in Saragossa. From a distinguished Aragonese family, he rose to the rank of general in the army and in 1760 was appointed ambassador to Poland. Aranda returned to Madrid in 1766 to quell a revolt there. He expelled the Jesuits from Spain, claiming that they were responsible for antimonarchical sentiments and conspiracies among the people and promoted a liberal policy. As president of the Council of State, he opposed the foreign policy of the statesman and royal favorite Manuel de Godoy (1767–1851); as a result Aranda was banished to Aragón in 1795.

ARAN ISLANDS, also Arana Naomh, group of three small islands, W Republic of Ireland, in the Atlantic Ocean, at the mouth of Galway Bay. The islands, part of county Galway, are Inishmore, the largest, Inishmaan, and Inisheer. Fishing has always been the main industry, and some islanders still use the fishing methods of their ancestors. The rugged life of these island fishermen was the subject of the play *Riders to the Sea* (1904), by the Irish dramatist John M. Synge.

Tourists are attracted to the islands by the customs of the islanders, many of whom still speak Gaelic and hold ceili, Irish folk dances. Other attractions are the beautiful beaches and historic landmarks of the area. Scattered throughout the islands are ruins of ancient fortifications, churches, and monasteries constructed in the early Christian era. Among them are the 9th-century Tempall Brecan and the House of Saint Edna, which was the most important religious settlement on Inishmore throughout the medieval period. Area, 47 sq km (18 sq mi).

ARANY, János (1817-82), Hungarian poet, who is regarded as one of the greatest poets of Hungary. He was born in Salonta (now in Romania). While working as a civil servant, he wrote his first poem, *The Lost Constitution,* a satirical epic about the lives of government officials. The first part of his great trilogy, *Toldi* (1847), an epic founded wholly upon Magyar traditions, won him popularity. In 1860 he moved to Pest and was appointed general secretary of the Hungarian Academy of Science in 1870.

Arany based many of his poems on Magyar legends and traditions, appealing strongly to the spirit of Hungarian national pride. His other notable works include *King Buda's Death* (1864; trans. 1936), an epic in 12 cantos; and the second and third parts of the *Toldi* cycle, *Toldi szerelme* (1879) and *Toldi's Eve* (1854; trans. 1914); and ballads.

ARAPAHO, North American Indian tribe of Algonquian linguistic stock, originally inhabiting what is now Minnesota and later the plains between the Yellowstone River and Rio Grande. At an unknown time the Arapaho formed a permanent alliance with the Cheyenne, but, unlike the Cheyenne, they were friendly toward white settlers. The Arapaho were a nomadic tribe whose art and religious ceremonies exhibited advanced characteristics of Plains Indian culture, especially in the sun dance (q.v.). The tribe now lives in settlements in three major divisions: the Northern Arapaho with the Shoshoni in Wyoming; the Southern Arapaho with the Cheyenne in Oklahoma; and the Gros Ventre, or Atsina, with the Assiniboin in Montana. *See also* AMERICAN INDIAN LANGUAGES; AMERICAN INDIANS.

ARAPAHOE PEAK, mountain, N Colorado, in the Front Range of the Rocky Mts., near Boulder; 4117 m (13,506 ft) high. On the face of the peak is an ice field known as Arapahoe Glacier.

ARARAT (Arm. *Masis;* Turk. *Ağri Daği;* Pers. *Kohi-nuh*), mountain, extreme E Turkey, near the border with Armenia and Iran. Except on the NW, where a spur nearly 2134 m (7000 ft) high merges with a long ridge, the mountain is completely isolated, being surrounded on all other sides by elevated plains ranging from about 760 to 1370 m (about 2500 to 4500 ft) above sea level. From an elevation of about 2680 m (about 8800 ft) Ararat rises in two peaks, known as Great Ararat (5165 m/16,946 ft) and Little Ararat (3914 m/12,840 ft). Above the 4267-m (14,000-ft) level, Great Ararat is perpetually covered with snow. Vegetation, consisting for the most part of grasses, is chiefly confined to the area between about 1525 and 3355 m (about 5000 and 11,000 ft). According to the Old Testament (see Gen. 8:4), Noah's ark landed on the "mountains of Ararat" after the deluge. Great Ararat was first climbed in modern times in 1829. On July 2, 1840, great masses of the mountain were torn loose by a violent earthquake. The resulting avalanche buried a village and a convent on its lower slopes. An American expedition ascended Ararat in the summer of 1949 in an unsuccessful search for evidence of the existence of Noah's ark. Recent expeditions have reported finding timbers that members believe to have come from the ark.

For further information on this topic, see the Bibliography in volume 28, section 867.

ARAS, also Araks (anc. *Araxes*), river, Asia, rising near Erzurum, Turkey, and flowing in a generally E direction into Armenia and Azerbaijan, where it joins the Kura R. before emptying into the Caspian Sea. The river forms the border between Turkey, Armenia, the Nakhichevan autonomous region, Iran, and Azerbaijan. The chief tributaries of the Aras, which is about 966 km (about 600 mi) long, are the Razdan and the Qara Su rivers. Traces of ancient canals and other evidence of the once dense population that inhabited the area have been discovered on the banks of the river.

ARAUCANIAN, name of several tribes of South American Indians of the Araucanian linguistic stock, inhabiting various areas of central and southern Chile and western Argentina. The principal surviving Araucanian tribes are the Mapuche, Huilliche, and Picunche. When first seen by outsiders, in the 16th century, the Araucanians lived in small villages and subsisted solely by hunting and fishing. They practiced little agriculture, growing only corn and potatoes. Today the chief occupations of the Araucanians are farming and cattle raising; many own their property. They are also skilled at fashioning beautiful silver ornaments, saddles, leatherwork, and pottery and at weaving blankets and shawls. Others are soldiers, teachers, and politicians.

Probably the fiercest and boldest of the South American Indians, the Araucanians waged relentless warfare in defense of their tribal domains for more than 200 years, repeatedly turning back the Spanish intruders. The capacity of the Araucanians to resist began to weaken late in the 18th century, but they did not finally submit until 1881. The first phase of their heroic struggle against the Spaniards is immortalized in *La Araucana* (1569–89), the famous epic poem by the Spanish soldier and writer Alonso de Ercilla y Zúñiga.

See AMERICAN INDIANS.

ARAUCARIA, common name for evergreen trees of the family Araucariaceae, in the order Pinales (*see* CONIFER), native to South America and Australasia. The family contains two genera with several trees of commercial importance. *Araucaria imbricata,* called also Chile pine and monkey puzzle, is a valuable timber tree native to the Chilean Andes, where it grows to a height of 45 m (150 ft). The trunk is straight and free from knots, yielding a beautifully veined, yellowish-white, hard wood and abundant resin. Like many pines, the young trees have branches almost from the ground, but the older ones have tall, naked stems with a crown of branches. The kauri pine, *Agathis australis,* of New Zealand, growing to 60 m (200 ft), yields valuable timber and resin.

ARAWAK, a once-predominant group of South American Indians of the Arawakan linguistic family, originally inhabiting an area that stretched from present-day Florida down through the islands of the West Indies and the coastal area of South America as far as southern Brazil. The Arawak were the first natives of the New World encountered by Christopher Columbus.

A number of Arawak tribes have been extinct for several hundred years. Those of the Lesser Antilles were subjugated in fighting with the Carib Indians in the late 15th century. The Arawak population in the West Indies fell from a probable 2 to 3 million to a few thousand by the early 16th century; by the end of that century island Arawak were extinct. This catastrophic mortality rate was due to the introduction of European diseases, damage to the Arawaks' food supplies, and Spanish brutality and enslavement.

Before the Spanish conquest, the large-island ecologies, offering bountiful harvests and abundant fish, combined with the compact and stable island populations, permitted the development of an elaborate political and social structure. A class of hereditary chiefs ruled three other classes, the lowest of which was composed of slaves. Conflict between classes was apparently minimal. In this matrilineal society, rulers were succeeded by their eldest sister's eldest son. Religion offered a hierarchy of deities parallel to the social structure.

The Arawak tribes of South America better survived European contact because their groups were smaller and more scattered. Their social structure was also matrilineal but much less complex. Mainland Arawak traded with the Dutch and English. In the 17th and 18th centuries they made a transition to plantation agriculture.

In the 20th century, the existing Arawak began to accept wage-paying jobs as a supplement to farming, hunting, and fishing. Although their present-day culture reflects various non-Arawak influences, this group has been noted since pre-Columbian times as skilled potters, weavers, and wood- and metalworkers. Today some 30,000 Arawak live in Guyana, with smaller numbers in Suriname and French Guiana. Arawakan-speaking groups are also widespread in other parts of South America.

See AMERICAN INDIAN LANGUAGES; AMERICAN INDIANS.

ARAXES. *See* ARAS.

ARBELA, BATTLE OF. *See* GAUGAMELA, BATTLE OF.

ARBITRATION, reference of a dispute to an impartial person or persons, called arbitrators, for a decision or award based on evidence and arguments presented by the disputants. The parties involved usually agree to resort to arbitration in lieu of court proceedings to resolve an existing dispute or any grievance that may arise between them. Arbitration may sometimes be compelled by law, particularly in connection with labor disputes involving public employees or employees of private companies invested with a public interest, such as utilities or railroads.

Most arbitration in the U.S. has involved labor or commercial disputes. In recent years, however, other uses of arbitration have gained acceptance, such as arbitration of medical malpractice claims and resolution of disputes among insurers in states with no-fault insurance or uninsured motorist programs. As worldwide trade and investment have increased, international commercial arbitration has become important both in planning international transactions and in resolving disputes when they arise.

Labor arbitration is concerned largely with disputes between employers and employees over interpretation or application of the terms of collective bargaining agreements, and occasionally with new contract terms. Commercial arbitration deals with disputes among private parties regarding contracts to produce, buy, sell, lease, or distribute goods, or to perform a business service.

It was formerly thought that so-called public law disputes, such as those arising under antitrust, securities, or patent laws, could not be arbitrated. Since 1982, however, disputes concerning validity or infringement of a U.S. patent are arbitrable by statute. The U.S. Supreme Court has approved enforcement of agreements to arbitrate cases involving claims under the securities laws, and (in international transactions) under the antitrust laws as well.

Labor Arbitration. In the 1947 Taft-Hartley Act, Congress declared that arbitration was the "desirable method for settlement of grievance disputes arising over the application or interpretation of an existing collective bargaining agreement" (*see* NATIONAL LABOR RELATIONS ACT). Building from that policy, the Supreme Court has created presumptions favoring a broad judicial interpretation of arbitral authority, and has severely limited the judiciary's role in reviewing arbitrators' awards.

Today the overwhelming majority of private-sector collective bargaining agreements provide for grievance arbitration, including cases of employee discipline and discharge. Such agreements typically leave to union discretion the choice of which claims to take to arbitration, but the union is subject to a legally enforceable "duty of fair representation." In recent years grievance arbitration has also been widely accepted in the public sector. Increasingly, too, compulsory arbitration to establish the terms of a new collective agreement has been used in the public sector.

Arbitrators generally are chosen because they are acceptable to both management and labor. Most are lawyers, economists, educators, or specialists in industrial relations. Some collective bargaining agreements provide for selection of arbitrators according to the procedures of the Federal Mediation and Conciliation Service, the American Arbitration Association, or a state or municipal public-sector labor agency.

Commercial Arbitration. In the U.S., commercial arbitration is used most often in the construction, garment, and textile industries; in cases involving insurance and negligence; in maritime disputes; and in controversies involving members of stock and commodity exchanges. All but six states have adopted modern arbitration statutes, and since 1925 the Federal Arbitration Act has governed arbitration of grievances arising out of maritime transactions and transactions in interstate or foreign commerce. These statutes provide that agreements may be made to arbitrate future as well as existing disputes; that the courts will not hear disputes subject to valid agreements to arbitrate; and that arbitral awards may be enforced in the courts. Such awards generally may be set aside only because of misconduct (such as an undisclosed conflict of interest) by an arbitrator. Agreements to arbitrate usually are contained in the arbitration clause of a contract; the Supreme Court has held that if there is a dispute about the validity or effectiveness of a contract containing such a clause, it is for the arbitrators—not the courts—to decide the issue.

Commercial arbitrators include business executives, lawyers, and other professionals who, as a public service, are willing to help resolve conflicts in their areas of expertise. In simple cases, a single arbitrator may hear a dispute; in cases in which the issues are complicated or the amount in dispute is substantial, it is common to provide for a panel of three arbitrators. Arbitrations are often conducted under the auspices of the American Arbitration Association or a specialized trade association.

See also INTERNATIONAL LABOR ORGANIZATION; LABOR, DEPARTMENT OF; LABOR RELATIONS.

International Arbitration. International arbitration is the settlement by a mutually acceptable third party of disputes between sovereign states. Modern international arbitration began with the conclusion of Jay's Treaty (1794) by Great Britain and the U.S. Numerous disputes were arbitrated during the 19th century, many involving these two countries. The most important disputes were settled in the Treaty of Ghent (1814) and in various treaties defining fishing rights in specific areas. The Treaty of Washington (1871) embodied arbitrations of the San Juan Boundary Dispute and of claims arising from the American Civil War. In Europe, the first important development in international arbitration in modern times was The Hague Conference of 1899, which resulted in the creation of the Permanent Court of Arbitration. Although reluctant to participate in many early international treaties, the U.S. continued to make individual arbitration treaties, especially in the years between World Wars I and II.

Today, international arbitration may be used to settle boundary disputes, controversies about interpretation of international agreements, and claims arising out of wartime damage. International commercial arbitration involves private parties and/or governments engaging in commercial activity. The International Bank for Reconstruction and Development, for example, sponsors the International Center for Settlement of Investment Disputes, to hear disputes between private investors and the countries in which their investments were made.

International commercial arbitration, like its counterpart in the U.S., proceeds on the basis of an arbitration clause contained in an export-import, investment, or similar contract between persons from different countries. Since neither party wishes to have future disputes adjudicated in the courts of the other party, arbitration in a neutral forum is a common solution. The arbitration clause usually provides for the manner of selecting arbitrators; sometimes provision is made for arbitration to be conducted under the supervision of an institution such as an international trade association.

Some 80 countries, including the U.S., the former Soviet republics, and all other major commercial nations outside Latin America, are parties to the UN Convention on the Recognition of Foreign Arbitral Awards. This convention enforces arbitral awards rendered in any contracting state, regardless of the nationalities of the parties to the dispute. Agreements to arbitrate are also enforceable, and a court will generally not hear a dispute that is governed by a valid agreement to arbitrate between persons from different contracting states.

Typically, international arbitrations are heard before three arbitrators, one appointed by each side and the third by mutual agreement or by designation of an administering body. Most arbitrators are jurists and are expected to support their award by full opinions. Centers for international arbitration are London, Paris, Zurich, Geneva, New York, Tokyo, Hong Kong, and (for East-West trade disputes) Stockholm.

See also INTERNATIONAL LAW. A.F.L. & D.G.C.

For further information on this topic, see the Bibliography in volume 28, sections 214, 248.

ARBOR DAY (Lat. *arbor,* "tree"), in the U.S., an annual tree-planting day for the beautification of towns or the forestation of empty tracts of land. It is generally observed in public schools in order

Dwarf arborvitae, Thuja occidentalis, *are grown in containers to a height of about 38 cm (about 15 in).*
© Barry L. Runk–Grant Heilman Photography

to stress the importance of forest preservation, and in some states it is a legal holiday. Only a few states have a fixed date for Arbor Day, which was introduced by Julius Sterling Morton (1832–1902), in Nebraska, in 1872.

ARBORVITAE (Lat., "tree of life"), common name for evergreen trees of the genus *Thuja,* of the family Cupressaceae (*see* CYPRESS), so named early in the 17th century because of the medicinal value ascribed to its balsamic resin. Extracts increase blood pressure and reduce fever. The leaves have a fragrant, balsamlike odor. The wood is reddish, light, and durable. Some of the larger species are valuable timber trees. The smaller species are cultivated in gardens and as wind screens for more tender plants.

The common, or American, arborvitae, *T. occidentalis,* often called white cedar, is found in the northeastern regions of North America, as far south as Virginia. It flourishes in moist, cool places and attains a height of 15 m (50 ft). The branches are horizontally expanded, compressed or flattened, and have small, scalelike leaves. The cones are small and obovate. The only other species native to North America is the giant arborvitae, *T. plicata,* found west of the Rocky Mts. from northern California to Alaska. Sometimes called red cedar or canoe cedar, it may attain a height of 60 m (200 ft) under favorable conditions, and the trunk may exceed 4.5 m (15 ft) in diameter.

The Oriental arborvitae of the Old World, *T. orientalis,* is smaller and less hardy than the American species. It has denser foliage, more nearly vertical branches, and larger, rougher, and more nearly spherical cones.

ARBUS, Diane, *née* NEMEROV (1923–71), American photographer of disturbing images of bizarre individuals. Arbus was born and lived in New York City. She worked first with her husband, the photographer Allan Arbus (1918–), and then alone. Arbus presented such subjects as twins, eccentric New Yorkers, circus people, and the insane in a manner that accentuated their grotesqueness or abnormality. Her work was published in magazines and the book *Diane Arbus* (1972) and shown at the Museum of Modern Art in New York City (1965, 1967, retrospective in 1972). A woman of extreme temperament, Arbus took her own life in 1971.

ARBUTHNOT, John (1667–1735), Scottish physician and wit, born in Arbuthnot, Kincardine, and educated at University College, University of Oxford. He was a successful physician and in 1705 was appointed physician in ordinary to Queen Anne of Great Britain. He is best remembered, however, as the witty companion and counselor of the British writers Jonathan Swift and Alexander Pope. His works include the essays *On Ailments* (1731) and *Concerning the Effects of Air on Human Bodies* (1732) and the satire *History of John Bull* (1712).

Trailing arbutus, Epigaea repens
© John Shaw–Bruce Coleman, Inc.

ARBUTUS, genus of small trees and shrubs of the family Ericaceae (*see* HEATH). It includes the madrona tree, *Arbutus menziesii,* of California and Oregon, and the strawberry tree, *A. unedo,* of Europe.

In the eastern U.S. a closely related genus, *Epigaea,* is called trailing arbutus. *E. repens* grows in sandy woods or in rocky soil in the shade of pines. The plant is called ground laurel in the southern states and mayflower in New England. The leaves are evergreen and the fragrant blossoms rose-colored or white, in small clusters.

ARC, in electricity. *See* ELECTRIC ARC.

ARC, in mathematics, a segment of a curve. An arc of a circle is often expressed in degrees and corresponds to the magnitude of the angle at the center of the circle that subtends (defines) the arc. When the length of an arc is equal to the radius of the circle of which the arc is part, the length is called one radian. *See* GEOMETRY; TRIGONOMETRY.

ARC, Jeanne d'. *See* JOAN OF ARC, SAINT.

ARCADE, in architecture, a row of arches, flat or curved, supported on columns, piers, or pilasters, used by architects since ancient Egyptian times. The Romans brought the use of arcades to its most sophisticated level, employing them to support tiers of seats in theaters, as in Rome's semicircular Theater of Marcellus (13 BC), for temple substructures, as in the immense Temple of Fortuna Primigenia (early 1st cent. BC) in Praeneste (now Palestrina), Italy; and for aqueducts, as in the triple-tiered Pont du Gard (late 1st cent. BC), near Nîmes, France. An arcade built against a wall or with its openings filled with masonry is called a blind arcade. *See also* ARCHITECTURE; ARCH AND VAULT.

ARCADIA, city, Los Angeles Co., SW California, a suburb W of Los Angeles, at the foot of the San Gabriel Mts.; inc. 1903. Primarily residential, it has some light industry. The Santa Anita Park racetrack and the Los Angeles Arboretum are in Arcadia. The city was laid out in 1888 and named for the region of ancient Greece that was known for its pastoral character. Pop. (1980) 45,994; (1990) 48,290.

ARCARO, Eddie, full name GEORGE EDWARD ARCARO (1916–), American jockey, born in Cincinnati, Ohio. After a short period as an exercise boy, he became a jockey, winning his first race in 1932. In a career that lasted until 1962, Arcaro rode in 24,092 races and won 4779, including 549 stakes races, at the time a record for Thoroughbred racing. He won the Kentucky Derby five times and the Preakness and Belmont Stakes six times each. Arcaro twice won the Triple Crown for 3-year-olds, with Whirlaway in 1941 and Citation in 1948. The horses he rode earned a total of $30,039,543, making Arcaro one of the greatest money-winning jockeys in the history of Thoroughbred racing.

ARCE, Manuel José (1786–1847), first president (1825–29) of the United Provinces of Central America, formed by the five countries of that region that refused annexation by Mexico after liberaton from Spain. He was born in San Salvador. Twice imprisoned for insurrection against the Spanish, Arce was appointed head of the Salvadorean army in 1821, and in 1825 he won the federation's presidency. Ruling first with liberal, then conservative, support, pleasing none, he was deposed by Francisco Morazán in 1829 and fled to Mexico; from there he led two abortive revolts (1831 and 1833). After the demise of the federation, he returned to El Salvador to run unsuccessfully for the presidency of that country. Exiled in 1843 for leading still another revolt, he finally returned to El Salvador in 1845.

ARCH. *See* ARCH AND VAULT.

ARCHAEBACTERIA, simple organisms that resemble ordinary bacteria (q.v.) in that they lack a well-formed nucleus and can therefore be characterized as procaryotes in the classification (q.v.) of living organisms. Their biochemistry differs in important ways from that of other bacteria, however, and some biologists place them in a kingdom of their own. According to these theories, archaebacteria may be ancestral to the main cellular body of eucaryotes, or organisms with well-formed cell nuclei, whereas ordinary bacteria are generally thought to be ancestral to the mitochondria and chloroplasts within eucaryotic cells.

ARCHAEOASTRONOMY, study of the varied astronomical achievements of ancient peoples, extending from prehistoric times to the advanced cultures of the Middle East and Latin America. Such study involves the combined efforts of astronomers, archaeologists, ethnographers, and other scientists to interpret the meaning of architectural remains and written records of astronomical significance. Such remains range from rock paintings, the so-called medicine wheels of native North Americans, and much larger megalithic structures, such as Great Britain's Stonehenge, to the sophisticated calendars developed by the Egyptians and Maya.

The remnants of cultures throughout the world give evidence of their concern with the complex regularity of the motions of the sun, moon, and stars and with unusual occurrences such as the appearance of a nova or comet in the sky. Besides the simple fact that the sky was a dominating feature of the human world in ancient times—a fact obscured for people in advanced modern civilizations by the prevalence of artificial lighting—the regularity of celestial events provided ancient peoples with the best means for bringing order to their understanding of the world. It enabled them to measure the passage of time, to predict the recurrence of seasonal events (an essential for agriculture), to undertake extensive navigations, and to develop the calendars needed for their complex societies.

The celestial orientations of the pyramids of Egypt and of various temples and structures of the Middle East and Europe first began to be studied scientifically in the late 18th and early 19th centuries. These efforts intensified greatly in the late 19th century with the work of the English astronomer Sir Joseph Norman Lockyer and others. Studies of Stonehenge and similar early megaliths have clearly indicated that these structures were oriented on celestial events such as the summer solstice. Temples and other constructions were also used to mark the phases of the moon and the rising of certain bright stars such as Sirius. In the New World the large, circular patterns of stone called medicine wheels, as well as the structures left by the Mound Builders, were similarly oriented on the summer solstice; and rock paintings appear to record such events as the AD 1054 supernova, now known as the Crab nebula.

The mode of ancient astronomical observations varied according to their location on the earth's surface. For example, in tropical regions such as Oceania, people recorded the directions for long sea journeys with structures based on the horizon system of coordinates, rather than on the ecliptic as in temperate zones. The degree of sophistication of these ancient systems is only now beginning to be realized.

ARCHAEOLOGICAL INSTITUTE OF AMERICA, society for the promotion and direction of archaeological investigation, the protection of endangered archaeological sites, and the dissemination of scholarly information to the general public. The institute was organized in Boston in 1879. It founded and maintains connections with the American School of Classical Studies in Athens (1881) and the American School of Classical Studies in Rome (1895). Other schools associated with the institute include the American Schools of Oriental Research, with headquarters in Jerusalem (1910; a branch was established in Baghdad in 1923); the School of American Research in Santa Fe, N.Mex. (1907); and the American Research Center in Egypt (1948). The institute publishes the *American Journal of Archaeology,* a scholarly quarterly, and *Archaeology,* a popular magazine issued six times a year, as well as career and counseling publications. Membership in the institute is open to all. The headquarters is in New York City, and 81 local chapters are maintained in the U.S. and Canada.

ARCHAEOLOGY (Gr. *archaios,* "old" or "ancient"; *logos,* "word," hence study or science of), literally, the study of old, or ancient, ways of human life. Many other definitions of archaeology, however, go beyond this. In the past those who were inclined toward materialism defined archaeology as the "systematic study of the material remains of past human life." Others emphasized the behavioral aspects and defended archaeology as the "reconstruction of the life of past peoples and the arrangement of this life to form a historical development." Adherents of the new archaeology define it as the "science of past cultures," or the "discipline that makes generalizations about past cultures."

Archaeology has always been involved in the writing of history, and in the New World it has often been considered an aspect of anthropology—the study of human beings and their cultures. Modern archaeology, however, is linked to many other fields. For example, to establish a chronology archaeologists often use techniques developed by researchers in other disciplines: radiocarbon dating, developed by atomic physicists; geological-dating procedures, developed by geologists; and techniques for evaluating fauna, developed by paleontologists. To reconstruct ancient ways of life, archaeologists also use techniques developed in the fields of sociology, demography, geography, economics, and political science.

HISTORY

The history of archaeology may be divided into six periods. During the first, which began in the Renaissance and extended to the end of the 18th century, antiquaries collected ancient works of art and other artifacts and speculated in an unsystematic way about their significance. About 1800, three events marked the beginning of a new period. One was Thomas Jefferson's report, pub-

Stonehenge, near Salisbury, England, is a prehistoric megalithic structure built for religious and astronomical purposes about 2000–1500 BC. Its four concentric rings of huge stones surround an altar. British Tourist Authority

The ruins of the frescoed, colonnaded palace (c. 1500 BC) at Knossos, Crete, suggest the splendors of the Mediterranean Bronze Age. Gidal–Monkmeyer Press

lished (1799) by the American Philosophical Society, on his excavations of mounds in Virginia and the well-reasoned conclusions he drew from this work. About the same time, in England, John Frere (1769–1846) began to recognize Paleolithic (Acheulean) hand axes and attempt to interpret them in light of ancient human behavior. The third event—and perhaps the most important, for it led to further advances—occurred in Denmark, where archaeologists recognized excavated artifacts as human products; moreover, a national museum was founded (1807). Danish studies—by Christian J. Thomsen (1788–1865) and J. J. A. Worsaae (1821–85)—led to the establishment of the three successive Stone, Bronze, and Iron ages. During this period, in France, Jacques Boucher de Perthes studied the Somme gravels, and, in south Devon, England, William Pengelly (1812–94) studied Paleolithic findings.

A new period began about 1859, when Charles Darwin and Alfred R. Wallace published their theories of organic evolution, with obvious implications for cultural evolution. Subsequently, basic studies of the Paleolithic, begun in France, led to the Paleolithic classification of Gabriel Mortillet (1821–98). At the same time excavations were made in the Middle East and the classical world, the most famous of which were those of Heinrich Schliemann at Troy and later in Greece. This again initiated studies by the Americans in mainland Greece, the French at Delos and Delphi, and the English in Crete and Egypt. Solid archaeological techniques and methods were developing as a result of research in Europe—work in northern Italy and Switzerland on the Swiss lake dwellers, diggings and analyses by Danes in the Baltic area, and the excavations of barrows, earthworks, and villages in England by Augustus H. Pitt-Rivers (1827–1900). Archaeologists were also beginning to work in America. One group was attempting to determine the identity of the Mound Builders (q.v.); another sought evidence of the Paleolithic period in the New World.

New Trends and Great Discoveries. Although archaeologists working in the Old World continued much as before, the trend in the New World changed radically about the turn of the century, ushering in a period that lasted until the Great Depression. The principal reason for this change was the influence of the American anthropologist Franz Boas, who criticized cultural evolutionary studies, both for their methods and for their lack of careful anthropological data collection. For archaeology this meant a need for meticulous stratigraphic studies, good field and digging techniques, and a knowledge of specific tribes or ethnic groups. During this period the classic studies of the U.S. Southwest began, culminating in the Pecos excavations of Alfred V. Kidder (1885–1963); basic Inuit (Eskimo) studies were undertaken by Danish archaeologists; shell mounds were dug in California; and the general sequence of events in the Valley of Mexico was established.

The Middle East, however, was the site of the largest archaeological projects of this period. Sir Leonard Woolley (1880–1960) dug at Ur, Sir Arthur Evans at Knossos, James H. Breasted and the Oriental Institute of Chicago in Iran, Howard Carter and the earl of Carnarvon in Egypt, and the French at Nineveh. Great archaeological treasures were discovered by these expeditions.

Simultaneously, research into the Paleolithic was moving ahead. Studies were conducted in the caves of France, and Paleolithic artifacts were turned up in China, Burma, India, Java, the Middle East, and Africa. The Lower Paleolithic was charted, the typology of lithic (stone) tools becoming the basis for classifications. Advances were made in the field of classical archaeology, and the Neolithic, Bronze, and Iron ages were investigated in many countries—the Danes and the British leading the way. New techniques, such as clay varve studies (based on annual deposition of silt), pollen analysis, fluorine tests, and aerial photography, were developed.

Charting Regional Chronologies. With the Great Depression, financial backing for overseas expeditions came to an end, and local and regional areas became the focus of archaeological research. In the Americas one group was concerned with finding evidence of human life in the New World before the end of the Ice Age. A plethora of new finds enabled them to set the date for the first humans in the Americas farther back.

Another archaeological focus in the Americas was establishing local and regional chronologies. This began in the U.S. under the federal Works Progress Administration, which sponsored local archaeological programs to relieve unemployment. One direct outgrowth was river-basin archaeology, which has led to great advances in dating the Great Plains cultures. Latin American governments also sponsored archaeological projects. Throughout the New World archaeologists established local and regional chronologies, and Willard F. Libby's development of the radiocarbon (C-14) dating method (c. 1946) helped place their conclusions on a firmer footing.

The New Archaeology. During this period, however, many archaeologists began to find historiography-oriented archaeology sterile. Some, such as the American anthropologist Walker W. Taylor (1913–), deplored the overemphasis on chronology and sought to use anthropological data about contemporary cultures to understand those of the past. Others—Albert C. Spaulding

Fieldwork by Washington State University archaeologists on the Snake River in 1969 yielded ruined dwellings and other artifacts of an ancient Nez Percé Indian camp.
Seth Beckerman—Editorial Photocolor Archives

(1914–), for example—demanded more sophisticated quantitative methods and techniques. Still others felt that archaeologists were not focusing sufficiently on theoretical objectives. Many young archaeologists of the 1950s sought to understand how and why cultural changes take place instead of simply describing and dating them. In their view, the ultimate goal of archaeology is to formulate laws of cultural change, thereby establishing it as a science. They believed that understanding the process of change in one area of archaeological research would yield generalizations that could be applied to other areas. The leader of this new movement was Lewis R. Binford (1930–), who began writing on the subject about 1960, ushering in yet another period—that of the new archaeology.

The basic characteristics of the new archaeology are the following: (1) explicit use of evolutionary theory; (2) employment of sophisticated cultural and ecological concepts, which often require an interdisciplinary approach in fieldwork and computer techniques in analysis; and (3) use of systems theory. Although relatively little theory has been formulated so far, the approach has great potential.

Remarkable archaeological achievements have been realized since 1960. In the New World, studies of early humans indicate that they may have begun coming to the landmass some 30,000 years ago. In the Old World, Louis and Mary Leakey and others have established that humans used tools 5 million years ago. Even more important, the various kinds of archaeologists—classical, anthropological, historical, and other kinds—have begun to communicate with one another, not only to improve their methodology but also to attack the problems of formulating laws of cultural change.

METHODS AND TECHNIQUES

The archaeologist's work may be divided into four successive stages: data collection, description and preliminary analysis, creation of cultural-historical integrations, and formation of hypotheses of cultural change.

Data Collection. The archaeologist's first task is to conduct archaeological reconnaissance in order to locate promising sites for the collection of data. Traditionally, archaeologists relied on accidental discoveries, historical research, and surveys on foot to find such sites. By the mid-20th century, aerial photography had become an important additional method of reconnaissance. Since the 1970s a number of sophisticated new techniques have been added, including the use of ground-penetrating radar, infrared sensors, electrical resistivity, proton magnetometers, and remote sensing by orbiting satellites. In the field of underwater archaeology, the introduction of new sonar and electronic sensing devices has resulted in a greatly enhanced ability to detect the ruins of sunken ships. In the search for buried

Harvard University archaeologists in Turkey clean a relief of a Roman river god unearthed at Sardis, the ancient capital of Lydia. This site, where excavations began in 1910, has yielded relics of several civilizations. Archaeological Exploration of Sardis

archaeological remains, the goal is to find sites that will yield a rich, stratified mix of artifacts. Ideally, the layers of objects will allow a clear chronology to be established and, given enough contextual information, the reconstruction of an entire cultural system for each historical level. The better the initial survey is, the easier are the excavation and field research. *See* AERIAL SURVEY.

This preliminary work leads directly to intensive data collection, accomplished primarily by digging. The purpose of excavation is twofold: to establish chronology and to make contextual observations. The old, reliable way of establishing a chronology was to dig stratified sites, preferably by peeling off superimposed occupation layers. Many other ways of obtaining relative, chronometric, or absolute dates have now been developed (see below). With interdisciplinary techniques, such data may be collected for any occupation site, stratified or not. Making contextual observations from occupational layers also requires careful excavation techniques, with particular attention to the location of each artifact and ecofact (preserved sample of ancient ecology). Such formation must be supplemented by environmental data, collected by means of interdisciplinary techniques. Preliminary collection of such data often begins with zoological, botanical, and geological surveys and with studies of the soil and climate in order to define the ecosystem and microenvironment within which the digging is to be done.

Description and Preliminary Analysis. Laboratory analysis and description usually follow the data collection, but some simultaneous work of this nature can greatly enhance the excavation. Preliminary analysis during data collection can reveal gaps in the chronology and contextual field and thus indicate where more data should be collected. The important analysis, however, usually comes afterward. Like data collection, it is twofold: chronological and contextual.

Defining the chronology. Although the use of interdisciplinary techniques may result in fine chronometric and temporal dimensions, the chronology must be basically determined by the artifact sequence in the specific stratigraphic contents. Stratigraphy, however, is not the only determinant of relative chronology. Dating artifacts by the geological age of their strata, by their association with sequentially aligned fossil animals or plant remains (such as pollen), or by association with datable historical artifacts are other ways of arriving at a relative chronology. Of course, in some cases, chronology can be established absolutely with radiocarbon dating, dendrochronology, thermoluminescence, archaeomagnetism, and clay varve dating. Mass spectrometry and atomic accelerators are being used to date artifacts and remains by radiometric methods (*see* DATING METHODS: *Radiometric Dating*).

Defining cultural contexts. The study of cultural contexts generally follows the determination of chronology and is a more complicated process. The purpose of studying cultural and ecological contexts is to reconstruct cultural and ecological systems. Each artifact is then considered not as a time marker but rather as a result of, and part of, human activity and is derived from a specific ecosystem.

The particular position of an artifact may be determined by relatively simple means—careful in situ excavation—but understanding exactly what activity produced it and from what part of the ecosystem it came is problematic. Interdisciplinary data collection may reveal where, and in what part of the ecosystem, the materials for the artifact were found, and—more important—it may establish a relationship between the culture and the ecosystem. Determining what activity produced the artifact is basically an attempt to reconstruct the prevailing technology. Each piece of garbage, botanical and zoological, indicates something about subsistence activities, the elements of the ecosystem, the seasonality of settlement patterns, trading habits, and so forth. The manner of burial and the contents of tombs imply much about the past, particularly in terms of kinship, rank, status, and religious activities, as do other features, such as fire pits and architectural remains. Each artifact reflects activities during the periods when humans occupied a site.

Creation of Cultural-Historical Integrations. Having all this material in hand, the archaeologist then attempts to synthesize the reconstructed regional chronologies into a sequence of cultures and ecosystems in major areas or interrelated regions. Too often, however, this becomes a mere static history of regions rather than a dynamic description of processes that can be analyzed to determine the causes of cultural change. In other words, it may reveal how such change happened but not why.

Formation of Hypotheses of Cultural Change. Ideally, working with hypotheses should be the next step. Only rarely, however, do archaeologists analyze the larger sequence of cultural systems to determine the causes of one system's change into another. The problem of forming hypotheses of cultural change has been extensively discussed, but little real work of this sort has yet been done. R.S.Ma.

A carved relief of a human-headed bull ornaments a portal at Calah (now Nimrud, Iraq), the capital city of the ancient Assyrian Empire. The city was founded by Ashurnasirpal II on the site of an earlier settlement. Silvio-Fiore–Shostal Associates

THE ARCHAEOLOGICAL RECORD

The preceding discussion has introduced the discipline of archaeology, its history, methods, and objectives. This section presents some conclusions that archaeologists have reached regarding the human past and describes some major sites and artifacts they have uncovered during the past century or two.

THE MIDDLE EAST

Since the beginning of systematic archaeological research, the Middle East, from Mesopotamia to Egypt, has been a principal area of investigation, and it is perhaps the region that has yielded the richest rewards.

Mesopotamia. Archaeological exploration in Mesopotamia began with the surveys of Babylon (1812) and Nineveh (1820) made by C. James Rich (1787–1820). His reports drew the French consul Paul Émile Botta to the ruins of Nineveh (q.v.) and nearby Khorsabad (in present-day Iraq) to dig for relics in 1843–45 and the British traveler Sir Austin H. Layard (1817–94) to Nineveh and Nimrud a few years later; both were supported by their governments. Simultaneously, Sir Henry C. Rawlinson and Edward Hincks (1792–1866), with aid from other scholars, were deciphering the Assyro-Babylonian cuneiform script. Thus, the written texts on the stone carvings and the thousands of clay tablets found at Nineveh could be read and the history of the kingdoms restored. Great palaces, with miles of sculptured reliefs, demonstrated the power of Assyrian kings previously known only from references in the Bible and in Greek writings. Excavations in the Assyrian palaces have continued sporadically to the present day.

Twelve seasons (1949–63) of digging by British archaeologists at Nimrud, Iraq, yielded hundreds of finely carved ivory panels—furniture decorations—the booty of Assyrian armies. A German team investigated (1902–14) the Assyrian capital, Ashur, and with great skill disentangled superimposed mud-brick temples and palaces that dated from the 3d century AD to the 3d millennium BC. These structures displayed the culture of early Assyria and its dependence on Babylonia, and historical information came from numerous inscriptions. Farther south another German team, led by Robert Koldewey (1855–1925), worked (1899–1914) at Babylon, revealing the city's plan in its heyday under Nebuchadnezzar II. The Ishtar Gate, covered with blue-glazed bricks and magic animals molded in relief, the temple of Marduk, the royal palace, city walls, and a Euphrates bridge were the principal discoveries. *See also* BABYLON.

In 1877 the French consul Ernest de Sarzec (1837–1901) found magnificent statues of the Sumerian ruler Gudea (c. 2144–2124 BC) at Lagash (Iraq), clues to the high culture there about 2130 BC. This kindled interest in Sumer (q.v.) and its civilization. At Nippur (Iraq) an American team began work in 1887, finding thousands of cuneiform tablets, notably literary compositions in Sumerian. The work of Sir Leonard Woolley at Ur (q.v.) in 1922–34 revealed splendidly equipped tombs of Sumerian kings (c. 2500 BC) and well-built houses (c. 1800 BC). At Mari (now Tell Hariri) on the mid-Euphrates, the French archaeologist André Parrot (1901–80) unearthed a great palace from about 1800 BC and buildings and sculpture of the 3d millenium. German discoveries at Uruk, or Erech (now Warka), since 1928 have disclosed the skill of architects and artisans of about 3500 BC, as well as the earliest writing known. Since World War II continuing work has enlarged knowledge of all periods, notably the earliest—about 6000–3000 BC—when the first settlements were made in Babylonia.

Research into the remains of the Parthian and Sassanid empires (c. 250 BC–AD 650) has recovered palatial buildings and temples at Hatra, Ctesiphon (q.v.), and Kish (all in Iraq). Islamic sites, such as Samarra and Wasit, have been excavated or surveyed, and those above ground have been restored.

Egypt. Modern knowledge of ancient Egypt began with the scholars Napoleon Bonaparte took to survey the country in his campaign of 1798. Their discovery of the Rosetta Stone (1799), a valuable relic (a heavy block of black basalt, now in the British Museum, London), bearing an inscription written in hieroglyphic, demotic, and in Greek characters, precipitated Jean François Champollion's decipherment (1822) of Egyptian hieroglyphics. Now the monuments could be understood, and surveys of those standing above ground were undertaken by Karl R. Lepsius and others; these are still valuable because the sites have since been damaged. At the same time large-scale collecting for private and public collections resulted in the loss of much information. In 1858 the Cairo Museum was founded, and treasure hunting was gradually controlled. Finally, in the 1880s Sir Flinders Petrie began to excavate systematically and interpret methodically all finds. Such works and more surveys continue in Egypt today.

Exploration in the south since 1960 has located sites where late Paleolithic people cultivated barley, the earliest attempts at farming the rich Nile soil. Subsequent Neolithic cultures brought true agriculture, pottery, and weaving, culminating in the so-called Tasian phase, which merged into the first metalworking period, the Badarian. It was during the Badarian that copper was first utilized and the red-polished, black-topped ware typical of early Egypt was first made. Petrie's excavation (1894–95) of 3000 graves at Naqada first brought to light the period just before the begin-

A small wooden model found in a tomb from the Middle kingdom. The figure at right is playing a stringed instrument, and the three at left are clapping in time and singing while their master and mistress listen. Federico Borromeo–Scala

Treasures in the tomb of the Egyptian pharaoh Tutankhamen near Thebes were numbered and cataloged by archaeologists who found the tomb in 1922.
Metropolitan Museum of Art, photograph by Harry Burton

ning of Egyptian history, about 3400 BC. Later studies distinguished the culture of the south from that of the north, where Asian influences—and possibly a different race—encouraged advances in pottery (painted with people and ships) and metalwork.

According to tradition, the southern king Menes united the land at the beginning of the dynastic age (c. 3100 BC). A series of slate palettes for cosmetics from that time bear elaborate carved battle and hunting scenes; chief among them is the Palette of King Narmer (fl. about 3100 BC), who may have been Menes. Similar carvings on stone and ivory mace-heads and handles reveal links with Mesopotamia, and the oldest hieroglyphic texts date from this time. With the first dynasties appear the earliest of Egypt's famous tombs, lavishly equipped for the future life of the dead. Cemeteries at Naqada, Abydos, and Saqqara shed light on the history and culture of this time. The large brick tombs (*mastabas*) at Saqqara gave place to stone pyramids, the first rising in steps, but later ones, such as that of Khufu (Cheops) at Giza, cased in smooth blocks. Robbed long ago, they yet tell of the skill and ability to move stone in those centuries. Gold-plated wooden furniture of Queen Hetepheres (fl. about 2600 BC), reburied in antiquity after a robbery, was brilliantly restored from a mass of fragments by George A. Reisner (1867–1942) of Harvard University in 1924–27. King Menkaure (r. about 2578–2553 BC) is known from the fine slate statue of him found by Reisner; it is now in Boston.

Egyptian archaeology has concentrated on tombs and temples, because most ancient town sites are still occupied. They are generally in the damp river valley, where perishable materials do not survive; burials were made in the desert, where the heat dries and preserves most things. Wooden models of domestic activities, left in tombs, join paintings, wall carvings, and tools buried with the dead to give a fuller view of ancient life than other civilizations afford. The tomb of King Tutankhamen (who reigned about 1334 to 1325 BC), is the richest in content and craftsmanship, but hundreds of other tombs, from the 1st Dynasty on, display the life-styles of rich and poor alike.

Near the royal tombs in the Valley of the Kings (q.v.) stood a village where the tomb carvers lived. Completely excavated, its 70 houses supplement the material from the tombs. Numerous discarded notes, scribbled on broken pottery or stone flakes, identify some of the carvers and their houses, telling of their work, their food, and their faith.

The eccentric religious ideas of Ikhnaton, the "heretic" pharaoh, led him to establish a new capital at Akhetaton (now Tell el-Amarna). A chance find of some 400 clay tablets, written in Babylonian, drew attention to the site in 1887. These tablets were letters concerning relations with the Middle East from about 1375 to 1330 BC. Excavation in the town has uncovered workers' cottages, which are better than many modern laborers enjoy, and some fine villas of the wealthy. Unusually naturalistic art forms characterize the period, as illustrated by the exquisite head of Nefertiti (fl. 1340 BC), Ikhnaton's queen. *See also* TELL EL-AMARNA.

Studies of the great temples of al-Karnak and Luxor have traced successive stages of building and alteration, frequently leading to the recovery of sculptured blocks reused by later builders. Such reuse created a mystery for modern scholars in the delta area. Ramses II and his successors lived at Pi-Ramesse in the delta. Early archaeologists first sought the town at Pelusium and then at Tanis, where quantities of sculptured stones with Ramses's name suggested it had stood. Tanis was the capital of the Hyksos kings (c. 1600 BC) and again of those who ruled from the 11th to the 8th century BC. None of the Ramses stones seemed to be in their true positions, however, and investigation suggested that they had been brought from Qantir, 29 km (18 mi) to the south, where Ramses II certainly had a palace; indeed, Qantir has been identified as the site of Pi-Ramesse. *See* KARNAK, AL-; LUXOR.

Archaeologists have traced imports from the Aegean from the 15th to the 13th century BC; association of Mycenean pottery with tombs of known Egyptian kings is vital for the study of early Greek archaeology, although not entirely satisfactory. Greek traders, mercenaries, and even tourists were in Egypt from the 7th century BC on, and they left various relics. With Alexander the Great's conquest, the Greek language began to replace Egyptian. Thousands of papyrus documents, dating from the following millennium, have been found in the towns around Faiyum Lake (Birket Qarun) near Cairo, abandoned when the irrigation system failed. Other sites have yielded thousands more. These papyruses vividly record every aspect of life in astonishing detail. They are also the source of the oldest copies of many famous Greek books and of the New Testament.

Syria and Palestine. Discoveries in Syria and Palestine are of particular importance for the study of the earliest settled human life. Remains of a Mesolithic community, the Natufian, have been unearthed in the Carmel Hills (1929–32), and a Natufian structure has also been found in the center of Jericho's ruins. With the advance from the Mesolithic to the Neolithic, farming communities arose, such as that at Mureybet on the mid-

A view of the ruins of the western palace at Masada, the royal citadel of Herod the Great, erected in the 1st century BC and destroyed by the Romans a century later.

Eric L. Brown–Monkmeyer Press

Euphrates, excavated in 1972–76. In some "pre-pottery" Neolithic centers, clay plaster faces, which were finely modeled on the skulls of the dead, were preserved in homes. During the subsequent "pottery" Neolithic (c. 6000–4000 BC), cultural impulses came primarily from the north and east, a situation that continued in the first metal-using phase, represented in Palestine by the sites of Ghassul in the Jordan Valley and others near Beersheba. Developed cities of the early Bronze Age have been uncovered on the mid-Euphrates at Byblos (q.v.) and in Palestine at Arad, Ai, Tell el-Farah, Jericho, and Tell Gath. All these cities had walls with closely placed square or semicircular towers. The magnificent brick palace at Ebla (q.v.) in Syria dates from the end of this period. The royal archives, written in Sumerian cuneiform on clay tablets, brilliantly illuminate Syrian history from about 2500 to 2200 BC. Seals and carvings in stone and wood clearly display local adaptations of classic Mesopotamian designs.

After a decline, associated by many scholars with movements of Amorite tribes, cities again flourished in the area from about 1900 to 1200 BC. French excavations since 1929 at Ugarit on the Syrian coast have provided a fine example of a major Canaanite city. Here, pottery from Cyprus, Crete, and Greece demonstrates the westward sea trade; other items show links with Egypt and Babylonia. Scribes wrote Egyptian on papyrus and Babylonian and Hurrian on clay tablets, and they adapted the idea of the alphabet, invented farther south, to their own cuneiform, producing a script of 30 signs. In this they wrote documents of every sort, including myths about their gods that give a unique picture of local religion.

Burned and ruined buildings bespeak the violent destruction of Ugarit and other late Bronze Age cities by the Sea People (including the Philistines), the Israelites, the Arameans, and other invaders, and then their resettlement (*see* BIBLICAL ARCHAEOLOGY). The following Iron Age has been much more intensively studied in Palestine than in Syria. At Hamath (Hama) on the Orontes (Asi) River, a Danish expedition in 1931–38 uncovered citadel buildings destroyed by Assyrian troops in 720 BC; the expedition found carved ivory and stonework. Farther north British Museum work at Carchemish produced stone slabs and a statue of the neo-Hittite style carved in the 9th century BC.

Monumental buildings of the Hellenistic-Roman age, still standing above ground in Syria-Palestine, have long drawn scholarly attention. At Petra, in Jordan, carved rock tombs exhibit a fusion of Oriental and Greek motifs in the capital of the Nabataeans (q.v.). Other mixtures can be seen in Palmyra, a trading center in Syria, where extensive excavations have been made; Roman town planning is evident here, as it is in numerous other towns of the region. Late Roman buildings, early Byzantine churches and synagogues, and later Muslim buildings are often adorned with pictorial mosaic floors. The Great Mosque of Damascus, incorporating the earlier cathedral, preserves mosaics on its walls. Early Muslim princes utilized the skills of local artisans, as found in the mosaic and stonework of the Umayyad villa (c. 720–44) at Khirbet al-Mafjar, near Jericho. Other villas and castles in the Syrian desert exemplify early Islamic architectural skills.

The state antiquities organizations of Syria, Lebanon, Jordan, and Israel sponsor excavations by their own staffs and qualified foreigners. Further discoveries are likely, especially in Syria.

Other Middle Eastern Areas. Turkey was the scene of one of the first famous archaeological excavations, when the German archaeologist Heinrich Schliemann worked at Troy (q.v.). Gold jewelry found by Schliemann, as well as some remarkable gold plate from tombs at Alaca Hüyük, attest to the high skills of early Bronze Age Anatolians. Observations by travelers led to the discovery of Hattusha (now Boğazköy, east of Ankara), the capital of the Hittite Empire (c. 1800–1200 BC). German archaeologists began excavations there in 1906, and work continues. Within the heavily fortified city were elaborate palaces and temples, some yielding thousands of clay tablets bearing texts in the Indo-European language of the Hittites.

Far older than Troy is Çatal Hüyük, investigated in 1961–65. Here, cattle-farming Mesolithic and Neolithic people built a town of small houses that were huddled together and could be entered by way of the roof. Several small shrines were adorned with plaster reliefs of mother-goddess and animal figures, and wall paintings showed hunting scenes. This and subsequent work, aided by advanced techniques for recovering plant remains, has opened a new stage in understanding early human settlement in Anatolia.

Arabia is archaeologically the least-known area. Paleolithic flints have been collected in many places, but little subsequent material has been found before pottery of the Mesopotamian Ubaid type (c. 4000 BC). A gap of some 3000 years intervenes before the next known era, when cities in the southwest grew rich on the trade in incense. Excavations in Aden and Yemen have revealed fine stone temples, South Arabian inscriptions, and metalwork, showing trade with Rome and India. A.R.M.

Carved stone reliefs decorate the Royal Gate of the Hittite capital of Hattusha located at Boğazköy, Turkey. The site also has many extensive temple complexes and numerous ornamented gateways.
John Elk III–Bruce Coleman, Inc.

EUROPE

The sequence of periods called the Neolithic, Copper Age, Bronze Age, and Iron Age describes an evolution of European civilization on the basis of the metal most conspicuously in use during each of them. This evolution took place at a somewhat faster pace and under different circumstances in the Greek-Aegean region than in the rest of Europe. The history of the former provides the correlative dates for the latter, where the Bronze Age lasted from about 2000 BC to roughly 700 BC.

Greece. The archaeology of Greece includes the study of the Bronze Age and still earlier phases (*see* AEGEAN CIVILIZATION; MINOAN CULTURE). These may be regarded as separate from, though clearly related to, the main historical era, beginning with the Iron Age. The archaeological periods of the Iron Age are the Protogeometric (c. 1050–900 BC) and the Geometric (c. 900–700 BC), both named for the style of pottery produced; the Archaic (c. 700–500 BC), named for the style of its art in comparison with that of the following period; the Classical (c. 500–330 BC), a period later revered for its artistic excellence and, thus, much imitated; and the Hellenistic (c. 330–50 BC), an age of aggressive spreading (and diluting) of Greek cultural and artistic ideas by Alexander the Great and his successors. During these periods, spanning about 1000 years, Greek creativity underwent a continual, remarkably unified development. Of particular note is sculpture displaying great psychological realism.

Geographically, the Protogeometric and Geometric periods encompass Greece proper and the Ionian (west) coast of Asia Minor. Near the end of the Geometric and during much of the Archaic period, the Greek city-states founded colonies, principally in Sicily, southern Italy (Magna Graecia), and the Black Sea region. The history of these settlements, on which the dating of the whole period is based, is traced through excavations of sites yielding Greek artifacts. In the later periods archaeological finds can sometimes be better correlated with the more abundant literary sources. During the Hellenistic period the city-states of Greece proper—except perhaps Athens—were superseded in importance by such new Hellenistic cities as Alexandria, Egypt, and Antioch, Syria.

The archaeology of the five periods involves the study of architecture, painting, sculpture, and objects in the allied arts, such as pottery, jewelry, seals, coins, utensils, and figurines. Greek architecture is based on the post-and-lintel system and reached its greatest glory in the temple, the gables of which often displayed relief or free-standing sculpture. By integrating the sculptured human figure and architecture, the Greeks enhanced both in an ideal way, the supreme example being the Parthenon, designed by Ictinus and Phidias. Other building types are of generally simple forms in harmony with natural surroundings, especially theaters cupped in hillsides. A two-story oblong, colonnaded building (stoa) was used in marketplaces or civic centers. Fresco

Gilded sheathing for a bow-and-arrow case and tarnished leg armor as they were found in the antechamber of the tomb of Philip II of Macedonia. Manolis Andronicus

painting flourished in Greece, but few examples have been preserved. The progress of drawing, however, may be seen in decorated pottery of all periods. *See also* GREEK ART AND ARCHITECTURE.

Rome. The first settlements on the site of Rome date from the Bronze Age in the 2d millennium BC. Remnants of timber buildings from the 8th century BC have been found on the Palatine Hill. During the 7th and 6th centuries, and especially under Etruscan rule (*see* ETRUSCAN CIVILIZATION), the Latin settlements on the Tiber were merged into the seven-hilled city of Rome, with temples, laid-out streets, and other public works, such as the *cloaca maxima* (central sewage system).

A major change occurred about 509 BC, when the Etruscans were expelled and a republic created. Rome then embarked on a policy of expansion that by the 2d century BC had established its rule from Spain and Africa to Macedonia. In the imperial period the frontiers were further extended to the north of England, to the Rhine and Danube valleys, and east as far as Assyria and Armenia. During these centuries Rome's Italic heritage continuously interacted with the cultural and artistic traditions of distant, unrelated peoples. The Romans absorbed a great deal from the older eastern cultures, particularly that of Greece; Greek architecture, painting, and sculpture were frequently adapted to Roman taste and needs. The Romans in turn gave much to the culturally diverse peoples of western and northern Europe.

For an understanding of the architecture of Republican Rome, excavations in Rome itself—especially in the Forum Romanum, in Ostia (the port of Rome), and in Praeneste and Cosa—have been most helpful. Herculaneum and Pompeii, cities buried under volcanic debris in AD 79, are an inexhaustible source of information about the transition from the Republican to the imperial era. By that time, as shown by archaeological studies, Roman art was becoming localized in provincial traditions, such as the Gallo-Roman, Romano-British, or Egypto-Roman, each with a strong regional flavor. This may be seen, for example, in mosaic patterns.

Roman archaeology involves, above all, a study of building types and techniques, fields in which the Romans were supremely inventive, and sculpture, in which they largely accepted foreign inspiration, although they showed great talent in the creation and political use of portraiture and historical relief. Perhaps their greatest contribution to civilization was the technique of constructing large buildings by creative variations on the arch principle, realized through the use of concrete. An example of this is the dome of the Pantheon (q.v.) in Rome. Even provincial cities that have been excavated reveal the Roman stamp in their layout, public baths, marketplaces, basilicas (courthouses), apartment blocks, aqueducts, and sewers. Objects of the allied arts, which were mass-produced in various centers, included glass, jewelry, pottery, and household utensils. The distribution of terra-cotta products with marker or merchant stamps has greatly facilitated the study of ancient trade routes. *See also* ROMAN ART AND ARCHITECTURE.

Other European Areas. As in Greece and Rome, the Bronze Age elsewhere in Europe was the great formative stage out of which patterns of later, more diversified cultures emerged. Owing to the absence of written records, the identification of specific peoples and cultures remains speculative, but however vague the historical contours, the group names used by classical authors for contemporary peoples are still useful: Celts for the inhabitants of western Europe, Germans for the inhabitants of central Europe, and Scythians for the tribes living on the steppes of southern Russia between the Carpathians and the Caucasus. Such architecture as these people had, even their fortifications, was of wood and proved to be ephemeral by Mediterranean standards. Painting and sculpture lay outside their interests, but artistic competence in metal artifacts was traditional, beginning in the Bronze Age. *See also* CELTS; GERMANIC PEOPLES; SCYTHIANS.

The type name Hallstatt (after a village in Austria) is used to designate the first stage (c. 750–450 BC) of Iron Age civilization in central and southwestern Europe. Excavation of barrow-type graves, or mounds, has revealed elaborate burials, richly defined by bowls, jewelry, and weapons made of metals, including luxury products imported from as far afield as Greece, and even chariots. Such burials suggest ostentation as well as social stratification. Native-style motifs, bespeaking simpler tastes, tend to be rectilinear.

The next stage, covering central and northwestern Europe, is called La Tène (c. 450–58 BC) after a lake site in Switzerland, where a cache of weapons, tools, and jewelry was found. Decoration on La Tène artifacts is a representational depiction of curvilinear motifs, such as palmettes and spirals, from the Mediterranean world. Together with expressionistic animal forms derived from Scythian art, these constitute a style important as a precursor of the "Barbarian" style that

The court of the House of the Mosaic of Neptune and Amphitrite at Herculaneum, Italy, is elaborately adorned with well-preserved mosaic paintings.
Editorial Photocolor Archives

flourished in the folk migration period during the early centuries of the Christian era. J.L.B.

ASIA

The archaeology of Asia, apart from the Middle East, is a relatively new field, but important work has been done on the continent since World War II, and investigations are continuing.

South Asia. Many sites from the Middle Pleistocene—that is, 100,000 to 1 million years old—have been found in South Asia. They have yielded numerous stone tools—roughly shaped hand axes, choppers, cleavers, and some flake implements—that were used by small hunting-gathering groups (the so-called Soan culture) to exploit local resources. Late Pleistocene hunter-gatherer settlements (15,000–100,000 years old) are found throughout the Indian subcontinent. Little is known of these late Soan culture groups, except their implements. They still used hand axes but relied more than before on small flake tools.

A hunting-gathering economy continued in many regions after the Pleistocene in settlements near rivers, lakes, and swamps. The inhabitants made small stone tools for cutting, scraping, piercing, and engraving. Dwellings were simple tents and wooden pole structures. At Langhnaj, near Ahmadabad, India, where several graves have been excavated, people exploited all local resources, but the prevalence of animal and fish remains shows that hunting was most important. Pottery and iron tools dating from the last Langhnaj occupation period also indicate interaction with technologically more sophisticated groups.

At Mehrgarh, Pakistan, the earliest domesticated plants (wheat, barley) and animals (cattle, sheep, goats) have been found in a village dating from before 6000 BC, suggesting that agriculture was independently developed on the subcontinent. People built mud-brick houses, buried their dead throughout the village, and made a wide variety of stone tools, personal ornaments (including copper beads), and baskets.

The early Bronze Age (4000–2500 BC) was characterized by different agricultural groups of the Amri, Kot Diji, and Sothi cultures. Each had its own distinctive style of pottery, and each made a variety of stone, bone, shell, metal, and ceramic objects. The people lived in small mud-brick villages, although a few settlements were large enough to be called towns. Contact between cultures was maintained by trade in shells, metals, and semiprecious stones. Although each culture had traits in common with the Indus Valley civilization (q.v.), none has been identified as its precursor.

The Indus Valley, or Harappan, civilization (2500–1700 BC) occupied the entire Indus River valley. Harappan villages and cities, such as Mohenjo-daro (q.v.), are characterized by similarities of artifacts, such as black-on-red pottery, jewelry, metal tools, stone weights, and stamp seals with script. All settlements featured public buildings and organized layout, although no definite examples of temples, palaces, or royal

A view of the great bath at Mohenjo-daro, one of the most advanced cities of the Indus Valley Civilization. The bath is thought to have been used for religious ablutions.
Douglass Waugh–Peter Arnold, Inc.

Some of the more than 6000 terra-cotta warriors and horses discovered in the tomb of Emperor Shih Huang Ti at Xi'an, Shaanxi Province, China. New China Pictures Co., Beijing, China

cemeteries have been found. After 2000 BC ecological changes forced the abandonment of many Indus Valley settlements, especially the cities; late Harappan culture was characterized by small farming villages. The typical artifacts were still made and showed increased regional variation, but stamp seals and the Harappan script seem to have become rare; no cities of this late period have been found.

The early historic period is characterized by iron tools and two new pottery types: Painted Gray Ware (1100–300 BC) and Northern Black Polished Ware (500–100 BC). The people who made the gray pottery lived mostly in villages, inhabiting wattle-and-daub and mud-brick houses. In some places their culture was contemporary with the late Harappan. During the Northern Black Polished Ware period the Mauryan Empire was established, and historical records supplement archaeological data.

China. Remains of the so-called *Homo erectus,* found at Zhoukoudian (Chou-k'outien), near Peking, in association with animal bones, stone tools, and hearths, have been dated up to 460,000 years old. This Pleistocene hunter-gatherer made tools for chopping, cutting, and scraping. Animal bones indicate that people ate mostly roasted deer meat, along with small amounts of larger animals; evidence of cannibalism has also been found. Plants were eaten as well, but not preserved.

Evidence of later Pleistocene hunter-gatherer groups in China is rare. Only a few sites, such as Sjaraosso-gol, have been found in the north. Some 30,000 years ago this area was occupied by groups that established camps near water sources. These people probably lived in tents, but only stone tools and animal remains have been preserved. Small stone tools mounted on handles were used for scraping and cutting. Bison was the main food animal, but larger animals were also hunted.

After the Pleistocene epoch modern environmental conditions triggered changes in the hunter-gatherer economy. Most groups became more sedentary and made better use of plants and riverine resources, such as fish, shellfish, and mollusks. From about 5000 to 2000 BC, regional cultures varied a great deal, reflecting their environmental conditions. In some areas groups practicing intense foraging persisted into the historic period, but in the Huang He (Hwang Ho, or Yellow River) valley, agriculture was developed.

Hunting, fishing, and gathering continued, but by 3500 BC domesticated millet, pigs, and fowl, and later sheep, goats, and cattle, were the main sources of food. The farming settlements of the Yang-shao culture (3950–1700 BC) are exemplified by Banpocun (Pan-p'o-ts'un) in Shaanxi (Shensi) Province. This large village was surrounded by a ditch and contained many semisubterranean wattle-and-daub dwellings. In the village center was a large, elaborate structure that may have been the home of an important person or perhaps a public building. Besides agriculture, the villagers practiced silkworm cultivation, pottery manufacture, textile production, and jade carving. Part-time craft specialization, suggesting the emergence of a separate class of artisans, is evident from the similarity of artifacts found in different villages.

After some complex social and political changes occurred among these agriculturalists, the Lung-shan culture (2000–1850 BC) emerged in North China. As in the Yang-shao culture, great similarity is found in the artifacts of Lung-shan villages, especially in their fine black pottery. Villages became larger and were occupied longer. Cultivation of the original crops continued, with increased use of rice. Large walls around settlements, as well as evidence of the manufacture of weapons and of violent deaths, suggest more frequent social conflicts. Writing appeared for the first time in the form of scapulimancy. The excellence of the crafted artifacts, the writing, the village walls, and the varying wealth of goods in its graves suggest that the Lung-shan culture was socially stratified.

Through internal changes the Lung-shan culture gradually developed into the first Chinese civilization—that of the Shang dynasty (c. 1766–c. 1027 BC). Most information about this period comes from sites near Zhengzhou (Chengchou). Under the Shang appear the first written records, monumental architecture, craft specialization, cities, and gross differences in social and political prestige. The Shang capital, Ao, had city walls enclosing noble residences; artisans and farmers lived outside. Suburban settlements were inhabited by specialized artisans, who made characteristic Chinese objects, among them elaborate articles of bronze.

Near Anyang, the administrative and ceremonial center of Xiaotun (Hsiao-t'un) and the royal cemetery at Xibeigang (Hsi-pei-kang) have been excavated. Thousands of oracle bones, found at these late Shang sites, provide more information about the culture. Spectacular art objects and other wealth, as well as the many human sacrifices associated with the royal cemetery, demonstrate the political and economic power of the nobility. The Shang was replaced by the Chou dynasty (c. 1027–256 BC), but the essential traits of Chinese civilization had been established.

Other Asian Countries. *Homo erectus* fossils found in Java, Indonesia, have been dated at about 2 million years old, but the cultural remains of this and later hunter-gatherers are limited to scattered finds of stone hand axes, choppers, and scrapers. Settlements of hunter-

Mummification was practiced by indigenous cultures in Luzon, the Philippines, about 1500 AD. Mummified remains were sealed in wooden coffins and deposited in burial caves.
Bruno Zehnder–Peter Arnold, Inc.

gatherers from between 10,000 and 15,000 years ago show that they grew wild yams and taro. Remains of possibly domesticated rice, found at Spirit Cave, Thailand, may date from before 6800 BC. Later evidence for early domestication of rice has been found at Non Nok Tha, Thailand. Also located at this site was a sophisticated bronze industry, dating from 3000 BC. At Ban Chiang, also in Thailand, demonstrable use of bronze dates from as early as 4500 BC. Excavated graves have yielded evidence that a stratified society had emerged in the region by 3000 BC.

Japan was inhabited during the Pleistocene, and many sites have revealed stone tools similar to those of contemporary Asian cultures. By the late Pleistocene hunter-gatherers were exploiting both land and sea resources. They lived in small villages of semiunderground houses associated with shell middens. The earliest pottery, possibly dating from 13,000 years ago, comes from such a village. Agriculture was unknown in Japan until rice was introduced about 600 BC. J.G.Sh.

THE AMERICAS

Archaeological studies in the New World have revealed five generally successive, although sometimes overlapping, stages of human life on the continents—the Lithic, the Archaic, the Formative, the Classic, and the Post-Classic.

The Lithic Stage. This earliest stage began with the first arrival of Asian hunters in the New World. Probably Mongoloids, the earliest arrivals began crossing the Bering Strait over an ice-age land bridge, possibly more than 30,000 years ago. Archaeological evidence suggests four waves of migration, although linguistic studies of modern tribes suggest three.

Archaeologists have been sharply divided over when these earliest people first arrived. Some maintain that there is no firm evidence of a human presence before 11,500 years ago, the age of spearpoints found near Clovis, N. Mex. Others consider that archaeological evidence from places such as the Meadowcroft Rockshelter in Pennsylvania and Monte Verde in Chile, which they date at 16,000 and 13,000 years ago respectively, establishes a pre-Clovis presence and lends credence to even older dates attributed to other artifacts of a more fragmentary nature.

From sparse, scattered finds, the tools of the Lithic stage show a general progression, over the course of some 20,000 years, from unifacial chipped stone and bone to bifacial leaf-shaped points and blades, to the fluted projectile points used by the Clovis people. Clovis points were used in killing mammoths and other big game until the close of the Pleistocene epoch, but in some places, such as Tierra del Fuego, the Lithic stage lasted into the Recent epoch, that is, until historic times.

Ceramic jug of Mixtec origin, from the Oaxaca region of modern southwestern Mexico. The Mixtec people produced superb examples of ceramic art.
Mexican National Tourist Council

The Archaic Stage. With the extinction of the megafauna and other Pleistocene animals, many groups abandoned big-game hunting and became collectors. This afforded them many choices for subsistence that often led to a seasonally scheduled way of life. Perhaps the most typical way of life at the Archaic stage was that adopted in the eastern U.S. between 9000 and 4000 years ago. Here, groups often settled along rivers, developing special techniques for hunting small and big game with darts propelled by spear-throwers. They also made use of aquatic resources, frequently using gill nets with sinkers. Seeds were collected as well and ground with milling stones. Many kinds of thumbnail end scrapers were used for a variety of tasks.

Somewhat akin to these specific groups were the collectors in the boreal forests of Canada and Alaska and along the Arctic coast as far as the Bering Strait. Invaders from Asia, they represented a new way of life in northern North America. Characteristic among their implements were various microblade tools made from tongue-shaped cores, similar to those often found in Siberia, Mongolia, and Japan. They hunted big game with spears and darts, garnered small game in traps, and fished in the lakes. People of this "Northwest Microblade" tradition, who lived mostly inland, contrasted with those living on the coast, who were of the "Small Tool" tradition. The latter also used delicately made microblade tools, arrow points, and other implements, but adapted them both to inland caribou hunting and to harpooning of marine animals.

During this stage, throughout both North and South America, many peoples adapted themselves to life on the seacoasts, and great shell mounds were formed. Obviously, however, many regional differences existed among these coastal Archaics. Groups on the northwest Pacific coast used ground slate and developed watercraft; those in California became seed and shellfish collectors; people on the U.S. Atlantic coast used decorated bone daggers, as well as ground slate, and buried their dead with elaborate ceremonies featuring red paint. In Mesoamerica some groups began making boats that may have brought them to the Antilles.

Others, such as those in Peru, exploited the inland coastal regions (*lomas*) in one season and the sea in another.

In general, the Archaic peoples of the U.S. southwestern desert, highland Mexico, and highland Peru contrasted sharply with the collectors described above. Although they too may be considered plant collectors, their environment contained potentially domesticable plants, and their seasonal round of activities, exploiting different environments, necessitated storage. Some of these peoples, consequently, began to cultivate and domesticate plants. Eventually, such horticultural practices led to agriculture and, with it, village life and pottery, all characteristics of the next stage—the Formative. In many areas, however, such as the tropical lowlands, California, the Great Basin of the U.S., and the pampas of Chile and Argentina, as well as the forests of northern Canada, people never developed the agricultural village life of the Formative but remained in an extended Archaic stage.

The Formative Stage. An early substage of the Formative is a period called Woodland, which lasted from about 500 BC to roughly AD 1000 and was characterized by ceremonialism; people of this period made burial mounds and used crude, often cord-marked pottery. The Woodland was followed, especially in the U.S. South and Southeast, by a second substage, distinguished by temple mounds, more advanced agriculture, incised pottery, and large palisaded villages, similar to those of the later Classic stage.

Perhaps the most typical culture of the Formative stage, however, is that of the Pueblo of the U.S. Southwest and their various predecessors, including the Cliff Dwellers (agricultural villagers, who planted corn, beans, and squash and made beautiful black-and-white and polychrome pottery with geometric designs). Among the

A view of one of the large pyramidal temple structures of Monte Albán, Mexico. The city, thought to have been built and inhabited by the Zapotec, was the dominant center of the Valley of Oaxaca from about 500 BC to about AD 500. Andrew Rakoczy–Dena

Skeleton and vessels in a museum reproduction of a painted tomb from Monte Albán, near Oaxaca, show the stylized art and burial customs of the Zapotec civilization of pre-Columbian Mexico. Bruce Coleman, Inc.

Pueblo the Formative stage lasted from about the beginning of the Christian era up until the present. *See also* CLIFF DWELLER.

Contemporaneous with the Pueblo in the eastern U.S. were people who used unpainted pottery and practiced subsistence agriculture. Although they grew the same plants, their farming was less intensive, and their villages were not built of stone or clay but of wood and bark.

Among the peoples of the Great Plains of the U.S. and Canada, the Formative stage started later than elsewhere, even after the time of Christ. These people also made crude, unpainted pottery, but many of them had little or no agriculture; their economy was based on buffalo hunting. Only along the Missouri River did large villages and agriculture develop just before historic times.

Farther north were other groups that appeared to be of the Formative stage but really were not. The Inuit, for example, used pottery, and both they and the Aleuts lived in villages, but instead of agriculture they developed a maritime economy based on whale hunting. The people on the northwest coast also looked toward the sea for their subsistence; they used even better seacraft and lived in plank-house villages. They had no pottery but are famous for their totem poles and other carved wooden objects. Because none of these groups had any agriculture—the major trait of the Formative stage—they were actually highly developed Archaics.

The real Formative stage was found mainly in and on both sides of Central America, in the nuclear area from Mexico to Peru. The peoples of this area developed village life, with permanent houses, distinctive pyramids, well-painted pottery, and clay figurines. They practiced a subsistence agriculture that included many other species besides their staples—corn, beans, and squash. In Mexico they grew amaranth, avocado, runner beans, and several other plants. In Central America, northern South America, and the Antilles manioc, or tapioca, was added to the three basics. In Peru potatoes, peanuts, and quinoa were cultivated, and the llama, alpaca, guinea

One of the many elaborately carved stone pillars, excellent examples of pre-Columbian art, that are found at the Mayan site of Copán in western Honduras.
D. Donne Bryant–Art Resource

pig, and Muscovy duck were all domesticated.

In the nuclear area all these developments of the Formative stage ripened in the more complex cultures of the later stages, but outside it—for example, to the south, in the Amazon, northern Chile, and Argentina—villagers remained who maintained the Formative way of life up to historic times.

The Classic Stage. Only in the nuclear area mentioned above did Formative peoples evolve into more complex cultures, forming not only villages but towns and occasional cities that required political organization of the chiefdom type. This demanded further division of labor, producing full-time specialists, not only in weaving (as in Peru), but in metallurgy (Colombia and Central America) and ornate stone architecture and sculpture (Guatemala and Mexico). Most of these advances were made from just before the time of Christ to AD 700–1100, but in Central America and northern South America this Classic stage lasted until the Spanish conquest.

The Post-Classic, or Imperial, Stage. Only in Mesoamerica (Mexico and Guatemala) and the Andean nuclear area (Peru, northern Boliva, and southern Ecuador) did native development reach the final stage, characterized by the rise of a state, or empire, and real civilization. The two best-known examples of this stage are the Aztec (q.v.) of Mexico and the Inca (q.v.) of Peru, but both had civilized predecessors and neighbors. The predecessors of the Aztecs were the Toltec; other civilized groups living at the same time were the Mixtec, the Zapotec, and the Maya (q.v.). In Peru the Huari and Chimú (q.v.) empires preceded the Inca. All displayed the basic characteristics of the Post-Classic stage: national states, cities, full-time specialists, class systems, complex economic and exchange machinery, monumental architecture, numbering systems, and intensive agriculture. Theirs was an urban civilization, the apogee of development in the New World that the Spanish saw and conquered in the 16th century. *See also* CHAVÍN DE HUANTAR; CHICHÉN ITZÁ; MACCHUPICCHU; MONTE ALBÁN; PALENQUE; TENOCHTITLÁN; TEOTIHUACÁN; TIAHUANACU; TULA. R.S.Ma.

AFRICA

Sub-Saharan Africa confronts archaeologists with a vast area, thousands of known living sites going back to the earliest human existence, and a host of problems concerning the genesis of human beings, tribal migrations, and manifold cultures. Yet an important source of data is lacking: Africans built with perishable wood and mud brick. Except in Ethiopia, Zimbabwe, and East Africa, archaeologists must work with only a portion of the evidence available to colleagues working, for example, in the Middle East.

Archaeologists working in East Africa, among whom the most prominent have been the paleoanthropologists Louis, Mary, and Richard Leakey, have uncovered evidence of the earliest known direct ancestors of modern humans. Among the most notable discoveries have been the 3.7 million-year-old partial skeleton of "Lucy," a female *Australopithecus afarensis,* the first humanlike species, found in Ethiopia in 1974; and the 1.8 million-year-old skeletal remains of a female *Homo habilis,* the first truly human species and the earliest to use tools, found in Tanzania in 1986. Hundreds of Stone Age sites have been

The most impressive remains of early American cultures in the Middle West are the religious mounds near Cahokia, Ill. The large central earthen structure, known as Monk's Mound, was used as a platform for wooden religious buildings. Illinois Department of Conservation

A view of the impressive stone walls of Great Zimbabwe, the center of an old commercial empire; its name was later given to the 20th-century Republic of Zimbabwe.
Shostal Associates

identified throughout Africa, but only a few have been thoroughly studied. The main concern with these and Iron Age sites has been dating by conventional and radiocarbon methods. Since 1960 some understanding has emerged of the interconnections between peoples and of the clues to their complex migrations.

In only a few late Iron Age locales in Africa are remains of stone buildings, monuments, and stelae preserved. One such is the ancient kingdom of Aksum. Elsewhere in Ethiopia structures of stone bear witness to a 1500-year evolution of society. Another area is southern Zimbabwe, where remnants of stone fortresses and villages are displayed on many hilltops. Great Zimbabwe, built by the Shona and Rozwi peoples (11th–18th cent. AD), with its huge dry stone walls, interconnected buildings, and conical towers, is the finest example of stone craft south of the Sudan. Muslim builders in East Africa have also left behind a history in stone, such as the abandoned city of Gedi (11th–16th cent. AD) in Kenya.

Archaeological finds elsewhere are more modest. Foundations of buildings have been uncovered in sites suspected to be the capitals of the Ghana and Kanem empires. Some of the many stone circles found in the Senegambia area have been excavated and human remains and artifacts discovered, dating from the 14th century. Pottery shards from many sites have enabled researchers to speculate about Bantu migrations. Nigeria has yielded much information and some of the

A terra-cotta head excavated from a shrine in Ife, Nigeria. Ife, the sacred city of the Yoruba people, was founded about 1300 and flourished until the 17th century.
Eliot Elisofon–Museum of African Art

world's great art. The Nok culture (c. 500 BC–AD 300) has been partly reconstructed on the basis of discoveries on the Bauchi Plateau in northern Nigeria. Many terra-cotta, stone, and bronze statues in a naturalistic style, along with numerous artifacts unearthed at Ife, confirm the high culture of the Yoruba. Bronzes from Benin provide a distinct record of that kingdom's past from the 14th century onward. Discoveries at Igbo-Ukwu in 1959 revealed the existence of a powerful forest kingdom in southern Nigeria as early as the 9th century AD. H.A.G.

See also ANTHROPOLOGY; CHRONOLOGY; and individual articles on most of the periods mentioned, such as STONE AGE; as well as history sections of articles on individual countries, such as EGYPT. For additional information on individal archaeologists, see biographies of those whose names are not followed by dates.

For further information on this topic, see the Bibliography in volume 28, sections 877–78.

ARCHAEOPTERYX, the first known bird, the remains of which were found in the 19th century in lithographic stone (a limestone of the Jurassic period) in Solnhofen, Bavaria, Germany. To date six fossil specimens have been found. The bird appears to have ranged from the size of a pigeon to that of a small crow. It had many characteristics of dinosaurs (*see* DINOSAUR). The vertebral column was extended so as to form a long tail, and quilled feathers grew from each vertebra. The entire body was covered with feathers. A striking intermediate between later birds and other small Mesozoic carnivorous dinosaurs, *Archaeopteryx* is one of the best examples of evolution. *See also* BIRD.

ARCHANGEL, an angel, or heavenly being, of higher rank than angels. In Jewish and Christian literature, the four best known are Michael, Gabriel, Raphael, and Uriel. In Islam, it is believed that four archangels guard the throne of Allah. According to Christian tradition, archangels belong to the eighth of nine choirs of angels. Arranged according to their importance, in descending order, these choirs are seraphim, cherubim, thrones, dominations, virtues, powers, principalities, archangels, and angels.

ARCHBISHOP, prelate having jurisdiction over an ecclesiastical province. He superintends certain activities of the other bishops in his province and also exercises episcopal authority in his own diocese. The two archbishops of the Church of England are those of Canterbury and York. The only archbishops in the U.S. are the 53 archbishops of the Roman Catholic church. The Roman Catholic archbishops of England and Wales are of Westminster, Southwark, Birmingham, and Liverpool. Scotland has two Roman Catholic archbishops, one of Saint Andrews and Edinburgh and one of Glasgow. Ireland has four, one each at Armagh, Dublin, Cashel, and Taum. The title of archbishop in the Orthodox churches is usually honorary.

ARCHDEACON, in Christian churches, an ecclesiastical dignitary with jurisdiction immediately subordinate to that of a bishop. The title was first used in the 3d century. Originally, the responsibilities of archdeacons were restricted to attending the bishop at the altar and at ordinations, assisting him in managing the revenues of the church, and directing the deacons in their duties. Beginning in the 5th century, archdeacons began to gain more powers. The archdeacon represented the bishop at councils, and he governed the diocese during the time between the death of a bishop and the election of a new one. In the Roman Catholic church, the office of archdeacon became less important after the Council of Trent, and its duties were discharged by the vicar-general. In the Church of England, each diocese has from two to four appointed archdeacons.

ARCHER, William (1856–1924), Scottish playwright and drama critic, born in Perth. He helped to bring contemporary achievements in Continental drama to the British theater. His translation of *The Pillars of Society,* by the Norwegian dramatist Henrik Ibsen, was produced in London in 1880, the first of Ibsen's dramas to be staged in England. Subsequently Archer translated and edited Ibsen's *Prose Dramas* (5 vol., 1890–91). He was the author himself of several plays, notably *The Green Goddess* (1923).

ARCHERY, art, practice, or skill of using a bow and arrow for hunting or warfare or as a sport. Modern bows, used to propel arrows, generally are constructed of wood, fiberglass, or graphite or carbon composites with a taut cord or string connecting the bent ends of the bow. Arrows are usually made of either aluminum or carbon graphite, pointed at one end and with flight-stabilizing feathers at the other end. A notch in this butt end is fitted to the bowstring. As the string is pulled back, the bow bends for maximum tension, and when the string is released, the arrow is propelled.

History. Some authorities date the origin of archery as early as the Aurignacian period, about 25,000 years before the modern era. The earliest people known to have used the bow and arrow were the ancient Egyptians, who adopted the weapon at least 5000 years ago. In the time of the earliest pharaohs, the Egyptians practiced archery in hunting, as well as in warfare against the ancient Persians, who were then equipped only with spears and slingshots. Soon after, however, the bow and arrow was used extensively in the ancient world. The Assyrians and Babylonians depended on the weapon, and the Old Testament refers several times to archery as a characteristic skill of the ancient Hebrews. The Romans owed much of their military superiority to armies of skilled archers. At the beginning of the medieval period the Romans were in turn defeated by the more highly skilled archers of the Goths, Huns, and Vandals.

During the Middle Ages the most notable European archers were the English. Medieval ballads celebrate their feats in hunting, fighting, and, for the first time in recorded history, sport. Outside Europe, in the same period, peoples of the Middle East excelled in archery. Accounts of European travelers during the Renaissance indicate that the bow and arrow was the most important weapon used throughout the Far East, the Americas, Central Africa, and the Arctic regions.

The introduction of gunpowder gradually made the bow and arrow obsolete, especially in western Europe. In the defeat of the Spanish Armada by the English in 1588, for example, 10,000 English troops were experimentally equipped with firearms, while the Spanish relied on archers; the success of the English forces played a major role in convincing military theorists that archery had become a relatively inefficient method of waging war. Nevertheless, peoples of the Far East employed archers in warfare as recently as the 19th century, and the use of the bow and arrow in hunting and intertribal fighting continues in central Africa and South America up to the present day.

Archery as a Sport. Archery has long been popular as an amateur sport, particularly in England. The oldest continuously held archery tournament still extant, known as the Ancient Scorton

Modern archers use high-precision bows with adjustable counterweights and tension regulators. Here, Denise Parker, a member of the 1988 bronze-medal-winning U.S. Olympic team, competes in a tournament. ©duomo–Tim Davis 1989

Arrow, was founded in Yorkshire in 1673; and about 1790 the Royal Toxophilite (Gr. *toxon,* "bow"; *philos,* "loving") Society was formed to advance the sport. The Grand National Archery Society, the official organization of British archery, was established in 1844, and it has conducted championship contests since that year. Archery as a sport was introduced in North America in the 17th century. The earliest organized body of archers in the U.S., known as the United Bowmen of Philadelphia, was active from 1828 to 1859, and the modern ruling body, the National Archery Association of the United States, was founded in Boston in 1879 as the National Association of Archers. Under the auspices of the association, the first annual archery tournament was held in Chicago in 1879.

Archery competition is divided into various categories, for example, target, field, and flight shooting. The main events of a target-shooting tournament are called rounds, and the number of arrows shot and the range of distance are specified. In U.S. tournaments, target faces are made of paper and pinned to straw mats. The target is circular and has a series of concentric rings around a solid center, or bull's-eye. The center of the bull's-eye is suspended 4 ft 3 in. (1.3 m) above the ground. Ranging outward from the bull's-eye, the colors of the rings are gold, red, blue, black, and white. The rings are assigned point values for arrows shot into them; from gold to white, the values range from 10 (in the center of the gold) to 1 (in the outer part of the white ring).

Field shooting simulates hunting game, with small targets placed in natural surroundings, and without aids to sighting. In flight shooting the object is distance traversed by the arrow rather than accuracy of the shot.

In recent years hunting with bow and arrow has become popular, and in many parts of the U.S. legal seasons have been established for taking deer in this manner.

ARCHES NATIONAL PARK, SE Utah, near Moab, established as a national monument in 1929, as a national park in 1971. The park consists of a desert region remarkable for its natural rock formations. The reddish sandstone has been eroded into fantastic sculptures, such as pinnacles, pedestals, windows, and giant arches. Of the more than 90 natural arches in the park, Landscape Arch is the largest, with a width of 89 m (291 ft) and a height of about 30 m (about 100 ft). Area, 297 sq km (114.7 sq mi).

ARCHIDAMUS II (d. 427 BC), king of Sparta (476–427 BC) in the years preceding the Peloponnesian War. He tried to avert the war, perhaps in part because of his friendship with the Athenian statesman Pericles. After war was declared, however, Archidamus led expeditions against the cities of Attica and Plataea during the first years of the struggle. He was succeeded by his son, Agis II (r. about 426–398 BC).

ARCHIDAMUS III (d. 338 BC), king of Sparta (360–338 BC). He led the Spartan forces during the reign of his father Agesilaus II against the army of Thebes under Epaminondas. During his own reign, his hostility to Thebes caused him to support Phocis, a country in northern Greece, in the second sacred war (355–346).

ARCHILOCHUS (fl. c. 710–676 BC), Greek poet, whose bitter satires scourged his enemies in a malicious and merciless fashion. Considered the first Greek lyric poet, he was also regarded as the creator of iambic poetry, the poetry of the passions and of biting raillery. Only fragments of his compositions have survived.

ARCHIMEDES (287–212 BC), preeminent Greek mathematician and inventor, who wrote important works on plane and solid geometry, arithmetic, and mechanics.

Archimedes was born in Syracuse, Sicily, and educated in Alexandria, Egypt. In pure mathematics he anticipated many of the discoveries of modern science, such as the integral calculus, through his studies of the areas and volumes of curved solid figures and the areas of plane figures. He also proved that the volume of a sphere is two-thirds the volume of a cylinder that circumscribes the sphere.

In mechanics, Archimedes defined the principle of the lever and is credited with inventing the compound pulley. During his stay in Egypt he invented the hydraulic screw for raising water from a lower to a higher level. He is best known for discovering the law of hydrostatics, often called Archimedes' principle, which states that a body immersed in fluid loses weight equal to the weight of the amount of fluid it displaces. This discovery is said to have been made as Archimedes stepped into his bath and perceived the displaced water overflowing.

Archimedes spent the major part of his life in Sicily, in and around Syracuse. He did not hold any public office but devoted his entire lifetime to research and experiment. During the Roman conquest of Sicily, however, he placed his gifts at the disposal of the state, and several of his mechanical devices were employed in the defense of Syracuse. Among the war machines attributed to him are the catapult and—perhaps legendary—a mirror system for focusing the sun's rays on the invaders' boats and igniting them.

After the capture of Syracuse during the Second Punic War, Archimedes was killed by a Roman soldier who found him drawing a mathematical diagram in the sand. It is said that Archimedes was so absorbed in calculation that he offended the intruder merely by remarking, "Do not disturb my diagrams." Several of his works on mathematics and mechanics survive, including *Floating Bodies, The Sand Reckoner, Measurement of the Circle, Spirals,* and *Sphere and Cylinder.* They all exhibit the rigor and imaginativeness of his mathematical thinking.

ARCHIPENKO, Alexander Porfiryevich (1887–1964), Russian-American sculptor, born in Kiev. He studied at the Kiev Art School and at the École des Beaux-Arts in Paris. He made Paris the center of his activities from 1908 to 1914; lived in Berlin from 1921 to 1923; and after 1923 made his home in the U.S., where he taught and lectured at various colleges and universities. From 1939 to 1955 he conducted a private school of fine arts in New York City. Archipenko was an experimenter and innovator in sculpture, deriving abstract forms from the human figure in some of the earliest cubist sculptures known, such as *Medrano* (1915, Guggenheim Museum, New York City). He developed a style that relies for its effect on the emphasis given to concavities and negative spaces, or voids.

Female Torso *by Alexander P. Archipenko.*
Metropolitan Museum of Art–Bequest of Charles F. Ikle

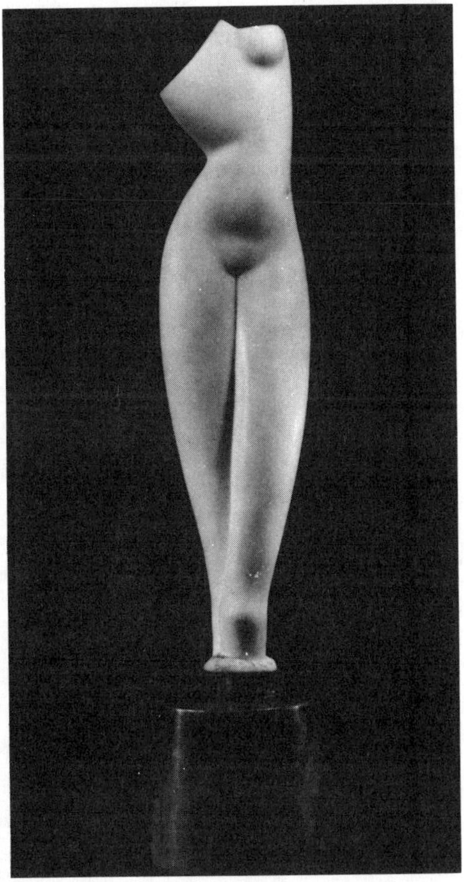

ARCHITECTURE, the practice of building design and its resulting products; customary usage refers only to those designs and structures that are culturally significant. Architecture is to building as literature is to the printed word. Vitruvius, a 1st-century BC Roman, wrote encyclopedically about architecture, and the English poet Sir Henry Wotton (1568–1639) was quoting him in his charmingly phrased dictum: "Well building hath three conditions: Commoditie, Firmenes, and Delight." More prosaically, one would say today that architecture must satisfy its intended uses, must be technically sound, and must convey aesthetic meaning. But the best buildings are often so well constructed that they outlast their original use. They then survive not only as beautiful objects, but as documents of the history of cultures, achievements in architecture that testify to the nature of the society that produced them. These achievements are never wholly the work of individuals. Architecture is a social art.

Architectural form is inevitably influenced by the technologies applied, but building technology is conservative and knowledge about it is cumulative. Precast concrete, for instance, has not rendered brick obsolete. Although design and construction have become highly sophisticated and are often computer directed, this complex apparatus rests on preindustrial traditions inherited from millennia during which most structures were lived in by the people who erected them. The technical demands on building remain the elemental ones—to exclude enemies, to circumvent gravity, and to avoid discomforts caused by an excess of heat or cold or by the intrusion of rain, wind, or vermin. This is no trivial assignment even with the best modern technology.

BUILDING MATERIALS

The availability of suitable materials fostered the crafts to exploit them and influenced the shapes of buildings. Large areas of the world were once forested, and their inhabitants developed carpentry. Although it has become relatively scarce, timber remains an important building material.

Many kinds of stone lend themselves to building. Stone and marble were chosen for important monuments because they are incombustible and can be expected to endure. Stone is also a sculptural material; stone architecture was often integral with stone sculpture. The use of stone has declined, however, because a number of other materials are more amenable to industrial use and assembly.

Some regions lack both timber and stone; their peoples used the earth itself, tamping certain mixtures into walls or forming them into bricks to be dried in the sun. Later they baked these substances in kilns, producing a range of bricks and tiles with greater durability.

Thus, early cultures used substances occurring in their environment and invented the tools, skills, and technologies to exploit a variety of materials, creating a legacy that continues to inform more industrialized methods.

Building with stones or bricks is called masonry. The elements cohere through sheer gravity or the use of mortar, first composed of lime and sand. The Romans found a natural cement that, combined with inert substances, produced concrete. They usually faced this with materials that would give a better finish. In the early 19th century a truly waterproof cement was developed, the key ingredient of modern concrete.

In the 19th century also, steel suddenly became abundant; rolling mills turned out shapes that could make structural frames stronger than the traditional wooden frames. Moreover, steel rods could be positioned in wet concrete so as to greatly improve the versatility of that material, giving impetus early in the 20th century to new forms facilitated by reinforced concrete construction. The subsequent profusion of aluminum and its anodized coatings provided cladding (surfacing) material that was lightweight and virtually maintenance free. Glass was known in prehistory and is celebrated for its contributions to Gothic architecture. Its quality and availability have been enormously enhanced by industrial processing, which has revolutionized the exploitation of natural light and transparency.

CONSTRUCTION

When masonry materials are stacked vertically, they are very stable; every part is undergoing compression. The real problem of construction, however, is spanning. Ways must be found to connect walls so as to provide a roof. The two basic approaches to spanning are post-and-lintel construction and arch, vault, and dome construction. In post-and-lintel construction, lintels, or beams, are laid horizontally across the tops of posts, or columns; additional horizontals span from beam to beam, forming decks that can become roofs or be occupied as floors. In arch, vault, and dome construction, the spanning element is curved rather than straight. In the flat plane of a wall, arches may be used in rows, supported by piers or columns to form an arcade (q.v.); for roofs or ceilings, a sequence of arches, one behind the other, may be used to form a half-cylinder (or barrel) vault; to span large centralized spaces, an arch may be rotated from its peak to form a hemispherical dome (*see* ARCH AND VAULT; DOME).

Post-and-lintel solutions can be executed in various materials, but gravity subjects the horizontal members to bending stress, in which parts of the member are in compression while others are in tension. Wood, steel, and reinforced concrete are efficient as beams, whereas masonry, because it lacks tensile components, requires much greater bulk and weight. Vaulting permits spanning without subjecting material to tension; thus, it can cover large areas with masonry or concrete. Its outward thrust, however, must be counteracted by abutment, or buttressing.

Trussing is an important structural device used to achieve spans with less weighty construction. Obviously, a frame composed of three end-connected members cannot change its shape, even if its joints could act as hinges. Fortunately, however, the principle of triangulation—attaching a horizontal tie beam to the bottom ends of two peaked rafters—can be extended indefinitely. Spanning systems of almost any shape can be subdivided into triangles, the sides of which can be made of any appropriate material—wood, rolled steel, or tubing—and assembled using suitable end connections. Each separate part is then subject only to either compressive or tensile stress. In the 18th century, mathematicians learned to apply their science to the behavior of structures, thus making it possible to determine the amounts of these stresses. This led to the development of space frames, which are simply trusses or other elements arrayed three-dimensionally.

Advances in the art of analyzing structural behavior resulted from the demand in the 19th century for great civil engineering structures: dams, bridges, and tunnels. It is now possible to enclose space with suspension structures—the obverse of vaulting, in that materials are in tension—or pneumatic structures, the skins of which are held in place by air pressure. Sophisticated analysis is particularly necessary in very tall structures, because wind loads and stresses that could be induced by earthquakes then become more important than gravity.

Architecture must also take into account the internal functional equipment of modern buildings. In recent decades, elaborate systems for vertical transportation, the control of temperature and humidity, forced ventilation, artificial lighting, sanitation, control of fire, and the distribution of electricity and other services have been developed. This has added to the cost of construction and has increased expectations of comfort and convenience.

In modern architectural terminology the word *program* denotes the purposes for which buildings are constructed. Certain broad purposes have always been discernible. The noblest works—temples, churches, mosques—celebrate the mysteries of religion and provide assembly places where gods can be propitiated or where the multitudes can be instructed in interpretations of belief and can participate in symbolic rituals. Another important purpose has been to provide physical security: Many of the world's most permanent structures were built with defense in mind.

Related to defense is the desire to create buildings that serve as status symbols. Kings and emperors insisted on palaces proclaiming power and wealth. People of privilege have always been the best clients of designers, artists, and artisans, and in their projects the best work of a given period is often represented. Today large corporations, governments, and universities play the role of patron in a less personal way.

A proliferation of building types reflects the complexity of modern life. More people live in mass housing and go to work in large office buildings; they spend their incomes in large shopping centers, send their children to many different kinds of schools, and when sick go to specialized hospitals and clinics. They linger in airports on the way to distant hotels and resorts. Each class of facility has accumulated experiences that contribute to the expertise needed by its designers.

The attention of clients, architects, and users is more and more focused on the overall qualities manifested by aggregates of buildings and parts of cities as being more significant than individual structures. As the total building stock grows, conserving buildings and adapting them for changes in use becomes more important. *See* CITY PLANNING.

AESTHETICS

The aesthetic response to architecture is complex. It involves all the issues already discussed, as well as other, more abstract qualities. An experience of architectural space is personal and psychological; it differs from that of sculpture or painting because the observer is in it. It is affected by associations the observer may have with the materials used and the way they have been assembled, and by the lighting conditions.

Structural logic may or may not have been dramatized. Elements such as windows, and their scale and rhythm, affect the observer, as do the interplay of geometrical form and the way space is articulated. Movement through a sequence of spaces has narrative force; no single point of view is adequately descriptive. The recurrence of thematic forms, appearing in varied guises and contexts, contributes to unity and creates feelings—relaxation and protection or stimulation and awe. Perhaps the key element is proportion—the relation of various dimensions to one another and their relation to human scale.

During the mid-19th century, architecture became institutionalized as a profession requiring formal preparation and subject to codes of performance. During this period connoisseurship—full academic training in the history of architecture and its aesthetics—was the designer's most important qualification. In every Western country the École des Beaux-Arts in Paris was accepted as the model for architectural education. Architecture was easily separated from engineering, which had pragmatic rather than aesthetic goals. Yet today the profession delivers not only aesthetic guidance but also a bewildering array of technical services requiring many specialized contributors. The architect strives to maintain the position of generalist, one who can take the long view while orchestrating the resolution of complex interrelated issues.

THE ANCIENT WORLD

For the convenience of Western readers, the architecture of the ancient world, of the Orient, and of the pre-Columbian Americas may be divided into two groups: indigenous architecture, or ways of building that appear to have developed independently in isolated, local cultural conditions; and classical architecture, the systems and building methods of Greece and Rome, which directly determined the course of Western architecture.

INDIGENOUS ARCHITECTURE

The oldest designed environments stable enough to have left traces date from the first development of cities.

Mesopotamia. This region, the greater part of modern Iraq, comprises the lower valleys of the Tigris and Euphrates rivers. The Assyrian city of Khorsabad, built of clay and brick in the reign of Sargon II (r. 722–705 BC), was excavated as early as 1842, and much of its general plan is known. It became the basis for the study of Mesopotamian architecture, because the far older cities of Babylon and Ur were not discovered and excavated until the late 19th and 20th centuries. *See* MESOPOTAMIAN ART AND ARCHITECTURE.

Early Persian architecture—influenced by the

Colonnade of the Temple of Amon (14th cent. BC), Luxor, has columns suggesting bundles of papyrus. Massive and closely spaced, they exemplify the awesome, monumental Egyptian style.
Editorial Photocolor Archives

Greeks, with whom the Persians were at war in the 5th century BC—left the great royal compound of Persepolis (518–460 BC), created by Darius the Great, and several nearby rock-cut tombs, all north of Shiraz in Iran. *See* IRANIAN ART AND ARCHITECTURE.

Egypt. The urban culture of Egypt also developed very early. Its political history was more stable, however, with strong continuity in the development and conservation of tradition. Also, granite, sandstone, and limestone were available in abundance. These circumstances, in a cultural system conferring enormous power on rulers and priests, made possible the erection, over a long period, of the most awesome of the world's ancient monuments.

Each Egyptian ruler was obsessed with constructing a tomb for himself more impressive and longer lasting than that of his predecessors. Before the 4th Dynasty (begins c. 2680 BC) Egyptian royal burial took the form of the mastaba, an archetypal rectangular mass of masonry. This evolved into the stepped pyramid and finally into the fully refined pyramid, of which the largest and best preserved are those of Khufu (built c. 2570 BC) and Khafre (c. 2530 BC) at Giza near Cairo. These immense monuments testify to the pharaohs' vast social control and also to the fascination of their architects with abstract, perfect geometrical forms, a concern that reappears frequently throughout history.

Egyptians built temples to dignify the ritual observances of those in power and to exclude others. Thus, they were built within walled enclosures, their great columned halls (hypostyles) turning inward, visible from a distance only as a sheer mass of masonry. A hierarchical linear sequence of spaces led to successively more privileged precincts. In this way was born the concept of the axis, which in the Egyptian temples was greatly extended by avenues of sphinxes in order to intensify the climactic experience of the approaching participants. The temples also introduce the monumental use of post-and-lintel construction in stone, in which massive columns are closely spaced and bear deep lintels.

The best-known Egyptian temples are in the mid-Nile area in the vicinity of the old capital, Thebes. Here are found the great temples of Luxor, al-Karnak, and Deir el-Bahri (15th–12th cent. BC) and Idfu (3d cent. BC). *See* EGYPTIAN ART AND ARCHITECTURE; TEMPLE.

India and Southeast Asia. Hindu traditions are rich in visual symbols; the early stone architecture of India was elaborately carved, more like sculpture than building, especially as the designers did not emphasize structural systems and rarely faced the task of enclosing large spaces.

India. The Indian commemorative monument takes the form of large hemispherical mounds called stupas, like the one built from the 3d to the 1st century BC, during Buddhist ascendancy, at Sanchi, near Bhopal in central India.

In the early period of monastery and temple building, shrines were sculpted out of the solid rock of cliffs. At sites such as Ellora and Ajanta, northeast of Bombay, are great series of these artificial caves carved over many centuries. As the art of temple building developed, construction by subtraction gave way to the more conventional method of adding stones to form a structure, always, however, with more concern for sculptural mass than for enclosed volume.

Hindu temples are found throughout India, especially in the south and east, which were less dominated by the Mughal rulers. Jainism, still a very successful cult, has its own temple tradition and continues to build on it. *See* INDIAN ART AND ARCHITECTURE.

Southeast Asia. In Southeast Asia a Buddhist temple is called a wat. The most famous of these, and perhaps also the largest known, is Angkor Wat in central Cambodia, built in the early 12th century under the long-dominant Khmer dynasty. A richly sculptured stone complex, it rises 61 m (200 ft) and is approached by a ceremonial bridge 183 m (600 ft) long that spans the surrounding moat.

Buddhist architectural traditions, sometimes coming via China, are strongly evident in Burma, Thailand, Malaysia, Java, and Sri Lanka. The rich temples and shrines of the Royal Palace compound in Bangkok are less than 200 years old, testifying to that culture's continuing vitality.

China and Japan. The cultures of China and Japan have shared many features, but each has used them according to its national temperament. The resultant architectures are quite different from each other in both form and purpose.

Chinese architecture. China has a traditional reverence toward ancestors; the stable and hierarchical life of the Chinese extended family is proverbial. It is reflected in the formality of the Chinese house, built in rectangular form, preferably at the northern end of a walled courtyard entered from the south, with auxiliary elements disposed in a symmetrical fashion on either side of the north-south axis. This pattern was the

The temples of Kandariya Mahadevo and Devi Jogadanta in Kajuraho, India, are decorated with elaborately carved sculptures. Borromeo–Editorial Photocolor Archives

The Imperial Palace in Peking, also known as the Forbidden City, was an immense complex of ceremonial halls, courtyards, and residential sections.

C. Moore–Editorial Photocolor Archives

point of departure for more lavish programs for mansions, monasteries, palaces, and, eventually, whole cities.

The city of Peking took form over a very long time, under various rulers. Two contiguous rectangles, the Inner City and the newer Outer City, each embrace several square kilometers. The Inner City contains the Imperial City, which in turn contains the Forbidden City, which sheltered the imperial court and the imperial family. The entire development adheres to symmetry along a strong north-south avenue—the apotheosis, on a grand urban scale, of the Chinese house.

Stone, brick, tile, and timber are available in both China and Japan. The most characteristic architectural forms in both countries are based on timber framing. In China, the wooden post carried on its top an openwork timber structure, a kind of inverted pyramid formed of layers of horizontal beams connected and supported by brackets and short posts to support the rafters and beams of a steep and heavy tile roof. The eaves extended well beyond column lines on cantilevers. The resulting archetype is rectangular in plan, usually one story high, with a prominent roof. *See* CHINESE ART AND ARCHITECTURE.

Japanese architecture. The Japanese house developed differently. The Japanese express a deep poetic response to nature, and their houses are more concerned with achieving a satisfying relationship with earth, water, rocks, and trees than with establishing a social order. This approach is epitomized in the Katsura Palace (1st half of the 17th cent.), designed and built by a master of the tea ceremony. Its constructions ramble in a seemingly casual way, but in reality constitute a carefully considered sequence always integrated with vistas to or from outdoor features.

Japan had already perfected timber prototypes early in its history. The Ise Shrine, on the coast southwest of Tokyo, dates from the 5th or 6th century; it is scrupulously rebuilt every 20 years. Its principal building, within a rectangular compound containing auxiliary structures, is a timber treasure house elevated on wooden posts buried in the ground and crowned by a massive roof of thatch. Lacking both bracketing and trussing, the ridge is supported by a beam or ridgepole held up by fat posts at the middle of each gabled end; the forked rafters, joining atop the ridgepole, exert no outward thrust. This tiny but beautifully proportioned and crafted monument is an excellent example of the understated subtlety of the art of Japan. *See* JAPANESE ART AND ARCHITECTURE.

Pre-Columbian architecture. The nomadic North American tribes left little permanent building, but the Pueblos of Sonora, Mexico, and of Arizona and New Mexico did build in stone and adobe. These cultures were already in decline by AD 1300; a number of impressive cliff dwellings and other villages remain as significant monuments. *See* AMERICAN INDIANS.

The Spanish conquistador Hernán Cortés encountered the Aztecs in 1519 and within two years had destroyed their capital city, Tenochtitlán, where Mexico City now stands. But he passed over the nearby center of the older Teotihuacán culture (200 BC–AD 750), which has now been extensively restored and excavated. Teotihuacán contains two immense pyramids—of the sun and of the moon—that recall those of Egypt. They are arranged, along with other monuments and plazas, on a north-south axis at least 3 km (2 mi) in length, and the complex is embedded in what was a vast city, laid out accurately in blocks. Monte Albán, near Oaxaca, was the center of another culture that flourished about the same time. Its imposing stone structures are set around a spacious plaza created by leveling the top of a mountain.

The Mayan civilization had existed for 2700 years when first confronted by the Spanish in the 17th century, but its greatest building periods fall within the 4th to the 11th century. The Maya occupied every part of the Yucatán Peninsula, the principal sites, in roughly the order of their development, being Copán (Honduras), Tikal (Guatemala), Palenque, Uxmal, Chichén Itzá, and Tulum (Mexico). The important ceremonial monuments found in these centers are of stone; although the enclosure of space has more emphasis than in other pre-Columbian cultures, the Mayans never mastered the true vault. Nevertheless, they created impressive structures through extensive earth moving and bold architectural sculpture either integral with the stone or as added stucco ornamentation. The so-called Governors' Palace at Uxmal, sited on a great artificial terrace, is a long, horizontal building, the proportions and ornamentation of which suggest the eye and hand of a master designer.

The Incas' thriving empire was centered high in the Andes of east-central Peru at Cuzco, which flourished from about 1200 to 1533, with other cities at nearby Sacsahuaman and Machu Picchu. Inca architecture lacks the sculptural genius of the Maya, but the masonry craftsmanship is unexcelled; enormous pieces of stone were transported over mountain terrain and fitted together with precision, in what is called cyclopean masonry. *See* PRE-COLUMBIAN ART AND ARCHITECTURE.

CLASSICAL ARCHITECTURE

The building systems and forms of ancient Greece and Rome are called classical architecture. Greek contributions in architecture, as in so much else, defy summarization. The architecture of the Roman Empire has pervaded Western architecture for more than two millennia.

Aegean Architecture. Helladic or Aegean architecture belongs to the Greek cultures that preceded the arrival in about 1000 BC of the Ionians and the Dorians. The Minoan culture (3000–1200 BC) flourished on the island of Crete; its principal site is the multichambered Palace of Minos at Knossos (1650–1500 BC) near Iráklion. On the Pelopónnisos near Argos are the fortress-palaces of Mycenae and Tiryns, and in Asia Minor the city of Troy—all of them excavated by the German archaeologist Heinrich Schliemann in the last quarter of the 19th century. Mycenae and Tiryns represent the Achaean culture, the subject of Homer's epic *Iliad* and *Odyssey*. See AEGEAN CIVILIZATION.

The Kinkaku (Golden Pavilion) in the Rokuon-ji temple compound in Kyoto, Japan, was constructed (1394–1427) during the Ashikaga period. It is decorated with gold leaf and reflected in an artificial lake bordered with elaborate stonework. Bob & Ira Spring

The Hephaesteion (5th cent. BC*) in Athens, with fluted Doric columns, shows the concern of Greek architects for gracefully proportioned temples in imposing settings.*
Michael Tzovaras–Editorial Photocolor Archives

Greek Architecture. The Greek temple emerged as the archetypal shrine of all time. Unlike the Egyptians, the Greeks put their walls inside to protect the cella and their columns on the outside, where they could articulate exterior space. Perhaps for the first time, the overriding concern is for the building seen as a beautiful object externally, while at the same time containing precious and sacred inner space. Greek architects have been praised for not crushing the viewer with overmonumentality; yet they found it appropriate to build temples on basically the same theme ranging in size from the tiny Temple of Nike Apteros (427–424 BC) of about 6 by 9 m (about 20 by 30 ft) on the Athens Acropolis to the gigantic Temple of Zeus (c. 500 BC) at Agrigento in Sicily, which covered more than 1 ha (more than 2 acres). The Greeks seldom arranged their monuments hierarchically along an axis, preferring to site their temples to be seen from several viewpoints in order to display the relation of ends to sides.

In successive efforts during many centuries the Greeks modified their earlier models. Concern for the profile of the building in space spurred designers toward perfection in the articulation of parts, and these parts became intellectualized as stylobate, base, shaft, capital, architrave, frieze, cornice, and pediment, each representing metaphorically its structural purpose.

The Greek orders. Two orders developed more or less concurrently. The Doric order predominated on the mainland and in the western colonies. The acknowledged Doric masterpiece is the Parthenon (448–432 BC) crowning the Athens Acropolis (*see* PARTHENON).

The Ionic order originated in the cities on the islands and coasts of Asia Minor, which were more exposed to Asian and Egyptian influences; it featured capitals with spiral volutes, a more slender shaft with quite different fluting, and an elaborate and curvilinear base. Most of the early examples are gone, but Ionic was used inside the Propylaea (begun 437 BC) and in the Erechtheum (begun 421 BC), both on the Athens Acropolis.

The Corinthian order, a later development, introduced Ionic capitals elaborated with acanthus leaves. It has the advantage of facing equally in four directions and is therefore more adaptable than Ionic for corners.

City planning was stimulated by the need to rebuild Dorian cities after the end (466 BC) of the Persian Wars and again by the challenge of new cities established (beginning 333 BC) by Alexander the Great. The plan of Miletus in Asia Minor is an early example of the gridiron block, and it provides a prototype for the disposition of the central public areas, with the significant municipal buildings related to the major civic open spaces. A typical Greek agora included a temple, a council house (*bouleuterion*), a theater, and gymnasiums, as well as porticoes giving shape to the edges of the open space. Greek domestic architecture transformed the Mycenaean megaron (hearthroom) into the house with rooms disposed about a small open court, or atrium, a theme later elaborated in Italy, Spain, and North Africa. *See* GREEK ART AND ARCHITECTURE; HOUSE.

Roman Architecture. Roman architecture continued the development now referred to as classical, but with quite different results. Unlike the tenuously allied Greek city-states, Rome became a powerful, well-organized empire that planted its constructions throughout the Mediterranean world, northward into Britain, and eastward into Asia Minor. Romans built great engineering works—roads, canals, bridges, and aqueducts. Their masonry was more varied; they used bricks and concrete freely, as well as stone, marble, and mosaic.

Use of the arch and vault introduced curved forms; curved walls produced a semicircular space, or apse, for terminating an axis. Cylindrical and spherical spaces became elements of design, well suited to the grandiose rooms appropriate to the Roman imperial scale.

The dome. Barrel or tunnel vaults are inherently limited in span, and they exert lateral thrust. Two Roman inventions of enormous importance overcame this. First was the dome, inherently more stable than the barrel vault because it is doubly curved, but also limited because it thrusts outward circumferentially. It was possible for Hadrian to rebuild (AD 118–28) the Pantheon in Rome with a dome 43 m (142 ft) above the floor, but only by encircling it with a massive hollow ring wall 6 m (20 ft) thick that encloses eight segments of curved units. Thus, a dome provides for a one-room building but cannot easily be combined with other domes to make a larger space.

The groin vault. The second important invention was the groin vault, formed by the intersection of two identical barrel vaults over a square plan. They intersect along ellipses that go diagonally to the corners of the square. Because the curvature is in more than one direction, each barrel tends to reinforce the other. The great advantage of the groin vault is that it can be placed on four piers (built to receive 45° thrust), leaving the sides of the square for windows or for continuity with adjoining spaces.

In the great Roman thermae (baths) and basilicas (law courts and markets), rows of square groin-vaulted bays (or units) provided vast rooms lighted by clerestory windows high on the long sides under the vaults.

The Romans introduced the commemorative or triumphal arch and the colosseum or stadium. They further developed the Greek theater and the Greek house; many excellent examples of houses were unearthed in the excavations of Pompeii and Herculaneum, towns that were buried in the violent eruption of Vesuvius in AD 79.

The Roman genius for grandiose urban design is seen in the plan of Rome, where each emperor left a new forum, complete with basilica, temple, and other features. Their plans are axially organized, but with greater complexity than heretofore seen. The most remarkable among the great complexes is Hadrian's Villa (AD 125–32) near Tivoli, which abounds in richly inventive plan forms.

The Greek orders (Doric, Ionic, Corinthian) were widely adopted and further elaborated. But the Romans ultimately trivialized them by applying them indiscriminately, usually in the form of engaged columns or pilasters with accompanying cornices, to both interior and exterior walls as a form of ornamentation. They lost in the process the orders' capacity to evoke a sense of the loads being sustained in post-and-lintel construction. *See* ROMAN ART AND ARCHITECTURE.

THE MEDIEVAL WORLD

Two major architectural developments were initiated by historic religious events. The first occurred in 312, when the Roman emperor Constantine I conferred recognition on Christianity, which led to the development of Christian architecture. The second, the promulgation of Islam in about 610 by the Prophet Muhammad, spawned Islamic architecture.

THE ARCHITECTURE OF CHRISTIANITY

Constantine's removal in 330 of the imperial capital to Byzantium, which became Constantinople (modern İstanbul), separated the Christian church into East and West and set in motion two divergent architectural developments—Early Christian and Byzantine—each taking as its point of departure a different Roman prototype.

Early Christian Architecture. The term Early Christian is given to the basilican architecture of the church prior to the reintroduction of vaulting about the year 1000. The surviving churches in Rome that most clearly evoke the Early Christian character are San Clemente (with its 4th-cent. choir furnishings), Sant' Agnese Fuori le Mura (rebuilt 630 and later), and Santa Sabina (422–32). While Byzantine architecture developed on the concept called the central church, assembled around a central dome like the Pantheon, the Western or Roman church—more concerned with congregational participation in the Mass—preferred the Roman basilica. Early models resembled large barns, with stone walls and timber roofs. The central part (nave) of this rectangular structure was supported on columns opening toward single or double flanking aisles of lower height. The difference in roof height permitted high windows, called clerestory windows, in the nave walls; at the end of the nave, opposite the entrance, was placed the altar (q.v.), backed by a large apse (also borrowed from Rome), in which the officiating clergy were seated.

The Eastern emperor Justinian I was in control of Ravenna during his reign (527-65). Some of the constructions there can be considered Byzantine, as they featured mosaic mural compositions in Byzantine style. Two of Ravenna's great churches, however—Sant' Apollinare Nuovo (c. 520) and Sant' Apollinare in Classe (c. 530-49)—are basilican in plan. *See* EARLY CHRISTIAN ART AND ARCHITECTURE.

Byzantine Architecture. Byzantine architecture has its early prototypes in San Vitale (526-47) in Ravenna and in Saint Sergius and Saint Bacchus (527) in Constantinople, both domed churches on an octagonal plan with surrounding aisles. But it was Justinian's great church at Constantinople, Hagia Sophia, or the Church of the Holy Wisdom (532-37), that demonstrated how to place a vast dome over a square plan. The solution was to place the dome on pendentives, or spherical triangles, that make a circle out of the square by rounding its corners.

The pendentive can be understood by visualizing its geometry. A square drawn on the ground has two circles, one circumscribed around it, the other inscribed within it. A hemisphere set on the larger circle is intersected by vertical planes rising from the sides of the square, forming four arches. A horizontal plane is then passed through the hemisphere at the tops of these arches, providing a ring on which is built the dome, which has a diameter equal to the circle inscribed within the square. The pendentives are spherical triangles, the remaining portions of the first, or outer, hemisphere.

At Hagia Sophia, two opposing arches on the central square open into semidomes, each pierced by three smaller radial semidomes, forming an oblong volume 31 m (100 ft) wide by 80 m (260 ft) long. The central dome rises out of this series of smaller spherical surfaces. An abundance of small windows, including a circle of them at the rim of the dome, provides a diffused light.

Byzantine figurative art developed a characteristic style; its architectural application took the form of mosaics (q.v.), great mural compositions executed in tiny pieces (tesserae) of colored marble and gilded glass, a technique presumed to have been borrowed from Persia.

Byzantine churches, each with a central dome opening into surrounding semidomes and other vault forms, and accompanied by the characteristic iconography, proliferated throughout the Byzantine Empire—Greece, the Balkans, Asia Minor, and parts of North Africa and Italy—and also influenced the design of churches in Western Christendom. Later churches are often miniaturizations of the original grandiose concept; their proportions emphasize vertical space, and the domes themselves become smaller. When Moscow became Christian, Europe was already into the Renaissance, but Moscow's Saint Basil's Cathedral (1500-60) shows how Byzantine domes finally became onion-shaped tops of towers, no longer relevant to interior space making. *See* BYZANTINE ART AND ARCHITECTURE.

The nave of St. Mark's Cathedral (11th cent.) in Venice, then a center of Byzantine trade with the West, has domes on pendentives and sumptuous mosaics in the Byzantine style. Scala–Editorial Photocolor Archives

Romanesque Architecture. A plan drawn on parchment of a now-vanished monastery in Saint Gall, Switzerland, shows that by the time of Charlemagne (742-814) the Benedictine monastic order had become a big departmentalized institution, but not until almost 1000 did church building come to life throughout the West. At first, the architects were all monks, for the monasteries supplied not only the material wealth but also the aggregated learning that made the new initiative possible.

The basilican plan used in earlier times needed elaboration to accommodate a new liturgy. The essential symbol of the cross was incorporated in the form of transepts, a cross axis (perhaps borrowed from Byzantium) that served to identify the choir (for the monks), as distinct from the nave (for the public). Beyond the choir, in a semicircular apse girded by the ambulatory (a semicircular extension of the aisles), stood the main altar, the focal point of the building. Subaltars, needed for the daily Mass required of many monks, were placed in the transepts and in the ambulatory. At the nave entrance were placed narthexes, vestibules and reception areas for pilgrims. Although many French churches—Saint Savin sur Gartempe (nave 1095–1115), Saint Sernin in Toulouse (c. 1080–1120), and Sainte Foy in Conques (begun 1050)—had barrel-vaulted naves, Saint Philibert in Tournus (950–1120) used transverse arches to support a series of barrel vaults, with windows high in the vertical plane at the ends of the vaults. Ultimately, the groin vault became the preferred solution, because it offered high windows together with a continuous longitudinal crown, as in Sainte Madeleine in Vézelay (1104) and Worms Cathedral (11th century) in Germany. The semicircular arches of the groin vault form a square in plan; thus, the nave consisted of a long series of square bays or segments. The smaller and lower vaults of the aisles were often doubled up, two to each nave bay, to conform to this configuration.

The nave of Amiens Cathedral (13th cent.), with its clustered columns soaring up into pointed, ribbed vaults, is a triumph of medieval Christian piety and the French High Gothic style. Scala–Editorial Photocolor Archives

The greatest monastic Romanesque church, Cluny III (1088–1121), did not survive the French Revolution but has been reconstructed in drawings; it was an immense double-aisled church almost 137 m (almost 450 ft) long, with 15 small chapels in transepts and ambulatory. Its design influenced Romanesque and Gothic churches in Burgundy and beyond. Another important stimulus to French Romanesque was the pilgrimage cult; a convergence of routes led over the western Pyrenees into Spain and thus to Santiago de Compostela, where the pilgrim could venerate the presumed relics of St. James. Along the routes to Spain, certain points were sanctified as pilgrimage stops, which led to the erection of splendid Romanesque churches at Autun (1120–32), Paray-le-Monial (c. 1100), Périgueux (1120), Conques (1050), Moissac (c. 1120), Clermont-Ferrand (1262), Saint Guilhem le Désert (1076), and others. *See* ROMANESQUE ART AND ARCHITECTURE.

Gothic Architecture. At the beginning of the 12th century, Romanesque was transformed into Gothic. Although the change was a response to a growing rationalism in Christian theology, it was also the result of technical developments in vaulting. To build a vault requires first a temporary carpentry structure, called centering, which supports the masonry until the shell has been completed and the mortar has set. Centering for the ordinary groin vault must be for an entire structural unit, or bay, with a resultant heavy structure resting on the floor. About 1100, the builders of Durham Cathedral in England invented a new method. They built two intersecting diagonal arches across the bay, on lighter centering perhaps supported high on the nave walls, and then found ways to fill out the shell resting on secondary centering. This gave a new geometric articulation—the ribbed vault. Ribs did not modify the structural characteristics of the groin vault, but they offered constructional advantage and emphatically changed the vault's appearance.

Another development was the pointed arch and vault. The main advantage was geometrical. Vaults of various proportions could cover a rectangular or even a trapezoidal bay, so that nave bays could correspond with the narrower aisle bays, and vaulting could proceed around the curved apse without interruption. Also, the nave walls containing clerestory windows could be

The Abbey of Mont-Saint-Michel (13th cent.) was placed for defense on a rocky isle off the north French coast. It combines massive fortification with the more delicate Gothic style. Editorial Photocolor Archives

pushed just as high as the crown of the vault. Soon this clerestory became all window, filled with tracery and stained glass that conferred a new luminosity on the interior.

With these advances, the master builders were encouraged to construct more elegant, higher, and apparently lighter structures. But the vaults had to be kept from spreading outward by restraint imposed near the base of the vaults, now high above the aisle roofs. The solution was another innovation, the flying buttress, a half arch leaning against the vault from the outside, with its base firmly set in a massive pier of its own.

This new style received its most intensive development in the Île-de-France. The abbey church of Saint Denis (1140–44), the royal mausoleum near Paris, became the first grandiose model. Bishops in prosperous northern cities were then drawn into competition for designers and artisans to outdo other cathedrals. The beginning dates of the major French examples are Laon, 1160; Paris, 1163; Chartres, 1194; Bourges, 1195; Reims, 1210; Amiens, 1220; and Beauvais, 1225. The beginning dates of English Gothic cathedrals are Canterbury, 1174; Lincoln, 1192; York Minster, 1261; and Exeter, 1280. The collapse of the Beauvais choir in 1284, however, indicated that structural limits had been reached. The transverse span of the nave vaults of these cathedrals was in the range of 9 to 15 m (30 to 50 ft), but the rebuilt Beauvais choir attained a height of 47 m (154 ft).

Although the finest medieval architecture was ecclesiastical, secular builders also constructed great buildings in the years 1000 to 1400. The medieval castle is a romantic symbol of feudalism; one of the most impressive and best-preserved examples is the Krak des Chevaliers (1131) in Jordan, built by the Knights Hospitalers at the time of the Crusades.

Military architecture was a defensive response to advances in the technology of warfare; the ability to withstand siege remained important. Fortifications sometimes embraced whole towns; important examples include Ávila in Spain, Aigues-Mortes and Carcassonne in France, Chester in England, and Visby in Sweden.

Urbanization increased on a large scale, brought about by the needs and desires of many groups, including the church and its monasteries, the nobles and kings, the craft guilds, and the merchants and bankers. The planning patterns that developed are quite different from the arbitrary geometry of Roman cities or of Renaissance theorists. Throughout northern Europe, where hardwood remained available until the Industrial Revolution, timber frame construction flourished. In half-timber construction, a quickly erected wood frame was infilled with wattle and daub (twigs and plaster) or brickwork. Monastic barns and municipal covered markets necessitated large braced wooden frames. The descendants of Vikings built the curiously beautiful stave churches in Norwegian valleys. In the Alps whole towns were built of horizontally interlocked wood timbers of square cross section. Brick architecture also flourished in many regions, notably Lombardy, northern Germany, Holland, and Denmark. *See* GOTHIC ART AND ARCHITECTURE.

The Architecture of Islam. The Islamic concept of a mosque as a place for ablutions and prayer differs from the idea of a Christian church, and the desert climates in which Islam first became established required protection from sun, wind, and sand. The initial prototype was a simple walled-in rectangle containing a fountain and surrounded with porticoes. A qibla, or wall toward Mecca, had in its center an apse, or mihrab, with a nearby pulpit, or minbar; the shelter at this end consisted of multiple arcades of transverse and lateral rows of columns. Structural elements were the arch and the dome; roofs were flat unless forced upward by vaults, and there were no high windows. The mosque had at least one tower, or minaret, from which the call to prayer was issued five times daily. The same basic plan is followed to this day.

Western and Middle Eastern Islamic architecture. The Great Mosque at al-Qayrawan in Tunisia was built in AD 670, but its well-preserved state today reflects construction of the period 817-902.

The oldest mosque in Iraq is at Samarra (847-52). It is now a brick ruin, but its curious cone-shaped minaret with outside spiral ramp survives. The Great Mosque at Córdoba in Spain covers 2.4 ha (6 acres) and was built in several stages from 786 to 965. It was converted to a Christian cathedral in 1236. Also in Spain is the Alhambra (1354-91) at Granada, one of the most dazzling examples of Islamic palace architecture; its courts and fountains have delighted visitors ever since its construction.

Over the centuries Islamic architecture borrowed extensively from other cultures. Beginning in 1453, the Ottoman Turks ruled from Constantinople. Sultan Suleiman I (the Magnificent) was a patron of arts and architecture. His architect, Sinan, knew the Byzantine traditions, and in his mosques he refined and elaborated on the great 6th-century prototype, Hagia Sophia. Sinan's masterpieces are the Suleimaniye (begun 1550) in İstanbul and the Selimiye (begun 1569) in Edirne.

Iran is renowned for brick masonry vaulting and for glazed ceramic veneers. The finest examples of Islamic architecture in Iran are found in Isfahan, the former capital. The enormous imperial mosque, the Masjid-i-Jami, represents several construction periods, beginning in the 15th century. Even more richly ornamented is the sumptuous Masjid-i-Shah (1585-1616), built to be part of the royal civic compound of Shah Abbas.

Islamic architecture in India. The Mughal peoples, who had embraced Islam, made incursions into India and established an empire there. Mughal architecture was based on Persian traditions, but developed in northwestern India in ways peculiar to that region. The earliest remaining

The Berber architecture of North Africa, here shown in the village of Takrouna, Tunisia, is characterized by thick walls, small windows, white painted exteriors, and numerous courtyards—all designed to minimize the scorching heat of the desert sun.
Klaus D. Francke–Peter Arnold, Inc.

One of the most distinctive mosques in Islamic architecture, the Masjid-i-Shah Mosque in Isfahan, Iran, is famous for its elaborate glazed tilework.
SEF–Editorial Photocolor Archives

mosque, the Qutb, near Delhi, was begun in 1195. It is impossible to separate Mughal religious architecture from that erected to glorify the Mughal Empire.

The great builders were the emperors of the 16th and 17th centuries. Their most impressive monuments are a succession of imperial tombs. Notable are the superbly architectonic tomb (1564–73) of Humayun in Delhi, the jewellike Itimad-ud-Daulah (1622–28) in Agra, and the beautifully proportioned and decorated Taj Mahal (1632–48), also in Agra. A typical tomb was a high central dome surrounded by smaller chambers arranged about two intersecting axes so that all four sides of the structure are alike. It is built on a raised platform overlooking a large formal garden, surrounded by a wall, with pavilions at the axial points.

Each of the 16th- and 17th-century Mughal emperors elaborated the huge forts at Lahore, Delhi, and Agra. These forts included living quarters, mosque, baths, public and private audience halls, and the harem. One compound, that of Fatehpur Sikri, was begun in 1571 and abandoned in 1585. *See* INDIAN ART AND ARCHITECTURE.

Islam forbade the representation of persons and animals; yet craftsmen created highly ornamented buildings. The motifs are geometrical designs, floral arabesques, and Arabic calligraphy. The materials are glazed tile, wood joinery and marquetry, marble, mosaic, sandstone, stucco carving, and white marble inlaid with dark marbles and gemstones. *See* ISLAMIC ART AND ARCHITECTURE.

THE NEW AGE

The cultural revolution in Western civilization now called the Renaissance brought about an entirely new age, not only in philosophy and literature but in the visual arts as well. In architecture, the principles and styles of ancient Greece and Rome were revived and reinterpreted, to remain dominant until the 20th century.

RENAISSANCE ARCHITECTURE

The Renaissance, literally meaning "rebirth," brought into being some of the most significant and admired works ever built. Beginning in Italy about 1400, it spread to the rest of Europe during the next 150 years.

Italian Renaissance Architecture. The families who governed rival cities in northern Italy in the 15th century—de Medici, Sforza, da Montefeltro, and others—had become wealthy enough through commerce to become patrons of the arts. People of leisure began to take serious scholarly interest in the neglected Latin culture—its literature, its art, and its architecture, whose ruins lay about them.

Early in the 15th century the city of Florence was in the process of completing its cathedral. Piers had already been erected to support a dome almost as large as that of the Pantheon in Rome. A proposal for its completion was submitted by Filippo Brunelleschi, who had studied Roman structural solutions. His constructed dome (1420–36) is derived from Rome but is different; it is of masonry, is octagonal, has inner and outer shells connected by ribs, is pointed and rises higher, and is crowned with a lantern.

Its drum with circular windows stands alone without buttressing, for the base contains a tension ring—huge stone blocks held together with iron clamps and topped with heavy iron chains. Two additional tension rings are contained within the dome's double shells. Brunelleschi stood at the threshold between Gothic and Renaissance. His Pazzi Chapel (begun c. 1441), also in Florence, is a clear statement of new principles of proportion and design.

A new type of urban building evolved at this time—the palazzo, or city residence of a prominent family. The palazzi were several stories high; rooms were grouped around a *cortile,* or courtyard; the outer walls of the palazzo were on the lot lines.

The Florentine architect Leon Battista Alberti, in his design for the Palazzo Rucellai (1446–51), employed in its facade three superposed classic orders, much as in the Roman Colosseum, except that he used pilasters instead of engaged columns. They seem to have been engraved in the wall plane; the resulting compartmentalization of the facade provides a logical setting for the windows. Alberti also published in 1485 the first book on architectural theory since Vitruvius, which became a major influence in promoting classicism.

In the 16th century, Rome became the leading center for the new architecture. The Milanese architect Donato Bramante practiced in Rome beginning in 1499. His Tempietto (1502), an elegantly proportioned circular temple in the courtyard of San Pietro in Montorio, was one of the earliest Renaissance structures in Rome.

The erection of a new basilica of Saint Peter in Vatican City was the most important of many 16th-century projects. In drawing the first plan (1503–06) Bramante rejected the Western basilica concept in favor of a Greek cross of equal arms with a central dome. Popes who came after Julius II, however, appointed other architects—notably Michelangelo and Carlo Maderno—and, when the church was completed in 1612, the Latin cross form had been imposed with a lengthened nave. Michelangelo's dome, ribbed and with a lantern, is a logical development from Brunelleschi's in Florence. It rises in a high oval and is the prototype not only for later churches but for many state capitol buildings in the U.S.

Toward the middle of the 16th century such leading architects as Michelangelo, Baldassare Peruzzi, Giulio Romano, and Giacomo da Vignola began to use the classical Roman elements in ways that did not conform to the rules that governed designs in the early Renaissance. Arches, columns, and entablatures came to be used as devices to introduce drama through depth recession, asymmetry, and unexpected proportions and scales. This tendency, called

The colonnaded court of the Ducal Palace of Urbino (15th cent.), an elegant space based on classical Roman models, is a masterpiece of Italian Renaissance style.
Luciano Laurano–Scala–Editorial Photocolor Archives

Mannerism (q.v.), is exemplified by Giulio's sophisticated Palazzo del Te (1526–34) at Mantua.

The architect Andrea Palladio practiced in the environs of Vicenza and Venice. Although he visited Rome, he did not wholly adopt the Mannerist approach. He specialized in villas for gentleman farmers. These villas explore all the variations on the classical norms: governing axis defined in the approach, single major entrance, single major interior space surrounded by smaller rooms, secondary functions extended in symmetrical arms, and careful attention to proportion. They were immortalized by Palladio's publication *The Four Books of Architecture* (1570; trans. 1738), in which drawings for them appear, with the dimensions written into the plans to emphasize Palladio's harmonic series of dimensions that govern the major proportions. These books later enabled Inigo Jones in England and Thomas Jefferson in Virginia to propagate Palladian principles among the gentleman farmers of their times. In two large Venetian churches, San Giorgio Maggiore (1565) and Il Redentore (1577), Palladio made important contributions toward the adaptation of classic ideas to the liturgical and formal traditions of Roman Catholicism.

Northern Renaissance Architecture. Renaissance ideas had spread rapidly to France by 1494. French royal policy was to attract Italian artists (beginning with Leonardo da Vinci in 1506) while at the same time encouraging and developing native talent. It is believed that the Italian architect Domenico da Cortona (fl. 1497–1549) designed the extraordinary Château de Chambord that Francis I built (1519–47) in the Loire Valley, which retains outward characteristics of a medieval castle. The French architects Jacques Androuet du Cerceau the Elder (c. 1520–c. 1584) and Philibert Delorme worked at Fontainebleau, and Delorme was architect for the Château d'Anet, where Benvenuto Cellini was employed as sculptor. In Paris, work on the Louvre was undertaken by Pierre Lescot (c. 1500–78) in 1546.

Philip II of Spain engaged Juan de Herrera and Juan Bautista de Toledo (d. 1567) as architects for his colossal Escorial (1563–84) near Madrid—half palace, half monastery. England was somewhat slower to change. Inigo Jones, its principal early Renaissance architect, visited Italy and emulated Palladio in such works as the Banqueting House (1619–22) in Whitehall, London. *See* RENAISSANCE ART AND ARCHITECTURE.

BAROQUE AND ROCOCO ARCHITECTURE

In early Renaissance and even Mannerist architecture, elements were combined in rather static compositions; classic design implies a serene balance among the several components, and spaces locked into the geometry of perspective. Unsatisfied with this, the baroque architects of the 17th century deployed classic elements in more complex ways, so that the identity of these elements was masked, and space became more ambiguous and more activated. Baroque movement is understood as that of the observer experiencing the work, and of the observer's eyes scanning an interior space or probing a long vista. Some of the later rococo works contain a richness of ornament, color, and imagery that, combined with a highly sophisticated handling of light, overwhelms the observer.

Italian Baroque Architecture. Italians were the pioneers of baroque; the best known was the architect-sculptor Gian Lorenzo Bernini, designer of the great oval plaza (begun 1656) in front of St. Peter's. Francesco Borromini produced two masterpieces, both on an intimate scale, in Rome. San Carlo alle Quattro Fontane (1638–41; facade completed 1667) distorts the dome on pendentives into a coffered ellipse to stretch the space into a longitudinal axis; its facade undulates, entablature and all. The plan of Sant'Ivo della Sapienza (begun 1642) is based on two intersecting equilateral triangles that produce six niches of alternating shapes; these shapes, defined by pilasters and ribs, rise through what would ordinarily be a dome, continuing the hexagonal concept from floor to lantern.

Guarino Guarini designed a church in Turin, San Lorenzo (1668–87), with eight intersecting ribs that offer interstices for letting in daylight. His even more astonishing Capella della Santa Sindone (Chapel of the Holy Shroud, 1667–94), also in Turin, has a cone-shaped hexagonal dome created by six segmental arches rising in eight staggered tiers.

French Baroque Architecture. Seventeenth-century French architects also designed baroque churches, one of their greatest being part of Les Invalides, Paris (1676–1706), by Jules Hardouin-Mansart. The best French talent, however, was absorbed in the secular service of Louis XIV and his government. The Château de Vaux-le-Vicomte (1657–61) is a grandiose ensemble representing the collaboration of the architect Louis Le Vau, the painter Charles Le Brun, and the landscape architect André Le Nôtre. The Sun King was so impressed that he engaged these designers to rebuild the Château de Versailles on a truly regal scale. The Palace of Versailles became the center of government and was continuously enlarged between 1667 and 1710. Bernini submitted designs for enlarging the Louvre in Paris, but Claude Perrault (1613–88) was finally awarded that commission (executed 1667–79).

The dome and paired columns of the Church of Les Invalides, Paris (1680–91), by Jules Hardouin-Mansart, exemplify French baroque architecture.
J. & M. Williamson–Air France

French architecture of *le grand siècle* lacks the exuberance of Italian baroque, but its designers achieved the epitome of elegance.

English Baroque Architecture. In England the rebuilding of London after the 1666 fire brought to prominence the many-talented Sir Christopher Wren, whose masterpiece is Saint Paul's Cathedral (1675–1710). He also designed or influenced the design of many other English churches. Among other innovations, Wren introduced the single square tower belfry with tall spire that became the hallmark of church architecture in England and the U.S.

Baroque Urban Design. Baroque thinking powerfully addressed the area of urban design. Michelangelo's Campidoglio (Capitol, 1538–64) in Rome had already provided a model for the public square, and villas such as Vignola's Villa Farnese (begun 1539) in Caprarola showed how these important buildings could extend axial ties into the townscape. Baroque church facades frequently had more to do with their accompanying piazzas than with the church interiors. Often, whole new towns were built on formal principles. Early in the 18th century Peter the Great brought Italian and French baroque architects to Russia to create Saint Petersburg. In the New World were built such large urban centers as Mexico City; Santiago, Chile; Antigua, Guatemala; Philadelphia; Savannah, Ga.; and Washington, D.C. *See* BAROQUE ART AND ARCHITECTURE.

Rococo Architecture. When Louis XIV died (1715), changes in the artistic climate led to the exuberant rococo style (q.v.). Once again the work of Italians—notably Guarini and Filippo Juvarra—provided the basis for a new thrust. The expression of royal grandeur has survived in Paris's Place de la Concorde (begun 1753) by Jacques Ange Gabriel and the great axis and plazas (1751–59) by Héré de Corny (1705–63) at Nancy. A more intimate and personal expression appears in Gabriel's Petit Trianon (1762-64) at Versailles. Rococo came to full flower, however, in Bavaria and Austria. The Austrian Benedictine Abbey (1748–54) at Ottobeuren by Johann Michael Fischer (1692–1766) is only one of a brilliant series of spectacular churches, monasteries, and palaces that includes Balthasar Neumann's opulent Vierzehnheiligen (Church of the Fourteen Saints, 1743–72) near Bamberg, Germany, and the Amalienburg Pavilion (1734–39) by the Flemish-born Bavarian architect François de Cuvilliés (1695–1768) in the park at Nymphenburg near Munich.

The many elaborate colonial churches found throughout Central and South America attest to the power and influence of the Roman Catholic church during baroque and rococo times. They include cathedrals in Mexico City, Guanajuato, and Oaxaca, Mexico; Antigua, Guatemala; Quito, Ecuador; Ouro Preto, Brazil; and Cuzco, Peru; as well as such northern missions as Sant' Xavier del Bac in Tucson, Ariz., and the chain of missions on the California coast. The Spanish architect José Churriguera developed an extremely elaborate decorative style that, transferred to Latin America and somewhat debased, was given the name Churrigueresque. *See* LATIN AMERICAN ART AND ARCHITECTURE.

Neoclassical Architecture. In many countries of northern Europe the elegance and dignity attainable through adherence to classic rules of composition retained appeal, while in central and southern Europe and Scandinavia, baroque and rococo ran their course. In England, the duke of Marlborough's great Blenheim Palace, designed

(1705) by Sir John Vanbrugh, emulated in rougher and reduced form the grandeur of Versailles.

A renewed interest in Palladio and his follower Inigo Jones emerged. Development of the resort city of Bath gave opportunities to John Wood and his son to apply Palladian classicism to the design of Queen's Square (1728), the Circus (1754–70), and finally the great Royal Crescent (1767–75), in all of which the individual houses were made to conform to an encompassing classic order. Robert Adam popularized classicism, expressing it notably through delicate stucco ornamentation. Historical scholarship became more precise, and true Greek architecture—including such pure examples of Doric as the Parthenon—became known to architects through the 1762 publication by James Stuart (1713–88) and Nicholas Revett (1720–1804) of *Antiquities of Athens.* These developments reinforced the grip of neoclassicism in England, and the resulting type of architecture became popularly known as the Georgian style (q.v.).

In what was to become the northeastern U.S., Peter Harrison (1716–75) and Samuel McIntyre (1757–1811) took their cues from English architects in their own version of Georgian architecture, which was called Federal after the U.S. won independence. In the Southeast, with an aristocracy predominantly rural, Thomas Jefferson, Benjamin Latrobe, and others derived their building style more directly from Palladio. Jefferson, whose early virtuosity had been demonstrated in Monticello (1770–84), was also moved by ancient Rome, and placed a version (1817–26) of the Pantheon at the head of his magnificent Lawn at the University of Virginia. *See* NEOCLASSICAL ART AND ARCHITECTURE.

THE INDUSTRIAL AGE

The Industrial Revolution, which began in England about 1760, led to radical changes at every level of civilization throughout the world. The growth of heavy industry brought a flood of new building materials—such as cast iron, steel, and glass—with which architects and engineers devised structures hitherto undreamed of in function, size, and form.

ECLECTIC REVIVALS

Disenchantment with baroque, with rococo, and even with neo-Palladianism turned late 18th-century designers and patrons toward the original Greek and Roman prototypes. Selective borrowing from another time and place became fashionable. Its Greek aspect was particularly strong in the young U.S. from the early years of the 19th century until about 1850. New settlements were given Greek names—Syracuse, Ithaca, Troy—and Doric and Ionic columns, entablatures, and pediments, mostly transmuted into white-painted wood, were applied to public buidings and important town houses in the style called Greek Revival (q.v.).

In France, the imperial cult of Napoleon steered architecture in a more Roman direction, as seen in the Church of the Madeleine (1807–42), a huge Roman temple in Paris. French architectural thought had been jolted at the turn of the century by the highly imaginative published projects of Étienne Louis Boullée (1728–99) and Claude Nicholas Ledoux (1736–1806). These men were inspired by the massive aspects of Egyptian and Roman work, but their monumental (and often impractical) compositions were innovative, and they are admired today as visionary architects.

The most original architect in England at the time was Sir John Soane; the museum he built as his own London house (1812–13) still excites astonishment for its inventive romantic virtuosity. Late English neoclassicism came to be seen as elitist; thus, for the new Houses of Parliament the authorities insisted on Gothic or Tudor Revival. The appointed architect, Sir Charles Barry, was not a Gothic expert, but he called into consultation an architect who was—A. W. N. Pugin, who became responsible for the details of this

Three crescents of stately Georgian row houses by John Wood and his son form the open green Circus in Bath, England. They are an outstanding example of 18th-century urban design. Judith Aronson–Peter Arnold, Inc.

vast monument (begun 1836). Pugin, in a short and contentious career, made a moral issue out of a return to the Gothic style. Other architects, however, felt free to select whatever elements from past cultures best fitted their programs—Gothic for Protestant churches, baroque for Roman Catholic churches, early Greek for banks, Palladian for institutions, early Renaissance for libraries, and Egyptian for cemeteries.

In the second half of the 19th century dislocations brought about by the Industrial Revolution became overwhelming. Many were shocked by the hideous new urban districts of factories and workers' housing and by the deterioration of public taste among the newly rich. For the new modes of transportation, canals, tunnels, bridges, and railroad stations, architects were employed only to provide a cultural veneer.

The Crystal Palace (1850–51; reconstructed 1852–54) in London, a vast but ephemeral exhibition hall, was the work of Sir Joseph Paxton, a man who had learned how to put iron and glass together in the design of large greenhouses. It demonstrated a hitherto undreamed-of kind of spatial beauty, and in its carefully planned building process, which included prefabricated standard parts, it foreshadowed industrialized building and the widespread use of cast iron and steel. *See* CRYSTAL PALACE.

Also important in its innovative use of metal was the great tower (1887–89) of Alexandre Gustave Eiffel (1832–1923) in Paris. In general, however, the most gifted architects of the time sought escape from their increasingly industrialized environment by further development of traditional themes and eclectic styles. Two contrasting but equally brilliantly conceived examples are Charles Garnier's sumptuous Paris Opéra (1861–75) and Henry Hobson Richardson's grandiose Trinity Church (1872–77) in Boston.

MODERN ARCHITECTURE

At the turn of the century, designers appeared who refused to work in borrowed styles. Antoni Gaudí in Barcelona, Spain, was the most original; his sinuous Casa Milá (1905–7) and the unfinished Iglesia di Sagrada Familia (Church of the Holy Family, 1883–1926) exhibit a search for new organic structural forms. His work has some affinity with the movement called Art Nouveau (q.v.), which had been inaugurated contemporaneously in Brussels and Paris. Charles Rennie Mackintosh, whose masterpiece is the Glasgow School of Art (1898–99), espoused a more austere version of Art Nouveau.

The Skyscraper. The Chicago architect Louis Sullivan, in his Wainwright Building (1890–91) in Saint Louis, Mo., his Guaranty Building (1895) in Buffalo, N.Y., and his Carson Pirie Scott Department Store (1899–1904) in Chicago, gave new expressive form to urban commercial buildings. His career converges with the so-called Chicago school (q.v.) of architects, whose challenge was to invent the skyscraper or high-rise building, facilitated by the introduction of the electric elevator and the sudden abundance of steel. They made a successful transition from the masonry bearing wall to the steel frame, which assumed all the load-bearing functions. The building's skeleton could be erected quickly and the remaining components hung on it to complete it, an immense advantage for high-rise buildings on busy city streets. Sullivan is memorable not only for his own work but for having provided the apprenticeship of Frank Lloyd Wright, America's greatest native architect, whose career extended 50 years beyond that of Sullivan. *See* AMERICAN ART AND ARCHITECTURE.

Reinforced Concrete. In France attention centered on reinforced concrete. Auguste Perret's apartment building (1902–3) in the Rue Franklin and his Théâtre des Champs-Élysées (1911–12), both in Paris, were early successes. Tony Garnier (1869–1948) had, during his studies in Rome, created a detailed design for an imaginary city with many buildings, all in concrete; its plans were published in 1917 as *La cité industrielle.* Vienna was the scene of work by Otto Wagner and by Adolf Loos, who worked in severe linear forms and proclaimed that "ornament is a crime." Peter Behrens, a founding member of the Deutscher Werkbund (German Craft Alliance), is revered as a German precursor of modern architecture. *See* MODERN ART AND ARCHITECTURE.

The Bauhaus. When the Bauhaus (q.v.) opened, the modern movement in architecture began to coalesce. The Bauhaus school (Weimar, 1919–25; Dessau, 1926–33) brought together architects, painters, and designers from several countries, all determined to formulate goals for the visual arts in the modern age. Its first director was Walter Gropius, who designed the innovative buildings for the move to Dessau; its second was Ludwig Mies van der Rohe. The new architecture demonstrated its virtues in new *Siedlungen* (low-cost housing) in Berlin and Frankfurt. An exhibition of housing types, the Weissenhof *Siedlung* (1927) in Stuttgart, brought together works by Mies, Gropius, the Dutch J. J. P. Oud, and the Swiss-French Le Corbusier; this milestone identified the movement with a better life for the common man. The chastely elegant German Pavilion (1929) by Mies for the Barcelona Exhibition, executed in such lavish materials as travertine, marble, onyx, and chrome-plated steel, asserted a strong, formal ar-

Crown Hall, designed by Ludwig Mies van der Rohe for the Illinois Institute of Technology, Chicago (1950–56), is a masterpiece of the sleek, rectilinear, glass-and-steel International Style. Dan Ryan—IIT

gument independent of any social goals. Gropius, his disciple Marcel Breuer, and Mies eventually established themselves in the U.S., where they enjoyed productive and influential decades—extending through the '70s for Breuer—as architects and teachers.

Le Corbusier, over a long career, exerted immense influence. His early publications championed a machine aesthetic and urged the replacement of traditional cities in favor of life and work in skyscrapers arranged regimentally in vast parks. His Villa Savoie (1929–30) in the French countryside downplays a sense of structure and materials in order to dramatize complexity of spacial organization and allow a subtle ambiguity between interior and exterior space. In the 1950s, with Jawaharlal Nehru as client, he laid out the new capital city of the Punjab, Chandigarh, and designed for it three monumental concrete government edifices standing in a vast plaza. In France he produced two unique religious buildings, the pilgrimage chapel at Ronchamp (1950–55) and the Dominican monastery of La Tourette (1957–61), both in concrete. Having abandoned the extreme rationalism of his early career, he manipulated form and light in these extraordinary structures for emotional response and dramatic effect.

Innovative Architecture. Such structural engineers as the Swiss Robert Maillart (1872–1940), the French Eugène Freyssinet (1879–1962), and the Italian Pier Luigi Nervi produced works in reinforced concrete that combined imagination with rationality to achieve aesthetic impact. Among architects the Danish Jørn Utzon (1918–73), in Australia's Sydney Opera House (1957–73), and the Finnish-American Eero Saarinen, in Dulles Airport (1960–62) near Washington, D.C., employed unusual structural solutions. From his base in Helsinki, the Finnish architect Alvar Aalto extended his oeuvre through more than four decades, refusing to celebrate the industrialized repetition of steel, concrete, glass, and aluminum, but molding spaces with utmost sophistication, great care in the distribution of light, and the use of materials—stone, wood, and copper—with familiar and sympathetic tactile qualities. The American Louis I. Kahn infused his designs with a transcendent monumentality recalling Roman classicism, as in the transformation of tunnel vaults into light-modulating girders in his Kimbell Art Museum (1972), located in Fort Worth, Tex.

The International Style. Despite these noteworthy exceptions—including such later works of Wright as New York City's Guggenheim Museum (completed 1959)—the style initiated by the Bauhaus architects and termed the International Style (q.v.) gradually prevailed after the 1930s. The theory and practice of the new style was introduced in the U.S. largely through the efforts of Philip Johnson, one of Gropius's students at Harvard University. In the hands of its most gifted exponents, such as Mies, the International Style was particularly well suited to large metropolitan apartment and office towers. The chaste elegance and subtle proportions of Mies's Lake Shore Drive Apartments (1951) in Chicago and (with Philip Johnson) his Seagram Building (1958) in New York City represent modernism at its finest. Many of his imitators, however, seized on its commercial potential; it proved extremely efficient for large-scale construction, in which the same module could be repeated indefinitely. Inner spaces became standardized, predictable, and profitable, and exteriors reflected the monotony of the interiors; the blank glass box became ubiquitous.

Assessing modernism after a half century in which it was dominant, commentators pointed out that even though it was embraced by big business and big government, the lay public never grew fond of it. At most an austere classicism was conceded to it, but this was achieved in a coldly impersonal and often overwhelming way. Modernism had cut off architecture's roots in the past by about 1930. Suddenly it became incorrect for a new building to show any resemblance to old ones; and for a period of time the study of historical styles almost disappeared from professional schools.

Postmodern Architecture. Between about 1965 and 1980 architects and critics began to espouse tendencies for which there is as yet no better designation than *postmodern.* Although postmodernism is not a cohesive movement based on a distinct set of principles, as was modernism, in general it can be said that the postmodernists value individuality, intimacy, complexity, and occasionally even humor.

Postmodern tendencies were given early expression in *Complexity and Contradiction in Architecture* (1966; rev. ed. 1977) by the American architect Robert Venturi (1925–). In this provocative work he defended vernacular architecture—for example, gas stations and fast-food restaurants—and attacked the modernist establishment with such satiric comments as "Less is a bore" (a play on Mies's well-known dictum "Less is more"). By the early 1980s, postmodernism had become the dominant trend in American architecture and an important phenomenon in Europe as well. Its success in the U.S. owed much to the influence of Philip Johnson, who had performed the same service for modernism 50 years earlier. His AT&T Building (1984) in New York City, with its Renaissance allusions and its pediment evoking Chippendale furniture, immediately became a landmark of postmodern design.

Other postmodern office towers built during the 1980s aspired to a similar high stylistic profile, recalling the great Art Deco skyscrapers of the 1920s and '30s or striving for an eccentric flamboyance of their own. Vivid color and other decorative elements were effectively used by Michael Graves (1934–) in several notable buildings, while Richard Meier (1934–) developed a more austere version of postmodernism, influenced by Le Corbusier, in his designs for museums and private houses. Outstanding American practitioners of postmodernism, in addition to Venturi, Johnson, Graves, and Meier, are Helmut Jahn (1940–), Charles Gwathmey (1938–), Charles Willard Moore (1925–), and Robert A. M. Stern (1939–).

Closely related to the postmodernist interest in historical styles was the historic preservation movement, which during the 1970s and '80s led to the renovation of many landmark older buildings and to a tendency to resist new architecture that seemed to threaten the scale or stylistic integrity of existing structures. The stark, confrontational approach of modernism has been replaced by a more inclusive sense of the architectural heritage that acknowledges and seeks to preserve the very finest achievements of every period.

For additional information on individual architects and designers, see biographies of those whose names are not followed by dates. *See also* AFRICAN ART AND ARCHITECTURE; CANADIAN ART AND ARCHITECTURE; INTERIOR DESIGN; OCEANIAN ART AND ARCHITECTURE; SEVEN WONDERS OF THE WORLD. L.B.A.

For further information on this topic, see the Bibliography in volume 28, sections 660–63; 676–79.

ARCH AND VAULT, a fundamental construction system in architecture used to span the space between walls, piers, or other supports and to create a roof or a ceiling. Until the 19th century the arch and vault were the only alternative to the far more limited and simpler post-and-lintel system supporting a flat or peaked beamed roof.

Arch. An arch, in construction, is a rigid span curving upward between two points of support. It appears in a variety of structures, such as an arcade (q.v.), formed by a row of arches, supported by load-bearing arches or a roof or a bridge, or as a single, freestanding triumphal or

MAJOR TYPES OF ARCH AND VAULT

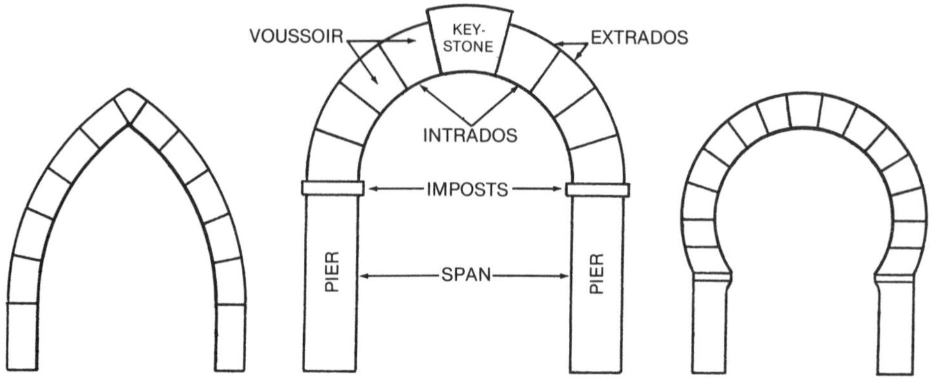

GOTHIC (POINTED) ARCH

ROUND (ROMAN) ARCH

HORSESHOE (ISLAMIC) ARCH

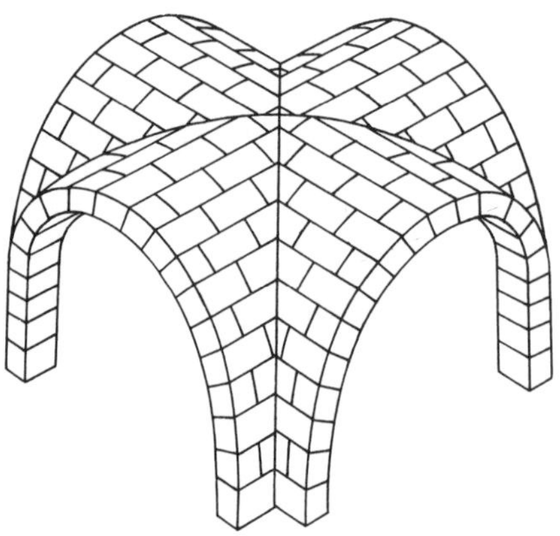

BARREL VAULT

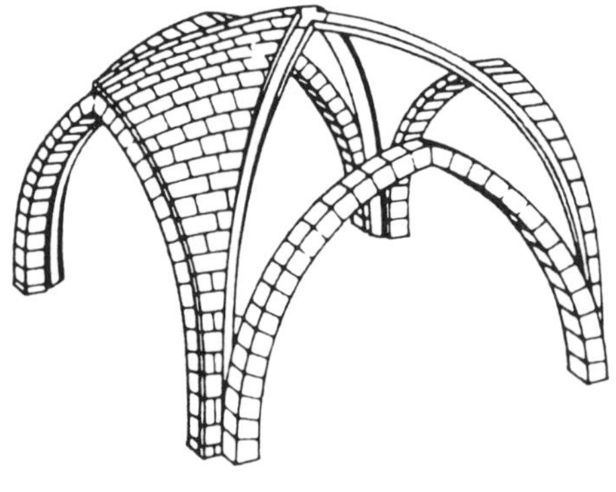

GOTHIC RIBBED VAULT

memorial arch. The traditional stone or brick arch, formed of many segments held in place by lateral thrust, was developed to connect a greater distance between two supports than a single horizontal beam, or lintel, could bridge. Since the 19th century, arches have also been made of single, curved spans of iron, steel, or reinforced concrete.

The masonry arch has many elements. Its supports may be walls, piers, or columns, and the capstones from which it springs are known as imposts. The upper part of the arch is the crown, the portions near the impost are the haunches, its wedge-shaped segments are voussoirs, and the central or crowning voussoir is the keystone. The inner edge of the arch is the intrados; the outer edge, the extrados; and the undersurface, the soffit. The molded band that often is found around the opening of the arch is the archivolt. The wall spaces on either side of an arch, or between adjacent arches, are spandrels. If the space between the arch and the lintel is filled in, the resulting flat surface is the tympanum.

Arches have been built since prehistoric times. Rude prototypes were made by leaning two slabs of rock together or by constructing a stepped, or corbeled, arch in which projecting elements from a wall rise in steps from the supports to meet in the center. The Egyptians, Babylonians, and Greeks used the arch, generally for secular structures, such as storerooms and sewers. The Assyrians built palaces with arched ceilings, and the Etruscans used arches in bridges, passageways, and gates. The Romans, however, were the first to develop the arch on a massive scale. They used the semicircular arch freely in secular structures such as amphitheaters, palaces, and aqueducts, but their temples usually had the post-and-lintel construction of Greek temples. The few vaulted exceptions, however, include the Pantheon (q.v.) in Rome.

During the Middle Ages, Byzantine architecture in the East and Romanesque architecture in the West retained the characteristic round Roman arch. Islamic architects developed a rich variety of pointed, scalloped, horseshoe, and ogee (S-curve) arches for mosques and palaces. In Moorish Spain, horseshoe arches were set on delicate columns, giving a characteristic airy effect. Gothic architecture in Western Europe was characterized by the pointed arch, which minimized outward thrust and thus made possible higher, thinner, window-filled walls, creating the lofty, spacious interiors of Gothic cathedrals. In the 20th century, arches of molded reinforced concrete based on the curve of a parabola have been used in all sorts of public structures.

Vault. A vault, in architecture, is an arch-shaped structure, usually of masonry, used as the ceiling of a room or other enclosed space, as the roof of a building, or as the support for a ceiling or roof. Masonry vaults are usually composed of wedge-shaped pieces called voussoirs, which are held in place, like the stones of an arch, by the pressure of the neighboring pieces. Because of the combined pressure of its components, any arch exerts an outward pressure at its base, and the base, therefore, must be so constructed as to withstand the outward as well as the downward thrust of the arch. This construction can be accomplished by using strong, heavy walls to support the arch or by supporting the walls with exterior structures, or buttresses. A temporary supporting structure must be erected within the vaulted area during construction, because a masonry vault does not become self-supporting until the central voussoirs or keystones are put in place.

A number of different types of vaults are used architecturally. The simplest of these is the barrel, or tunnel, vault, the roof of which is shaped like half a cylinder and is supported by straight walls. The annular vault is similar to the barrel vault, except that the passage within it is not straight but curved, giving the entire structure the appearance of a portion of a ring. A groined vault is formed by the intersection of two vaults of the barrel type, usually at right angles to each other. The junctures at which the two vaults meet are elliptical ridges, called groins. In the simplest form of groined vault, the two conjoined vaults are of the same size and the floor of the vault is square; if the vaults are of different sizes, however, the floor of the vault is rectangular and the two areas of the ceiling between the groins are of unequal shape and size.

A dome (q.v.) is a spherical vault resting on a circular base wall. Pendentives are portions of spherical vaults, or spherical triangles, placed in the corners of square or other polygonal structures to form a circular base for a dome above. More complicated vaults include ribbed vaults,

Horseshoe-shaped brick arches, characteristic of Islamic architecture, give an airy effect in the 9th-century Grand Mosque in Kairouan, Tunisia. They rest on older Roman columns. Tunisian National Tourist Office

in which the inner vault surface is subdivided by a number of independent supporting arches, or ribs. A further refinement is the fan vault, most common in English late Gothic structures, in which the ribs are multiplied and grouped in the shape of an open fan.

See also ARCHITECTURE; GOTHIC ART AND ARCHITECTURE; ISLAMIC ART AND ARCHITECTURE; ROMAN ART AND ARCHITECTURE; ROMANESQUE ART AND ARCHITECTURE.

ARCIMBOLDO, Giuseppe (c. 1530–93), Italian Mannerist painter, whose witty allegorical compositions foreshadowed 20th-century surrealist art. He began as a designer of stained glass and tapestry in his native Milan; in 1562 he moved to Prague and then to Vienna, where he became painter to the Habsburg court. Arcimboldo invented a portrait type consisting of painted foliage, flowers, fruit, and the like composed to form a human likeness. Some are satiric portraits of court personages, and others are allegorical personifications.

ARCTIC, THE *or* **ARCTIC REGIONS,** large, cold area around the North Pole. The Arctic is not a clearly defined area: It includes the Arctic Ocean (q.v.), many islands, and parts of the mainlands of North America, Asia, and Europe.

Scientists define the Arctic in three major ways—first, as the area N of the Arctic Circle (lat 66°30′ N); second, as the region N of the 10° C (50° F) summer isotherm—on a map, a line drawn through locations with an average annual temperature of 0° C (32° F) or less and a mean temperature for the warmest summer month of 10° C (50° F); and third, as the region N of the tree line—on a map, a line connecting points beyond which trees do not grow. The second and third definitions enclose roughly the same territory, which is somewhat larger than the region bounded by the Arctic Circle, and will be used as the basis for this article.

The largest Arctic land areas are in Canada, Russia, Greenland (Kalâtdlit-Nunât), Scandinavia, Iceland, Alaska, and Svalbard and other islands.

THE NATURAL ENVIRONMENT

Unlike Antarctica, an ice-covered continental plateau surrounded by oceans, the Arctic has a central ocean almost enclosed by land. One large gap exists between Greenland and Scandinavia, and much smaller breaks are among the Canadian Arctic Islands and at the Bering Strait, which separates Alaska and Siberia.

The principal geological elements of the Arctic include parts of three ancient landmasses, composed predominantly of granite and gneiss, which are called shields—the Baltic-Scandinavian-Russian Shield, the Angara Shield or Siberian Platform (in N central Siberia), and the Canadian Shield (including all the Canadian Arctic except for the Queen Elizabeth Islands). Several regions, such as most of Greenland, are permanently ice covered, and extensive coastal plains are along much of N Siberia, parts of the NW mainland and islands of Canada, and the North Slope of Alaska. Mountain ranges are in the E Arctic region of Canada (notably on Baffin Island), in Yukon Territory, in N Alaska, in coastal Greenland, in Iceland, and in NE Siberia.

Rivers and Lakes. Low precipitation is characteristic of the Arctic, so large and elaborate river and lake systems are rare. In many places, however, permafrost (permanently frozen subsoil) restricts the downward drainage of meltwater from snow, and the water accumulates on the surface as shallow lakes, ponds, and marshes. In addition, rivers from more humid regions flow seaward across the dry Arctic terrain. Several large rivers are in the Russian Arctic, and the Mackenzie and Yukon rivers are in North America.

Climate. Winter in the Arctic is long and cold, and summer is short and cool. The Arctic Circle marks the border of a zone in which the sun never rises during at least one day in winter and never sets during at least one day in summer. The number of days when the sun is or is not visible during the entire day increases toward the N. Latitude, which determines the length of daylight, influences climate, but nearby areas contrast sharply. For instance, on the Greenland ice cap average midwinter temperatures are −33° C (−27.4° F), whereas adjacent coastal settlements, the climate of which is moderated by the relatively warm ocean, typically have a mean temperature of −7° C (19.4° F) in the same period. The North Pole is not the coldest spot in the Arctic, because its climate is moderated by the ocean. Oymyakon, in NE Siberia, holds the record low temperature of −68° C (−90.4° F). The coldest recorded temperature for North America is −65° C (−85° F), at Snag, in Yukon Territory. The characteristically low precipitation averages less than 250 mm (less than 10 in) per year, the moisture being received in almost all locations. Despite their distance from industrialized areas, the polar regions are sometimes blanketed by a smoglike haze.

See also AURORA.

Vegetation and Wildlife. The Arctic is not a frozen desert devoid of life on land or sea, even during the cold, dark winter months. Spring brings a phenomenal resurgence of plant and animal life. Low temperatures are not always the critical element—moisture, the type of soil, and available solar energy are also extremely important. Some

A tongue of the huge continental glacier that blankets the island of Greenland flows slowly toward the Arctic Ocean. Francisco Erize–Bruce Coleman, Inc.

animals adapt well to Arctic conditions; for instance, a number of species of mammals and birds carry additional insulation, such as fat, in cold months.

The Arctic has more than 400 species of flowering plants. The vast stretches of tundra that cover the plains and coastal regions consist of low creeping shrubs, grasses, thick growths of lichens and mosses, and herbs and sedges.

Abundant animal life inhabits the Arctic, both on land and in the sea. Arctic mammals include polar bear, Arctic fox, ermine, marten, Arctic wolf, wolverine, walrus, seal, caribou, reindeer (domesticated caribou), musk-ox, lemming, Arctic hare, and many species of whale.

Birds are plentiful throughout the Arctic Regions. The guillemot and little auk nest by the thousands along cliffs. Ravens, snow buntings, and sandpipers have been seen in the remotest N land regions, as have the snowy owl and the gyrfalcon. Various species of gull, including the jaeger, also range far to the N. Among other characteristic Arctic birds are the eider duck, teal, loon, petrel, puffin, and ptarmigan. Insects, found in the Arctic wherever vegetation exists, include bees and wasps, flies, butterflies and moths, beetles, and grasshoppers. Coastal waters are relatively rich in such fish as cod, flatfish, halibut, salmon, and trout. A large variety of invertebrates have been observed in Arctic seas.

Mineral Resources. Large deposits of several important minerals occur in the Arctic Regions. Among them are petroleum and natural gas, iron ore, nickel, lead, zinc, coal, uranium, tin, diamonds, gold, and cryolite.

THE PEOPLE

Long before Europeans reached the Arctic, much of the region had a scattered population; Iceland was a notable exception. The indigenous peoples were of many ethnic groups, using various languages, but all had originated in Asia. They had migrated for thousands of years. The Inuit (Eskimo) had eventually reached the Atlantic Ocean in E Greenland, and the Lapps (Saami) had reached Norway.

In the Arctic areas of Russia today exist about 20 national groups. These include the Komi, or Zyrian, numbering about 250,000 and occupying Arctic areas of European Russia; the Yakut, numbering about 300,000 and living mainly in the Lena R. Basin; the Tungus, numbering about 70,000 and inhabiting a large region E of the Yenisey R.; the Yukaghir, numbering about 1000 and dwelling chiefly between the Yana and Indigirka rivers; and the Chukchi, numbering about 15,000 and inhabiting extreme NE Siberia. In the Arctic areas of North America are three main ethnic groups—the Aleut, Indians, and Inuit—of which about 65,000 live in N Canada and about 51,000 in Alaska. The Aleut mostly inhabit the region of the Bering Sea; the Indians generally occupy grasslands; and the Inuit live mainly in N Alaska, N Canada, and coastal areas of Greenland.

All the indigenous residents of the Arctic originally depended entirely on hunting or fishing, or both, and employed natural materials for their

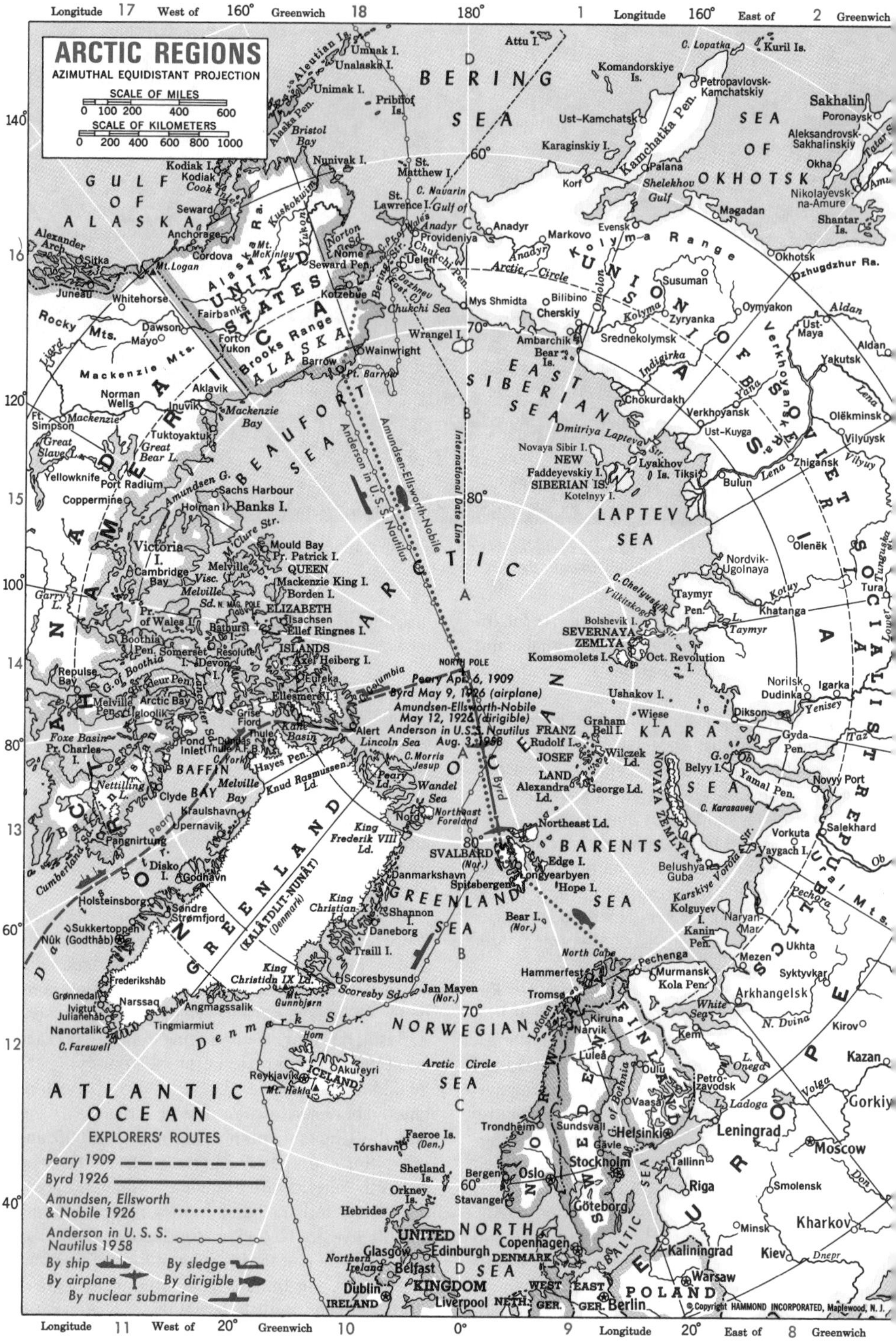
ARCTIC REGIONS
AZIMUTHAL EQUIDISTANT PROJECTION
SCALE OF MILES
0 100 200 400 600
SCALE OF KILOMETERS
0 200 400 600 800 1000
Longitude 17 West of 160° Greenwich 18 180° 1 Longitude 160° East of 2 Greenwich
Longitude 11 West of 20° Greenwich 10 0° 9 Longitude 20° East of 8 Greenwich
BERING SEA
SEA OF OKHOTSK
GULF OF ALASKA
BEAUFORT SEA
EAST SIBERIAN SEA
LAPTEV SEA
ARCTIC OCEAN
KARA SEA
BARENTS SEA
GREENLAND SEA
NORWEGIAN SEA
NORTH SEA
BALTIC SEA
ATLANTIC OCEAN
UNITED STATES
CANADA
ALASKA
GREENLAND (KALÂTDLIT-NUNÂT) (Denmark)
UNION OF SOVIET SOCIALIST REPUBLICS
EUROPE
ICELAND
NORWAY
SWEDEN
FINLAND
UNITED KINGDOM
IRELAND
POLAND
NORTH POLE
Peary Apr. 6, 1909
Byrd May 9, 1926 (airplane)
Amundsen-Ellsworth-Nobile May 12, 1926 (dirigible)
Anderson in U.S.S. Nautilus Aug. 3, 1958
International Date Line
Arctic Circle
EXPLORERS' ROUTES
Peary 1909
Byrd 1926
Amundsen, Ellsworth & Nobile 1926
Anderson in U. S. S. Nautilus 1958
By ship
By sledge
By airplane
By dirigible
By nuclear submarine
© Copyright HAMMOND INCORPORATED, Maplewood, N. J.

INDEX TO MAP OF ARCTIC REGIONS

Their spring migration completed, nomadic Lapps from Kautokeino, in northern Norway, make summer camp beside the Arctic Ocean. B & C Alexander–Bruce Coleman, Inc.

clothing, tools, homes, and vehicles. Articles were well designed and skillfully made, and some were artistically decorated. Well known are the Inuit kayak, parka, and harpoon.

The Arctic has also been settled by persons from more S areas. Norwegians and Russians reached the seacoast of N Europe about 1100 years ago, when the Norse were also settling Iceland. In recent times, scientists, miners, and missionaries have established communities in the Arctic Regions.

In the Arctic areas of Alaska, Canada, and Greenland are no large cities, the biggest generally having fewer than 10,000 inhabitants. In the Arctic regions of Scandinavia and Russia, however, are several communities of considerable size, such as Murmansk and Norilsk, in Russia, and Tromsø, in Norway. Reykjavík, Iceland, is an important urban center.

PATTERNS OF ECONOMIC DEVELOPMENT

Economic activity in most of the Arctic Regions is limited to obtaining and processing natural resources, especially fish and minerals.

Agriculture. The Arctic environment is generally unfavorable to the production of food by cultivation or animal husbandry. Reindeer herding, however, is important in N Scandinavia and Russia and to a lesser extent in the Arctic areas of Alaska, Canada, and Greenland. Sheep are raised in SW Greenland and in Iceland. Dairy farming to supply nearby communities is widespread; almost 1 million cattle are in northern Russia alone.

Fishing. Fish taken from rivers and lakes are important for the diet of people living in the Arctic Regions. Russia has highly developed river fisheries serving the local population as well as customers in distant cities. The Arctic Ocean is among the world's most important fishing grounds, and many countries send fishing boats to it. Large amounts of cod and shrimp are caught off W Greenland.

Mining. The recovery of minerals is an important industry in several parts of the Arctic Regions. In Russia, nickel, iron ore, and apatite are produced on the Kola Peninsula, and diamonds are mined in the Lena R. valley. Other major mineral products in the Russian Arctic include gold, tin, coal, mica, and tungsten. Sweden has produced iron ore at Kiruna and elsewhere N of the Arctic Circle since about 1900, and Norway has an important iron-ore mine on its N coast at Kirkenes.

Lead, zinc, and molybdenum are produced in Greenland, which formerly recovered much cryolite at Ivigtut. Large coal mines are on Spitsbergen, one of the islands of Svalbard. Mineral products of the Canadian Arctic include uranium, copper, nickel, lead, zinc, asbestos, iron ore, petroleum, and natural gas. Large-scale production of petroleum on the Arctic North Slope of Alaska began in 1977. A proposal in 1987 by the Reagan administration to open up the Arctic National Wildlife Refuge to oil development met with strong opposition from various environmental organizations.

Manufacturing. The North American Arctic is not of major manufacturing importance, except for raw-material processing. Costs of labor and transportation are too high for general manufacturing. Russia, however, has several important industrial areas in the N. These include the Kola Peninsula, the Pechora R. valley, the Yenisey R. valley, and the Lena R. valley near Yakutsk. Raw materials are processed in the Canadian Arctic, and Greenland and Iceland have a variety of small-scale manufacturing industries.

Transportation. Land and water transportation in the Arctic Regions are handicapped by year-round or seasonal obstruction by ice. Few roads serve the area, although some important arteries are in mainland Canada, in northern Russia, and in N parts of Norway and Sweden. Coastal shipping is significant in several regions of the Arctic, notably in Russia, Scandinavia, Alaska, and Canada. Icebreakers clear shipping lanes in winter. Russia has a good river navigation system in summer. Air transportation is of great importance. Airports serve several communities, and "bush" airlines link isolated communities and mining operations with larger centers.

EXPLORATION OF THE ARCTIC REGIONS

The Greeks of the 4th century BC were aware of the Arctic Regions, parts of which had by then been settled by Inuit and Indians. Early in the 9th century AD, Irish monks established a colony in Iceland. Vikings (q.v.), or Norsemen, from Scandinavia reached there later in the century. About 982 the Norse explorer Eric the Red sighted and named Greenland. During the next four centuries, Norsemen probably visited the Canadian Arctic.

Subsequent Arctic exploration was largely motivated by the European need for sea routes to the Orient—the Northeast Passage (q.v.) along N Asia and the Northwest Passage (q.v.) through the Arctic islands of North America. In 1553 the English navigator Sir Hugh Willoughby (fl. 1528–54) initiated the search for the Northeast Passage. His companion, Richard Chancellor (d. 1556), reached the site of modern Arkhangelsk (Eng. Archangel), on the White Sea, thus opening a new route to commerce.

The search for the Northwest Passage began when the English explorer Sir Martin Frobisher reached the Canadian Arctic in 1576; in 1587 John Davis sailed through part of what became known as Davis Strait, between Greenland and Baffin Island. In 1610 Henry Hudson sighted the bay that was later named for him; it was explored in 1612–13 by Sir Thomas Button (fl. 1612–34) from Wales. William Baffin, an Englishman, explored what came to be called Baffin Bay in 1616, reaching lat 77°45′ N, a record maintained for 200 years.

In the Arctic spring, an Inuit (Eskimo) dogsled makes its way over meltwater and ice floes near Tuktoyaktut, in Canada's Northwest Territories.
Nicholas DeVore III–Bruce Coleman, Inc.

Russian exploration of the coast of the Siberian Arctic was promoted by Czar Peter the Great in the early 18th century. He employed the Danish navigator Vitus Jonassen Bering, who in 1728 discovered the strait that bears his name.

As part of a renewed effort to find the Northwest Passage, the British government in 1818 organized the first of several Arctic explorations under Sir William Edward Parry, who in 1819 reached Melville Island in the Canadian Arctic. In 1845 Sir John Franklin led a British expedition toward the Bering Strait from Lancaster Sound, an arm of Baffin Bay. His two ships were trapped by ice during 1846, and he died the following year. The crews abandoned the ships, and all perished. The tragedy led to many search parties, beginning in 1848. Adolf Erik Nordenskjöld of Sweden, aboard the *Vega,* in 1878–79 became the first to complete the Northeast Passage.

The first official U.S. Arctic expedition, in 1881–82, was part of the first International Polar Year. Under the command of Lt. Adolphus W. Greely, it was based at Lady Franklin Bay, on Ellesmere Island, and made observations on magnetic and meteorological phenomena. In 1884, when relief vessels finally arrived, 17 members of the expedition had perished from cold and starvation.

The Greenland ice cap was crossed for the first time in 1888 by the Norwegian explorer Fridtjof Nansen. In September 1893, Nansen attempted to cross the North Pole in the ship *Fram,* which entered the pack ice near the New Siberian Islands. The vessel attained lat 86°14′ N, short of the North Pole, in August 1896.

Between 1886 and 1909 the American explorer Robert Edwin Peary headed several expeditions to the Arctic by way of Baffin Bay. He reached Cape Morris Jesup (on Greenland), the northernmost land point in the Arctic, in 1900 and on April 21, 1906, during an attempt to reach the North Pole, attained lat 87°6′ N. On April 6, 1909, he finally reached the North Pole by dogsled over pack ice from Grant Land in N Ellesmere Island. Some controversy continues to surround his claim to have reached the Pole. The first voyage by ship through the Northwest Passage was accomplished in 1903–6 by the Norwegian explorer Roald Amundsen.

In 1906 the Canadian-born American anthropologist Vilhjalmur Stefansson lived with the Inuit near the Mackenzie R. delta. Between 1908 and 1912 Stefansson and Rudolph Anderson (1876–1961) traveled in the Coronation Gulf-Victoria Island area, also to study the Inuit. From 1913 to 1918 Stefansson commanded the Canadian Arctic Expedition, discovering new land in the Arctic Archipelago.

In May 1926 the U.S. explorer Richard E. Byrd, along with the aviator Floyd Bennett, reached the North Pole by airplane. A few days later Amundsen, Lincoln Ellsworth, and Umberto Nobile (1885–1978) completed a flight of more than 70 hours in the dirigible *Norge,* from Spitsbergen (Svalbard), Norway, across the North Pole to Alaska, some 5460 km (about 3390 mi); and in 1928 the Australian explorer Sir George Wilkins flew from Point Barrow, Alaska, to Spitsbergen.

In 1932 the Soviet Union established the Northern Sea Route Administration to open commercial shipping through the Northeast Passage and to develop Siberian resources. Four Soviet scientists led by I. D. Papanin (1894–1986) drifted for nine months in 1937 on NP 1, a small ice floe, studying the ocean, and they subsequently set up temporary scientific stations on the drifting ice. By 1981 the USSR had established about 26 such stations and had also made many briefer landings on the Arctic Ocean ice for scientific purposes. During the summer of 1938, the Soviet pilots V. P. Chkalov (1904–38) and M. M. Gromov (1899–1985) made nonstop flights over the North Pole, to Vancouver, Wash., and to San Jacinto, Calif., in single-engine aircraft.

During World War II, several air bases and meteorological stations were established in Alaska, the Canadian Arctic, and Greenland, and in 1947 a scientific station was founded at Point Barrow,

Robert E. Peary and his dogs aboard the Roosevelt *during an expedition in 1905–6 to reach the North Pole.*
UPI

Alaska. In 1951 the U.S. Navy undertook Project Ski Jump in the Beaufort Sea, making many sea-ice landings. The first U.S. station on drifting ice was established early in 1952 by Joseph O. Fletcher (1920–).

Travel under the ice, long foreseen by Stefansson and Wilkins, became a reality in 1958, when the nuclear-powered USS *Nautilus* became the first submarine to traverse the Arctic Ocean. It went from the Bering Strait to Iceland via the North Pole in four days. Scientific activity in the Arctic Regions increased greatly during the International Geophysical Year (IGY) of 1957–58. The program involved several nations, which together operated more than 300 stations.

By the late 1970s, traditional exploration had been largely replaced by systematic data gathering and scientific research. Access had been greatly improved by airplane, submarine, icebreaker, and new overland transportation methods, and earth satellites and automatic instruments had taken over much of the task of routine information collecting. The centennial of the *Vega* voyage of 1878–79 was marked by a major research program by the Swedish icebreaker *Ymer* and an international scientific team working between the Barents Sea and NE Greenland. In the early 1980s, an international team of scientists pursued a long-term study of the Greenland ice cap by analyzing ice cores obtained by drilling from the surface to depths of about 2036 m (about 6680 ft). In 1986, on Axel Heiberg Island in the Canadian Arctic, the largest fossil forest yet found in the Arctic was dated at about 45 million years old, raising interesting questions about changing environmental conditions there in the geological past.

For additional information on individuals mentioned, see biographies of those whose names are not followed by dates.

For further information on this topic, see the Bibliography in volume 28, sections 1252–54.

ARCTIC CIRCLE, parallel of latitude on the surface of the earth at 66°30′ N. It marks the S limit of the area in which the sun does not rise on the winter solstice (about December 21) or set on the summer solstice (about June 21). Periods of continuous day or night increase from one day at the Arctic Circle to six months at the North Pole (*see* SOLSTICE).

ARCTIC OCEAN, variously identified as the smallest of four world oceans or as a virtually landlocked arm of the Atlantic Ocean. It extends from the North Pole S to the shores of Europe, Asia, and North America.

Boundaries and Size. The surface waters of the Arctic Ocean mingle with those of the Pacific Ocean through the Bering Strait, by way of a narrow and shallow channel, which has a depth of about 55 m (about 180 ft). More important is the mixing of Arctic waters with those of the Atlantic Ocean across a system of submarine ridges that span the great distances from S Norway to Greenland and from Greenland to Baffin Island at depths of about 500 to 700 m (about 1640 to 2300 ft). Emptying into the Arctic Ocean are the Ob, Yenisey, and Lena rivers in Asia and the Mackenzie R. in North America. The total surface area of the Arctic Ocean, including its major subdivisions—the North Polar Sea (the main portion), the Norwegian Sea, the North Sea, and the Barents Sea—is about 14 million sq km (about 5.4 million sq mi).

Structural Features. Approximately one-third of the Arctic Ocean is underlain by continental shelf, which includes a broad shelf N of Eurasia and the narrower shelves of North America and Greenland. Seaward of the continental shelves lies the Arctic Basin proper, which is subdivided into a set of three parallel ridges and four basins (or deeps). These features have only been discovered and explored since the late 1940s. The Lomonosov Ridge, the major ridge, cuts the North Polar Sea almost in half, extending as a submarine bridge 1700 km (1060 mi) from Siberia to the NW tip of Greenland. Parallel to it are two shorter ridges: the Alpha Ridge on the North American side, defining the Canada and Makarov basins, and the Mid-Ocean Ridge on the Eurasian side, defining the Nansen and Fram basins. The mean depth of the Arctic Ocean is only about 1500 m (about 4900 ft) because of the vast shallow expanses on the continental shelves. The deepest Arctic sounding is 5450 m (17,880 ft).

Islands. The islands of the Arctic Ocean lie on the continental shelves. To the NE of Norway lies Svalbard (Spitsbergen); to the E are Franz Josef Land, Novaya Zemlya, Severnaya Zemlya, the New Siberian Islands, and Wrangel Island, all of which are located N of Russia. The numerous islands of the Canadian Archipelago extend N and E from the Canadian mainland to Greenland, the largest island of the Arctic Ocean.

Ice. Three forms of ice are found in the Arctic Ocean: land ice, river ice, and sea ice. Land ice enters the ocean in the form of icebergs, which are created (primarily along the coasts of Greenland) when pieces of glaciers break off. The freezing of fresh water, and its subsequent transport into the ocean by rivers, produces nearshore concentrations of river ice over small areas of the Siberian and North American shelves. Sea ice (formed by the freezing of seawater) is the most extensive form of ice in the Arctic Ocean. In winter a permanent cap of sea ice covers all of the ocean surface, except for the area NE of Iceland and N of Scandinavia. In summer the ice cover shrinks to expose narrow bands of relatively open water along the coasts of most of Siberia, Alaska, and Canada. The ice cap is composed of pieces of ice that pile up and are pressed (hence, the name *pack ice*) in ridges or hummocks that may be more than 10 m (33 ft) in depth.

Resources. Fish, in commercially exploitable quantities, are found only in the warmer marginal seas, notably in the North Sea (herring, cod, and flounder) and the Barents Sea (primarily cod). Sea mammals, including various species of seal and whale, were hunted to near extinction before being protected by quotas in the 20th century. Tin is actively mined off the coast of E Siberia, and petroleum and natural gas are extracted N of Alaska and Canada and in the North Sea.

J.P.P.

For further information on this topic, see the Bibliography in volume 28, section 424.

ARCTOTIS, genus of annual plants, of the family Asteraceae (*see* COMPOSITE FLOWERS), native to southern Africa. They are grown in the U.S. in gardens that have good soil and sun. Arctotis blossoms last throughout the summer and autumn. The most common species is *Arctotis stoechadifolia,* also known as the African daisy. It grows to a height of more than 60 cm (24 in) and bears composite flowers up to 7 cm (3 in) in diameter with white rays and blue centers. The flowers close each night and open again the following morning. Two dwarf forms, *A. breviscarpa* and *A. gumbletoni,* have orange flowers.

ARCTURUS, fourth brightest star in the sky, with a visual magnitude (q.v.) of –0.05. An orange star in the northern constellation Boötes, Arcturus is about 40 light-years from the sun. Because it lies relatively nearby, its diameter has been measured; it is about 23 times that of the sun. Arcturus is one of the first stars to have its actual motion in the sky detected, through comparisons with its relative position in ancient charts.

ARDABIL *or* **ARDEBIL,** city, NW Iran, in East Azerbaijan Province. The city is on a plateau about 1525 m (about 5000 ft) above sea level. Because of a healthful climate and the warm mineral springs in the vicinity, Ardabil was a favorite home of the rulers of Persia. Points of interest in the city include the tomb of Ismail I (1486–1524), founder of the Safawid dynasty (1502–1736) of Persian shahs, and the home (now a Muslim shrine) of the Persian saint Safi-al-Din (1252–1334). During the Middle Ages the city was important because it was near the Lenkoran-Tabriz caravan route. Pop. (1986) 281,973.

ARDASHIR I (fl. 3d cent. AD), king of Persia (224–41), founder of the Sassanid dynasty and grandson of Sassan, for whom the dynasty was named. Ardashir's father made himself ruler of a district in Persia as vassal of the Arsacid king of Parthia. After his father's death in 212, Ardashir took over the district, killed his brothers, warred against neighboring vassals, and, in 224, finally defeated the king of Parthia, Artabanus V (r. about 213–24), at the Battle of Hormuz. Ardashir then assumed the title of king of kings and tried to rebuild a unified Persian empire after the model of the ancient Achaemenids. He made Zoroastrianism the national religion, built a new capital at Ctesiphon on the Tigris River, and, on the site of the ancient city of Seleucia, built the city of Weh-Ardashir. His last years were spent in unsuccessful wars against the Roman Empire. He was succeeded by his son, Shapur I (r. 241–72). Worshiped as a god in his own day, Ardashir was later the subject of countless legends among the Persians. His sculptured image, identified by an inscription in the Greek and Pahlavi languages, was found on the site of Persepolis.

ARDASHIR II (fl. 4th century AD), king of Persia (379–83). He was the ruler of Adiabene and became king of Persia at the age of 70. A weak ruler, he was deposed after a quarrel with the court nobles.

ARDASHIR III (621–30), king of Persia (628–30). He became king at the age of seven during a time of trouble after Khosrau II was murdered. Ardashir himself was killed two years later.

ARDENNES, in ancient times, the name given to a vast forest lying between the Rhine and Sambre rivers; in modern times, the name given to a hilly and wooded region extending from France through SE Belgium and the Grand Duchy of Luxembourg to the Rhineland in Germany. The Ardennes region covers most of the French department of Ardennes, most of the Belgian province of Luxembourg, and part of the Grand Duchy of Luxembourg. The hills, sloping gradually in a NW direction toward the plains of Flanders, are rarely above 488 m (1600 ft) high. Large sections of the Ardennes consist of gently undulating plateaus, with oak and beech trees; other areas are marshy and covered with heath. The region is rich in timber and minerals. Large deposits of coal and iron are mined in the NW and are important in the Belgian economy. Lead, antimony, and manganese are also found here. Cattle and sheep are raised extensively.

ARDENNES, BATTLE OF, an inconclusive battle of World War I, fought in the Ardennes region of France. French armies, which had been positioned in the region of Stenay and along the Sambre River to meet the German threat from the east, began an offensive on Aug. 20, 1914. As a result of serious tactical errors, the French Third Army, headed by Gen. Joseph Jacques Césaire Joffre, suffered heavy casualties. The German command failed to take advantage of its superior position, and between August 23 and 25 both the French and German armies withdrew.

ARDMORE, city, seat of Carter Co., S Oklahoma, near the Red R.; inc. 1898. An agricultural trade center and manufacturing hub, with petroleum products, processed foods, motor-vehicle tires, and electronic equipment being produced here. Cultural institutions include the Charles B. Goddard Center for the Visual and Performing Arts, Carter County Historic Museum, and the Eliza Cruce Doll Museum. Ardmore is a gateway to a large recreational area, including Lakes Murray and Texoma and the Arbuckle Mts. The city was founded in 1887 as a railroad station and is named for Ardmore, Pa. Pop. (1980) 23,689; (1990) 23,079.

AREA, in mathematics, the size of an enclosed region, given in terms of the square of a designated unit of length. Formulas for the areas of simple geometric figures include a^2 for a square, where a is a side; ab for a rectangle, where a and b are two adjacent sides; and πr^2 for a circle, where r is the radius.

ARECIBO, town, Arecibo Municipality, N Puerto Rico, a port of entry on the Atlantic Ocean at the mouth of the Río Grande de Arecibo; chartered as a town 1616. The town is a commercial, manufacturing, and shipping center. Products include rum, refined sugar, machinery, and clothing. The Inter-American University of Puerto Rico Arecibo Branch (1957) is here. One of the world's largest fixed-radio telescopes is located S of the town, and several hydroelectric facilities are nearby. The community was settled in 1556. Pop. (1980) 48,779; (1990) 49,545.

ARECIBO OBSERVATORY, large, stationary radio telescope, with attendant facilities, that is part of Cornell University's National Astronomy and Ionosphere Center. The telescope, located 15 km (9 mi) south of Arecibo on the northern coast of Puerto Rico, is a bowl-shaped dish set into a natural hollow. The dish, 305 m (1000 ft) wide, consists of nearly 40,000 individual reflecting panels attached to a network of steel cables. The panels focus incoming radio waves from outer space onto a detecting platform suspended above the dish. The platform can be adjusted to enable the telescope to observe the sky from 43° north to 6° south. It can also transmit signals and has been used for radar-reflection studies of the moon. A smaller radio telescope, used along with the main dish for interferometric studies, is located north of the observatory; it is 30 m (98 ft) wide.

The observatory was completed by Cornell University in 1963 and is operated under contract with the National Science Foundation. The telescope is used for studying the earth's upper and middle atmospheres as well as radio sources in deep space. It has also been used to search for radio signals that would indicate the existence of extraterrestrial life. *See* EXOBIOLOGY; RADAR ASTRONOMY; RADIO ASTRONOMY.

ARENDT, Hannah (1906–75), German-born American political philosopher, noted for her writings on totalitarianism and the Jews.

Arendt was born in Hannover, on Oct. 14, 1906. After studies at three universities, she received her Ph.D. degree from the University of Heidelberg at the age of 22. In 1933 she went to France to escape the Nazis and then, in 1941, fled to the U.S., becoming a naturalized U.S. citizen in 1951. In New York City she worked as an editor and held key positions in several Jewish organizations. Following the publication of her widely acclaimed *Origins of Totalitarianism* (1951), Arendt became a university professor and lecturer at such schools as the University of California at Berkeley, Princeton University, and the University of Chicago. She died in New York City on Dec. 4, 1975. Among her many other writings are *The Human Condition* (1958) and *Eichmann in Jerusalem* (1963).

AREOPAGUS, name of both a low, rocky hill west of the Acropolis in Athens and of an ancient court that convened there. The court, a council of nobles, met in the open; accuser and accused stood on platforms cut from the rock.

The Areopagus could call any government official to testify, and, because decisions of the court were final, its indirect power over the state is thought to have been considerable. Under the Athenian lawgiver Draco (fl. 650–621 BC), the Areopagus heard cases of murder. Another Athenian lawgiver, Solon, initiated a constitution in the 6th century BC that empowered the court to try officials and private citizens for moral offenses and acts contrary to the well-being of the community. Under Solon, however, the Areopagus could no longer take a direct part in administration and legislation. Despite this curtailment of its authority, the court retained its prestige after Athens was conquered by Rome in the 2d century BC.

In Greek mythology, the Areopagus acquitted Orestes of blood guilt in the murder of his mother Clytemnestra. At this trial Athena, the goddess of wisdom, supposedly presided. The Areopagus is important in the history of Christianity as the place where St. Paul preached his sermon to the Athenians (see Acts 17:19 ff.). G.E.D.

The Plaza de Armas, Arequipa, with its twin-spired cathedral (1612) and the snow-capped volcano El Misti. Jacques Jangoux–Peter Arnold, Inc.

AREQUIPA, city, S Peru, capital of Arequipa Department, near Mollendo. Located on the Pan-American Highway, the city is the commercial center for N Bolivia and W Brazil. Extensive trade in cotton, wheat, rice, and sugar is carried on in the city through railway connections with the seaport town of Mollendo. The chief industry is the grading and packing of alpaca wool. Arequipa has a mild, dry climate and is located in a beautiful mountain valley surrounded by several peaks, the highest of which is El Misti (5852 m/19,199 ft above sea level), notable for a perfectly shaped snowcapped cone. The city was founded in 1540 by the Spanish explorer Francisco Pizarro. The old city was virtually destroyed by an earthquake in 1868 and has been completely rebuilt. Pop. (1981) 447,431.

ARES, in Greek mythology, god of war and son of Zeus, king of the gods, and his wife, Hera. The Romans identified him with Mars, also a god of war. Aggressive and sanguinary, Ares personified the brutal nature of war. He was unpopular with both gods and humans. Among the deities associated with Ares were his consort, Aphrodite, goddess of love, and such minor deities as Deimos (Fear) and Phobos (Rout), who accompanied him in battle. Although fierce and warlike, Ares was not invincible, even against mortals.

The worship of Ares, believed to have originated in Thrace, was not extensive in ancient Greece, and where it existed, it lacked social or moral significance. Ares was an ancestral deity of Thebes and had a temple at Athens, at the foot of the Areopagus, or Hill of Ares.

ARETHUSA, in Greek mythology, a wood nymph, the favorite of the nature goddess Artemis. One day, while Arethusa was bathing in a stream belonging to the river god Alpheus, Alpheus appeared and proclaimed his love for her. Arethusa fled under the ocean to the island of Ortygia, where Artemis transformed her into a fountain. But Alpheus pursued her beneath the sea and was himself changed into a river whose waters united with those of the fountain. In ancient times, it was thought that the Alpheus River ran under the sea from Greece and emerged in the fountain of Arethusa in the Sicilian harbor of Syracuse.

ARETINO, Pietro (1492–1556), Italian poet, born in Arezzo. Banished from his native town for having written a satirical sonnet on papal indulgences, he moved to Rome, where he won the favor of Pope Leo X for his brilliance and wit. Aretino's vicious satire won him many enemies, who were able to force him to leave Rome when he published some lewd sonnets. He was supported for a time by the Italian patron of the arts Giovanni delle Bande Nere (1498–1526). In 1527

Aretino settled in Venice. Known as the Scourge of Princes, he was feared by those who wished to avoid his ridicule and fawned upon by those who wished to gain his favor. Among the rulers who showered fortunes on him were Holy Roman Emperor Charles V and King Francis I of France. Aretino's poetical works include five comedies and a tragedy.

AREZZO (anc. *Arretium*), city, central Italy, capital of Arezzo Province, in Tuscany Region. Arezzo is an agricultural market; manufactures include silk and other textiles, musical instruments, and machinery. It was originally an Etruscan town and was famous for terra-cotta pottery. A free commune in the 11th century, Arezzo came under the rule of Florence in 1384. It is the birthplace of the poet Petrarch, the satirist Pietro Aretino, and the artist and writer Giorgio Vasari. Pop. (1990 est.) 91,500.

ARGALI, common name for the largest species of wild sheep, *Ovis ammon,* which inhabit the high mountains and plateaus of Central Asia. The 12 known varieties range in color from buff to brown in summer, turning pale to white in winter. The immense, deeply ridged horns of the rams curl downward and then distinctively spiral outward, often making more than one complete turn.

The largest of the argali, the Siberian, stands about 1 m (about 4 ft) high at the shoulder and may weigh up to 159 kg (350 lb). Its massive horns measure as much as 41 cm (16 in) in circumference at the base and reach 1 m (4 ft) in length. The horns of the smaller but equally magnificent Pamir argali, *O. poli,* reach the spectacular length of 2.8 m (about 75 in). This long-haired subspecies, found in the Pamir plateau in Turkestan, was first described by Marco Polo and is also known as Marco Polo sheep.

See also SHEEP.

ARGELANDER, Friedrich Wilhelm August (1799–1875), German astronomer, born in Memel, Prussia (now Klaipėda, Lithuania), and educated at the University of Königsberg (now Kaliningrad). In 1837 he accepted the chair of astronomy at the University of Bonn, and he remained there until his death. At Bonn he completed his greatest achievement: cataloging the position and brightness of more than 324,000 stars of magnitude greater than 9.5 from the North Pole to 2° south of the equator. This catalog is known as the BDM, or *Bonner Durchmusterung* (Ger. *durch,* "through"; *mustern,* "to inspect"). Among Argelander's other achievements were the calculation (1837) of the motion of the sun in space; the development of a system of magnitudes for describing the brightness of stars too dim to be seen by the naked eye; and the development of the system still in use for naming various stars.

ARGENTEUIL, city, N France, in Val d'Oise Department, on the Seine R., near Paris. It is a major industrial center; manufactures include aerospace and electrical equipment, rubber goods, and pharmaceuticals. The Seamless Tunic, said to have been worn by Christ, is in the Basilica of Saint Denis here. Argenteuil grew around a convent founded in the 7th century. Héloïse (c. 1098–1164) became prioress of the convent (early 12th cent.) during her tragic romance with the philosopher Peter Abelard. Pop. (1982) 96,045.

ARGENTINA *or* **ARGENTINE REPUBLIC,** federal republic, S South America, bounded on the N by Bolivia and Paraguay; on the E by Brazil, Uruguay, and the Atlantic Ocean; on the S by the Atlantic Ocean and Chile; and on the W by Chile. The country occupies most of the S portion of the continent of South America and is somewhat triangular in shape, with the base in the N and the apex at Punta Dungeness, the SE extremity of the continental mainland. The length of Argentina in a N to S direction is about 3330 km (about 2070 mi); its extreme width is about 1384 km (about 860 mi). The country includes the Tierra del Fuego (q.v.) territory, which comprises the E half of the Isla Grande de Tierra del Fuego and a number of adjacent islands to the E, including Isla de los Estados. The area of Argentina is 2,766,889 sq km (1,068,302 sq mi); it is the second largest South American country, Brazil ranking first in area. Argentina, however, claims a total of 2,808,602 sq km (1,084,120 sq mi), including the Falkland Islands (q.v.), or Islas Malvinas, and other sparsely settled S Atlantic islands, as well as part of Antarctica. The Argentine coastline measures 2665 km (1656 mi) in length.

LAND AND RESOURCES

Argentina comprises a diverse territory of mountains, upland areas, and plains. The W boundaries of the country fall entirely within the Andes, the great mountain system of the South American continent. For considerable stretches the continental divide demarcates the Argentine-Chilean frontier. The Patagonian Andes, which form a natural boundary between Argentina and Chile, are one of the lesser ranges, seldom exceeding about 3660 m (about 12,000 ft) in elevation. From the N extremity of this range to the Bolivian frontier, the W part of Argentina is occupied by the main Andean cordillera, with a number of peaks above about 6400 m (about 21,000 ft). Aconcagua (q.v.) (6959 m/22,831 ft), the highest of these peaks, is the greatest elevation in the world outside Central Asia. Other noteworthy

The Andes, viewed from the southern Argentinian province of Santa Cruz. Argentina has within its borders or shares with Chile 16 Andean peaks exceeding 6100 m (about 20,000 ft) in height.
Des & Jen Bartlett–Bruce Coleman, Inc.

peaks are Ojos del Salado (6880 m/22,572 ft) and Tupungato (6800 m/22,310 ft), on the border between Argentina and Chile, and Mercedario (6770 m/22,211 ft). Several parallel ranges and spurs of the Andes project deeply into NW Argentina. The only other highlands of consequence in Argentina is the Sierra de Córdoba, situated in the central portion of the country. Its highest peak is Champaquí (2850 m/9350 ft).

Eastward from the base of the Andean system, the terrain of Argentina consists almost entirely of a flat or gently undulating plain. This plain slopes gradually from an elevation of about 610 m (about 2000 ft) to sea level. In the N the Argentine plains consist of the S portion of the South American region known as the Chaco. The Pampas (q.v.), treeless plains that include the most productive agricultural sections of the country, extend nearly 1600 km (about 1000 mi) S from the Chaco. In Patagonia (q.v.), S of the Pampas, the terrain consists largely of arid, desolate steppes.

Rivers and Lakes. The chief rivers of Argentina are the Paraná, which traverses the N central portion of the country; the Uruguay, which forms part of the boundary with Uruguay; the Paraguay, which is the main affluent of the Paraná; and the Río de la Plata (*see* PLATA, RÍO DE LA), the great estuary formed by the confluence of the Paraná and the Uruguay rivers. The Paraná-Uruguay system is navigable for nearly 3200 km (about 2000 mi). A famed scenic attraction, the Iguaçu Falls (*see* IGUAÇU), is on the river of the same name, a tributary of the Paraná. Other important rivers of Argentina are the Río Colorado, the Río Salado, and the Río Negro. In the area between the Río Salado and the Río Colorado and in the Chaco region, some large rivers empty into swamps and marshes or disappear into sinks. The hydrography of the country includes numerous lakes, particularly among the foothills of the Patagonian Andes. The best known are those in the alpine lake country around the resort town of Bariloche.

Climate. Temperate climatic conditions prevail throughout most of Argentina, except for a small tropical area in the NE and the subtropical Chaco in the N. In the vicinity of Buenos Aires the average annual temperature is a mild 16.1° C (61° F). The January and July averages for this area are, respectively, 23.3° C (74° F) and 9.4° C (49° F). At the N extremity of the Pampas the average annual temperature is about 16.9° C (about 62.5° F). The annual average at the S extremity of the Pampas is about 16° C (about 60° F). Considerably higher temperatures prevail near the tropic of Capricorn in the N. The annual average in this region is 23.3° C (74° F), and extremes as high as 45° C (113° F) are occasionally recorded. Climatic conditions are generally cold in the higher Andes, Patagonia, and Tierra del Fuego. In the W section of Patagonia winter temperatures average about 0° C (32° F). In most coastal areas, however, the ocean exerts a moderating influence on temperatures.

Precipitation in Argentina is marked by wide regional variations. More than 152 cm (60 in) fall annually in the extreme N, but conditions gradually become semiarid to the S and W. In the vi-

INDEX TO MAP OF ARGENTINA

Provinces

Buenos Aires . . . . D 4
Catamarca. . . . . C 2
Chaco . . . . D 2
Chubut . . . . C 5
Córdoba . . . . D 3
Corrientes . . . . E 2
Distrito Federal (fed. dist.). . . . . H 7
Entre Ríos . . . . E 3
Formosa . . . . D 1
Jujuy . . . . C 1
La Pampa . . . . C 4
La Rioja. . . . . C 2
Mendoza . . . . C 4
Misiones . . . . F 2
Neuquén . . . . C 4
Río Negro . . . . C 5
Salta . . . . D 1
San Juan. . . . . C 3
San Luis . . . . C 3
Santa Cruz . . . . C 6
Santa Fe . . . . D 3
Santiago del Estero . . . . D 2
Tierra del Fuego, Antártida e Islas del Atlántico Sur (terr.). . . C 7
Tucumán. . . . . C 2

Cities and Towns

Abra Pampa . . . . C 1
Acevedo. . . . . F 6
Adolfo Alsina . . . . D 4
Aguaray. . . . . D 1
Aguilares. . . . . C 2
Albardón . . . . C 3
Alberti . . . . G 7
Alcaraz . . . . G 5
Alcorta. . . . . F 6
Alejandra . . . . F 5
Allen . . . . C 4
Alpachiri . . . . D 4
Alta Gracia . . . . D 3
Aluminé. . . . . B 4
Alvear . . . . E 2
Ameghino . . . . D 3
Aminga . . . . C 2
Añatuya. . . . . C 2
Anchorena . . . . C 4
Andalgalá . . . . C 2
Anguil . . . . D 4
Apóstoles . . . . E 2
Arrecifes . . . . F 7
Arroyo Seco . . . . F 6
Ascension . . . . F 7
Avellaneda . . . . G 7
Ayacucho . . . . E 4
Azul . . . . E 4
Bahía Blanca. . . . . D 4
Bahía Thetis . . . . C 7
Baigorrita. . . . . F 7
Balcarce . . . . E 4
Balnearia. . . . . D 3
Bandera. . . . . D 2
Baradero . . . . G 6
Bariloche (San Carlos de Bariloche). . . . . . . B 5
Barrancas . . . . F 6
Barranqueras . . . . E 2
Barreal. . . . . C 3
Basavilbaso. . . . . G 6
Beazley . . . . C 3
Belén . . . . C 2
Bella Vista . . . . D 2
Bella Vista . . . . E 2
Bell Ville . . . . D 3
Bernardo de Irigoyen . . . F 6
Bernasconi . . . . D 4
Bolívar . . . . D 4
Bovril . . . . G 5
Bragado. . . . . F 7
Buenos Aires (cap.) . . . . H 7
Bustinza. . . . . F 6
Buta-Ranquil . . . . C 4
Cafayate . . . . C 2
Calafate . . . . B 7
Calchaquí . . . . F 5
Caleufú . . . . D 4
Camarones . . . . D 5
Campana. . . . . G 7
Cañada de Gómez . . . . . F 6
Canals . . . . D 3
Captain Bermúdez . . . . . F 6
Carabelas . . . . F 6
Carcarañá . . . . F 6
Carlos Casares . . . . F 7
Carlos Tejedor . . . . D 4
Carmen de Areco . . . . . . F 7
Carmen de Patagones . . D 5
Carmensa . . . . C 4
Casilda. . . . . F 6
Castelli. . . . . D 2
Castelli. . . . . H 7
Catamarca. . . . . C 2
Caucete. . . . . C 3
Cayasta . . . . F 5
Cayastacito . . . . F 5
Ceres. . . . . D 2
Chabás . . . . F 6
Chacabuco . . . . F 7
Chamical. . . . . C 3
Charadai . . . . D 2
Charata . . . . D 2
Chepes . . . . C 3
Chicoana. . . . . C 2
Chilecito . . . . C 2
Chivilcoy . . . . F 7
Choele-Choel . . . . C 4
Chos-Malal . . . . C 4
Chumbicha . . . . C 2
Cinco Saltos . . . . C 4
Cipolletti . . . . C 4
Clorinda. . . . . E 2
Colón . . . . F 6
Colón. . . . . G 6
Colonia Elisa . . . . E 2
Colonia las Heras. . . . . . C 6
Comandante Fontana . . D 2
Comandante Luis Piedrabuena . . . . C 6
Comodoro Rivadavia . . . C 6
Concepción . . . . C 2
Concepción. . . . . E 2
Concepción de la Sierra . . . . E 2
Concepción del Uruguay. . . . . G 6
Concordia . . . . G 5
Copacabana . . . . C 2
Córdoba . . . . D 3
Coronda. . . . . F 6
Coronel Bogado . . . . F 6
Coronel Brandsen . . . . . H 7
Coronel Dorrego . . . . . . D 4
Coronel Moldes . . . . C 2
Coronel Pringles. . . . . . . D 4
Coronel Suárez. . . . . D 4
Coronel Vidal . . . . E 4
Corral de Bustos . . . . . . D 3
Corrientes . . . . E 2
Cosquín . . . . D 3
Crespo . . . . F 6
Cruz del Eje . . . . C 3
Cuadro Nacional . . . . . . C 3
Curuzú Cuatiá . . . . G 5
Cutral-Có. . . . . C 4
Daireaux . . . . D 4
Deán Funes. . . . . D 3
Díaz . . . . F 6
Doblas . . . . D 4
Dolavón. . . . . C 5
Dolores . . . . E 4
Dudignac. . . . . F 7
Eduardo Castex . . . . D 4
El Bolsón. . . . . B 5
Eldorado . . . . F 2
Elisa. . . . . F 5
El Milagro . . . . C 3
Elortondo. . . . . F 6
El Quebrachal. . . . . D 2
El Turbio . . . . B 7
Embarcación. . . . . D 1
Emilio Ayarza . . . . F 7
Empedrado . . . . E 2
Ensenada . . . . H 7
Escobar. . . . . G 7
Esperanza . . . . F 5
Esquel . . . . B 5
Esquina. . . . . G 5
Famatina . . . . C 2
Federación . . . . G 5
Felipe Yofré . . . . G 4
Fernández. . . . . D 2
Fiambalá . . . . C 2
Firmat. . . . . F 6
Formosa . . . . E 2
French . . . . F 7
Frías. . . . . D 2
Gaiman . . . . C 5
Gálvez . . . . F 6
Gastre . . . . C 5
General Acha . . . . C 4
General Alvear . . . . F 7
General Alvear . . . . C 3
General Arenales . . . . . F 7
General Belgrano. . . . . . G 7
General Conesa . . . . C 5
General Galarza . . . . G 6
General Güemes. . . . . . . D 1
General Guido . . . . E 4
General José de San Martín. . . . . E 2
General Juan Madariaga . . . . E 4
General La Madrid . . . . . D 4
General Las Heras. . . . . G 7
General Lavalle. . . . . E 4
General O'Brien . . . . F 7
General Paz . . . . E 2
General Paz . . . . H 7
General Pico. . . . . D 4
General Ramírez . . . . . . F 6
General Roca . . . . C 4
General San Martín . . . . D 4
General San Martín . . . . G 7
General Viamonte . . . . . F 7
General Villegas . . . . . . D 4
Gobernador Crespo . . . . F 5
Gobernador Gregores . . C 6
Governador Mansilla . . . G 6
Godoy Cruz. . . . . C 3
Goya . . . . G 4
Gualeguay. . . . . G 6
Gualeguaychú . . . . G 6
Guandacol . . . . C 2
Guardia Mitre . . . . D 5
Hasenkamp . . . . F 5
Helvecia. . . . . F 5
Hernandarias. . . . . F 5
Hernández. . . . . F 6
Hernando . . . . D 3
Herradura . . . . E 2
Herrera . . . . D 2
Huanqueros. . . . . F 5
Huinca Renancó. . . . . . . D 3
Humahuaca. . . . . C 1
Humberto island . . . . . . F 5
Ibarreta . . . . D 2
Ibicuy. . . . . G 6
Icaño . . . . C 2
Icaño . . . . D 2
Ingeniero Huergo . . . . . C 4
Ingeniero Jacobacci. . . . C 5
Ingeniero Luiggi . . . . . . D 4
Intendente Alvear . . . . . D 4
Itatí. . . . . E 2
Ituzaingó . . . . E 2
Jáchal . . . . C 3
Jesús María. . . . . D 3
Joaquín V. Gonzáles . . . D 2
José de San Martín . . . . B 5
José M. Micheo . . . . G 7
Juárez . . . . D 4
Jujuy . . . . C 1
Juncal . . . . F 6
Junín . . . . F 7
Junín de los Andes . . . . B 4
La Banda. . . . . D 2
Laboulaye . . . . D 3
La Carlota . . . . D 3
La Clarita . . . . G 5
La Cruz . . . . E 2
La Cumbre . . . . C 3
La Falda . . . . D 3
La Gallareta. . . . . F 5
Laguna Paiva . . . . F 5
Lanús . . . . H 7
La Paz. . . . . C 3
La Paz. . . . . G 5
La Pelada . . . . F 5
La Plata. . . . . H 7
Laprida . . . . D 4
La Quiaca . . . . C 1
La Rioja. . . . . C 2
Larroque . . . . G 6
Las Flores . . . . E 4
Las Lajas. . . . . B 4
Las Lomitas . . . . D 1
Las Palmas . . . . E 2
Las Rosas . . . . F 6
Las Termas . . . . D 2
Las Varillas . . . . D 3
La Toma . . . . C 3
Lavalle. . . . . G 4
Lezama . . . . H 7
Liberador General San Martín. . . . . D 1
Lincoln. . . . . F 7
Lobería . . . . E 4
Lobos . . . . G 7
Lomas de Zamora . . . . . G 7
López. . . . . F 6
Lucas González . . . . G 6
Luján. . . . . G 7
Lules . . . . C 2
Macachín . . . . D 4
Maciel . . . . F 6
Magdalena . . . . H 7
Maipú. . . . . E 4
Makallé . . . . E 2
Malabrigo. . . . . F 4
Malargüe . . . . C 4
Maquinchao . . . . C 5
Marcos Juárez . . . . D 3
Mar del Plata. . . . . E 4
Margarita . . . . F 5
Mariano I. Loza. . . . . . . G 4
Máximo Paz. . . . . F 6
Mburucuyá . . . . E 2
Médanos . . . . D 4
Médanos . . . . G 6
Media Agua. . . . . C 3
Melincué . . . . F 6
Mendoza . . . . C 3
Mercedes . . . . C 3
Mercedes . . . . G 4
Mercedes . . . . G 7
Merlo . . . . G 7
Metán . . . . D 2
Miguel Riglos . . . . D 4
Miramar . . . . E 4
Moisés Ville. . . . . E 5
Monte Caseros . . . . G 5
Monte Comán . . . . C 3
Monte Quemado. . . . . . . D 2
Monteros. . . . . C 2
Morteros . . . . D 3
Navarro . . . . G 7
Necochea . . . . E 4
Nelson . . . . F 5
Neuquén . . . . C 4
Nogoyá . . . . F 6
Norquincó . . . . B 5
Nueve de Julio . . . . F 7
Oberá. . . . . F 2
Olavarría . . . . D 4
Oliva . . . . D 3
Olta . . . . C 3
Ordoqui . . . . F 7
Palo Santo. . . . . E 2
Pampa del Infierno. . . . . D 2
Paraná . . . . F 6
Paso de los Libres . . . . . E 2
Paso Flores. . . . . C 5
Pátquia . . . . C 3

ARGENTINA
CONIC PROJECTION
SCALE OF MILES
0 50 100 200 300
SCALE OF KILOMETERS
0 50 100 200 300
Capitals of Countries
Capitals of Provinces
International Boundaries
Boundaries of Provinces
B
C
D
E
F
G
70°
65°
60°
55°
50°
25°
30°
35°
1
2
3
Tropic of Capricorn
BOLIVIA
PARAGUAY
BRAZIL
URUGUAY
OCEAN
JUJUY
SALTA
FORMOSA
CHACO
TUCUMAN
SANTIAGO DEL ESTERO
CATAMARCA
LA RIOJA
SAN JUAN
CORDOBA
SANTA FE
CORRIENTES
MISIONES
ENTRE RÍOS
SAN LUIS
MENDOZA
BUENOS AIRES
LA PAMPA
Asunción
SANTIAGO
MONTEVIDEO
BUENOS AIRES
La Plata
Córdoba
Rosario
Mendoza
S. Miguel de Tucumán
Salta
Jujuy
Santa Fe
Paraná
Corrientes
Resistencia
Posadas
Formosa
Santiago del Estero
La Rioja
San Juan
San Luis
Santa Rosa
Antofagasta
Valparaíso
Concepción
Porto Alegre
Río de la Plata
Lagoa dos Patos
Lagoa Mirim
Chaco Boreal
Chaco Central
Chaco Austral
Salar de Atacama
Puna de Atacama
Mar Chiquita
Salinas Grandes

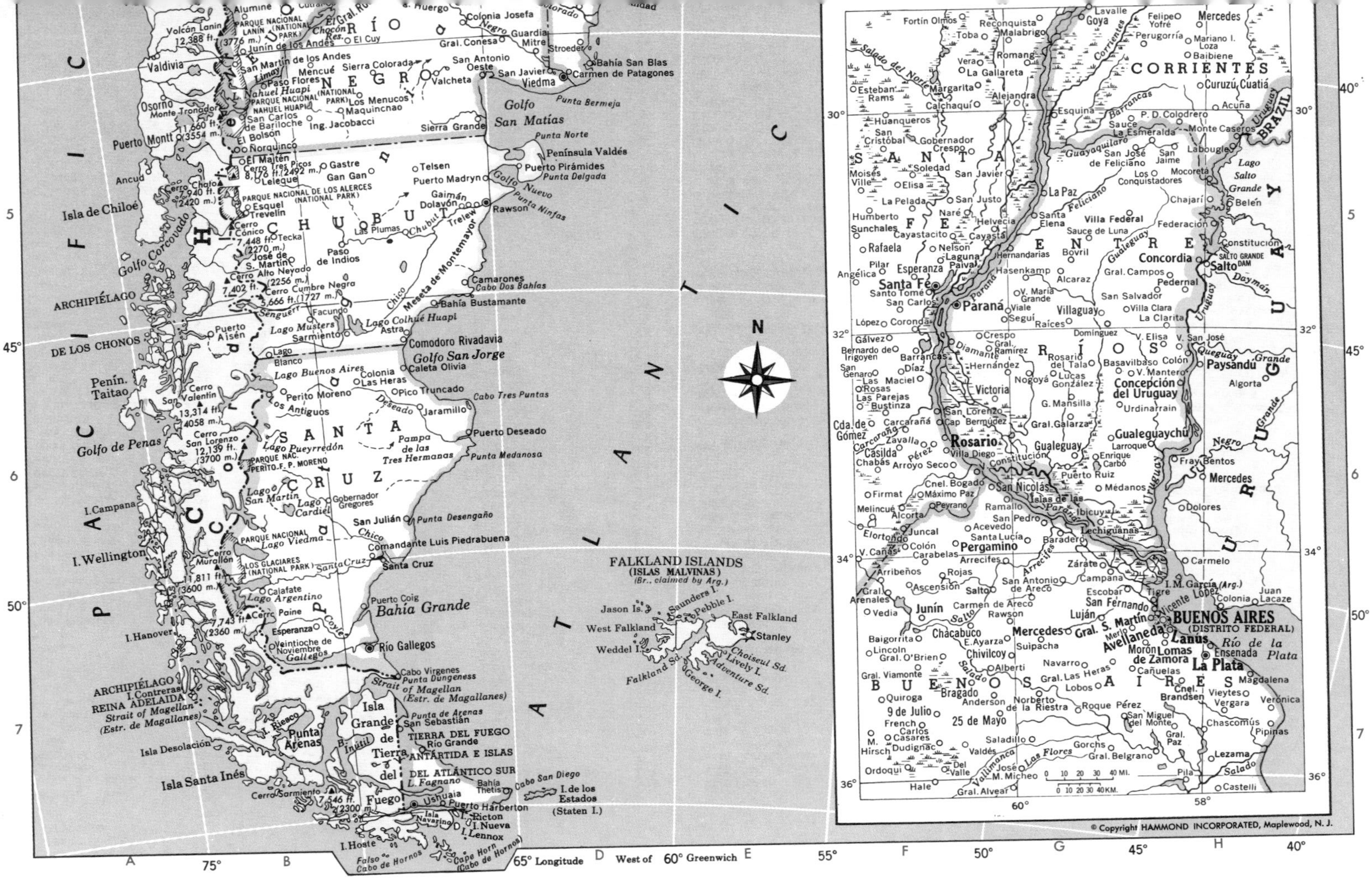
PACIFIC
ATLANTIC
CHUBUT
SANTA CRUZ
RÍO NEGRO
CORRIENTES
SANTA FE
ENTRE RÍOS
BUENOS AIRES
URUGUAY
BRAZIL
FALKLAND ISLANDS
(ISLAS MALVINAS)
(Br., claimed by Arg.)
West Falkland
East Falkland
Stanley
Golfo San Matías
Golfo San Jorge
Bahía Grande
Golfo de Penas
Isla de Chiloé
ARCHIPIÉLAGO DE LOS CHONOS
Strait of Magellan
(Estr. de Magallanes)
Isla Grande de Tierra del Fuego
TIERRA DEL FUEGO
ANTÁRTIDA E ISLAS
DEL ATLÁNTICO SUR
I. de los Estados
(Staten I.)
Cape Horn
(Cabo de Hornos)
Comodoro Rivadavia
Puerto Deseado
Río Gallegos
Punta Arenas
Ushuaia
Rawson
Viedma
Puerto Montt
Valdivia
Osorno
Santa Fe
Paraná
Rosario
Concordia
Paysandú
Concepción del Uruguay
Gualeguaychú
BUENOS AIRES
(DISTRITO FEDERAL)
La Plata
Río de la Plata
Pergamino
Junín
Mercedes
65° Longitude
West of 60° Greenwich
A B D E F G H
75° 55° 50° 45° 40°
0 10 20 30 40 MI.
0 10 20 30 40 KM.

Index to Map of Argentina

Other Features

cinity of Buenos Aires annual rainfall is about 102 cm (about 40 in).

Natural Resources. The traditional wealth of Argentina lies in its vast grasslands and Pampas, which are used for extensive grazing and grain production; but Argentine mineral resources, especially offshore deposits of petroleum and natural gas, have assumed increasing importance in recent decades.

Plants and Animals. The indigenous vegetation of Argentina varies greatly with the different climate and topographical regions of the country. The warm and moist NE area supports tropical plants, including such trees as the palm, rosewood, lignum vitae, jacaranda, and red quebracho (a source of tannin). Grasses are the principal variety of indigenous vegetation in the Pampas. Trees, excluding such imported drought-resistant varieties as the eucalyptus, sycamore, and acacia, are practically nonexistent in this region and in most of Patagonia. The chief types of vegetation in Patagonia are herbs, shrubs, grasses, and brambles. The Andean foothills of Patagonia and parts of Tierra del Fuego, however, possess flourishing growths of conifers, notably fir, cypress, pine, and cedar. Cacti and other thorny plants predominate in the arid Andean regions of NW Argentina.

In the N the fauna is most diverse and abundant. The mammals in these regions include the monkey (several species), jaguar, puma, ocelot, anteater, tapir, peccary, and raccoon. Indigenous birds include the flamingo and various hummingbirds and parrots. In the Pampas are the armadillo, fox, marten, wildcat, hare, deer, American ostrich or rhea, hawk, falcon, heron, plover, and partridge; some of these animals are also found in Patagonia. The cold Andean regions are the habitat of the llama, guanaco, vicuña, alpaca, and condor. Fish abound in coastal waters, lakes, and streams.

Soils. The soils of Argentina vary greatly in fertility and suitability for agriculture, and water is scarce in many areas outside the NE and the humid Pampas. The Pampas, which are largely made up of a fine sand, clay, and silt almost wholly free from pebbles and rocks, are ideal for the cultivation of cereal. In contrast, the gravelly soil of most of Patagonia, in S Argentina, is useless for growing crops. The natural grasslands of this region are used primarily as pasture for sheep. Most of the N Andean foothill region is unsuitable for farming, but several oases favor fruit culture. In part of the Chaco an unusually saline soil is believed to be responsible for the abundance of the tannin-rich quebracho trees.

POPULATION

About 85% of the population is of European origin. Unlike most Latin American countries, Argentina has relatively few mestizos (persons of mixed European and Indian ancestry), although their number has increased in recent times.

Argentine cowboys of the northwestern province of Salta. In Salta the gaucho traditions are staunchly upheld, and equestrian skills are regularly displayed in competitions. Francisco Erize–Bruce Coleman, Inc.

An aerial view of Buenos Aires with its superb harbor in the background. The Argentine capital is known as one of the great cities of the southern hemisphere.
Walter S. Clark

European immigration continues to be officially encouraged; from 1850 to 1940, some 6,608,700 Europeans settled in the country. Spanish and Italian immigrants have predominated, with significant numbers of French, British, German, Russian, Polish, Syrian, and other South American immigrants. More than one-third of the population lives in or around Buenos Aires; about 85% of the people live in urban areas.

Population Characteristics. According to the 1980 census the population of Argentina was 27,949,480, an increase of about 20% over 1970. The estimated population in 1989 was 32,425,000; the overall population density was about 12 persons per sq km (about 30 per sq mi).

Political Divisions. Argentina comprises 22 provinces; the self-governing Federal District, which consists of the city of Buenos Aires and several suburbs; and the national territory of the Argentine part of Tierra del Fuego, the Argentine-claimed sector of Antarctica, and several South Atlantic islands.

The provinces are grouped into five major areas: the Atlantic Coastal, or Littoral, provinces, comprising Buenos Aires (excluding the city of Buenos Aires), Chaco, Corrientes, Entre Ríos, Formosa, Misiones, and Santa Fe; the Northern provinces, comprising Jujuy, Salta, Santiago del Estero, and Tucumán; the Central provinces, comprising Córdoba, La Pampa, and San Luis; the provinces of the Andes, or Andina, comprising Catamarca, La Rioja, Mendoza, Neuquén, and San Juan; and the Patagonian provinces, comprising Chubut, Río Negro, and Santa Cruz.

A number of nations, including the U.S., do not recognize the Argentine claim to the vast sector of Antarctica, between long 25° W and 74° W, and to a number of South Atlantic islands.

Principal Cities. The capital and largest city is Buenos Aires (q.v.). Other important cities are Córdoba (pop., 1980 prelim. 990,007), a major manufacturing and university city; the river port of Rosario (greater city, 935,471); La Plata (473,233), capital of Buenos Aires Province; Mar del Plata (423,989), a resort city at the mouth of the Rio de la Plata; San Miguel de Tucumán

(392,888), a diversified manufacturing center; Salta (265,632), famous for its colonial architecture; and Mendoza (118,427), hub of an important agricultural and wine-growing region.

Language. Spanish is the national tongue and is spoken by the overwhelming majority of Argentines. A number of Indian languages are still spoken as well.

Religion. Roman Catholics make up over 90% of the population. Jews and Protestants account for another 2% each; a number of other Christian and non-Christian religions are practiced, but several faiths and sects are banned as "injurious to public order." By law, the president and vice-president of Argentina must be Roman Catholic.

EDUCATION AND CULTURE

Argentina is a nation with a rich Spanish heritage, strongly influenced since the 19th century by European, notably Italian, immigration. A lively interest is maintained in the nation's history, particularly as symbolized by the gaucho (cowboy). In the fine arts, the most important model has been France; only in folk art has there been significant influence from native Indian cultures.

Education. Primary education is free and compulsory from ages 6 to 14. In the mid-1980s about 4.8 million pupils attended primary schools; 1.9 million attended secondary and vocational schools. More than 900,000 were enrolled in colleges and universities. Argentina's literacy rate of about 95% is one of the highest in Latin America.

Argentina has 24 national universities and many state and private universities. The principal institution is the University of Buenos Aires (1821). Other major national universities are located in Córdoba (1613), La Plata (1905), San Miguel de Tucumán (1914), and Rosario (1968).

Libraries and Museums. The leading library of Argentina is the National Library (1810) in Buenos Aires, which has about 1.9 million volumes. Prominent among the many museums in Buenos Aires are the Argentine Museum of Natural Sciences, the National Museum of Fine Arts, and such private collections as the International Art Gallery. The Museum of La Plata is famous for its collections of reptile fossils.

Literature. Argentine literature, originally a derivative form of Spanish literature, took on a markedly nationalistic flavor in the 19th century. The poem *Fausto* (1866), by Estanisláo del Campo (1834–80), is a gaucho version of the Faust legend; *Martín Fierro* (1872), a narrative poem on gaucho life by José Hernández (1834–86), is considered by many the national epic of Argentina; and finally, the sociological essay *Facundo* (1845; trans. 1868), by Domingo Faustino Sarmiento, is a study of how the rural life of the Argentine Pampas helped shape the national character.

Twentieth-century Argentine literature has produced the celebrated *Shadows in the Pampas* (1926; trans. 1935), a novel by Ricardo Guiraldes (1886–1927); *Hopscotch* (1963; trans. 1966), a novel by Julio Cortázar; *The Kiss of the Spider Woman* (1976; trans. 1979), a novel by Manuel Puig (1932–90); and the stories of Ernesto Sábato (1911–). Eduardo Mallea, a novelist who wrote on existentialist themes, and Jorge Luis Borges, internationally renowned for his fantasies, are major contemporary figures. The best-known poet is Leopoldo Lugones (1874–1938), who wrote both symbolist and naturalist verse.

Art. Painting in the 19th century was dominated by gaucho themes and scenes of town life. Prilidiano Pueyrredón (1823–70) was the principal artist of the period. Painters of the 20th century include the realist Cesareo Bernaldo de Quirós (1879–1968); Benito Quinquela Martín (1890–1977), painter of port life in Buenos Aires; the cubist Emilio Pettoruti (1884–1965); and Raul Soldi (1905–). The works of the sculptor Rogelio Yrurtia (1879–1920) are widely known.

Music. The most important components of traditional Argentine music are the gaucho folk song and folk dance; Indian music from the N provinces; European influences; and, to a minor extent, African music. The tango, which developed in Buenos Aires and became a favorite ballroom dance throughout much of the world, is perhaps Argentina's most famous contribution to modern music. Astor Piazzolla (1921–92), a prolific tango composer, bandleader, and performer, incorporated jazz and classical influences in his works.

Symphonic music and opera are important features of cultural activity. The National Symphony Orchestra is based in Buenos Aires, and the opera company of the city is housed in the Colón Theater, built in 1908. The Colón opera has achieved an international reputation for excellence. Leading figures in the classical music field are three brothers, José María Castro (1892–1964), Juan José Castro (1895–1968), and Washington Castro (1909–), all conductors and composers. Alberto Williams (1862–1952), the founder of the Buenos Aires Conservatory, was the best known of all Argentine composers. Alberto Ginastera is well known for his symphonic, ballet, operatic, and piano music, which is popular throughout the world.

Communications. A postal service extending to the entire country is maintained by the government. More than 3.6 million telephones are in use. In the late 1980s some 21.6 million radio receivers were in use in Argentina, and television receivers numbered about 7.2 million.

More than 200 daily newspapers are published in Argentina, although the principal ones are published in Buenos Aires and circulate throughout the country. *La Prensa* and *La Nación,* with circulations of about 65,000 and 211,000, respectively, are famed internationally for their independent views and objectivity. Other leading Buenos Aires papers are *Clarín* (daily circulation 480,000) and *La Razón* (180,000). The provincial capitals and other secondary centers all have daily papers with strong local followings. A number of magazines containing both news and features are published in Buenos Aires and circulate throughout the country.

ECONOMY

The Argentine economy is based primarily on the production of agricultural products and the raising of livestock, but manufacturing and mining industries have shown marked growth in recent decades. Argentina is one of the world's leading cattle- and grain-producing regions; the country's main manufacturing enterprises are meat-packing and flour-milling plants. Argentina's estimated national budget in 1987 called for revenue of about $7.1 billion and expenditure of $9.5 billion.

Agriculture. In normal years, Argentina raises enough agricultural products not only to fill domestic needs but also to export surpluses to foreign markets. Of Argentina's land area of about 280 million ha (about 692 million acres), slightly more than 50% is used for pasturing cattle and sheep herds, less than 22% for woodland, and about 4% for permanent crops; about 13% of the country's land area is arable. The Pampas is the most important agricultural zone of the country, producing wheat and cereal grains. Irrigated areas, from the Río Negro N through Mendoza, San Juan, Tucumán, and Jujuy, are rich sources of fruit, sugarcane, and wine grapes.

Livestock raising and slaughtering are major enterprises in Argentina, as are the refrigeration and processing of meat and animal products; total annual meat production exceeds 3.4 million metric tons. In the late 1980s, there were some 50.8 million head of cattle, 29.2 million sheep, and 4.1 million pigs in Argentina. In addition, there were about 3.1 million horses; Argentine horses have won an international reputation as racehorses and polo ponies.

Despite declines during the 1980s, livestock export still plays an important role in foreign

Cattle raising in Argentina. The pampas are world famous as an excellent grazing area for cattle, and few countries surpass Argentina in livestock production.

Bjorn Bolstad–Peter Arnold, Inc.

Harvesting grapes in an Argentinian vineyard. They will be used in wine making.
Loren McIntyre–Woodfin Camp & Associates

trade. Earnings from meat, hides, and skins in 1989 were about $1.1 billion, or about 11% of total export earnings. Argentina has long ranked as a world leader in the export of raw meat. Cooked and canned meats are increasingly important exports.

Large quantities of wool are produced and exported; in the late 1980s, about 138,000 metric tons of wool were produced per year, out of a world total of about 3.12 million metric tons. About 40% of all sheep in Argentina are raised in the Patagonia region.

Wheat is the most important crop. Argentina is among the major producers of wheat in the world. In the late 1980s, the annual wheat crop totaled about 7.8 million metric tons. Other major crops were corn (9.2 million metric tons), barley (266,000), and oats (620,000).

Other major field crops include soybeans, sorghum, flaxseed, sunflower seeds, sugarcane, cotton, potatoes, rice, maté, peanuts, and tobacco, as well as a considerable crop of grapes, oranges, lemons, and grapefruit.

Forestry and Fishing. Situated mainly in mountain areas distant from centers of population, the 59,500,000 ha (147,027,000 acres) of woodland are relatively unused. Among the most exploited woods are elm and willow, for cellulose production; white quebracho, for fuel; red quebracho, for tannin (used for tanning leather); and cedar, for the manufacture of furniture. Other economically important woods are oak, araucaria, pine, and cypress.

Argentina's fisheries, potentially highly productive, have not been fully exploited, although production increased steadily in the 1960s and '70s. In the late 1980s the annual catch was about 560,000 metric tons, mostly hake, anchovy, mackerel, and dorado.

Mining. Although the country has a variety of mineral deposits, including petroleum, coal, and various metals, mining has been relatively unimportant. In recent decades, however, production of petroleum and coal, in particular, has increased significantly. In terms of value, the chief mineral product is petroleum. In the late 1980s annual production of crude petroleum was 157.3 million barrels, furnishing virtually all of the country's needs; offshore reserves are expected to boost production levels. Relatively small quantities of gold, silver, copper, lead, zinc, iron, tin, tungsten, mica, and limestone are mined.

Manufacturing. Most industry is centered in Buenos Aires. About 20% of the national labor force is employed by manufacturing establishments. The country's oldest and largest industry is the processing and packaging of foodstuffs. The textile industry ranks second. Other major industries produce rubber goods (both natural and synthetic), cement, chemicals, plastics, and petroleum products. Steel production is rapidly expanding; in the mid-1980s yearly steel production totaled about 2.6 million metric tons, and the automotive industry produced 175,000 motor vehicles.

Energy. Most rivers and falls with potential energy are located far from industrial centers, but despite these technical limitations water resources are being developed in Argentina at a rapid rate. Major hydroelectric projects undertaken in the 1970s and '80s were located in N Patagonia, on the Paraná R., and on the Uruguay R. (in cooperation with Uruguay). Overall, 52.2 billion kwh of electricity were produced yearly in Argentina in the late 1980s, of which 42% came from hydroelectric installations. Nuclear power accounted for 12%, and conventional thermal plants for the remaining 46%.

Currency and Banking. Formerly, Argentina's monetary system was based on the peso oro ("gold peso"), although no gold coins actually circulated. The peso moneda nacional (called the paper peso and consisting of 100 centavos) was the currency in use. Rampant inflation in the 1970s and early 1980s rapidly depreciated the value of the peso, and in June 1985 a new currency, the austral (equal to 1000 pesos), was introduced as part of an ambitious program to control inflation. When this failed, the peso (equal to 10,000 australs) was restored in January 1992, at an exchange rate of 1 peso = U.S.$1.

The Central Bank, which was established in 1935 and came under government control in 1949, functions as the national bank and has the sole right to issue currency. In the mid-1980s, 30 other banks were government owned, and about 160 commercial banks were in the private sector.

Commerce and Trade. The trade balance tends to be favorable to Argentina when world demand for food is high. In the late 1980s, Argentina's balance of trade continued to be strongly favorable; annual imports were about $3.9 billion and exports $9.6 billion. The U.S. was the leading supplier of imports and a major outlet for Argentine exports. Principal imports are machinery and electrical equipment; iron, iron manufactures, and other metals; chemicals; mineral fuels and oils; and paper and food products. The major exports are cereals, oilseeds, meat, wool, hides, dairy products, transportation equipment, and forest products (notably tannin and tung oil).

Transportation. The Argentine railroad system, which has been owned and operated by the government since 1948, has a total length of about 34,500 km (about 21,435 mi). Two different gauges are used. Two lines crossing the Andes provide a connection with points in Chile; railroad links also connect Argentina with Bolivia, Paraguay, Uruguay, and Brazil.

Argentina is well served by international airlines; the national airline, Aerolíneas Argentinas; and several smaller internal lines. About 3100 km (about 1900 mi) of waterways are provided by navigable rivers, especially those in the Río de la Plata region. The combined length of all roads and highways is about 211,370 km (about 131,340 mi). A railroad tunnel through the Andes has provided facilities for motor vehicles since its expansion in 1940. In the mid-1980s some 3.9 million passenger cars and 1.4 million commercial vehicles were registered.

Labor. In the late 1980s the total labor force numbered about 11.8 million. Most of Argentina's 1100 labor unions are affiliated with the Confederación General del Trabajo (General Labor Confederation), known as the CGT. The right to unionize, suspended in 1976, was restored in 1982, and the labor movement embraced some 213 million workers by the late 1980s.

GOVERNMENT

The constitution of 1853, in the preamble and in much of the text, reflects the ideals and aims of the U.S. Constitution. A new constitution was passed in 1949, only to be rescinded in 1956. All constitutional provisions were suspended in 1966 following a military take-over. After another military coup in 1976, the constitution of 1853 was again suspended, but it was reinstated when Argentina returned to civilian rule in 1983.

Central Government. According to the constitution of 1853, Argentina is a federal republic headed by a president, who is assisted by a council of ministers. Legislative powers are vested in a national congress consisting of a Senate and a House of Deputies. The president and vice-president each serve for a single 6-year term. From 1976 through 1983, when constitutional government resumed, the Junta Militar, comprising the military chiefs of staff, was the supreme organ of state, with the power of appointing and dismissing the president.

The constitution of 1853 permits the suspension of parliamentary government and civil liberties should the president deem that a national emergency requires a "state of siege." This provision has been invoked frequently in Argentine history.

Health and Welfare. The National Institute of Social Welfare has administered most Argentine welfare programs since its founding in 1944. Health services are provided to workers by the various unions and to others by free hospital clinics. Medical standards are relatively high in the cities, and efforts are constantly being made

Ushuaia, on the Beagle Channel in the southern part of Argentinian Tierra del Fuego, is the southernmost city in the world. Editorial Photocolor Archives

to improve medical facilities located in outlying rural areas.

Legislature. The organization of the legislature of Argentina is similar to that of the U.S. The Argentine national congress consists of a lower chamber, the 254-member House of Deputies, and an upper chamber, the 46-member Senate. Deputies are directly elected to 4-year terms; senators are chosen by provincial legislatures for terms of 9 years. Voting is compulsory for all citizens 18 years of age or older. Proportional representation in national elections was initiated in 1962.

Local Government. Under the constitution, the provinces of Argentina elect their own governors and legislatures. During periods when the constitution has been suspended, provincial governors have been appointed by the central government.

Judiciary. Federal courts include the supreme court, 17 appellate courts, and district and territorial courts on the local levels. The provincial court systems are similarly organized, comprising supreme, appellate, and lower courts.

Defense. The Argentine military establishment is one of the most modern and best equipped in Latin America and has historically played a prominent part in national affairs. The army is a national militia, with service compulsory for all able-bodied male citizens between the ages of 18 and 45. Up to 14 months of full-time duty are required. The army has a strength of about 55,000 men. The navy consists of an aircraft carrier, six missile-equipped destroyers, and a number of lighter ships and submarines; it has a strength of about 25,000 men. The air force, with 15,000 men, has about 200 combat aircraft, including jet fighters and bombers.

HISTORY

In February 1516, the Spanish navigator Juan Díaz de Solís (1470?–1516), then engaged in search of a southwest passage to the East Indies, piloted his vessel into the great estuary now known as the Río de la Plata and claimed the surrounding region in the name of Spain. Sebastian Cabot, an Italian navigator in the service of Spain, visited the estuary in 1526. In search of food and supplies, he and his men ascended the river later called the Paraná to a point near the site of modern Rosario. They constructed a fort and then pushed up the river as far as the region now occupied by Paraguay. Cabot, who remained in the river basin for nearly four years, obtained from the natives quantities of silver (Span. *la plata*), a name that was soon applied to the river system and most of the region watered by it.

Early Settlements. Colonization was begun in 1535 by the Spanish soldier Pedro de Mendoza (1487?–1537). In February 1536, Mendoza, who had been appointed military governor of the entire continent south of the Río de la Plata, founded Buenos Aires. In its efforts to establish a permanent colony, his expedition encountered severe hardships, chiefly because of difficulties in obtaining food. Hostile natives forced the abandonment of this settlement five years later.

In 1538 Domingo Martínez de Irala (1486–1557?), one of Mendoza's lieutenants, founded Asunción (now the capital of Paraguay), which was the first permanent settlement in the La Plata region. From their base at Asunción, the Spanish gradually won control over the territory between the Paraná and Paraguay rivers. The small herds of livestock brought from Spain had meanwhile multiplied and spread over the Pampas, creating the conditions for a stable agricultural economy.

Santiago del Estero, the first permanent settlement on what is now Argentine soil, was established in 1553 by Spanish settlers from Peru. Santa Fe was founded in 1573, and in 1580 the resettlement of Buenos Aires was begun. In 1620 the entire La Plata region was attached to the viceroyalty of Peru for administrative purposes. Because of the restrictive commercial policies of the Spanish government, colonization of the La Plata region proceeded slowly during the next 100 years. Buenos Aires, the center of a flourishing trade in smuggled goods, grew steadily. By the middle of the 18th century, its population numbered close to 20,000. In 1776 the territory occupied by present-day Argentina, Bolivia, Paraguay, and Uruguay was separated from Peru and incorporated as the viceroyalty of La Plata.

Patriotic Awakening. In June 1806, Buenos Aires was attacked by a British fleet under the command of Adm. Home Riggs Popham (1762–1820). The viceroy offered no defense against the attack, which was made without authorization by the British government. The invaders occupied the city but were expelled by a citizen army the following August. An expeditionary force subsequently dispatched by the British government against Buenos Aires was compelled to capitulate in 1807. These events had far-reaching consequences; the colonial patriots, imbued with confidence in their fighting ability, soon became active in the independence movement that had begun to develop in Spanish South America.

Revolutionary sentiment in La Plata reached its peak in the period following the deposing (1808) of King Ferdinand VII of Spain by Napoleon. The people of Buenos Aires refused to recognize Joseph Bonaparte, Napoleon's brother, who was then installed on the Spanish throne. On May 25, 1810, they overthrew the viceregal government and installed a provisional governing council in the name of Ferdinand VII. The provisional government shortly broke with the representatives of Ferdinand and launched an energetic campaign to revolutionize the La Plata hinterland. This campaign ended in failure. Several signal victories, however, were won over invading royalist armies in 1812–13. The liberated part of the viceroyalty was divided into 14 provinces in 1813. In 1814 the brilliant military leader José de San Martín took command of the northern army, which later struck decisive blows against Spanish rule in Chile and Peru.

The United Provinces. During 1814 and 1815 sentiment crystallized in the liberated area, which was nominally still subject to the Spanish crown, in favor of absolute independence. Representatives of the various provinces convened at Tucumán in March 1816. On the following July 9 the delegates proclaimed independence from Spanish rule and declared the formation of the United Provinces of South America (later United Provinces of the Río de la Plata). Although a so-called supreme director was appointed to head the new state, the congress was unable to reach agreement on a form of government. Many of the delegates, particularly those from the city and province of Buenos Aires, favored the creation of a constitutional monarchy. This position, which was later modified in favor of a highly centralized republican system, met vigorous opposition from the delegates of the other provinces, who favored a federal system of government. Friction between the two factions mounted steadily, culminating in a civil war in 1819. Peace was restored in 1820, but the central issue, formation of a stable government, remained unresolved. Throughout most of the following decade a state of anarchy, further compounded by war (1825–27) with Brazil, prevailed in the United Provinces. Brazil was defeated in the conflict, a result of rival claims to Uruguay, which emerged as an independent state.

The national political turmoil lessened appreciably after the election (1829) of Gen. Juan Manuel de Rosas as governor of Buenos Aires Province. A federalist, Rosas cemented friendly relations with other provinces, thereby winning broad popular support. He rapidly extended his authority over the United Provinces, which became known as the Argentine Confederation, and during his rule all opposition groups were crushed or driven underground.

Republican Government. The dictatorial regime of Rosas was overthrown in 1852 by a revolutionary group led by Gen. Justo Urquiza (1800–70), a former governor of Entre Ríos Province, who received assistance from Uruguay and Brazil. In 1853 a federal constitution was adopted, and Urquiza became first president of the Argentine Republic. Buenos Aires Province, refusing to adhere to the new constitution, proclaimed independence in 1854. The mutual hostility of the two states flared into war in 1859. The Argentine Republic won a quick victory in this conflict, and in

October 1859, Buenos Aires agreed to join the federation. The province was, however, the center of another rebellion against the central government in 1861. Headed by Gen. Bartolomé Mitre, the rebels defeated the national army in September of that year. The president of the republic resigned on November 5. In May of the next year a national convention elected Mitre to the presidency and designated the city of Buenos Aires as the national capital. With these events, Buenos Aires Province, the wealthiest and most populous in the union, achieved temporary hegemony over the remainder of the nation.

Turmoil in Uruguay brought on a Paraguayan invasion of Argentine territory in 1865, beginning the bloody War of the Triple Alliance, which ended in complete victory for Argentina, Brazil, and Uruguay in 1870. During the next decade the conquest of the Pampas as far as the Río Negro was completed and the threat of hostile Indians from that direction eliminated. This so-called War of the Desert (1879–80), directed by Gen. Julio A. Roca, opened up vast new areas for grazing and farming. In 1880 Roca, who opposed the ascendency of Buenos Aires in national affairs, was elected to the presidency. In the aftermath of his victory, the city of Buenos Aires was separated from the province and established as a federal district and national capital. A long-standing boundary dispute with Chile was settled in 1881; through this agreement Argentina acquired the title to the eastern half of Tierra del Fuego. In 1895 a boundary dispute with Brazil was submitted to arbitration by the U.S., which awarded about 65,000 sq km (about 25,000 sq mi) of territory to Argentina. The country became involved in a serious controversy with Chile regarding the Patagonian frontier in 1899. This dispute was finally settled in 1902, with Great Britain acting as arbitrator.

In the half century following 1880, Argentina made remarkable economic and social progress. During the first decade of the 20th century the country emerged as one of the leading nations of South America. It began to figure prominently in hemispheric affairs and, in 1914, helped to mediate a serious dispute between the U.S. and Mexico. Argentina remained neutral during World War I but played a major role as supplier of foodstuffs to the Allies.

Depression and Turmoil. The world economic crisis that began in 1929 had serious repercussions in Argentina. Unemployment and other hardships caused profound social and political unrest. Economic conditions improved substantially during the administration of Gen. Augustín Justo (1876–1943), but political turbulence intensified, culminating (1933–34) in an unsuccessful Radical uprising. In the period preceding the presidential elections of 1937, Fascist organizations became increasingly active. In May 1936, following the organization of a left-wing Popular Front, the Argentine right-wing parties united in a so-called National Front. This organization, which openly advocated establishment of a dictatorship, successfully supported the finance minister, Roberto M. Ortiz (1886–1942), for the presidency. Contrary to the expectations and demands of his supporters, however, Ortiz took vigorous steps to strengthen democracy in Argentina. Countermeasures were adopted against the subversive activities of German agents, who had become extremely active after the victory of National Socialism in Germany. The corrupt electoral machinery of the country was overhauled. Ortiz proclaimed neutrality after the outbreak of World War II, but he subsequently cooperated closely with the other American republics on matters of hemispheric defense.

World War II. In July 1940, President Ortiz, unable to function because of illness, designated Vice-President Ramón S. Castillo (1873–1944) as acting president. A Conservative, Castillo broke with the foreign and domestic policies of his predecessor. At the Pan-American Defense Conference, held at Rio de Janeiro in January 1942, shortly after the Japanese attack on Pearl Harbor, Argentina and Chile were the only American nations to refuse to sever relations with the Axis powers.

Castillo, who had officially succeeded to the presidency following the resignation of Ortiz in June 1942, was removed from office one year later by a military group headed by Gen. Arturo Rawson (1884–1952), who favored severance of relations with Germany and Japan. On the eve of his assumption of office as provisional president, however, Rawson's associates forced him to resign. The provisional presidency went to Gen. Pedro Ramírez (1884–1962), one of the leaders of the revolt. Ramírez shortly abolished all political parties, suppressed opposition newspapers, and generally stifled the remnants of democracy in Argentina. In January 1944, in a complete reversal of foreign policy, his government broke diplomatic relations with Japan and Germany.

Fearful that war with Germany was imminent, a military junta, the so-called Colonels, forced Ramírez from office on Feb. 24, 1944. The central figure in the junta was Col. Juan Domingo Perón, chief of labor relations in the Ramírez regime. Despite protestations of sympathy with the Allied cause, the government continued the policy of suppression of democratic activity and of har-

Gen. Juan and Eva Perón amid a throng of their supporters and admirers during the heady days of the mid-1940s. UPI

boring German agents. In July the U.S. government accused Argentina of aiding the Axis powers. Finally, on March 27, 1945, when Allied victory in Europe was assured, the country declared war on Germany and Japan. In the following month the government signed the Act of Chapultepec, a compact among American nations for mutual aid against aggressors. Argentina, with U.S. sponsorship, became a charter member of the UN in June. Shortly afterward, it was announced that elections would be held early in 1946.

The Perón Era. Revival of political activity in Argentina was marked by the appearance of a new grouping, the Peronistas. Formally organized as the Labor party, with Perón as its candidate for the presidency, this group found its main support among the most depressed sections of the agricultural and industrial working class. The Peronistas campaigned among these workers, popularly known as *descamisados* (Span., "shirtless ones"), with promises of land, higher wages, and social security. The elections, held on February 24, resulted in a decisive victory for Perón over his opponent, the candidate of a progressive coalition.

In October 1945, Perón married the former actress Eva Duarte, who, as first lady of Argentina, managed labor relations and social services for her husband's government until her death in 1952. Adored by the masses, whom she manipulated with consummate skill, she was, as much as anyone, responsible for the popular following of the Perón regime. In October 1946, President Perón promulgated an ambitious five-year plan for the expansion of the economy. During 1947 he deported a number of German agents and expropriated about 60 German firms. After these moves, relations between Argentina and the U.S. improved steadily.

New constitution. In March 1949, Perón promulgated a new constitution permitting the president of the republic to succeed himself in office. Taking advantage of the new law, the Peronista party in July 1949 renominated Perón as its presidential candidate for 1952. As a result the opposition parties and press became increasingly critical of the government. The Peronista majority in the congress retaliated (September) with legislation providing prison terms for persons who showed "disrespect" for government leaders. Many opponents of the regime were jailed in subsequent months. The congress shortly instituted other retaliatory measures, notably suppression of the opposition press.

La Prensa, a leading independent daily newspaper, was suppressed in March 1951. In the following month congress approved legislation expropriating the paper. Severe restrictions were imposed on the anti-Peronista parties in the campaign preceding the national elections, which took place in November 1951, instead of February 1952, the originally scheduled date. President Perón was reelected by a large majority, and Peronista candidates won 135 of the 149 seats in the house of deputies.

Second term. In January 1953 the government inaugurated a second five-year plan. The plan emphasized increased agricultural output instead of all-out industrialization, which had been the goal of the first five-year plan. During 1953 Argentina concluded important economic and trade agreements with several countries, notably Great Britain, the Soviet Union, and Chile. Foreign commercial transactions in 1953 produced a favorable balance of trade, the first since 1950; but inflationary pressures, which had resulted in an increase in the cost of living of more than 200 percent since 1948, did not lessen.

In November 1954, Perón accused a group of Roman Catholic clergymen of "fostering agitation" against the government. Despite church opposition, the government proposed and secured enactment during the next two months of legislation legalizing absolute divorce, granting all benefits of legitimacy to children borne out of wedlock, and legalizing prostitution. The schism between church and state widened steadily in the succeeding months.

Overthrow. On June 16, 1955, dissident elements of the Argentine navy and its air arm launched a rebellion in Buenos Aires. The army remained loyal, however, and the uprising was quickly crushed. Tension increased during the next few weeks, as factions within the government and the military maneuvered for position. Finally, on September 16, insurgent groupings in all three branches of the armed forces staged a concerted rebellion; after three days of civil war, during which approximately 4000 persons were killed, Perón resigned and took refuge on a Paraguayan gunboat in Buenos Aires Harbor. On September 20 the insurgent leader Maj. Gen. Eduardo Lonardi (1896-1956) took office as provisional president, promising to restore democratic government. Perón went into exile, first in Paraguay and later in Spain.

Provisional Presidents. In less than two months the Lonardi government was itself overthrown in a bloodless coup d'etat led by Maj. Gen. Pedro Eugenio Aramburu (1903-70). The announced reason for the revolt was the unwillingness of Lonardi to suppress Peronism, especially in the army and among the workers. Aramburu abrogated the 1949 constitution and restored the liberal charter of 1853. Under the latter, a president may not succeed himself. A Peronist revolt was crushed in June 1956. Thousands were arrested, and 38 alleged Peronistas were executed. Scores of persons were subsequently imprisoned on charges of plotting to overthrow the new regime.

Elections to a constitutional assembly were held in July. The moderate Radical party, headed by Ricardo Balbín (1904-81), received the most votes, closely followed by the somewhat leftist Intransigent Radical party under Arturo Frondizi (1908-). The Peronistas, forbidden to function as a party, were instructed by their exiled leader to cast blank ballots. Blanks, which were encouraged also by some minor groups, exceeded the votes of any single party and constituted about one-fourth of the total cast.

Elected Presidents. The constituent assembly, which opened in Santa Fe in September, unanimously readopted the constitution of 1853 after the Intransigent Radicals and some others withdrew. When general elections were held in February 1958, Frondizi won the presidency with Peronist and Communist support, and his Intransigent Radical party won a majority in the legislature. Representative government was restored on May 1.

Despite labor unrest and continual rises in living costs, a degree of economic stability was achieved in early 1959 with the aid of substantial foreign loans and credits; by 1960, loans from U.S. public and private agencies alone amounted to $1 billion.

Frondizi's popularity declined markedly throughout 1961. In elections held in March 1962, Peronistas, again permitted electoral participation, polled about 35 percent of the total vote. Although Frondizi forbade five successful Peronist candidates from assuming the provincial governorships they had won, he was deposed at the end of the month by military leaders critical of his leniency toward Peronism. José María Guido (1910-75), as president of the Senate, became Frondizi's constitutional successor.

His government, however, was dominated by the armed forces. Both Peronistas and Communists were barred from the national elections of July 1963, in which Arturo Illía (1901-83), a moderate of the People's Radical party, was elected president. Illía announced a program of national recovery and regulation of foreign investment and tried to control rising prices, shortages, and labor unrest by fixing prices and setting minimum-wage laws.

Military Rule. In elections in 1965, Peronist candidates made significant gains, although Illía's party retained a 71-seat plurality in the lower house. Labor unrest continued into 1966, and the Peronistas continued to win victories in by-elections. The result was a military coup in June 1966. The junta that then took control named succeeding presidents, the third of whom, Gen. Alejandro Augustín Lanusse (1918–), took office in 1971.

In the early months of his regime, Lanusse began moving toward a return to civilian rule. He announced an economic program designed to hold down the inflationary spiral and scheduled national elections for March 1973. In 1972, however, the country became increasingly torn by violence, including strikes, student riots, and terrorist activities. The economy too was headed for a new crisis. The Peronistas had grown increasingly vocal, and they now nominated Perón for the presidency. He remained in Spain until after the date set for candidates to be resident in Argentina, however, and Hector J. Cámpora (1909–80) was nominated in his place.

Return and Death of Perón. Peronistas swept the elections in March 1973, and Cámpora was inaugurated as president on May 25. Terrorism escalated, now joined by rightist vigilantes, with numerous kidnappings, soaring ransom demands, and killings. Divisions between moderate and leftist Peronistas also brought widespread violence. On June 20, when Perón returned to Buenos Aires, a riot resulted in approximately 380 casualties.

A month later Cámpora resigned, and in September Perón was elected president, with more than 61 percent of the votes. His third wife, Isabel, was elected vice-president.

The strain, however, proved too much for the aging Perón. He died on July 1, 1974, and his wife succeeded him, becoming the first woman chief executive of a modern Latin American state. During her presidency, political and economic conditions deteriorated rapidly. In 1975 terrorist activities by right- and left-wing groups resulted in the deaths of more than 700 people. The cost of living increased by 335 percent, and strikes and demonstrations for higher wages were frequent. After repeated cabinet crises and an abortive air force rebellion in December 1975, a military junta led by the army commander, Lt. Gen. Jorge Rafael Videla, seized power on March 24, 1976. The junta dissolved the legislature, imposed martial law, and ruled by decree.

Military Rule and the Falklands War. For the first few months after the military takeover, terrorism remained rampant, but it waned somewhat after the Videla government launched its own terror campaign against political opponents. In 1977 the Argentine Commission for Human Rights, in Geneva, blamed the regime for 2300 political murders, some 10,000 political arrests, and 20,000 to 30,000 disappearances.

President Raúl Alfonsín arrives for his first official day at work. The office had been occupied by a military government for more than seven years. UPI/Bettmann Newsphotos

The economy remained chaotic. Videla was succeeded as president (March 1981) by Field Marshal Roberto Viola (1924–), himself deposed in December 1981 by the commander in chief of the army, Gen. Leopoldo Galtieri (1926–). Galtieri's government rallied the country behind it in April 1982 by forcibly occupying the British-held Falkland Islands (called Islas Malvinas by the Argentines). A shooting war ensued with Great Britain in May and June, ending with the British recapture of the islands. The discredited Galtieri was replaced by Maj. Gen. Reynaldo Bignone (1928–).

With an unprecedented international debt and inflation at more than 900 percent, Argentina held its first presidential election in a decade in October 1983. The winner was the candidate of the Radical party, Raúl Alfonsín (1927–). Under Alfonsín, the armed forces were reorganized; former military and political leaders were charged with human rights abuses; the foreign debt was restructured; fiscal reforms (including a new currency) were introduced; and a treaty to resolve a dispute with Chile over three Beagle Channel islands was approved. Inflation remained unchecked, however, and in May 1989 the Peronist candidate, Carlos Saúl Menem (1930–), was elected president. With Argentina's economy deteriorating rapidly, Menem took office in July, five months ahead of schedule, and imposed an austerity program.

For further information on this topic, see the Bibliography in volume 28, sections 666, 726, 847, 1231–33, 1236.

ARGENTINA, La, professional name of ANTONIA MERCÉ (1890–1936), Argentine-born Spanish dancer, who was the single greatest influence in the 20th-century renaissance of Spanish dance. Born in Buenos Aires and reared in Spain, she studied under her Spanish-born parents, both professional dancers. Trained in classical ballet, La Argentina was première danseuse at the Madrid Opera at age 11 but left when she was 14 to study the regional dances of Spain. Transforming these into an art of great plasticity and vitality, she toured widely and eventually won acceptance for her dance as a theatrical art form.

ARGENTINE (Lat. *argentum,* "silver"), common name for fishes of the genus *Argentina,* sometimes extended to other fishes of the same family, Argentinidae. They are small, smeltlike, deep-sea fishes abundant off the coasts of Europe and off both coasts of America. Argentines, named for their silvery luster, are major food fishes.

ARGO, also Argo Navis, in ancient astronomy, constellation in the southern hemisphere, extending from Canis Major to the Southern Cross and including part of the Milky Way. Representing *Argo,* the ship of the Argonauts, the constellation has been reclassified as separate constellations by modern astronomers. The main divisions are Carina (the Keel), Puppis (the Stern), and Vela (the Sails). Canopus, the principal star in the constellation, is the second brightest star in the heavens.

ARGON, gaseous element, symbol Ar, one of the noble gases (q.v.) in group 18 (or VIIIa) of the periodic table (*see* PERIODIC LAW); at.no. 18, at.wt. 39.948. Argon melts at −189.3° C (−308.2° F) and boils at −185.86° C (−302.55° F).

Argon is composed of monatomic molecules and is colorless and odorless. It constitutes 0.93 percent of the atmosphere. Argon was discovered (1894) by the British scientists Sir William Ramsay and Baron Rayleigh. They were led to this discovery by a discrepancy between the density of supposedly pure nitrogen, prepared from air, and actually pure nitrogen, prepared from ammonium nitrate.

Argon is produced commercially by the fractional distillation of liquid air. It is used in large quantities to fill electric light bulbs. If air is left in incandescent bulbs, the filament burns; if the bulb is evacuated, as was formerly done, the tungsten filament tends to evaporate, blackening the inside of the bulb. To prevent this evaporation, the bulb may be filled with nitrogen, which is the least expensive gas for the purpose, or argon, which is better, as it is a poorer conductor of heat and so cools the filament less.

Argon is also used in one type of neon lamp. Whereas pure neon gives a red light, argon gives a blue light. Argon tubes require a lower voltage than neon tubes, and for this reason small amounts of argon are sometimes mixed with neon. Argon is also used in electric-arc technology, in gas lasers, and in arc welding. *See* LASER; WELDING.

ARGONAUTS, in Greek mythology, the band of heroes who sailed on the ship *Argo* to obtain the Golden Fleece. The leader of the expedition was Jason, son of Aeson, king of Iolcus in Thessaly. Aeson was deposed by his half brother Pelias, who then tried to prevent Jason from claiming the throne. To this end, he persuaded Jason to undertake the dangerous quest for the Golden Fleece, which was held by Aeëtes, king of Colchis, a region located at the eastern end of the Euxine (Black) Sea. Jason assembled 50 of the noblest young men of Greece to accompany him on the voyage. The group chosen included Hercules, Orpheus, Castor and Pollux, and Peleus.

The *Argo* sailed from Iolcus to the island of Lemnos, and on to the Euxine Sea by way of

Mysia, an area east of the Aegean Sea, and Thrace. Early in the voyage the crew lost Hercules, who left the ship to search for Hylas, his friend and armor bearer. The Argonauts saved a Thracian king, Phineus, from starvation caused by the Harpies, flying creatures with heads of women, who were carrying off and befouling his food. In gratitude, Phineus told them how to pass through the Symplegades, the rocks that guarded the entrance to the Euxine Sea by clashing against each other when anything went between them. As Phineus had instructed them, the Argonauts released a dove that flew between the Symplegades. As the rocks clanged together and began to return to their positions, the *Argo* sailed swiftly through.

When the ship finally reached Colchis, Aeëtes refused to relinquish the fleece unless Jason could first yoke and plow a field with two fire-breathing, brass-hoofed bulls. He was then to sow a field with dragon teeth and vanquish the armed men that would spring up from them. Helped by Aeëtes' daughter, the sorceress Medea, who had fallen in love with him, Jason accomplished these tasks and carried off the fleece. Medea, fleeing with him, slew her brother, Apsyrtus, to delay the pursuit of her father. On the homeward voyage the *Argo* safely passed between the six-headed monster Scylla and the whirlpool Charybdis. Sea nymphs, sent by the goddess Hera, saved the ship from destruction in a storm off the coast of Libya. From there the *Argo* sailed to Crete and then home to Iolcus.

ARGONNE, also Argonne Forest, wooded plateau region, NE France, lying between the Meuse and Aisne rivers, and occupying parts of the departments of Ardennes, Marne, and Meuse. The region extends from the Belgian frontier SE to the vicinity of Verdun, a distance of about 71 km (about 44 mi). It has an average width of about 16 km (about 10 mi). The Aire R. and smaller streams flow through the region. Elevations average about 350 m (about 1150 ft), and steep cliffs delineate the river valleys in the E portion of the region. These, together with brush woods and forests, make the region a natural defense bastion. In 1792, during the French Revolution, the French general Charles François Dumouriez (1739–1823) conducted a successful campaign against the Prussians led by Charles William Ferdinand, duke of Brunswick (1735–1806), on the Argonne; it ended in the decisive French victory of Valmy. In 1870, during the Franco-Prussian War, the Argonne was the scene of the retreat of the French army under Marshal MacMahon from Beaumont to Sedan. The Argonne region was also the site of a major battle of World War I.

ARGONNE, BATTLE OF THE, often Meuse-Argonne offensive, major battle of World War I, fought in the fall of 1918 between the U.S. First Army, which included the XVII French Corps, and strong units of the German army. The battle was part of a general Allied offensive against the Hindenburg line, the highly fortified German defense positions in western Europe. To weaken these positions in the Argonne region of France was the immediate objective of the First Army; the secondary objective was to capture the chief German supply line, extending through Sedan and Mézières (both in France). On September 22, after a victory at Saint-Mihiel, France, the First Army, under the command of Gen. John J. Pershing, began to move into the Argonne sector. By September 25, the line of the First Army extended from Regneville-Sur-Meuse, opposite Samogneux, in a southwesterly direction 32.2 km (20 mi) to La Harazée in the Argonne Forest above the valley of the Biesme River. This line was assigned to three army corps, the I, the III, and the V. Nine divisions formed the front line, and three were in reserve. French forces lay west of the Aisne River, and on the east the U.S. position was flanked by French troops under U.S. command. Opposed to the U.S. forces were the German Fifth Army, with eight divisions, part of the German Third Army, and about eight divisions in reserve.

U.S. operations were conducted in three stages, the first of which lasted from September 26 to October 1 and drove a salient about 11 km (about 7 mi) deep into enemy positions before the Hindenburg line. During the second stage, which lasted from October 4 to 16, the First Army crossed the Aire River and captured all major German defense positions in the Argonne region. The third, or pursuit, stage lasted from November 1 to 10.

In the Argonne offensive, more than 1,200,000 U.S. troops were concentrated for the advance; of that number, 60,000 took an active part in the battle, which extended over an area of 1295 sq km (500 sq mi). U.S. casualties in the entire Battle of the Argonne were 117,000 killed or wounded. German losses were 94,000 killed or wounded, 26,000 captured by U.S. forces, and 30,000 captured by the French. The battle caused the final breakdown of German resistance and helped bring about the German request for an armistice, which was granted on Nov. 11, 1918.

ARGONNE NATIONAL LABORATORY, a U.S. center for research in nuclear and high-energy physics, located at Argonne, Ill., near Chicago. It was founded in 1946 and is operated by the University of Chicago and Argonne Universities

Great argus pheasant, Argusianus argus, *can attain a length of 2 m (6.5 ft).*
© Tom McHugh–Photo Researchers, Inc.

Association for the U.S. Department of Energy (originally for the Atomic Energy Commission). The staff of about 5000 conducts research in the peaceful uses of nuclear energy and related environmental problems. The first experimental boiling water reactor was constructed here in 1956. Current facilities include breeder reactors and an intense pulsed neutron source. Its proton accelerator, called the zero-gradient synchrotron, or ZGS, was shut down in 1970. *See* PARTICLE ACCELERATORS.

ARGOS, city, central Greece, in the Pelopónnisos Region, near Corinth. Argos dates from the Bronze Age and is believed to be the oldest city in Greece. In the Homeric Age, Argos was reputedly ruled by the warrior Diomedes. The city subsequently became part of the Mycenaean civilization. In historic times, specifically during the reign of King Pheidon (fl. 7th cent. BC), Argos was the most powerful city-state in the Pelopónnisos. After a disastrous protracted struggle with Sparta in the 5th century BC, Argos lost power and influence. In 229 BC it joined the Achaean League, and it became part of the Roman province of Achaea in 146 BC. During the late Middle Ages Argos was part of the Byzantine Empire. The Turks held the city from 1460 until 1830. In the 1820s, during the Greek struggle for independence, the city served briefly as the seat of the Greek National Assembly. A Turkish army sacked the city in 1825. The present city is an important railway junction and is noted for the ruins of a temple to the Greek goddess Hera. Pop. (1981) 20,702.

ARGUS, in Greek mythology, a 100-eyed giant (also called Panoptes) who was assigned by the goddess Hera, wife of Zeus, to guard Io, of whom she was jealous. Zeus, who favored his mistress Io, changed her into a heifer to protect her from Hera. The god Hermes, dispatched by Zeus to rescue Io, slew Argus by lulling his eyes to sleep with music and then severing his head. In one version of the story, Argus subsequently became a peacock; in another, Hera transplanted his eyes onto the peacock's tail.

Argus was also the name of the builder of the *Argo,* the ship that carried Greek hero Jason in his quest for the Golden Fleece (*see* ARGONAUTS). Also known by the name Argus was the old dog of Odysseus, Greek leader during the Trojan War. When his master returned after 19 years, Argus recognized him and promptly died.

ARGUS PHEASANT, common name for *Argusianus argus,* of the family Phasianidae (*see* PHEASANT). The argus pheasant is named after the 100-eyed mythological creature Argus, because of the many eye-like iridescent spots on the inner wing feathers of the male. Although the bird is not much larger than a large chicken when divested of its plumage, the total length, including the tail feathers, is more than 1.5 m (5 ft). The tail consists of 12 feathers, of which the two middle ones are very long. The plumage of both sexes is simple and dull in color except for the male's beautiful inner wing feathers. In both sexes the bill is nearly as long as the rest of the head, and the sides of the head and neck have almost no feathers. The argus pheasant lives in jungles of the Malay Peninsula, Sumatra, and Borneo.

ARGYLL, Archibald Campbell, 5th Earl of (1530–73), Scottish general and statesman. He was a supporter of Mary, queen of Scots, and was implicated in the murder in 1567 of her husband Henry Stuart, Lord Darnley. In 1568 Argyll, commanding the army of the queen, was defeated at Langside by the forces of the regent of Scotland, James Stuart, earl of Moray (1531?–70). Argyll later made peace with Moray and was made lord high chancellor of Scotland in 1572.

ARGYLL, Archibald Campbell, 1st Marquess and 8th Earl of (1598–1661), Scottish statesman, great-grandson of the 5th earl. A Puritan, he was a leader of the Covenanters, and at the onset of the first phase of the English Revolution, he forced Charles I, king of England, to submit to the demands of the Scottish Parliament. In 1645 Argyll and his forces were defeated at Inverlochy by Scottish Royalist nobles led by James Graham Montrose. After the execution of Charles I in 1649, Argyll invited Charles II to Scotland and crowned him king of Scotland at Scone in 1651. In 1660, upon the restoration of Charles II as king of England, Argyll was arrested on a charge of having collaborated with the Commonwealth leader Oliver Cromwell in the latter's invasion of Scotland in 1650. Argyll was tried by the Scottish Parliament and was convicted and beheaded.

ARGYLL, Archibald Campbell, 9th Earl of (1629–85), Scottish nobleman, son of the 8th earl. During the second phase of the English Revolution, he fought for Charles II against Oliver Cromwell at Dunbar, Scotland, in 1650. After the Restoration, Argyll increasingly criticized the government. Subsequently, he was arrested for treason and his estates were seized. He escaped to the Netherlands, where he joined the conspiracy to capture the English throne for James Scott, duke of Monmouth. Argyll led an invasion of Scotland in support of Monmouth in 1685, but was captured and beheaded.

ARGYLL, Archibald Campbell, 10th Earl and 1st Duke of (1651?–1703), Scottish nobleman, son of the 9th earl. During the Glorious Revolution (1688) he helped the Dutch royal couple to gain the thrones of the British Isles as William III and Mary II. Argyll recovered the lands that had been seized from his father and had been denied Argyll by the deposed monarch James II, king of England. Argyll was instrumental in the submission of the Scottish nobles to the joint sovereigns; in 1701 he was rewarded with a dukedom.

ARGYLL, John Campbell, 2d Duke of (1678–1743), Scottish soldier and statesman, son of the first duke. He distinguished himself as a soldier, fighting under John Churchill, 1st duke of Marlborough, at the Battle of Malplaquet (France) during the War of the Spanish Succession. Later, as high commissioner, Argyll furthered the union of England and Scotland. In his political activities he several times changed his views and alternated in favor and disfavor at court. He was made duke of Greenwich in the English peerage in 1719.

ARGYLLSHIRE, former county, W Scotland; Inveraray was the county town. The county, largely mountainous and unarable with a deeply indented Atlantic coastline, included numerous islands. Among the more important islands, which belong to the Inner Hebrides, are Mull, Islay, and Iona; the Celtic missionary St. Columba founded an abbey on Iona in the 6th century. The history of Argyllshire after the 15th century is associated with that of the noble Scottish family of Campbell. In 1975 Argyllshire was divided between the newly created Highland and Strathclyde (qq.v.) regions.

ÅRHUS, also Aarhus, city, central Denmark, capital of Århus Co., on the Jutland Peninsula and Århus Bay (an arm of the Kattegat). It is a seaport and has major shipbuilding and petroleum-refining industries; other manufactures include machinery, transportation equipment, processed food, and beer. Among the points of interest in the city are Saint Clement's Cathedral (begun 13th cent., largely rebuilt 15th cent.); Vor Frue Church (begun 11th cent.); the Old Town (Den Gamle By), an outdoor museum of medieval buildings; and the city hall (1938-42). Århus University (1928) is in the city.

Århus became an episcopal see in 948 and prospered under a succession of notable Roman Catholic bishops in the 14th and 15th centuries. It declined after the Reformation (16th cent.), but it was revived in the 19th century as a shipping and manufacturing center. Pop. (1988 est.) 258,000.

ARIA, musical composition for solo voice with instrumental accompaniment, usually part of an opera, oratorio, or cantata. It provides a lyrical pause in the dramatic action, during which a character can comment on some aspect of the drama. Often it is also a difficult piece designed to display the singer's skill.

The aria originated in Italy in the late 16th century as a short solo song, particularly a strophic song (that is, having the same music for each stanza of text). Early 17th-century composers developed the "strophic-bass" aria, in which, for each stanza, the bass remained constant but the melody was varied. Strophic-bass arias were soon adopted by early opera composers such as the Italian Claudio Monteverdi.

Shortly before 1650 a new aria form appeared, which dominated operatic music until about 1750. This was the *da capo* aria, written in three sections: ABA. To indicate the repeated A section, composers simply wrote the direction *da capo* (Ital., "from the beginning") after the B section. The *da capo* aria developed into a long musical structure with the B section usually in a contrasting but related key. An instrumental introduction usually preceded the A section, and an instrumental interlude separated the A and B sections. Singers took advantage of the repeated A section as a vehicle for virtuosic improvised variations. Alessandro Scarlatti, the celebrated Italian opera composer, helped establish the nearly universal use of the *da capo* aria. Later the 18th-century German-born composer George Frideric Handel used it extensively in his operas and oratorios, and his contemporary Johann Sebastian Bach used it in his oratorios and cantatas.

In the late 18th century, operatic reformers such as the German Christoph Willibald Gluck, reacting against the *da capo* aria, employed a variety of aria forms. Wolfgang Amadeus Mozart and others often used arias with two contrasting sections, and the one-section cavatina also became popular. The romanticism of the 19th century fostered wide variety in aria forms. In the late 19th century Richard Wagner dispensed with the aria almost completely in his mature works, favoring a continuous span of music rather than a separation of action and lyrical comment. Although many 20th-century opera composers follow Wagner's example, others use arias of many different formats.

ARIADNE, in Greek mythology, the daughter of Minos, king of Crete, and Pasiphaë, daughter of Helios, the sun god. The hero Theseus came to Crete from Athens with a band of 14 young men to slay the Minotaur, a monster, half bull, half human, that was confined in the mazes of the Labyrinth. When Ariadne saw Theseus, she fell in love with him and offered to help him if he would promise to take her back to Athens and marry her. She then gave him a ball of thread, which she had obtained from Daedalus, the inventor and designer of the labyrinth. Fastening one end to the door and unwinding the thread as he went along, Theseus was able to find and kill the Minotaur and then to escape from the maze by rewinding the thread.

Taking Ariadne with them, Theseus and his companions fled over the seas toward Athens. On the way they stopped at the island of Naxos. According to one legend, Theseus deserted Ariadne, sailing without her while she was asleep on the island; the god Dionysus found her and comforted her. According to another legend, Theseus set Ariadne ashore to recover from seasickness while he returned to the ship to do some necessary work. A strong wind then carried him out to sea. When he was finally able to return, he found that Ariadne had died.

ARIANISM, a Christian heresy of the 4th century that denied the full divinity of Jesus Christ. It was named for its author, Arius (256–336). A native of Libya, Arius studied at the theological school of Lucian of Antioch (d. 312), where other supporters of the Arian heresy were also trained. After he was ordained a priest in Alexandria, Arius became involved (319) in a controversy with his bishop concerning the divinity of Christ. Arius was finally exiled (325) to Illyria because of his beliefs, but debate over his doctrine soon engulfed the whole church and agitated it for more than half a century. Although his doctrine was eventually outlawed (379) throughout the Roman Empire by Emperor Theodosius I, it survived for two centuries longer among the barbarian tribes that had been converted to Christianity by Arian bishops.

Arius taught that God is unbegotten and without beginning. The Son, the Second Person of the Trinity (q.v.), therefore, because he is begotten, cannot be God in the same sense that the Father is. The Son was not generated from the divine substance of the Father; he did not exist from all eternity, but was created out of nothing like all other creatures, and exists by the will of the Father. In other words, the relationship of the Son to the Father is not natural, but adoptive.

The teaching of Arius was condemned in 325 at the first ecumenical council at Nicaea (*see* NICAEA, COUNCILS OF). The 318 bishops assembled there drafted a creed which stated that the Son of God was "begotten not made," and consubstantial (Gr. *homoousios,* "of the same substance") with the Father; that is, the Son was part of the Trinity, not of creation (*see* NICENE CREED). Previously, no creed had been universally accepted by all churches. The status of the new creed as dogma was confirmed by bans aganst the teaching of Arius.

Despite its condemnation, the teaching of Arius did not die. In part this was due to the interference of imperial politics. Under the influence of the Greek church historian Eusebius of Caesarea, whose orthodoxy had also been questioned, Emperor Constantine I recalled Arius from exile about 334. Soon after, two influential people came to the support of Arianism: The next emperor, Constantius II, was attracted to the Arian doctrine; the bishop and theologian Eusebuis of Nicomedia, later patriarch of Constantinople, become an Arian leader.

By 359 Arianism had prevailed and was the official faith of the empire. Quarreling among themselves, however, the Arians divided into two parties. The semi-Arians consisted mostly of conservative eastern bishops, who basically agreed with the Nicene Creed but were hesitant about the unscriptural term *homoousios* (consubstantial) used in the creed. The neo-Arians said that the Son was of a different essence (Gr. *heteroousios*) from, or unlike (Gr. *anomoios*), the Father. This group also included the Pneumatomachi (combatants against the Spirit), who said that the Holy Spirit (q.v.) is a creature like the Son. With the death of Constantius II in 361, and the reign of Valens, who persecuted the semi-Arians, the way was opened for the final victory of Nicene orthodoxy, recognized by Emperor Theodosius in 379 and reaffirmed at the second ecumenical council (Constantinople I) held in 381.

See CONSTANTINOPLE, COUNCILS OF. *See also* ATHANASIUS, SAINT. M.Sn.

ARIAS, Arnulfo (1901–88), president of Panama (1940–41, 1949–51, and 1968). Born into one of Panama's leading families, he was trained in medicine at Harvard University but never practiced. He led the U.S.-based Acción Comunal, which initiated a coup in 1931, and the following year helped elect his brother, Harmodio (1886–1962), to the presidency. He subsequently served as ambassador to several European countries.

Elected to his first presidential term in 1940, Arias soon rewrote the constitution, presiding over a pro-Fascist regime. Ousted in 1941 and exiled until 1945, he ran again for the presidency in 1948 and lost, but he was declared the winner the following year. His authoritarianism led to his removal from office in 1951. Having lost a bid for the presidency in 1964, he was elected a third time in 1968 but was overthrown after only 11 days in office. He made an unsuccessful presidential race in 1984.

ARICA, city, N Chile, in Tarapacá Province, on the Pacific Ocean. It is a major seaport and transportation center for N Chile, Bolivia, and the adjacent Tacna region of Peru. The Pan-American Highway passes through the city, which is also served by an international airport. Copper, tin, sulfur, and citrus fruit are major exports. The city was founded in 1570 as San Marcos de Arica. It was a seaport of Peru until 1880, when it was occupied by Chile during the War of the Pacific (1879–83). Chilean control, recognized in the Treaty of Ancón (1883), was confirmed in 1929 by an agreement resolving the long-standing Tacna-Arica Dispute. Pop. (1987 est.) 169,774.

ARIES (Lat., "the ram"), in astronomy and astrology, a zodiacal constellation, that is, one of the constellations on the ecliptic, the annual path of the sun through the heavens. The brightest star in this constellation, Hamal, is a second-magnitude star.

ARIOSTO, Ludovico (1474–1533), Italian poet, born in Reggio nell'Emilia. At an early age he wrote comedies that were favorably noticed by Ippolito I, cardinal d'Este (1479–1520). From 1503 to 1517 Ariosto was one of Ippolito's courtiers. He then entered the service of the cardinal's brother, Alfonso I, duke of Ferrara (1486–1534). Aristo's greatest poem, the *Orlando Furioso* (1st version, 1516; final version, 1532), is ostensibly a continuation of the unfinished epic poem *Orlando Innamorato* (1487), by the Italian poet Matteo Maria Boiardo. Actually, the poem is a tribute to the patrons of Ariosto, the Este family, and its real hero is Ruggiero d'Este, the legendary founder of the house. Many critics consider it among the finest epics written because of its vigor and exalted style. Ariosto's other works include comedies such as *La Lena* (The Wind, 1529), as well as odes, satires, and sonnets.

ARISTA, Mariano (1802–55), Mexican soldier and statesman, born in San Luis Potosí. He received a military education and served in the Spanish army until June 1821, when he joined the Mexican independence movement. He was subsequently promoted through various grades to the rank of general, but was exiled during Santa Anna's presidency from 1833 to 1836. In 1846, during the Mexican War, fought against the U.S., an army under his command was defeated in the battles of Palo Alto and Resaca de la Palma by American forces under Gen. Zachary Taylor. Arista served as minister of war in the administration of President José Joaquín Herrera (1792–1854) from 1848 to 1851, when he succeeded Herrera in the presidency. A conservative coalition forced his resignation in January 1853, and shortly thereafter he was exiled again.

ARISTAEUS, in Greek mythology, son of the god Apollo and the nymph Cyrene. He was worshiped as the protector of hunters, herdsmen, and flocks and as the inventor of beekeeping and olive culture. When Aristaeus tried to seduce Eurydice, the wife of the celebrated musician Orpheus, she fled from him and received a fatal snake bite. The nymphs punished him by causing all of his bees to die; but he appeased the nymphs with a sacrifice of cattle, from whose carcasses emerged new swarms of bees. Aristaeus was learned in the arts of healing and prophecy, and he wandered over many lands sharing his knowledge and curing the sick. He was widely honored as a beneficent god and was often represented as a youthful shepherd carrying a lamb.

ARISTARCHUS OF SAMOS (c. 310–250 BC), Greek astronomer of the Alexandrian school. He was the first to assert that the earth revolved around the sun, thus completing the cosmology of the followers of the Greek philosopher and mathematician Pythagoras, who, in the 6th century BC, had propounded the theory that the earth is spherical and rotates on its own axis. The study of these correct hypotheses was later abandoned and was not revived until the 16th century. In his treatise *On the Dimensions and Distances of the Sun and Moon,* Aristarchus explained his discovery of a method of estimating the relative distances of these bodies from the earth. Although his method was essentially correct, his estimates were wrong because of his inadequate knowledge of mathematics and his lack of modern instruments.

ARISTIDES, called The Just (c. 530–468 BC), Athenian statesman and general. He was one of the ten Greek leaders at the Battle of Marathon in 490 BC at which the Greeks defeated the Persian forces led by King Darius I. In 483 Aristides was banished from Athens because of a long-standing conflict with the Athenian general and statesman Themistocles over the latter's naval policy. Three years later, however, when the Persians again invaded Greece under their king Xerxes I, Aristides was recalled from exile. In 479 BC he led the victorious Athenian army against the Persians at the Battle of Plataea, and in the following year he took a prominent part in the formation of the confederacy of Greek city-states known as the Delian League. Aristides remained a leading figure until his death.

ARISTIPPUS (c. 435–c. 360 BC), Greek philosopher, who studied with Socrates in Athens and founded the Cyrenaic school of hedonism. He held that pleasure is the greatest good and pain the least. Virtue, then, is the capacity to enjoy pleasure and eschew pain. Aristippus maintained that people should dedicate their lives to the pursuit of pleasure, but that they should also exercise judgment and restraint to keep dangerous impulses in check.

ARISTOBULUS I (140?–103 BC), king of Judea (104–103 BC), son of the high priest John Hyrcanus (fl. 135–104 BC); he was the first of the Hasmonean (Maccabean) family to assume the royal title. He annexed Ituraea (in present-day Lebanon) and forced its inhabitants to adopt Judaism. During part of his brief reign, he shared the throne with his brother, Antigonus I.

ARISTOBULUS II (d. 48 BC), last Hasmonean king of Judea (67–63 BC). He was the son of Alexander Jannaeus, king of Judea, and his queen, Salome Alexandra. On the death of Salome Alexandra, the succession was disputed between Aristobulus and his brother Hyrcanus II. In the ensuing civil war Roman forces led by Pompey the Great intervened, ending Hasmonean rule (63 BC). In 60 BC Pompey took Aristobulus to Rome as his prisoner and made Hyrcanus high priest of Judea. Julius Caesar released Aristobulus and sent him back to Judea with two legions, but on the way there Aristobulus was poisoned by followers of Pompey.

ARISTOCRACY (Gr. *aristos,* "best"; *kratos,* "power"), form of government in which the sovereign power is vested in a small number of citizens who are theoretically the best qualified to rule, as opposed to monarchy, in which the supreme authority is vested in one person, and to democracy, in which the ultimate authority is exercised by the entire body of citizens or their representatives. In an aristocracy, although the power of government is wielded by a few, theoretically the administration of government is carried on for the welfare of the many. Whenever the interests of the people as a whole are made subservient to the selfish interests of the rulers, aristocracy becomes a form of government known as oligarchy.

Athens, before the period of the Persian wars of the 5th century BC, and Sparta, during practically its entire history, were aristocracies. The same was true of Rome during the period of the Republic, lasting from the 6th to the 1st century BC. During the Middle Ages no true aristocracy existed, for although political power reposed in the hands of a few, each feudal lord was sole master in his own domain. In England, the government from the accession of the house of Hanover in 1714 through the 19th century, although parliamentary in form, was in fact an aristocracy, since king and Parliament alike were under the control of a few great Whig families.

At present the term *aristocracy* is used loosely and in a great variety of combinations to denote a select few with superiority in various categories, for example, an aristocracy of birth, of wealth, or of intellect.

ARISTOPHANES (c. 448–385 BC), Athenian playwright, considered one of the greatest writers of comedy in literary history. His plays have been produced through the centuries and, because of their wit, comic invention, and poetic language, have remained popular.

Aristophanes is believed to have been born in the deme, or township, of Cydathenaeum, in Athens, the son of one Philippos. He was, presumably, well educated and may have had property on the island of Aegina. He had three sons, Philippos, Araros, and Nikostratos, all of whom were comic poets.

Aristophanes was noted for his conservatism. He favored aristocratic rather than democratic rule and the established philosophical and theological ideas rather than the new ideas of the Sophists. In his opposition to new ideas, however, Aristophanes did not distinguish between destructive and progressive ideas. His opposition to novelty and reform was more emotional than intellectual. Aristophanes wrote more than 40 plays, of which 11 are extant. His first three plays were produced under pseudonyms. One of these was *The Acharnians* (425 BC), a plea for ending the war with Sparta. *The Knights* (424 BC), the first of the plays of Aristophanes to be presented under his own name, is a devastating satire about the Athenian politician and military leader Cleon, champion of the democratic forces and leader of the war party. *The Clouds* (423 BC) is a satire on the Greek philosopher Socrates, whose penetrating analysis of established values Aristophanes considered inimical to the interests of the state. In *The Wasps* (422 BC) Aristophanes satirized the courts of justice of the day, and in *The Peace* (421 BC) he again argued for peace between Athens and Sparta. *The Birds* (414 BC) ridicules the Athenian fondness for litigation. *Lysistrata* (411 BC), another satire on war in which women strike for peace by practicing celibacy, is his most famous work. *Thesmorphoriazusae* (411 BC) and *The Frogs* (405 BC) include attacks on Euripedes. *Ecclesiazusa* (393 BC) is a satire on the idea of communal ownership of property, and *Plutus* (388 BC) reduced to absurdity the concept of redistribution of wealth in Athens. These works, basically fantasies, were written in a form less strict than that of contemporary tragedy; they include dialogue scenes, long choral harangues, lyric passages, and a great deal of music and dance.

The plays of Aristophanes exerted considerable influence on English satire, notably that of Ben Jonson in the 17th century and Henry Fielding in the 18th century.

ARISTOTLE (384–322 BC), Greek philosopher and scientist, who shares with Plato the distinction of being the most famous of ancient philosophers.

Aristotle was born at Stagira, in Macedonia, the son of a physician to the royal court. At the age of 17, he went to Athens to study at Plato's Academy. He remained there for about 20 years, as a student and then as a teacher.

When Plato died in 347 BC, Aristotle moved to Assos, a city in Asia Minor, where a friend of his, Hermias (d. 345 BC), was ruler. There he counseled Hermias and married his niece and adopted daughter, Pythias. After Hermias was captured and executed by the Persians, Aristotle went to Pella, the Macedonian capital, where he became the tutor of the king's young son Alexander, later known as Alexander the Great. In 335, when Alexander became king, Aristotle returned to Athens and established his own school, the Lyceum. Because much of the discussion in his school took place while teachers and students were walking about the Lyceum grounds, Aristotle's school came to be known as the Peripatetic ("walking" or "strolling") school. Upon the death of Alexander in 323 BC, strong anti-Macedonian feeling developed in Athens, and Aristotle retired to a family estate in Euboea. He died there the following year.

Works. Aristotle, like Plato, made regular use of the dialogue in his earliest years at the Academy, but lacking Plato's imaginative gifts, he probably never found the form congenial. Apart from a few fragments in the works of later writers, his dialogues have been wholly lost. Aristotle also wrote some short technical notes, such as a dictionary of philosophic terms and a summary of the doctrines of Pythagoras. Of these, only a few brief excerpts have survived. Still extant, however, are Aristotle's lecture notes for carefully outlined courses treating almost every branch of knowledge and art. The texts on which Aristotle's reputation rests are largely based on these lecture notes, which were collected and arranged by later editors.

Among the texts are treatises on logic, called *Organon* ("instrument"), because they provide the means by which positive knowledge is to be attained. His works on natural science include *Physics,* which gives a vast amount of information on astronomy, meteorology, plants, and animals. His writings on the nature, scope, and properties of being, which Aristotle called *First Philosophy* (*Protē philosophia*), were given the title *Metaphysics* in the first published edition of his works (c. 60 BC), because in that edition they followed *Physics.* His treatment of the Prime Mover, or first cause, as pure intellect, perfect in unity, immutable, and, as he said, "the thought of thought," is given in the *Metaphysics.* To his son Nicomachus he dedicated his work on ethics, called the *Nicomachean Ethics.* Other essential works include his *Rhetoric,* his *Poetics* (which survives in incomplete form), and his *Politics* (also incomplete).

Methods. Perhaps because of the influence of his father's medical profession, Aristotle's philosophy laid its principal stress on biology, in contrast to Plato's emphasis on mathematics. Aristotle regarded the world as made up of individuals (substances) occurring in fixed natural kinds (species). Each individual has its built-in specific pattern of development and grows toward proper self-realization as a specimen of its type. Growth, purpose, and direction are thus built into nature. Although science studies general kinds, according to Aristotle, these kinds find their existence in particular individuals. Science and philosophy must therefore balance, not simply choose between, the claims of empiricism (observation and sense experience) and formalism (rational deduction).

One of the most distinctive of Aristotle's

Aristotle Contemplating the Bust of Homer, a work painted in 1653 by the Dutch master Rembrandt.
Metropolitan Museum of Art

philosophic contributions was a new notion of causality. Each thing or event, he thought, has more than one "reason" that helps to explain what, why, and where it is. Earlier Greek thinkers had tended to assume that only one sort of cause can be really explanatory; Aristotle proposed four. (The word Aristotle uses, *aition,* "a responsible, explanatory factor" is not synonymous with the word *cause* in its modern sense.)

These four causes are the material cause, the matter out of which a thing is made; the efficient cause, the source of motion, generation, or change; the formal cause, which is the species, kind, or type; and the final cause, the goal, or full development, of an individual, or the intended function of a construction or invention. Thus, a young lion is made up of tissues and organs, its material cause; the efficient cause is its parents, who generated it; the formal cause is its species, lion; and its final cause is its built-in drive toward maturity. In different contexts, the same four causes apply analogically. Thus, the material cause of a statue is the marble from which it was carved; the efficient cause is the sculptor; the formal cause is the shape the sculptor realized—Hermes, perhaps; and the final cause is its function, to be a work of fine art.

In each context, Aristotle insists that something can be better understood when its causes can be stated in specific terms rather than in general terms. Thus, it is more informative to know that a "sculptor" made the statue than to know that an "artist" made it; and even more informative to know that "Polycleitus" chiseled it rather than simply that a "sculptor" did so.

Aristotle thought his causal pattern was the ideal key for organizing knowledge. His lecture notes present impressive evidence of the power of this scheme.

Doctrines. Some of the principal aspects of Aristotle's thought can be seen in the following summary of his doctrines, or theories.

Physics, or natural philosophy. In astronomy, Aristotle proposed a finite, spherical universe, with the earth at its center. The central region is made up of four elements: earth, air, fire, and water. In Aristotle's physics, each of these four elements has a proper place, determined by its relative heaviness, its "specific gravity." Each moves naturally in a straight line—earth down, fire up—toward its proper place, where it will be at rest. Thus, terrestrial motion is always linear and always comes to a halt. The heavens, however, move naturally and endlessly in a complex circular motion. The heavens, therefore, must be made of a fifth, and different element, which he called *aither.* A superior element, *aither* is incapable of any change other than change of place in a circular movement. Aristotle's theory that linear motion always takes place through a resisting medium is in fact valid for all observable terrestrial motions. Aristotle also held that heavier bodies of a given material fall faster than lighter ones when their shapes are the same; this mistaken view was accepted as fact until Galileo proved otherwise.

Biology. In zoology, Aristotle proposed a fixed set of natural kinds ("species"), each reproducing true to type. An exception occurs, Aristotle thought, when some "very low" worms and flies come from rotting fruit or manure by "spontaneous generation." The typical life cycles are epicycles: The same pattern repeats, but through a linear succession of individuals. These processes are therefore intermediate between the changeless circles of the heavens and the simple linear movements of the terrestrial elements. The species form a scale from simple (worms and flies at the bottom) to complex (human beings at the top), but evolution is not possible.

Aristotelian psychology. For Aristotle, psychology was a study of the soul. Insisting that form (the essence, or unchanging characteristic element in an object) and matter (the common undifferentiated substratum of things) always exist together, Aristotle defined a soul as a "kind of functioning of a body organized so that it can support vital functions." In considering the soul as essentially associated with the body, he challenged the Pythagorean doctrine that the soul is a spiritual entity imprisoned in the body. Aristotle's doctrine is a synthesis of the earlier notion that the soul does not exist apart from the body and of the Platonic notion of a soul as a separate, nonphysical entity. Whether any part of the human soul is immortal, and, if so, whether its immortality is personal, are not entirely clear in his treatise *On the Soul.*

Through the functioning of the soul, the moral and intellectual aspects of humanity are developed. Aristotle argued that human insight in its highest form (*nous poetikos,* "active mind") is not reducible to a mechanical physical process. Such insight, however, presupposes an individual "passive mind" that does not appear to transcend physical nature. Aristotle clearly stated the relationship between human insight and the senses in what has become a slogan of empiricism—the view that knowledge is grounded in sense experience. "There is nothing in the intellect," he wrote, "that was not first in the senses."

Ethics. It seemed to Aristotle that the individual's freedom of choice made an absolutely accurate analysis of human affairs impossible. "Practical science," then, such as politics or ethics, was called science only by courtesy and analogy. The inherent limitations on practical science are made clear in Aristotle's concepts of human nature and self-realization. Human nature certainly involves, for everyone, a capacity for forming habits; but the habits that a particular individual forms depend on that individual's culture and repeated personal choices. All human beings want "happiness," an active, engaged realization of their innate capacities, but this goal can be achieved in a multiplicity of ways.

Aristotle's *Nicomachean Ethics* is an analysis of character and intelligence as they relate to happiness. Aristotle distinguished two kinds of "virtue," or human excellence: moral and intellectual. Moral virtue is an expression of character, formed by habits reflecting repeated choices. A moral virtue is always a mean between two less desirable extremes. Courage, for example, is a mean between cowardice and thoughtless rashness; generosity, between extravagance and parsimony. Intellectual virtues are not subject to this doctrine of the mean. Aristotle argued for an elitist ethics: Full excellence can be realized only by the mature male adult of the upper class, not by women, or children, or barbarians (non-Greeks), or salaried "mechanics" (manual workers) from whom, indeed, Aristotle proposed to take away voting rights.

In politics, many forms of human association can obviously be found; which one is suitable depends on circumstances, such as the natural resources, cultural traditions, industry, and literacy of each community. Aristotle did not regard politics as a study of ideal states in some abstract form, but rather as an examination of the way in which ideals, laws, customs, and property interrelate in actual cases. He thus approved the contemporary institution of slavery but tempered his acceptance by insisting that masters should not abuse their authority, inasmuch as the interests of master and slave are the same. The Lyceum library contained a collection of 158 constitutions of the Greek and other states. Aristotle himself wrote the *Constitution of Athens* as part of the collection, and after being lost, this description was rediscovered in a papyrus copy in 1890. Historians have found the work of great value in reconstructing many phases of the history of Athens.

Logic. In logic, Aristotle developed rules for chains of reasoning that would, if followed, never lead from true premises to false conclusions (validity rules). In reasoning, the basic links are syllogisms: pairs of propositions that, taken together, give a new conclusion. For example, "All humans are mortal" and "All Greeks are humans" yield the valid conclusion "All Greeks are mortal." Science results from constructing more complex systems of reasoning. In his logic, Aristotle distinguished between dialectic and analytic. Dialectic, he held, only tests opinions for their logical consistency; analytic works deductively from principles resting on experience and precise observation. This is clearly an intended break with Plato's Academy, where dialectic was supposed to be the only proper method for science and philosophy alike.

Metaphysics. In his metaphysics, Aristotle argued for the existence of a divine being, described as the Prime Mover, who is responsible for the unity and purposefulness of nature. God is perfect and therefore the aspiration of all things in the world, because all things desire to share perfection. Other movers exist as well—the intelligent movers of the planets and stars (Aristotle suggested that the number of these is "either 55 or 47"). The Prime Mover, or God, described by Aristotle is not very suitable for religious purposes, as many later philosophers and theologians have observed. Aristotle limited his "theology," however, to what he believed science requires and can establish.

Influence. Aristotle's works were lost in the West after the decline of Rome. During the 9th century AD, Arab scholars introduced Aristotle, in Arabic translation, to the Islamic world. The 12th-century Spanish-Arab philosopher Averroës is the best known of the Arabic scholars who studied and commented on Aristotle. In the 13th century, the Latin West renewed its interest in Aristotle's work, and St. Thomas Aquinas found in it a philosophical foundation for Christian thought. Church officials at first questioned Aquinas's use of Aristotle; in the early stages of its rediscovery, Aristotle's philosophy was regarded with some suspicion, largely because his teachings were thought to lead to a materialistic view of the world. Nevertheless, the work of Aquinas was accepted, and the later philosophy of scholasticism (q.v.) continued the philosophical tradition based on Aquinas's adaptation of Aristotelian thought.

The influence of Aristotle's philosophy has been pervasive; it has even helped to shape modern language and common sense. His doctrine of the Prime Mover as final cause played an important role in theology. Until the 20th century, logic meant Aristotle's logic. Until the Renaissance, and even later, astronomers and poets alike admired his concept of the universe. Zoology rested on Aristotle's work until Charles Darwin modified the doctrine of the changelessness of species in the 19th century. In the 20th century a new appreciation has developed of Aristotle's method and its relevance to education, literary criticism, the analysis of human action, and political analysis.

Not only the discipline of zoology, but the world of learning as a whole, seems to amply justify Darwin's remark that the intellectual heroes of his own time "were mere schoolboys compared to old Aristotle."

For a discussion of the *Poetics, see* DRAMA AND DRAMATIC ARTS. *See also* LOGIC; METAPHYSICS; PHILOSOPHY. R.S.B.

For further information on this person, see the section Biographies in the Bibliography in volume 28.

ARITHMETIC, literally, the art of counting. The word, in its oldest Greek form, comes from the word *arithmētikē,* which combines the ideas of two words in Greek, *arithmos,* meaning "number," and *technē,* referring to an art or skill. For the history of arithmetic and mathematics, *see* MATHEMATICS.

The numbers used for counting are called the positive integers. They are generated by adding 1 to each number in an unending series, so that each number in the sequence is one more than its immediate predecessor. Different civilizations throughout history have developed different kinds of number systems (q.v.). One of the most common is the one used in all modern cultures, in which objects are counted in groups of ten. Called the base 10, or decimal, system, it is the one that is used in this article.

In the base 10 system, integers are represented by digits expressing various powers of 10. For example, take the number 1534. Every digit in this number has its own place value, and the place values increase by another power of 10 as they move to the left. The first place value is a unit value (here, 4); the second place value is 10 (here, 3 × 10, or 30); the third place value is 10 × 10, or 100 (here, 5 × 100, or 500); and the fourth place value is 10 × 10 × 10, or 1000 (here, 1 × 1000, or 1000).

FUNDAMENTAL DEFINITIONS AND LAWS

Arithmetic is concerned with the ways in which numbers can be combined through addition, subtraction, multiplication, and division. The word *number* also includes negative numbers, fractions, and algebraic irrational numbers. For a summary of the laws of addition, multiplication, and distribution, *see* ALGEBRA.

Addition. The arithmetic operation of addition is indicated by the plus sign (+) and is basically a means of counting by increments greater than 1. For example, four apples and five apples could be added by putting them together and then counting them individually from 1 to 9. Addition, however, makes it possible to add, or compute, sums more readily. The simplest combinations of sums must be memorized. The following table represents the sums of any two digits from 0 to 9:

	0	1	2	3	4	5	6	7	8	9
0	0	1	2	3	4	5	6	7	8	9
1	1	2	3	4	5	6	7	8	9	10
2	2	3	4	5	6	7	8	9	10	11
3	3	4	5	6	7	8	9	10	11	12
4	4	5	6	7	8	9	10	11	12	13
5	5	6	7	8	9	10	11	12	13	14
6	6	7	8	9	10	11	12	13	14	15
7	7	8	9	10	11	12	13	14	15	16
8	8	9	10	11	12	13	14	15	16	17
9	9	10	11	12	13	14	15	16	17	18

To find the sum of any two numbers between 0 and 9, locate the first of the numbers in the vertical column at the left of the table and the other number in the horizontal row at the top. The sum is the number in the body of the table at the intersection of the particular row and column that have been selected.

Arithmetic also makes it possible to add long lists of large numbers by applying simple rules that make the work quite easy. For example, it would be possible to add 27 + 32 + 49 by first counting to 27, then counting 32 more times after 27, and then another 49 times beyond that to get the total, or sum. But if the numbers are listed one under another so that all the units are in a line, all the tens are in a line, and so on, the addition is relatively simple:

$$\begin{array}{rrl} \text{tens} & \text{units} & \\ 2 & 7 & \text{(addend)} \\ 3 & 2 & \text{(addend)} \\ +\ 4 & 9 & \text{(addend)} \\ \hline & & \text{(sum)} \end{array}$$

First the units (7 + 2 + 9) are added; they total 18. Then the digits in the tens place (2 + 3 + 4) are added; they total 9, but this means 9 *tens,* or 90. This can now be written as

$$\begin{array}{rl} 27 & \\ 32 & \\ +\ 49 & \\ \hline 18 & \text{(total of the units)} \\ 90 & \text{(total of the tens)} \\ \hline 108 & \end{array}$$

In the last step, the total of the units is added to the total of the tens. This procedure may be shortened by carrying the 1 of 18, which stands for one ten, over to the tens column and adding it directly with the digits there.

$$\begin{array}{rl} 1 & \text{(carried from the 18 of the units total)} \\ 27 & \\ 32 & \\ +49 & \\ \hline 8 & \end{array}$$

The digits in the tens column are added, and the sum 108 is the result. Similarly, in adding numbers with three or more places, numbers may be carried to the hundreds, thousands, or higher places.

Subtraction. The arithmetic operation of subtraction is indicated by the minus sign (−) and is the opposite, or inverse, operation to addition. Again, it is possible to subtract 23 from 66 by counting backward from 66 or by taking away 23 items from a collection of 66 until one reaches the remainder of 43. The rules of arithmetic for subtraction, however, provide a much simpler method for obtaining the answer. First the numbers are aligned under one another, units under units, tens under tens:

$$\begin{array}{rl} 66 & \text{(minuend)} \\ -23 & \text{(subtrahend)} \\ \hline 43 & \text{(remainder)} \end{array}$$

Subtraction is a bit more complicated if digits of the subtrahend are larger than those of the minuend. This can be handled in a manner analogous to carrying, but known as borrowing in subtraction. For example, to subtract 46 from 92

$$\begin{array}{r} 92 \\ -46 \\ \hline \end{array}$$

10 can be borrowed from the tens column—that is, from the 9 of 92—leaving 8 in the tens column.The 10 is brought over to the units column and added to the 2 already there, giving 12 (notated $^{1}2$) in that column from which 6 can now be subtracted:

$$\begin{array}{rl} {}^{8}\not{9}\ {}^{1}2 & \text{(the 1 has been borrowed from the 9 in the tens column)} \\ -4\ \ 6 & \\ \hline 6 & \end{array}$$

The subtraction is completed by carrying out the difference in the tens column, that is, by taking 4 away from 8 to give 4; the answer is 46.

Negative Numbers. As long as smaller numbers are being subtracted from larger ones, carrying out the operation of subtraction in arithmetic is not difficult. But if the subtrahend is larger than the minuend, the only way to produce an answer, or remainder, is to introduce the concept of negative numbers.

Negative numbers may be most easily visualized by considering the familiar numbers of arithmetic, the positive integers, arranged in a line and increasing in a positive direction. Negative numbers are reached by proceeding away from 0 in the opposite direction. The following number line represents both positive and negative numbers:

negative direction — positive direction

−4 −3 −2 −1 0 +1 +2 +3 +4

If 4 is subtracted from 2, written symbolically as 2 − 4, four units are counted backward from +2, and −2 is reached—the difference when 4 is subtracted from 2. Rules for basic arithmetic operations involving negative numbers are given at the end of this section, following the laws of basic arithmetic operations.

Multiplication. The arithmetic operation of multiplication is indicated by the times sign (×). Sometimes a dot is used to indicate the multiplication of two or more numbers, and sometimes parentheses are used. For example, 3 × 4, 3 · 4, and (3)(4) all indicate the product of 3 times 4. Multiplication is simply repeated addition. The expression 3 × 4 means that 3 is to be added to itself four times; or, similarly, that 4 is to be added to itself three times. In either case, the answer is the same. When large numbers are involved, however, such repeated addition is tedious, and thus arithmetic provides procedures for simplifying the operations. As in addition, it is necessary to know the basic multiples of the integers between 0 and 9, which are provided in the following table:

	0	1	2	3	4	5	6	7	8	9
0	0	0	0	0	0	0	0	0	0	0
1	0	1	2	3	4	5	6	7	8	9
2	0	2	4	6	8	10	12	14	16	18
3	0	3	6	9	12	15	18	21	24	27
4	0	4	8	12	16	20	24	28	32	36
5	0	5	10	15	20	25	30	35	40	45
6	0	6	12	18	24	30	36	42	48	54
7	0	7	14	21	28	35	42	49	56	63
8	0	8	16	24	32	40	48	56	64	72
9	0	9	18	27	36	45	54	63	72	81

To find the product of any two numbers between 0 and 9, locate the first of the numbers in the vertical column at the left of the table and the second number in the horizontal row at the top of the table. The product is then the number in the body of the table at the intersection of the column and row in question. For example, 7 × 8 = 56.

In order to multiply two numbers, the units, tens, hundreds, and so on, are aligned, as in the following example.

```
 386 (multiplicand)
×  4 (multiplier)
────
     (product)
```

Each digit of the multiplicand is then multiplied by the multiplier, in this case, 4. The results of all these multiplications are then added together, giving the product 1544:

```
  386
×   4
─────
   24 (4×6 in the units place)
  320 (4×8 in the tens place, or 4×80)
 1200 (4×3 in the hundreds place, or 4×300)
─────
 1544
```

This operation can be shortened by carrying tens and hundreds, as in addition:

```
   2
 386
×  4
────
   4
```

The 6 is multiplied by 4, giving 24; the 4 is written in the units place in the product and the 2, which stands for 2 tens, or 20, is carried. The 8 in the tens place is now multiplied by 4, giving 32, to which 2 is added, giving 34. (Actually, 80 has been multiplied by 4, giving 320, and the 20, which had been carried, is then added to 320.) The 4 is written down in the tens place, and the 3 (which stands for 3 hundreds) is carried and placed over the hundreds column. To finish, the 3 in the hundreds place of the multiplicand is multiplied by 4, giving 12 (actually 1200), and the 3 that was carried is added to give 15 (actually 1500):

```
  32
 386
×  4
────
1544
```

For larger multipliers, an analogous procedure may be followed. For example, the following product is begun by carrying out multiplication by the unit 3 of the multiplier:

```
  22
  579 (multiplicand)
×  63 (multiplier)
─────
 1737 (partial product)
```

The 9 is next multiplied by 6, giving 54, and the 4 is placed under the number 3 in the tens place of the partial product. This is done because the digit 6 in the multiplier is in the tens place and actually represents 60. The 5 is carried as usual. The 7 in the tens place of the multiplicand is multiplied by the 6, giving 42, and the carried 5 is added, giving 47 (really 6 times 70, plus 50, giving 470). Now the 7 is written in the hundreds place (directly to the left of the 4 in the tens place), and the 4 is carried. The rest of the multiplication is straightforward, and the total product is obtained by adding the two partial products:

```
  45
  579 (multiplicand)
×  63 (multiplier)
─────
 1737 (partial product)
3474  (partial product)
─────
36477 (total product)
```

For each digit in the multiplier there will be a line for each partial product obtained as the units, tens, hundreds, and so on are multiplied out. Each successive partial product is placed one digit to the left of the partial product above it, corresponding to the position of the digit being multiplied in the multiplier. Thus, in the above example, the partial product of 6 times 579 yields 3474, and the 4 in the digits place must be written in the tens place for the partial product. This is because the multiplier is really 60, not 6; the entire partial product is actually a multiple of 10,

34740, which would of course produce the same alignment:

$$\begin{array}{r} 579 \\ \times\ 63 \\ \hline 1737 \\ 34740 \\ \hline 36477 \end{array}$$

Superscript numbers (raised numbers) are employed to notate the multiplication of a number by itself. For example $5 \cdot 5$ is notated 5^2 and is termed "five squared." Similarly, $5 \cdot 5 \cdot 5 = 5^3$, or five cubed.

Division. The arithmetic operation of division is the opposite, or inverse, operation to multiplication. Using the example of 12 divided by 4, division may be indicated by the division sign ($12 \div 4$), a bar ($\frac{12}{4}$), a slash (12/4), or the notation $4\overline{)12}$.

Basically, division is the arithmetic operation that determines how many times a given number is contained in another as a multiple. For example, 4 is contained three times in 12; thus, 12 divided by 4 is 3, or 12/4 is 3, or

$$\begin{array}{r} 3 \\ 4\overline{)12} \end{array} \qquad \begin{array}{r} \text{quotient} \\ \text{divisor}\overline{)\text{dividend}} \end{array}$$

Many divisions may be carried out by inspection, but more complicated cases require a procedure known as long division. For example, in the quotient $3918 \div 6$, or $6\overline{)3918}$, the number 6 will not divide 3 one or more times, but 6 will go into 39 at least six times and less than seven times (6×6 is 36). The number 6 is therefore written in the quotient over the 9 in the dividend, 3918, and 36 (the product of the divisor, 6, and the first number of the quotient, 6) is written under the 39 and subtracted from it, yielding 3.

What has actually been determined thus far in this process of long division is that 3918 contains 600 6s, and that 318 is left when these are taken away. Long division is a repetition of a cycle of simple operations, an iterative process that is much used in modern computing science (*see* ALGORITHM). Thus in the next step of the division process, the 1 in the dividend is brought down and written to the right of the 3 to give 31:

$$\begin{array}{r} 6 \\ 6\overline{)\ 3918} \\ -36 \\ \hline 31 \end{array}$$

The 6 in the divisor will go into 31 at least five times and less than six times (6×5 is 30). The 5 is then written to the right of the 6 in the quotient, above the 1 in the dividend. The product, 5×6, or 30, is placed under the 31 and subtracted from it, yielding 1. The 8 from the dividend is brought down and written to the right of the 1 to give 18. The 6 in the divisor will go into 18 exactly three times, so the number 3 is written in the quotient above the 8 in the dividend:

$$\begin{array}{r} 653 \\ 6\overline{)\ 3918} \\ -36 \\ \hline 31 \\ -30 \\ \hline 18 \\ -18 \\ \hline 00 \end{array}$$

The answer to how many times 6 will divide 3918 is 653. This can be easily verified by multiplying 6×653; this proof should yield the dividend 3918.

Remainders. Had the dividend been 3923, the last subtraction would not have yielded 00, but would have left a remainder of 5. Such a remainder must then be incorporated into the answer as a fraction—a fraction of the divisor, in this case 6, leaving a fractional remainder of $\frac{5}{6}$:

$$\begin{array}{r} 653\ \frac{5}{6} \\ 6\overline{)3923}\phantom{\ \frac{5}{6}} \\ 36\phantom{\ \frac{5}{6}} \\ \hline 32\phantom{\ \frac{5}{6}} \\ 30\phantom{\ \frac{5}{6}} \\ \hline 23\phantom{\ \frac{5}{6}} \\ 18\phantom{\ \frac{5}{6}} \\ \hline 5\phantom{\ \frac{5}{6}} \end{array}$$

Again, it is easily verified, by multiplication (see below, under fractions), that $6 \cdot (653\frac{5}{6})$ is 3923.

Long division. Long division is an arithmetic procedure whereby larger divisors may be dealt with in carrying out divisions. The method is basically analogous to the shorter method for division described above. For example, in dividing 3626 by 25

$$25\overline{)3626}$$

25 will go into 36 once; therefore, a 1 is placed over the 6 in 36. The 25 is multiplied by 1, and this product (25) is written under the 36 and subtracted from it, yielding 11. The 2 is then brought down to give 112:

$$\begin{array}{r} 1 \\ 25\overline{)\ 3626} \\ -25 \\ \hline 112 \end{array}$$

Because 25 will go into 112 at most four times, a 4

is written next to the 1 in the quotient, over the 2 in the dividend. The divisor is multiplied by 4, and the product, 100, is written under the 112 and subtracted from it, yielding 12. The 6 is brought down to give 126. Because 25 will go into 126 five times, with a remainder of 1, the answer is

$$\begin{array}{r} 145\,\frac{1}{25} \\ 25\,\overline{)\,3626} \\ -25 \\ \hline 112 \\ -100 \\ \hline 126 \\ -125 \\ \hline 1 \end{array}$$

Operations with Negative Numbers. Before it is possible to deal adequately with arithmetic operations involving negative numbers, the concept of absolute value must be introduced. Given any number, whether positive or negative, the absolute value of that number is the value of the number regardless of its sign. Thus, the absolute value of $+5$ is 5, and the absolute value of -5 is also 5. In symbolic notation, the absolute value of any number a is written as $|a|$ and defined as follows: The absolute value of a is a if a is positive, and the absolute value of a is $-a$ if a is negative. In the following discussion, inequality signs are used. The symbol $>$ means greater than; $\geq$ means greater than or equal to. Similarly, $<$ means less than; $\leq$ means less than or equal to. The symbol $\neq$ means not equal to. For example, the expression $a \geq 0$ is read "a is greater than or equal to zero."

$$|a| = a \text{ if } a \geq 0; \quad |7| = |7|$$
$$|a| = -a \text{ if } a < 0; \quad |-9| = -(-9) = +9$$

By referring once again to the number line, which includes both positive and negative numbers, it is easy to see that the sum of any two negative numbers will be negative and that the sum will simply be the total of the absolute values of the two numbers, but negative:

$$(-5) + (-6) = -11$$

If, however, the signs of the two numbers are opposite, then it is necessary to proceed more cautiously.

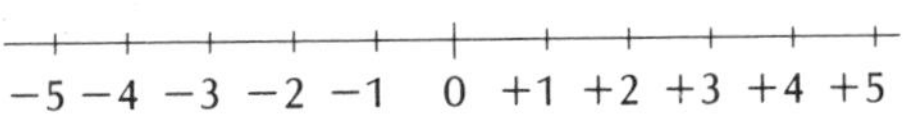

To add -4 and $+2$, for example, it is clear that by beginning at -4 and adding 2 by moving two units to the right in the positive direction, the result will be -2 (the answer is the difference between the absolute values of the two numbers with the result taking the sign of the larger). The result must be negative because in terms of absolute value, $|-4| > |+2|$. The answer, however, is obtained by calculating the difference between the absolute values 4 and 2. Similarly, to add -3 and $+7$, beginning at -3 and moving seven units to the right produces $+4$. This may now be summarized conveniently in two rules:

Rule 1. If two numbers of like sign are to be added, the absolute values of the two numbers are added, and the answer is given the sign of the numbers in question:

$$(+6) + (+7) = +13; \quad (-4) + (-8) = -12$$

Rule 2. If two numbers of different sign are to be added, their absolute values are ascertained, and the smaller number is subtracted from the larger. The result is given the sign of the number with the larger absolute value:

$$(-5) + (+6) = +1; \quad (-8) + (+5) = -3$$

The subtraction of negative numbers is easier to visualize by referring again to the number line. Subtracting one number from another indicates a reversal of direction from addition. To subtract 5 from 7, for example, begin at 7 and move in the negative direction five units, reaching $+2$ as the answer. Similarly, to subtract -2 from 5, start at 5 and move in the opposite direction from -2, that is to say, in the positive direction, two units to $+7$. Subtraction basically indicates that one is to change the sign, or direction, of the number in question. For example,

$$6 - (-3) = 6 + (+3) = +9$$

Subtraction problems are best converted to problems in addition; following rules 1 and 2 above, the addition is then carried out as indicated. For subtraction, the following rule applies:

Rule 3. Whenever subtraction is indicated, change the subtraction to addition after changing the sign of the number following the subtraction sign, and then add, using the above rules for addition:

$$(+4) - (+7) = (+4) + (-7) = -3$$
$$(-4) - (-6) = (-4) + (+6) = +2$$

Multiplication of negative numbers is carried out using the following two conventions:

Rule 4. To multiply two numbers of the same sign, multiply their absolute values and give the resulting product a positive sign:

$$(+7)(+2) = +14$$
$$(-6)(-5) = +30$$

Rule 5. To multiply two numbers of different sign, multiply their absolute values and give the resulting product a negative sign:

$$(-3)(+6) = -18; \quad (+5)(-3) = -15$$

Division is the inverse operation of multiplication; therefore, dividing signed numbers involves rules similar to those for multiplication.

Rule 6. To divide two numbers of the same sign, divide their absolute values and give the resulting quotient a positive sign:

$$(-6)/(-3) = +2; \quad (+4)/(+2) = +2$$

Rule 7. To divide two numbers of different sign, divide their absolute values and give the resulting quotient a negative sign:

$$(10)/(-5) = -2; \quad (-9)/(+3) = -3$$

If a number carries no explicit sign with it, it is assumed to be positive.

THEORY OF DIVISORS

Before discussing fractions, some additional remarks must be made about several other classes of numbers: An even number is any number divisible by 2. An odd number is any number not divisible by 2. A prime number is any integer greater than 1 that is divisible only by itself. Examples of prime numbers are 2, 3, 5, 7, 11, 13, 17, 19. . . . The only even prime number is 2. All integers that are not prime are said to be composite, but all composite numbers can be written as the product of prime numbers.

The Fundamental Theorem of Arithmetic. "Every integer greater than 1 that is not a prime number is the product of one and only one set of prime numbers." This theorem was first proved rigorously by the German mathematician Carl Friedrich Gauss. Given a number such as 14, the theorem states that it may be written uniquely as the product of primes, in this case, $14 = 2 \cdot 7$. Similarly, $50 = 2 \cdot 5 \cdot 5 = 2 \cdot 5^2$. By factoring numbers into their prime components, both their least common multiple and their greatest common divisor can be found.

Least Common Multiple. The least common multiple (LCM) of any two (or more) numbers is the least number into which each number will divide evenly. The LCM will contain the maximum number of prime factors of all primes appearing in each of the given numbers. For example, to find the LCM for the three numbers 27, 63, and 75, each number is first factored: $27 = 3^3$, $63 = 3^2 \cdot 7$, and $75 = 3 \cdot 5^2$. The LCM must contain at least factors of 3^3, 7, and 5^2; thus, $3^3 \cdot 7 \cdot 5^2 = 4725$ is the least number into which 27, 63, and 75 will all divide evenly.

Greatest Common Divisor. The largest factor common to a given set of numbers is called the highest common factor (HCF) or greatest common divisor (GCD). For example, given 9, 15, and 27, the GCD is 3, which can readily be seen by examining the prime factorization of each number: $9 = 3^2$, $15 = 3 \cdot 5$, $27 = 3^3$; the only factor common to each number is 3.

FRACTIONS

Numbers representing parts of a whole are called rational numbers, or fractions. Simple fractions are familiar: a dime is $\frac{1}{10}$ of a dollar; $\frac{1}{4}$ of a pie plus $\frac{1}{2}$ of a pie is $\frac{3}{4}$ of a pie; and so on. In general, fractions may be expressed as the quotient of two integers a and b.:

$$\frac{a \text{ (numerator)}}{b \text{ (denominator)}}$$

A fraction is said to be reduced to lowest terms if neither the numerator nor the denominator has a factor in common. For example, $\frac{6}{8}$ is not a fraction reduced to lowest terms because both 6 and 8 contain factors of 2: $\frac{6}{8} = (2 \cdot 3)/(2 \cdot 4)$; $\frac{3}{4}$, however, is a fraction reduced to lowest terms.

Cancellation Law of Multiplication. If a/c is a fraction, and $b \neq 0$, then $(a \cdot b)/(c \cdot b) = a/c$. Two types of fractions exist, proper and improper. A proper fraction is one in which the numerator is less than the denominator; $\frac{2}{3}$, $-\frac{7}{8}$, and $\frac{16}{19}$ are all proper fractions. An improper fraction is one in which the numerator is larger than the denominator; $\frac{3}{2}$, $-\frac{8}{4}$, and $\frac{7}{3}$ are improper fractions. Improper fractions can be converted to mixed fractions or whole numbers (for example, $\frac{3}{2} = 1\frac{1}{2}$, $-\frac{8}{4} = -2$, and $\frac{7}{3} = 2\frac{1}{3}$) by dividing the numerator by the denominator and expressing any remainder as a fraction of the denominator.

Adding and Subtracting Fractions. In order to add or subtract fractions the denominators of which are the same, the numerators are added or subtracted, just as for integers, and the result is expressed as a fraction of the denominator. The result is reduced to lowest terms. For example,

$$\frac{2}{3} + \frac{4}{3} = \frac{2+4}{3} = \frac{6}{3} = 2$$

$$\frac{5}{8} - \frac{1}{8} = \frac{5-1}{8} = \frac{4}{8} = \frac{1}{2}$$

Only fractions of equal denominators may be added or subtracted as they stand. If the denominators are unequal, a common denominator must be found. The least common denominator (LCD), in fact, will always be the least common multiple (LCM) of the denominators in question. For example, in the expression $\frac{2}{3} + \frac{3}{4}$, the denominators 3 and 4 are different, but the LCM of 3 and 4 is 12. Thus, to add $\frac{2}{3}$ and $\frac{3}{4}$, the fractions must be changed into those with 12 as a common denominator. Because both the numerator and denominator can be multiplied by the same number without changing the value of the fractions, it is apparent that

$$\frac{2}{3} = \frac{2 \cdot 4}{3 \cdot 4} = \frac{8}{12}; \frac{3}{4} = \frac{3 \cdot 3}{4 \cdot 3} = \frac{9}{12}$$

Now it is possible to add

$$\frac{2}{3} + \frac{3}{4} = \frac{8}{12} + \frac{9}{12} = \frac{8+9}{12} = \frac{17}{12} = 1\frac{5}{12}$$

Similarly,

$$\frac{7}{10} - \frac{3}{5} = \frac{7}{10} - \frac{3 \cdot 2}{5 \cdot 2} = \frac{7}{10} - \frac{6}{10} = \frac{1}{10}$$

Multiplying Fractions. Given two fractions $\frac{a}{b}$ and $\frac{c}{d}$, multiplication is straightforward: numerators are multiplied together and denominators are multiplied together, so that

$$\frac{a}{b} \cdot \frac{c}{d} = \frac{a \cdot c}{b \cdot d}$$

For example,

$$\frac{6}{5} \cdot \frac{2}{3} = \frac{12}{15} = \frac{4}{5}$$

The answer must always be reduced to the lowest terms. Similarly,

$$(-\frac{2}{3})(\frac{4}{5}) = -\frac{8}{15}$$

The rules for multiplying signed fractions are the same as those for multiplying signed integers. The same is true for the rules governing addition, subtraction, and division of signed fractions.

Dividing Fractions. The division of fractions is most easily understood in terms of reciprocals. Given any number a, $a \neq 0$, the reciprocal of a is $\frac{1}{a}$. This is also called the inverse of a and may be written as a^{-1}. Note that $a(\frac{1}{a}) = 1$.

To carry out the following division

$$\frac{a}{b} \div \frac{c}{d}, \text{ or } \quad \frac{\frac{a}{b}}{\frac{c}{d}}$$

both the numerator and the denominator can be multiplied by the same nonzero number without affecting the value of the original number. Both-numerator and denominator in the above example are multiplied by $\frac{d}{c}$:

$$\frac{\frac{a}{b} \cdot \frac{d}{c}}{\frac{c}{d} \cdot \frac{d}{c}} = \frac{\frac{a}{b} \cdot \frac{d}{c}}{\frac{cd}{cd}} = \frac{\frac{a}{b} \cdot \frac{d}{c}}{1} = \frac{ad}{bc}$$

This division is equivalent to multiplying the numerator $\frac{a}{b}$ by the reciprocal of the denominator $\frac{c}{d}$, that is by $\frac{d}{c}$.

The following two examples illustrate the general procedure outlined above:

$$\frac{2}{3} \div \frac{5}{8} = \frac{\frac{2}{3}}{\frac{5}{8}} = \frac{2}{3} \cdot \frac{8}{5} = \frac{16}{15} = 1\frac{1}{15}$$

Note that $\frac{8}{5}$ is the reciprocal of the denominator $\frac{5}{8}$.

$$\frac{2}{3} \div (-\frac{4}{5}) = \frac{\frac{2}{3}}{-\frac{4}{5}} = (\frac{2}{3})(-\frac{5}{4}) = -\frac{10}{12} = -\frac{5}{6}$$

Note that $-\frac{5}{4}$ is the reciprocal of $-\frac{4}{5}$. In general, division by a fraction is equivalent to multiplication by its reciprocal:

$$\frac{1}{\frac{a}{b}} = \frac{1\ (b/a)}{\frac{a}{b}(b/a)} = \frac{1\ (b/a)}{\frac{ab}{ab}} = \frac{1\ (b/a)}{1} = \frac{b}{a}$$

For example,

$$1 \div \frac{3}{2} = 1 \cdot \frac{2}{3} = \frac{2}{3}$$

Zero (0) has no reciprocal. This follows because the reciprocal of any number a is a number $(\frac{1}{a})$ such that $a(\frac{1}{a}) = 1$. To say that zero has no reciprocal is to say that no number $(\frac{1}{a})$ exists such that $0(\frac{1}{a}) = 1$. This is obvious, since no number exists that can be multiplied by zero to give $1{:}0.r = 0$, whatever r may be.

DECIMALS

The idea of place values can be extended to accommodate fractions. Instead of writing $\frac{2}{10}$, or two-tenths, a decimal point (.) can be introduced so that 0.2 can represent the fraction. Just as places to the left of the decimal represent units, tens, hundreds, and so on, those to the right of the decimal represent places for tenths $(\frac{1}{10})$, hundredths $(\frac{1}{100})$, thousandths $(\frac{1}{1000})$, and so forth. These are decreasing powers of ten, which can be represented as 10^{-1}, 10^{-2}, 10^{-3}, and so on. In general, a number such as 5428.632 is called a decimal fraction in which 0.632 represents

$$6(10^{-1})+3(10^{-2})+2(10^{-3})$$

tenths hundredths thousandths

This number is read as follows: "five thousand four hundred twenty-eight and six hundred thirty-two thousandths."

Addition and Subtraction. In a number system based on the number 10, because places to both the left and right of the decimal point represent powers of ten, addition and subtraction of decimal fractions are handled in the same manner as described for integers. The decimal point, however, must always be aligned, so that tens are under tens, units under units, tenths under tenths, and so on, ensuring that each value is being added to or subtracted from a similar value at every step. For example, to add 365.289 and 32.4, the decimals are aligned, and then the numbers are added beginning at the right and moving to the left.

$$\begin{array}{r} 365.289 \\ +\ 32.4 \\ \hline \end{array}$$

The addition of zeros to the right of a number does not change the number; filling in the number of places helps ensure that the same number of places exist to the right of the decimal point for all numbers being added or subtracted:

$$\begin{array}{r} 365.289 \\ +\ 32.400 \\ \hline 397.689 \end{array}$$

Subtraction with decimals proceeds in much the same way as addition: Zeros are added to give both numbers the same number of places to the right of the decimal. The numbers are then subtracted as usual.

Multiplication. Multiplying decimals is similar to multiplying integers, except that the values of the decimal points must be kept in mind. For example, in multiplying 0.3 and 0.5, visualizing the process involved is easier if each of these decimals is converted to common fractions and then multiplied.

$$\frac{3}{10} \times \frac{5}{10} = \frac{3 \cdot 5}{10 \cdot 10} = \frac{15}{100} = 0.15$$

The 15, of course, is the direct value of the product of 3 and 5, but the placement of the decimal point is determined by the fact that 0.3 and 0.5 each represent one decimal place, for a total of two decimal places that must be represented in the answer; thus, the product is 0.15.

Another example will serve to make this concept even clearer. Multiply (0.2) and (0.3). The product of the two numbers is 6, but since 0.2 and 0.3 each has one decimal place, the product must have a total of two decimal places. This can be achieved by placing the decimal point two places to the left in the product: 0.06. The following rule governs the multiplication of decimal fractions:

Decimal fractions are multiplied as if they were integers. The decimal point is then placed at the appropriate place in the product so that the number of places there is the same as the total number of decimal places in the multiplier and multiplicand. For example:

$$\begin{array}{r} 0.259 \\ \times\ 0.12 \\ \hline 518 \\ 259 \\ \hline 3108 \end{array}$$

Because the multiplicand has three decimal places and the multiplier has two, the product must have a total of five decimal places. Counting five places to the left from the digit farthest to the right (digit 8 of the final product), the answer must be 0.03108.

One final example will also illustrate the importance of counting the proper number of decimal places in determining products of decimal fractions. Multiply .001 and .002. The multiplication of the digits is simple: the answer is 2. There are, however, three decimal places in the multiplier, and three in the mulitplicand, giving a total of six places that must be preserved in the product. Six places must be counted to the left of the 2, and the answer is 0.000002.

Division. Like multiplication, the division of decimal fractions follows the same procedures used to divide integers, except that care must be taken to determine the proper placement of decimal points in the quotients. Dividing a decimal fraction by a whole number is straightforward: The decimal point is placed in the quotient directly above the decimal point in the dividend, and the division is performed as usual.

$$\begin{array}{r} 3.38 \\ 7\overline{)\ 23.66} \\ -21 \\ \hline 26 \\ -21 \\ \hline 56 \\ -56 \\ \hline 00 \end{array}$$

In cases where the divisor is also a decimal fraction, the problem is converted to one in which the divisor is an integer; division may then proceed as in the above example. To divide 14 by 0.7, for example, the divisor is converted to an integer by multiplying it by 10: (0.7)(10) = 7. The dividend must then be multiplied by an equal amount, that is by 10, to preserve value of the division. This may be understood more easily by considering what division means. In the above example the division can be rewritten as a fraction, $\frac{14}{0.7}$. Multiplying both numerator and denominator by the same amount will not change the value of the fraction:

$$\frac{14}{0.7} = \frac{14(10)}{0.7(10)} = \frac{140}{7}$$

Similarly, the division of 2.675 by 0.23 can be considered in the form 2.675/0.23. This can be converted to a division involving an integer divisor, namely, 23, if both numerator and denominator are multiplied by 100:

$$\frac{2.675}{0.23} = \frac{2.675(100)}{0.23(100)} = \frac{267.5}{23}$$

The following rule for the division of decimal fractions summarizes the above concisely:

Any division of a decimal fraction by another decimal fraction may be converted into a straightforward division with an integer divisor by moving the decimal point as many places to the right in the divisor as is necessary to make it an integer. The decimal point in the dividend is then moved an equal number of places to the right, and zeros are added if necessary. The division is carried out as usual, the decimal point in the quotient being placed directly over the new decimal point in the dividend. For example, in the division $.002\overline{)21.5}$, the decimal point in the divisor is moved three places to the right, giving the integer 2. The decimal point in the dividend is moved three places to the right as well, giving $2\overline{)21500}$. The division is then carried out as usual. The quotient in this case is 10750.

See also MATHEMATICAL SYMBOLS; MATHEMATICS, NEW; NUMBER; POWER; ROOT. J.W.D.

For further information on this topic, see the Bibliography in volume 28, sections 367, 370.

ARITHMETIC PROGRESSION, series of numbers that increase or diminish by a common difference so that any number in the series is the arithmetic mean, or average, of the numbers preceding and following it (*see also* GEOMETRIC PROGRESSION; SEQUENCE AND SERIES). The numbers 7, 10, 13, 16, 19, 22 form an arithmetic progression, as do the numbers 12, $10\frac{1}{2}$, 9, $7\frac{1}{2}$, 6. The natural numbers 1, 2, 3, 4 form an arithmetic progression in which the difference is 1. To find the sum of any such progression, multiply the sum of the first and last terms by half the number of terms. Thus, the sum of the first ten natural numbers is $(1 + 10) \times (10 \div 2) = 55$.

The general arithmetic progression is a, $a + d$, $a + 2d$, $a + 3d$, . . . in which the first term, a, and the common difference, d, are arbitrary numbers. The nth term of this progression (often denoted by the term a_n) is given by the formula $a_n = a + (n - 1)\, d$, and the sum of the first n terms is $\frac{1}{2}n[2a + (n - 1)d]$, or $\frac{1}{2}n(a + a_n)$.

ARIZONA, one of the Mountain states of the U.S., bounded on the N by Utah, on the E by New Mexico, on the S by Mexico, and on the W by California and Nevada. The Colorado R. forms much of the W boundary.

Arizona entered the Union on Feb. 14, 1912, as the 48th state. Once primarily a mining and agricultural area, the state developed a diversified economy after 1950 and in the 1990s was an important producer of high-technology items, notably in the Phoenix region. Arizona also enjoys successful copper-mining, cotton-growing, and tourist industries. The name of the state is derived from an Indian word *(arizonac)* believed to mean "place of the small spring." Arizona is called the Grand Canyon State.

LAND AND RESOURCES

Arizona is the sixth largest U.S. state, with an area of 295,276 sq km (114,006 sq mi). It encompasses terrain that ranges in elevation from 21 m (70 ft) above sea level, along the Colorado R. near Yuma, to 3851 m (12,633 ft), atop Humphreys Peak, in the San Francisco Mts. N of Flagstaff. The approximate mean elevation is 1251 m (4100 ft). The state is roughly rectangular in shape, and its extreme dimensions are about 635 km (about 395 mi) from N to S and about 555 km (about 345 mi) from E to W. The federal government owns 42% of Arizona's land area.

Physical Geography. Arizona can be divided into three geographic regions—the Sonoran Desert, in the SW; the Colorado Plateau, in the N; and the Mexican Highland, mainly in the central and SE parts of the state.

The Sonoran Desert, also known as the Gila Desert, is an arid area consisting mostly of broad stream-carved valleys, with isolated mountains rising above the alluvial soil deposited by floodwaters of modern and ancient streams. Ranges in the region include the Big Horn, Castle Dome, Gila Bend, Harcuvar, and Maricopa mountains. The S edge of the Colorado Plateau region, which contains a number of level plateaus and several mountains and deep gorges, is marked by the Mogollon Rim, which has elevations ranging between about 2000 and 2500 m (about 6560 and 8200 ft). From the edge of the plateau the land slopes gently to the N; higher elevations are in the NE. In the W part of the region lies the spectacular Grand Canyon, in the center is the

The Grand Canyon, a view from the south (lower) rim. The mile-deep sculptured gorge in northern Arizona is among the natural wonders of the world.
M. P. L. Fogden–Bruce Coleman, Inc.

Painted Desert, along the Little Colorado R.; and in the SE is the Petrified Forest. Between the Sonoran Desert and the Colorado Plateau is the Mexican Highland, a series of valleys and mountains taking in lofty areas such as the White Mts. near the border with New Mexico.

Rivers and Lakes. Virtually all of Arizona is drained by the Colorado R. and its tributaries, notably the Little Colorado and Gila. The waters of the Salt, Santa Cruz, San Pedro, and Verde rivers join the Gila before entering the Colorado. Many of Arizona's smaller rivers do not flow year-round, but only after periods of considerable rainfall.

Dams along the Colorado have created several large, elongated lakes, such as Powell, Mead, Mohave, and Havasu, all of which lie partly in neighboring states. Similar artificial lakes are on the Gila, Salt, and Verde rivers.

Climate. Because of the variety of Arizona's topography, the average annual temperature and precipitation vary widely. Nevertheless, the state can be divided into three distinct climatic zones. The arid Sonoran Desert is hot in summer but experiences frost in most winters. Most of the Sonoran Desert receives less than about 200 m (about 8 in) of precipitation each year. The Colorado Plateau region is hot and relatively dry in summer and windy and cold in winter. In most parts of the region annual precipitation is less than 400 mm (about 16 in). The Mexican Highland region receives significant precipitation in both the summer and the winter, and yearly precipitation in lofty sections can reach about 760 mm (about 30 in). Temperatures in summer are appreciably lower than in the Sonoran Desert, and temperatures on winter nights are generally below freezing (0° C/32° F). The recorded temperature in Arizona has ranged from −40° C (−40° F), in 1971 near McNary, to 52.8° C (127° F), in 1905 at Parker.

Plants and Animals. In most parts of Arizona the amount of natural vegetation varies proportionately with the amount of precipitation. The sparsely covered Sonoran Desert is known for its cacti, including the organ-pipe cactus, the giant saguaro cactus, and the cholla cactus. Also found the region are many types of wild flowers, creosote bushes, mesquite, ocotillo, and yucca. At higher elevations in the state, forests of piñon and juniper occur below the commercial timber zone, where white and silver fir, Douglas fir, ponderosa pine, birch, ash, and elder grow. Altogether, nearly 25% of Arizona is covered with forest, approximately one-fifth of which contains commercially useful timber.

Big game animals in Arizona include large numbers of white-tailed deer and mule deer and some elk, antelope, and bighorn sheep. Buffalo roam freely in the N part of the state, and bear are found in remote areas. Smaller animals, such as the mountain lion, badger, beaver, otter, raccoon, muskrat, and weasel, live in mountain districts. The peccary, or javelina, a type of wild pig,

INDEX TO MAP OF ARIZONA

Cities and Towns

⊙ County seat

Other Features

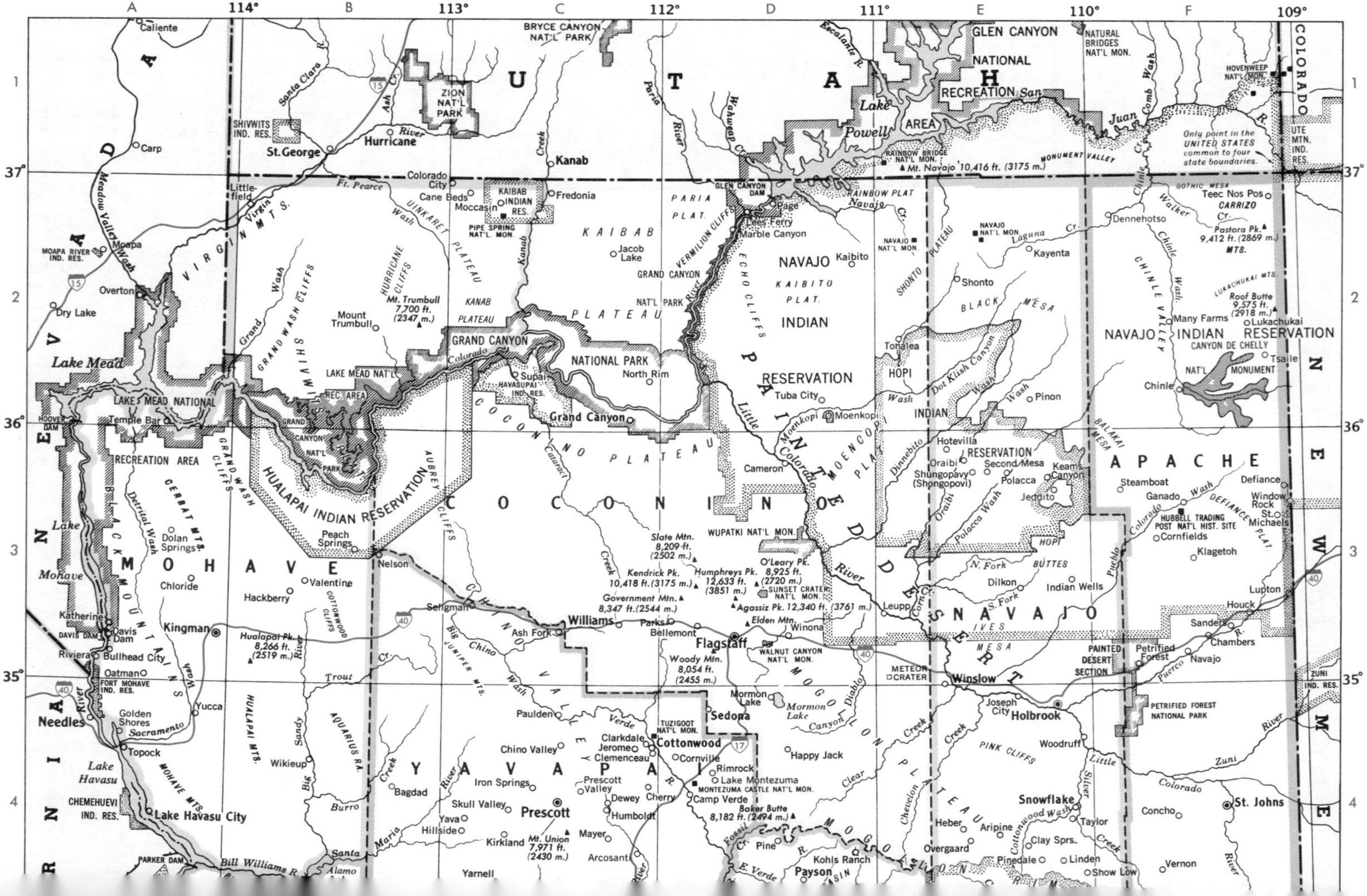

114°
113°
112°
111°
110°
109°
37°
36°
35°
UTAH
NEVADA
NEW MEXICO
COLORADO
ARIZONA
GLEN CANYON NATIONAL RECREATION AREA
NATURAL BRIDGES NAT'L MON.
HOVENWEEP NAT'L MON.
BRYCE CANYON NAT'L PARK
ZION NAT'L PARK
SHIVWITS IND. RES.
St. George
Hurricane
Kanab
Fredonia
KAIBAB INDIAN RES.
PIPE SPRING NAT'L. MON.
Colorado City
Cane Beds
Moccasin
Lake Powell
RAINBOW BRIDGE NAT'L MON.
Mt. Navajo 10,416 ft. (3175 m.)
MONUMENT VALLEY
Only point in the UNITED STATES common to four state boundaries.
UTE MTN. IND. RES.
GLEN CANYON DAM
Page
Lees Ferry
Marble Canyon
KAIBAB PLATEAU
Jacob Lake
GRAND CANYON NAT'L PARK
GRAND CANYON NATIONAL PARK
North Rim
Grand Canyon
Supai
HAVASUPAI IND. RES.
Mt. Trumbull 7,700 ft. (2347 m.)
Mount Trumbull
LAKE MEAD NAT'L REC. AREA
LAKE MEAD NATIONAL RECREATION AREA
Lake Mead
HOOVER DAM
Temple Bar
HUALAPAI INDIAN RESERVATION
Peach Springs
Nelson
Valentine
Hackberry
Kingman
Chloride
Dolan Springs
CERBAT MTS.
MOHAVE
Lake Mohave
Katherine
DAVIS DAM
Davis Dam
Bullhead City
Riviera
Oatman
FORT MOHAVE IND. RES.
Needles
Golden Shores
Topock
Yucca
Lake Havasu
CHEMEHUEVI IND. RES.
Lake Havasu City
PARKER DAM
Hualapai Pk. 8,266 ft. (2519 m.)
HUALAPAI MTS.
AQUARIUS RA.
Wikieup
Caliente
Carp
Moapa
MOAPA RIVER IND. RES.
Overton
Dry Lake
Littlefield
VIRGIN MTS.
COCONINO
COCONINO PLATEAU
Slate Mtn. 8,209 ft. (2502 m.)
Kendrick Pk. 10,418 ft. (3175 m.)
Humphreys Pk. 12,633 ft. (3851 m.)
O'Leary Pk. 8,925 ft. (2720 m.)
SUNSET CRATER NAT'L MON.
Agassiz Pk. 12,340 ft. (3761 m.)
Government Mtn. 8,347 ft. (2544 m.)
WUPATKI NAT'L MON.
Elden Mtn.
Seligman
Williams
Ash Fork
Parks
Bellemont
Flagstaff
Winona
WALNUT CANYON NAT'L MON.
Woody Mtn. 8,054 ft. (2455 m.)
Cameron
Tuba City
Moenkopi
NAVAJO INDIAN RESERVATION
KAIBITO PLAT.
Kaibito
PAINTED DESERT
HOPI INDIAN RESERVATION
Tonalea
Shonto
Kayenta
Pinon
BLACK MESA
NAVAJO NAT'L MON.
Hotevilla
Oraibi
Shungopavy (Shongopovi)
Second Mesa
Polacca
Keams Canyon
Jeddito
Dilkon
Indian Wells
Leupp
METEOR CRATER
Winslow
Joseph City
Holbrook
PAINTED DESERT SECTION
PETRIFIED FOREST NATIONAL PARK
Petrified Forest
Navajo
Chambers
Sanders
Houck
Lupton
APACHE
Steamboat
Ganado
HUBBELL TRADING POST NAT'L HIST. SITE
Cornfields
Klagetoh
Defiance
Window Rock
St. Michaels
CANYON DE CHELLY NAT'L MONUMENT
Chinle
Many Farms
Lukachukai
Roof Butte 9,575 ft. (2918 m.)
Tsaile
Teec Nos Pos
Pastora Pk. 9,412 ft. (2869 m.)
Dennehotso
ZUNI IND. RES.
St. Johns
Concho
Vernon
Snowflake
Taylor
Woodruff
Clay Sprs.
Linden
Show Low
Pinedale
Heber
Aripine
Overgaard
MOGOLLON PLATEAU
Happy Jack
Mormon Lake
Sedona
TUZIGOOT NAT'L MON.
Cottonwood
Cornville
Clarkdale
Jerome
Clemenceau
Rimrock
Lake Montezuma
MONTEZUMA CASTLE NAT'L MON.
Camp Verde
Baker Butte 8,182 ft. (2494 m.)
Pine
Kohls Ranch
Payson
YAVAPAI
Chino Valley
Paulden
Prescott Valley
Dewey
Cherry
Humboldt
Prescott
Mayer
Mt. Union 7,971 ft. (2430 m.)
Iron Springs
Skull Valley
Kirkland
Yava
Hillside
Bagdad
Yarnell
Arcosanti

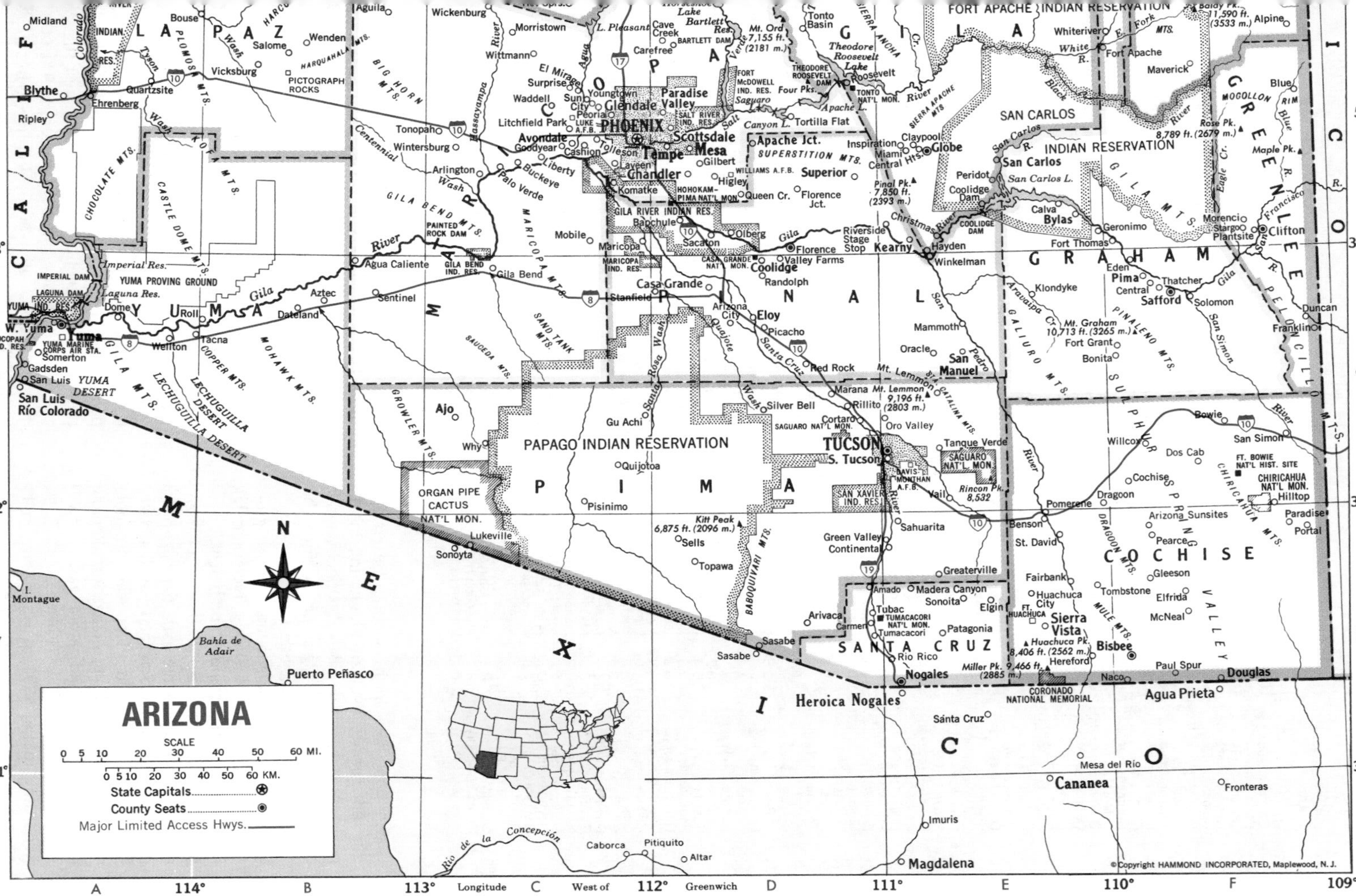

ARIZONA
SCALE
0 5 10 20 30 40 50 60 MI.
0 5 10 20 30 40 50 60 KM.
State Capitals
County Seats
Major Limited Access Hwys.
PHOENIX
Tucson
Yuma
Flagstaff
Glendale
Scottsdale
Tempe
Mesa
Chandler
Casa Grande
Coolidge
Eloy
Florence
Globe
San Carlos
Safford
Clifton
Nogales
Bisbee
Douglas
Sierra Vista
Benson
Willcox
Ajo
Sells
Gila Bend
Buckeye
Wickenburg
Quartzsite
Blythe
San Luis
Río Colorado
Puerto Peñasco
Heroica Nogales
Agua Prieta
Cananea
Magdalena
Caborca
PAPAGO INDIAN RESERVATION
SAN CARLOS INDIAN RESERVATION
FORT APACHE INDIAN RESERVATION
GILA RIVER INDIAN RES.
YUMA PROVING GROUND
ORGAN PIPE CACTUS NAT'L MON.
SAGUARO NAT'L MON.
CORONADO NATIONAL MEMORIAL
LA PAZ
YUMA
MARICOPA
PINAL
PIMA
GILA
GRAHAM
GREENLEE
COCHISE
SANTA CRUZ
CALIFORNIA
MEXICO
YUMA DESERT
LECHUGUILLA DESERT
Bahía de Adair
Longitude West of Greenwich
114°
113°
112°
111°
110°
109°
33°
32°
31°
A B C D E F
5 6 7
©Copyright HAMMOND INCORPORATED, Maplewood, N.J.

ARIZONA

index to Map of Arizona

Chocolate (mts.)	A 5
Clear (creek)	D 4
Coconino (plat.)	C 3
Cocopah Indian Res.	A 6
Colorado (river)	A 5
Colorado River Indian Res.	A 5
Coolidge (dam)	E 3
Copper (mts.)	B 6
Corn (creek)	E 3
Coronado National Mem.	E 7
Cottonwood (cliffs)	B 3
Cottonwood Wash (dry river)	E 4
Davis (dam)	A 3
Davis-Monthan Air Force Base	E 6
Defiance (plat.)	F 3
Detrital Wash (dry river)	A 3
Diablo (canyon)	D 4
Dinnebito Wash (dry river)	E 3
Dot Klish (canyon)	E 2
Dragoon (mts.)	F 7
Eagle (creek)	F 5
East Verde (river)	D 4
Echo (cliffs)	D 2
Elden (mt.)	D 3
Fort Apache Indian Res.	E 5
Fort Bowie National Hist. Site	F 6
Fort McDowell Indian Res.	D 5
Fort Mohave Indian Res.	A 4
Fort Pearce Wash (creek)	B 2
Fossil (creek)	D 4
Four (peaks)	D 5
Galiuro (mts.)	E 6
Gila (mts.)	A 6
Gila (mts.)	F 5
Gila (river)	B 6
Gila Bend (mts.)	B 5
Gila Bend Indian Res.	C 6
Gila River Indian Res.	C 5
Glen Canyon (dam)	D 2
Gothic (mesa)	F 2
Government (mt.)	C 3
Graham (mt.)	F 6
Grand Canyon National Park	C 2
Grand Wash (cliffs)	B 3
Grand Wash (dry riv.)	B 2
Greens (peak)	F 4
Growler (mts.)	B 6
Harcuvar (mts.)	B 5
Harquahala (mts.)	B 5
Hassayampa (river)	C 5
Havasu (lake)	A 4
Havasupai Indian Res.	C 2
Hohokam Pima National Mon.	D 5
Hoover (dam)	A 2
Hopi (buttes)	E 3
Hopi Indian Res.	E 2
Horseshoe (lake)	D 5
Hot Springs National Park	D 4
Huachuca (peak)	E 7
Hualapai (mts.)	B 4
Hualapai (peak)	B 3
Hualapai Indian Res.	B 3
Hubbell Trading Post National Hist. Site	F 3
Humphreys (peak)	D 3
Hurricane Cliffs (cliffs)	B 2
Imperial (dam)	A 6
Imperial (res.)	A 6
Ives (mesa)	E 3
Juniper (mts.)	C 3
Kaibab (plat.)	C 2
Kaibab Indian Res.	C 2
Kaibito (plat.)	D 2
Kanab (creek)	C 2
Kanab (plat.)	C 2
Kellogg (mt.)	E 6
Kendrick (peak)	D 3
Kitt (peak)	D 7
Kofa (mts)	B 5
Laguna (creek)	E 2
Laguna (dam)	A 6
Laguna (res.)	A 6
Lake Mead National Recreational Area	A 2
Lechuguilla (desert)	B 6
Lemmon (mt.)	E 6
Little Colorado (river)	D 3
Lukachukai (mts.)	F 2
Luke Air Force Base	C 5
Maple (peak)	F 5
Maricopa (mts.)	C 5
Maricopa Indian Res.	C 6
Mazatzal (peak)	D 4
Mead (lake)	A 2
Meteor Crater	E 3
Miller (peak)	E 7
Moencopi (plat.)	D 3
Moenkopi Wash (dry river)	D 2
Mogollon (plat.)	D 4
Mogollon Rim (cliffs)	F 5
Mohave (lake)	A 3
Mohave (mts.)	A 4
Mohawk (mts.)	B 6
Montezuma (lake)	D 4
Montezuma Castle National Mon.	D 4
Mormon (lake)	D 4
Mule (mts.)	E 7
Navajo (creek)	D 2
Navajo Indian Res.	D 2
Navajo National Mon.	E 2
Navajo Ordnance Depot	D 3
O'Leary (peak)	D 3
Oraibi Wash (dry river)	E 3
Ord (mt.)	D 5
Organ Pipe Cactus National Mon.	C 6
Painted (desert)	D 2
Painted Desert (Park)	F 3
Painted Rock (dam)	C 5
Papago Indian Res.	C 6
Paria (plateau)	D 2
Paria (river)	D 1
Parker (dam)	A 4
Pastora (peak)	F 2
Peloncillo (mts.)	F 6
Petrified Forest National Park	F 4
Pictograph Rocks	B 5
Pinal (peak)	E 5
Pinaleno (mts.)	F 6
Pink (cliffs)	E 4
Pipe Spring National Mon.	C 2
Pleasant (lake)	C 5
Plomosa (mts.)	A 5
Polacca Wash (dry river)	E 3
Powell (lake)	E 1
Pueblo Colorado Wash (dry river)	F 3
Puerco (river)	F 3
Quajote Wash (dry river)	D 6
Rainbow (plat.)	D 2
Rincon (peak)	E 6
Roof (butte)	F 2
Rose (peak)	F 5
Sacramento Wash (dry river)	A 4
Saguaro (lake)	D 5
Saquaro National Mon.	E 6
Salt (river)	D 5
Salt River Indian Res.	D 5
San Carlos (lake)	E 5
San Carlos (river)	E 5
San Carlos Indian Res.	E 5
Sand Tank (mts.)	C 6
San Francisco (river)	F 5
San Pedro (river)	E 6
San Simon (river)	F 6
Santa Catalina (mts.)	E 6
Santa Cruz (river)	D 6
Santa Maria (river)	B 4
Santa Rose Wash (dry river)	D 6
San Xavier Indian Res.	D 6
Sauceda (mts.)	C 6
Shivwits (plat.)	B 2
Shonto (plat.)	E 2
Sierra Ancha (mts.)	D 5
Sierra Apache (mts.)	E 5
Silver (creek)	E 4
Slate (mt.)	D 3
Sonoran Desert	B 5
Sulphur Spring (valley)	F 6
Sunset Crater National Mon.	D 3
Superstition (mts.)	D 5
Theodore Roosevelt (dam)	D 5
Theodore Roosevelt (lake)	D 5
Tonto (basin)	D 4
Tonto (creek)	D 4
Tonto National Mon.	D 5
Trout (creek)	B 3
Trumbull (mt.)	B 2
Tumacacori National Mon.	E 7
Tuzigoot National Mon.	D 4
Tyson Wash (dry river)	A 5
Uinkaret (plat.)	B 2
Union (mt.)	C 4
Verde (river)	D 5
Vermilion (cliffs)	D 2
Virgin (mts.)	A 2
Virgin (river)	B 2
Walker (creek)	F 2
Walnut Canyon National Mon.	D 3
White (mts.)	F 5
White (river)	E 5
Williams Air Force Base	D 5
Woody (mt.)	D 3
Wupatki National Mon.	D 3
Yavapai Indian Res.	C 4
Yuma (desert)	A 6
Yuma Marine Corps Air Station	A 6
Yuma Proving Ground	A 6
Zuni (river)	F 4

is also found here. In the Sonoran Desert, many different species of lizard (including the Gila monster), spiders, and snakes abound. Eagles, vultures, hawks, and owls are among Arizona's birds of prey; game birds include wild turkey, which are limited to the higher mountains, dove, grouse, and quail. Fish in the state's rivers and lakes include trout, bass, crappie, and bluegill.

Mineral Resources. Arizona contains a variety of minerals, including large-scale deposits of low-grade copper ore, coal, sand and gravel, and stone. Other minerals are gold, silver, lead, tin, molybdenum, zinc, vanadium, manganese, mercury, uranium, petroleum, and natural gas. R.W.D.

POPULATION

According to the 1990 census, Arizona had 3,665,228 inhabitants, an increase of 34.8% over 1980; Arizona was the third fastest growing state in the U.S., after Nevada and Alaska. The average population density in 1990 was 12 people per sq km (32 per sq mi). Whites made up 80.8% of the population and blacks 3%. There were also 203,009 American Indians (5.6% of the total). The two major Indian groups were the Navajo (*see* NAVAJO INDIANS) and the Hopi (q.v.); California and Oklahoma were the only states with larger Indian populations. Some 688,338 persons, about 19% of the total population, were of Hispanic background. Mostly of Mexican descent, Hispanics were concentrated in the S half of the state. Roman Catholics made up the largest single religious group, accounting for 23.9% of the population, followed by Baptists (11.6%), Methodists (6.6%), and Mormons (4.9%). In 1990, about 88% of the people of Arizona lived in areas defined as urban, and the rest lived in rural areas. The state's largest cities were Phoenix, the capital; Tucson; Mesa; Glendale; Tempe; and Scottsdale.

EDUCATION AND CULTURAL ACTIVITY

Arizona has a comprehensive statewide educational system. Many of the state's cultural institutions are concentrated in its major cities, notably Tucson and Phoenix.

Education. Although the first schools in Arizona were established by Spanish missionaries in the 17th century, the area's first public school was not opened until 1864, in Prescott. By the late 1980s Arizona had 1026 public elementary and secondary schools with a total yearly enrollment of 451,300 elementary pupils and 156,300 secondary students. In addition, some 35,500 students attended private schools.

Arizona State University, the state's oldest institution of higher education, was established in 1885 in Tempe. By the late 1980s Arizona had 37 colleges and universities with a total annual enrollment of approximately 252,600 students. Besides Arizona State, notable schools included Northern Arizona University (1899), in Flagstaff; the University of Arizona, in Tucson; and Navajo Community College (1969), in Tsaile, the first U.S. college to be established on an Indian reservation.

Cultural Institutions. Many of Arizona's foremost museums are located in Tucson and Phoenix. The Arizona Historical Society, Tucson Museum of Art, the University of Arizona Museum of Art, Arizona State Museum, and Arizona-Sonora Desert Museum are in Tucson, and the Arizona Mineral Museum, Phoenix Art Museum, Heard Museum, and Pueblo Grande Museum are in Phoenix. Tucson is also the site of the Flandrau Science Center and Planetarium, the Arizona Opera Company, and the Tucson Symphony Orchestra. Phoenix contains the Desert Botanical Garden, the Phoenix Zoo, and the Phoenix Symphony Orchestra. Three museums of special interest are the Navajo Tribal Museum, in Window Rock; the Mohave Museum of History and Arts, in Kingman; and the Colorado River Indian Tribes Museum, in Parker.

Historical Sites. A number of Arizona's historical sites include remains of early Indian cultures. Among these are Canyon de Chelly, Casa Grande, Montezuma Castle, Navajo, and Wupatki national monuments. Dating from more recent times are Hubbell Trading Post National Historic Site, near Ganado, a still-active post for trade with Indians; London Bridge, transported from England, in Lake Havasu City; the Old Governor's Mansion, completed in 1864, in Prescott; and Mission San Xavier del Bac, established in 1700, in Tucson.

The high-rise downtown area of Tucson, Arizona's second-largest city, is an important commercial center. The city's high altitude and abundant sunshine make it a popular resort as well. George Hunter–Shostal/Superstock

ARIZONA

DATE OF STATEHOOD: February 14, 1912; 48th state

CAPITAL:	**Phoenix**
MOTTO:	***Ditat Deus*** **(God enriches)**
NICKNAME:	**Grand Canyon State**
STATE SONG:	**"Arizona" (words by Margaret R. Clifford; music by Maurice Blumenthal)**
STATE TREE:	**Paloverde**
STATE FLOWER:	**Saguaro cactus blossom**
STATE BIRD:	**Cactus wren**
POPULATION (1990):	**3,665,228; 24th among the states**
AREA:	**295,276 sq km (114,006 sq mi); 6th largest state; includes 943 sq km (364 sq mi) of inland water**
HIGHEST POINT:	**Humphreys Peak, 3853 m (12,633 ft)**
LOWEST POINT:	**21 m (70 ft), along the Colorado River**
ELECTORAL VOTES:	**8**
U.S. CONGRESS:	**2 senators; 6 representatives**

POPULATION OF ARIZONA SINCE 1870

Year of Census	Population	Classified As Urban
1870	10,000	30%
1890	88,000	9%
1910	204,000	31%
1930	436,000	34%
1940	499,000	35%
1950	750,000	55%
1960	1,302,000	75%
1980	2,718,000	84%
1990	3,665,228	87%

POPULATION OF TEN LARGEST CITIES

	1990 Census	1980 Census
Phoenix	983,403	789,704
Tucson	405,390	330,537
Mesa	288,091	152,453
Glendale	148,134	96,988
Tempe	141,865	106,743
Scottsdale	130,069	88,412
Chandler	90,533	29,673
Yuma	54,923	42,433
Peoria	50,618	12,251
Flagstaff	45,857	34,641

CLIMATE	PHOENIX	FLAGSTAFF
Average January temperature range	3.3° to 18.3° C (38° to 65° F)	–10° to 5° C (14° to 41° F)
Average July temperature range	25.6° to 40.6° C (78° to 105° F)	10° to 27.2° C (50° to 81° F)
Average annual temperature	21.1° C (70° F)	7.2° C (45° F)
Average annual precipitation	178 mm (7 in)	483 mm (19 in)
Average annual snowfall	negligible	2261 mm (89 in)
Mean number of days per year with appreciable precipitation	35	76
Average daily relative humidity	27%	39%
Mean number of clear days per year	214	170

NATURAL REGIONS OF ARIZONA

PRINCIPAL PRODUCTS OF ARIZONA

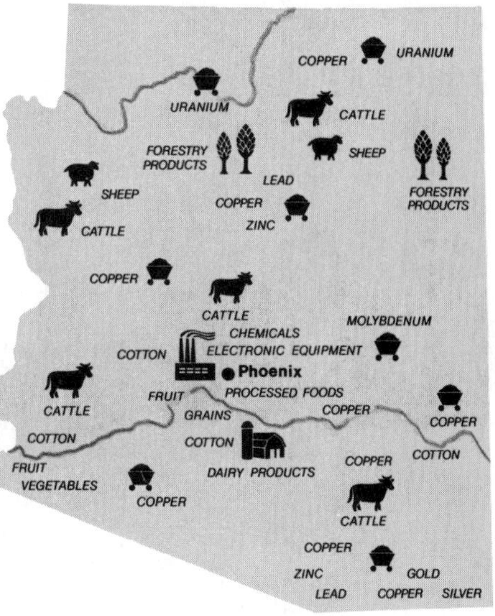

ECONOMY

State budget	general revenue $7.0 billion
	general expenditure $7.5 billion
	accumulated debt $2.2 billion
State and local taxes, per capita	$1921
Personal income, per capita	$13,461
Population below poverty level	15.7%
Assets, insured commercial banks (43)	$26.4 billion
Labor force (civilian nonfarm)	1,457,000
Employed in services	27%
Employed in wholesale and retail trade	25%
Employed in government	17%
Employed in manufacturing	13%

	Quantity Produced	Value
FARM PRODUCTS		**$1.9 billion**
Crops		**$1.1 billion**
Cotton	221,000 metric tons	$221 million
Vegetables	711,000 metric tons	$147 million
Hay	1.3 million metric tons	$141 million
Citrus fruits	283,000 metric tons	$108 million
Lettuce	677,000 metric tons	$102 million
Livestock and Livestock Products		**$819 million**
Cattle	217,000 metric tons	$348 million
Milk	739,000 metric tons	$231 million
MINERALS		**$3.0 billion†**
Copper	898,000 metric tons	$2.6 billion
Coal	10.8 million metric tons	N/A
Sand, gravel	30.8 million metric tons	$134 million
Gold	2800 kg	$34 million
Silver	170 metric tons	$30 million

†Excluding coal

	Annual Payroll
MANUFACTURING	**$5.2 billion**
Transportation equipment	$1.1 billion
Electronic equipment	$1.1 billion
Instruments and related products	$540 million
Industrial machinery and equipment	$385 million
Printing and publishing	$342 million
Primary metals	$208 million
Fabricated metal products	$188 million
Food and kindred products	$164 million
Stone, clay, and glass products	$162 million
OTHER	**$25.6 billion**
Services	$7.0 billion
Government	$6.9 billion
Retail trade	$3.3 billion
Finance, insurance, and real estate	$2.1 billion
Transportation, communications, and public utilities	$1.9 billion
Construction	$1.8 billion
Wholesale trade	$1.7 billion

ANNUAL GROSS STATE PRODUCT

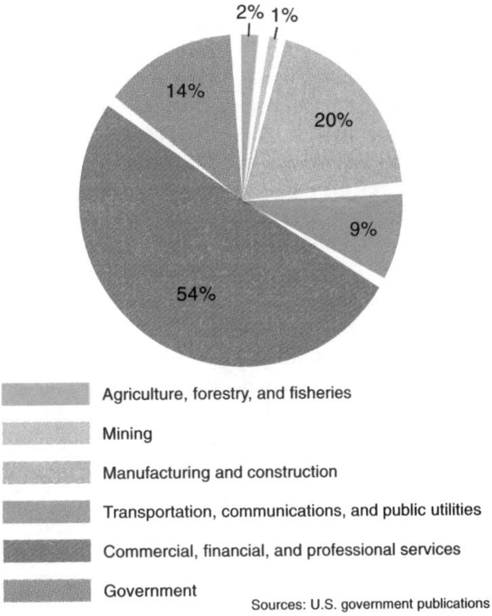

Sources: U.S. government publications

Navajo Indians herding sheep in Monument Valley, northeastern Arizona. The strange rock formations behind them are indicative of the spectacular scenery that abounds in this mountain state. **W. Bayer–Bruce Coleman, Inc.**

Sports and Recreation. Arizona's mountains, parks, rivers, and lakes provide ideal conditions for hunting, fishing, camping, hiking, boating, swimming, skiing, and horseback riding. Among Arizona's favorite outdoor spots are the Glen Canyon and Lake Mead national recreation areas.

Communications. In the early 1990s Arizona had 73 AM and 76 FM radiobroadcasting stations and 27 television stations. The state's first radio station, KFAD in Phoenix, was licensed in 1922. KPHO-TV in Phoenix, the first commercial television station, began operation in 1949. The *Weekly Arizonian,* Arizona's first newspaper, was initially published in Tubac in 1859. By the early 1990s Arizona had 20 daily newspapers with a total daily circulation of about 737,400 copies. Influential dailies include the *Arizona Republic* and the *Phoenix Gazette,* in Phoenix, and the *Arizona Daily Star* and *Tucson Citizen,* in Tucson.

GOVERNMENT AND POLITICS

Arizona is governed under its original constitution, adopted in 1911 and put into effect in 1912, as amended. An amendment to the constitution may be proposed by the legislature, by a voters' initiative, or by a constitutional convention. To be adopted, a proposed amendment must be approved by a majority of the persons voting on the issue in an election.

Executive. The chief executive of Arizona is a governor, who is popularly elected to a 4-year term and may be reelected any number of times. The same regulations apply to the secretary of state, who succeeds the governor should the latter resign, die, or be removed from office. Other elected state officers include the attorney general, treasurer, superintendent of public instruction, mine inspector, and the corporation commissioner.

Legislature. The bicameral Arizona legislature is made up of a senate and a house of representatives. The 30 members of the senate and the 60 members of the house are elected to serve 2-year terms.

Judiciary. Arizona's highest court, the supreme court, is composed of 5 justices who serve 6-year terms. The intermediate court of appeals has 21 judges who serve 6-year terms, and the major trial courts, the superior courts, have 116 judges who serve 4-year terms. Supreme court justices and court of appeals judges are appointed by the governor.

Local Government. Arizona has 15 counties and 86 municipalities. Most counties are governed by either a three- or five-member elected board of supervisors. Many cities employ the council-manager form of government.

National Representation. Arizona elects two senators and six representatives to the U.S. Congress. The state has eight electoral votes in presidential elections.

Politics. In both state and national elections Arizona was a stronghold of the Democratic party from the advent of statehood until the early 1950s. The election of a conservative Republican, Barry M. Goldwater, to the U.S. Senate in 1952 marked the emergence of a Republican trend that continued into the 1980s. In 1988 Republican Gov. Evan Mecham (1925–), found guilty by the Arizona senate on two charges of official misconduct, became the first U.S. governor to be impeached and removed from office since 1929.

ECONOMY

In the 20th century Arizona has experienced remarkable economic growth, developing from a region of scattered mining, ranching, and cotton-growing operations into a state with a diversified modern economy. In the early 1990s the chief employers were commercial firms, government agencies, service industries (especially health services), and manufacturing concerns.

Agriculture. Arizona has some 8000 farms, averaging about 1820 ha (about 4500 acres)—the highest such average of any U.S. state. About 58% of the annual farm income derives from the sale of crops, and the rest comes from sales of livestock and livestock products. The most valuable agricultural commodities are cattle, cotton, dairy products, vegetables, and hay. Citrus fruits and lettuce are also significant sources of income.

Crop farming in Arizona depends almost entirely on irrigation. Most cultivated land is in the S, especially in the Salt R. valley, near Phoenix. Citrus fruit, particularly oranges and grapefruit, market vegetables, and alfalfa all occupy much farmland around Phoenix, but the leading cash crop in the region is cotton, which occupies more than 40% of the entire state's cropland. Elsewhere in Arizona productive agricultural land is found along the upper Gila R., in several basins between Phoenix and Tucson, and near the lower Colorado R. In the Colorado Plateau region of N Arizona are numerous large ranches on which livestock is raised, but few crop farms.

Forestry and Fishing. Arizona has a relatively small lumbering industry, the annual cut being composed almost exclusively of softwoods such as ponderosa pine, yellow pine, and Douglas fir. Numerous lumbering operations are situated near Flagstaff. Commercial fishing in the state is negligible; most of the catch is taken by people fishing for recreation.

Mining. Arizona is the leading U.S. state in copper production, usually accounting for more than half of the country's annual output. Copper mines are located in the S half of the state, mostly situated between the Salt R. and the Mexican border. One of Arizona's largest copper mines is an open-pit operation at Morenci, and a very big underground copper mine is located at San Manuel, NE of Tucson. Gold and silver ores exist in the S Arizona mountains and are frequently recovered in conjunction with copper extraction, as is molybdenum. Coal is found in a number of areas on the Colorado Plateau and is mined in considerable quantity in the Black Mesa region of the NE. Other minerals produced in significant

Bisbee, Ariz., has been an important center for the mining of metals, notably copper, since the prospecting days of the 1870s. Worked-out copper mines are now open to visitors. Arizona Office of Tourism

quantities include sand and gravel, stone, lead, and tin.

Manufacturing. Beginning in the 1940s Arizona's manufacturing capacity increased markedly, and in the late 1980s firms engaged in manufacturing accounted for more than $22 billion in annual sales and employed more than 180,000 workers. Leading types of manufactures are transport equipment, electronic items, instruments and related products, industrial machinery, and primary metal and fabricated metal goods. Arizona's most visible manufacturing concerns are the great copper concentrators, located adjacent to every important mine. In addition, the state has several big copper smelters. Large factories producing electronic equipment are located in and around Phoenix and Tucson.

Tourism. The tourist industry annually contributes more than $6.8 billion to the economy of Arizona. The state's best-known attractions are in the Colorado Plateau region in the N, where the dramatic landscape in Grand Canyon National Park (q.v.) is the most famous lure. More than 3.5 million persons visit the Grand Canyon each year, and most of them also spend some time at other N Arizona attractions, which include Petrified Forest National Park (q.v.), the Navajo and Hopi Indian reservations, the Anasazi Indian ruins in Canyon de Chelly National Monument (q.v.), and skiing areas near Flagstaff. To the W, Lakes Mead and Havasu, both on the Colorado R., combine varied water-sport opportunities with clear desert air; in S Arizona the mission ruins at Tumacacori National Historical Park (q.v.), the giant cacti in Saguaro National Monument, and countless mountain trails draw many visitors.

Transportation. Despite the presence of vast desert expanses, deep canyons, and numerous mountains, buttes, and mesas, Arizona has a well-knit transportation network. The state is served by about 2870 km (about 1785 mi) of operated railroad track, including parts of two major transcontinental railroad lines. Arizona has some 83,060 km (some 51,610 mi) of roads, and hard-surfaced routes serve all communities of significant size. Major road hubs are Phoenix, Tucson, and Flagstaff. Arizona has 181 airports, of which the busiest serve the Phoenix and Tucson areas; there are also 90 heliports.

Energy. About half of Arizona's electricity is generated in thermal plants using coal or natural gas; another 12% comes from hydroelectric plants, and 33% from nuclear installations. The state draws power from such major hydroelectric facilities as Glen Canyon, Hoover, Davis, and Parker dams, all on the Colorado R. Power plants in Arizona have an aggregate electricity generating capacity of about 14.9 million kw and produce some 62.3 billion kwh of electricity each year. M.E.B.

HISTORY

Long before its discovery by Europeans, the region comprising present-day Arizona was inhabited by culturally advanced tribes of Indians. The ruins of irrigation canals and aqueducts, cities, and fortifications built by these ancient peoples are scattered throughout the valleys and canyons of the state. The first European known to have visited the region was the Franciscan missionary and explorer Marcos de Niza (c. 1495–1558), leader of an expedition (1539) from Mexico City. The Spanish explorer Francisco Vásquez de Coronado, impressed by de Niza's accounts of riches in the area, led another expedition from Mexico in 1540. Members of that group crossed the Colorado River and came upon the Grand Canyon.

Inspired by reports of mineral wealth in Arizona, other explorers followed, but the hostility of the Indians discouraged attempts at colonization. The Spanish government made the region part of New Spain in 1598. Christianity and Spanish culture were introduced to the Indians by the Jesuit missionary Eusebio Francisco Kino, who was active also in northern Mexico. Among the missions Kino founded in Arizona was San José de Tumacacori (now a national historical site). Other Jesuit missions were founded during the first half of the 18th century, and in 1776 the Spaniards established a presidio at Tucson. As a result of a serious Indian uprising in 1802, the disorders attending the successful Mexican revolt (1821) against Spain, and another Indian uprising in 1827, almost all of the Spanish Arizona settlements and missions were abandoned.

American settlers, traders, and explorers, however, had begun to move into the region. During the Mexican War (1846–48) U.S. troops seized control of Arizona and adjoining New Mexico. Under the terms of the Treaty of Guadalupe Hidalgo, the agreement terminating the war, Mexico ceded all of Arizona and New Mexico north of the Gila River to the U.S. The section south of the Gila was acquired by the U.S. through the Gadsden Purchase in 1853. In 1863 Arizona, until then a part of the territory of New Mexico, was established as a separate territory. Serious Indian uprisings occurred in the territory during the American Civil War and at sporadic intervals until 1896.

The U.S. Congress rejected an application by Arizona for statehood in 1891. Legislation admitting Arizona and New Mexico as a single state was enacted by Congress twice between 1904

The White House Pueblo in Canyon de Chelly National Monument, northeastern Arizona. It constitutes the ruins of a cliff village first occupied about the 11th century.
Arizona Office of Tourism

and 1906, but the measure failed (1906) to win the approval of the Arizona electorate. In January 1910, Congress authorized the territory to hold a constitutional convention for the purpose of drafting a state constitution. The convention completed its work in December 1910, and the document was ratified in February 1911. Shortly thereafter Congress passed a resolution conferring statehood on Arizona. President William Taft vetoed the resolution because the proposed state constitution provided for the recall of elective judges. In August, Congress and the president approved a resolution making the admission of Arizona to the Union conditional upon the elimination of the constitutional provision for recall. The state's electorate endorsed the amendment on December 12, and on Feb. 14, 1912, Taft signed the proclamation admitting Arizona as the 48th state. On Nov. 5, 1912, the voters restored the provision for recall to the constitution.

A series of federal irrigation projects, especially those of the 1930s, accelerated Arizona's development, which increased sharply with the post-World War II demand for the state's chief products—copper, cattle, and cotton.

In 1948, Arizona Indians won the right to vote and began to enjoy some economic gains. In 1969 the first college on an Indian reservation, Navajo Community College, opened in Tsaile.

Arizona's warm, dry climate and diverse recreational lands have, since the early 1950s, attracted both a great number of new residents and a heavy stream of tourists. A commensurate increase in social and consumer services, followed by expanding industry, has dramatically affected the state's economic and political profile. As the population of Arizona nearly tripled between 1960 and 1990, the state aquired a national reputation for conservatism in politics and for probusiness policies that favored rapid growth.

Increased real estate development has led to a degradation of air quality, depletion of freshwater resources, and encroachment on the state's unique desert and forest reserves. Pollution controls, land-use restrictions, and water conservation measures have been only sporadically effective. The Central Arizona Project, extending 541 km (336 mi) and built at a cost of $3.7 billion, began supplying Colorado R. water by pipeline to Phoenix in 1985 and Tucson in 1991.

For further information on this topic, see the Bibliography in volume 28, sections 1212, 1217.

ARIZONA, UNIVERSITY OF, land-grant state-controlled institution of higher learning, in Tucson, Ariz. It was chartered in 1885 and opened for instruction in 1891. It offers courses in liberal arts, in fine arts, and in agriculture, architecture, astronomy, business and management, education, engineering, home economics, law, medicine, mining, music, nursing, and pharmacy. The degrees of bachelor, master, and doctor are conferred. The university maintains ten agricultural-research centers, and its archaeological field school provides research experience and training opportunities at prehistoric sites away from campus. Notable facilities on the campus in Tucson include the Steward Observatory, a mineralogical museum, and the Arizona State Museum.

ARK. *See* DELUGE.

ARKANSAS, one of the West South Central states of the U.S., bounded on the N and NE by Missouri, on the E by Tennessee and Mississippi, on the S by Louisiana, on the SW by Texas, and on the W by Oklahoma. The Mississippi R. forms virtually the entire E boundary.

Arkansas entered the Union as the 25th state on June 15, 1836. A slaveholding state, it was part of the Confederacy during the American Civil War. Long known as an agricultural state with diverse mineral resources, Arkansas by the 1990s had an economy that was dominated by the manufacturing and service sectors. The name of the state is taken from the Arkansas R., which was named for the Arkansa Indians; the *s* was added as a plural, and the French pronunciation was retained. Arkansas is called the Land of Opportunity.

LAND AND RESOURCES

Arkansas, with an area of 137,742 sq km (53,182 sq mi), is the 29th largest state in the U.S; 7.1% of the land is owned by the federal government. Arkansas is roughly square in shape, although narrower in the S, and its extreme dimensions are about 355 km (about 220 mi) from both N to S and E to W. Elevations range from 17 m (55 ft) along the Ouachita R., near the Louisiana border, to a maximum of 839 m (2753 ft) at Magazine Mt. The mean elevation is about 198 m (650 ft).

Physical Geography. The physical landscape of Arkansas consists of heavily wooded mountains in much of the N and W and plateaus and low-lying plains in the E and S. The Ozark Plateau covers much of N Arkansas, from the Oklahoma border to the Ozark escarpment on the E. It is a land of rugged hills and valleys and of upland forests interspersed with rich farmland. Above the S section of the plateau rise the Boston Mts. The Arkansas Valley separates the Ozark Plateau from the Ouachita Mts. Although the valley is primarily a lowland, some mountains rise from its floor. It is a prosperous farming and mining area. The Ouachita Mts. to the S are composed of E–W-trending ridges that are separated by narrow valleys. The region is a major source of timber and is also known for its hot springs.

The West Gulf Coastal Plain cuts a wide swath through SW Arkansas. It is part of the great coastal plain that extends N from the Gulf of Mexico. Soils of clay loams mixed with gravel make the area relatively fertile for farming and for the commercial growth of pine trees. The Mississippi Alluvial Plain occupies approximately the E one-third of the state. Rich alluvial soils have been deposited here over thousands of

About one-half of Arkansas is wooded, and many tourists are drawn to its peaks and forests. Shown here is Falling Water Creek in Ozark National Forest.
Peter B. Kaplan–Photo Researchers, Inc.

INDEX TO MAP OF ARKANSAS

Cities and Towns

⊙ County seat

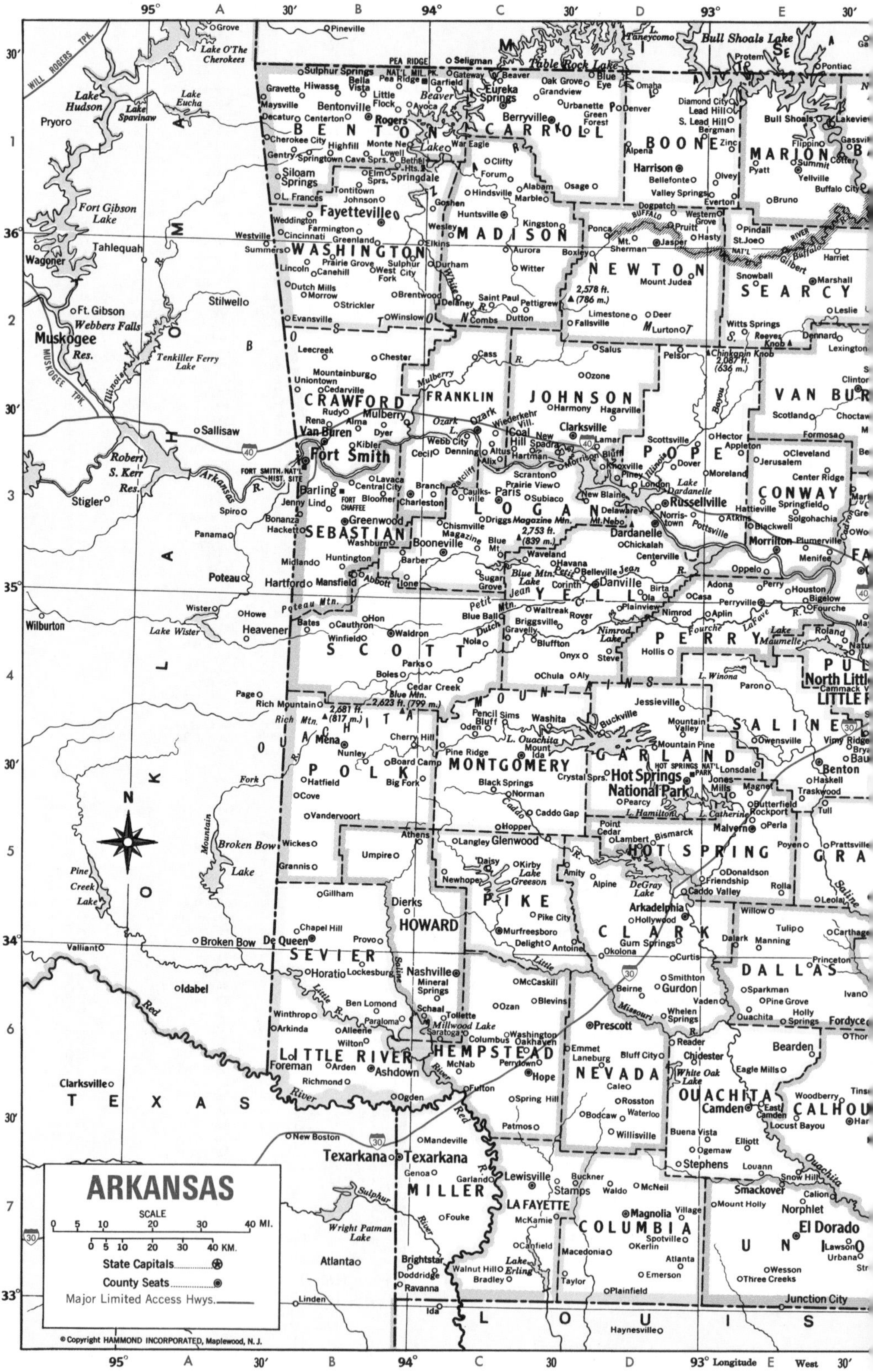
ARKANSAS
SCALE
0 5 10 20 30 40 MI.
0 5 10 20 30 40 KM.
State Capitals
County Seats
Major Limited Access Hwys.
© Copyright HAMMOND INCORPORATED, Maplewood, N. J.
95° A 30′ B 94° C 30′ D 93° E 30′
95° A 30′ B 94° C 30 D 93° Longitude E West 30′
30′
1
36°
2
30′
3
35°
4
30′
5
34°
6
30′
7
33°
BENTON
CARROLL
BOONE
MARION
WASHINGTON
MADISON
NEWTON
SEARCY
CRAWFORD
FRANKLIN
JOHNSON
VAN BUREN
POPE
CONWAY
SEBASTIAN
LOGAN
YELL
PERRY
SCOTT
SALINE
GARLAND
POLK
MONTGOMERY
HOT SPRING
GRANT
HOWARD
PIKE
CLARK
SEVIER
DALLAS
LITTLE RIVER
HEMPSTEAD
NEVADA
OUACHITA
CALHOUN
MILLER
LA FAYETTE
COLUMBIA
UNION
OKLAHOMA
TEXAS
LOUISIANA
MISSOURI
Bull Shoals Lake
Table Rock Lake
L. Taneycomo
Beaver Lake
Lake O'The Cherokees
Lake Hudson
Lake Eucha
Lake Spavinaw
Fort Gibson Lake
Tenkiller Ferry Lake
Webbers Falls Res.
Robert S. Kerr Res.
Lake Wister
Broken Bow Lake
Pine Creek Lake
Lake Dardanelle
Lake Ouachita
L. Hamilton
L. Catherine
DeGray Lake
Lake Greeson
Millwood Lake
Wright Patman Lake
Lake Erling
White Oak Lake
L. Winona
Lake Maumelle
Blue Mtn. Lake
Nimrod Lake
Arkansas R.
Red River
Ouachita R.
Little Missouri R.
Sulphur River
Buffalo
Ouachita Mtns.
Magazine Mtn. 2,753 ft. (839 m.)
Mt. Nebo
2,578 ft. (786 m.)
Chinkapin Knob 2,087 ft. (636 m.)
Rich Mtn. 2,681 ft. (817 m.)
Blue Mtn. 2,623 ft. (799 m.)
PEA RIDGE NAT'L MIL. PK.
FORT SMITH NAT'L HIST. SITE
FORT CHAFFEE
HOT SPRINGS NAT'L PARK
WILL ROGERS TPK.
MUSKOGEE TPK.
Pineville
Grove
Seligman
Bentonville
Rogers
Springdale
Fayetteville
Eureka Springs
Berryville
Harrison
Jasper
Huntsville
Marshall
Yellville
Clarksville
Ozark
Van Buren
Fort Smith
Paris
Booneville
Russellville
Dardanelle
Danville
Morrilton
Perryville
Waldron
Mena
Mount Ida
Hot Springs National Park
Benton
Malvern
Glenwood
Murfreesboro
Arkadelphia
Nashville
De Queen
Ashdown
Hope
Prescott
Camden
El Dorado
Magnolia
Lewisville
Texarkana
Fordyce
North Little Rock
Little Rock
Muskogee
Tahlequah
Stilwell
Sallisaw
Poteau
Wilburton
Idabel
Broken Bow
Clarksville
Stigler
Pryor
Wagoner

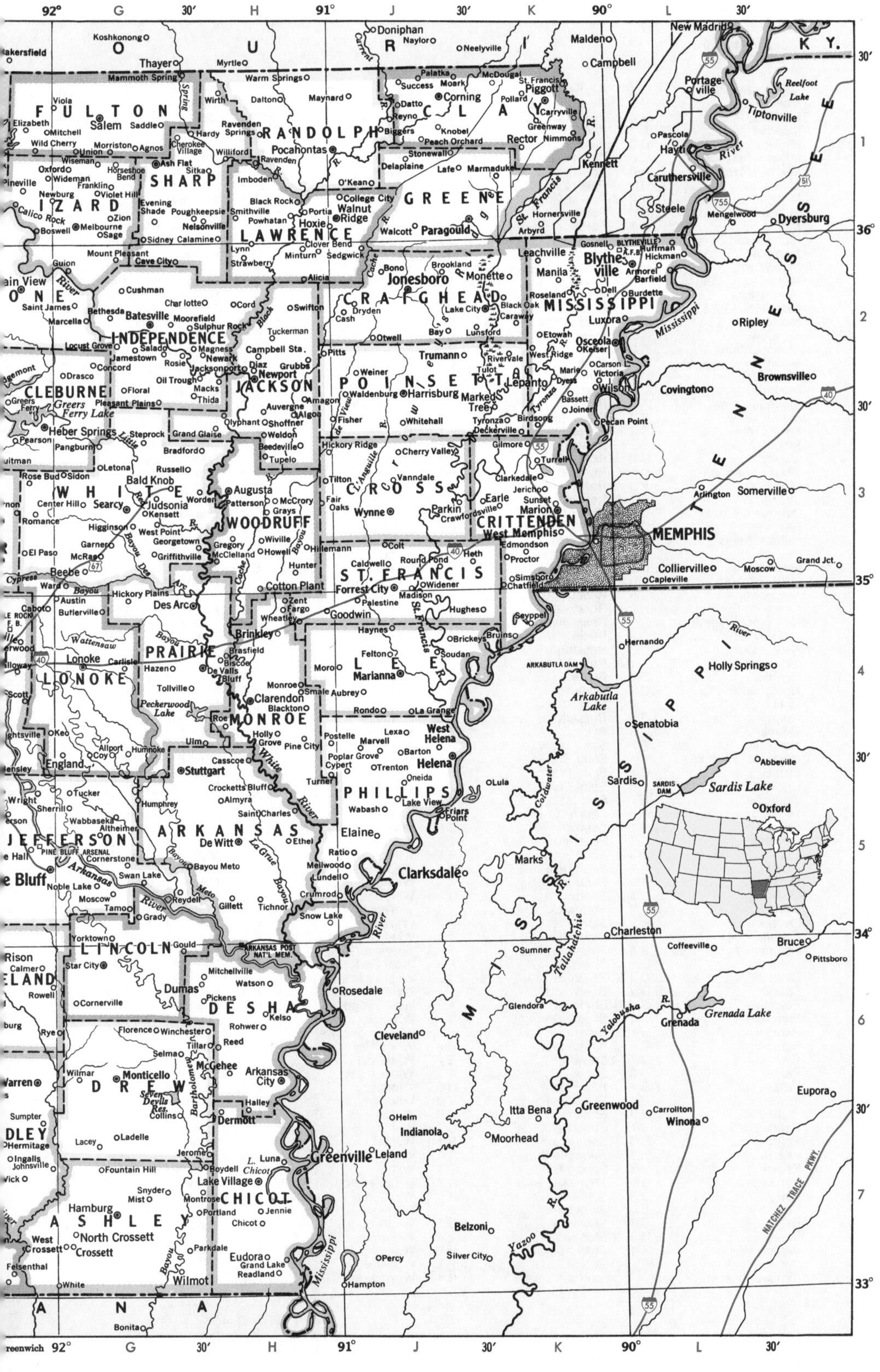
92°
G
30′
H
91°
J
30′
K
90°
L
30′
30′
1
36°
2
30′
3
35°
4
30′
5
34°
6
30′
7
33°
Greenwich 92°
Bakersfield
Koshkonong
O U R I
Doniphan
Naylor
Current
Neelyville
Malden
New Madrid
K Y.
Campbell
Thayer
Myrtle
Mammoth Spring
Warm Springs
Palatka
McDougal
St. Francis
Piggott
Success
Moark
Corning
Pollard
Carryville
Portage ville
Reelfoot Lake
Tiptonville
Viola
FULTON
Salem
Saddle
Elizabeth
Mitchell
Wild Cherry
Morriston
Agnos
Union
Wirth
Dalton
Maynard
Hardy
Ravenden Springs
RANDOLPH
Datto
Reyno
CLAY
Biggers
Knobel
Peach Orchard
Greenway
Rector
Nimmons
Pascola
Hayti
Pocahontas
Cherokee Village
Williford
Ravenden
Stonewall
Delaplaine
Lafe
Marmaduke
Kennett
Caruthersville
Wiseman
Oxford
Wideman
Horseshoe Bend
Franklin
Ash Flat
SHARP
Sitka
Imboden
O'Kean
Pineville
Newburg
Violet Hill
IZARD
Calico Rock
Zion
Boswell
Melbourne
Sage
Evening Shade
Poughkeepsie
Nelsonville
Sidney
Calamine
Black Rock
Smithville
Powhatan
Portia
Walnut Ridge
College City
Hoxie
GREENE
LAWRENCE
Walcott
Paragould
Hornersville
Arbyrd
Steele
Mengelwood
Dyersburg
River
St. Francis R.
Guion
Mount Pleasant
Cave City
Lynn
Strawberry
Clover Bend
Minturn
Sedgwick
Alicia
Cache
Bono
Jonesboro
Brookland
Monette
Leachville
Manila
Gosnell
BLYTHEVILLE A.F.B.
Blytheville
Huffman
Hickman
Armorel
Barfield
Dell
Burdette
Mountain View
STONE
Saint James
Marcella
Cushman
Bethesda
Batesville
Charlotte
Moorefield
Sulphur Rock
Cord
Black
Swifton
CRAIGHEAD
Dryden
Cash
Lake City
Black Oak
Caraway
Roseland
MISSISSIPPI
Luxora
Ripley
INDEPENDENCE
Locust Grove
Salado
Magness
Newark
Jamestown
Tuckerman
Campbell Sta.
Pitts
Otwell
Bay
Lunsford
Etowah
Osceola
Keiser
West Ridge
Concord
Drasco
Rosie
Jacksonport
Diaz
Newport
Grubbs
Trumann
Rivervale
Tulot
Marie
Dyess
Carson L.
Victoria
Wilson
Brownsville
Covington
CLEBURNE
Floral
Oil Trough
Macks
Thida
JACKSON
Weiner
Waldenburg
Harrisburg
POINSETT
Marked Tree
Lepanto
Greers Ferry
Greers Ferry Lake
Pleasant Plains
Amagon
Auvergne
Algoa
Fisher
Whitehall
Tyronza
Birdsong
Deckerville
Bassett
Joiner
Pecan Point
Heber Springs
Steprock
Grand Glaise
Olyphant
Shoffner
Weldon
Beedeville
Tupelo
Hickory Ridge
Cherry Valley
Gilmore
Turrell
Pearson
Pangburn
Bradford
Little
Letona
Russell
Rose Bud
Sidon
WHITE
Bald Knob
Judsonia
Center Hill
Searcy
Kensett
Romance
Augusta
Patterson
Worden
McCrory
Grays
WOODRUFF
Tilton
Fair Oaks
Wynne
CROSS
Vanndale
Parkin
Crawfordsville
Earle
Clarkedale
Jericho
Sunset
Marion
CRITTENDEN
West Memphis
MEMPHIS
Arlington
Somerville
Higginson
West Point
Georgetown
Griffithville
Gregory
McClelland
Wiville
Howell
Hillemann
Colt
Edmondson
Proctor
El Paso
Garner
McRae
Beebe
Round Pond
Caldwell
Heth
ST. FRANCIS
Forrest City
Widener
Madison
Palestine
Hughes
Collierville
Moscow
Grand Jct.
Capleville
Simsboro
Chatfield
Hunter
Cotton Plant
Cypress
Ward
Austin
Cabot
Butlerville
Hickory Plains
Des Arc
Zent
Fargo
Wheatley
Goodwin
Brinkley
Haynes
Brickeys
Bruins
Seyppel
Hernando
Wattensaw
Lonoke
Carlisle
PRAIRIE
Brasfield
Biscoe
De Valls Bluff
Hazen
Felton
Moro
LEE
Marianna
Soudan
ARKABUTLA DAM
Arkabutla Lake
Holly Springs
LONOKE
Tollville
Monroe
Clarendon
Smale
Aubrey
Blackton
Peckerwood Lake
Roe
MONROE
Rondo
La Grange
Senatobia
Scott
Keo
Holly Grove
Pine City
Lexa
Marvell
Postelle
West Helena
Helena
Barton
Allport
Coy
Humnoke
Ulm
England
Stuttgart
Casscoe
Poplar Grove
Cypert
Trenton
Oneida
Abbeville
Sardis
SARDIS DAM
Sardis Lake
Oxford
Lula
Tucker
Wright
Sherrill
Humphrey
Crocketts Bluff
Almyra
Saint Charles
Turner
PHILLIPS
Wabash
Lake View
Friars Point
Coldwater
Wabbaseka
Altheimer
JEFFERSON
ARKANSAS
De Witt
Ethel
Elaine
PINE BLUFF ARSENAL
Cornerstone
Ratio
Pine Bluff
Noble Lake
Swan Lake
Bayou Meto
La Grue
Mellwood
Lundell
Clarksdale
Marks
Moscow
Tamo
Reydell
Gillett
Tichnor
Crumrod
Grady
Snow Lake
Tallahatchie R.
Yorktown
LINCOLN
Gould
ARKANSAS POST NAT'L MEM.
Sumner
Charleston
Coffeeville
Bruce
Pittsboro
Rison
Calmer
CLEVELAND
Star City
Mitchellville
Watson
Rowell
Dumas
Pickens
Rosedale
Cornerville
DESHA
Kelso
Glendora
Yalobusha R.
Grenada
Grenada Lake
Rye
Florence
Winchester
Rohwer
Tillar
Reed
Cleveland
Selma
McGehee
Wilmar
Monticello
DREW
Seven Devils Res.
Collins
Arkansas City
Bartholomew
Warren
Halley
Eupora
Sumpter
Dermott
Helm
Itta Bena
Greenwood
Carrollton
Winona
BRADLEY
Hermitage
Lacey
Ladelle
Jerome
Indianola
Moorhead
Ingalls
Johnsville
Fountain Hill
Boydell
L. Chicot
Luna
Greenville
Leland
Wick
Snyder
Mist
Lake Village
Montrose
CHICOT
Portland
Jennie
Chicot
NATCHEZ TRACE PKWY.
Yazoo R.
Hamburg
ASHLEY
North Crossett
Crossett
West Crossett
Belzoni
Parkdale
Eudora
Grand Lake
Readland
Silver City
Percy
Felsenthal
White
Wilmot
Mississippi
Hampton
LOUISIANA
Bonita
MISSISSIPPI
TENNESSEE
River
55
40
51
755
67
Greenwich 92°
G
30′
H
91°
J
30′
K
90°
L
30′

Index to Map of Arkansas

Place	Map key
Melbourne ⊙	G 1
Mellwood	H 5
Mena ⊙	B 4
Menifee	E 3
Midland	B 3
Mineral Springs	C 6
Mitchellville	H 6
Moark	J 1
Monette	K 2
Monroe	H 4
Monte Ne	B 1
Monticello ⊙	G 6
Montrose	H 7
Moorefield	H 2
Moro	H 4
Morganton	F 3
Morrilton ⊙	E 3
Morrow	B 2
Moscow	G 5
Mountainburg	B 2
Mountain Home ⊙	F 1
Mountain Pine	D 4
Mountain Valley	D 4
Mountain View ⊙	F 2
Mount Holly	E 7
Mount Ida ⊙	C 4
Mount Judea	D 2
Mount Pleasant	G 2
Mount Sherman	D 1
Mount Vernon	F 3
Mulberry	B 2
Murfreesboro ⊙	C 5
Nashville ⊙	C 6
Natural Steps	F 4
Newark	H 2
New Blaine	D 3
New Edinburg	F 6
Newhope	C 5
Newport ⊙	H 2
New Rocky Comfort (Foreman)	B 6
New Spadra	C 3
Nimmons	K 1
Nimrod	D 4
Noble Lake	G 5
Nola	C 4
Norfolk	F 1
Norman	C 5
Norphlet	E 7
North Little Rock	F 4
Oak Grove	C 1
Ogden	B 6
Ogemaw	E 7
Oil Trough	G 2
O'Kean	J 1
Okolona	D 5
Ola	D 3
Olvey	E 1
Omaha	D 1
Oneida	J 5
Oppelo	E 3
Osceola ⊙	K 2
Otwell	J 2
Owensville	E 4
Oxford	G 1
Ozark ⊙	C 3
Ozone	D 2
Palestine	J 4
Pangburn	G 3
Paragould ⊙	J 1
Paris ⊙	C 3
Parkdale	G 7
Parkin	J 3
Parks	B 4
Paron	E 4
Patterson	H 3
Peach Orchard	J 1
Pearcy	D 5
Pea Ridge	B 1
Pecan Point	L 3
Perla	G 5
Perry	E 3
Perryville ⊙	E 3
Pettigrew	C 2
Pickens	H 6
Piggott ⊙	K 1
Pindall	E 1
Pine Bluff ⊙	F 5
Plainfield	D 7
Plainview	D 4
Pleasant Plains	G 2
Plumerville	E 3
Pocahontas ⊙	H 1
Pollard	K 1
Poplar Grove	J 4
Portia	H 1
Portland	H 7
Pottsville	D 3
Poughkeepsie	H 1
Powhatan	H 1
Poyen	E 5
Prairie Grove	B 2
Prairie View	C 3
Prattsville	F 5
Prescott ⊙	D 6
Proctor	K 3
Pyatt	E 1
Quitman	F 3
Ratcliff	C 3
Ratio	J 5
Ravenden	H 1
Ravenden Springs	H 1
Reader	D 6
Rector	K 1
Redfield	F 5
Reed	H 6
Reyno	J 1
Richmond	B 6
Rison ⊙	F 6
Rivervale	K 2
Rockport	E 5
Roe	H 4
Rogers	B 1
Roland	E 4
Rondo	J 4
Rose Bud	F 3
Rosie	G 2
Rosston	D 6
Round Pond	J 3
Rover	D 4
Rudy	B 2
Russell	G 3
Russellville ⊙	D 3
Rye	F 6
Sage	G 1
Saint Charles	H 5
Saint Francis	K 1
Saint Paul	C 2
Salado	G 2
Salem ⊙	G 1
Schaal	C 6
Scotland	E 2
Scott	F 4
Scottsville	D 3
Scranton	C 3
Searcy ⊙	G 3
Sedgwick	J 2
Selma	G 6
Seyppel	K 4
Shannon Hills	F 4
Sheridan ⊙	F 5
Sherrill	G 5
Sherwood	F 4
Shirley	F 2
Siloam Springs	B 1
Simsboro	K 3
Smackover	E 7
Snowball	E 2
Snow Hill	E 7
Snow Lake	H 5
Solgohachia	E 3
Sparkman	E 6
Spotville	D 7
Springdale	B 1
Springfield	E 3
Spring Hill	C 6
Stamps	D 7
Star City ⊙	G 6
Stephens	E 7
Steprock	G 3
Stonewall	J 1
Strawberry	H 2
Strong	F 7
Stuttgart ⊙	H 4
Sublaco	C 3
Success	J 1
Sugar Grove	C 3
Sulphur Rock	H 2
Sulphur Springs	B 1
Summers	A 2
Summit	E 1
Sunset	K 3
Sweet Home	F 4
Swifton	H 2
Tamo	G 5
Taylor	D 7
Texarkana ⊙	C 7
Thornton	F 6
Three Creeks	E 7
Tillar	H 6
Timbo	F 2
Tinsman	F 6
Tollette	C 6
Tontitown	B 1
Traskwood	E 5
Trumann	J 2
Tucker	G 5
Tuckerman	H 2
Tulip	E 5
Tull	E 5
Tulot	K 2
Tupelo	H 3
Turner	H 5
Turrell	K 3
Tyronza	K 3
Ulm	H 4
Uniontown	B 2
Urbana	E 7
Valley Springs	D 1
Van Buren ⊙	B 3
Vandervoort	B 5
Vanndale	J 3
Victoria	K 2
Village	D 7
Vilonia	F 3
Vimy Ridge	F 4
Viola	G 1
Wabash	J 5
Wabbaseka	G 5
Waldenburg	J 2
Waldo	D 7
Waldron ⊙	B 4
Walnut Ridge ⊙	J 1
Ward	F 3
Warren ⊙	F 6
Washburn	B 3
Washington	C 6
Waterloo	D 6
Watson	H 6
Waveland	C 3
Webb City	C 3
Weddington	B 1
Weiner	J 2
Weldon	H 3
Wesley	C 1
Wesson	E 7
West Crossett	F 7
Western Grove	D 1
West Fork	B 2
West Helena	J 4
West Memphis	K 3
West Ridge	K 2
Wheatley	H 4
Whelen Springs	D 6
White Hall	F 5
Whitehall	J 3
Wickes	B 5
Widener	J 3
Williford	H 1
Willow	E 5
Wilmar	G 6
Wilmot	G 7
Wilson	K 2
Wilton	B 6
Winchester	G 6
Winfield	B 4
Winslow	B 2
Winthrop	B 6
Wiseman	G 1
Woodson	F 4
Wooster	F 3
Wrightsville	F 4
Wynne ⊙	J 3
Yellville ⊙	E 1
Zion	G 1

⊙ County seat

Other Features

Feature	Map key
Arkansas (river)	G 5
Arkansas Post Nat'l Mem.	H 6
Bartholomew (bayou)	G 7
Bayou Bodcau (res.)	C 7
Beaver (lake)	C 1
Black (river)	H 2
Blue Mountain (lake)	C 3
Blytheville AFB	L 2
Boston (mts.)	B 2
Buffalo (river)	F 2
Buffalo Nat'l River	D 1
Bull Shoals (lake)	E 1
Cache (river)	H 3
Caddo (river)	D 5
Cadron (creek)	F 3
Catherine (lake)	E 5
Chicot (lake)	H 7
Chinkapin Knob (mt.)	E 2
Crowley's Ridge (mt.)	J 2
Current (river)	J 1
Cypres (bayou)	F 3
Dardanelle (lake)	D 3
DeGray (lake)	D 5
Des Arc (bayou)	G 3
De View (bayou)	J 3
Dutch (creek)	C 4
Erling (lake)	C 7
Fort Chaffee	B 3
Fort Smith Nat'l Hist. Site	B 3
Fourche La Fave (river)	D 4
Greers Ferry (lake)	F 2
Greeson (lake)	C 5
Hamilton (lake)	D 5
Hot Springs Nat'l Park	D 4
Illinois (bayou)	D 3
La Grue (bayou)	H 5
Little (river)	B 6
Little Missouri (river)	D 6
Little Red (river)	G 3
Little Rock AFB	F 4
Magazine (mt.)	C 3
Maumelle (lake)	E 4
Meto (bayou)	H 5
Millwood (lake)	C 6
Mississippi (river)	L 2
Moro (creek)	F 6
Mulberry (river)	C 2
Nebo (mt.)	D 3
Nimrod (lake)	D 4
Norfolk (lake)	F 1
Ouachita (lake)	C 4
Ouachita (mts.)	C 4
Ouachita (river)	E 7
Ozark (plat.)	C 1
Pea Ridge Nat'l Mil. Pk.	B 1
Peckerwood (lake)	G 4
Petit Jean (mt.)	C 3
Pine Bluff Arsenal	F 5
Poteau (mt.)	B 4
Red (river)	C 6
Rich (mt.)	B 4
Saint Francis (river)	J 4
Saline (river)	B 6
Saline (river)	F 5
Seven Devils (res.)	G 6
Spring (river)	H 1
Sulphur (river)	B 7
Table Rock (lake)	D 1
Tyronza (river)	K 2
Wattensaw (bayou)	G 4
White (river)	C 2
White Oak (lake)	D 6
Winona (lake)	E 4

years by the Mississippi R. during flood stages. Levees have been constructed to protect the farmland of the area from flooding.

Rivers and Lakes. The Mississippi R. and its major tributary, the Arkansas R., drain most of the state. The majority of rivers flow W or SW to either of these and include the Little Missouri, Ouachita, Saline, and Red rivers in the S and the Saint Francis, Black, and White rivers in the N. A number of oxbow lakes (abandoned river meanders) have been formed along the Mississippi R.; Lake Chicot is the largest of these. Most of the large lakes of Arkansas, however, are artificial. They include Dardanelle Reservoir on the Arkansas R. and Lakes Ouachita, Catherine, and Hamilton in the Ouachita Mts. Bull Shoals Lake and Lakes Beaver and Table Rock are located in the Ozark Plateau.

Climate. Arkansas has a humid subtropical climate; winters are mild and summers hot, particularly in the lowland areas. The average annual temperatures range from about 14.4° C (about 58° F) in the NW to 18.9° C (66° F) in the lowlands. The highest recorded temperature in the state was 48.9° C (120° F), at Ozark in 1936; the lowest, −33.9° C (−29° F), at Gravette in 1905. Precipitation is well distributed through the year, with a slight concentration in the spring months. Average annual precipitation ranges from about 1000 mm (about 40 in) in the Ozark Plateau to nearly 1400 mm (about 55 in) in the S plains. Occasional droughts may occur in the N and W.

Plants and Animals. Forests cover about one-half of the total land area of Arkansas. Pine forests are found mainly in the SW part of the state; E areas are covered by a great variety of hardwoods, including ash, buckeye, hackberry, hawthorn, hickory, maple, oak, and cherry. Arkansas is also known for its flowering trees and shrubs such as dogwood, azalea, and redbud and for its wild flowers and ferns.

The mountains of the state are the habitat of a variety of small mammals, including mink, raccoon, skunk, weasel, and woodchuck. The plains are the home of deer, rabbit, fox, and bobcat. Birdlife thrives throughout the state and includes pheasant, duck, goose, turkey, and such songbirds as cardinal, robin, mockingbird, phoebe, and whippoorwill. Among the freshwater fish here are bass, catfish, perch, and sturgeon.

Mineral Resources. Arkansas is rich in mineral resources, chief among which are petroleum and natural gas in the SW, coal in the Arkansas Valley, and bauxite near Little Rock. The state also contains commercial quantities of granite, gypsum, marble, mercury, soapstone, vanadium, and bromine. Murfreesboro in the SW has become famous as a source of diamonds. J.F.R.

POPULATION

According to the 1990 census, Arkansas had 2,350,725 inhabitants, an increase of 2.8% over 1980. The average population density in 1990 was 17 people per sq km (44 per sq mi). Whites made up 82.7% of the population and blacks 15.9%; additional population groups included 12,733 American Indians, Eskmos, and Aleuts and 12,530 Asians and Pacific Islanders. Nearly 20,000 Arkansas residents were of Hispanic origin. Baptists accounted for 42.2% of the population in 1990, and Methodists comprised 8.8%. About 54% of the people of Arkansas lived in areas defined as urban, and the rest lived in rural areas. The state's largest cities were Little Rock, the capital; Fort Smith; North Little Rock; Pine Bluff; Jonesboro; and Fayetteville.

EDUCATION AND CULTURAL ACTIVITY

Arkansas has a diversity of educational and cultural institutions; the foremost of these, however, are located in the major cities.

Education. Although the state legislature passed an act in 1843 enabling a system of common schools to be established, free schools for all children were not provided until 1868. By the late 1980s Arkansas had 1094 public schools with a combined annual enrollment of 311,100 elementary pupils and 123,900 secondary students. About 23,100 students attended private schools. In the same period Arkansas had 37 institutions of higher education with a total yearly enrollment of some 88,600 students. Among the most notable of these schools were the University of Arkansas (1871), with branches in Fayetteville, Little Rock, Monticello, and Pine Bluff; Arkansas College (1872), in Batesville; Arkansas State University (1909), in State University, near Jonesboro; Arkansas Baptist College (1884), in Little Rock; University of the Ozarks (1834), in Clarksville; Harding University (1924), in Searcy; Henderson State University (1890), in Arkadelphia; and Hendrix College (1876) and the University of Central Arkansas (1907), in Conway.

Cultural Institutions. Arkansas contains a variety of museums, including the Arkansas Arts Center, in Little Rock; the Southeast Arkansas Arts and Science Center, in Pine Bluff; the University of Arkansas Museum, in Fayetteville; the Fort Smith Art Center, in Fort Smith; and the Arkansas State University Art Gallery, in State University. Of special interest are the Saunders Memorial Museum, exhibiting an outstanding collection of pistols and rifles, in Berryville; and the Miles Musical Museum, which displays old musical instruments and Indian relics, in Eureka Springs. The Arkansas Symphony Orchestra is based in Little Rock.

ARKANSAS

ARKANSAS

DATE OF STATEHOOD: June 15, 1836; 25th state

CAPITAL:	**Little Rock**
MOTTO:	***Regnat populus*** **(The people rule)**
NICKNAME:	**Land of Opportunity**
STATE SONG:	**"Arkansas" (words and music by Eva Ware Barnett)**
STATE TREE:	**Pine**
STATE FLOWER:	**Apple blossom**
STATE BIRD:	**Mockingbird**
POPULATION (1990):	**2,350,725; 33d among the states**
AREA:	**137,742 sq km (53,182 sq mi); 29th largest state; includes 2867 sq km (1107 sq mi) of inland water**
HIGHEST POINT:	**Magazine Mt., 839 m (2753 ft)**
LOWEST POINT:	**17 m (55 ft), along the Ouachita River**
ELECTORAL VOTES:	**6**
U.S. CONGRESS:	**2 senators; 4 representatives**

POPULATION OF ARKANSAS SINCE 1810

Year of Census	Population	Classified As Urban
1810	1,000	0%
1830	30,000	0%
1860	435,000	1%
1880	803,000	4%
1900	1,312,000	9%
1920	1,752,000	17%
1940	1,949,000	22%
1960	1,786,000	43%
1980	2,286,000	52%
1990	2,350,725	54%

POPULATION OF TEN LARGEST CITIES

	1990 Census	1980 Census
Little Rock	175,795	158,461
Fort Smith	72,798	71,626
North Little Rock	61,741	64,288
Pine Bluff	57,140	56,636
Jonesboro	46,535	31,530
Fayetteville	42,099	36,608
Hot Springs	32,462	35,781
Springdale	29,941	23,458
Jacksonville	29,101	27,589
West Memphis	28,259	28,138

CLIMATE	LITTLE ROCK	FORT SMITH
Average January temperature range	−1.7° to 10° C (29° to 50° F)	−2.2° to 10° C (28° to 50° F)
Average July temperature range	21.1° to 33.9° C (70° to 93° F)	21.7° to 34.4° C (71° to 94° F)
Average annual temperature	16.1° C (61° F)	16.1° C (61° F)
Average annual precipitation	1245 mm (49 in)	1067 mm (42 in)
Average annual snowfall	127 mm (5 in)	127 mm (5 in)
Mean number of days per year with appreciable precipitation	103	95
Average daily relative humidity	71%	69%
Mean number of clear days per year	120	124

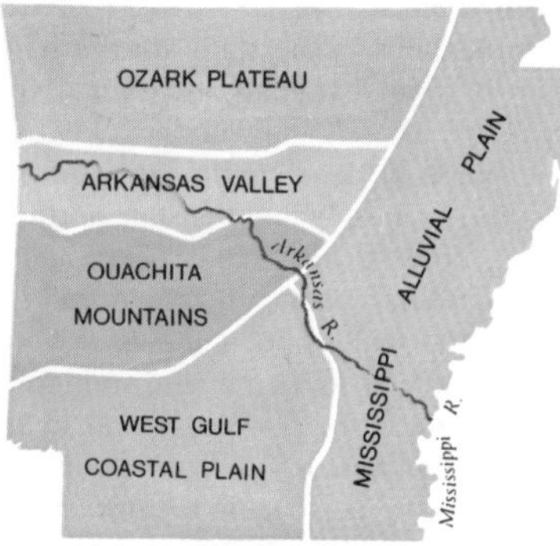

NATURAL REGIONS OF ARKANSAS

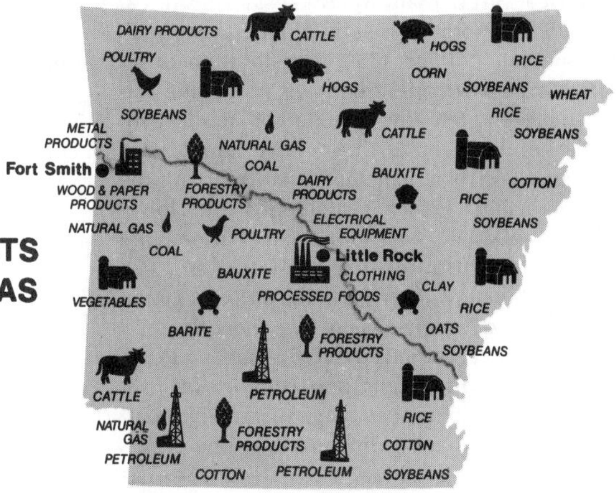

PRINCIPAL PRODUCTS OF ARKANSAS

ECONOMY

State budget	general revenue $4.1 billion
	general expenditure $3.9 billion
	accumulated debt $1.7 billion
State and local taxes, per capita	$1273
Personal income, per capita	$10,520
Population below poverty level	19.1%
Assets, insured commercial banks (257)	$19.5 billion
Labor force (civilian nonfarm)	892,000
Employed in manufacturing	26%
Employed in wholesale and retail trade	23%
Employed in services	20%
Employed in government	17%

	Quantity Produced	Value
FARM PRODUCTS		**$4.3 billion**
Crops		**$1.6 billion**
Soybeans	2.5 million metric tons	$547 million
Rice	3.0 million metric tons	$476 million
Cotton	239,000 metric tons	$345 million
Wheat	1.3 million metric tons	$152 million
Livestock and Livestock Products		**$2.7 billion**
Chickens (broilers)	1.8 million metric tons	$1.4 billion
Cattle	268,000 metric tons	$426 million
Eggs	3.6 billion	$261 million
Turkeys	206,000 metric tons	$186 million
Hogs	143,000 metric tons	$156 million
Milk	357,000 metric tons	$123 million
MINERALS		**$1.0 billion**
Natural gas	4.8 billion cu m	$406 million
Petroleum	11.4 million barrels	$197 million
Bromine	N/A	N/A
Stone	17.0 million metric tons	$78 million
Sand, gravel	7.3 million metric tons	$31 million

	Annual Payroll
FORESTRY	**$9 MILLION**
MANUFACTURING	**$4.2 billion**
Food and kindred products	$625 million
Paper and allied products	$409 million
Electronic equipment	$395 million
Fabricated metal products	$387 million
Industrial machinery and equipment	$354 million

MANUFACTURING (cont.)	
Lumber and wood products	$302 million
Rubber and plastics products	$233 million
Transportation equipment	$223 million
Printing and publishing	$196 million
Primary metals	$192 million
OTHER	**$11.1 billion**
Government	$3.2 billion
Services	$2.7 billion
Retail trade	$1.6 billion
Transportation, communications, and public utilities	$1.1 billion
Wholesale trade	$895 million
Finance, insurance, and real estate	$733 million
Construction	$522 million

ANNUAL GROSS STATE PRODUCT

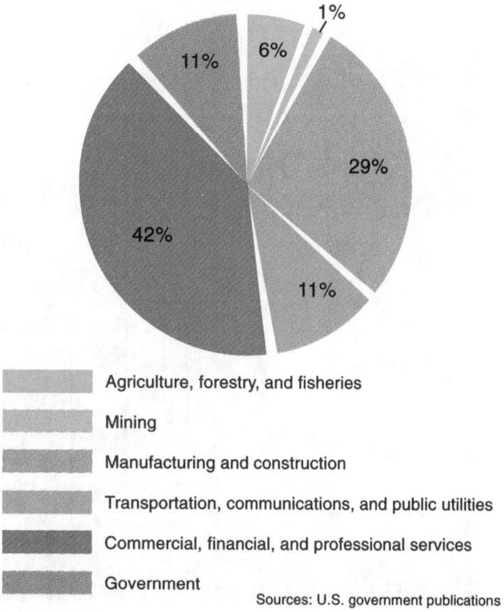

Sources: U.S. government publications

Historical Sites. Many of Arkansas's historical sites commemorate the early pioneer days, such as Mountain Village 1890, a restoration of an early Ozark town, in Bull Shoals; Fort Smith National Historic Site, including a U.S. military installation built in 1817, in Fort Smith; and Arkansas Post National Memorial, marking the first permanent French settlement in the lower Mississippi Valley, near Gillett. Also of note are the Old State House, in Little Rock, and Pea Ridge National Military Park, the site of a Union victory in the American Civil War, near Rogers.

Sports and Recreation. Arkansas's parks, forests, and lakes provide ample opportunities for fishing, hunting, hiking, camping, swimming, boating, and horseback riding. Among the state's most popular recreational areas are Hot Springs National Park, with numerous mineral thermal springs; Ouachita National Forest; Ozark National Forest; Saint Francis National Forest; and Bull Shoals State Park.

Communications. In the early 1990s Arkansas had 99 AM and 129 FM radiobroadcasting stations and 21 television stations. The state's first radio station, WOK, in Pine Bluff, was licensed in 1920. KATV, in Little Rock, Arkansas's first commercial television station, began operation in 1953. The *Arkansas Gazette,* the state's first newspaper, was initially published in Arkansas Post in 1819. By the early 1990s Arkansas had 32 daily newspapers with a total daily circulation of about 566,000. Influential dailies included the *Arkansas Democrat-Gazette,* in Little Rock, and the *Southwest Times Record,* in Fort Smith.

GOVERNMENT AND POLITICS

Arkansas is governed under a constitution adopted in 1874, as amended. Four earlier constitutions had been adopted in 1836, 1861, 1864, and 1868. An amendment to the constitution may be proposed by the state legislature, by a constitutional convention, or by initiative. To become effective an amendment must be approved by a majority of the persons voting on the issue in an election.

Executive. The chief executive of Arkansas is a governor, who (effective 1984) is popularly elected to a 4-year term and who may be reelected any number of times. The same is true of the lieutenant governor, who succeeds the governor should the latter resign, die, or be removed from office. Other elected state officers include the secretary

Hot Springs National Park, central Arkansas. The spa annually attracts thousands of visitors, who come to "take the waters." **Arkansas Dept. of Parks and Tourism**

A mechanical cotton picker at Lake Village, in southeastern Arkansas. Arkansas is one of the top cotton-producing states. Arkansas Dept. of Parks and Tourism

of state, attorney general, treasurer, auditor, and land commissioner.

Legislature. The bicameral Arkansas General Assembly is composed of a senate and a house of representatives. The 35 members of the senate serve 4-year terms, and the 100 members of the house serve 2-year terms.

Judiciary. Arkansas's highest court, the state supreme court, is composed of 7 justices elected to serve 8-year terms. The intermediate court of appeals has 6 judges, also elected to 8-year terms. There are 32 chancery court judges serving 4-year terms, 33 circuit court judges (6-year terms), and 33 chancery probate court judges (4-year terms).

Local Government. Arkansas has 75 counties, each of which is administered by a county judge. Other elected county officials include the treasurer, assessor, sheriff, clerk, coroner, surveyor, and collector.

National Representation. Arkansas elects two senators and four representatives to the U.S. Congress. The state has six electoral votes in presidential elections.

Politics. From the Reconstruction period through the mid-1960s Arkansas was, in both state and national elections, a Democratic party stronghold. In 1966, however, a Republican, Winthrop Rockefeller, won the state governorship. In 1968 George C. Wallace (American Independent) became the first non-Democratic presidential candidate to carry the state in almost 100 years. Since then, the Republican and Democratic parties have each experienced success in presidential, congressional, and gubernatorial races, but the Democrats have consistently controlled both houses of the state legislature. As governor of Arkansas (1979–81, 1983–), Bill Clinton (1946–) dominated state politics throughout the 1980s.

ECONOMY

By most standards, Arkansas is one of the poorest states in the U.S. Although real personal income per capita in Arkansas rose by more than 1% annually during the 1980s, the state figure of $10,520 in 1990 was 27% below the U.S. average.

Arkansas has been described historically as part of the Cotton Belt. In recent years, however, this designation has become somewhat misleading. Although cotton remains a leading crop, natural gas and petroleum, broiler chickens, cattle, soybeans, and rice are far more important to the economy. Manufacturing and services together account for two-thirds of the gross state product.

Agriculture. Farming accounts for about 5% of the annual gross state product. The combination of a long growing season, plentiful rainfall, and rich alluvial soils has helped to make the state a national leader in the production of rice, soybeans, and cotton; these crops are grown primarily in the Mississippi Valley and the lowlands of the tributary rivers. Significant quantities of wheat, hay, sorghum, spinach, peaches, and tomatoes are also grown. Arkansas is an important producer of cattle, hogs, eggs, and turkeys and ranks first in the nation in the production of commercial broilers; livestock and livestock products account for over 60% of the state's farm income. Arkansas has about 46,000 farms averaging 136 ha (337 acres).

Forestry. The state's timber resources are considerable. The principal types of lumber are oak, hickory, cypress, and especially pine, which is harvested increasingly from tree farms maintained by large corporations. About two-thirds of the annual timber cut is pine; the remainder consists of hardwoods.

Mining. The mining industry accounts for about 1% of the gross state product. Arkansas usually ranks first in the nation in the production of bromine. Bauxite deposits, which are concentrated in central Arkansas, are no longer mined commercially. Significant quantities of coal, petroleum, limestone, barite, and silica are mined, as well as small quantities of industrial diamonds.

Manufacturing. Since 1960 manufacturing employment has grown steadily, reaching a total in the late 1980s of about 230,000 jobs. Manufacturing enterprises account for about one-fourth of the gross state product. Most of the principal manufactured items are fabricated from the state's diverse raw materials; these include food products, petrochemicals, paper and wood products, and apparel and textiles. Electronic equipment is also a major manufacture. The principal industrial areas are found in or near the major cities. The region of Little Rock and North Little Rock is the state's industrial heart. Other important manufacturing centers are Fort Smith, Pine Bluff, El Dorado, and Fayetteville.

Tourism. More than 16 million people visit Arkansas each year, producing more than $2.4 billion for the state economy. Visitors are attracted to the areas in the state administered by the National Park Service, such as Hot Springs National Park and Fort Smith National Historic Site, as well as some 25 state parks. The state also maintains numerous recreation areas, many of which provide opportunities for fishing, boating, camping, and sightseeing.

Transportation. Arkansas has a network of about 124,055 km (about 77,085 mi) of federal, state, and local roads, including 847 km (526 mi) of interstate highways. The state is served by a system of about 3975 km (about 2470 mi) of operated railroad track. Railroads handle freight almost exclusively. An extensive inland waterway network comprises four rivers: the Mississippi, Arkansas, White, and Ouachita. Year-round barge service is available on all four rivers. The McClellan-Kerr Arkansas River Navigation System provides a navigable channel between the Mississippi R. and Tulsa, Okla. Little Rock, on the Arkansas R., is a port of entry; Fort Smith and Pine Bluff are also river ports. Arkansas has more than 160 airports; the principal ones are located in Little Rock, Hot Springs, Fort Smith, and Fayetteville.

Energy. The electric generating plants of Arkansas have a total capacity of 9.6 million kw and produce about 37.1 billion kwh of electricity annually. About 30% of the electricity is generated in nuclear power plants, about 60% in conventional steam-powered plants, and the remainder in hydroelectric installations. R.G.Bo.

HISTORY

Arkansas was named for the Arkansa, or Quapaw, Indians, one of the most numerous of the tribes that occupied the region before the coming of white settlers. Other Indian groups in the area included the Osage, Caddo, Cherokee, and Choctaw. Arkansas was explored by a Spanish expedition under Hernando de Soto in 1541. The French followed in the 17th century, and in 1686 Henri de Tonty founded a trading station at Arkansas Post, near the confluence of the Arkansas and Mississippi rivers. The region formed part of the area named Louisiana by the French explorer Robert Cavelier, sieur de La Salle, in 1682. Americans began to settle Arkansas during the late 18th century; the U.S. acquired it from France as part of the Louisiana Purchase in 1803.

Statehood and the Antebellum Period. In 1812 Arkansas was made a county of the newly established Missouri Territory. Many veterans of the War of 1812 settled in the region during the next decade. In 1819 the U.S. Congress granted Arkansas territorial status. The next year, when Little Rock was founded, the population of the territory numbered 14,273. Increasing numbers of cotton farmers migrated to the territory, bringing slaves with them, and by 1830 the population totaled 30,388. Exploitation of forest resources and the introduction of steamboat transportation further added to the growth, and by 1860, 24 years after Arkansas became a state, the population was 435,450, including 111,307 slaves.

Despite the numerical strength and political influence of the slave owners, considerable antisecessionist sentiment developed in Arkansas during the critical period preceding the outbreak of the American Civil War. The advocates of secession prevailed, however, after the rebellion began, and Arkansas was part of the Confederacy from 1861 to 1865.

Post–Civil War Period and the 20th Century. The period of Reconstruction in Arkansas was marked by acute economic distress and fierce political rivalries, graft, corruption, and mounting indebtedness. From 1868 to 1874, however, beginnings were made in railroad building, public schools were founded, and the University of Arkansas was established.

After Reconstruction, Arkansas became a stronghold of the Democratic party in both state

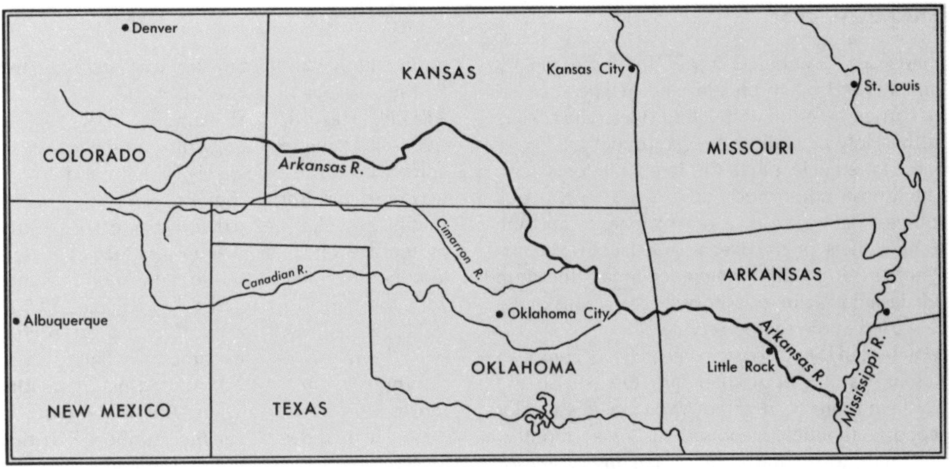

The Arkansas River and its chief tributaries. Marion Davis

and national politics, despite the development during the 1880s and '90s of a strong third-party movement based on general agrarian discontent.

Noteworthy economic events included the discovery of bauxite near Little Rock in 1887, the development of oil fields in southern Arkansas beginning with a well near El Dorado in 1921, and the establishment of the Arkansas Industrial Development Commission in 1955.

In 1957 Gov. Orval Faubus (1910-) called out the Arkansas National Guard to prevent court-ordered integration at Little Rock Central High School. President Dwight Eisenhower sent federal troops to enforce the law, and the black students were admitted to Central. The state's solidarity with the Democratic party was broken with the election of Winthrop Rockefeller, a Republican, as governor in 1966. The Arkansas River navigation system, completed in 1970, opened up a water route between the Mississippi River and Oklahoma, promoting industrial expansion in several Arkansas River ports along the waterway. Voters in 1980 rejected a proposed new state constitution, but in 1984 they extended the terms of the governor and other state officials from two years to four. In the 1970s and '80s the state promoted development of the cattle and poultry industries, bringing prosperity to some areas but also controversy over increased pollution. J.E.Gr.

For further information on this topic, see the Bibliography in volume 28, section 1195.

ARKANSAS, river, western U.S., a major tributary of the Mississippi R., 2334 km (1450 mi) long. Rising in central Colorado, in the Sawatch Range of the Rocky Mts., at an altitude of about 4270 m (about 14,000 ft), the river flows generally E and forms a turbulent stream passing over rocky beds and through deep canyons such as the Royal Gorge. As it flows through the plains of Kansas, the river broadens to a wider, less turgid stream until it enters Oklahoma; at that point it receives two chief tributaries, the Cimarron and the Canadian rivers. Except for a large N bend in Kansas, the Arkansas R. follows a SE course, merging with the Mississippi R. above Arkansas City, Ark. The water levels of the river are extremely variable, and several dams have been built for flood control and irrigation and to create hydroelectric power; one of the most impressive, the John Martin Dam in SE Colorado, was built in 1948. The Arkansas River Navigation System, completed in the early 1970s, made the river navigable to Tulsa, Okla.

ARKANSAS, UNIVERSITY OF, state-controlled institution of higher learning, with campuses in Fayetteville, Little Rock, Monticello, and Pine Bluff, Ark. The university was founded in Fayetteville in 1871 as Arkansas Industrial University, a land-grant college. The present name was adopted in 1899. Courses of instruction include arts and sciences, agriculture, architecture, home economics, business administration, education, engineering, medicine, and law. An agricultural experiment station, bureau of business and economic research, engineering experiment station, industrial research and extension center, and the Barton Institute for Medical Research are affiliated with the university. The degrees of bachelor, master, and doctor in the arts and sciences, as well as the appropriate professional degrees, are conferred. The main campus library in Fayetteville includes a unique collection of Arkansas and American folklore.

ARK OF THE COVENANT, in Judaism, sacred repository. Mentioned frequently in the Bible, the ark is described in Exod. 25 as a chest of acacia wood. It was known also as the Ark of the Law, the Ark of the Testimony, or the Ark of God. The chest was 2.5 cubits (3 ft 9 in) in length and 1.5 cubits (2 ft 3 in) in breadth and height; it could be carried by poles at the long sides. The ark lay in the Holy of Holies, the sacrosanct enclosure of the tabernacle and of the Temple in Jerusalem. The chest contained, according to various sources, Aaron's rod, a pot of manna, and the stone tablets of the Decalogue (*see* TEN COMMANDMENTS). In the synagogues today, the term *ark* designates the repository for the scrolls of the Law used in the sacred service.

ARKHANGELSK, also Archangel, city, N European Russia, capital of Arkhangelsk Oblast, on the Northern Dvina R., near the White Sea. It is a major seaport, although icebound in winter months. The city is also a trade and processing center for an important timber-producing region. A maritime school, a forestry institute, and a regional museum are located here.

Arkhangelsk was the chief Russian seaport from its founding (1584) as Novo-Kholmogory until the building of the Baltic port of Saint Petersburg in 1703. It received its present name in 1613. The city declined in the 18th century, but trade revived at the end of the 19th century, when a railroad to Moscow was completed. During World Wars I and II Arkhangelsk was a major port of entry for Allied aid. The city resisted Bolshevik rule during 1918–20 and was a stronghold of the White Army, supported by Allied forces. Pop. (1987 est.) 416,000.

ARKWRIGHT, Sir Richard (1732–92), British inventor and cotton manufacturer, who designed a spinning frame in which the cotton fiber was spun into thread.

Arkwright was born in Preston, Lancashire, England. His machine was put to practical use in Preston in 1768. The hand-spinning workers, who supposed that their means of subsistence would be destroyed by competition from the machine, compelled the inventor to move to Nottingham, where he entered into partnership with the British cotton spinner Jedediah Strutt (1726–97), the inventor of the stocking frame. In 1769 Arkwright took out a patent for his spinning machine and set up his first mill, in which the power was supplied by horses. In 1771 he established at Cromford a larger mill driven by waterpower. His success was due also to his system of management and division of labor, which became the model for the factory system, then in the process of development.

Arkwright was compelled to enter numerous patent suits, but after several years of litigation, a jury in the Court of King's Bench decided against him in 1785, and his patent was annulled. Despite this, Arkwright continued to be successful in cotton manufacture and was later knighted by King George III of Great Britain.

ARLEN, Harold, real name HYMAN ARLUCK (1905–86), American songwriter, arranger, and pianist, who wrote extensively for films and Broadway musicals. Born in Buffalo, N.Y., Arlen began singing and playing the piano at an early age and by the age of 15 had begun a career as an entertainer. He later moved to New York City and, with the American lyricist Ted Koehler (1894–1973), wrote revues for the Cotton Club in Harlem. From this period comes his famed song "Stormy Weather" (1932). Among his many film scores, the best known is *The Wizard of Oz* (1939); it includes "Over the Rainbow," written for the American singer Judy Garland.

ARLES (anc. *Arelas* or *Arelate*), city, S France, in Bouches-du-Rhône Department, on the Rhône R., in Provence. It is a port (linked to the Mediterranean Sea by canal) and a farm-trade and manufacturing center. Products include processed food, textiles, and chemicals. Points of interest include a Roman amphitheater, which held about 26,000 persons; a Roman obelisk, retrieved from the Rhône R. and now in the Place de la République; the ruins of a Roman theater, in which were found many works of art including the statue *Venus of Arles* (Louvre, Paris); the palace of the Roman emperor Constantine I; and the Romanesque Church of Saint Trophime.

During the last century BC, Arelas, as the city was then called, emerged as one of the chief commercial centers of the Roman Empire. An episcopal see from the 4th century until 1790, it was the site of several important ecclesiastical councils, including the Council of Arles (314), which condemned Donatism (q. v.). After the collapse (476 AD) of the Roman Empire of the West, Arles was seized by the Visigoths and then by the Ostrogoths. In 730, while ruled by the Merovingian dynasty, it was plundered by Muslim invaders. In 879 Arles was made the seat of the kingdom of Provence, and in 933 it became the capital of the kingdom of Arles, more often called the kingdom of Burgundy. After 1246, it was included in Provence. Several painters, including Vincent van Gogh, had been active here. Pop. (1982) 50,772.

ARLINGTON, town, Middlesex Co., NE Massachusetts, on the Mystic R.; settled in the 1630s as Menotomy, inc. 1807 as West Cambridge. It is a residential suburb of Boston with some light manufacturing. The town was renamed Arlington (for Arlington, Va.) in 1867. It was the site of a skirmish (April 19, 1775) that followed the Battle of Concord in the American Revolution. Pop. (1980) 48,219; (1990) 44,630.

ARLINGTON, city, Tarrant Co., N Texas, on the Trinity R. and Lake Arlington, between Dallas and Fort Worth; inc. 1920. It is a manufacturing and distribution center. Products include motor vehicles, aircraft, farm equipment, fabricated plastics, electronic components, printed materials, and processed food. The city is the site of the University of Texas at Arlington (1895), the huge Six Flags over Texas amusement park, a water-theme park, and Arlington Stadium, home of the Texas Rangers baseball team. It was founded in 1875 and is named for Arlington, Va. After the arrival of the railroad in 1876, it grew as a cotton-ginning and truck-farming center. Large-scale industrialization began in the early 1950s. Pop. (1980) 160,123; (1990) 261,721.

ARLINGTON, county, NE Virginia, on the Potomac R., opposite Washington, D.C. It is a residential suburb of Washington and contains many U.S. government offices, notably the Pentagon, headquarters of the Department of Defense. Washington National Airport, Arlington National Cemetery, and Fort Myer Military Reservation are here. Educational institutions include Marymount University (1950).

Capt. John Smith, the English colonist, explored the region of modern Arlington Co. in 1608. It became part of the huge Fairfax land grant and in about 1700 was divided into 15 plantations. It was ceded to the U.S. government in 1791 as part of the new national capital; because Washington failed to expand across the Potomac, the land was returned to Virginia in 1846. During the American Civil War it was occupied by Union troops. In 1920 the county was separated from the city of Alexandria and was named for Arlington House, the home here of the Confederate general Robert E. Lee. Pop. (1980) 152,599; (1990) 170,936.

ARLINGTON HEIGHTS, village, Cook and Lake counties, NE Illinois, a suburb of Chicago; settled 1836, inc. 1887. Manufactures include machinery, electronic equipment, printed materials, motor-vehicle parts, and pharmaceuticals. Arlington International Racecourse is nearby. Pop. (1980) 66,116; (1990) 75,460.

ARLINGTON NATIONAL CEMETERY, federal burial ground, NE Virginia, administered by the U.S. Army. The site, on the Potomac R. across from Washington, D.C., occupies more than 170 ha (420 acres) and contains more than 90,000 graves. Most of those interred here were members of the U.S. Armed Forces killed in battle. Among the monuments on the grounds are the Tomb of the Unknown Soldier, the Arlington Memorial Amphitheater, and Arlington House, also known as the Custis-Lee Mansion.

U.S. Army honor guard at Arlington National Cemetery.
© 1985 Disario–The Stock Market

In 1861, after the outbreak of the American Civil War, the mansion and grounds were confiscated from the owner, the Confederate general Robert E. Lee, by the Union government. The house was converted to a hospital, and in 1864 the grounds were first used as a military cemetery. After the Civil War the U.S. Supreme Court ruled that the house was the property of George Washington Custis Lee (1832–1913), son of Robert E. Lee. He sold it to the federal government in 1883. Famous Americans buried in the cemetery include the political leader and editor William Jennings Bryan, Presidents William H. Taft and John F. Kennedy, the political leader Robert F. Kennedy, Generals Philip H. Sheridan and John J. Pershing, the army surgeon and bacteriologist Maj. Walter Reed, and the explorer Adm. Robert E. Peary.

ARMADA, SPANISH, fleet assembled and dispatched by King Philip II of Spain in an unsuccessful attempt to invade England in 1588. The defeat of the armada was one of the great achievements of Queen Elizabeth I and helped bring about the subsequent decline of the Spanish Empire.

The mission of the armada combined political and religious aims. Politically, it grew out of King Philip's inability to suppress a revolt of his Protestant subjects in the Netherlands, begun in 1566, which morally as well as materially was aided by the English. By 1586 Philip had decided that he would be unable to defeat the Dutch without first mastering England. At the same time he hoped to resolve the long-standing religious rivalry between Protestant England and Roman Catholic Spain by dethroning Elizabeth and reconverting England to Catholicism. He therefore evolved a plan to conquer the English.

The defeat of the Spanish Armada, 1588 (from a 1739 engraving), with portraits of the English commanders. Granger Collection

The scheme called for coordinating a fleet sailing from Spain with an army from the Netherlands for a simultaneous invasion of England. To lead the force of 130 ships, transporting nearly 30,000 men, Philip appointed Alonso Pérez de Guzmán, duke of Medina-Sidonia (1550–1615). The English, aware of the plan, tried to prevent the armada from sailing by attacking it at Cádiz in 1587, and they succeeded in delaying it for nearly a year.

By July 1588, however, the armada had sailed. It was first sighted off Cornwall on July 29, and a larger English fleet, commanded by Lord Howard (later 1st earl of Nottingham), intercepted it near Plymouth. For the next week, Howard, with his faster, smaller, and more maneuverable ships, attacked the Spanish in battles off Plymouth, Portland Bill, and the Isle of Wight. Unable to break the armada's formation, however, the English waited for a chance to strike a decisive blow.

The opportunity came when the armada anchored near Calais, hoping to join with the troops scheduled to sail from the Netherlands. Howard then ordered fire ships sent against the armada, producing panic that broke the Spanish formation. In the ensuing Battle of Gravelines (August 8) the English defeated the armada. Unable to sail against the wind back through the English Channel, the Spaniards were forced to sail north around Scotland to return home. Only 76 of the original 130 ships reached Spain, and most of these were in poor condition.

The failure of the armada did not end the war between England and Spain, which lasted until 1604. It did, however, stimulate English nationalism, secure Protestantism as England's state religion, and create the trust in English seamanship that for centuries was the first line of the nation's defense. For Spain, in contrast, it was a demoralizing defeat that nearly bankrupted the treasury.

R.Po.

For further information on this topic, see the Bibliography in volume 28, section 903.

ARMADILLO, armored mammal of the family Dasypodidae, related to the anteaters and sloths in the order Edentata. The peba, or nine-banded armadillo (*Dasypus novemcinctus*), is found in South and Central America and in Texas, southern Oklahoma, Louisiana, Arkansas, Mississippi, and parts of Florida. The six-banded armadillo, or peludo (*Euphractus sexcinctus*); the tree-banded armadillo, or apar (*Tolypeutes t. cinctus*); and the giant armadillo (*Priodontes giganteus*) are among the commoner South American species. They vary in size from the giant armadillo, which is almost 1 m (about 3 ft) long excluding the tail, to species only about 15 cm (about 6 in) long when fully grown.

The bony plate that protects the animal against predators is formed by the ossification of the greater part of the skin. In some species even the tail is so protected. In most species except the giant armadillo, the shoulders and rump are each covered by a single large shield, and the middle of the body is covered by transverse bands that are movable and articulated, so that the animal can contract and curl up to cover its unprotected abdomen; the nine-banded armadillo can roll itself into a ball.

Despite short legs, the armadillo moves rela-

Giant armadillo, Priodontes giganteus
New York Zoological Society

tively quickly, and with its strong feet and thick claws it can burrow with considerable speed. It is nocturnal in habit and feeds on insects and worms and sometimes on carrion. The flesh is palatable and is used for food. Fossil remains of gigantic extinct armadillos have been found in the Pleistocene strata of South America.

The survival of several species, including the giant and the three-banded armadillos, is now in doubt because of hunting and encroachment on habitat (*see* ENDANGERED SPECIES).

ARMAGEDDON, battlefield described in the Bible in Rev. 16:16 as the scene of the predicted final struggle between good and evil. The name may be taken from that of the battlefield Megiddo (see Judg. 5:19) in the Plain of Esdraelon, well known because of the many battles that were fought there between the Israelites and their enemies during the biblical period. Hence, the term has been applied to any great conflict or slaughter.

ARMAGH, former county, Ulster Province, S Northern Ireland; Armagh was the county town. Armagh comprised a lowland area in the N and a hilly upland area in the S. The economy was based on agriculture, notably fruit growing, and light industry. Armagh was made a county in 1586 and was colonized by English Protestant settlers during the 17th century. County Armagh ceased to exist as an administrative unit in 1973.

ARMAGH, town, S Northern Ireland, administrative center of Armagh District. It is a market center and transportation junction with some light industry, notably linen weaving. It is the seat of archbishops of the Roman Catholic church and the Protestant Church of Ireland, and it has two cathedrals. In the town are a museum and the famous Armagh Astronomy Center, which has a planetarium and an observatory (1790). In the 5th century AD St. Patrick founded a church here on the site of a fort, Ard Macha, thus marking the community's emergence as the ecclesiastical capital of Ireland. Pop. Armagh District (1982 est.) 47,500.

ARMENIA, independent republic, E Europe, bordered on the N by Georgia, on the E by Azerbaijan, on the S by Iran and Turkey, and on the W by Turkey.

The Republic of Armenia, formerly the ARMENIAN SOVIET SOCIALIST REPUBLIC (1936–90), occupies the northwestern part of the historic region of Armenia, which comprised southern Caucasia and northeastern Asia Minor; the southwestern part of the historic region now belongs to Turkey, and the southeastern part to Iran. Area of the republic, about 29,800 sq km (about 11,500 sq mi).

For map of this area, *see* UNION OF SOVIET SOCIALIST REPUBLICS.

LAND AND RESOURCES

Armenia is a landlocked country of plateaus traversed by mountain ranges and valleys. There is little forest land. The rivers, notably the Aras and its tributary the Razdan, are utilized to irrigate the fertile valleys. Lake Sevan, Armenia's largest lake, is drained by the Razdan.

Climate. The climate is generally continental, with cold winters and warm summers. There is little rainfall, and many areas are subject to periodic drought.

Natural Resources. Armenia has deposits of copper, gold, zinc, and molybdenum ores, all of which are being exploited. Marble, granite, and other building materials are also quarried.

POPULATION

About 90% of the people are ethnic Armenians; there are also Russian, Kurdish, and Azerbaijani minorities. The geographical origins of the Armenians are obscure, but ethnologically they are classified as Caucasoid, linguistically as Indo-European. According to some authorities, their ancestors include the aboriginal people of the region; the Chaldeans, who occupied it late in the 2d millennium BC; and later invaders. The republic has a total population of 3,580,000 (1991 est.)

Principal Cities. Yerevan, the capital and chief industrial and cultural center, has a population of 1,300,000 (1991 est.); other major cities are Kirovakan, with about 160,000 residents, and Kumayry (formerly Leninakan), with about 120,000.

ECONOMY

Armenia's many rivers provide not only irrigation for agriculture but also hydroelectric power for industrial plants.

Agriculture. Farm produce includes grapes, olives, figs, and other fruit, grown in the valleys, and wheat, tobacco, and sugar beets, grown at higher altitudes. Sheep, cattle, pigs, and poultry are also raised.

Mining and Manufacturing. Armenian industries process local mineral resources, which include copper, zinc, and molybdenum ores. Other manufactures are chemicals, fertilizer, textiles, aluminum, and wine.

GOVERNMENT

A new constitution was adopted in April 1978. The parliament, with 259 members, is the nation's central governing body; the parliamentary chairman is also president of the republic.

HISTORY

The country known since ancient times as Armenia has a long and turbulent history.

Persian Conquest. The name Armenia first appeared in the Behistun inscription of Darius I, king of Persia about 521 BC. In 612 BC the country had been conquered by Media, which ruled it until 549 BC. Cyrus the Great, founder of the Persian Empire, seized Armenia in 549 BC, whereupon it became a satrapy of Persia. Some years after the death (323 BC) of Alexander the Great, who had conquered Persia, Armenia became independent. Antiochus III, king of Syria, conquered it in 212 BC and divided it into two satrapies under Armenian princes. These satrapies were independent kingdoms from 190 BC until 94 BC, when Tigranes the Great (c. 140–55 BC), king of Armenia, reunited them under his rule. Tigranes conquered parts of Asia Minor and Mesopotamia, but was beaten by the Romans in 69 BC. As a result, Armenia became a satellite of Rome.

In the struggles between Rome and the Parthians, who had become masters of Persia, Armenia remained neutral and autonomous whenever possible. When the Sassanid Persians overthrew the Parthians in the 3d century AD, they seized Armenia, but the Arsacid king Tiridates III (238–314), with the aid of Roman emperor Diocletian, liberated the country. Tiridates was converted to Christianity in 303 and established a state church some 20 years before Roman emperor Constantine made Christianity the official religion of the Roman Empire.

Christian Armenia. As a center of Christianity, Armenia opposed the Zoroastrian Persians after the 4th century. The conquest of Persia by the Arabs in 642 was followed by their overlordship in Armenia. In 653, however, the Arab caliph chose an Armenian prince to administer the country, designating him patrician of Armenia. In time the patricians became virtual kings, and in 886 the Bagratuni dynasty reestablished the Armenian kingdom, and ruled the country during the 9th and 10th centuries. Many churches and vast irrigation works survive from that era.

The major enemies of medieval Armenia were the Byzantine Empire and the Seljuks, who overran the country in the 11th century. Constant warfare drove many Armenians to seek homes elsewhere; one group founded a kingdom called Lesser Armenia, which included the ancient region of Cilicia, in 1082; it lasted until 1375.

A Country Divided. About 1240 Armenia was invaded by the Mongols, who ruled it until the early 15th century. A period of confusion, during which Iran for a short time controlled Armenia, ended when the Ottomans conquered most of the region in the 16th century. Thereafter it suffered ceaseless warfare between Turkey and Iran. The Armenians remaining in the Iranian-controlled part were removed to another part of the country early in the 17th century, while those in the Turkish part, after the fall of Constantinople in 1453, were reorganized under the leadership of an Armenian bishop. They were given a large degree of religious, cultural, and political autonomy. Yet, Russian conquests in Caucasia in the 19th century were welcomed by the Armenians. After the Russians captured part of the region in 1828–29, most Armenians moved into the Russian-conquered area. At first the Russians welcomed them, possibly hoping that a friendly attitude would make them their allies.

Turkish Atrocities. Similar considerations of power politics involved Great Britain in Armenian affairs. In order to offset the role assumed by Russia as protector of Armenian Christendom, the British undertook to act as protector of the Armenians in Turkey, which was at that time under British influence. As a result of such foreign intervention, factions appeared among the Armenians, stimulating the development of nationalism, but directing it along divergent paths. Part of the Armenian leadership emphasized loyalty to Turkey, but other groups engaged in activities the Turks considered subversive. Turkish reprisals took the form of atrocities that shocked the world, including massacres of an estimated 200,000 Armenians in 1896 alone. Meanwhile the Russians, disturbed by the effect among Armenians of British propaganda against them, forbade the Armenians to speak their own language and to have their own schools and churches. They also deported various nationalist leaders to Siberia. British "protection" proved worthless.

During World War I Armenia became a battleground for Russian and Turkish armies. Between January and August 1916, the Russians conquered the greater part of Turkish Armenia, but the revolution in 1917 forced their withdrawal, and the Turks reoccupied the country.

As the war raged on, Turkish atrocities against Armenians increased, leading the government of the U.S. to send a formal note of protest to Turkey on Feb. 17, 1916. Deaths attributed to massacres and famine reached an estimated total of 800,000 during the war period. Many Armenians fled, seeking homes in other lands, including the U.S.; about 200,000 found refuge in Russia.

Modern Armenia. On May 26, 1918, Armenians formerly under czarist rule established the Armenian Autonomous Republic, which was recognized by the Allies in 1920.

During the Greco-Turkish war of 1920–22 the Armenians sided with the Greeks, and again the victorious Turks inflicted severe reprisals on them. In addition, the Turks invaded the republic, which they had refused to recognize. A settlement was finally reached in 1921, by which the Republic of Armenia ceded about half its Caucasian lands to the Turks. In 1922 the Armenian Republic joined with the Soviet Socialist republics of Azerbaijan and Georgia to form the Transcaucasian SFSR, which became one of the four original republics of the USSR. A separate Armenian SSR was formed in 1936. Claims of discrimination against the Armenian minority still residing in the Azerbaijan SSR in the late 1980s led to mass demonstrations and widespread sectarian fighting in both Armenia and Azerbaijan. In 1990 the Supreme Soviet of Armenia declared that the country was a sovereign republic and elected Levon A. Ter-Petrosyan (1945–), leader of the Armenian National Movement, as its president. In a referendum held on September 21, 1991, Armenia's voters approved a declaration of independence from the USSR. Two months later the new republic became a founding member of the Commonwealth of Independent States (q.v.).

For further information on this topic, see the Bibliography in volume 28, section 1056.

ARMENIAN CHURCH, one of the oldest branches of the Christian faith. The earliest authentic accounts of the introduction of Christianity into Armenia date from the apostolic work of St. Gregory the Illuminator (c. 240–330), who, in 303, converted King Tiridates III (238–314) and members of his court. Christianity was strengthened in Armenia by the translation of the Bible into the Armenian language by the Armenian monk and scholar St. Mesrob (350?–439). Following the ecclesiastical controversy concerning the twofold nature of Christ, the Armenian Christians refused to accept the decisions of the Council of Chalcedon and formed a separate church, sometimes referred to as the Gregorian church. In 1439 a union with the Roman Catholic church was accepted by some members of the Armenian church. This was later repudiated, but a group of Armenian Catholics accept papal supremacy and the authority of the Catholic Armenian patriarchate of Sis or Cilicia (in Beirut, Lebanon), which was set up in 1742. They use an Armenian rite. The remaining larger portion of the Armenian church is headed by its catholicos, who resides at Echmiadzin, a monastery near Yerevan in Armenia. He is nominally in authority over the Armenian patriarchs of Jerusalem and Constantinople (that is, residing in Istanbul, Turkey). The monastery has been the ecclesiastical metropolis of the Armenian nation since the 4th century; it is said to be the oldest monastic foundation in the Christian world.

The older branch of the Armenian church in the U.S., the Armenian Church of North America, has been under the jurisdiction of the See of Echmiadzin since 1887. In 1957 this diocese joined the National Council of Churches. According to the most recent statistics the diocese had more than 450,000 members in about 66 churches. Another diocese, which left the parent American body in 1932, recognized the authority of the See of Cilicia in 1957. Known as the Armenian Apostolic Church of America, it claimed a membership of 225,000 in about 27 churches.

ARMENIAN LANGUAGE, Indo-European language, spoken by Armenians in Turkey and the Republic of Armenia, and in Armenian settlements elsewhere in the Middle East, Europe, and the U.S. Because of the presence of many words borrowed in ancient times from Iranian, Armenian was long believed to be an Iranian dialect. Modern scholarship, however, has firmly established it as an independent branch of the Indo-European languages (q.v.), although it diverged in striking ways from the presumed parent language.

Armenian is known to have replaced the earlier languages of the historical Armenian region (*see* ARMENIA) by at least the 7th century BC, and it may have been influenced by the languages it replaced. In 410 AD, according to tradition, Armenian acquired an alphabet invented by St. Mesrob (350?–439), a monk and scholar. A literature appeared by the 5th century, and the written language of that era, called Grabar or Classical Armenian, with various changes remained the literary language until the 19th century. Meanwhile, the spoken language developed independently; many dialects appeared, not all mutually intelligible. A nationalist movement in the 19th century led to the creation of two slightly different modern literary dialects that are closer to the spoken language: Eastern or Yerevan Armenian (the official language of the Armenian Republic) and Western or Turkish Armenian.

Armenian has many harsh combinations of consonants and is particularly rich in affricative sounds (such as *f, h, th*). Both Classical Armenian and the modern spoken and literary dialects have a complicated system of noun declension, with six or seven cases (but no grammatical gender). The old verb inflections in general have been replaced by modern forms that require auxiliary verbs (comparable to English "he will go"), and negative verbs are conjugated differently than positive ones are. Grammatically, early forms of Armenian had much in common with Greek, but Modern Armenian appears, after centuries of geographical proximity, to have absorbed some grammatical influences from Turkish (for instance, postpositions instead of prepositions).

For further information on this topic, see the Bibliography in volume 28, section 350.

ARMENIAN LITERATURE, works written in the Armenian language. Before the introduction of Christianity into Armenia in the 3d century AD, Armenian literature was Assyrian or Medo-Persian in character. After that date, however, the language, literature, and finally the alphabet of Greece appeared in Armenian writing, although eastern Armenia retained the Syriac alphabet. The translation of the Bible into Classical Armenian, traditionally ascribed to the monk and scholar St. Mesrob (350?–439), and his systematization of the Armenian alphabet in 410 opened a period of literary activity in the 5th century known as the Golden Age of Armenian literature. The principal Armenian writers of this age were translators. Other authors were the philosopher Eznik of Golp, or Kolb, who wrote *Refutation of the Sects,* especially valuable for its account of the Zoroastrian and Manichaean religions; Moses of Chorene (c. 407–92), reputed author of a geography and of a history of Armenia; and the preacher Eliseus (d. 480), author of *History of Vardan and of the Battles of the Armenians.*

Arab rule over Armenia, lasting through most of the 6th to the 10th century, caused a decline in the production of literature in Armenia. In the 10th century Thomas of Ardsruni (fl. 936), an important historian, appeared, as did the poet and bishop Gregory Narek (951–1003). In the 12th century the patriarch Nerses the Gracious (1098–1173), poet, theologian, and historian, wrote prayers and hymns still in use. New literary forms began to appear in the 13th century, but for the next four centuries Classical Armenian literature was confined to the monasteries. A body of literature in the contemporary or vernacular language, however, was produced by such poet-minstrels as Sayat-Nova (1712–95) in the 18th century.

During the 18th century Armenian congregations were established in many cities in Europe, as well as in Asia. A special impetus toward the preservation of Armenian literature was given by the establishment in 1717 of a college and convent on the island of San Lazzaro near Venice by the Armenian prelate Mechitar da Petro (1676–1749). In Venice, and at another congregation established later in Vienna, Mechitarist monks are still producing literature in Armenian.

Beginning about 1850 a modern school of Armenian writers came into existence, especially in the Russian and Turkish parts of the country; the members of this school wrote exclusively in the dialects of Modern Armenian. This movement produced works in every literary form, though none of its writers won an international reputation; the movement is also responsible for important collections of Armenian folklore. After the founding of the Armenian SSR in 1936, literature in Armenian was encouraged and carefully monitored by the Soviet government. The most successful field for the Armenian writer in the 20th century was journalism, with many periodicals written in Armenian being published in various parts of the world.

ARMENIAN SOVIET SOCIALIST REPUBLIC. *See* ARMENIA.

ARMILLARY SPHERE, ancient astronomical instrument that shows the principal divisions of the heavens and the motion of celestial bodies. It consists of a number of graduated brass rings representing the chief celestial circles, such as the meridian, equator, ecliptic horizon, tropics, and colures (circles that intersect each other at right angles at the Poles). The instrument was probably invented about 255 BC by the Greek astronomer Eratosthenes. Armillary spheres were used until the 17th century.

ARMINIANISM, a doctrine in Christianity, formulated in the 17th century, which declares that human free will can exist without limiting God's power or contradicting the Bible. Named for the Dutch Calvinist Jacobus Arminius (1560–1609), the doctrine gradually became a liberal alternative to the more rigid belief in predestination held by High Calvinists in Holland and elsewhere (*see* CALVINISM; PREDESTINATION).

Arminius, who studied in Geneva under the French Protestant theologian Theodore Beza, returned to his native Holland and was a professor of theology (1603–9) at the University of Leiden. He believed predestination was biblical and true—that God had intended some persons for heaven and others for hell, as indicated by Jesus' reference to "sheep and goats." But he focused on God's love more than on God's power in speaking of election, the process by which God chose those intended for heaven.

After Arminius died, a group of ministers who sympathized with his views developed a systematic and rational theology based on his teachings. In their declaration, a remonstrance issued in 1610, the Arminians argued that election was conditioned by faith, that grace could be rejected, that the work of Christ was intended for all persons, and that it was possible for believers to fall from grace.

At the Synod of Dort or Dordrecht (1618–19), the High Calvinists prevailed over the Arminian party and condemned the Remonstrants. The Synod of Dort declared that Christ's work was meant only for those elect to salvation, that people believing could not fall from grace, and that God's election depended on no conditions. Remonstrants were not tolerated at all in Holland until 1630, and then not fully until 1795. They have, however, continued an Arminian tradition in the Netherlands into the late 20th century.

The British theologian John Wesley studied and affirmed the work of Arminius in his Methodist movement during the 18th century in England. American Methodists for the most part have leaned toward the theology of the Remonstrants. In popular expression Arminianism has come to mean that no predestination exists and people are free to follow or reject the gospel.

L.B.W.

ARMINIUS (18 BC?–AD 19), chief of the Cherusci, a Teutonic tribe inhabiting parts of what are now the states of Brunswick and Hannover, Germany. German nationalists of the 19th century celebrated him as a national hero, under the name of Hermann, for having freed Germany from Roman control. He served in the Roman army (AD 1–6), obtaining Roman citizenship and an insight into the arts of war and policy as practiced by the Romans. Returning home about AD 7, he found his people oppressed by the Roman governor Publius Quintilius Varus (fl. 13 BC–AD 9). Arminius organized a rebellion of the Cherusci, annihilating three Roman legions in the Battle of Teutoburg Forest in AD 9 and forcing the Romans back to the Rhine River. The defeat of his legions led Varus to commit suicide. In AD 15 the Romans, under the general Germanicus Caesar, invaded Germany and in AD 16 defeated Arminius. Germanicus was recalled to Rome, however, and the advantages of his victories were lost. After this time, no Roman army ventured to penetrate the interior of Germany. After the expulsion of the Romans, internal feuds broke out among the Teutonic tribes, and Arminius was slain by his relatives. A colossal statue of him was set up in 1875 near the spot where he defeated Varus.

ARMISTICE DAY. *See* VETERANS DAY.

ARMOR, any equipment of various materials, but generally of metal, used to protect a body in combat. The oldest of protective devices is the shield; the earliest body armor was a wide belt to protect the abdomen.

Ancient Armor. In ancient Egypt (c. 3000 BC) this belt was developed into a wraparound garment extending from armpits to knees, reinforced by quilting, and held up by shoulder straps. In Syria (c. 1400 BC) the national costume, a sleeved shirt, was reinforced with bronze scales and used as armor for charioteers, who with both hands occupied were unable to hold a shield. The scales were sewn onto a fabric backing or were laced together in flexible rows of lamellae. Helmets, in the form of tight-fitting caps of beaten copper, were first used by the Sumerians (c. 3000 BC). Assyrian helmets were conical bronze caps with small earflaps.

Greek and Roman Armor. Both scale and lamellar armor were taken over by the Scythians and the Greeks. Greek armor was a wraparound of reinforced quilts with wide shoulder flaps; its lower part was a skirt of loose strips, or *pteryges.* A cuirass, or *thorax,* of hammered bronze plates realistically embossed to portray the muscles of a naked torso was also worn to protect chest and back. Greek body armor was completed by bronze greaves, that is, a covering for the lower legs, and by a round oxhide shield. Helmets were designed to enclose the entire head; in their perfected form only a Y-shaped opening for eye-slits and for breathing was left.

The cuirass (*lorica*) worn by Roman soldiers was a modification of Greek armor and existed in three basic versions: *lorica squamata,* with bronze scales on a leather backing; *lorica hamata,* made of mail, that is, of interlinked iron rings; and *lorica segmentata,* constructed of horizontally overlapping iron plates. Roman helmets, of bronze or iron, had movable cheek pieces. The large rectangular Roman shield made greaves superfluous.

Early Medieval Armor. Roman technology survived in the armament of the most typical figure of the European Middle Ages, the knight. By the 11th century a knight's armor consisted of a thigh-length shirt of mail (known as a hauberk) with elbow-length sleeves and a conical helmet with nose guard. In the 12th century the mail shirt gained an attached hood (coif), and the sleeves were full length, terminating in mittens. Mail chausses protected the legs. A mail shirt, containing up to 250,000 metal rings, might weigh about 11 kg (about 25 lb). Mail offers resistance to sword cuts, but it can be penetrated by the points of spears or arrows and its too yielding against a heavy blow. A padded undergarment, or acton, and a shield were, therefore, essential as shock breakers.

In the 11th century it became acceptable battle technique to charge with the lance couched, that is, held under the right armpit. The left, or shield, side of the knight was always turned to the

German armor for man and horse, dated 1548.

enemy. The former oval-shaped shield was, therefore, modified to an elongated form with a sharp lower point, to protect the horseman from eyes to knee, but this protection locked the fighter in too rigid a position. After a face-covering visor was developed and added to the helmet, the upper part of the shield was cut straight; and after solid knee protectors and greaves of plate had been developed, the lower point of the shield was shortened. Since the visor made the knight's face unrecognizable, identifying marks had to be placed on his shield, the most convenient surface. This was the origin of heraldry (q.v.). Crusaders wore a sleeveless surcoat over their mail armor as protection against the hot sun; these surcoats too became emblazoned with heraldic emblems and were known as coats of arms.

Bolts released by the improved crossbows introduced in the first quarter of the 14th century were able to penetrate mail with ease. Armor with deflecting surfaces, therefore, became necessary. This was achieved, about 1350, by the development of full plate defenses for arms and legs and body armor made of small plates riveted inside the surcoat, known as a coat of plates or brigandine. The loose-fitting mail shirt was slipped on over the head, but the coat of plates had to be tight-fitting and opened in front. The fighting position was with the left, shield-protected side toward the enemy; to deflect spear points and sword blades, therefore, the coat of plates had to be buckled with its left side overlapping the right. (For this reason, men's jackets are still buttoned left over right.)

Later Medieval Armor. The fully articulated plate armor developed in the first half of the 15th century is called Gothic, because of its emphasis on vertical lines and its spiky silhouette reminiscent of Gothic architecture. About 1500 the style changed, with the more rounded shapes characteristic of Renaissance style dominant; a variant favored in Germany for its additional strength (the so-called Maximilian armor, after the emperor Maximilian I) had fluted surfaces, like corrugated iron.

In the construction of armor the weight problem was crucial; armor was supposed to give maximum protection with minimal weight. A full suit of battle armor was not to exceed about 29 kg (about 65 lb); such a suit, well articulated and fitted to the body, was expected to give a knight full mobility so that he might mount a horse without stirrups in an emergency. Tournament (q.v.) armor was up to twice as heavy, safety rather than mobility being the prime consideration.

Armor-making centers were located in Milan and Brescia, Italy; Augsburg, Nuremberg, and Landshut, Germany; Innsbruck, Austria; Paris and Tours, France; and Antwerp and Brussels, Belgium. Metal armor was expensive and thus restricted to the wealthy warrior. Some reigning princes (notably in Burgundy, France, and England) had court armories of their own, mainly for the manufacture of elaborate suits of armor to be used as diplomatic presents. Armor as a status symbol was enhanced by decoration. Surface ornamentation by etching and gilding did not lower its defensive value (gilding was actually a rust-proofing device), but highly embossed plates defeated the purpose of armor as a deflecting surface. The embossed parade armors popular in the 16th century were strictly body jewelry, made by specialist artisans.

Non-European Armor. Best known among non-European armor is that of the Japanese samurai; these feudal warriors wore wraparound lamellar armor with shoulder flaps and skirt akin to the ancient Greek pattern. Such protective costumes were worn in Japan until 1876, and in Tibet similar armor was worn into the 20th century. Nonmetallic versions of bone or wood lamellae were worn by the Chukchi in Kamchatka, the Inuit (Eskimo) in Alaska, and the Iroquois in New York State (at the time of European contact). Excavations in China have yielded clay statues of warriors, dating from the 3d century BC, represented as wearing lamellar armor of a pattern similar to the Roman *lorica segmentata.* In India, Persia, and Turkey, armor consisted primarily of mail, sometimes reinforced with small rectangular plates. Helmets were pointed, with movable cheek pieces and a neck guard (in Turkey), or with a camail, a hanging curtainlike piece of mail to protect neck and chest (in Persia).

In Mexico, at the time of the Spanish conquest, quilted jackets were worn by the Aztecs and other Indians; these garments were so efficient against flint-tipped arrows that the invading Spaniards soon adopted them for their own use. Similar quilted armor and helmets reinforced with basketwork were the equipment of the Inca warriors of Peru. The Plains Indians of North America had breastplates made of bone tubes arranged in rows, but most tribes both in North and South America wore little body armor. Even the armored Iroquois used such gear not for offensive warfare but in combat waged in the defense of their villages.

Decline of Armor. While a knight in full armor was almost invulnerable to pointed or edged weapons, the impact of a soft lead bullet could break an armor plate. Thus, as guns and gunpowder replaced older weaponry, armor began to be modified. Thicker plates afforded needed protection against bullets but greatly increased the weight of the armor. For this reason, by the late 16th century, overall protection was sacrificed in favor of partial armor; by the mid-17th century only the cuirass and helmet survived. In the 18th and 19th centuries cuirasses were still used—as protection against sword cuts.

Modern Use of Armor. During World War I a soldier's body was effectively protected inside a trench or foxhole, but steel helmets were required as protection against shrapnel; the first such helmets were introduced by the German army in 1915. Armor in the form of steel helmets and flak jackets is still used in modern warfare. Aside from military use, armor in the form of visored helmets, bulletproof vests, and shields is indispensable in modern times for special police work. Armor has its place too in more peaceful, though hazardous, occupations and recreations. Hard hats (a form of helmet) are worn by miners and construction workers, and—sometimes with elaborate additional protective devices—in many contact sports. H.N.

For further information on this topic, see the Bibliography in volume 28, section 28.

ARMORED CAR. *See* TANK.

ARMORICA, ancient name of the coastal area between the Seine and Loire rivers in what is now France. Its original Celtic inhabitants were conquered by the Romans in the 1st century BC, but, unlike the rest of Gaul, Armorica was never fully Romanized. In the 5th century AD it was settled by Celtic tribes from Britain and from that time on was called Brittany.

ARMORY SHOW, art exhibition in New York City in 1913 that was the first major showing of avant-garde works in the U.S. *See* AMERICAN ART AND ARCHITECTURE.

ARMOUR, Philip Danforth (1832-1901), American meat packer, born in Stockbridge, N.Y. In 1863 he became head of the pork-packing firm of Armour, Plankington & Co. He acquired a large interest in the grain business belonging to his brother Herman Ossian Armour (1837-1901) and added a pork-packing plant to it in 1868. In 1870 the two companies merged as Armour & Co. Philip Armour became head of the firm in 1875. He was a pioneer in the use of refrigeration and in the canning of meat. In 1892 he founded and endowed the Armour Institute of Technology in Chicago.

ARMS, HERALDIC. *See* HERALDRY.

ARMS CONTROL, INTERNATIONAL, attempts through treaties, proclamations, convention, and tacit agreement to limit the destructiveness of war by controlling the acquisition and use of weapons and military technology.

Historically, war appears an integral part of human affairs. In three millennia of recorded history, less than 300 years have been free of armed conflict; yet people have always recognized the folly, waste, brutality, and inhumanity of warfare and have continually attempted to limit its devastation and the spread of increasingly destructive weapons.

History. One of the earliest formal attempts to limit the scope of warfare was organized by the Amphictyonic League (q.v.), a quasi-religious alliance of most of the Greek tribes, formed before the 7th century BC. League members were pledged to restrain their actions in war against other members; thus, for example, they were barred from cutting a besieged city's water supply. The league was empowered to impose sanctions on violating members, including fines and punitive expeditions, and could levy troops and raise funds from its members for this purpose.

The Middle Ages. Because arms technology remained nearly static from the 3d century BC to the Middle Ages, few attempts were made to control the spread of new weapons. In feudal societies, such as those of medieval Europe or Japan, laws and customs developed to keep weapons a monopoly of the military classes and to suppress arms that might democratize warfare. These customs tended to disappear as soon as some power saw a decisive advantage in the use of a new weapon.

In medieval Europe the Roman Catholic church attempted to use its power as a supranational organization to limit both new weapons and the intensity of warfare. The Peace of God, instituted in 990, protected ecclesiastical property, defenseless noncombatants, and the agrarian base of the economy from the ravages of war. In 1139 the Second Lateral Council prohibited the use of the crossbow against Christians, although not against infidels (*see* TRUCE OF GOD).

Early modern period. Firearms widened the scope of war and increased the potential for violence, culminating in the devastation of central Europe in the Thirty Years' War (1618–48). Widespread revulsion against the horrors of that conflict led to attempts in many countries to mitigate the brutality of warfare by limiting combat to recognized armed forces, by formulating conventions for the humane treatment of prisoners and wounded, and by organizing logistics to end supply by pillage. These rules prevailed throughout the 18th century, making war a relatively limited and civilized "game of kings." Many utopian plans for the total abolition of war were also formulated during this period by such men as Jean Jacques Rousseau and Charles Castel, Abbé de St. Pierre (1658–1743). Frederick the Great of Prussia commented that all these plans needed to succeed was the cooperation of all the kings of Europe.

The rise of mass armies during the revolutionary and Napoleonic Wars (1792–1815) again enlarged the size and devastation of war; yet throughout that period no attempts were made to reduce or limit national arsenals other than those imposed by the victors upon the vanquished. The one exception was the Rush-Bagot Treaty (1817), under which Great Britain and the U.S. reduced, equalized, and eventually eliminated their naval forces on the Great Lakes.

The Hague conferences. In the 19th century the manufacturing capabilities created by the Industrial Revolution were duly applied to the production of war matériel. Technological innovation led to the development of rifled artillery, breech-loading rifles, machine guns, and other weapons that revolutionized warfare. The resources of entire nations could now be turned to war, making possible conflicts of unprecedented scale and destructiveness. Although many government leaders saw the arms buildup in Europe as potentially disastrous, nothing was done to reduce armaments until the First Hague Disarmament Conference of 1899.

The First Hague Conference was convened at the initiative of Czar Nicholas II of Russia for the purpose of controlling arms development and ameliorating the conditions of warfare. Twenty-six nations attended the conference, which codified the laws and customs of land warfare, defined the status of belligerents, and drafted regulations on the treatment of prisoners, wounded, and neutrals. It also banned aerial bombardment (by balloons), dumdum (expansion) bullets, and the use of poison gas. Most important, it established a court for the arbitration of international disputes (although this court had no enforcement powers). *See* PERMANENT COURT OF ARBITRATION.

The Second Hague Disarmament Conference

of 1907 was marked more by discord than discourse, a sign of the deteriorating world situation. It did further the cause of mediation and arbitration of disputes by establishing additional courts to arbitrate cases involving ship's cargoes seized during war and resolution of international debts. A Third Hague Conference was scheduled for 1915. Ironically, World War I caused its abandonment. *See* HAGUE CONFERENCES.

Modern International Agreements. After the carnage of World War I the international climate was more receptive to the idea of arms control. During the years between the two world wars many formal arms control conferences were held and many treaties were drawn up.

The Covenant of the League of Nations established criteria for reducing world armaments. The league's Council was to establish reasonable limits on the military forces of each country and submit them for consideration to the member governments. Members of the league were also called upon to limit the private manufacture of arms and munitions and to exchange information on the size and status of their military establishments and arms industries. The league's lack of enforcement capability, however, made compliance strictly voluntary.

Washington Conference. In 1921–22 the Washington Naval Conference was held to establish stable relationships among the naval forces of the various powers. Three treaties were enacted at the conference: the Four-Power Treaty, the Five-Power Treaty, and the Nine-Power Treaty. By the terms of the first, France, Great Britain, Japan, and the U.S. agreed to respect the status quo in the fortification of Pacific possessions and promised consultation in the event of a dispute. An associated agreement was signed with the Netherlands regarding the Dutch East Indies. The second treaty focused on arms limitations. A 5–5–3–1.7–1.7 ratio was established between U.S., British, Japanese, French, and Italian battle-ships. That is, for every 5 U.S. and British battle-ships, Japan was allowed 3 and France and Italy were allowed 1.7. Maximum total tonnage was limited, as well as specification of a maximum single-ship tonnage of 35,000 tons. A ten-year moratorium on a battleship building (except to fill out the treaty) and a limit on the size and armament were also included. The third treaty was an attempt to accommodate the signatories' interests in China.

Geneva Conference and the Kellogg-Briand Pact. In 1925, a convention in Geneva banned the use of toxic gas in warfare. By World War II most of the Great Powers, except Japan and the U.S., were signatories. (Japan signed it in 1970 and the U.S. in 1974.) This accord has been observed by most of the signatories, although Italy used gas in Ethiopia in 1936.

In 1928, the Kellogg-Briand Pact, initiated by France and the U.S., was signed by 63 nations. The pact renounced war as an instrument of foreign policy. It made no provisions, however, for enforcing compliance, and many nations only signed it with sweeping qualifications. Its effect on international affairs was nil.

The fate of disarmament in the 1930s. In 1930 a naval conference was held in London to amend the Washington Conference treaties. Its most important effect was to change the U.S.-Japanese battleship ratio to 5–3.5. It also extended the battleship moratorium through 1936.

In 1932, after nearly ten years of preliminary discussions, a World Disarmament Conference was held in Geneva under the auspices of the League of Nations. The keystone of the conference was the so-called Hoover Plan—proposals put forth by the U.S., based on the concept of qualitative disarmament, that is, the progressive elimination of offensive weapons. The result was to have been an increasingly unfavorable ratio between offensive and defensive power. Qualifications imposed by many of the major nations, however, diluted the Hoover Plan until little remained but a statement of principles.

A final naval conference was held in London in 1936. There the U.S. and Great Britain reaffirmed the naval limitation treaties, with an acceleration clause (that is, one providing for proportional increase in the U.S. to British ratio) to counteract any German or Japanese violations. The Japanese, increasingly militaristic and fearful of American and British superiority, withdrew from further negotiations. This was the last major arms control conference before World War II.

Control of the Means for Mass Destruction. After World War II considerable support again developed for arms control and for alternatives to military conflict in international relations. The UN Charter was designed to permit a supranational agency to enforce peace, avoiding many of the weaknesses of the League of Nations covenant. Thus, Article 11 of the charter states that the General Assembly may consider the general principle of disarmament and the regulation of armaments. The Security Council, under Article 26, is required to submit plans for a system of armament regulation. A military staff committee is established, under Article 47, to assist the Security Council in this task.

Atomic arms race. The development of the fission bomb by the U.S. toward the end of World War II brought with it the capability of devastating whole civilizations. While the U.S. still maintained a monopoly on nuclear weapons, it made overtures in the UN for the control and elimination of atomic energy for military purposes. In June 1946, Bernard Baruch presented a plan to the UN Atomic Energy Commission, calling for the abolition of nuclear weapons, international control over the processing of nuclear materials, full sharing of all scientific and technological information concerning atomic energy, and safeguards to ensure that atomic energy would be used only for civilian purposes. The Soviet government, which insisted on the destruction of existing atomic weapons as a precondition for UN control, vetoed the Baruch Plan in the Security Council.

In 1949 the Soviet Union exploded an atomic weapon of its own, ending the U.S. monopoly. The possibility of a nuclear war was now present, because relations between the Soviet Union and the West were tense (*see* COLD WAR). Both the U.S. and the Soviet Union were engaged in a race to develop thermonuclear (hydrogen) devices, which have many times the destructive power of fission bombs. These weapons raised the possibility of ending all life on earth in all-out war. Since 1954, when the Soviet Union exploded its first H-bomb, the primary concern of arms control has been to reduce nuclear arsenals and prevent the proliferation of nuclear weapons technology.

Agreements limiting nuclear weapons. In 1957 the International Atomic Energy Commission was established to oversee the development and spread of nuclear technology and materials. Two years later a treaty was negotiated to demilitarize the Antarctic and to prohibit the detonation or storage of nuclear weapons there. Both the U.S. and the USSR were among the signatories.

In 1961 the UN General Assembly passed the Joint Statement of Agreed Principles for Disarmament Negotiations. It was followed (1963) by a treaty that bound the U.S., Great Britain, and the Soviet Union not to test nuclear weapons in space, in the atmosphere, and underwater. In 1967 another treaty between the same nations limited the military use of outer space to reconnaissance only. The deployment of nuclear weapons in orbit was expressly prohibited. A second treaty in 1967 banned nuclear weapons from Latin America.

One of the most important agreements on arms control is the Nuclear Nonproliferation Treaty (1968). Signatories pledge to restrict the

An ominous mushroom cloud forms after the detonation of a nuclear device–the equivalent of 10,000 tons of TNT– in the Nevada desert in September 1957. UPI

The signing of the nuclear test ban treaty in Moscow 1963. Signatories, from left to right, are U.S. Secretary of State Dean Rusk, Soviet Foreign Minister Andrey Gromyko, and British Foreign Secretary Sir Alec Douglas-Home. Centered behind them are U.S. Senator Hubert H. Humphrey, U.S. Ambassador to the UN Adlai Stevenson, UN Secretary General U Thant, and Soviet Premier Nikita Khrushchev. UPI

development, deployment, and testing of nuclear weapons to ensure the nontransference of weapons, materials, or technology to nonnuclear states. Among recognized nuclear powers, France, India, and China have not accepted it.

In the late 1960s, negotiations known as the Strategic Arms Limitation Talks (q.v.), or SALT, were initiated between the USSR and the U.S. on the regulation of their strategic weapons arsenals. The SALT I negotiations resulted in a series of agreements, in May 1972, limiting the size and composition of the two nations' nuclear weaponry. That same year a treaty was signed barring nuclear weapons from the seafloor, and an Executive Agreement Covering Certain Offensive Systems was ratified that placed limits on the sizes and numbers of specific weapons systems. SALT II talks were held from 1972 to 1979, but the resulting treaty went unratified by the U.S. Senate, as U.S.-Soviet relations deteriorated.

Planned negotiations toward a comprehensive test ban were canceled by U.S. President Ronald Reagan in 1981. During the early 1980s, controversy surrounded the successful effort by the U.S. to place ballistic missiles on the territory of some of its Western European allies; opposition within West Germany played a part in unseating Chancellor Helmut Schmidt in 1982. In 1983, U.S. antinuclear groups rallied to support a bilateral arms freeze, and U.S. Roman Catholic bishops approved a pastoral letter with a similar aim.

U.S.-Soviet arms negotiations resumed in 1985. At a summit meeting in Washington in December 1987, President Reagan and Soviet leader Mikhail Gorbachev signed a treaty banning intermediate-range nuclear forces (INF), including many of those the U.S. had placed in Western Europe several years earlier. The treaty called for the destruction of all U.S. and Soviet missiles with ranges of about 500–5500 km (about 300–3400 mi) and established a 13-year verification program. The INF treaty was ratified by the U.S. Senate and the Soviet Presidium in May 1988.

Nonnuclear weapons agreements. In addition to nuclear weapons, technology offers the possibility of producing chemical and bacteriological weapons capable of mass destruction, as well as more lethal conventional weapons. In 1977 a resolution of the Diplomatic Conference on the Reaffirmation and Development of Humanitarian Law Applicable to Armed Conflict banned the use against civilians of certain area-effect conventional weapons, such as booby traps, landmines, and napalm. Because these weapons do not, by definition, discriminate between combatants and noncombatants, any action short of complete prohibition is meaningless.

Agreements to limit chemical and biological weapons have also been enacted (the first, the Geneva Convention, in 1925). In 1972 a convention was signed by the U.S., the USSR, and most other nations to prohibit the development, production, and stockpiling of biological and toxin weapons. Despite the treaties, however, both the U.S. and the USSR were accused of continuing research and development in this area, and at least eight other nations were suspected of developing such weapons. Prompted by the use (1987–88) of poison gas by Iraq in its war against Iran, and by U.S. allegations of the building of a chemical weapons plant in Libya in 1988, representatives of more than 140 nations met in Paris in January 1989. They reaffirmed the previous conventions and called for a treaty that would ban all such weapons. The office of the secretary-general of the UN was empowered to investigate suspected chemical weapons use.

Another convention, signed in 1977, prohibits military or other hostile use of genetic engineering or environmental modification techniques. As advances are made in these fields, the importance of such agreements will increase.

Cold War Aftermath. As the 1990s began, the U.S. and the USSR continued to negotiate arms control accords. In May 1990, Gorbachev and U.S. President George Bush approved a treaty to end production and reduce stockpiles of chemical weapons, and in July 1991 the two men signed an agreement requiring substantial cuts in their nations' strategic nuclear arsenals. Both sides also moved to reduce conventional weapons and to continue phased withdrawal of their forces from Europe. The collapse of the Soviet Union during late 1991 raised complex new problems for arms control negotiators. Several of the former Soviet republics announced plans to maintain their own separate armed forces. In addition, strategic nuclear weapons were located at sites in Russia, Ukraine, Kazakhstan, and Belarus (Belorussia), and virtually all the other republics had tactical nuclear weapons on their soil. The establishment, in December, of the Commonwealth of Independent States (q.v.), with a single unified command over strategic weapons, calmed immediate fears. The U.S. and its allies expressed concern, however, that the breakup of the USSR might hasten the spread of sophisticated weapons to the Middle East, the Indian subcontinent, and other world trouble spots.

E.N.L.

For further information on this topic, see the Bibliography in volume 28, sections 195–96, 556.

ARMSTRONG, Edwin Howard (1890–1954), American inventor and electrical engineer, born in New York City, and educated at Columbia University, where he became professor of electrical engineering in 1936. Armstrong made two contributions of great importance to the development of radio. The regenerative circuit, which he invented in 1912, revolutionized radio by amplifying weak signals with fidelity. Frequency modulation, which he developed in the 1930s, is a means to eliminate static in radiobroadcasting.

ARMSTRONG, (Daniel) Louis "Satchmo" (1900–71), American jazz musician, one of the most influential figures in the history of jazz.

Armstrong was born July 4, 1900, in New Orleans, La., and was largely self-educated. He learned to play the bugle, clarinet, and cornet and took trumpet lessons from the noted jazz artist Joe ("King") Oliver. In 1917 Armstrong made

Louis Armstrong Columbia Records

his professional debut as a trumpeter with the band of "Kid" Ory (1886–1973) in New Orleans. In 1922 he joined Oliver's Creole Jazz Band in Chicago, then the center of American jazz, and except for a year (1924–25) with Fletcher Henderson in New York City, he remained in Chicago until 1929. Armstrong organized his own band in 1925. Within the next few years he won recognition as one of the foremost jazz trumpet players of all time and as an outstanding jazz vocalist. He appeared in several motion pictures, including *Cabin in the Sky* (1943), *Jam Session* (1944), *High Society* (1956), and *The Five Pennies* (1959). Among his recordings, which total about 1500, are "Ain't Misbehavin'," "I Can't Give You Anything but Love," and "Tiger Rag." His own compositions include "I've Got a Heart Full of Rhythm" and "Wild Man Blues." Armstrong's autobiography is *Satchmo, My Life in New Orleans* (1954). He died on July 6, 1971, in New York City.

For further information on this person, see the section Biographies in the Bibliography in volume 28.

ARMSTRONG, Neil Alden (1930–), American astronaut, born in Wapakoneta, Ohio. He served as a pilot in the U.S. Navy during the Korean War. After graduating (1955) from Purdue University, he joined the National Aeronautics and Space Administration, then known as the National Advisory Committee for Aeronautics, serving as a civilian test pilot at Edwards Air Force Base, Lancaster, Calif. In 1962 he became the first civilian to enter the astronaut-training program. In March 1966, Armstrong was command pilot of the *Gemini 8* mission, which accomplished the first physical joining of two orbiting spacecraft. In July 1969, Armstrong, as commander of the *Apollo 11* lunar mission, became the first person to set foot on the moon. His companions on the mission were Edwin E. Aldrin, Jr., and Michael Collins. In 1971 he became professor of aerospace engineering at the University of Cincinnati. Following the fatal explosion of the space shuttle *Challenger* in January 1986, Armstrong was appointed deputy chief of the presidential commission set up to investigate the disaster.

ARMSTRONG, Samuel Chapman (1839–93), American soldier and educator, born in Hawaii, and educated at Oahu College and Williams College. In 1862, after the outbreak of the American Civil War, he joined the Union army. In 1864 he was commissioned colonel of a black regiment, which he commanded for two years. In 1866 he was promoted to the rank of brigadier general. In Hampton, Va., in 1868 he founded, for the education of blacks, the Hampton Normal and Agricultural Institute, now Hampton University, and served as its president until his death.

ARMY, military land forces of a nation, assembled, drilled, disciplined, and equipped for offense and defense in maneuvers in warfare. The term may refer either to the entire body of military personnel in a nation, or to a specific unit under a military commander.

The composition of armies often reflects the attitudes toward war of the civilizations and societies they represent. In ancient Greece, for example, men up to the age of 60 were expected to serve. More importance was attached to military than to civil office. In ancient Rome, the citizen-soldier army of the Republic changed to a professional force as social conditions changed and the Republic gave way to the empire.

RISE OF ANCIENT ARMIES

In prehistoric and early historic times, armies as such did not exist; armed forces consisted of groups engaged sporadically in combat for the purpose of defending or acquiring land desired for hunting or pasture. The rise of permanent settlements, however, in the Tigris-Euphrates Valley and along the Nile, was paralleled by the employment of citizen-soldiers to protect them.

Ancient Middle East. In Mesopotamia standing armies of spearmen and bowmen were created as early as 3200 BC, and about 2500 BC warfare was revolutionized with the introduction of chariots drawn by asses and horses (*see* CAVALRY). In Egypt, Sesostris I (r. 1962–1928 BC) maintained a regular army—well equipped, disciplined, and salaried. He divided his kingdom into 36 military provinces, established a national militia, allocated land for the support of the military, and used this army both offensively and defensively. In the mid-6th century BC, the Persians, under Cyrus the Great, refined the concept of the standing army by promoting the deployment of both infantry and cavalry and establishing a system of discipline.

Greece. The Greek city-states maintained bodies of militia capable of being united into one great army. The superior organization and strict discipline of these citizen-soldiers, or hoplites, helped achieve the great victories won at such battles as Marathon and Plataea during the Persian Wars of the 5th century BC.

In the mid-6th century BC, the Spartans introduced the concept of the phalanx, the first important tactical formation. Primarily defensive in its original form, it consisted of eight rows of heavily armored shield-bearing spearmen standing shoulder to shoulder in rectangular ranks. Although capable of withstanding cavalry charges, it was slow in attack and awkward in traversing difficult terrain. In contrast, the Athenians developed the use of cavalry to provide a cover in front of the army and to harass the enemy's rear.

In the 4th century BC, Philip II of Macedonia established a large standing army in which he added cavalry forces to the phalanx and introduced the use of the long pike. His son, Alexander the Great, who destroyed the Persian Empire, organized the first army supply system and established light infantry as a link between phalanx and cavalry. The use of archers, light catapults (*see* CATAPULT), siege engines, a tactical smoke- and sound-signal system, and a medical service were important contributions to a more sophisticated army organization.

Rome. The genius of the Carthaginian general Hannibal enabled his army to cross the Alps from France into Italy by means of masterly feats of logistics. In his march on Rome during the Second Punic War, Hannibal transported 30,000 men, horses, and elephants and inflicted a stunning defeat on the Romans at the Battle of Cannae in 216 BC by enveloping and destroying their army. (The Carthaginian attempt to control the western Mediterranean ended when the Roman legions finally conquered Carthage in 146 BC.) About 200 BC Rome had instituted for the first time a conscription of all able-bodied men between 17 and 46 years of age. A rigid physical training program for those selected in early childhood to become soldiers ensured a superior state

Ancient Roman war machine that propelled arrows by means of a spring attachment. Bettmann Archive

of readiness, especially for men chosen to serve in the legions. The campaigns of these celebrated units of foot soldiers and cavalry—organized in three lines of small phalanxes called maniples or cohorts—were expedited by the great Roman military engineering skills that provided the necessary roads, bridges, and forts.

The relaxation of army discipline and the drafting of slaves and criminals into the service, together with problems caused by incursions of Teutonic tribes and by internal social dissent, necessitated far-reaching military reforms, achieved under the consul Gaius Marius. In 104 BC wealthy and part-time soldiers were replaced by a professional army, recruited for a 20-year period. The maneuverability of the legions was balanced by a system of fixed fortifications, which were the key defenses of the far-flung Roman provinces.

The Far East. The legendary Chinese general Sun Tzu (fl. 6th cent. BC) wrote the earliest military treatise, *The Art of War* (c. 500 BC). In it he described Chinese weapons, command systems, communications, discipline, grade distinctions, strategy, and logistics. Although in later centuries Chinese and Japanese military organization was comparable to that of their Middle Eastern and European contemporaries, the Asian invention of stirrups (by or before the 2d cent. BC) had revolutionized mounted warfare by making chariots obsolete. The Battle of Adrianapole (AD 378), in which Huns, Alans, Goths, and Spartans annihilated the Romans, demonstrated the superiority of cavalry to infantry forces.

With a semimobile circle of wagons acting as a base of operations, the Mongol conqueror Genghis Khan in 1190 spearheaded Mongolian advances from the Gobi Desert into the heart of Europe. Their conquests, accomplished with relatively small armies but innovative military skill, relied on a basic formation of 10,000 mounted warriors, the *touman.* Sixty percent of this force was lightly protected; 40 percent was armored. Special weapons included hurled missiles, fire, and explosives. Communication was by signal flags and drumbeats. The Mongolian hordes lived off the country, and their tactical deployment relied on surprise attacks, thrusts at the enemy's flank and rear that preceded heavy cavalry assaults.

RISE OF MODERN ARMIES

The fall of Rome in the 5th century and the barbarian invasions that followed formed the background to the development of the feudal system and the disappearance for several centuries of large standing armies in Europe.

Middle Ages. Feudalism was based on a concept of local defense, each baron or landowner governing land that had been given him by the king, and each lord having his own personal protective forces recruited from among men who worked for him. In return, each lord and his men were pledged to annual service to the monarch and could be called on in special instances, as in the defense of Christendom, during the Crusades. National armies thus began to appear again. The Crusades emphasized the need for organization and discipline in opposing a common enemy; as a result, large forces of foot soldiers were constituted. Although the introduction of gunpowder (q.v.), supported by the use of crossbows (*see* CROSSBOW) and other weapons, changed the character of war, the ambition of the individual knight engaging in personal combat with his sword diminished the effective utilization of the army as a unified force.

Throughout Europe during the 14th century, when firearms were introduced (*see* ARTILLERY), mercenary professional soldiers were recruited by the highest bidder. Such companies, varying in strength from tens to thousands, were the forerunners of modern professional armies. The present Swiss Guard (q.v.) of the Vatican is a direct successor of a 15th-century mercenary company. Among other extant survivors of the mercenary army, one of the most renowned is the French foreign legion (*see* FOREIGN LEGION), organized in 1831 for service outside France and composed of diverse ethnic groups. It has seen service in combat all over the world.

16th–18th Century Armies. Spain is considered the first modern European country to have established a standing army. The nucleus of this 16th-century force was four infantry regiments of 7000 men bearing pikes and firearms.

Sweden under King Gustav II Adolph conscripted an army to serve in the Thirty Years' War. The king improved military efficiency by organizing six or more 150-man companies into regiments and combat brigades and enforcing strict discipline, which in turn made possible increased mobility. Artillery was integrated into the cavalry and infantry formations.

Under Louis XIV, the French army organized a quartermaster department to perform supply functions, and training and inspection of the troops were standardized. By 1678 France's standing forces numbered more than 200,000 soldiers. Marshal Sébastien Le Prestre de Vauban (1633–1707) designed a system for attacking fortified places, improved a system of defensive fortification, and created the first modern corps of engineers (*see* FORTIFICATION AND SIEGE WARFARE).

Britain's first regular army, established by the Lord Protector Oliver Cromwell in 1645, consisted of 14,000 infantry and 7600 mounted men and heavy artillery. The use of the "ring" bayonet (invented c. 1689), attached by loose rings to the muzzle of a flintlock musket, enabled John Churchill, 1st duke of Marlborough, to dispense with pikemen and increase the number of musketeers (*see* BAYONET). Infantrymen thus became self-sufficient.

The techniques of modern warfare were greatly advanced in the 18th century by the theories and strategems of the great military leader Frederick the Great of Prussia. Under his guidance the Prussian army was formed into one of

A view of the French army under Napoleon in Vienna, Austria, in 1809. The French army was the first to introduce conscription and compulsory military training.
Anne S. K. Brown Military Collection

Frederick William I, king of Prussia, inspecting the pride of his army, the giant guards. Bettmann Archive

the most efficient forces known up to that time. **Napoleon.** The army of the French Revolution possessed a mobile, well-equipped artillery branch and an infantry with a high degree of morale. The military engineer Lazare Carnot in 1792 instituted a nationwide draft of citizens into the first all-arms divisions (infantry, artillery, and cavalry) whose aim was the total destruction of the enemy. In 1798, under Napoleon, military conscription was made compulsory by law. Every male between 21 and 25 years of age was liable to four years of service. Napoleon's initial contribution to the citizen army of France was in the area of artillery improvements. Subsequently, he established himself as perhaps the world's foremost military strategist, able to muster an army of between 200,000 and 500,000 men and to demonstrate that this massive force could move speedily, along separate roads, live off the land without fixed depots, and in concentrated units take an enemy by surprise. Napoleonic campaigns are classics that are still studied.

Origin and Development of the U.S. Army. Colonial militias were the first American forces to do battle with the British. Their lack of reliability, however, caused Congress, at the urging of George Washington, to create the Continental army on June 14, 1775. With the raising of ten companies, the army achieved a maximum strength of 35,000 men in November 1778. On June 2, 1784, however, Congress abolished the army on the basis that "standing armies in time of peace are inconsistent with the principles of republican government. . . ." In 1789 the War Department was established to oversee and administer military forces. After the war Congress again authorized a small standing army to guard U.S. frontiers, and in 1802 it established the United States Military Academy (q.v.) at West Point to train regular army officers. State militias, however, provided the main manpower resource during the American Civil War—when military conscription was first adopted and then abolished. Until World War I, and the establishment of the draft, federalized state troops and volunteers provided the manpower needed in times of crisis. The first peacetime conscription was instituted in 1940, continued throughout the Korean and Vietnam wars, and ended on Jan. 27, 1973; the Military Selective Service Act expired June 30, 1973. Since that time military power has been dependent on an all-volunteer force. *See* CONSCRIPTION; SELECTIVE SERVICE; UNITED STATES ARMY.

The Changing Army. The Women's Army Auxiliary Corps of the U.S., authorized by an act of Congress on May 14, 1942, was renamed the Women's Army Corps (q.v.), or WAC, on July 1, 1943. WAC personnel served with the army ground-aid and service forces, as well as in the administrative and technical services and in the General Staff Corps. The first overseas WAC contingent reached North Africa in January 1943. At its peak in 1945, the corps had a strength of more than 100,000; in 1948 the corps was accorded permanent status in both the regular army and the organized Army Reserve Corps.

Although blacks had served in the armed forces since colonial times, they were relegated to segregated units and assigned service as opposed to combat duties. In 1948 President Harry Truman signed an executive order for the integration of blacks into all branches of the armed forces, and the process of desegregation of the military was begun. *See* BLACKS IN THE AMERICAS.

The importance of guerrilla warfare (q.v.) was demonstrated on all fronts during World War II. The subsequent spread of nationalistic or ideological "brushfire wars" further promoted the use of guerrilla tactics and strategy. World War II also demonstrated the operational utility of airborne troops; such units were first used by the USSR against Finland in 1939–40 and then by the Germans in Denmark, Norway, Belgium, and France. Mountain warfare was employed on a wide front between Italy and Austria-Hungary in World War I, involving specially trained alpine troops using skis. In World War II the Germans used mountain divisions in their campaign in Norway; and Soviet troops versed in winter warfare played a critical role during the war.

Modern counterparts of the mercenary armies of former centuries are the 20th-century international armies such as the 15-nation force that fought in Korea in 1950–53 under the aegis of the UN, and the many UN peacekeeping forces in the Congo, Lebanon, and the Middle East.

Armies of the Future. Technical demands made of individual soldiers will require that a small elite of well-trained volunteers exist to operate under conditions of peace or limited war, this corps to be reinforced by large numbers of conscripted soldiers performing traditional functions during large-scale operations. Women, now assigned to service and combat-support branches,

The functions of the modern army include many nonmilitary procedures, such as the debris removal and land-clearing operations being conducted here by a U.S. Army Emergency Operations crew. U.S. Army

will increasingly be assigned to infantry, cavalry, armor, and engineer units in the field. It can also be projected that military professional and technical skill will be increasingly utilized in meeting civilian needs.

See also WARFARE. E.A.W.

For further information on this topic, see the Bibliography in volume 28, sections 278, 281, 285.

ARMY, DEPARTMENT OF THE, one of the three major components of the U.S. Department of Defense. It was created by the National Security Act of 1947 to succeed the Department of War, which had been established in 1789. The department is headed by the secretary of the army, a civilian who is appointed by the president and functions under the direction of the secretary of defense. The secretary of the army is responsible for the conduct of all affairs of the army, including those necessary for its training, operations, administration, logistical support and maintenance, welfare, preparedness, and effectiveness. The secretary is also responsible for the administration of civil functions, such as the maintenance of Arlington and Soldiers' Home National Cemeteries, and for the civil works program of the Army Corps of Engineers.

Military assistance and advice are provided by the Army Staff, headed by the chief of staff, who serves as the army member of the Joint Chiefs of Staff. The chief of staff is a principal adviser to the president, to the National Security Council, and to the secretary of defense.

Various acts of Congress and executive orders have increased the scope of department responsibilities beyond exclusively military matters. Thus, the department now administers programs aimed at protecting the environment, flood control, and water resource development. The army also may be called on to provide natural disaster relief assistance and emergency medical air transportation service.

ARMY, UNITED STATES. *See* UNITED STATES ARMY.

ARMY ANT. *See* ANT.

ARMY CORPS OF ENGINEERS, principal engineering component of the U.S. Army, dating to June 16, 1775, when the Continental Congress authorized a chief engineer and two assistants for the army. They prepared the fortifications for the Battle of Bunker Hill. The engineers were permanently organized into a corps in 1802.

Originally, the duties of the Corps of Engineers were strictly military: combat engineering, coastal fortification, topographical surveying, and mapmaking. The scarcity of trained civil engineers led Congress to pass the General Survey Act in 1824, to allow army engineers to undertake nonmilitary duties, such as canal, road, and railroad surveys; lighthouse construction; and river and harbor improvements. The corps also planned and built important public buildings in Washington, D.C., among them the Capitol of the United States, Lincoln Memorial, Library of Congress, and Washington Monument (qq.v.). For the construction of the Panama Canal (q.v.), the chief engineer and many aides were selected from the Corps of Engineers. During World War II the corps built the Alaska Highway (q.v.) and was involved in the construction of nuclear production plants used in the Manhattan Project leading to the first atomic bomb.

The present work of the corps is divided between military and civil projects. The military program currently includes construction for the army and air force and environmental restoration of areas contaminated by toxic wastes. The civil program centers on development of water resources, including navigation improvement, hydroelectric power, flood control, recreation, and conservation of fish and wildlife. The corps also provides emergency assistance in the wake of disasters such as floods. Its traditional combat engineering functions, such as clearance of minefields, construction of field fortifications, and erection of bridges in theaters of operations, are carried out by engineers assigned to various U.S. Army combat units.

ARMY MATÉRIEL COMMAND, UNITED STATES. *See* UNITED STATES ARMY.

ARMYWORM, common name for the larvae of any of several American species of moths of the family Noctuidae that travel in groups from one area of vegetation to another, particularly *Pseudaletia unipuncta.* The specific name (Lat. *unus,* "one"; *punctum,* "a point") refers to the single white spot on each front wing of the adult moth, which is otherwise uniformly a dull brown color; it has a wingspread of about 4 cm (about 1.5 in). The caterpillar, which is almost 5 cm (2 in) long when fully grown, is green, with three yellowish stripes down the back and a darker stripe on each side. The caterpillars feed chiefly on grasses and are usually most troublesome in cornfields. They feed only at night; by day they hide in the sod or among the inner leaves. When they have completely stripped an area, they march in a group to another plot. They are periodically abundant in most of the U.S. east of the Rocky Mountains. In the southern U.S. six generations may occur in a season. *See also* CUTWORM.

ARNAUD, Henri (1641–1721), Waldensian pastor and soldier, born in France, and educated in Basel and Geneva. Encouraged and probably aided by English Protestants, Arnaud undertook to return those Waldenses (Christian dissenters) who had been expatriated by Victor Amadeus (1666–1732), duke of Savoy, to their homes in Piedmont. In 1689 he led about 1000 exiles into the Piedmont Valley, where they withstood attacks by the allied armies of France and Savoy. Soon afterward, war broke out between France and Piedmont, and the Waldenses were permitted to live at peace in their native valleys; from 1690 to 1697 Arnaud and his troops fought against the French. After the war, however, Piedmont and France once more united against the Waldenses, and Arnaud was exiled. He spent the remainder of his life as a pastor in Württemberg. He wrote *Histoire de la glorieuse rentrée des Vaudois dans leurs vallées* (History of the Glorious Return of the Waldenses to Their Valleys, 1710).

ARNAULD, Antoine (1612–94), known as the Great Arnauld, the most famous French exponent of Jansenism (q.v.), a 17th- and 18th-century Roman Catholic theological movement of rigorous and unorthodox tendencies.

Born in Paris, Arnauld studied law and theology at the Sorbonne. As a student he came under the influence of the French theologian Jean Duvergier de Hauranne, abbot of Saint-Cyran and one of the founders of the Jansenist movement. Arnauld was ordained a priest in 1641 and made a member of the Society of the Sorbonne in 1643. In the latter year his *De la fréquente communion* (About Frequent Communion), a basic exposition of Jansenist principles, was published. The work antagonized the Jesuits, with whom Arnauld engaged in bitter controversy for the remainder of his life.

For some time Arnauld was a member of the Jansenist community in Port Royal, near Paris. The Jesuits succeeded in bringing about his expulsion from the Sorbonne in 1656 and, despite the protection of Louis XIV of France, forced him into exile in Belgium in 1679. Undaunted, Arnauld continued to issue a barrage of polemical writings against numerous adversaries, including freethinkers and the Calvinists.

ARNDT, Ernst Moritz (1769–1860), German patriot and writer, born on the island of Rügen, and educated at the universities of Greifswald and Jena. When Napoleon invaded Prussia in 1806, Arndt went into exile, producing, under the general title of *Der Geist der Zeit* (The Spirit of the Times), a series of stirring polemics against the French emperor, and writing German patriotic songs. After the expulsion of the French, Arndt returned to Germany, but he fell into disfavor with the Prussian government because of his liberal views. In 1840, on the accession of the liberal monarch Frederick William IV to the Prussian throne, he was restored to favor. For the last 20 years of his life he was professor of history at the University of Bonn.

ARNE, Thomas Augustine (1710–78), English composer of dramatic music, whose style became a model for nearly a century of English music. During his lifetime he was overshadowed by the presence in his native London of the German-born composer George Frideric Handel. Arne's best works include the masques *Comus* (1738), *The Judgement of Paris* (1740), and *Alfred* (1740), which contains the British patriotic song "Rule, Britannia"; and his songs for a 1740 series of Shakespearean comedies.

ARNHEM, city, E Netherlands, capital of Gelderland Province, on the Lower Rhine R., near Utrecht. Arnhem is an industrial and commercial center, with a large trade in grain and with plants engaged in the manufacture of precision instruments, paper, mirrors, and wood products. Among the principal points of interest in Arnhem are the Groote Kerk (Great Church), dating from the 15th century, and the town hall, another 15th-century edifice. In medieval times Arnhem was a member of the Hanseatic League. The city came under the authority of the States-General, the parliament of the Dutch Republic, in 1585. It remained under Dutch rule, except for periods of French occupation from 1672 to 1674 and from 1795 to 1813, until World War II. In May 1940, Arnhem was occupied by German troops. It was recaptured by the Allies in 1944. Pop. (1986 est.) 128,000.

ARNIM, Achim von (1781–1831), German writer. With his brother-in-law, the German romantic Clemens Brentano, he compiled three volumes of folk poems, *Des Knaben Wunderhorn* (The Boy's Magic Horn, 1805–8), which stand as his memorial. His novellas show an interest in the supernatural and influenced novelists in the romantic tradition. *Die Kronenwächter* (The Guardians of the Crown, 1817) helped launch the historical novel in Germany.

ARNIM, Bettina von, *née* ELISABETH BRENTANO (1785–1859), German writer. Sister of the romantic Clemens Brentano and wife of his associate Achim von Arnim, she published her correspondence with famous people, such as the German writer Johann Wolfgang von Goethe. In *Goethe's Correspondence with a Child* (1835; trans. 1837) she added imaginative touches to the letters, making them almost fiction. Later she dropped romanticism for liberal and political treatises, as in *Dies Buch gehört dem König* (This Book Is for the King, 1843).

ARNO, river, central Italy, in Tuscany. From the source of the river on Mt. Falterona in the Apennines, the Arno flows generally W for about 225 km (about 140 mi), past the cities of Florence and Pisa, to the Ligurian Sea. Navigation by barges is possible as far as Florence, but it requires caution against the sudden floods that sometimes swell the stream.

ARNOLD, Benedict (1741–1801), American military leader, who distinguished himself during the first phase of the American Revolution, but later betrayed the American cause.

Arnold was born on Jan. 14, 1741, in Norwich, Conn. Both his parents were of long-established, well-respected New England families. He was apprenticed to an apothecary in his youth but, preferring the battlefield to a druggist's life, he enlisted in the militia during the French and Indian War. When his father died in 1761, Arnold moved to New Haven, Conn., where he became a druggist, selling potions and books. In 1764 he expanded his prosperous enterprises into shipping and trade with Canada and the West Indies. Commercial success brought election to a militia captaincy in 1775.

Service in the Continental Army. As a militia colonel, Arnold joined with Ethan Allen to take Fort Ticonderoga from the British at the beginning of the American Revolution (1775). Military supplies from the fort were a boon for George Washington's ill-equipped American forces besieging Boston. Later the same year Arnold led a brave but unsuccessful assault on British Québec and was promoted to brigadier general; enemy reinforcements subsequently forced his retreat to Lake Champlain.

On the lake Arnold was defeated (1776) by a British naval attack, but his delaying tactics thwarted an enemy drive to New York City, which would have divided the colonies. His leadership in the Battle of Ridgefield, Conn. (April 1777), won him a belated promotion to the rank of major general. During the crucial Saratoga campaigns in New York in the summer and fall of 1777, his relief of Fort Stanwix and his courageous and imaginative battlefield leadership contributed decisively to an American victory.

Benedict Arnold

Treason. After he became commander of Philadelphia in 1778, he met and married Margaret Shippen (1760–1804) the following year and with her squandered money on an extravagant social life among the Loyalist families of Philadelphia. Needing money, he then began a 16-month treasonable correspondence with the British commander in chief, Sir Henry Clinton. As commandant of West Point, key to the Hudson River valley, Arnold agreed in 1780 to surrender the fort to the enemy in return for a royal commission in the British army and a sum of money. The capture of Clinton's envoy, Maj. John André, exposed the plot, and Arnold fled to the enemy.

Arnold's anger and treachery were stimulated by the following: the promotion of junior officers over him; charges by Pennsylvania authorities that he had violated military regulations, which culminated in his court-martial; the need for ready money to reimburse wartime expenses and to pay for his Philadelphia extravagances; and his distaste for the Franco-American alliance (he distrusted Roman Catholic France and had not forgotten the French and Indian War).

Work for the British. As a brigadier general in the British army, Arnold conducted raids in Virginia (1780) along the James River to Richmond and, later, to Petersburg. In 1781, to divert a projected French and American attack on British forces in the south, Arnold's marauding expeditions shifted to New London, Conn., where he, in effect, raided former neighbors. There he burned more than 150 buildings, and his troops massacred American militia at Fort Griswold, near New London.

In December 1780 Arnold and his family sailed to England, where he advised British officials on the conduct of the war. With the Revolution's military conclusion (1781) and the ouster of his English political supporters, the unpopular traitor was excluded from active military service in the British army. His commercial enterprises proved unsuccessful, and for his treason he received less than one-third the money he had sought. After enduring years of British scorn, he died in London, on June 14, 1801.

Evaluation. Scholars have not found that Arnold was a callous soldier, but they disparage his character—not simply because he was a traitor, but

rather because he frequently made himself the measure of all things while trampling the moral standards of others. He compounded his arrogance by personalizing disagreements, oversimplifying complex problems, and browbeating opponents. Despite his offensive personality and self-serving nature, Arnold continues to fascinate because he was a patriot and hero-turned-traitor.
R.S.

ARNOLD, Matthew (1822-88), English poet, whose work is representative of Victorian intellectual concerns and who was the foremost literary critic of his age.

Arnold was born in Laleham, Middlesex, on Dec. 24, 1822, the son of Thomas Arnold, famous headmaster of Rugby School. In 1840, while a student at Rugby, young Arnold won the prize for poetry with his "Alaric at Rome." Subsequently he attended Balliol College, University of Oxford, where, in 1843, his poem "Cromwell" won the Newdigate prize.

Matthew Arnold

After a period spent teaching the classics at Rugby, Arnold served as an inspector of schools from 1851 to 1886. From 1857 to 1867, he was also professor of poetry at Oxford. Arnold visited the Continent repeatedly in the interests of education and journeyed twice to the U.S. as a lecturer, in 1883 and 1886. He died in Liverpool on April 15, 1888.

A meditative, elegiac tone is characteristic of Arnold's poetry, notably "Empedocles on Etna" (1852), "The Scholar-Gipsy" (1853), "Sohrab and Rustum" (1853), "Thyrsis" (1866), "Rugby Chapel" (1867), "Dover Beach" (1867), and "Westminster Abbey" (1882). Arnold's philosophical despair and sense of isolation are best expressed in the following lines from "Stanzas from the Grande Chartreuse" (1855):

> Wandering between two worlds, one dead,
> The other powerless to be born,
> With nowhere yet to rest my head,
> Like these, on earth I wait forlorn.

Despite his religious doubts, Arnold wrote several pieces seeking to establish the essential truth of Christianity against conventional dogmatism. He also defended culture against scientific materialism in his collection of essays *Culture and Anarchy* (1867-68). His most influential literary criticism is found in essays such as "The Function of Criticism at the Present Time" (1865) and "The Study of Poetry" (1880).

ARNOLD, Thomas (1795-1842), British educator, born on the Isle of Wight, England, and educated at the Winchester School and the University of Oxford. In 1818 he was ordained a deacon in the Church of England. Arnold was headmaster of Rugby School from 1828 to 1842. Under his leadership, the school rose to considerable prominence. Although he was concerned with character development and the encouragement of Christian principles, his major interest was in academic excellence. He tried to instill in the students a desire for knowledge and to provide them with the means to pursue it. Arnold added modern languages, mathematics, history, poetry, and philosophy to Rugby's classical curriculum. His changes influenced the reorganization of the entire English public school system of education. In 1841 he was appointed professor of modern history at Oxford. His principal works include a *History of Rome* (3 vol., 1838-43), his Oxford *Lectures of Modern History* (1842), and a posthumously published *History of the Later Roman Commonwealth* (1845). He was the father of Matthew Arnold, eminent British poet and critic.

ARNOLD OF BRESCIA (c. 1100-c. 1155), Italian religious and political reformer and monk, born in Brescia. After studying theology in Paris, where he may have come under the influence of the French philosopher and theologian Peter Abelard, he returned to Brescia and preached against the corruption and greed of the Roman Catholic clergy. Opposed to the ownership of land by the church, he led the citizens of Brescia in rebellion against the authority of Pope Innocent II (r. 1130-43) and as a result was exiled to France in 1139. Accused by St. Bernard of Clairvaux of being a follower of Abelard, Arnold was condemned by the Council of Sens in 1140 and forced into exile in Zürich. He was compelled to leave Zürich in 1145 as a result of further accusations against him by St. Bernard. Arnold moved to Rome, where he aided in exiling Pope Eugene III. There, under the protection of the insurgent nobility, Arnold reorganized the government of Rome. The pope excommunicated Arnold and returned to Rome, but Arnold retained his popular following in the city, thereby avoiding additional reprisals. In 1155, however, following the interdict placed on the city by Pope Adrian IV, Arnold fled Rome. Arrested by order of Frederick I, the Holy Roman emperor, he was returned to Rome, condemned to death, and hanged.

ARNOLFO DI CAMBIO (c. 1245–c. 1302), Italian late Gothic architect and sculptor, born near Siena. Following his apprenticeship to the sculptor Nicola Pisano, Arnolfo worked in Rome, Orvieto, and other cities, carving many tombs, altar canopies, and fountains. About 1294 he began work on Florence Cathedral; construction continued for over a century after his death. Arnolfo's sculptures for the cathedral facade, now dispersed to several museums, harmonize ancient Roman forms and late Gothic motifs in a style heralding the Renaissance.

ARNSBERG, town, W central Germany, in North Rhine-Westphalia, located on a tributary of the upper Ruhr R., in the wooded uplands of the Sauerland. It is a popular resort for the great Ruhr industrial area to the W and a regional transportation and manufacturing center. Founded in the 11th century, Arnsberg retains many old streets and medieval buildings. Pop. (1989 est.) 73,900.

ARNULF (d. 899), king of Germany (887–99) and Holy Roman emperor (896–99). He was an illegitimate son of the East Frankish ruler Carloman (828–80), who was a great-grandson of Charlemagne. In 887 Arnulf led the revolt that forced Charles III (The Fat), king of France and Holy Roman emperor, to abdicate and was elected king of the East Franks, that is, of Germany. In 891 he repulsed the Vikings, who were invading his kingdom. He campaigned in Italy in 894 and again in 895–96. In early 896, he captured Rome and was crowned Holy Roman emperor, the last Carolingian to be so invested.

AROMATIC COMPOUNDS, large group of organic chemical compounds that usually contain closed rings of carbon atoms. Some aromatic rings, however, may also contain an oxygen or a nitrogen atom. The term was originally restricted to the coal tar product benzene and its derivatives, but it now includes about half of all organic compounds, the remaining half being classified as aliphatic compounds.

Important aromatic compounds include all hormones and vitamins except vitamin C; virtually all flavorings, perfumes, and organic dyes, synthetic and natural; those alkaloids that are not alicyclic (aliphatic bases such as putrescine are sometimes incorrectly classified as alkaloids); some substances of military importance, such as TNT and tear gas; many drugs; and a wide variety of other substances.

Certain derivatives of aromatic compounds have special properties and special names. For example, the addition of the hydroxyl group to an aromatic hydrocarbon yields a phenol.

See also HYDROCARBONS. For a general discussion of organic compounds, *see* CHEMISTRY, ORGANIC.

AROOSTOOK, river, NE Maine and W New Brunswick, Canada, about 225 km (about 140 mi) long. It rises in Piscataquis Co., Maine, and flows NE before joining the Saint John R. just beyond the Canadian border. The river drains a fertile potato-growing region in Maine. The lower basin of the Aroostook was a disputed area in the Aroostook War (1838–39), a bloodless controversy between the U.S. and Great Britain over a part of the boundary between the NE United States and present-day Canada. The controversy was resolved in 1842 by the Webster-Ashburton Treaty.

ARP, Jean *or* **Hans** (1887–1966), avant-garde French sculptor, painter, and poet, born Sept. 16, 1887, in Strasbourg. Arp studied art in Weimar and Paris between 1905 and 1909 and then painted in Switzerland for several years. By 1912 he had become associated with the Blaue Reiter (Blue Rider), a group of expressionist artists in Munich. Arp's work during the 1915–16 period consisted of angularly patterned, totally abstract tapestries and drawings. In 1916 Arp helped found the revolutionary Dadaist school of artists in Zürich. In 1917 Arp's style of art changed to the familiar abstract, curvilinear forms of his later work. In 1924 Arp moved to Paris, where he was associated with the surrealists and produced painted wooden bas-reliefs and humorous cut-cardboard constructions. In the 1930s, Arp began to work in freestanding sculpture, carving and molding a variety of substances. An example of his smooth, biomorphic forms is *Human Concretion* (1935; cast stone version, 1949, Museum of Modern Art, New York City). He also worked at various times in gouache, collage, engraving, and lithography. Throughout his career, he wrote both poetry and essays. Arp was bilingual and called himself Jean when writing in French and Hans when writing in German.

ÁRPÁD (869–907), semilegendary national hero of Hungary. In 895 or 896 Árpád led the Magyars, a nomadic people of uncertain origin, into the ancient country of Pannonia. He greatly extended his conquests by continuous and successful warfare with the Bulgar, Wallachians, and Moravians. The Árpád dynasty ruled Hungary as dukes from 889 to 1000 and as kings from that year until the male line became extinct with the death of Andrew III (c. 1265–1301). Árpád is the subject of many Hungarian folk songs and legends.

ARQUEBUS. *See* HARQUEBUS.

ARRAH, city, NE India, in Bihar State, capital of Shahabad District, on the Son Canal, near Patna. It is the trading center of a farming region that produces grain, oilseeds, and sugarcane. In 1857, during the Sepoy Mutiny, a small group of Europeans and loyal Indians successfully defended an isolated dwelling in the city against a large force of mutineers. Pop. (1981 prelim.) 124,614.

ARRAIGNMENT, in the law of Great Britain and the U.S., the bringing of a person who has been formally accused of a crime before the court that has jurisdiction to try the person to answer the accusations of the indictment. After the accused is identified, the indictment is read, and he or she must plead guilty or not guilty. The arraignment always follows the indictment and may be regarded as the first stage in the trial of the accused. If the indictment is for a felony, the personal presence of the accused is necessary in the courts of most states of the U.S. In misdemeanor cases, however, the accused need not be personally present at the arraignment as long as an attorney appears in court for the accused. After the arraignment is completed, the court may grant the accused time in which to answer the indictment.

The answer of the defendant must take one of three forms: a plea of guilty or not guilty; an application to the court to dismiss the indictment because of some defect in form; or a demurrer, that is, an assertion that the facts alleged in the indictment are not such as to constitute a crime. Defendants who refuse to answer the indictment are deemed to have pleaded not guilty.

Human Lunar Spectral (Torso of a Giant), *in bronze, is the work of Jean Arp, who is also famous as a painter.*
Hirshhorn Museum & Sculpture Garden, Smithsonian Institution

ARRAN, island, W Scotland, in the Firth of Clyde, part of Strathclyde region. The island is mountainous, reaching a maximum elevation of 874 m (2866 ft), and the wild and rugged breakers of the N shore attract both geologists and tourists. The island also is noted for beautiful glens and picturesque waterfalls. Places of interest include a ruined castle on the N part of the island and the caves on the SW in which the liberator of Scotland, Robert Bruce, is believed to have taken refuge from the English in 1307. The industries of the island include fishing, raising sheep and cattle, and growing oats and potatoes. Area, about 433 sq km (about 169 sq mi).

ARRAS, city, N France, capital of Pas-de-Calais Department, on the Scarpe R. It is a farm-trade, manufacturing, and transportation center, and its products include metal goods, machinery, and clothing.

Arras is of Gallo-Roman origin, and it was an important seat of banking and trade in the 12th century. The city became the capital of the province of Artois in 1237, and it subsequently came under French, Burgundian, Austrian, and Spanish rule. The Treaty of Arras, ending hostilities between Burgundy and France, was signed here in 1435. During the Middle Ages, the city was noted for its beautiful tapestries, and from the 17th to the 19th century it was known for its lace. Because of its strategic location, Arras was the scene of several battles in World War I. It was badly damaged in World War II. Pop. (1982) 45,364.

ARRAS, BATTLES OF, five major engagements fought between military forces of the Allied and Central powers during World War I in and around Arras, administrative center of the department of Pas-de-Calais in northern France and a strategic railroad junction.

First Battle of Arras, fought during September and October 1914. German troops occupied the town on September 1. French forces recaptured and began to fortify it on September 18. Heavy German counterattacks throughout October were repulsed, but on October 24 the French were forced to yield Vimy Ridge, a strategic location about 16 km (about 10 mi) north of the town.

Second Battle of Arras, also called the Battle of Artois, fought during June and July 1915. It began as a French offensive to relieve German pressure on the town. The fighting was severe, and by June 23 most of the German trenches and dugouts before Arras had been captured. Early in July the French cleared the communications between Arras and Béthune and captured the nearby towns of Souchez and Neuville-Saint-Vaast. Total French casualties during the first two battles of Arras were 113,000 men. German losses were approximately the same.

Third Battle of Arras, fought during April and May 1917. Sir Douglas Haig, commander of the British Expeditionary Forces in France, had decided to capture Vimy Ridge before a general offensive against Ypres (or Ieper). With Vimy Ridge in German possession during such an offensive, Haig's forces would have been open to German counteroffensive from the Arras district. The attack against Vimy Ridge began on April 9, and the Germans were cleared from the position the following day. Violent attacks and counterattacks were carried out by both sides throughout the remainder of April and in May. Allied forces captured Gavrell, Guémappe, and important positions east of Lens, and strengthened considerably their entire position around Arras.

Fourth Battle of Arras, fought in March 1918. It began when German armies under the command of Gen. Karl von Bülow (1846-1921) attempted to break through the Allied front at Arras. The Allied armies were forced to retreat in a sector north of Arras, but the attack exhausted 15 German divisions. Haig considered the German offensive a failure.

Fifth Battle of Arras, fought during August and September 1918. The Allies had decided to capture the German railways running south and southwest from the town of Douai. On August 26 British and Canadian forces attacked along a 9-km (5.5-mi) front directly east of Arras, carrying the German positions after severe fighting. A German counterattack was repulsed, and the Allied advance continued during the following day. German losses, including 18,850 prisoners and 200 guns, were heavy in this battle, which resulted in the establishment of an Allied sector before Cambrai.

ARREST, the process of taking a person into custody, usually carried out by a duly appointed law enforcement officer. Arrest can be classified as criminal or civil. Criminal arrest is generally the first step in a series of legal actions taken against a person suspected of committing a crime, in order to bring that person to court for judgment. Civil arrest, infrequently used today, is designed to compel an individual to fulfill some legal obligation at the order of a court. Certain privileged persons, such as representatives of foreign governments, are not liable to arrest in either civil or criminal proceedings.

Criminal Arrest. A person may be arrested when there is probable cause to believe that he or she has committed a crime; when an indictment has been handed down by a grand jury; or when parole or probation has been violated in any way. The court may then issue an arrest warrant, which is served by a police officer or other court-appointed individual. The warrant must specify clearly the nature of the offense with which the party arrested is charged.

In most cases, however, arrests are made by police officers without warrants when they apprehend a suspect during the commission of a crime or when they have sufficient reason to believe that a person is guilty of a criminal offense. Civilian arrests are sometimes made by one who is not an officer of the law when a felony is committed in that person's presence. Private individuals and, occasionally, arresting officers may be subject to suit for false arrest if the accused party is acquitted.

Since the 1960s, the rights of a person facing arrest in the U.S. have been protected by several landmark decisions of the U.S. Supreme Court. The best known is the case of *Miranda* v. *Arizona* (1966), in which the Court ruled that the suspect must be informed by the arresting officer of his or her constitutional rights, including the right to remain silent and the right to have an attorney present during questioning. After an arrest is made the suspect is taken to a police station to be booked. *See* CRIMINAL PROCEDURE.

Civil Arrest. According to the old common law of England, a debtor was considered guilty of a breach of the peace and was subject to forcible arrest and imprisonment. The severity of the law was gradually mitigated, until, by the 19th century, imprisonment for debt had been abolished in Great Britain and the U.S. In some civil actions, however, a party is still subject to arrest. As a rule, these actions are either of a quasi-criminal nature, such as the recovery of a fine or penalty, or are brought to redress wrongs to person or property.

ARRHENIUS, Svante August (1859-1927), Swedish chemist, who helped lay the foundations of modern chemistry. Born in Wijk, near Uppsala, he was educated at the University of Uppsala and received his Ph.D. in 1884. While still a student, he undertook the study of the conductivities of electrolytic (charge-conducting) solutions. In his doctoral thesis he formulated the theory of electrolytic dissociation, also called the ionic theory. Arrhenius pointed out that, although the molecules of those chemical compounds that have solutions able to conduct an electric current are broken down in solution into electrically charged particles called ions, such dissociation is practically complete even when no passage of electric current occurs. He also stated that the degree of dissociation increases as the solution becomes more dilute—an observation later found to apply only to weak electrolytes. His theory of electrolytic dissociation was at first ignored but was later generally accepted and finally became one of the cornerstones of modern physical chemistry and electrochemistry.

In 1889 Arrhenius also observed that the speed of chemical reactions increases markedly when the temperature is increased, at a rate proportional to the concentration of the activated molecules. Arrhenius became professor of chemistry at the University of Stockholm in 1895 and director of the Nobel Institute of Physical Chemistry in 1905. His awards and honors include the 1903 Nobel Prize in chemistry. He wrote works on physical and biological chemistry, electrochemistry, and astronomy. In the last-named area, he is noted for his suggestion that life on earth, and presumably elsewhere, originated from living spores driven through space by the pressure of light. *See* IONIZATION.

ARRIAN, full name FLAVIUS ARRIANUS (c. 95–180), Greek historian, born in Nicomedia, Bithynia (now İzmit, Turkey). In his youth, he lived at Nicopolis, Epirus (now Preveza, Greece), where he was a pupil of the Greek Stoic philosopher Epictetus. He served as governor of Capadocia (131–37) and later as archon, or chief magistrate, of Athens. Arrian's works, influenced by those of Xenophon, include the *Anabasis of Alexander,* an authoritative biography of Alexander the Great; *Indica,* about the voyage of Alexander's fleet; and fragments of the discourses of Epictetus.

ARROWHEAD, common name for any of the aquatic plants of the genus *Sagittaria,* of the family Alismataceae (*see* WATER PLANTAIN). They are distinguished by unisexual flowers, having three sepals and three colored petals, with numerous stamens and carpels. Arrowheads are native to many climates, from the Tropics to the cold regions. About 30 species are known. Several species and

American arrowhead, Sagittaria latifolia

many varieties are found in North American waters. The common arrowhead of Europe, *S. sagittifolia,* and the common arrowhead of America, *S. latifolia,* have leaves that are usually elongated and triangular, with the basal lobes bent downward, resembling an arrowhead.

ARROWROOT, common name for a variety of nutritious starch extracted from the roots of certain plants growing in tropical countries or the plants from which such starch is obtained. The true arrowroot plant, *Maranta arundinacea,* is a native of tropical America, especially Florida, and is extensively cultivated in the West Indies. It grows up to 2 m (6 ft) high. An acre of arrowroot yields about 6 metric tons of rhizomes, or fleshy roots, from which about 1 metric ton of starch is obtained. Arrowroot, more easily digested than other forms of starch, is also obtained from other plants of the same family, Marantaceae. Florida arrowroot is in part prepared from *Zamia integrifolia,* a cycad (q.v.).

ARROWWORM, common name for small, transparent, free-swimming marine animals constituting the phylum Chaetognatha. They are 1 to 8 cm (0.5 to 4 in) long, arrow-shaped, and streamlined, with one or two pairs of lateral fins and a caudal fin that propel the body forward in rapid, darting movements. The rounded head bears a set of bristles on each side, used in catching small animals. A retractable hood can be drawn over the bristles and mouth, which streamlines the head while swimming. Almost all arrowworms live in the open ocean waters. They occur in great numbers along coasts and continental shelves, where they constitute an important part of the food web (q.v.) as predators and as food for other animals. Arrowworms locate prey by detecting vibrations. All are hermaphrodites, containing both ovaries and testes, and some can fertilize themselves. The phylum is not very diverse, having only about 50 species in a few families. Arrowworms are quite unlike any other animals, but possibly may be related to echinoderms and chordates.

ARSENIC, metalloid element, symbol As, in group 15 (or Va) of the periodic table (*see* PERIODIC LAW); at.no. 33, at.wt. 74.92. When arsenic is heated, it sublimes, passing directly from solid to gaseous form at 613° C (1135° F). A common form of arsenic is gray, metallic in appearance, and has a sp.gr. of 5.7. A yellow, nonmetallic form also exists and has a sp.gr. of 2.0.

Properties and Occurrence. Chemically, the element is intermediate between metals and nonmetals. Its properties lie, in general, in the middle of the series formed by the family of the elements nitrogen, phosphorus, arsenic, antimony, and bismuth. Arsenic ranks about 52nd in natural abundance among the elements in crustal rocks.

Arsenic has been known since ancient times. The pure element can be easily prepared by heating a common ore called arsenopyrite (q.v.), FeAsS. Other common minerals are realgar, As_2S_2; orpiment, As_2S_3; and arsenic trioxide, As_2O_3; occasionally the pure element is found in nature. Arsenic occurs frequently in place of some of the sulfur in the sulfides that are the principal ores of many of the heavy metals. When these ores are roasted, the arsenic sublimes and may be collected from the dust in the flues as a by-product.

Uses. Arsenic is used in large quantities in the manufacture of glass to eliminate a green color caused by impurities of iron compounds. A typical charge in a glass furnace contains 0.5 percent of arsenic trioxide. Arsenic is sometimes added to lead to harden it and is also used in the manufacture of such military poison gases as lewisite and adamsite. Until the introduction of penicillin, arsenic was of great importance in the treatment of syphilis. In other medicinal uses, it has been displaced by sulfa drugs or antibiotics. Lead arsenate, calcium arsenate, and Paris green are used extensively as insecticides. Certain arsenic compounds, such as gallium arsenide (GaAs), are used as semiconductors. GaAs is also used as a laser material. Arsenic disulfide, As_2S_2, also known as red orpiment and ruby arsenic, is used as a pigment in the manufacture of fireworks and paints.

Arsenic is poisonous in doses significantly larger than 65 mg (1 grain), and the poisoning may arise from a single large dose or from repeated small doses, as, for example, inhalation of arsenical gases or dust. On the other hand, some persons, notably the so-called "arsenic eaters" of the mountains of southern Austria, have found that arsenic has a tonic effect and have built up a tolerance for it, so that they can ingest each day an amount that would normally be a fatal dose. This tolerance, however, does not protect them against the same amount of arsenic administered hypodermically.

A reliable test that can detect the presence of minute amounts of arsenic is often important, because arsenic is a violent poison and is widely used and therefore a frequent contaminant. The Marsh test, named for its inventor, the English chemist James Marsh (1794–1846), supplies a simple method for detecting traces of arsenic. The substance to be tested is placed in a hydrogen generator and any arsenic present is converted to arsine (AsH_3), which mixes with the evolved hydrogen. If the stream of hydrogen is heated as it passes through a glass tube, the arsine decomposes, and metallic arsenic is deposited in the tube. Minute amounts cause an appreciable stain; as little as 0.1 mg (0.000003 oz) of arsenic or antimony can be detected by using the Marsh test.

ARSENOPYRITE, mineral composed of iron sulfarsenide, FeAsS, used as an ore of arsenic. It crystallizes in the monoclinic system in prismatic crystals and has a hardness (q.v.) ranging from 5.5 to 6 and a sp.gr. of 5.92 to 6.22. It is opaque and silver-white in color, with a metallic luster. Arsenopyrite is the most common mineral containing arsenic and is found in considerable abundance in southeastern Germany, in areas of England and Bolivia, and in parts of the U.S. It is often associated with other sulfide ores of tin, tungsten, silver, gold, cobalt, and nickel.

ARSINOË I (fl. 282–247 BC), first wife of Ptolemy II, king of Egypt, and the mother of Ptolemy III. She was the daughter of King Lysimachus (c. 355–c. 281 BC) of Thrace. About 278 BC her husband, having accused her of complicity in a plot against his life, banished her to Coptos, in Upper Egypt. Shortly afterward, Ptolemy II married his sister, Arsinoë II, who had previously been married to King Lysimachus, and thus had been both stepmother and sister-in-law of Arsinoë I.

ARSINOË II (316–271 BC), Egyptian queen of the Ptolemaic dynasty, the daughter of King Ptolemy I. After the death of her first husband, King Lysimachus (c. 355–c. 281 BC) of Thrace, she married her brother, Ptolemy II, in accordance with Egyptian royal custom. She soon became the real ruler of the country. Coinage was issued in her name, and she was given divine status. After her death Ptolemy built a shrine to her in Alexandria, and many cities were named for her.

ARSON, in the law of Great Britain and the U.S., the act of willfully and maliciously setting fire to a house, building, or other property. Under common law, arson was the willful and malicious burning of the house of another person and was considered a felony punishable by death. The penalty for arson now consists of differing periods of penal servitude or simple imprisonment. If the act results directly or indirectly in the death of a person, it is treated according to the modern definition of murder. The act of burning one's own house to defraud an insurer or destroy the property of another on the premises was also a crime, usually a misdemeanor, in common law; in some states of the U.S., however, this act is now defined as a lower degree of arson and consequently is punished less severely. Under the penal statutes of some states, including New York, arson in the first degree is setting fire to any building in which a human being is present.

ART, a disciplined activity that may be limited to skill or expanded to include a distinctive way of looking at the world. The word *art* is derived from the Latin *ars,* meaning "skill." Basically, art is skill at performing an orderly set of specialized actions, as, for example, the art of gardening or of playing chess. The liberal arts are fundamentally verbal and mathematical skills, although the term includes wider applications.

Art in its broader meaning, however, involves both skill and creative imagination in such areas as the literary arts, the performing arts, and the visual arts. Art in this sense may be effective in many ways. It may serve a practical purpose, as when a church shelters worshipers, a march inspires soldiers, or a play conveys a moral message. It may amuse, frighten, seduce, or elevate. It may, moreover, be therapeutic to the artist who creates it. Essentially, however, art is a skill that provides artist and public with an experience of beauty.

Fine Arts and Decorative Arts. Traditionally, in most societies, art has combined practical and aesthetic functions. Since the 18th century in the West, however, a more sophisticated public has distinguished between art that is more purely aesthetic and art that is also practical. The fine, or major arts (Fr. *beaux arts*)—including literature, music, dance, painting, sculpture, and architecture—are concerned primarily with aesthetics. The decorative, applied, or so-called minor arts, such as pottery, metalwork, furniture, tapestry, and enamel, are useful arts and for a time were demoted to the rank of crafts. Because the École des Beaux-Arts in Paris taught only the major visual arts, the terms *art* was sometimes narrowed to mean only drawing, painting, and sculpture. Since the mid-20th century, however, greater appreciation of non-Western and folk traditions and of individual work in a mechanized society has tended to blur the old distinction. Both categories are equally valued as art.

Art and Science. Both art and science require technical skill. Both artist and scientist try to create order out of the seemingly random and multifarious experiences of the world. Both try to understand and appreciate the world and to convey their experience to others. An essential difference, however, exists: The scientist studies quantitative sense perceptions in order to discover laws or concepts that are universally true. The artist selects qualitative perceptions and arranges them to express personal understanding. Whereas further investigation may cause a scientific law to be invalidated, a work of art, despite changes in the artist's view or the public taste, has permanent validity as an aesthetic statement at a particular time and place.

The Artist in the World. Although artists may be unique geniuses impelled by their own creative energies, they are also very much products of their societies. A society must provide sufficient wealth and leisure to enable the public or an institution to pay a professional artist, as did Sumerian priests and Renaissance princes. An amateur artist must have free time, as, for example, a farmer who carves or embroiders in winter, or an office worker who paints on Sunday. Even the choice to be an artist may be culturally influenced. In many traditional societies, artists, like other people, customarily followed their father's profession, as did certain Japanese families of actors and painters and the musical dynasties of 18th-century Europe.

The physical resources of a society affect the medium in which an artist works. In stoneless Mesopotamia, Sumerian architects built in brick. Nomadic Asian herders wove wool from their flocks into rugs. Medieval European painters worked on wood panels, plaster walls, stained-glass windows, or parchment books in an era before paper was known in the West. Mass production and world trade have given 20th-century artists an enormous range of materials.

An artist's medium affects the style of the work. Thus, a sculptor must treat stone differently from wood; a musician achieves different effects with drums than with violins; a writer must meet certain demands of poetry that are irrelevant to the novel. Local tradition also affects art styles. Pottery design in one area and period may be geometric, in another, naturalistic. Indian tradition prescribed close curled hair in depictions of the Buddha, just as Western tradition decreed a blue robe for the Madonna. Eastern artists paid no heed to scientific perspective, which was a major concern of painters in the European Renaissance.

In addition, the subject of art is largely dictated by the society that supports it. In ancient Egypt, dominated by state and religion, painting, sculpture, and architecture glorified the pharaoh and life after death. In pious medieval Europe, most visual arts and theater had Christian themes. In 20th-century totalitarian countries, art must serve the state. In most Western countries artists have greater freedom to choose the subjects they please. Sometimes, as in abstract painting and absolute music, the form of the work becomes its subject.

The status of artists in the West has changed over the centuries. In classical and medieval times, poets and other writers who used mental skills were usually ranked above actors, dancers, musicians, painters, and sculptors who used physical skills. From the Renaissance on, as all aspects of the human personality came to be valued, those skilled in the visual and performing arts gradually gained greater recognition. Today art in all its categories is considered an essential area of human achievement, and its many, varied creators are ranked among the first citizens of the world.

For art theory *see* AESTHETICS; CRITICISM, LITERARY. For art technique and history *see* ARCHITECTURE; COSTUME; DANCE; DRAMA AND DRAMATIC ARTS; MUSIC; MUSIC, WESTERN; NOVEL; PAINTING; POETRY; POTTERY; SCULPTURE. See also articles on individual artists, dancers, musicians, and writers.

For further information on this topic, see the Bibliography in volume 28, sections 28, 642-80, 712-15.

ART, PHILOSOPHY OF. *See* AESTHETICS.

ARTAUD, Antonin (1896-1948), French writer and actor, born and educated in Marseilles. He went to Paris in 1920 and became a stage and screen performer. In 1927 he cofounded the Théâtre Alfred Jarry, where he produced several plays, including his own *The Cenci* (1935), an illustration of his concept of the *theater of cruelty.* He used this term to define a new theater that minimized the spoken word and relied instead on a combination of physical movement and gesture, nonspecific sounds, and the elimination of conventional spatial arrangements and sets. Their senses thus violated, spectators would be forced to confront the inner, primal self, stripped of its civilized veneer. Hindered by lifelong physical and mental illness, Artaud was unable to implement his theories. His book *The Theatre and Its Double* (1938; trans. 1958) describes theatrical modes that later, however, became identifying traits of the ensemble theater movement; the theater of the absurd; and the epic, environmental, and ritual theater. *See also* DRAMA AND DRAMATIC ARTS.

ART CONSERVATION AND RESTORATION, actions taken to examine, preserve, and restore to their original condition objects of historic and artistic merit. An art conservator examines an object to determine the materials of construction and the causes of their deterioration or alteration. The conservator preserves the object by preventing or retarding deterioration and restores it by correcting deterioration or any alteration made by someone other than the original artist.

From the moment an art object is completed by the artist it undergoes physical and chemical changes, such as the drying of oil paints, perhaps accompanied by color alteration, and the changes in dimension of materials containing moisture. When these changes become undesirably noticeable, deterioration is well under way. The principal causes of unwanted change are too much or too little humidity, light, heat and cold, polluted atmosphere, biological infestations, neglect, contact with contaminating objects, and inherent incompatibility of materials. Excessive moisture makes wood swell, makes paper become limp, and makes organic substances develop mold. Insufficient moisture causes wood and ivory to warp and crack, and leather and paper to become brittle. Too bright light fades watercolors and textiles and accelerates their photochemical deterioration. Freezing and overheating may cause fracturing of stone, plaster, and glass. Insects, rodents, molds, and bacteria can destroy organic materials—textiles, leather, paper, and wood. Art objects placed in contact with chemically reactive materials can be damaged, as, for example, a drawing on good rag paper mounted under a wood-pulp mat, or colors in a collage, which darken as a result of the oxidation of poor-quality glue. Many materials change through oxidation, or reaction to air pollutants. For instance, in sulfur-laden air (resulting from the burning of fuel oil and coal) limestone, marble, and murals on lime plaster walls may all be changed from calcite to gypsum, which expands and flakes away.

Because all art objects are unique and give aesthetic pleasure to the beholder, they are much valued by the individual collector and by the art-minded public. Each country takes pride in its historic and artistic monuments. In recent years the public has become more aware of the need to preserve its past through conservation of that small percentage of human creative genius that survives. Museums have set up conservation and scientific laboratories for the study, authentication, and preservation of their treasures. Universities have established graduate training programs in art conservation, which offer courses in art history and in the science and techniques of examination and treatment of art objects. National laboratories have been established in many countries, as have governmental agencies concerned with the preservation of the world's artistic heritage.

Archaeologists have also become more aware of the need to preserve what they find. At many sites trained conservators examine and treat objects recovered from the earth or the sea. Some archaeologists employ architects and engineers to reconstruct monuments that were buried in antiquity.

Architecture. The architectural past has become a concern of governments, foundations, historical societies, and private citizens. Many old public buildings and noteworthy houses have been placed on registers of national monuments or have been designated as landmarks. Professional architectural preservationists study the materials and construction techniques used in old buildings. Many such structures may be preserved intact; the exteriors of others may be kept intact while the interiors are adapted to a new function, as, for example, the conversion of large private estates to museums. Houses are often furnished in keeping with their period to re-create a harmonious entity or a historic setting.

Decorative Arts and Sculpture. Furniture, ceramics, textiles, and many other types of artifacts require the attention of various specialists. Some study these objects to determine materials, methods and date of manufacture, and authenticity. Carbon-14 dating is frequently used to determine the age of organic materials. Thermoluminescent dating may be used to obtain the firing date of a ceramic object or, from its clay core material, the casting date of a bronze.

Conservators are taught the use of adhesives to reassemble broken objects and the methods used to clean marble, ivory, and other materials. Conservators of metal objects learn to recognize genuine old patina or the effects of corrosion. They treat such problems as bronze disease—a chemical reaction involving bronze, the chloride ion found in most burials, water, and oxygen—that eventually may cause bronze to crumble.

Textile conservators must be able to analyze fibers, weaves, and deterioration problems and be prepared to consolidate, clean, reweave, and mount fragile materials on auxiliary supports in preparation for storage or exhibition.

The specialist who conserves sculpture must understand the problems involved in preserving marble, limestone, granite, and other hard stones, and ceramics, metals, plastics, woods, papers, and fabrics.

Conservation of this panel painting consisted in first covering the face with a protective coating. The painting was then transferred from its deteriorated wood backing to a new masonite support. Last, the protective facing material was removed with swabs and special solvent.

L. J. Majewski–Conservation Center, New York University

Art on Paper. The conservation of works of art containing paper—watercolors, drawings, prints, photographs, posters, documents, books, constructions, collages, and sculpture—presents special problems. Paper is fibrous material containing cellulose—flax, cotton, jute, hemp, the inner bark of mulberry or other trees, and pulverized wood—felted together in thin sheets. The greater the amount of pure alpha cellulose present, the more permanent is the paper. Wood-pulp papers such as newsprint contain many impurities, which cause them to turn brown and become brittle and acidic. The paper conservator must analyze the types of fibers in a particular paper as well as diagnose the deterioration problems and treat them. Treatment may include deacidification, washing, bleaching, lining, laminating, matting, removing old restoration, and providing proper storage or exhibition conditions.

Painting. Perhaps the area of conservation that receives most attention and arouses most controversy is that of painting. A painting is a multilayered structure usually consisting of the following: (1) the support, that is, the wall, panel, canvas, or other foundation; (2) the ground, or preparation applied to the support to render it more receptive to paint; (3) the design, or paint layers; (4) the protective coating, or varnish. One or more of these layers may need attention. The canvas may be brittle and torn; the ground may be detached from the support; the paint film may be flaking, cracking, or changing color; and the varnish may be covered with grime or have oxidized to a dark brown. The conservator first examines the painting in detail, using the stereomicroscope, ultraviolet and infrared illumination, and special viewers; in the process, the painting may be photographed to record all findings. It may also be X-rayed to reveal changes made by the artist or by previous restorers.

Treatment usually begins with consolidation, that is, repairing or strengthening the support and reattaching loose paint. Cleaning is a delicate operation involving removal of grimy or discolored varnish and of disfiguring restorations. It is accomplished with solvents that are carefully tested in small areas. Most old paintings have some damaged areas, which must be filled with a gesso-type substance to the original surface level and then inpainted without touching any of the original paint. The conservator's objective is to preserve the work, prolong its life, and restore it to the intent of its creator. L.J.M.

For further information on this topic, see the Bibliography in volume 28, section 644.

ART DECO, style of design popular in the 1920s and '30s. It was used primarily in furniture, jewelry, textiles, and interior decor. Its sleek, streamlined forms connote elegance and sophistication. Although the movement began about 1910, the term Art Deco was not applied to it until 1925, when it was coined for the title of the seminal Paris design exhibition, Exposition Internationale des Arts Décoratifs et Industriels Modernes.

Art Deco grew out of a conscious effort to simplify the elaborate turn-of-the-century Art Nouveau (q.v.) style, to make it more responsive to the new machine-age ideals of speed and glamour. Two of Art Deco's earliest practitioners were the couturier Paul Poiret (1879–1944) and the jeweler and glassmaker René Lalique; their designs featured delicate unconstricted, flowing lines. Further important influences were the Russian ballet producer Sergey Diaghilev's Ballets Russes, with its Oriental stage decor and exotic colors; King Tutankhamen's tomb (opened in 1922), which created a vogue for Egyptian motifs; and cubism, with its elegantly geometric aesthetic. Leading designers of the 1920s and '30s were Jacques Émile Ruhlmann (1879–1933) in furniture, Jean Dunand (1877–1942) in lacquerwork, Jean Puiforcat (1897–1945) in silver, and Lalique in jewelry.

Art Deco became steadily more geometric and linear as objects were increasingly mass-produced and as the U.S. supplanted France as the spiritual center of the movement. It found ex-

The Prometheus Fountain, sculpted by Paul Manship and installed in 1934, is the centerpiece of Rockefeller Center, an Art Deco landmark in New York City.
Vance Henry–Taurus Photo

pression in objects as diverse as locomotives, skyscrapers, roadside diners, radio cabinets, jukeboxes, and advertising displays. Principal European monuments of Art Deco were Ruhlmann's Paris exhibition rooms, Le Pavillon d'un Collectioneur (1925), and the grand salon (c. 1930) of the French liner *Normandie,* with lighting and decor by Lalique. Primary examples of Art Deco in the U.S. are the interior of Radio City Music Hall (1931) in New York City, designed by Donald Deskey (1894–1989); and William van Alen's (1882–1954) Chrysler Building (1930, New York City), with its sleek aluminum-banded facades and arched and pointed spire.

Art Deco declined after 1935 but has enjoyed a significant revival since the 1960s. *See also* FURNITURE; GLASS; INTERIOR DESIGN.

ARTEMIS, in Greek mythology, one of the principal goddesses, counterpart of the Roman goddess Diana. She was the daughter of the god Zeus and Leto and the twin sister of the god Apollo. She was chief hunter to the gods and goddess of hunting and of wild animals, especially bears. Artemis was also the goddess of childbirth, of nature, and of the harvest. As the moon goddess, she was sometimes identified with the goddesses Selene and Hecate.

Although traditionally the friend and protector of youth, especially young women, Artemis prevented the Greeks from sailing to Troy during the Trojan War until they sacrificed a maiden to her. According to some accounts, just before the sacrifice, she rescued the victim, Iphigenia. Like Apollo, Artemis was armed with a bow and arrows, which she often used to punish mortals who angered her. In other legends, she is praised for giving young women who died in childbirth a swift and painless death.

ARTERIOSCLEROSIS. *See* ARTERY.

ARTERY, one of the tubular vessels that conveys blood from the heart to the tissues of the body. Two arteries have direct connection with the heart: (1) the aorta, which, with its branches, conveys oxygenated blood from the left ventricle to every part of the body; and (2) the pulmonary artery, which conveys blood from the right ventricle to the lungs, whence it is returned bearing oxygen to the left side of the heart (*see* HEART: *Structure and Function*). Arteries in their ultimate minute branchings are connected with the veins by capillaries. They are named usually from the part of the body where they are found, as the brachial (arm) or the metacarpal (wrist) artery; or from the organ which they supply, as the hepatic (liver) or the ovarian artery. The facial artery is the branch of the external carotid artery that passes up over the lower jaw and supplies the superficial portion of the face; the hemorrhoidal arteries are three vessels that supply the lower end of the rectum; the intercostal arteries are the arteries that supply the space between the ribs; the lingual artery is the branch of the external carotid artery that supplies the tongue. The arteries expand and then constrict with each beat of the heart, a rhythmic movement that may be felt as the pulse (q.v.).

Disorders of the arteries may involve inflammation (q.v.), infection, or degeneration of the walls of the arterial blood vessels. The most common arterial disease, and the one which is most often a contributory cause of death, particularly in old people, is arteriosclerosis, known popularly as hardening of the arteries. The hardening usually is preceded by atherosclerosis, an accumulation of fatty deposits on the inner lining of the arterial wall. The deposits reduce the normal flow of the blood through the artery. One of the substances associated with atherosclerosis is cholesterol (q.v.). As arteriosclerosis progresses, calcium is deposited and scar tissue develops, causing the wall to lose its elasticity. Localized dilatation of the arterial wall, called an aneurysm, may also develop. Arteriosclerosis may affect any or all of the arteries of the body. If the blood vessels supplying the heart muscle are affected, the disease may lead to a painful condition known as angina pectoris (q.v.). *See* HEART: *Heart Diseases.*

The presence of arteriosclerosis in the wall of an artery can precipitate formation of a clot, or thrombus. Treatment consists of clot-dissolving enzymes called urokinase and streptokinase, which were approved for medical use in 1979. Studies indicate that compounds such as aspirin (q.v.) and sulfinpyrazone, which inhibit platelet reactivity, may act to prevent formation of a thrombus, but whether they can or should be taken in tolerable quantities over a long period of time for this purpose has not yet been determined.

Embolism (q.v.) is the name given to the obstruction of an artery by a clot carried to it from another part of the body. Such floating clots may be caused by arteriosclerosis, but are most commonly a consequence of the detachment of a mass of fibrin from a diseased heart. Any artery may be obstructed by embolism; the consequences are most serious in the brain, the retina, and the limbs. In the larger arteries of the brain, embolism causes stroke (q.v.).

ARTESIAN WELL, well bored down to the point, usually at great depth, at which the water pressure is so great that the water is forced out at the surface. The name is derived from the French region of Artois, where the oldest well in Europe was bored in 1126.

ARTEVELDE, Jacob van (c. 1295–1345), known as the Brewer of Ghent, Flemish statesman and political leader, born in Ghent of a wealthy commercial family. He married twice and amassed a fortune, probably in the brewing industry. Artevelde rose to prominence during the early stages of the Hundred Years' War. Fearful that hostilities between France and England would hurt the prosperity of Ghent, he entered political life in 1337. He proposed an alliance with Bruges, Ypres, and other Flemish towns in order to show neutrality. Artevelde served as captain general of Ghent from that time until his death. Neutrality was eventually broken, and the towns took the side of the English in 1340. In that year, Artevelde persuaded the federation to recognize King Edward III of England as sovereign of France and overlord of Flanders. Flemish trade and industry flourished under Artevelde's semidictatorial rule. In 1345, however, rumors that he planned to recognize the son of Edward III as count of Flanders caused a popular uprising in Ghent, and Artevelde was killed by an angry mob.

ART FORGERY, the intent to deceive, usually for financial gain, by proffering an art object as representing something other than what it is. Art forgery has many subdivisions, such as the deliberate imitation offered as an original; a genuine old object that has been altered by partial repainting or reworking to give it greater value; early copies not initially intended to deceive but later passed off as originals; the pastiche made up of original parts that do not go together; and workshop artifacts attributed to the master.

Notable Forgers. Throughout history art forgeries have been made whenever creative works have been considered valuable for a collection. The Romans copied Greek original sculptures, and many of the copies have at some time or other been considered originals. Today these copies are in museums, valued for what they are. Coins have been counterfeited since they were first minted by King Gyges of Lydia (d. about 648 BC) about 670 BC. Sometimes molds were made of originals and copies produced by castings. At other times original dies were used to strike an unauthorized issue. Various Byzantine emperors debased their coinage with base alloys—a form of deception—and coins were even produced in base metals and gilded to be passed off as solid gold. Jean de France, duc de Berry (1340–1416), an art patron and coin collector, had modern copies made of old Dutch and French coins to fill in gaps in his collection. The Italian artists Giovanni Cavino and Pirro Ligorio (c. 1500–83) were master coin counterfeiters of the 16th century. Even the great Michelangelo forged an "antique" marble cupid for his patron, Lorenzo de Medici. In the 18th century a forger produced a marble head of Julius Caesar that had been purchased by London's British Museum in 1818 as being authentic.

Perhaps the most prolific production of art forgeries has occurred in the 19th and 20th centuries during periods of avid collecting, when profits for a successful deception have been enormous. The Louvre Museum in Paris bought its gold Tiara of Saïtaphernes for 200,000 gold francs and declared it a genuine work of the 3d century BC, although it had been made in 1880 by the goldsmith Israel Ruchomovsky of Odessa, Russia. He was commissioned to execute a number of works in the antique manner by unscrupulous dealers, who then sold the objects as antiquities. The Italian artist Giovanni Bastianini (1830–68), in the third quarter of the 19th century, executed in good faith a number of fine sculptures in the manner of Donatello, Verrocchio, Mino de Fiesole, and other Italian old masters, which were subsequently sold as genuine to—among others—the Louvre and the Victoria and Albert Museum in London.

Perhaps the most famous master forger of all time was Alceo Dossena (1878–1936), who successfully produced sculptures of such high quality that they were accepted as genuine by many art critics, museum directors, and famous collectors. Apparently Dossena, a master artist, did not know he was defrauding a third party, as he merely supplied work in various styles—archaic, Greek, Hellenistic, Roman, Gothic, and Renaissance. When he discovered that a *Madonna and Child* he had sold for 50,000 lire was in turn sold for 3 million lire, he stepped forward and proclaimed that the works were modern.

Of almost equal notoriety is the story of Hans van Meegeren (1884–1947); he painted a number of fake Vermeers and Pieter de Hoochs that were accepted as genuine by eminent art critics and sold to important collectors and museums for fabulous sums. When he was accused of collaborating with the enemy in having sold, through an intermediary, Vermeer's *The Woman Taken in Adultery* to Hermann Göring during World War II, he was able to prove the "Vermeer" was by his own hand; van Meegeren was sent to prison for one year.

In recent years skillful forgeries of paintings by Vincent van Gogh, Paul Cézanne, Pablo Picasso, and other modern masters have appeared. Often these are declared fake by art historians, frequently after a technical examination.

Detecting Forgeries. By use of special illumination such as ultraviolet black light, infrared photography, and X-ray radiographs, inconsistencies and changes in paintings may be detected. Instrumental analyses may reveal anachronisms in a work of art, and techniques such as carbon-14 dating, thermoluminescence dating, and dendrochronology (tree-ring dating) are all helpful in detecting forgeries in works of art.

The dates when many pigments were introduced into the artist's palette are known; thus, if the 18th-century pigments Prussian blue and zinc white appear in a painting purported to be of an earlier date, then the work is obviously a forgery. Paint extending over an old crackle pattern may be evidence of repainting. Signatures are often changed by a forger; frequently, the binocular microscope is used to detect the alteration. Radiographs will reveal changes made by the original artist as well as those made on an old object by a forger. Pottery from archaeological sites is often "restored" from pieces that do not belong together by filing down edges of similar pieces from a second object. These, and fills of plaster or other materials, may show up in the X-ray.

The best detector of a false work of art, however, is the trained human eye. For example, a banker who is thoroughly familiar with printed currency can detect counterfeit money just by casual scrutiny, just as a fraudulent signature on a check is glaringly obvious when compared with a true signature. The detection of forgeries should be carried out jointly by art historians, art conservators, and scientists who have specialized in analysis of art and archaeological materials.

See also ART CONSERVATION AND RESTORATION.

L.J.M.

ART GALLERY, a building, hall, or room used for the public exhibition of art objects; often the term is interchangeable with *museum,* as in the case, for example, of the Walters Art Gallery, a museum in Baltimore, Md. In a more limited sense, however, an art gallery is a private commercial establishment offering works of art for sale. To this end, special exhibitions may be held. Many artists have formal arrangements with galleries that act as their agents or dealers, showing their works and taking a percentage of the selling price.

ARTHRITIS, inflammation of a joint. Over 100 different diseases can produce arthritis. In its most common and troubling forms, arthritis may occur in one or more joints of the body and is usually a long-term condition that may progressively disable and handicap.

Osteoarthritis, the most common form, affects an estimated 16 million people in the U.S., especially women; it is a usually mild, sometimes painful disease occurring primarily with advancing age, when degenerative changes alter the structure of the joints. Symptoms may be relieved and the condition controlled with drugs, exercises, and other measures, sometimes including orthopedic surgery.

Rheumatoid arthritis is by far the most serious, painful, and potentially crippling form; it is chronic, is characterized by flare-ups and remissions, and affects one million in the U.S., mostly women, but even children. Rheumatoid arthritis attacks the joints primarily but may affect supporting connective tissues throughout the body, causing fever, weakness, fatigue, and deformity. The cause is not known, but a hereditary predisposition and an environmental agent, such as a virus, are suspected. Although no cure has been discovered, the disease can be controlled. Pain-relieving and anti-inflammatory drugs are used, as well as programs of exercise, rest, heat, and assistive devices to maintain joint motion and function. Aspirin (q.v.) is the drug most widely used in treating the disease. Severe cases may be treated with gold compounds or the drugs hydroxychloroquine or penicillamine. Disability in advanced cases can be markedly reduced, and surgery is often effective in correcting deformities.

Inflammation of the joints can also be caused by gout, rheumatic fever (qq.v.), or ankylosing spondylitis, a disease affecting the spine.

Most forms of arthritis respond to a new class of drugs called nonsteroidal anti-inflammatory drugs, which inhibit synthesis of prostaglandins.

REV. BY F.C.M.

ARTHROPOD, term for invertebrate (q.v.) animals having an external skeleton and jointed appendages, such as crustaceans, insects, and spiders. The phylum they constitute, the Arthropoda (Gr. *arthron,* "joint"; podes, "feet"), is the largest in the animal kingdom, with about 875,000 known species found in almost all habitats.

Characteristics. Early arthropods were probably much like their presumed ancestors, annelids (*see* ANNELID). The body was long, soft, and had many segments, all much alike and each equipped with a pair of limbs. Subsequently the surface of the body became hardened to form an external skeleton (exoskeleton). This development had many protective advantages, but also some drawbacks. For example, an exoskeleton has to be shed (molted) if growth is to occur, and during this process the animal is soft and vulnerable. The strength and some other properties of an exoskeleton also diminish with size, so that arthropods do not grow very large. Lobsters can reach a weight of about 20 kg (44 lb), but terrestrial arthropods, unsupported by water, never grow that large. Their exoskeleton protects them from becoming dehydrated; however, special provisions for breathing are necessary, such as tubes (tracheae) that deliver air directly to the body tissues.

An arthropod's body surface bears a wide variety of sense organs, many of which are quite different from those of vertebrates. Sense organs include one to many pairs of eyes, either simple or compound or both, and often antennae that serve as organs of touch and taste. The nervous system of an arthropod is fairly complicated, but is limited by its comparatively small size.

Evolution. The evolution of arthropods has been noteworthy for the numerous variations on the basic body plan, with such organs as wings allowing a great variety in ways of life. A distinct trend can be observed toward a reduction in number of segments and limbs and toward their specialization and elaboration. Distinct body regions are formed from combinations of segments; limbs used in walking become longer, more effective in locomotion, and concentrated near the head, whereas other limbs assume new functions such as chewing or sensing the environment. The life cycle also undergoes specialization, with different stages adapted to different circumstances. Often a pronounced change in form—called metamorphosis—takes place, in which the young, or larva, differs greatly from the adult, or imago. Such evolutionary changes, which have sometimes been described as leading from "lower" to "advanced" arthropods, actually have occurred time and again in separate groups. A few authorities therefore hold that arthropods do not constitute a unit descended from a common ancestor and propose that they be divided into various phyla.

Classification. About nine classes of living arthropods are recognized, and these fall into a few larger assemblages. Three classes are presumably transitional from annelids, as is shown by their soft bodies: the Tardigrada (water bears), which are tiny, simple animals; the Pentastomida, which are parasites; and the Onychophora, which superficially resemble caterpillars and live in moist places on land, mainly in the southern hemisphere. The class Myriapoda ("countless legs") consists of the centipedes and millipedes, along with a few other animals. Members of the class Insecta (insects) have six pairs of walking legs and are often winged. (Some zoologists put onychophorans in a group with myriapods and insects, because all are basically terrestrial and have a single pair of antennae.)

The class Crustacea (crustaceans), which is largely marine (though not uncommon on land) and abounds in fresh water, includes such animals as lobsters, shrimps, and crabs. Crustaceans have two pairs of antennae.

Three classes of arthropods are grouped as chelicerates because of their specialized mouthparts, called chelicerae; antennae are absent. The Pycnogonida (sea spiders) have long legs and suck the juices of marine animals. The only living representative of the class Merostomata is the horseshoe crab. The class Arachnida contains forms such as spiders, scorpions, ticks, and mites, which are primarily terrestrial. Of the extinct groups of arthropods, the trilobites, class Trilobitomorpha, are the best known.

See ANIMAL; ARACHNID; CENTIPEDE; CRUSTACEAN; HORSESHOE CRAB; INSECT; MILLIPEDE. M.T.G.

For further information on this topic, see the Bibliography in volume 28, sections 464, 466.

ARTHUR (fl. 6th cent.), semilegendary king of the Britons who fought against the invading Anglo-Saxons. Although some historians consider him a mythical figure, there is reason to believe that a historical Arthur may have led the long resistance of the Britons against the invaders. According to legend, Arthur was the son of Uther Pendragon, king of Britain. Kept in obscurity during childhood, he was suddenly presented to the people as their king. He proved a wise and valiant ruler. He gathered a great company of knights in his court; problems of precedence were avoided by the use of a round table at gatherings.

With his queen, Guinevere, he maintained a magnificent court at Caerleon-upon-Usk (perhaps the legendary Camelot) on the southern border of Wales, where the Britons longest maintained their hold. His wars and victories extended to the continent of Europe, where he successfully defied the forces of the Roman Empire until he was called home because of the acts of his nephew Mordred, who had rebelled and seized his kingdom. In the final battle of Camlan, in southwestern England, the king and the traitor both fell, pierced by each other's spears. Arthur was mysteriously carried away to the mythical island of Avalon to be healed of his "grievous wound." The first allusion to Arthur is in the Welsh poem *Y Gododdin* (c. 600). He is again mentioned in *Historia Britonum* (c. 850) of the Welsh historian Nennius (fl. about 800); the *Annales Cambriae,* in a 10th-century manuscript, mentions him, giving 537 as the date of his death; and the fully developed legend appears in the *Historia Regum Britanniae* (c. 1139) of the English chronicler Geoffrey of Monmouth.

See also ARTHURIAN LEGEND.

ARTHUR, Chester Alan (1830-86), 21st president of the U.S. (1881-85), who rose above a background of political corruption to head a reform-oriented administration that enacted the first comprehensive U.S. civil service legislation.

Early Career. Arthur was born in Fairfield, Vt., on Oct. 5, 1830, the son of a poor country preacher. He graduated from Union College in Schenectady, N.Y., taught school, and then studied law and opened a practice in New York City before the American Civil War. A moderate abolitionist, he defended several runaway slaves and was an early activist in the New York Republican party. With the coming of the war, Arthur became New York's quartermaster-general in charge of supplying the state's volunteers with equipment. He performed this huge administrative task with efficiency and scrupulous honesty, earning an important place for himself in the state Republican organization, which was dominated by the so-called Stalwart faction. In 1871 he became collector of the Port of New York. Arthur administered the collection of customs with his usual care and honesty while directing his approximately 1000 employees in doing political work for the state Republican party and its leader, Senator Roscoe Conkling.

Arthur's position became difficult when the federal government investigaed the Custom House and issued an order banning civil servants from managing political affairs. When Arthur ignored the order at Conkling's request, President Rutherford B. Hayes had Arthur and his naval officer, Alonzo B. Cornell (1832-1904), removed from office. But Arthur retained the support of the New York party, and when James A. Garfield was nominated for president in 1880, his managers chose Arthur as their vice-presidential candidate to placate the Conkling faction. After Garfield's election, Arthur became his ally in a dispute with Conkling. Garfield died, the victim of an assassin, on Sept. 19, 1881, and Arthur became president.

The Presidency. Arthur as president put his Stalwart friends behind him, committing his administration to moderate reforms and maintaining the dignity of his office. He renovated the White House with his own ample funds (he had invested his money wisely over the years) and entertained in an opulent but tasteful style. He gradually changed Garfield's cabinet, but his own administration never took on any distinctive tone. He supported the civil service reform bill that became law in 1883, but never became fully identified with it in the public mind. Similarly, he worked toward the first downward revision of the tariff since the Civil War, but the bill,

Chester Alan Arthur Clarence Hornung

achieved in 1883, scarcely made a dent in the structure of protection. He vigorously prosecuted frauds uncovered during the Garfield administration, but the government failed to gain convictions. Arthur vetoed a Chinese exclusion bill that clearly violated a treaty with China and also vetoed a wasteful rivers and harbors bill, which Congress promptly passed over his veto.

Arthur succeeded in gaining respect as president, but he generated little political enthusiasm. And, unknown to his contemporaries, he was dying of kidney failure. He effectively hid his illness from the public and even made desultory attempts at the Republican nomination for 1884, but this was probably only because of intense pride. Leaving office in 1885, honored but unlamented, he died of nephritis on Nov. 18, 1886.

Summary. Arthur's career was representative of a major transition in Gilded Age politics. He lived through, and in many ways represented, the rise of intense factionalism, its collapse in the late 1870s and early '80s, and its legacy in a more bureaucratic and cautiously reformist Republican party that emerged in the 1880s. R.D.Ma.

For further information on this person, see the section Biographies in the Bibliography in volume 28.

ARTHURIAN LEGEND, group of tales (in several languages) that developed in the Middle Ages concerning Arthur (q.v.), semihistorical king of the Britons, and his knights. The legend is a complex weaving of ancient Celtic mythology with later traditions around a core of possible historical authenticity.

The earliest references to Arthur are found in Welsh sources—the poem, *Y Gododdin* (c. 600), histories, written in Latin, in the 9th and 10th centuries, and tales in the Welsh story collection *The Mabinogion* (c. 1100). In one of these tales Arthur's wife, Guinevere, and his knights Kay, Bedivere, and Gawain make their appearance. The earliest continuous Arthurian narrative is in the *Historia Regum Britanniae* (c. 1139) by the English writer Geoffrey of Monmouth. Here Arthur is identified as the son of the British king Uther Pendragon, and his counselor Merlin is introduced. The *Historia* mentions the isle of Avalon, where Arthur went to recover from wounds after his last battle, and it tells of Guinevere's infidelity and the rebellion instigated by Arthur's nephew Mordred.

All later developments of the Arthurian legend are based on Geoffrey's work. Thus, the first English Arthurian story is in the poet Layamon's *Roman de Brut* (1205), an English version of Geoffrey's *Historia*. Arthur is depicted as a warrior on an epic scale; and the story of his magic sword Excalibur, which only he could extract from a rock, is included for the first time.

Queen Guinevere *(1858), by William Morris.*
Tate Gallery, London/Art Resource, New York

An Arthurian tradition also developed in Europe, probably based on stories handed down from the Celts who immigrated to Brittany in the 5th and 6th centuries. By 1100 Arthurian romances were known as far away as Italy. Inspired by chivalry and courtly love, they are more concerned with the exploits of Arthur's knights than with Arthur himself.

The oldest of the French Arthurian romances is a series of 12th-century poems by Chrétien de Troyes. One introduces Lancelot, Arthur's chief knight and his rival for Guinevere's love; another poem about Percival (see below) is the earliest story of the search for the Holy Grail, which from then on was incorporated into the legend. Chrétien's work had great influence on later Arthurian romance, particularly early German versions, such as *Erec* and *Iwein,* by the 12th-century poet Hartmann von Aue (c. 1170-c. 1235), and the epic *Parzifal* (c. 1210), by Wolfram von Eschenback. By the early 13th century the story of Tristram and Iseult (or Tristan and Isolde), from another Celtic tradition, was added to the Arthurian legend.

English Arthurian romances, dating from the 13th and 14th centuries, concerned individual knights—Percival and Galahad, the Grail knights, and especially Gawain. The culminating masterpiece of these was the anonymously written *Sir Gawain and the Green Knight* (c. 1370). A number of these Arthurian tales were retold, in English prose, by Sir Thomas Malory in his *Morte d'Arthur* (1485). On this book the poet Alfred Tennyson based his *Idylls of the King* (1859–85), an allegorical treatment of Victorian society.

Many other writers have adapted the stories of Arthur and his knights and their great court at Camelot to contemporary tastes and themes. The poet Edmund Spenser used Arthur, as the perfect knight, in his epic allegory of Elizabethan society, *The Faerie Queene* (1590–99). Mark Twain contrasted New England progressivism with medieval society in his *A Connecticut Yankee at King Arthur's Court* (1880). *The Once and Future King* (4 vol., 1939-58), by the English author T. H. White, remains a widely read modern version of the legend. Music, too, shows the abiding interest in Arthurian stories—from the German composer Richard Wagner's *Parsifal* (1882) to the Broadway musical *Camelot* (1960), by Alan Jay Lerner and Frederick Loewe.

ARTICHOKE, common name for a plant, *Cynara scolymus,* of the family Asteraceae (*see* COMPOSITE FLOWERS); also the flower head of the plant, used as a table vegetable. The artichoke grows wild in the south of Europe and is cultivated in the U.S., primarily in California. The leaves proceed from the base of the stem and are

Artichoke, Cynara scolymus. Left: Edible floral bud. Right: Flowering plant.

long and somewhat spiny. The stem is up to 1 m (3 ft) high, branched, with large heads of violet-colored (sometimes white), thistlelike flowers at the summits of the branches. The thickened receptacle (heart) and fleshy bases of the scales (leaves) of the immature flower are the portions eaten.

ARTICHOKE, JERUSALEM, common name for a tuberous-rooted perennial sunflower (q.v.), *Helianthus tuberosus,* of the family Asteraceae (*see* COMPOSITE FLOWERS), growing stems up to 3 m (10 ft) high and closely resembling the common sunflower. It is cultivated for its tubers, which are used as a table vegetable, as feed for livestock, and as a source of inulin and levulose (*see* FRUCTOSE). The name Jerusalem is derived from the Italian *girasole,* meaning "sunflower."

ARTICLES OF CONFEDERATION, the compact made by the 13 original colonies that set up a permanent central government for the U.S. The document, consisting of a preamble and 13 articles, was the basic law of the country from its adoption in 1781 until 1789, when it was superseded by the U.S. Constitution.

The Articles of Confederation were proposed by the Second Continental Congress in 1776 and were drafted by a committee headed by the American statesman John Dickinson. The first draft provided for a strong central government, but this was not satisfactory to a Congress concerned with states' rights. The revised draft, adopted by the Continental Congress on Nov. 15, 1777, called for a government that theoretically possessed many powers but was actually subordinate to the states. The major controversies involved in the drafting and passage of the document concerned states' rights, representation, funding of the government, and control of the western lands beyond the borders of the new nation. The articles were finally ratified by all 13 states and took effect on March 1, 1781.

Under the articles, the nation was a league of sovereign states, each with a single vote. The Congress, or central government, made up of delegates chosen by the states, was given the power to conduct foreign affairs, make treaties, declare war, maintain an army and a navy, coin money, and establish post offices. Measures passed by Congress, however, required the approval of 9 of the 13 states. The Congress was severely limited in its powers. It could not raise money by collecting taxes; it had no control over foreign commerce; it could pass laws but could not force the states to comply with them. Thus, the government was dependent on the willingness of the various states to carry out its measures, and often the states refused to cooperate. In addition, the articles were virtually impossible to amend, so problems could not be corrected. These defects provided an insurmountable barrier to effective constitutional government. The nation's leaders realized that a stronger central administration was needed if the U.S. was to survive. In 1787 the Constitutional Convention met in Philadelphia to draw up a constitution, which was adopted in 1789.

ARTIFICIAL INSEMINATION, originally, the process in which male gametes, the spermatozoa, are collected and introduced artificially into the female genital tract for the purpose of fertilization (*see* REPRODUCTION: *Sexual Reproduction:* Insemination). Other artificial methods for achieving fertilization have since been devised. Artificial insemination was first developed for breeding cattle and horses. Spermatozoa are collected from a chosen male and frozen, then thawed and used to impregnate females.

Frozen human spermatozoa are now also used for insemination—most often from an anonymous male donor when a couple wishes to have a child but the husband is infertile. Use of frozen spermatozoa leads to pregnancy about 60 percent of the time, whereas freshly collected semen has a much higher success rate of about 90 percent. Neither method is known to result in an increase in birth defects, but frozen semen often becomes unusable after a long time.

A different method of artificial insemination is the mixing of sperm and ovum in a nutrient medium outside the woman's body, followed by implanting the fertilized egg into her uterus. This technique is used when a woman's fallopian tubes (*see* FALLOPIAN TUBE) are blocked, and, as a result, the spermatozoa cannot reach the ovum. The first baby born as a result of such a procedure was the English "test-tube baby," Mary Louise Brown, in 1979. In 1984 a further advance in this procedure was reported from Australia, with the embryo first being frozen for two months before it was successfully implanted. Yet another method was used that same year, in which the ovum was first fertilized within one woman's uterus and then transferred to the body of another woman. Eggs can now also be removed from a woman's ovaries and placed in her fallopian tubes along with her husband's sperm; normal fertilization then follows. Controversies have arisen over the legal and ethical status of some of these procedures, which have been widely used.

ARTIFICIAL INTELLIGENCE (AI), a term that in its broadest sense would indicate the ability of an artifact to perform the same kinds of functions that characterize human thought. The possibility of developing some such artifact has intrigued human beings since ancient times. With the growth of modern science, the search for AI has taken two major directions: psychological and physiological research into the nature of human thought, and the technological development of increasingly sophisticated computing systems.

In the latter sense, the term AI has been applied to computer systems and programs capable of performing tasks more complex than straightforward programming, although still far from the realm of actual thought. The most important fields of research in this area are information processing, pattern recognition, game-playing computers, and applied fields such as medical diagnosis. Current research in information processing deals with programs that enable a computer to understand written or spoken information and to produce summaries, answer specific questions, or redistribute information to users interested in specific areas of this information. Essential to such programs is the ability of the system to generate grammatically correct sentences and to establish linkages between words, ideas, and associations with other ideas. Research has shown that whereas the logic of language structure—its syntax—submits to programming, the problem of meaning, or semantics, lies far deeper, in the direction of true AI.

In medicine, programs have been developed that analyze the disease symptoms, medical history, and laboratory test results of a patient, and then suggest a diagnosis to the physician. The diagnostic program is an example of so-called expert systems—programs designed to perform tasks in specialized areas as a human would. Expert systems take computers a step beyond straightforward programming, being based on a technique called rule-based inference, in which preestablished rule systems are used to process the data. Despite their sophistication, systems still do not approach the complexity of true intelligent thought.

Many scientists remain doubtful that true AI can ever be developed. The operation of the human mind is still little understood, and computer design may remain essentially incapable of analogously duplicating those unknown, complex processes. Various routes are being used in the effort to reach the goal of true AI. One approach is to apply the concept of parallel processing—interlinked and concurrent computer operations. Another is to create networks of experimental computer chips, called silicon neurons, that mimic data-processing functions of brain cells. Using analog technology, the transistors in these chips emulate nerve-cell membranes in order to operate at the speed of neurons.

For further information on this topic, see the Bibliography in volume 28, section 3.

ARTIFICIAL LIMB. *See* PROSTHETICS.

ARTIFICIAL ORGANS. *See* individual articles on body organs.

ARTIFICIAL RESPIRATION, forcing of air into and out of the lungs of one person by another person or by mechanical means. It is usually employed during suspension of natural respiration caused by disease, such as poliomyelitis or cardiac failure; by electric shock; by an overdose of depressive drugs such as morphine, barbiturates, or alcohol; or by suffocation resulting from drowning, breathing noxious gases, or blockage of the respiratory tract. If the brain is deprived of oxygen for five minutes, it may be permanently damaged; slightly longer periods without oxygen usually result in death. The exception is drowning in very cold water, in which the body's oxygen demand is greatly reduced; persons have been revived after being submerged for one-half hour in cold water.

Human Intervention. Because of the danger of even short periods without oxygen, artificial respiration should always be started immediately. The mouth-to-mouth method, shown to be superior to the back-pressure and arm-lift procedure, is now recommended by the American Red Cross. In the mouth-to-mouth method the unconscious person is placed on his or her back with the head tilted as far back as possible to prevent the tongue from blocking the air passages. The victim's nose is then pinched shut, and the reviver's mouth is placed tightly over the victim's and gives four quick, deep breaths. If breathing does not resume, the reviver proceeds to give one breath each five seconds, allowing the air to come out of the victim's lungs between breaths. This is continued until the victim resumes breathing or until trained help arrives. If the unconscious person is a baby or small child, both the mouth and nose are covered with the reviver's mouth, and small puffs of air are breathed out to the victim at the rate of one every three seconds.

To restore breathing to a person who is choking, a rescuer gives four quick blows between the shoulder blades with the heel of the hand. If this does not dislodge the obstruction, the rescuer uses the stomach thrust, popularly called the Heimlich maneuver after its developer, the American physician Henry Jay Heimlich (1920-). The rescuer places the side of the fist against the victim's stomach, below the ribs and above the navel. Then, using the other hand, she or he thrusts the fist up into the stomach forcefully four times. With children, a rescuer first turns the child head-down and slaps the back. In using the Heimlich maneuver with children, only the first, and not the second hand, is used.

A type of respiratory first aid that requires special training is called cardiopulmonary resuscitation (CPR). In this procedure, which is used for a person who has had a heart attack, the reviver breathes for the victim and at the same time performs external massage on the person's chest to keep blood moving through the body. This technique is more easily done by two trained persons, one performing each maneuver. *See also* First Aid.

Respirators. Mechanical devices for the administration of artificial respiration include a portable resuscitator used by police and fire departments and the iron lung for persons whose respiratory nerves were destroyed by poliomyelitis (q.v.). The iron lung consists of a large tank that encloses all the patient's body except the head. A motor varies the pressure inside the tank to cause air to move into and out of the patient's lungs. An external respirator called a heart-lung machine is used to maintain oxygen saturation in the blood during open-heart surgery. Severe breathing difficulties may require help from a mechanical ventilator, which forces air into the lungs by way of a tube inserted into the upper airway through the nose, mouth, or a slit in the trachea. Comatose patients dependent on such a respirator for more than 30 days may not resume spontaneous breathing. In the much-publicized case of Karen Anne Quinlan (1954–85) in 1976, the New Jersey Supreme Court ruled that a mechanical respirator could be disconnected under certain conditions so that the comatose patient could "die with dignity." Normal breathing resumed, and the patient lived; nevertheless a precedent was established for the removal of life-support respirators in the absence of electrical activity in the brain cortex.

ARTIGAS, José Gervasio (1764–1850), Uruguayan soldier and national hero, born in Montevideo. Early in his career he became captain of a corps in the Spanish provincial service. He remained loyal to Spain for some time after the outbreak of the insurrection against Spanish rule in the Rio de la Plata viceroyalty. In 1811, however, he joined the revolutionary forces and became the first leader of the fight for Uruguayan independence. The patriot units under his command won a series of victories over the Spanish, but the victories did not result in independence for Uruguay. In 1813 he organized an independent force of gauchos, or cattle drivers, and tried to force the Buenos Aires junta to recognize Uruguay as one of a federation of La Plata states. He failed in this effort, but he liberated Montevideo from Buenos Aires control in 1815, thereby ensuring Uruguayan independence. Artigas then became ruler of Uruguay. He was defeated in 1817 by the Portuguese, who seized Montevideo. After another Portuguese victory over his army, in 1820, he went into permanent exile in Paraguay.

ARTILLERY, general military term referring to large weapons and rocket launchers. Artillery also describes the section or branch of an army that employs these weapons.

The Romans and others in the ancient world used catapults and ballistae as artillery to hurl rocks and other projectiles at enemy fortifications and formations. The first gunpowder weapons appeared in Europe early in the 14th century. Firing rocks, iron balls, or large, arrow-shaped bolts, artillery was often more successful in creating fear in enemy ranks than in inflicting actual damage. The first artillery pieces were notoriously unreliable. A gunner's life was especially hazardous, as artillery had a tendency to explode upon firing. Advances in casting gun barrels or tubes improved effectiveness and the artillery quickly earned a preeminent place in the major armies of the time.

Initially, land artillery was divided into three types: the gun, mortar, and howitzer (which shares some characteristics of both guns and mortars). Traditionally, the term *cannon* has been synonymous with guns and howitzers.

Guns. The gun is a long-tubed cannon that fires a projectile at a high velocity in a flat arc or trajectory. At first the damage it inflicted was the result of the weight of the projectile and its speed. Later developments included special shot for use against ships and canister, or case, shot—antipersonnel shells that filled the air with flying metal. In modern war, the projectile carries a high explosive charge that bursts on contact or after it penetrates the target. Projectiles to pierce armor are designed to transmit great force against a small section of the target. Shrapnel (q.v.) shells, the main artillery projectile through World War I, were filled with metal balls and could be set to explode at a predetermined time. The introduction of rifling (spiral grooves) to smoothbore cannons in the mid-19th century gave guns greater accuracy. A projectile fired through a rifled tube spins on its long axis generating a gyroscopic force that stabilizes its flight. The substitution of breech-loading for muzzle-loading allowed weapons to be loaded more quickly and fired more often. Today guns are used on modern warships and armored combat vehicles or tanks. *See* CANNON; *see also* PROJECTILE.

Mortars. The mortar, perhaps the first form of gunpowder weapon, is a smoothbore piece with a short barrel; it fires its shells in a high arc. Instead of relying primarily on the velocity of the projectile to penetrate obstacles, the shells pass over and fall behind them. At first, mortars caused damage by the weight of their shells alone; often heavy rocks were their sole ammunition. Before long, hollow shells filled with powder were used. These had fuses that were either lit before firing or that lit when the charge went off. The projectiles could be set to explode just before reaching the ground, giving a shrapnel effect. Charges set to go off after the shells embedded themselves in the ground could destroy protected arsenals, undermine walls, or collapse trenches. Modern mortars, still muzzle-loaded, consist of a light tube into which shells with propellant charges attached are dropped. Mortars are particularly suited to guerrilla warfare. Their high-angle fire is effective against small targets concealed in difficult terrain; they are easily transported and simple to operate.

Howitzers. Originally a compromise weapon, the howitzer used a medium-length tube to fire a mid-velocity projectile along a curved trajectory. By firing at a low angle, howitzers could achieve adequate range; at a high angle, they had the effects of a mortar. With modern artillery, differences between guns and howitzers are less distinct. Howitzers are now equipped with longer tubes and fire a variety of munitions at ranges formerly covered by field guns. Light howitzers usually are mounted on a wheeled carriage that can be towed by a small truck, airlifted by helicopter, or dropped from an airplane with a parachute. With advances in accuracy and lethality, these weapons are more efficient than heavy howitzers and field guns.

Rockets. At the beginning of the 19th century a fourth type of artillery weapon came into use. Although the employment of the rocket (q.v.) to stampede the opposing ranks' horses or elephants may be ancient, it was in 1804 that Sir William Congreve (1772–1828), an English ordnance officer and inventor, adapted the skyrocket to modern warfare. The use of a metal casing and a centered tail gave it greater durability and increased range and made it easier to launch. Before World War II the weapon found only sporadic battlefield use. By the end of that conflict, rocket-type artillery included unguided antiaircraft weapons; recoilless rifles; and the German V-2 rocket with a range of 350 km (220 mi), which left the earth's atmosphere during its high-arc flight to the target. Modern rockets can

Chinook helicopters transport 155 mm-howitzers of the 8th Artillery Regiment of the U.S. Army's 101st Airborne Division. They were preparing for the ground offensive in northern Saudi Arabia near the Iraqi border in February 1991. Bill Gentile–Sipa Press

be fired in rapid succession from multiple rocket launchers. These weapons can, accurately and at great ranges, launch free rockets and guided missiles (q.v.) armed with warheads.

Artillery Deployment. Changes in weaponry produced changes in warfare tactics. Guns and mortars were at first used primarily against fortified cities because their great weight prevented them from being used in mobile warfare. Not until the late 15th century did the French effectively use wheeled cannon in battle. For nearly another three centuries artillery was attached to the infantry forces. From Napoleon's time, artillery came into its own as a mobile supporting force in warfare. Used in batteries of many guns, massed fire was employed to destroy attacking enemy formations or disrupt defending forces before launching an attack. Mobile horse-drawn artillery could be shifted from place to place on a battlefield.

During World War I, massed artillery fire denied both sides the ability to maneuver forces, a condition that led to a stalemate of trench warfare. World War II saw a return to maneuver tactics with the advent of tanks and tracked personnel carriers, but the artillery has continued to be the most destructive force on the battlefield.

Recent Developments. In recent conflicts such as the wars in Korea and Vietnam, artillery has provided the preponderance of fire support for ground forces. Cannon artillery delivers close-in supporting fire with antiarmor and antipersonnel munitions. Examples include laser-guided projectiles that can destroy moving tanks and munitions that dispense antipersonnel/antiarmor bomblets. "Beehive" projectiles are canisters filled with hundreds of small darts that are employed against massed personnel at close range. U.S. Army medium howitzers are capable of firing chemical and nuclear munitions along with scatterable mines. Artillery rockets and missiles can cover battlefields out to extended distances with conventional and nuclear fire. Recent advances in on-board computers and self-locating capabilities enable modern cannons and rocket launchers to use so-called shoot-and-scoot tactics: individual cannons and launchers now move autonomously around the battlefield, stopping to shoot, and then quickly moving to a new firing position. In the near future, artillery cannon and launchers will deliver what are called "smart" munitions. These are projectiles and warheads that can locate and home-in on stationary or moving targets using sophisticated sensors and seekers. These munitions are referred to as "fire-and-forget" because they do not have to be updated in flight. Conventional smart munitions, along with nuclear capability, will ensure the artillery an even greater importance in the armies of the future. E.C.C.

For further information on this topic, see the Bibliography in volume 28, section 282.

ARTILLERY COMPANY, ANCIENT AND HONORABLE, oldest military organization in the U.S., established in Boston, Massachusetts Bay Colony, in 1637 as the Military Company of Boston. It was composed of the leading citizens of Boston and adjacent towns. The company took an active part in the American Revolution. Although its functions are now mainly social, the company holds military drills and participates in various ceremonial events. Headquarters is in Boston.

ARTIODACTYL (Gr. *artios,* "even"; *dactylos,* "finger" or "toe"), any member of the order of hoofed mammals, Artiodactyla, including cattle, pigs, goats, giraffes, camels, deer, antelopes, and hippopotamuses. A majority of species in the order are native to Africa, but they are well represented in North and South America, Europe, and Asia. Australia has no native artiodactyls.

Artiodactyls support their weight on the tips of two toes. Their remote ancestors had five toes. Through evolutionary modification, the first toe has disappeared; the second and fifth toes are only vestigial (nonfunctional) remnants and are located higher up on the foot than the terminal toes on which the animals stand. The vestigial toes, sometimes called dewclaws, serve no purpose except in pigs and caribou, preventing them from sinking into soft ground. Each of the two large, supporting toes of artiodactyls—the third and fourth—terminates in a hoof. The deceptive appearance of these two hooves gave rise to the biblical term *cloven hoof,* which suggests erroneously that the two hooves derive from a single large hoof. The hippopotamus, unique among artiodactyls, has four toes of equal size and width.

Artiodactyls feed almost exclusively on vegetation, and although they lack upper incisors and upper canine teeth, they have a pad in the upper jaw against which the lower teeth can operate. Although most males have horns or antlers, artiodactyls rely mainly on speed and keen senses to protect them from predators.

Artiodactyla was first classified as a separate order by the British comparative anatomist Richard Owen (1804–92) in 1847. The order has three suborders, the Suiformes, Tylopoda, and Ruminantia. The Suiformes are all those that do not chew cud, such as pigs. The Tylopoda, or cud chewers, include camels and llamas. The Ruminantia are true cud chewers with no upper front teeth. They consist of the Tragulina, which are represented by the chevrotains (small, hornless, deerlike animals) and antelope, cattle, deer, and giraffe.

The posters of the Czech-born designer Alphonse Mucha, such as this one for a play starring Sarah Bernhardt, exemplify many Art Nouveau characteristics: "whiplash" curves in the costume and the background; the twisted, exaggerated pose; opulent accoutrements such as the jeweled belt and dagger; and grotesque motifs such as the dragon. Joseph Martin–Scala

ART NOUVEAU, literally "new art," a complex and innovative European art movement of the last two decades of the 1800s and the first decade of the 1900s. It found expression in a wide range of art forms—architecture, interior design, furniture, posters, glass, pottery, textiles (qq.v.), and book illustration—and was characterized by its devotion to curving and undulating lines, often referred to as whiplash lines. The term Art Nouveau is derived from Maison de l'Art Nouveau, a Paris shop opened in 1896 by the dealer Siegfried Bing (1838–1905).

Art Nouveau had its roots in the Arts and Crafts movement (q.v.) in England (founded in 1861 by the designer William Morris), which vehemently rejected the sterile revival styles in contemporaneous architecture and the graceless examples of applied art that resulted from mass-production techniques. Art Nouveau took up and elaborated the Arts and Crafts manifesto, calling for the creation of a completely new style with no reference to current or revivalist styles. Art Nouveau borrowed motifs from sources as varied as Japanese prints, Gothic architecture, and the symbolic paintings of the English poet and artist William Blake to create a highly decorative style with strong elements of fantasy.

The earliest examples of Art Nouveau are usually considered the work of the English architect Arthur Mackmurdo (1851–1942), particularly a chair designed in 1882 and an engraved frontispiece for a book (*Wren's Early Churches*) in 1883, both of which exhibit the sinuous flowing lines that were to become Art Nouveau hallmarks. The fabric designs sold by Arthur Liberty (1843–1917) in his famous London shop (founded 1875) and the illustrations of Aubrey Beardsley—particularly those for the periodical *The Yellow Book* (1894) and for the English writer Oscar Wilde's *Salomé* (1894)—carried English Art Nouveau to its height. Annual exhibitions of the Arts and Crafts Exhibition Society, beginning in 1888, helped disseminate the style, and a new magazine, *The Studio* (founded 1893), helped spread it to Europe.

Art Nouveau first appeared in Belgium with the work of the architects Victor Horta and Henri van de Velde; their designs for townhouses proliferated, with elegantly twining wrought-iron staircases, balconies, gates, and wall decorations. In France, the style was most evident in the work of the architect Hector Guimard (particularly the exotic Parisian Métro subway entrances, 1898–1901), the glassmaker Émile Gallé (1846–1904), the furniture designer Louis Majorelle (1859–1926), and the poster artist Alphonse Mucha; it was also fashionable in interior decor, notably at Maxim's Restaurant in Paris. In Munich, as the Jugendstil ("youth style"), and in Vienna, as the Sezessionstil, it permeated applied art and magazine illustration and reached a peak in the paintings of Gustav Klimt and the furniture and architectural designs of Josef Hoffmann. In the U.S., the leading figure was Louis Comfort Tiffany, whose shimmering Favrile-glass vases and stained-glass lampshades were fantasies of iridescence. In Spain, Art Nouveau had perhaps its most original practitioner, Antoni Gaudí; his highly idiosyncratic parks and apartment buildings in Barcelona have no straight lines and give the impression of being natural organisms that have sprung from the earth.

Art Nouveau was in decline by 1910 and did not outlive World War I, being succeeded by the sleekly elegant Art Deco (q.v.) style. It had never been a popular or widespread style, since the best works were costly and unsuited to mass manufacture, and it fell into disfavor until its rediscovery in the 1960s. Art Nouveau was, however, a pivotal development in the history of art, particularly in architecture. By clearing away the moribund influences of the 19th century, its practitioners helped prepare the way for the advent of modern art and architecture.

ARTOIS, former province in northern France, almost corresponding with the modern department of Pas-de-Calais. The provincial capital was Arras. Both the province and its capital were named for the Atrebates, an ancient Gallic tribe that lived in the area. Artois belonged to the counts of Flanders during the Middle Ages. In 1237 Louis IX, king of France, made it a county. It was a possession of Burgundy, of Austria, and then of Spain until 1640, when King Louis XIII of France conquered it.

In World War I, Artois was the scene of an Allied offensive intended to dislodge the Germans from strategic centers, such as the city of Lens in the northern part of the region. Arras was the springboard of the attack, which lasted from May to July 1915. Casualties were high on both sides. The French took Lens in June, but the Germans regained their earlier holdings and continued to threaten Arras until the unsuccessful German offensive and subsequent retreat of 1918, when Lens was finally taken by the Allies.

ARTS AND CRAFTS MOVEMENT, art movement of the last half of the 19th century that strove to revitalize handicrafts and applied arts during an era of increasing mass production.

The movement coalesced in 1861, when the English designer William Morris founded the firm of Morris, Marshall, & Faulkner. Arguing that the true basis of art lay in the crafts, Morris and his followers attacked the sterility and ugliness of machine-made products; his firm promoted handmade textiles, books, wallpaper, and furniture. Around him grew a circle of other artisans, notably the architects Philip Webb (1831–1915) and C. F. A. Voysey (known for his "cottage" style), the cabinetmaker Ernest Gimson (1864–1919), the potter William De Morgan (1839–1917), and the designers Walter Crane and C. R. Ashbee (1863–1942). The Arts and Crafts Exhibition Society (founded 1888) and the magazines *The Studio* and *Hobby Horse* provided forums for the dissemination of the movement's ideas.

In Scotland, Glasgow became a lively center of the movement in the 1890s, under the leadership of the brilliantly innovative architect Charles Rennie Mackintosh. In Vienna, the movement was the inspiration for the craft-oriented Wiener Werkstätte (Vienna Workshop). In the U.S. it led to the establishment of notable craft workshops and exhibition societies, while the mission style in furniture and architecture carried arts and crafts ideals up to the years of World War I.

The movement was the principal forerunner of the Art Nouveau (q.v.) style, and, in its emphasis on plain materials and surfaces, it was one of the dominant sources of 20th-century modernism.

See also BOOKBINDING; FURNITURE; POTTERY.

ARTSYBASHEV, Mikhail Petrovich (1878–1927), Russian novelist, born in Ukraine. His series of short stories, begun in 1901, dramatize Russian revolutionary movements. His major work, the macabre, erotic novel *Sanine* (1907; trans. 1915), achieved sensational but short-lived acclaim. In 1921 Artsybashev's works were banned, and he was exiled from the Soviet Union. His other writings include the novel *The Breaking Point* (1912; trans. 1915) and the play *War* (1917; trans. 1918).

ARUBA, island, West Indies, in the Caribbean Sea, near the Paraguaná Peninsula of Venezuela. The island, one of the Lesser Antilles islands, was granted home rule by the Netherlands in 1986 (*see* NETHERLANDS ANTILLES). It is about 30 km (about 19 mi) long and about 8 km (about 5 mi) wide. Tourism and the refining of crude oil, which is imported from Venezuela, are the chief industries. Oranjestad, at the W end of the island, is the principal town and the seat of the University of Aruba. Aruba is scheduled to achieve independence in 1996. Area, 193 sq km (75 sq mi); pop. (1988 est.) 62,500.

ARUM, common name for the family Araceae, comprising about 2000 species of mostly herbaceous flowering plants, and for its representative genus *Arum.* The family is worldwide in distribution, and several species produce edible,

Green jack-in-the-pulpit, Arisaema triphyllum

starch-rich underground stems (*see* TARO). Many are grown as ornamentals.

The arum, or aroid, family consists primarily of herbs with a distinctive inflorescence (flower cluster): a large, often showy bract (the spathe) subtending and sometimes surrounding the spadix, a group of small, individually inconspicuous flowers borne on an elongated axis. Foul scents emitted by some inflorescences attract carrion flies, which then become trapped within the spathe and carry out pollination.

The aroid family is mainly tropical, although some Temperate Zone members occur, including the jack-in-the-pulpit, *Arisaema triphyllum,* and skunk cabbage, *Symplocarpus foetidus.* Of the 100 or so genera in the family, more than half are cultivated, mostly for their attractive foliage or spathes. Many are successful houseplants because they are preadapted to severe conditions, being derived from tropical epiphytes, plants that grow on others for support but not for nutrients. The epiphytic habitat is similar to the home environment; it is shaded, far from the ground, and thus low in humidity, and it depends on watering from rains rather than from moisture in the soil. Among well-known aroids are *Anthurium* (including *A. andraeanum,* flame lily), *Caladium, Colocasia* (elephant's ear), *Monstera, Philodendron,* and *Zantedeschia* (garden calla).

The family belongs to the order Arales, which also contains the duckweed family, Lemnaceae, small aquatic herbs that often float on the water's surface. The smallest plant known, *Wolffia,* scarcely 1 mm (about 4/100 in) in length, belongs to this group. A third family, Acoraceae, contains the genus *Acorus,* formerly placed in the family Araceae.

Plants of the order Arales are members of the class Liliopsida (*see* MONOCOTS) in the division Magnoliophyta (*see* ANGIOSPERM). M.R.C.

ARUNDEL, Thomas (1353–1414), English prelate, born in Sussex of a noble family. He was made bishop of Ely in 1374, archbishop of York in 1388, and archbishop of Canterbury in 1396. He served as lord chancellor three times during the reign of Richard II, king of England, but in 1397 he was exiled for working to depose the king. When Henry of Bolingbroke successfully revolted against Richard and became King Henry IV of England, Arundel returned as archbishop of Canterbury and crowned (1399) the new king. He vigorously guarded the rights and property of the church against attempts by Parliament to limit them; he was also active in the persecution of the Lollards (q.v.).

ARUSHA, city, NE Tanzania, capital of Arusha Region, on the slopes of Mt. Meru. It is a manufacturing center and the processing and shipping hub of a region in which pyrethrum, sisal, and coffee are produced. Manufactures include plastics, radios, and meerschaum pipes. The city is the terminus of a railroad that links it to the Indian Ocean ports of Tanga, Tanzania, and Mombasa, Kenya. Arusha also serves as a tourist gateway to Olduvai Gorge and the scenic national parks of N Tanzania. Located here is the Tropical Pesticides Research Institute (1962). Pop. (1978 est.) 88,155.

ARUWIMI, river, NE Zaire, rising W of Lake Albert and flowing SW to the Congo R., at Basoko. The river, 998 km (620 mi) long, is known as the Ituri in its upper course, where it traverses the Ituri Forest, a dense tropical forest inhabited by Mbuti Pygmies and Bantu-speaking Africans. The lower Aruwimi is navigable to Yambuya, near Banalia. Sir Henry M. Stanley, an Anglo-American, explored much of the river in 1887–88.

ARVADA, city, Jefferson and Adams counties, central Colorado, a residential suburb of Denver; settled 1868, inc. as a city 1963. It was a farming and flour-milling center until the 1940s, when large-scale housing construction began. Communications and aerospace research and production also form a large portion of the city's economic base. Pop. (1980) 84,576; (1990) 89,235.

ARYABHATA, also Aryabhatta (476–550?), Hindu astronomer and mathematician, born in Pataliputra (modern Patna, India). He was known to the Arabs as Arjehir, and his writings had considerable influence on Arabic science. Aryabhata held that the earth rotates on its axis, and he gave the correct explanation of eclipses of the sun and the moon. In mathematics he solved the quadratic equation, although many of his geometric formulas were incorrect. His only extant work is the *Aryabhatiya,* a series of astronomical and mathematical rules and propositions, written in Sanskrit verse.

ARYAN LANGUAGES. *See* INDO-EUROPEAN LANGUAGES.

ARYA SAMAJ (Skt., "Assembly of the Ancient Nobles"), Hindu religious sect founded in 1875 by Swami Dayananda Sarasvati. An attempt to reform Hinduism by synthesizing ancient Eastern ideas (the Vedas) with modern Western ideas (natural sciences), it argued that the Vedas, the earliest Hindu scriptures, were the only revelation from God and that they were the basis of all science. All Hindus were exhorted to return to the Vedas and to preach them throughout the world. The actual text of the *Rig-Veda,* one of the four collections of the Vedas, was reinterpreted loosely, to explain many anachronisms (such as steam engines) and incorporate much post-Vedic thought. After the founder's death in 1883, the Arya Samaj split into two sections, one with headquarters at Lahore, the other at Hardwar. W.D.O.

ASAHIKAWA, city, Japan, central Hokkaido Island, in Hokkaido Prefecture, in the scenic upper Ishikari R. valley. The city is a rail junction in a rice-growing and lumbering area, and machinery, textiles, chemicals, ceramic goods, wood pulp, and sake are manufactured here. Daisetsu-Zan National Park is nearby. The name of the city is sometimes spelled Asahigawa. Pop. (1988 est.) 362,500.

ASAMA *or* **ASAMAYAMA,** volcano, Japan, central Honshu Island, 2542 m (8340 ft) high, the largest active in the country. The earliest recorded eruption occurred in 1650. A severe eruption in 1783 destroyed several villages and primeval forest. Since then it has only erupted in showers of ashes and stones. Its crater is circular in shape and measures about 1.2 km (about 0.75 mi) in circumference.

ASANSOL, city, NE India, in West Bengal State, in the Damodar R. valley. A rail junction, the city is the center of the Raniganj coalfield. Industries include iron and steel milling and the manufacture of bricks, tile, and furniture. Asansol is also the site of an electrical engineering works and one of the principal locomotive shops in India. Coal mines and aluminum-extraction plants are nearby. Pop. (1981 prelim., greater city) 365,371.

ASBESTOS (Gr. *a-,* "not"; *sbestos,* "extinguishable"), the fibrous form of several minerals and hydrous silicates of magnesium. The name may also be applied to the fibrous forms of calcium and iron. Asbestos fibers can be molded or woven into various fabrics. Because it is nonflammable and a poor heat conductor, asbestos has been widely used to make fireproof products such as safety clothing for fire fighters and insulation products such as hot-water piping. The first recorded use of the word *asbestos* is by Pliny the Elder in the 1st century AD, although the substance itself was known as early as the 2d century BC. The Romans made cremation cloths and wicks from it, and centuries later Marco Polo noted its usefulness as cloth.

Asbestos is of two principal classes, the amphiboles and the serpentines, the former of relatively minor importance. Chrysotile, in the serpentine class, constitutes about 95 percent of the world supply of asbestos, of which three-fourths is mined in Québec. Other large deposits exist in South Africa. In the U.S., California, Vermont, and Arizona are the leading asbestos-producing states; however, the majority of U.S. deposits are of no commercial value.

Asbestos is obtainable by various underground mining methods, but the most common method is open-pit mining. Only about 6 percent of the mined ore contains usable fibers.

The fibers are separated from the ore by crushing, air suction, and vibrating screens, and in the process are sorted into different lengths, or grades. The most widely used method of grading, the Québec Standard Test Method, divides the fibers into seven groups, the longest in group one and the shortest, called milled asbestos, in group seven. The length of the fibers, as well as the chemical composition of the ore, determines the kind of product that can be made from the asbestos. The longer fibers have been used in fabrics, commonly with cotton or rayon, and the shorter ones for molded goods, such as pipes and gaskets.

Asbestos has been used in building-construction materials, textiles, missile and jet parts, asphalt and caulking compounds and paints, and in friction products such as brake linings. Exposure to asbestos fibers and dust, however, can cause asbestosis, a disease of the lungs caused by the inhalation of asbestos particles, and, after a latent period of up to 30 years and more, various cancers, especially lung cancer and mesothelioma, which is an inoperable cancer of the chest and abdominal lining (*see* OCCUPATIONAL AND ENVIRONMENTAL DISEASES). At present no wholly satisfactory substitutes are available for asbestos in many of its applications;

because of health risks posed by asbestos use, however, research into replacements has been accelerated. In 1986 the Environmental Protection Agency proposed an immediate ban on the major uses of asbestos and a complete ban on all asbestos products within the next decade.

ASBURY, Francis (1745–1816), first Methodist bishop ordained in America, born in Handsworth, Stafford Co., England, and largely self-educated. At the age of 18, he became a local preacher, and three years later was received by the evangelist John Wesley into the itinerant Methodist ministry. In October 1771, a few years after the establishment of the first Methodist church in America, Asbury came to Philadelphia as a missionary. At that time, the small number of Methodists in America lived in the middle colonies. Although Methodists were suspected of loyalty to Great Britain during the Revolution, Asbury sympathized with the American cause and became a citizen of Delaware. Because of his persuasive preaching and skillful organization, Methodist membership grew rapidly during the 1770s. In 1784 the several Wesleyan societies in the U.S. were organized into the Methodist Episcopal church, and Asbury and the British missionary Thomas Coke were elected joint superintendents. The next year Asbury assumed the title of bishop and devoted himself to preaching and supervising Methodist organization.

It is estimated that during his ministry Asbury traveled more than 434,522 km (270,000 mi), visiting every part of the country; he preached more than 16,000 sermons, ordained more than 4000 ministers, and presided at 224 conferences. The excellent organization and phenomenal growth of Methodism in the U.S. are due largely to his labors. Asbury's only written works are his journals (3 vol.; 1821).

ASBURY PARK, city, Monmouth Co., E New Jersey, on the Atlantic Ocean; inc. 1897. The city is a resort and convention center and contains some light industry; products include electronic equipment, printed materials, and textiles. The community was founded in 1870–71 as a summer resort for temperance advocates and is named for the Methodist Episcopal bishop Francis Asbury. Pop. (1980) 17,015; (1990) 16,799.

ASCALON. *See* ASHQELON.

ASCAP. *See* AMERICAN SOCIETY OF COMPOSERS, AUTHORS, AND PUBLISHERS.

ASCARIS, genus of parasitic worms in the nematode phylum (*see* ROUNDWORM). *Ascaris lumbricoides* is one of the four roundworms that infest humans, especially children. It lodges in the intestines, sometimes working its way into other parts of the body. It measures 15 to 25 cm (6 to 10 in) in length, is of a whitish color, and is pointed at both ends. The eggs develop in water or damp earth, and the embryos are probably directly swallowed. The worms can be expelled by means of purgatives. The genus includes many species that infest domestic and farm animals.

ASCENSION, small island, volcanic in origin, situated in the South Atlantic Ocean about midway between Africa and South America. It is part of the British dependency of Saint Helena. Ascension was discovered by the Portuguese in 1501, but it was uninhabited until the exile of Napoleon to St. Helena Island in 1815, when the British established a garrison here to guard against his escape. In 1922 the island was annexed to St. Helena. It served as a refueling base for U.S. aircraft in World War II. The U.S. built a station here in 1957 as a post for observing guided missiles. Huge numbers of sea turtles and sooty terns breed on the island. Georgetown is the main settlement. Area, 88 sq km (34 sq mi); pop. (1982) 1625.

ASCENSION, in Christian belief, the departure of Jesus Christ from the earth 40 days after his resurrection from the dead. The event is described as occurring in the presence of the apostles; Christ was lifted up and a cloud took him out of their sight. In some New Testament passages (see Mark 16:19–20; Luke 24:50–51; Acts 1:1–14) the ascension is represented as an observed historical fact. Other passages (see 1 Pet. 3:22; 1 Tim. 3:16, Heb. 4:14) stress its theological dimension. Its significance seems to center on the glorification of Christ and its service as a sign that his earthly mission had been fulfilled.

The Feast of the Ascension, one of the great festivals of Christianity, is observed on Thursday, 40 days after Easter. Artists have often depicted the theme in one of three ways: Christ ascending upon clouds toward the outstretched hand of God the Father, Christ being carried by angels, or Christ ascending by his own power.

ASCETICISM (Gr. *askesis,* "exercise"), practice of self-denial and renunciation of worldly pleasure in order to attain a higher degree of spirituality, intellectuality, or self-awareness. Among the ancient Greeks, the term originally denoted the training practiced by athletes and soldiers. In Greek philosophy, the adherents of Cynicism (*see* CYNICS) and Stoicism (q.v.) adopted the practice of mastering desire and passion. Asceticism is practiced to some extent by the adherents of every religion. It often requires abstinence from food, drink, or sexual activity, as in fasting or celibacy (q.v.). It may also require physical pain or discomfort, such as endurance of extreme heat or cold or self-punishment (*see* FLAGEL-

LANTS; SUFISM). It may require withdrawal from the material world to a life of meditation, as in the practice of Yoga (q.v.). *See also* BUDDHISM; HINDUISM; MONASTICISM; PENANCE.

ASCH, Sholem (1880–1957), Russian-born American writer, born in Kutno, Poland (then part of Russia), and educated at a rabbinical college. He moved to the U.S. in 1914. Early in his literary career Asch wrote in Hebrew; later he wrote primarily in Yiddish. All his important writings were published in English translation. *Salvation* (1934), probably his most significant work, expresses his faith, which transcends any religious creed. His success came largely from his ability to treat biblical figures in a style that was both reverential and realistic. The novels of Asch include *The Apostle* (1943), a life of St. Paul; *East River* (1946), about Jewish life in New York City; *Mary* (1949); and *Moses* (1951).

ASCHAM, Roger (1515–68), English scholar and author, born in Kirby Wiske, Yorkshire, and educated at Saint John's College, University of Cambridge. In 1540 he became the first professor of Greek at Cambridge. He published a popular treatise on archery called *Toxophilus* (1545). This work, which was a defense of physical recreation for scholars, was dedicated to King Henry VIII of England. The essay pleased the king, who granted the author an annual pension. Ascham was appointed tutor to Princess Elizabeth, later Queen Elizabeth I, in 1548. His instruction was at least partially responsible for her proficiency in Latin and Greek and her lifelong love of the classics. In 1550 Ascham traveled through Europe with a diplomatic mission. Thus, he was able to visit schools and scholars on the Continent. After returning to England in 1553, he became Latin secretary to the new queen, Mary I. Upon her death in 1558, he was appointed secretary to Queen Elizabeth, a post he held for the remainder of his life. Ascham, a major intellectual figure in Tudor England, was the author of several scholarly writings, including *The Scholemaster* (pub. posthumously, 1570).

ASCHELMINTHES, phylum or superphylum of common but inconspicuous, often microscopic worms. The name, which means "sac worm," refers to the aschelminth's fluid-filled cavity that serves as a kind of skeleton and that is called a pseudocoelom because it lacks the epithelial lining found in the coelom of more advanced animals. The body also lacks a circulatory system, but has a gut and anus.

Aschelminthes frequently live in water or soil or as parasites of plants or animals. The classes (or phyla) include Nematoda (roundworms), Nematomorpha (hairworms), Kinorhyncha, Gastrotricha, Rotifera (wheel animalcules, or rotifers), and Priapulida. Other pseudocoelomates that are probably closely related to the aschelminthes are the spiny-headed worm and the moss animals (qq.v.).

See also ANIMAL. M.T.G.

ASCLEPIADES (fl. 1st cent. BC), Greek physician, native of the ancient country of Bithynia in Asia Minor. He was a teacher of oratory in Rome, but later took up the practice of medicine. He believed that the movement of atoms in the body caused disease, and he advocated baths, dieting, exercise, and massage as cures. His numerous followers founded a school of medicine known as the Methodical.

ASCLEPIUS, in Greek mythology, the god of medicine. He was a son of the god Apollo and Coronis, a beautiful maiden of Thessaly. Angry because Coronis was unfaithful to him, Apollo killed her and took his infant son to the centaur Chiron to be raised. Asclepius learned all that Chiron knew about the art of healing and soon became a great physician. Because he committed the unpardonable sin of raising a man from the

A Roman statue of Asclepius, the Greek god of medicine, often represented with a staff and serpent.

dead, the god Zeus killed him with a thunderbolt. For hundreds of years after his death, the sick visited the many temples built in his honor. There they offered sacrifices and prayed to Asclepius, who, they believed, would come to them in dreams and prescribe cures for their illnesses.

ASCOMYCOTA. *See* FUNGI.

ASCORBIC ACID. *See* VITAMIN.

ASGARD, in Norse mythology, the abode of the gods. Access to Asgard was possible only by crossing the bridge Bifrost (the rainbow). Asgard was divided into 12 or more realms in which each principal god had his own luxurious mansion of gold or silver. The most important palace was Valhalla, the home of Odin, the chief of the gods.

ASH, solid residue of combustion. If combustion has been complete, the ash will be entirely inorganic.

The ash from wood or similar plant material generally consists principally of sodium carbonate and potassium carbonate; for centuries wood ash was the principal source of potassium for making such chemicals as saltpeter. As recently as World War I, it was an important potassium source for the U.S. The ash content of dry wood varies from 2 percent by weight for balsa to 0.2 percent for redwood (sequoia).

The ash of animal bones consists primarily of calcium phosphate. For many years bones were a principal source of phosphorus, and ground bone, or bone meal, is still used as fertilizer for its phosphorus and calcium content. Mineral deposits of calcium phosphate are now exploited, but much of this was formed from the bones of prehistoric animals. Ash from the burning of sea plants is a common source of iodine.

The content of ash in coal varies from as little as 3 percent by weight for some subbituminous coal to as much as 28 percent for some cannel coal. Its composition may also vary greatly; coal ash contains sodium and potassium carbonates and large quantities of silicate in combination with a wide variety of metals. The composition of the ash determines the fusion point of the ash, that is, the temperature at which it forms clinker, or slag. This may vary from below 1093° C (2000° F) to above 1649° C (3000° F), the lower fusion temperatures generally being found in coal with high silica content.

All the inorganic constituents of food are referred to collectively as ash, although some of them can actually be volatilized by burning the food. Such ash contains the minerals essential to the maintenance of life, of which the most important are calcium, chlorine, iodine, iron, phosphorus, potassium, sodium, and sulfur.

White ash, Fraxinus americana

ASH, common name for any member of the genus *Fraxinus,* of the family Oleaceae (*see* OLIVE), comprising about 70 species of mostly northern temperate trees and shrubs. Ashes are valued for timber and ornament. Characteristic of the group are the small, inconspicuous greenish flowers, usually borne in clusters with or without sepals and petals. These appear in early spring and produce dry, single-winged fruits called samaras. The finely toothed leaves are opposite on the stems and are compound, bearing an odd number of leaflets. The white, or American, ash (*F. americana*), European ash (*F. excelsior*), and Siebold ash (*F. sieboldiana*) of Asia are valuable sources of woods used in cabinetry. The flowering, or manna, ash (*F. ornus*), notable for its long petals, is cultivated in Mediterranean regions for its sweet gum (*see* MANNA). In North America, ashes have been subject for several years to a disease that usually kills a stricken tree in ten years. No preventative has been found for the disease, which may be caused by a leafhopper-borne mycoplasma.

Mountain ash is an unrelated tree of family Rosaceae (*see* ROSE). The prickly ash, also called Hercules'-club, belongs to the family Rutaceae (*see* RUE).

ASHANTI, Negroid people of the Twi (Tshi) linguistic stock, living principally in the Ashanti region of Ghana. In anthropology the Ashanti people are generally classified as a pure Negroid racial type. The people are composed of numerous tribes, notably the Juabin, Mampon, Ofinsu, Nkwanta, Adansi, Daniassi, Nsuta, and Kumasi. Features of Ashanti tribal organization include ruling chieftains and common ownership of land. Ashanti religion is a mixture of animism and ancestor worship, and until relatively recent times human sacrifice was practiced. Renowned as warriors and as artisans—especially in cotton weaving, pottery making, and the manufacture of gold and silver ornaments—the Ashanti also are skillful farmers.

ASHANTI, administrative region, central Ghana. The population of the region is predominantly Ashanti; the capital and largest city is Kumasi. Commercial products include cacao, timber, and bauxite.

The Ashanti tribes, which had confederated into a kingdom early in the 18th century, sought to extend their dominion over the Fanti tribes of the coast. From 1807 to 1826 their intrusions involved them in wars with Great Britain, which had established forts along the coast in Fanti territory. Traditional enmity with the Fanti and the refusal of the British to yield up a fugitive slave led to the Ashanti-British war of 1873–74, during which Kumasi was burned. Years of turmoil followed. Prempeh I (1872–1931), who was chosen king, or paramount chief, in 1888, was defeated and captured in 1896 after a series of wars against Great Britain and later was exiled to the Seychelles Islands. Ashanti was annexed to the Gold Coast Colony in 1901. Great Britain continued to rule through tribal chiefs, however, and Prempeh was finally restored to the position of paramount chief in 1926 in recognition of the loyalty of the Ashanti people to the Allies in World War I. From 1934, when the government of the Gold Coast Colony was reorganized, until 1957, when Ashanti was included in the newly formed country of Ghana, Ashanti was administered by a chief commissioner. Area, 25,123 sq km (9700 sq mi); pop. (1984) 2,090,100.

ASHCAN SCHOOL. *See* AMERICAN ART AND ARCHITECTURE.

ASHE, Arthur Robert, Jr. (1943–), American tennis player, born in Richmond, Va. In 1966, upon his graduation from the University of California at Los Angeles, Ashe was commissioned second lieutenant in the U.S. Army Reserve and during his period of active service was stationed at the U.S. Military Academy. He was the first black to win a major men's tennis tournament. Among his important tournament championships are the U.S. national intercollegiate (1965), the U.S. clay-court (1967), and the first U.S. open (1968). In 1969 Ashe became a professional player. In 1975 he won the Wimbledon (England) and the World Court championships and in 1977 the Australian Open Doubles. As the result of a heart condition, Ashe retired from competition in 1980. He is the author of *A Hard Road to Glory: A History of the Afro-American Athlete* (3 vols., 1989).

ASHEVILLE, city, seat of Buncombe Co., W North Carolina, at the confluence of the French Broad and Swannanoa rivers; inc. 1882. Situated on a high plateau between the Blue Ridge and Great Smoky mountains, Asheville is a commercial and manufacturing center and a mountain resort. Manufactures in the city include textiles, electronic equipment, precision instruments, forest products, and processed food. The city is headquarters for the Blue Ridge Parkway and three national forests. Tourist attractions include the boyhood home of the American writer Thomas Wolfe, and Biltmore, a large estate built by the American agriculturist and philanthropist George W. Vanderbilt (1862–1914). The University of North Carolina at Asheville (1927) and a community college are located here. Asheville is named for Samuel Ashe (1725–1813), who was governor of North Carolina in the 1790s. Pop. (1980) 53,281; (1990) 61,607.

ASHI (352–427), rabbi and Hebrew scholar, born in Babylon. At an early age he became the head of the rabbinical school in Sura, Babylonia. He is known primarily for his attempt to gather the discussions of the rabbis on the Mishnah (sayings and decisions of rabbis before the 3d cent.) into a compilation known as the Gemara. The Gemara and the Mishnah together constitute the body of Jewish law, the Talmud. Although he worked at this task for more than 50 years, it was left for his successors to complete.

ASHIKAGA, Japanese family that occupied the office of shogun ("great general") from 1338 to 1573; this time is called the Muromachi period, because the shogun's palace was in the Muromachi district of Kyoto. The dynasty's founder, Takauji (1305–58), rebelled against Emperor Daigo II (1287–1339), setting up a rival emperor at Kyoto in 1336. Civil war continued until 1392, when one of Daigo's successors renounced his claim to the throne. The Ashikaga then tried to reunify the country, but were unable to control fully the daimyo (local feudal lords). Wars among the daimyo became common by the 16th century, which is known as the Epoch of a Warring Country. The Ashikaga shogunate was finally brought down by the daimyo Oda Nobunaga.

ASHIKAGA, city, Japan, central Honshu Island, in Tochigi Prefecture. The city has an extensive trade in cotton and silk textiles. Famous for an academy of Chinese learning, believed to have been founded in the 9th century, it contains a vast library of Chinese literature and is a world-famous center of Chinese culture and Confucianism. Pop. (1987 est.) 168,200.

ASHKELON. *See* ASHQELON.

ASHKENAZIM, one of the two major groupings of Jews by geographical origin and the corresponding cultural tradition. The term distinguishes the medieval Jewish communities of central and eastern Europe and their descendants from those of the Iberian Peninsula and North Africa, known as Sephardim. In the 10th century, the biblical eponym Ashkenaz (see Gen. 10:3) was used by Jews as the Hebrew name for Germany, where a distinctive Jewish community was emerging. From the Rhineland, Ashkenazic Jews moved eastward into Poland during the 15th and 16th centuries; many of them migrated to North America and Israel during the 19th and 20th centuries. Most American Jews today are descendants of eastern European Ashkenazim. The Ashkenazim and Sephardim differ in their laws, customs, liturgy, and language. Yiddish (Judeo-German) is the traditional vernacular of the Ashkenazim; that of the Sephardim is Ladino (Judeo-Castilian). Today, about 85 percent of all Jews are Ashkenazim.
R.S.S.

ASHKHABAD, city, SW Turkmenistan, capital of the country, situated in an oasis near the Kara-Kum Desert and the border with Iran. It is known for its handwoven carpets; other manufactures include pumps, engines, glass, and textiles. Ashkhabad is the site of the Turkmen Academy of Sciences, a university, and a museum of fine arts. The city developed around a Russian fortress built in 1881 at the junction of caravan routes; major growth began when it became (1885) a station on the Trans-Caspian Railroad. In 1948 the city was almost totally destroyed by an earthquake. Pop. (1987 est.) 382,000.

ASHLAND, city, Boyd Co., NE Kentucky, on the Ohio R., part of a tristate metropolitan area also embracing Ironton, Ohio, and Huntington, W.Va.; inc. as a city 1870. Ashland is a commercial, manufacturing, and transportation center situated in a coal, clay, natural gas, and lumber producing region. Products of the city include iron and steel, coke, petroleum products, clothing, leather goods, and mining equipment. A community college is here. Settled in 1815, the community was known as Poage Settlement until 1850, when it was renamed for Ashland, the Lexington, Ky., home of the U.S. statesman Henry Clay. Pop. (1980) 27,064; (1990) 23,622.

ASHQELON, town of ancient Palestine, on the Mediterranean Sea. The site, which is marked by ruins, adjoins modern Ashqelon, a seaside resort in Israel, near Tel Aviv-Jaffa. Ashqelon was one of the five chief cities of the Philistines from about 1200 to 900 BC. It paid tribute to Solomon, king of Israel, and later fell to various invaders of Palestine. In 1099 European Crusaders under the French soldier Godfrey of Bouillon captured the city from the Arabs. Soon reconquered by the Muslims, it was taken in 1153, during the Second Crusade, by Baldwin III, king of Jerusalem. The Egyptian sultan Saladin recaptured it in 1187 but abandoned it four years later, first dismantling the fortifications. The destruction of the old city was completed in 1270 by the Mameluke sultan Baybars I. The name is also spelled Ashkelon or Ascalon. Pop. (1980) of modern Ashqelon, 53,100.

ASHTABULA, city, Ashtabula Co., NE Ohio, on Lake Erie, at the mouth of the Ashtabula R.; inc. as a city 1891. A port of entry on the Saint Lawrence Seaway, the city is an important transportation center for iron ore and coal. Major manufactures include fiberglass, plastics, and rubber products. A branch of Kent State University is located here as well as the Hubbard House, the end of the line on the underground railroad. The community was settled in 1801, and its name is derived from an Algonquian Indian term probably meaning "river of many fish." Pop. (1980) 23,449; (1990) 21,633.

ASHTON, Sir Frederick William Mallandaine (1904–88), British dancer and choreographer, who led the Royal Ballet to its esteemed international reputation. Born in Guayaquil, Ecuador, he saw the Russian ballerina Anna Pavlova perform when he was a child, and as a result traveled in the early 1920s to London, where he studied under the Russian-born choreographer Léonide Massine and the British dancer Marie Rambert. Ashton's first choreographies were encouraged and influenced by Rambert and the Russian-born choreographer Bronislava Nijinska (1891–1972). When he joined the Vic-Wells Ballet (later the Royal Ballet) in 1935, he not only established himself as an eminent choreographer and dancer but also began a long association with the British ballerina Margot Fonteyn, who created leading roles for many of his ballets. He was director of the Royal Ballet from 1963 to 1970, during which time some of his important creations were *Marguerite and Armand* (1963), which established the partnership of Fonteyn with the Soviet-born dancer Rudolf Nureyev; *Monotones* (1965–66); and *Enigma Variations* (1968). Later works include the solo for the British dancer Lynn Seymour (1939–), *Five Brahms Waltzes in the Manner of Isadora Duncan* (1975–76), and *Month in the Country* (1976).

ASHTON-WARNER, Sylvia (1905–84), New Zealand teacher and writer. She started writing while teaching Maori youngsters, the descendants of the original Polynesian inhabitants. Her early novels, *Spinster* (1958) and *Incense to Idols* (1960), bordered on the flamboyant, but the forceful, sensitive women portrayed in her novels attracted many readers. She received worldwide recognition with *Teacher* (1963), an account of her innovative teaching methods. After teaching in the U.S., she wrote *Spearpoint, "Teacher" in America* (1972), a critical commentary on television-influenced educational developments in the U.S.

ASHTORETH. *See* ASTARTE.

ASHUR, also Assur or Ashshur, earliest capital of Assyria, on the western bank of the Tigris River, south of Nineveh. The modern village of ash-Sharqat, Iraq, is on the site of Ashur. Systematic excavations of the ruins of Ashur were first undertaken in 1903–13. The city wall, according to an inscription, was built by Kikia, a king reigning probably in the earlier part of the 3d millennium BC. Enlarged by various rulers of Assyria, Ashur was a great center of the religious and political life of the nation. Even after Calah (modern Nimrud, Iraq) was made the seat of government about 880 BC and Nineveh became the new capital of the empire about 705 BC, the Assyrian monarchs still continued their building operations in Ashur. The city was destroyed by the Medes in 614 BC.

ASHURBANIPAL (r. 669–627 BC), last great monarch of the Assyrian Empire. He inherited a wide realm stretching from northern Egypt to Persia, and before 652 BC he had expanded this area to include southern Egypt and western Anatolia.

The king in a chariot. Relief from the palace of the Assyrian king Ashurbanipal in Nineveh; now in the Louvre, Paris. © Giraudon–Art Resource

Assyrian literature and art reached its height during his reign. He was one of the rare ancient Middle Eastern rulers who was literate, and his scribes amassed the first systematically collected library in that area; it included scholarly and literary texts and works on magic. His royal residences, especially at Nineveh, were decorated with magnificent reliefs depicting scenes of war, wild-animal hunts, and everyday palace life.

Although the Assyrian Empire reached its greatest extent under Ashurbanipal, the first signs of its decline also appeared during his reign. In 652 BC, his brother, Shamash-shum-ukin, led a revolt that gained widespread support among the Babylonians, Arameans, Elamites, and Arabs. It took Ashurbanipal four years to subdue Babylonia and at least three years more to punish the other rebels. This extensive military effort exhausted the resources of Assyria, and for most of its remaining decades as an imperial power it was confined to fighting defensive actions and border skirmishes. J.A.B.

ASHURNASIRPAL I, king of Assyria (1050–1031 BC), grandson of the great king Tiglath-pileser I (r. 1115–1076 BC). Ashurnasirpal, whose name means "Ashur Is Guardian of the Son," ruled at a time when the Assyrian state was hard pressed by invading nomadic tribes and its territory was greatly reduced. In a surviving inscription, he prays for help from the goddess Ishtar, describing the tribulations of his time and calling himself the Sorrowful One.

ASHURNASIRPAL II, king of Assyria (884–859 BC). He extended Assyrian power north to the borders of Urartu (now in eastern Turkey) and west as far as the Mediterranean Sea. The Phoenician city-states of Tyre, Byblos, and Sidon paid tribute to him in 867 BC. About 880 BC he rebuilt Calah (modern Nimrud, Iraq), using enemy captives as labor, and made it his capital. In inscriptions found at Calah, he describes his conquests in brutal detail, boasting of the cruel punishments he inflicted on his defeated enemies. Although he did not attack his powerful neighbors, Urartu and Babylonia, he began the era of expansion in which Assyria conquered the Middle East.

ASH WEDNESDAY, in Christian churches, the first day of the penitential season of Lent, so called from the ceremony of placing ashes on the forehead as a sign of penitence. This custom, probably introduced by Pope Gregory I, has been universal since the Synod of Benevento (1091). In the Roman Catholic church, ashes obtained from burned palm branches of the previous Palm Sunday are blessed before mass on Ash Wednesday. The priest places the blessed ashes on the fore-

A view of the Himalaya in Nepal, showing Mt. Everest, the highest peak in the world. The Himalaya stretch from Pakistan to China and give rise to many of the greatest rivers of Asia.
Suzanne J. Engelmann

heads of the officiating priests, the clergy, and the congregation, while reciting over each one the following formula: "Remember that you are dust, and unto dust you shall return."

ASIA, the largest of the earth's seven continents. With outlying islands, it covers an estimated 44,936,000 sq km (17,350,000 sq mi), or about one-third of the world's total land area. Its peoples account for three-fifths of the world's population; in the late 1980s, Asia had more than 3.1 billion inhabitants.

Lying almost entirely in the northern hemisphere, Asia is bounded on the N by the Arctic Ocean, on the E by the Bering Strait and the Pacific Ocean, on the S by the Indian Ocean, and on the SW by the Red and Mediterranean seas. On the W, the conventional boundary between Europe and Asia is drawn at the Ural Mts., continuing S to the Caspian Sea, then W along the Caucasus Mts. to the Black Sea. Many geographers prefer to regard the landmass formed by Europe and Asia as a single continent—Eurasia.

The continental mainland stretches from the S end of the Malay Peninsula to Cape Chelyuskin in Siberia. Its westernmost point is Cape Baba in NW Turkey, and its easternmost point is Cape Dezhnev in NE Siberia. The continent's greatest width from E to W is about 8500 km (about 5300 mi). In Asia are found both the lowest and highest points on the earth's surface, namely, the shore of the Dead Sea (395 m/1296 ft below sea level) and Mt. Everest (8848 m/29,028 ft).

To the SE of the mainland is an array of archipelagoes and islands, extending E to the Oceanic and Australian realms. Among these islands are those of Indonesia and the Philippines, including Sumatra, Java, Celebes, Borneo, and New Guinea. To the N lie Taiwan, the islands of Japan, and Sakhalin. In the Indian Ocean are Sri Lanka and smaller island groups such as the Maldives and the Andaman and Nicobar islands.

Because of its vast size and diverse character, Asia is divided for convenience into five major realms. These are as follows: former Soviet Asia, including Siberia, Central Asia (the former Central Asian USSR), and the Caucasus; East Asia, including China, Mongolia, Korea, and Japan; Southeast Asia, including Burma, Thailand, Cambodia, Laos, Vietnam, Malaysia, Singapore, Indonesia, Brunei, and the Philippines; South Asia, including India, Bangladesh, Pakistan, Sri Lanka, Nepal, and Bhutan; and Southwest Asia, including Afghanistan, Iran, Iraq, Turkey, Syria, Lebanon, Israel, Jordan, Saudi Arabia, and the other states of the Arabian Peninsula. The continent may also be divided into two cultural realms: that which is Asian in culture (East Asia, Southeast Asia, and South Asia) and that which is not (former Soviet Asia and Southwest Asia).

THE NATURAL ENVIRONMENT

Unlike the other continents, Asia has an interior that consists of mountains, plateaus, and intervening structural basins. The highland core, located somewhat S of the geometric center of the continent, is composed of the Himalaya and associated ranges and the Tibetan Plateau. Around this central core are arrayed four major plateau regions (Siberia, E China, S India, and the Arabian Peninsula) and several great structural basins and river plains.

Geological History. According to the theory of plate tectonics, the earth's surface crust consists of a number of huge continental plates and a number of equally large oceanic plates, most of which are in continuous motion. Of these, the largest is the Eurasian continental plate. Portions of this plate are composed of the most ancient rocks found on earth, those of the Precambrian age (4.65 billion to 570 million years ago), which are found today in the Angara Shield of E Siberia, in much of the Arabian Peninsula, and in India S of the Indo-Gangetic lowland.

During most of the Paleozoic and Mesozoic eras (570 to 65 million years ago), a huge sea known as the Tethys covered much of the interior of Eurasia and laid down thick deposits, which in time were converted into the sedimentary and metamorphosed formations. Approximately 30 million years ago, the subcontinent of India, which had broken off from SE Africa and drifted NE, began to thrust under the Eurasian continental plate, creating an enormous "deep" that later filled with sediments to form the Indo-Gangetic lowland. At the same time it generated tremendous pressure, causing the S continental margin to crumple into a series of great mountain ranges, of which the Himalaya is the most conspicuous.

Plate-tectonics theory also helps explain the formation of the arcuate (arc-shaped) ranges, peninsulas, and archipelagoes, as well as the volcanic activity and tectonic instability of East and Southeast Asia. In East Asia the primary force results from the underthrusting of the westward-moving Pacific plate against the Eurasian continental plate. Japan, Taiwan and the Ryukyus, and the Philippines are products of these forces. In Southeast Asia, the situation is complicated by the relative movements of the Pacific and Indian Ocean plates, and that movement helps explain the N-S trending highlands of mainland Southeast Asia and the volcanic activity that characterizes most of the Indonesian Archipelago.

Physiographic Regions. Asia's physiographic system focuses on the Pamir Knot, a towering plateau region known as the Roof of the World, located where the borders of India, China, Tajikistan, Pakistan, and Afghanistan converge; several peaks here exceed 6100 m (20,000 ft). Spiraling out from the Pamirs to the W are the Hindu Kush and their extension across N Iran, the Elburz Mts., and beyond the latter the Caucasus ranges, between the Caspian and the Black seas, and the Pontic Mts. along the Black Sea in Turkey. To the SE are the Great Himalaya, paralleled by lesser but still great ranges to the N and S of them. Together these ranges form an imposing E-W arc, some 2500 km (about 1550 mi) in length, containing numerous peaks of well more than 6100 m (20,000 ft), including Mt. Everest. To the E and NE of the Pamirs extends the high Karako-ram Range, which leads into the Kunlun Mts., and a branch, the Altun Shan; this line of mountains continues E at lower elevations as the Nan Ling (Nan Shan) to become the Qin Ling (Ch'in Ling) of North China, which marks a major cli-

The mountains of Guilin (Kuei-lin), China, are mentioned in many Chinese legends. Although they appear to be volcanic in origin, they are actually the result of massive earth upthrusts.

Suzanne J. Engelmann

matic divide between N and S China. Between the Himalayan system and the Karakoram-Kunlun ranges lies the Tibetan Plateau, which has average elevations of about 3660 to 4570 m (about 12,000 to 15,000 ft). Extending NE from the Pamirs is the great Tien Shan, also with peaks rising above 6100 m (20,000 ft) but diminishing in height as it approaches the borders of Outer Mongolia. To the NE, the Altai Mts. extend into Mongolia, and beyond them are the Sayan, Yablonovy, and Stanovoy ranges of E Siberia; the last two, however, are not part of the highland core.

Several major structural basins are found to the N of the central mountain core. Farthest N, located between the Tien Shan and the Altai Mts., lies the Dzungarian Basin; to the S of this, between the Tien Shan and the Karakoram and Kunlun, lies the vast Tarim Basin in which is found one of the largest middle-latitude deserts, the Takla Makan; and embraced by the Kunlun and Altun Shan is the deep Qaidam (Tsaidam) Basin.

Soil types also vary enormously. Siberia is overlain by acidic forest soils characteristic of the tundra and taiga; permafrost is common here, and drainage is usually poor. These soils merge into dark grassland, steppe, and desert soils across a vast band that extends from N China to the Black Sea and into Southwest Asia; the dark steppe soils, among the most fertile in Asia, are found in N central China and SW Siberia. In E and S Asia, the most valuable soils for agriculture are the alluvial soils that have been deposited in the lower valleys of the great rivers; these soils make up most of Asia's intensively used agricultural land. In low-latitude regions are found mature tropical soils, which are of generally low fertility; these mature soils grade, to the N, into soils with a higher humus content that are somewhat more fertile.

Drainage. The highland core of Asia might be likened to the hub of a colossal wheel, the spokes of which are great rivers that flow out in all directions. Seven of these are among the dozen longest rivers in the world. Flowing N from the N margin and NE extensions of the highland core to the icebound Arctic Ocean are the Lena, Yenisey, and Ob rivers. These rivers flow across vast alluvial plains underlain by permafrost. To the W, flowing from the slopes of the Tien Shan and the Pamirs themselves, are rivers such as the Ili, the Syrdarya, and the Amu Darya, which drain into interior seas—Lake Balkhash in the case of the Ili, the Aral Sea for the other two. These rivers, along with the Volga and lesser streams in N Tibet, W China, and S Mongolia, constitute the great interior drainage basin of Asia with an area of about 10 million sq km (about 4 million sq mi).

In the S, the SE, and the E, the great rivers flow through vast lowlands. Clockwise from SW to NE these rivers are the Indus, Ganges, Brahmaputra, Salween, Mekong, Yangtze, Huang He (Yellow), and Amur, all of which are snow- and glacier-fed and rise either well within, or along the margins of, the highland core.

Lake Baykal, in southern Siberia, is the largest freshwater lake in Asia and the deepest freshwater body of water in the world. Dieter Blum–Peter Arnold, Inc.

INDEX TO MAP OF ASIA

ARCTIC OCEAN
PACIFIC OCEAN
ATLANTIC OCEAN
NORWEGIAN SEA
BARENTS SEA
KARA SEA
LAPTEV SEA
EAST SIBERIAN SEA
CHUKCHI SEA
BERING SEA
SEA OF OKHOTSK
SEA OF JAPAN
YELLOW SEA
NORTH SEA
BALTIC SEA
BLACK SEA
CASPIAN SEA
MEDITERRANEAN SEA
ADRIATIC SEA
AEGEAN SEA
RED SEA
Bay of Biscay
WHITE SEA
UNION OF SOVIET SOCIALIST REPUBLICS
RUSSIAN SOVIET FEDERATED SOCIALIST REPUBLIC
KAZAKH S.S.R.
UZBEK S.S.R.
TURKMEN S.S.R.
KIRGIZ S.S.R.
TADZHIK S.S.R.
MONGOLIA
Inner Mongolia
NORTH AMERICA
UNITED STATES
ALASKA
NORWAY
SWEDEN
FINLAND
DENMARK
UNITED KINGDOM
IRELAND
NETH.
BELG.
LUX.
FRANCE
SWITZ.
AUSTRIA
CZECH.
HUNGARY
ROMANIA
BULGARIA
YUGOSLAVIA
ALB.
GREECE
ITALY
SPAIN
POLAND
EAST GER.
WEST GER.
TURKEY
SYRIA
LEB.
ISRAEL
JORDAN
CYPRUS
EGYPT
IRAQ
IRAN
KUWAIT
SAUDI ARABIA
AFGHANISTAN
N. KOREA
S. KOREA
JAPAN
Moscow
Leningrad
Kiev
Kharkov
Minsk
Riga
Tallinn
Helsinki
Stockholm
Oslo
Copenhagen
Berlin
Warsaw
Prague
Vienna
Budapest
Bucharest
Sofia
Belgrade
Paris
London
Brussels
Bonn
Rome
Milan
Istanbul
Ankara
Tehran
Baghdad
Kabul
Tashkent
Alma-Ata
Novosibirsk
Omsk
Sverdlovsk
Perm
Irkutsk
Ulan Bator (Ulaanbaatar)
Peking (Beijing)
Tianjin
Seoul
Tokyo
Osaka
Vladivostok
Magadan
Petropavlovsk-Kamchatskiy
Murmansk
Arkhangelsk
Volgograd
Rostov
Baku
Tbilisi
Yerevan
Kuybyshev
Gorkiy
Kazan
Chelyabinsk
Karaganda
Krasnoyarsk
Yakutsk
Verkhoyansk Range
Cherskiy Range
Kolyma Range
Stanovoy Range
Yablonovyy Range
Dzhugdzhur Range
Great Khingan Range
Sikhote-Alin Range
Koryak Ra.
Tien Shan
Kunlun Shan
Qilian Shan
Takla Makan
Gobi
Caucasus
Lake Baikal
Balkhash
ARAL SEA
Ob
Yenisey
Lena
Irtysh
Volga
Don
Dnepr
Amur
KURIL ISLANDS
NEW SIBERIAN IS.
SEVERNAYA ZEMLYA
Novaya Zemlya
FRANZ JOSEF LAND
SVALBARD
Spitsbergen
Bear I.
Jan Mayen
Faeroe Is.
Arctic Circle
North Pole
Longitude East of Greenwich

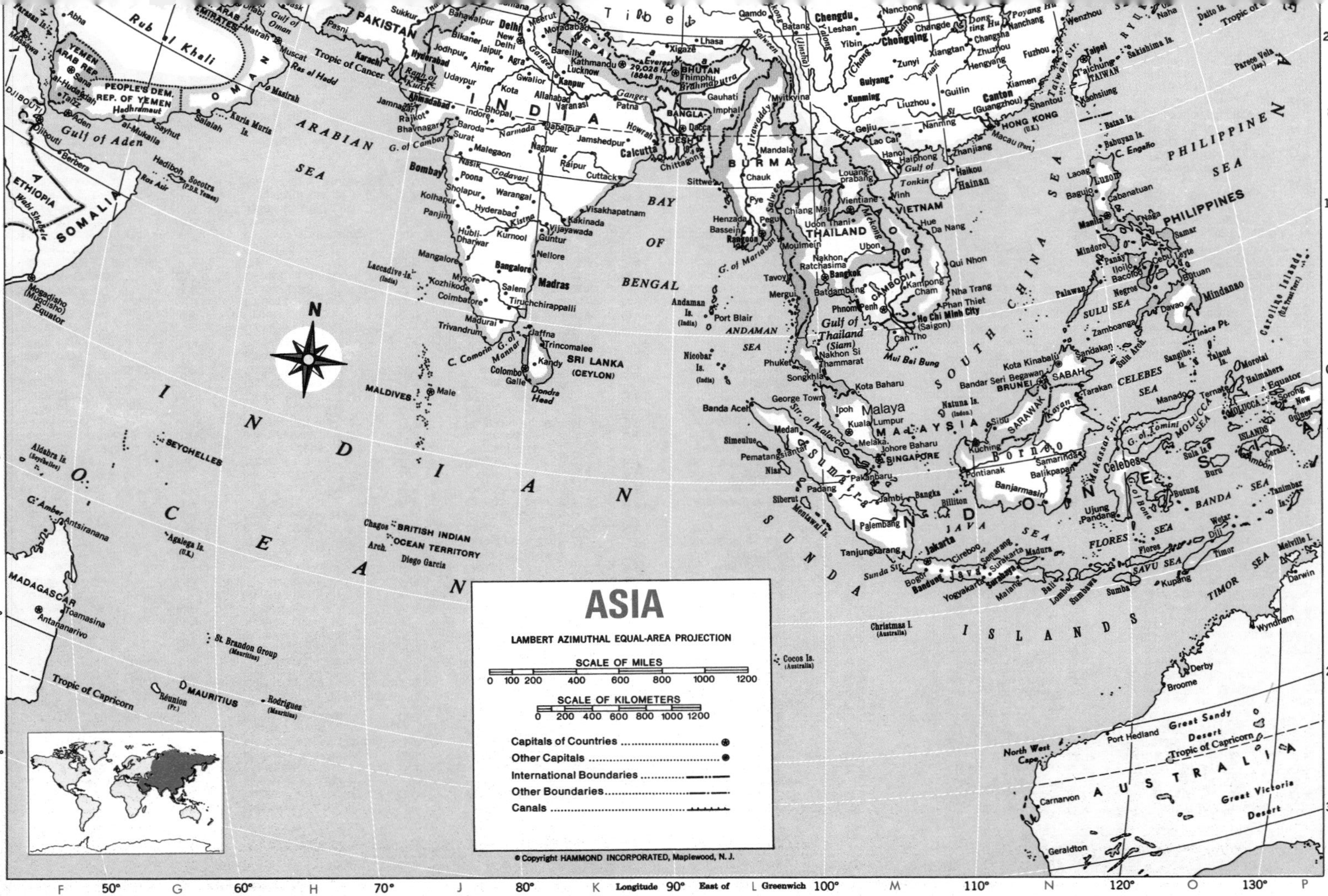

ASIA
LAMBERT AZIMUTHAL EQUAL-AREA PROJECTION
SCALE OF MILES
0 100 200 400 600 800 1000 1200
SCALE OF KILOMETERS
0 200 400 600 800 1000 1200
Capitals of Countries
Other Capitals
International Boundaries
Other Boundaries
Canals
© Copyright HAMMOND INCORPORATED, Maplewood, N. J.
Longitude 90° East of Greenwich
INDIAN OCEAN
ARABIAN SEA
BAY OF BENGAL
SOUTH CHINA SEA
PHILIPPINE SEA
ANDAMAN SEA
SULU SEA
CELEBES SEA
JAVA SEA
BANDA SEA
FLORES SEA
SAVU SEA
TIMOR SEA
SUNDA ISLANDS
INDIA
PAKISTAN
NEPAL
BHUTAN
BANGLADESH
BURMA
THAILAND
LAOS
CAMBODIA
VIETNAM
MALAYSIA
SINGAPORE
BRUNEI
INDONESIA
PHILIPPINES
SRI LANKA (CEYLON)
MALDIVES
SEYCHELLES
MAURITIUS
MADAGASCAR
SOMALIA
ETHIOPIA
DJIBOUTI
YEMEN ARAB REP.
PEOPLE'S DEM. REP. OF YEMEN
OMAN
BRITISH INDIAN OCEAN TERRITORY
AUSTRALIA
Tropic of Cancer
Equator
Tropic of Capricorn

Index to Map of Asia

Mt. Fuji, Japan's celebrated sacred volcano.

Climate. The climate of the continent is as varied as its surface configuration. Climates in Asia range from that of the equatorial rainforest to that of the Arctic tundra. For the most part, the N part of Asia is dominated by movement of polar continental air masses that travel from W Siberia to the N Pacific. Winters here are long and harsh, summers are short and cool, and the annual precipitation is light. A similar climate is characteristic of the Tibetan Plateau and other uplands. The interior regions have middle-latitude desert or semiarid climates, with harsh winters and warm summers and an average annual precipitation of less than 230 mm (less than 9 in).

The S and E margins of the continent, however, are characterized by monsoonal air movements (*see* MONSOON) from the cold interior E and S in winter and from the oceans N toward the warmer land in summer. For the most part the margins of Asia have cool to cold, dry winters and hot, humid summers, with a strong concentration of rainfall in the summer months. Although the term *monsoonal* is applied to all E and S Asia's climates, the true monsoon is characteristic only of part of the Indian subcontinent and Burma; in these areas average annual rainfall exceeds 2000 mm (more than 79 in). In other parts of S and E Asia, rainfall is either less heavily concentrated in the summer or evenly distributed throughout the year. Most of E Asia experiences flows of maritime air from the W Pacific in the form of a monsoon effect. In places where orographic factors (that is, mountains) intervene, the winter is likely to be wet, as is the case along the E coasts of portions of the Philippines, Vietnam, and Malaysia and in parts of S India. The coastal areas of E Asia are also subject to destructive typhoons, which originate in the W Pacific and the N part of the South China Sea.

Southwest Asia falls into a different climatic regime, characteristic of much of the Mediterranean area and dominated by a high-pressure belt of dry, relatively stable air masses that move slowly from W to E, bringing winter rainfall and then passing into N India. The average annual rainfall is light, and semiarid steppe and desert climates prevail. This climate regime extends into the NW Indian Peninsula.

Vegetation. Vegetation in Asia is extraordinarily diverse, bearing an intimate relation to the many varieties of soil and climate. In the far N reaches of the continent, in Siberia, tundra and taiga vegetation predominate. The former consists primarily of mosses and lichens; the latter is a largely coniferous forest consisting of pine, fir, and spruce. South of the taiga, grasslands occur in great E-W bands. These blend to the S into a desert scrub where aridity increases, as in the intermontane basins of the highland core and its peripheries, and in much of Southwest Asia.

In South, Southeast, and East Asia, equatorial rain forest predominates in the lowest latitudes, where heavy precipitation is characteristic throughout the year. The luxuriant evergreen rain forest is characterized by numerous species, including teak, jackfruit, eucalyptus, oak, and various species of bamboo and palm. Farther N of the equator lies a more open tropical forest, often called monsoonal, and this in turn merges to the N into subtropical evergreen forest, as in S China and Japan. In the middle latitudes mixed forests of deciduous and coniferous trees pre-

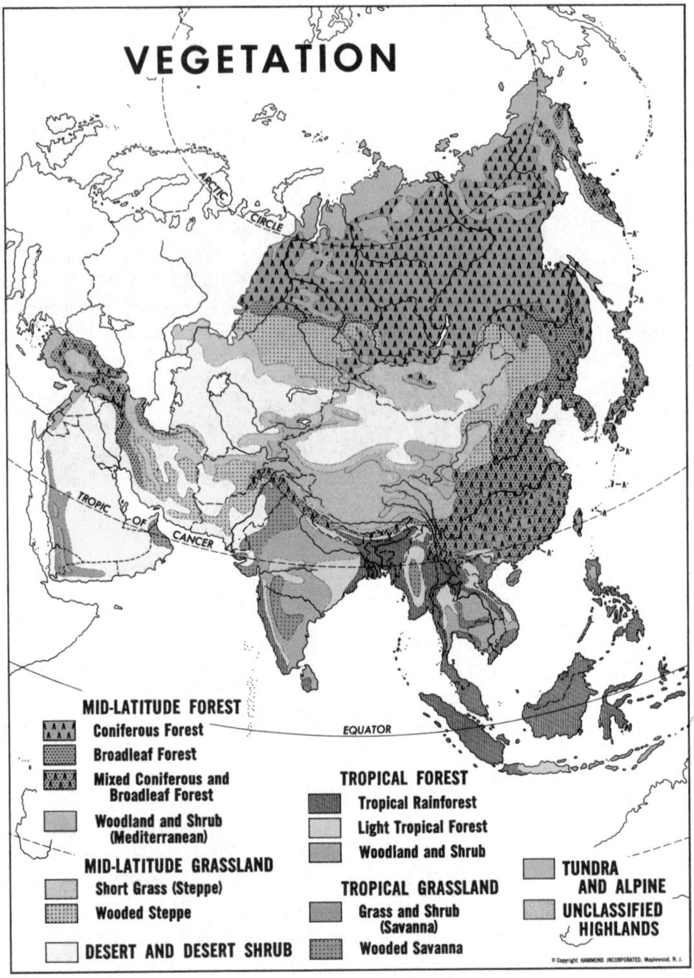

dominate, and these merge, to the N, with the region of coniferous forests.

Animal Life. The fauna of the continent are as diversified as its climates, terrain, and vegetation. The N regions are rich in furbearers, such as the brown bear, otter, lynx, sable, ermine, and wolf, in addition to a vast array of birdlife. The steppe and semiarid regions support antelope and numerous species of burrowing animals such as hare and field mice. Freshwater fish are found in all parts of the continent, and Lake Baykal is notable for its distinctive fauna. Wild sheep and goats are found in the highlands, and Tibet is the home of the wild yak. Wildlife is scarcer in the hot dry regions of Southwest Asia and in parts of South Asia, where the most famous indigenous animal, the Asian lion, is virtually extinct. Jackals and hyenas, however, are common in these regions. In the more humid regions of E and SE Asia, native animal life has been much diminished by centuries of human occupance. Monkeys, however, are ubiquitous in the S areas, and the Indian tiger is still found in small numbers in parts of South and Southeast Asia. Birdlife, snakes, and lizards abound here, and various types of crocodiles are widely distributed. Wild apes such as the gibbon and the scarce orangutan are found in Southeast Asia. Many types of deer and antelope also live in less well-populated areas such as Borneo, where flying squirrels and tree rats are numerous. Among the animals of unusual interest are the rare Southeast Asian rhinoceros, the Asian elephant, the tapir, the anteater, and the wild buffalo of India and Southeast Asia.

Mineral Resources. Asia is enormously rich in known mineral resources, even though much of the continent—Tibet, for instance—has not yet been explored geologically. Coal exists in great abundance in Siberia and N China, in NE India, and in lesser deposits elsewhere. Petroleum and natural gas also are well distributed, but with the greatest concentrations at the head of the Persian Gulf, in parts of Indonesia, in N and interior China, and on the shores of the Caspian Sea. Large offshore reserves are believed to exist as well along the coasts of China, Indonesia, Malaysia, and W India. Metallic minerals are relatively scarce in Southwest Asia, except in Turkey, which is a major chromium producer. Elsewhere on the continent metallic ores of various kinds are well distributed; China and Siberia in particular are well endowed. Malaysia, Thailand, and Indonesia are extremely rich in tin, and India is rich in iron and manganese ores. Other important mineral resources include gold, silver, uranium, copper, lead, and zinc; gemstones, such as diamonds, are found in Siberia, and sapphires and rubies occur in South and Southeast Asia.

THE PEOPLE

The peoples of Asia are more diverse than those of any other continent, and they are highly concentrated in a small proportion of the total area, chiefly in S and E Asia. Population densities in the N and interior areas are low by any standard, as are those in most parts of Southwest Asia. In East Asia, Southeast Asia, and most of South Asia, people are crowded onto relatively small areas of riverine lowlands, where population densities often exceed 3900 persons per sq km (about 1500 per sq mi). In China, for example, 90% of the population is concentrated in the E third of the country. Even in highly industrialized Japan most of the populace is concentrated in small lowlands where the largest cities are also located.

Ethnology and Languages. Mongoloid peoples are predominant in East Asia and mainland Southeast Asia, but Malayo-Polynesian stock prevails in the archipelagoes of Southeast Asia. In South Asia, about two-thirds of the population consists of Caucasoid stocks resembling the peoples of the Middle East; Caucasoid peoples also dominate in Southwest Asia and in much of former Central Asian USSR. In S India darker-skinned people speaking Dravidian languages are the dominant group. Mongoloid peoples inhabit the Himalayan and Tibetan area and extend through Mongolia into E Siberia. The primary ethnic group in Siberia, however, is Caucasoid, of European origin.

Ethnicity rather than race is a more meaningful approach to the population diversity of Asia. Sinitic culture, and cultures that are influenced by China but possess their own languages, are characteristic of East Asia; these peoples include the Chinese, Tibetans, Mongols, Koreans, and Japanese. Southeast Asia is more diversified, although peninsular and archipelagic Southeast Asia is mainly Malay. Burmese, Thai, Vietnamese, and Khmer inhabit mainland Southeast Asia along with a number of other ethnolinguistic groups. In South Asia, the peoples residing in the N speak a variety of Hindi-related Indo-Aryan languages; but in the S the Dravidian languages are most important. In Southwest Asia, Persian (Farsi), Arabic, Turkish, and Hebrew are the important languages identifying various ethnic groups. Turkic speakers also are numerous in former Soviet Central Asia and in W China, although Russian is by far the principal language in Siberia.

CHIEF POLITICAL DIVISIONS OF ASIA

Political Unit	Political Status
Afghanistan	Republic
Bahrain	Emirate
Bangladesh	Republic within Commonwealth of Nations
Bhutan	Monarchy
Brunei	Sultanate
Burma (Myanmar)	Republic
Cambodia (Kampuchea)	Republic
China, People's Republic of	Republic
China, Republic of (Taiwan)	Republic
Cyprus	Republic within Commonwealth of Nations
Hong Kong	British dependency
India	Republic within Commonwealth of Nations
Indonesia	Republic
Iran	Republic
Iraq	Republic
Israel	Republic
Japan	Constitutional monarchy
Jordan	Constitutional monarchy
Kazakhstan*	Republic
Korea, Democratic People's Republic of (North Korea)	Republic
Korea, Republic of (South Korea)	Republic
Kuwait	Constitutional emirate
Kyrgyzstan*	Republic
Laos	Republic
Lebanon	Republic
Macau (Macao)	Portuguese dependency
Malaysia	Constitutional monarchy within Commonwealth of Nations
Maldives	Republic
Mongolian People's Republic	Republic
Nepal	Constitutional monarchy
Oman	Sultanate
Pakistan	Republic
Philippines	Republic
Qatar	Constitutional emirate
Russia (Asian part)*	Part of Russian Republic
Saudi Arabia	Monarchy
Singapore	Republic within Commonwealth of Nations
Sri Lanka (Ceylon)	Republic within Commonwealth of Nations
Syria	Republic
Tajikistan*	Republic
Thailand	Constitutional monarchy
Turkey (Asian part)	Part of republic of Turkey
Turkmenistan*	Republic
United Arab Emirates	Federal state
Uzbekistan*	Republic
Vietnam	Republic
Yemen	Republic

*Member of Commonwealth of Independent States

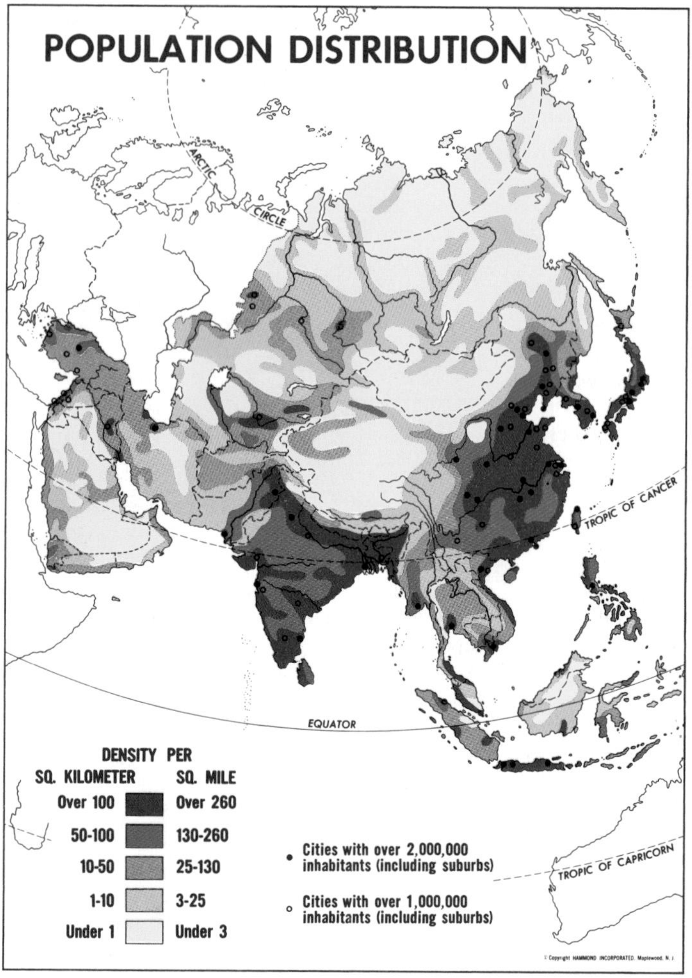

Demography. The total population of the continent exceeds 3.1 billion. East Asia alone contains about 1.3 billion people, Southeast Asia about 450 million, South Asia about 1.1 billion, Southwest Asia about 200 million, and former Soviet Asia at least 100 million. The overall population density of 71 persons per sq km (182 per sq mi) is the second highest of any continent, but the population is unevenly distributed.

For the most part the people of Asia are rural dwellers, but urbanization has proceeded rapidly in recent decades. The urban population accounts for a majority in Japan, Taiwan, South Korea, Singapore, Hong Kong, Jordan, Syria, Israel, Iran, Iraq, Saudi Arabia, Kuwait, and United Arab Emirates. The Philippines and Malaysia also have relatively large urban populations. Except in the Sinitic world and in parts of Southwest Asia, the large city is an innovation associated with the expansion of European colonization from the beginnings of the 16th century. The margins of South and Southeast Asia are dotted with large cities that developed as a result of European economic and political domination; among these are Karachi, Bombay, Goa, Colombo, Madras, Calcutta, Rangoon (Yangon), George Town (Pinang), Kuala Lumpur, Singapore, Jakarta, Surabaya, Manila, Ho Chi Minh City (formerly Saigon), Phnom Penh, and Hanoi. Only Bangkok is not a former colonial center, but it resembles the others in most other respects. Even in China, many of the larger coastal cities were strongly influenced by the European impact. In Japan, modern urbanism was a recent phenomenon, but more than 75% of the population now is urban. In most other countries the urban population ranges between 20% and 40%. In Southwest Asia, ancient traditions of city building were reinforced by Muslim culture, giving rise to cities such as Tehran, Baghdad, Damascus, Jerusalem, and Istanbul; modern urbanization is reflected in such cities as Tel Aviv-Jaffa, Beirut, and Ankara. Still, in some Southwest Asian countries urban populations are a small proportion of the whole. Nevertheless, Asia accounts for more than half the world's urban population, and that proportion will increase in the future because Asian cities are growing at twice the rate of the overall populations.

The urban growth reflects both immigration and rapid population growth in most countries. The annual rate of population increase for the continent as a whole is about 1.8%. Several countries have significantly lower growth rates; these include Japan, China, Taiwan, and Singapore. Although the demographic forecast is for large and rapid population increases in Asia, declining growth rates in China, the Philippines, and India suggest that a population explosion is unlikely. The populations in all Asian countries are young, however, and that means continued population growth for a long period, as well as large numbers of entrants into the labor market each year in countries ill prepared to provide them with employment.

Religion. Asia fostered all the principal religions of the world and many minor ones as well. Judaism, Christianity, and Islam originated in Southwest Asia; Buddhism and Hinduism in India; and the so-called Chinese religion, composed of Confucian and Taoist elements, as well as ancestor worship, in China. Although its historical impact, both direct and indirect, was great, Christianity is today practiced by only a small number of Asians (most notably in the Philippines and South Korea). Buddhism has virtually disappeared from India but, in two quite different forms, extends through interior Asia and into Southeast Asia, where it is the main religion of Burma, Thailand, Cambodia, and Laos; it also is important in Japan, Vietnam, and China. Islam dominates in Southwest Asia and is of major importance

In Kyoto, Japan, a Buddhist procession marches past the Heian Shrine during Jidai Matsuri, *the Festival of the Ages. The city, in southern Honshu, is a center of Buddhist worship and is noted for many ancient temples and shrines, monuments of great artistic and architectural skill. For more than a thousand years Kyoto was the capital of Japan, and it is still the cultural heart of the country.*

George Holton–Photo Researchers, Inc.

The ornately decorated Wat Arun is one of many Buddhist temples in Bangkok, Thailand. Buddhism represents one of the most important cultural forces in Southeast Asia, where it remains the predominant religion. M. P. Kahl–Bruce Coleman, Inc.

in South Asia, where both Pakistan and Bangladesh are predominantly Muslim. Indonesia, in Southeast Asia, is also predominantly Muslim. Several Southwest Asian cities are important centers of religious pilgrimage, most prominently Mecca, Medina, and Jerusalem.

PATTERNS OF ECONOMIC DEVELOPMENT

Most of Asia is economically underdeveloped. The majority of the continent's population is employed in agriculture, but most agricultural activity is characterized by low yields and low labor productivity. Relatively few people in Asia are employed in manufacturing. In general, urban centers and their industries are not well integrated economically with the rural sector. Transportation systems, both within countries and between them, are poorly developed.

A number of exceptions exist, and they are important. Japan has successfully modernized its economy, as have Taiwan, South Korea, Singapore, and, to a lesser extent, Malaysia and Thailand. All these have shown rates of economic growth of more than 5% per year, well beyond their rates of population growth. The Southwest Asian states with large petroleum resources also have done well, although not in the distribution of income.

Agriculture. Less than one-third of Asia's land is in agricultural use. In general the basic unit of production is the village rather than the farm. In South, Southeast, and East Asia agriculture is characterized by small landholdings in alluvial lowlands, too many people on too little land, production largely for subsistence, high rates of tenancy (except in the Communist countries), a heavy dependence on cereals and other food staples, and premodern technologies. Rice is the food-staple crop of South, Southeast, and East Asia. It is usually grown under wet conditions. In South and Southeast Asia, yields are extremely low, controlled irrigation facilities are poorly developed, and double-cropping is seldom practiced. Irrigation schemes in India have helped stabilize annual yields and increase overall production. The example of Japan has shown that small farms and wet-rice agriculture can enormously increase yields and production through the introduction of new high-yielding varieties, careful water management, the application of fertilizers, and the elimination of landlordism.

Despite a wide distribution of new high-yielding varieties of wet rice in many parts of South and Southeast Asia since the late 1960s (the so-called green revolution), production has not risen as hoped. The average rice yields in India, Thailand, and Burma are only one-third that of Japan. In India, however, high-yielding varieties of wheat, developed in Mexico, have had, in certain areas, an impressive impact on wheat yields, the country's second crop.

Also practiced in the lower latitudes, and in marked contrast with the predominantly subsistence types of agriculture, is large-scale estate agriculture, which produces crops for export, such as rubber, palm oil, coconut products, tea, pineapples, and abaca fiber. Estate production originated during the colonial period in South and Southeast Asia, and many estates remain under foreign ownership and control. Most of the same crops, however, are grown in substantial quantities on small holdings.

In East Asia agriculture is based on wet-paddy cultivation to a latitude of about 35° N in China and about 40° N elsewhere. In contrast to Southeast Asia, yields here are high, double-cropping is common, irrigation is highly controlled, and fertilizer inputs are extremely high, especially in Japan. North of the Huai R. in China, rice gives way to wheat and other dry grains, especially sorghum and corn, all cultivated in a form of intensive horticulture characteristic of Chinese agriculture. Although China's rural population has been organized into large managerial entities known as communes, cultivation is still basically carried on at the village level within the commune. Swine, poultry, and fish (in ponds) are raised in both the N and S where possible, but the raising of dairy and beef cattle is common only in Japan and Korea.

In the drier interior regions, some dry-farming of grains is practiced, and the raising of cattle, sheep, and horses is important. Oasis-type agriculture is found in favored locations in W China and in Central Asia. Dry-farming of grains, nomadic herding, and some irrigated oasis-type cultivation are also characteristic of Southwest Asia. For the most part, however, productivity levels are low.

Forestry and Fishing. Lumbering is an important industry in most Southeast Asian countries, especially in Malaysia, the Philippines, and Thailand, teak being the most important product in the lat-

A farmer in Thailand crosses an irrigation canal that serves his rice fields. Improved irrigation methods have made it possible to raise a second crop of rice during the dry season, thus doubling productivity.
United Nations

Chinese peasant women cleaning rice seedlings. Sovfoto

ter country. Forest gathering and shifting cultivation in forested interfluvial areas are widespread activities in Southeast Asia, as they are also in the more remote parts of humid South Asia and S China. In India and China, however, the original forest cover has long since been removed in the more heavily populated areas. In Japan, lumbering is a major industry, and large areas of planted stands, chiefly conifer, have replaced much of the indigenous vegetation. Siberian timber reserves are enormous and have been as yet relatively little tapped.

Marine fisheries are extremely important in Asia. Japan is the world's leading fishing country, and China is not far behind. The fishing industry is also important in Russia, Thailand, Indonesia, and the Philippines. Pisciculture, the raising of pond fish, is also an important activity, especially in China. Although fishing in the poor countries is largely for domestic consumption, emphasis has increasingly been placed on exports of dried, frozen, and canned fish.

Mining. Mining also is an important activity in most Asian countries, and it is a major export industry in several: manganese in India; tin in Malaysia, Thailand, and Indonesia (which, combined, produce most of the world's supply of this metal); and chromium ore in the Philippines. The most important Asian mineral export, however, is petroleum. Southwest Asia contains the world's largest reserves of oil outside the former USSR, and most of the production is exported. Indonesia, and more recently China and Malaysia, are also exporters. In South Asia modest petroleum and natural-gas deposits are exploited in Bangladesh, Pakistan, and off the W coast of India. Coal mining is important in China, E Siberia, NE India, Iran, and Turkey. Other significant mineral products include iron, manganese, and tungsten in China; sulfur, zinc, and molybdenum in Japan; and gold in Siberia.

Manufacturing. Manufacturing is relatively poorly developed. Japan is the great exception, with a highly diversified industrial sector that employs about 25% of the labor force. Other than Japan, the two major manufacturing countries in Asia are China and India, each of which has a large manufacturing sector. Manufacturing in China is concentrated in S Manchuria; in the ports of Shanghai, Tientsin, Tsingtao, and Wuhan; and in selected interior regions where raw materials are available. China's steel production is comparable to that of Great Britain, although production on a per capita basis remains low. Manufacturing in India is heavily concentrated in and near Calcutta, in the Bombay area, in the central peninsula, and in a number of other resource-advantaged areas. India is now a major industrial power, but its manufacturing sector employs only about 10% of the working population, while China's employs about 15%. Since the 1960s industry, especially light manufacturing, has developed rapidly in such countries as Taiwan, South Korea, Thailand, Malaysia, Singapore, and the Philippines. In other countries, industries tend to be associated with the processing of local agricultural, mineral, and forest raw materials, with light manufacturing for domestic markets, and with the assembly of machinery and vehicles imported from other countries. The trend in many Asian countries is to establish manufacturing industries geared to export, thereby taking advantage of the relatively inexpensive labor; notable examples are the electronic-equipment and clothing-manufacture industries of South Korea and Taiwan.

Energy. Although overall energy production has increased greatly since the 1960s, energy consumption per capita remains extremely low in most Asian countries. The more economically developed countries have moderate to high consumption levels. These include the former Soviet republics, Japan, Taiwan, South Korea, Singapore, Hong Kong, Malaysia, Kuwait, and Saudi Arabia. Energy sources are, in many regions, dependent on local resources. In Southwest Asia few alternatives to petroleum exist as an energy source. Hydroelectric potentials are immense in India, and about half of the electricity generated in that country comes from waterpower. Nonetheless, much of the energy consumed in rural India continues to be derived from the burning of dung and brushwood. In Southeast Asia, oil production is substantial in certain countries such as Indonesia and Brunei, but waterpower and fuel wood are the chief domestic sources of energy. Both China and Japan have shown that small-scale hydroelectric plants can be effective providers of energy to small towns and rural areas. China is reported to have some 90,000 small run-of-stream (not dammed) hydroelectric plants in operation, chiefly in S China, in addition to some 20 large plants. Nonetheless, coal remains China's chief energy source. In Japan petroleum is the largest energy source, and almost all of it is imported. The area of former Soviet Asia is immensely rich in hydro-electric potentials that have only recently begun to be tapped.

Transportation. In most of Asia transportation systems are poorly developed. No comprehensive continental land transportation system exists. Few railways cross international boundaries, and where they do, as between China and the former Soviet republics, they are underused. Much the same is true of roads, and, for the most part, navigable rivers are also not international routes of transportation, the Amur R., between Russia and China, being a major exception. Most of Asia's international communication is by sea and by air. All major Asian ports are connected with each other by both liner and tramper shipping services. Port facilities are varied, but few ports other than those in Japan, Hong Kong, and Singapore can handle large cargo. Singapore and Hong Kong are particularly important as entrepôts, to which small shipments are brought from a vast hinterland by small vessels and then shipped abroad. Air services link all major cities. Tokyo is the most important Asian air center, and Bangkok is the second, by virtue of its crossroads location in Southeast Asia.

Domestic transportation in most countries is also limited. Rural settlements are poorly connected with one another or with larger towns. Highways are few, and rural roads are usually unpaved. Japan, Taiwan, South Korea, Malaysia, and much of the Philippines are the exceptions. Where navigable, rivers are often the main highways of commerce, but not all countries have them. In China the Yangtze R. has long been the

Hazarara tribesmen enter the city of Kabul on horseback. UPI

E-W transportation artery, and it is connected by canal with the North China Plain. In Southeast Asia the Mekong, Menam, and Irrawaddy rivers all have acted as the spatial integrators of national territories. In India, however, the rivers have been much less important.

The continent's chief modern transportation medium is the railroad. Japan has a dense railroad network, and China, which possesses the world's sixth longest railroad system, had by the mid-1970s linked all of its major manufacturing centers and provincial capitals into one vast network. Korea and Taiwan also are well served. The countries of Southeast Asia, except for Thailand and Malaysia, and those of Southwest Asia have railroad systems that are small and truncated. In South Asia an integrated railroad system, originally built by the British, was divided by the political separation of India, Pakistan, and Bangladesh. Former Soviet Asia is crossed by the Trans-Caspian and Turk-Sib railroads in Central Asia and by the Trans-Siberian Railroad and the Baykal-Amur Mainline.

Trade. As a whole, the continent of Asia enters into world trade to a greater degree than either Africa or South America. A very high proportion of this trade is extracontinental. The important exceptions are the flow of oil from the Persian Gulf to Japan; the lesser flows from Indonesia and Brunei to Japan; the trade of China with Japan and with Southeast Asia; and, above all, the flow of raw materials to Japan, chiefly from Southeast Asia, and the return flood of Japanese manufactured goods to Southeast Asia. Japan ranks among the world leaders in the value of international trade, but only about a third of this is with other Asian countries. China and India both have a large value international trade, also chiefly outside the continent. Malaysia and Indonesia are major traders in raw materials. In per capita terms, however, all countries other than Japan, Taiwan, Korea, Malaysia, and Singapore, the major Southwest Asian oil exporters, and some former Soviet republics rank low on the world scale of international trade. N.S.G.

HISTORY

While Africa, for lack of other knowledge, is generally regarded as the birthplace of the human species, Asia is believed to be the cradle of civilization. Yet this civilization was not one and uniform, for the sheer size of the Asian mainland made it almost inevitable that several different civilizations would arise, independent of one another. The following historical survey attempts to show the interactions, collisions, and successions of these civilizations in continental terms. For additional information on countries or regions mentioned, see the history sections of articles on the individual Asian countries. *See also* ASSYRIA; BABYLONIA; INDUS VALLEY CIVILIZATION; MESOPOTAMIA; MIDDLE EAST; PERSIA; SIBERIA; SUMER.

Ancient Civilizations. The earliest known civilizations arose in the great river valleys of southwest Asia, northwest India, and northern China, and despite their differences, all had certain common features. All were agricultural societies that needed advanced social and political structures to maintain irrigation and flood-control systems. Raiding nomadic herders also forced the farmers in all of them to live in walled cities for defense and to entrust their protection to an aristocratic class of leaders. The invention of the plow about 3000 BC reduced the need for farm labor, freeing workers to become artisans. Increased yield from the land and the work of the artisans in turn provided trade items, and trade brought exchanges between cultures.

Mesopotamia. The land that fostered the Sumer-Akkad culture of the Tigris-Euphrates Valley—that is, Mesopotamia—is often called the cradle of civilization. By 3000 BC, the Sumerians irrigated their fields from precisely measured canals, used bronze as well as polished stone tools, made textiles and wheel-turned pottery, built great temples and palaces, and traveled in wheeled carts and sailing ships. Their accurate calendars predicted seasons, and their cuneiform writing was an international script until the 4th century BC. They worshiped a sun god, and they lived by written laws.

Although the Sumer-Akkad Kingdom fell to northern invaders, Mesopotamia remained the center of western Asian civilization until the 6th century BC. Most important of the later rulers were the Babylonians (c. 1900–1600 BC), the Assyrians (9th–7th cent. BC), and the Chaldeans (7th–6th cent. BC). It was the Chaldean Nebuchadnezzar II who destroyed Jerusalem and deported the Jews. (Already, however, Judaism was a major religious force.) After 1600 BC, nomads from Central Asia swept into Babylonia, sometimes to destroy but overall to build and advance the civilization founded by the Sumerians.

Indian civilizations. By 2300 BC, an advanced civilization in the Indus Valley of northwest India traded its cotton and textiles with Mesopotamia. As in Mesopotamia, irrigation produced crop surpluses and required an advanced social and political system. The two major cities, Mohenjo-daro (q.v.) and Harappa, had straight streets lined with large, two-story homes equipped with plumbing. The Indus peoples had written languages, used wheeled carts, and exhibited a high level of creativity in their art, jewelry, and toys.

The Great Wall of China was begun before the 3d century BC*, as fortification against barbarian invaders from the north.*

Kurt Scholz–Shostal/Superstock

Waves of tall, fair-haired Aryans from Central Asia destroyed the Indus cities between 1500 and 1200 BC, afterward settling in the Ganges Valley of northeast India. They spoke Sanskrit, an Indo-European language related to Persian, Greek, and Latin. Still nomadic, they lived in tribal groups headed by rajas. Like their Aryan relatives in Homeric Greece, they fought in horse-drawn chariots and composed an epic literature, the Vedas.

Between 900 and 500 BC, the Indo-Aryans—that is, people speaking Indic languages—settled into city-states under absolute monarchs. They depended on irrigated farming, including rice culture (possibly imported from Southeast Asia). Their Hindu religion, as embodied in the Vedas, provided for an elaborate caste system that stratified society.

Roots of Chinese civilization. A river basin also nurtured the early Chinese. Between 3000 and 1600 BC, the Huang He (Yellow River) plain sustained large communities of farmers who raised silkworms and spun silk thread and cloth, which they sent across the camel trails of Central Asia. They had an advanced society, but written records did not appear until the 16th century BC under the Shang dynasty. The Shang ruled over a number of kings of walled city-states. They cooperated to repulse the raiding northern nomads, who then dislodged other tribes, setting off a chain of migrations such as that of the Aryans into India.

The Chou, who displaced the Shang, continued the feudal organization. Under the Eastern Chou (770–256 BC), China advanced in political, economic, and social life. Chinese territory more than doubled to include south Manchuria and the Yangtze River Basin, with probably the highest population concentration in the world. The Chou used iron weapons, expanded irrigation, and built roads and canals to improve communication and commerce. An educated civil service replaced hereditary officials. Three major strands of Chinese thought crystallized: Confucianism, Taoism, and Legalism. *See* CHINESE PHILOSOPHY.

Major Ancient States. In the 11 centuries from 500 BC to AD 600, the early civilizations expanded and interacted. Expansionist rulers such as Alexander the Great facilitated the cultural exchange. The aggressive Manchurian nomads also caused tribal migrations that brought masses of people into the orbit of civilization. By AD 500 the major world religions and philosophies, with the exception of Islam, had spread far from their places of origin.

Cultural interaction. An early expansionist, Cyrus the Great, unified the Iranian descendants of the nomadic Aryans into the kingdom of Persia. He then built the Achaemenid Persian Empire (c. 550–330 BC), which spread Persian culture from the Mediterranean to the Indus River. The third Achaemenid king, Darius I, centralized the empire's government and supported Zoroastrian worship of Ahura-Mazda, god of light. *See* ZOROASTRIANISM.

By 330 BC the Persian Empire had been conquered by Alexander the Great, who dreamed of merging Eastern and Western cultures. Although Alexander's early death interrupted this plan, his generals planted Greek culture in the three kingdoms they made of his empire. The Seleucids ruled the Asian sector, which early broke into several states. One of these, Bactria (q.v.), straddled the east-west and north-south trade routes across which Chinese silk and Indian cotton traveled to Greece and Rome in return for glass, manufactured items, and gold. Elements of Greek culture were channeled through Bactria across Asia. Even after nomadic tribes from Central Asia conquered Bactria, Greek influences prevailed, for the new Kushan rulers absorbed Hellenistic culture. Through the 1st century AD, Greek was the international language of business and diplomacy. By this time, Hellenized Romans were entrenched in western Asia, from which the Eastern Roman Empire developed.

Although Greek influences were strong, much of southwestern and Central Asia and north India were actually dominated by Persians under two great dynasties—the Arsacids (c. 250 BC–AD 226) and the Sassanids (AD 226–651)—who spread Persian culture widely. Persian ladies' costumes and cosmetics, for example, were copied throughout Asia, and Persian architecture, art, and religion moved both east and west. Both the Arsacids and the Sassanids dominated the transcontinental trade, the terminus of which was in the Eastern Roman, later the Byzantine, Empire.

Indian expansionism. North India was also conquered by Persians, invaded by Alexander the Great, and ruled by Greek kings and by former "barbarians" from Central Asia. As international contacts grew, elements of Indian culture spread widely. Both Hinduism and Buddhism may have influenced Greek philosophers. Indians, in turn, felt strong foreign influences, as evidenced by the Greek-style Gandharan Buddha images of the Kushan period. After the Kushans conquered north India in the 1st century AD, they became Indianized, converted to Buddhism, and encouraged its growth in the Central Asian city-states and in China.

Although foreigners dominated north India for long periods, two native dynasties gained imperial status—the Maurya (322–185 BC), whose

Sriringam, on an island in the Cauvery River in Madras Province, India, is famous for its group of temples dedicated to the Hindu god Vishnu. Shown are the two monumental gate towers, or gopurams, *that give access to the precincts of one of the temples. Built in the 17th century, the shrine is visited by pilgrims in great numbers.* Ian Graham–Photo Researchers, Inc.

greatest ruler, Asoka, sent Buddhist missionaries throughout India and Asia; and the Gupta (c. 320–c. 535), under whom Indian art, architecture, and civilization reached a pinnacle.

Small native kingdoms also ruled central and south India. The Tamil peoples of the south first colonized Southeast Asia in the early centuries AD. From these colonies grew the native Indianized kingdoms of Champa (modern central Vietnam) and Funan (modern Cambodia) and lesser states in Thailand, Burma, Malaya, and the Indonesian islands.

Spread of Chinese civilization. Ambitious emperors of the Han dynasty (206 BC–AD 220) spread Chinese hegemony west across the wide Tarim River Basin. They built military outposts along the enlarged Great Wall and the edges of the desert to protect the long trade caravans against raiding nomad tribesmen. Persian, Arab, and Indian traders frequented the Han capital, and the Eastern (Later) Han probably had direct contact with Rome.

In 105 BC, the Han colonized northern Korea, and Chinese culture shaped the indigenous Korean kingdoms of Koguryo, Silla, Pakche, and Kaya. To the south, the Chinese Sinicized Vietnam, which they directly ruled for 1000 years.

The Han reached new heights in literature, especially after the discovery of papermaking, and in pottery, sculpture, painting, and music. Their engineers built roads and canals comparable to those of the Romans, and the prosperous urbanized society tried to live by Confucian moral ideals.

As the Han declined, frontier tribesmen were emboldened in their attacks. In the early centuries AD, waves of Turkic, Mongol, and Hunnish invaders set off tribal movements that pushed through Central Asia, into Europe (*see* HUNS), and eventually to Rome itself. Many Chinese fled south, where a Chinese state ruled by a series of dynasties formed in the Yangtze Valley. Despite troubled times, however, Chinese civilization advanced, with Buddhism and native Taoism the dominant religions. Although Chinese rule over Korea ended, Chinese influence remained strong during Korea's period of the Three Kingdoms (4th–7th cent.). The Koreans became Buddhists, and they used Chinese characters for writing and the Chinese Confucian system of government.

This Chinese culture spread from Korea to the island kingdom of Japan, ruled by the Yamato clan, which traced its origins to a legendary sun god. Becoming expansionist, the Japanese conquered parts of Korea in the 4th century but were driven out again two centuries later. By that time the Japanese had embraced Buddhism.

Muslim and Mongol Ascendancy. From the 7th to the 15th century, two forces dominated Asian events: the spread of the new religion of Islam and the expansion of the Mongols, who conquered much of Asia and threatened Europe. The Mongols warred with and, on occasion, accepted and thus strengthened Islam.

Rise and spread of Islam. In 7th-century Arabia, the Prophet of Islam, Muhammad, claimed to have received the will of Allah (God) through the angel Gabriel. Muhammad's teachings, collected into the Koran, provided the framework of Islamic governments. To spread the word of Allah, Muhammad set Arab tribes on the road to conquest. He and his successors, the Umayyad caliphs (*see* CALIPHATE), expanded Islam from India to Spain. The Umayyads and the subsequent Abbasids presided from their respective centers in Damascus and Baghdad over the Islamic states, whose culture combined Byzantine, Persian, Babylonian, and Indian elements. A major link between them was the Arabic language, which all shared through the Koran.

The later Abbasids became puppets of their Seljuk Turk soldiers from Central Asia, who threatened Christian Byzantium. Combined with the closing off of Christian holy places in Palestine, this threat touched off 300 years of Crusades (q.v.), which brought great European armies to western Asia. The Crusaders failed to dislodge the Muslims, but they took back to Europe many elements of Islamic culture.

When the Mongols captured Baghdad in 1258, ending the Abbasid theocracy, Islam had already taken root in India. Muslim traders introduced it in 711 to a country still suffering from the Hunnish invasions, which had been interrupted by the benevolent and cultured rule of the native Harsha (r. 606–47). Muslim Turks and Afghans repeatedly raided India, destroying Hindu and Buddhist centers, until the foundation of the Delhi sultanate (q.v.). Although slowed by Mongol invasions, the sultanate continued Muslim expansion in India.

While Muslim fanatics were nearly destroying Indian Buddhism, Indian traders and missionaries carried both Buddhism and Hinduism throughout Southeast Asia. There the kingdom of Champa (*see* CHAMPA, KINGDOM OF) fought both the Sinicized Vietnamese, to their north, and the Indianized Khmers of Angkor (modern Cambodia), to their west. Angkor's advanced civilization with its great stone temples was itself doomed to fall to the Thai, who were pushed out of South China by the Mongols. The Buddhist kingdom of Pagan in Burma felt the direct Mongol force.

In Malaya and the East Indian islands, the Buddhist Sri Vijaya kingdom of Sumatra (*see* SRI VIJAYA, KINGDOM OF) rivaled the Sailendras of Java, who were also Hindu and Buddhist temple builders. They were followed in turn by the Indianized Singosari and Majapahit kingdoms (*see* MAJAPAHIT, KINGDOM OF), whose commerce by the 15th century was dominated by Indian Muslim traders. Although Malaya and the islands thus became Muslim, Buddhism persisted in Burma, Thailand, and Cambodia.

Chinese orbit and Mongol ascendancy. Islam failed to convert the countries within the Chinese orbit, possibly because China experienced a cultural renaissance under the T'ang dynasty (618–906). Chinese T'ang influence reached from Japan to the Tarim Basin, where China blocked Islam. The T'ang fostered Confucian government, but Buddhism flourished, spawning new sects such as the Ch'an (Zen), which appealed to the Japanese. The subsequent Sung dynasty (960–1279) was pushed out of the north by Khitan and Jurchin tribes and out of the south by Mongols.

In Korea, meanwhile, the united Silla Kingdom (660–935), which was allied with the T'ang, continued Korean borrowing of Chinese culture and religion. The succeeding Koryo dynasty (935–1392), like the Chinese Sung, was beset by Khitans and Jurchens before falling to the Mongols. As Mongol power declined, a Korean general founded the Yi dynasty (1392–1910).

China's renaissance also affected the Japanese, who intensified their adoption of Chinese culture. The 7th-century Taika and 8th-century Taiho edicts adopted Chinese government and socioeconomic ideas. The court copied Chinese rituals and customs, and Buddhism spread Chinese ideas countrywide. As the provincial nobility grew stronger, the Fujiwara (q.v.) clan gained control. During their rule, known as the Heian period (794–1185), the Japanese court achieved an extreme of luxury, as poetry writing, music, dancing, painting, landscape gardening, and perfume smelling became the primary activities of the courtiers. Ending this dilettantism, the Minamoto clan became military dictators (shoguns) and ruled at Kamakura, while powerless emperors reigned at Kyoto (1185–1333). Repulsing two Mongol invasions so weakened Kamakura that power was seized by the Ashikaga (q.v.), under whom Japan fell into feudal anarchy.

The Mongols who dominated Asia for two centuries originated in the vast Asian steppeland. They came to power under Genghis Khan, who adroitly used espionage, trickery, terror, and talented men of all races to conquer western and North China and Central Asia. His sons and grandsons expanded the Mongol Empire (q.v.) into Turkestan, Iran, and Russia. After North China and Korea fell, Kublai Khan conquered the south, where he ended the Sung rule and proclaimed the Yüan dynasty (1279–1368).

Mongol expeditions against Southeast Asia were doomed by the tropical climate, and naval attacks against Java and Japan failed. The use of foreign officials, corruption, heavy taxes, flood, famine, and banditry led to the overthrow of the Mongols by the Ming (1368–1644). During their ascendancy, however, the Mongols accelerated cultural exchanges by maintaining an open, thriving intercontinental trade and by encouraging foreigners such as Marco Polo to serve in the Mongol court in China.

Rise of Colonialism. With the fall of the Mongols, rival Asian empires contended for power: the Ottoman Turks, the Iranians, the Mughals of India, and the Chinese under the Ming and Ch'ing. The political disintegration closed overland trade. Then, as Europe's new national states entered an era of exploration and colonialism, the Ottoman Turks cut off the western end of the sea route to the East. The resulting international competition for trade subjected Asia to European encroachment.

Post-Mongol empires. The Muslim Ottomans, who thus hastened European expansion, had conquered the remains of the Seljuk and Byzantine empires and moved north into Europe. They then took Constantinople, Syria, and the holy cities of Islam, Mecca and Medina. After 1566, however, there were few strong sultans, and as Ottoman power declined, their empire became subject to European rivalries.

Iran revived under the Safavid dynasty (1502–1736) but then became a battlefield for Turks, Russians, and Afghans. The subsequent Kajar dynasty (1794–1925) was a pawn in European power struggles.

As did Turkey and Iran, Muslim India experienced an early renaissance under the Mughal dynasty (1526–1858), which claimed descent from Tamerlane and Genghis Khan. Religious toleration and political unity grew during the long reign of the third emperor, Akbar. Later, however, India fell into warring Muslim, Hindu, and Sikh states while weak emperors reigned in Delhi. Into this power vacuum moved the empire-building Europeans.

Colonial expansion. By the mid-19th century, the major colonial powers in Asia were Great Britain and Russia. The Dutch controlled the East Indies (modern Indonesia) and the lucrative spice trade, which they had wrested from the Portuguese; Spain ruled the Philippines; and the French had a toehold in Indochina. The Portuguese, who had been first to bypass the Turks by sailing around Africa, had lost most of their Asian strongholds. Asia was torn by the rivalry between the great powers. In India, for example, during the Anglo-French wars of the 18th century, both sides used Indian soldiers (sepoys).

After defeating the French in the late 18th century, the British expanded in India, annexing some states, offering protection to others, until—by 1850—they controlled the entire subcontinent. Indian discontent with British rule exploded in the Sepoy Mutiny (q.v.) of 1857. Although bloodily suppressed, the mutiny brought reforms that perpetuated British control for nearly another century.

From India, the British moved into Burma and Malaya. Two Anglo-Burmese wars (1824–26 and 1852) cost Burma its seacoast. The British extended protection over Muslim states of the Malay Peninsula and took direct possession of the important trade centers of Singapore, Penang, and Malacca. Although Britain also threatened Siam, the Thai kingdom bargained its claims to several Malay states in order to retain its own independence.

The French lost India, but they gained influence in Indochina. After 1400, Vietnam had broken into two states, but it was reunited in the 19th century by the southern Nguyen dynasty, who used French military assistance. The Nguyen move into Cambodia and Laos, and their persecution of Christians, led to French annexations in the south and the extension of French protection over Cambodia.

Russian expansion into Asia far surpassed that of the British in area and was much earlier completed. By 1632, Russian traders and cossacks had reached the Pacific. Soldiers and officials followed, building forts and collecting tribute from native tribes. Russia advanced into Turkestan in 1750 and secured claims to the Caucasus by 1828.

Breaking down the doors. China's experience with the Europeans in this period was quite different. A thriving trade between Europe and China marked both the early Ming and early Ch'ing (1644–1912) dynasties. The early Ming added tributaries and sent great fleets as far as Africa, showing superiority over all European nations. But then they withdrew into themselves until pirates ravaged the Chinese coast while Confucianist officials bickered at court.

In this crisis, a Sinicized Manchu tribe seized Peking and proclaimed the Ch'ing dynasty. Their great emperor K'ang Hsi expanded China, met with scholarly missionaries, and welcomed trade, which grew despite China's treatment of foreigners as inferiors and the confinement of them to Canton and Macao. Over Chinese protests, opium became a major trade item in Canton, where the British predominated. In the mid-19th century, disagreement over opium sales brought armed clashes between the Chinese and foreigners, clashes that forced China to open other ports, cede Hong Kong to Britain and Amur Province to Russia, accept Western equality, and grant other trade and diplomatic concessions. While still independent, China was humbled by the European "barbarians."

The impact of Western trade hit Japan near the close of its anarchic Ashikaga shogunate, which was ended by a military triumvirate in 1573. Toyotomi Hideyoshi, the brilliant general of the group, completed Japan's reunification in 1587 with the aid of Portuguese guns and military advice. He then unleashed his forces on Korea, but was turned back by a coalition of Chinese Ming and Korean forces. Under the Tokugawa (q.v.) clan, who succeeded to the shogunate, the Japanese faced the full impact of foreign influences, which they viewed with fear and suspicion.

First had come the Portuguese and Spanish, accompanied by missionaries who spread Christianity through the islands. Fearing that the missionaries were forerunners of foreign invasion, the shoguns banned Christianity, and, when the Europeans ignored the ban, they were expelled from Japan. Western trade stopped, except with the Dutch, who avoided missionary activities and helped suppress a Christian rebellion. For two peaceful centuries, the Dutch were Japan's sole link with the West.

Foreigners knocked vainly on Japan's door until 1854, when an American mission under Matthew Perry secured a treaty opening consular relations. In 1858, the first consul, Townsend Harris, concluded a trade treaty.

Korea's Yi dynasty also shut off Western trade and persecuted Christians. As tributary to China, Korea expected protection, but when 19th-century Europeans forced China's doors, Korea only shut its own more tightly.

Imperial Expansion and Modernization. Colonialism and imperialism brought new problems to Asians, who were previously used to absorbing invaders. The new sea invaders came to trade; but as their technical and military superiority grew, they sought economic and political control.

Techniques of Western exploitation. In establishing this supremacy the European colonizers generally took the gradual approach. Requests for trade were followed by demands for forts and land to protect the trade, and for concessions to exploit local resources. Government and military advisers were then pressed on local rulers. Weaker rulers were offered protection, which in time involved some control. Sometimes, as in the East Indies, tribute was demanded, payable in trade goods. In nations such as Iran and China, rival powers carved out spheres of interest. The ultimate result was annexation and direct rule.

The imperialists built railroads, roads, canals, and some schools, but they also invested in plantations, oil wells, and other enterprises linked with the world economy. Most of the profits went abroad. Meanwhile, population growth brought fragmentation of farms, urbanization, and demoralizing social problems.

Except in Japan and Siam, traditional Asian institutions were too slow in borrowing Western techniques or ideologies to prevent humiliating exploitation, unequal treaties, or foreign rule. By World War II, nationalism and socialism had spread among the Western-educated native elite, and movements for self-government and independence emerged everywhere. The colonial

A village of sampan houseboats in Hong Kong.

governments, however, usually responded too slowly to the rising expectations these movements generated.

Responses to imperialism. The training of native armies and the education of an elite produced internal forces that destroyed the existing dynasties and prompted reform and modernization. In the Ottoman Empire and Iran, for example, foreign-trained army officers seized power. They aroused nationalism and ruthlessly promoted modernization.

Native participation in the colonial government of India broadened gradually, but the pace never satisfied Indian aspirations. Indian schools, teaching liberal ideas, produced more graduates than there were jobs. Rising discontent found voice in 1889 in the Indian National Congress (q.v.) and in 1905 in the rival Muslim League. Britain's failure to grant the expected dominion status after World War I stimulated a Hindu independence movement led by Mohandas K. Gandhi, and in 1935 the Muslim League under Muhammad Ali Jinnah demanded a separate Muslim state.

Nationalism and dissent also grew in Southeast Asia. In Burma, fully annexed in 1881, the use of Indians to exploit resources aroused local agitation led by Buddhist monks and students. Although the Dutch ended crown rule in the East Indies in 1867 and granted reforms and increased autonomy, dissidence grew, stimulated by Muslim leaders and Dutch repression. In the Philippine Islands, annexed by the U.S. in 1898, nationalistic activities paralleled growing self-government. France completed annexing or asserting protectorates over Indochina by 1885. Although Laos and Cambodia accepted French rule, Vietnamese nationalists agitated for independence.

As China suffered foreign exploitation plus revolutions and natural disasters, many Chinese believed the Ch'ing had lost their mandate to rule. They doubted, however, that any dynasty could cope with Western technology and ideologies without modifying or eliminating China's Confucian system. China's defeat by Japan in 1894 further exposed its helplessness and stimulated dissent. A revolution in 1911 ended the Ch'ing dynasty, but idealistic republicans such as Sun Yat-sen were pushed aside by generals. During World War I, China disintegrated into warlord rule.

Mistreatment of China at the peace conference aroused its educated youth. Some became republican nationalists, while others looked to communism and the new Soviet Union. A long civil war followed between the nationalist Kuomintang (q.v.) under Chiang Kai-shek and the Communists under Mao Zedong (Mao Tse-tung). They were unable to unite, even against Japanese invaders, who by 1941 had advanced from their puppet state in Manchuria deep into China proper.

Maintaining independence. Siam retained independence thanks to two progressive kings, Mongkut (1804–68) and Chulalongkorn. Constitutional monarchy came in 1932, but subsequent coups brought military dictatorships and a new name, Thailand, symbolizing its nationalism.

Japan prevented foreign encroachment by rapid modernization. The government built factories and sold them to private companies. Universal conscription ended the samurais' military monopoly, and in the new army even peasants became officers. The Meiji constitution of 1889, giving universal male suffrage, forced leaders to seek popular support.

Japan's victory over Russia in 1904–5 made all Asians proud and prepared Japan to become a colonial power by annexing Korea in 1910. World War I stopped European exports and helped Japan expand its foreign markets, but the depression of the 1930s led ambitious young officers to press for ultranationalist policies. They initiated heavy arms expansion, the conquest of Manchuria, invasions of China and Southeast Asia, and, in 1940, alliance with Hitler and Mussolini, who accepted Japan's plans for a "new order" in East Asia.

Independence and Conflict. World War II catapulted Asia into world prominence as Japan's rapid conquests revealed the vulnerability of the Western powers. India became an Allied staging area, and in southwestern Asia, the Allies occupied strategic areas to protect supply routes. The eventual Allied victory further stimulated the expectations for independence and modernization.

Intensified nationalism. By the end of the 1950s, militant independence movements, fueled by intensified nationalism, had largely ended colonial rule in Asia. But major differences persisted. On the Indian subcontinent, religious separatism created Muslim Pakistan alongside the republic of India. In 1971, Pakistan was itself subdivided when its eastern section broke away under the name of Bangladesh. Border disputes embittered Pakistani-Indian relations as Pakistan produced a series of autocratic military rulers, while India maintained a parliamentary democracy.

In southwestern Asia, religious and territorial nationalism created the Jewish state of Israel. Hostilities between Israel and its Arab neighbors—Egypt, Syria, Iraq, and Jordan—disrupted world trade by closing the Suez Canal (1956–57,

Farmers in southern Vietnam plow their rice field with simple ox-drawn equipment. Rice is a staple crop in most of the countries of Asia, both as food for the people and as a commodity important to the economy. James Pickerell–Black Star

1967–75), while Israel occupied large tracts of Arab land. Palestinian Arab refugees from Israel formed the Palestine Liberation Organization (q.v.) and demanded return of their homeland. Peace efforts led to an Israeli-Egyptian treaty in 1979, but solution of the Israeli-Arab differences remained elusive.

The Asian Middle East was divided into numerous states, each subject to internal stresses. Iran, for example, experienced a nationalistic outburst in the 1950s under its charismatic prime minister, Mohammed Mossadegh, who nationalized the oil industry. Twenty-five years later, a religious and political nationalistic surge deposed the U.S.-supported Shah Muhammad Riza Pahlavi. As the conservative Islamic government floundered, militants seized the U.S. embassy, initiating a long international crisis, while Iraq seized the opportunity to launch a bloody, costly, and ultimately inconclusive border war. Iraq occupied Kuwait in 1990, but the Persian Gulf War (q.v.) of 1991 restored Kuwaiti independence.

Ideological confrontation. Postwar rivalry between Communist and non-Communist ideologies was part of the global contest between the U.S. and USSR that ended with the dissolution of the Soviet Union in 1991. Communism appealed to Asians eager for independence, participatory government, and social reforms. The victory of the Soviet-supported People's Republic of China in 1949 and the retreat of the U.S.-backed Nationalists to Taiwan was the first major Communist triumph. It was tempered by continued UN recognition of the Republic of China on Taiwan. Under Mao Zedong the Chinese Communists (until 1960 backed by the USSR) experimented with radical socialistic programs, ending in the destructive Cultural Revolution of 1966–69. As Sino-Soviet differences grew, the U.S. began diplomatic contacts. The People's Republic was given China's seat at the UN in 1971, and in 1979 the U.S. recognized it as China's only government.

In 1975, Communist forces also won in Vietnam, when the Democratic Republic of Vietnam in the north, aided by the USSR and China, defeated the U.S.-supported Republic of Vietnam in the south. A by-product of the Communist victories in Cambodia and Laos as well as Vietnam was a mass migration of refugees to other countries of Asia, Europe, and America.

In other locations, Communist forces lost. The new independent government of the Philippines crushed the Communist Hukbalahaps (Huks), and the Malays, with British help, contained their Communist guerrillas. Indonesia's Communist party, which thrived under independence leader Sukarno, was suppressed in 1965. The resulting massacre mingled ideological with nationalistic motivations, for many Indonesian Communists were ethnic Chinese.

In Korea, which had been divided by Soviet and American occupation forces, the Communist north invaded the south in 1950. As UN forces repulsed the North Korean troops, Communist Chinese intervention brought a stalemate and an uneasy truce.

The strategic position and resources of the Asian Middle East thrust the area into the ideological contest. An early Soviet attempt to occupy northern Iran failed, but later the USSR gained influence in Iraq, Syria, and Yemen. The

Arab-Israeli conflict also inclined many Arab nationalists to favor the Soviet Union. From 1979 to 1989, Soviet troops occupied Afghanistan, sending some 3 million Afghan refugees into Pakistan.

No Asian country was untouched by the confrontation. The failure of Turkey's government to stop leftist-inspired riots and assassinations or to curb inflation brought a military coup in 1980. During most of the 1970s and 1980s, India sided with the Soviets on many foreign policy issues, and Pakistan looked toward China and the U.S. While postwar Japan maintained the democratic reforms of the U.S. occupation, Communists gained power in labor unions and student groups.

Economic expansion. Economic and industrial expansion made some Asian areas into world leaders in wealth and industrial output. During the 1970s, Japan outpaced the U.S. in automobile, steel, and electronic production, and South Korea and Taiwan prospered as they expanded manufacturing and exports.

In southwestern Asia, oil exports produced huge wealth. Although large sums ended in private hands, much poured into social and modernization programs. Thousands of students who studied abroad returned to demand more rapid change than governments or conservative religious elements could accommodate. Such a climate preceded the Iranian revolution of 1979.

Oil also became a potent political weapon. During the Yom Kippur War (q.v.), Arab producers denied oil to countries supporting Israel. The oil-exporting nations, acting together, so escalated crude-oil prices during the late 1970s that oil-importing countries suffered severe inflation with concurrent recession. The Iran-Iraq war of the 1980s, which at first appeared to threaten oil output, actually had the effect of reducing oil prices because it fostered disunity among the oil-producing countries of the Middle East.

Just as the Persian Gulf conflicts disrupted the Iranian and Iraqi economies, so Vietnam suffered from the long war between north and south, as did Laos and Cambodia from internal upheavals. China was set back by its break with the USSR and by the Cultural Revolution, but after its accord with the U.S., it again stressed industrialization.

Despite conflicting ambitions and ideologies, and local problems, wide sectors of Asia in the 1980s enjoyed economic growth, increased democracy, and improved living standards.

For additional information on historical figures, see biographies of those whose names are not followed by dates. Ch.A.B.

For further information on this topic, see the Bibliography in volume 28, sections 119–28, 131, 871, 1065–1102.

ASIA MINOR, region of the ancient world, roughly corresponding to present Asian Turkey, or the peninsula of Anatolia. Some of the earliest Neolithic settlements in the Middle East have been found in Asia Minor. One of the most important, at Çatal Hüyük, near present Konya, dates from as early as 9000 BC.

Early Indigenous States. Of the Anatolian cultures of the succeeding Bronze Age, the most important was that of the Hittites (q.v.), about 1900–1200 BC, which originated in the central plateau. At its widest extent, the Hittite Empire covered most of Asia Minor and rivaled Egypt as a Middle Eastern power. It was destroyed by invaders known as the Sea Peoples, who swept over Asia Minor and Syria toward the end of the 12th century BC. The destruction of the western Anatolian city of Troy, an event celebrated in ancient Greek legends, probably occurred during these invasions.

One of the Sea Peoples, the Phrygians, established a kingdom that became the dominant Anatolian power in the 9th and 8th centuries BC. Their king, Midas, was credited by the Greeks with the power to change anything he touched into gold. Hittite culture survived in Carchemish, Milid (present-day Malatya, Turkey), and other small states in eastern Asia Minor until about 700 BC. During this same period the Greeks founded Miletus, Ephesus, and Priene and a number of other cities in Ionia, an area along the Aegean coast. About 700 BC the Phrygian kingdom was overrun and destroyed by the Cimmerians, a nomadic people who thereafter lived in western Asia Minor. In the 7th century BC the Lydians also appeared near the Aegean coast, where they founded a kingdom, the capital of which was Sardis. According to Greek writers, they were the first people to coin money. Their last king, Croesus, fabled for his wealth, was overthrown by the Persians under Cyrus the Great in 546 BC.

Foreign Rule. From the mid-6th century to 333 BC most of Asia Minor belonged to the Persian Empire, although the Greek cities frequently enjoyed a considerable degree of autonomy. In the 4th century BC Persian power declined, and after 333 BC it was supplanted by the Macedonian Empire of Alexander the Great. After Alexander's death, his realm was divided among his followers, Asia Minor falling to the Seleucid kings of Syria, except for Lycia and Caria on the south coast, which were governed by the Ptolemies of Egypt. In the 3d century BC, Bithynia and Pontus in the north and Cappadocia in the east became independent; Celtic invaders settled in central Asia Minor, in an area thenceforth known as Galatia; and the kingdom of Pergamum was established on the Aegean coast. In the 2d and 1st centuries BC, Asia Minor was gradually conquered by the Romans. For the most part the region prospered under Roman rule, and its cities flourished as centers of Greek culture.

Medieval and Modern Times. After the division of the Roman Empire in the 4th century AD, Asia Minor became part of the Eastern Roman, or Byzantine, Empire, the capital of which was Constantinople, or Byzantium, located on the European side of the Bosporus, just across from the west coast of Anatolia. During the 8th and 9th centuries the free peasantry of Anatolia provided recruits for the imperial army and were the main bulwark of the Byzantine state. During the 11th century Asia Minor was invaded by the Seljuk Turks, and the eastern part of the region became predominantly Turkish in character. In the 14th and 15th centuries the Ottoman Turks conquered the whole peninsula, and it remained part of the Ottoman Empire until the establishment of the republic of Turkey in 1923. M.S.C.

ASIMOV, Isaac (1920–92), prolific American writer, esteemed for his science fiction and for his popular works in all branches of science. Asimov was born in Petrovichi, Russia. His family immigrated to the U.S. when he was three years old and settled in Brooklyn, N.Y. His encounters with science-fiction magazines led him to follow the dual careers of writing and science. He entered Columbia University at the age of 15 and at 18 sold his first story to *Amazing Stories.*

After serving in World War II, Asimov earned a Ph.D. at Columbia in 1948; he taught (1949–58) biochemistry at the Boston University School of Medicine. His first science-fiction novel, *Pebble in the Sky,* appeared in 1950, and his first science book, a biochemistry text written with two colleagues, in 1953. Asimov turned to writing full time in 1958. He authored some 500 books for young and adult readers, extending beyond science and science fiction to include mystery stories, humor, history, and several volumes on the Bible and Shakespeare. Among his best-known science-fiction works are *I, Robot* (1950); *The Foundation Trilogy* (1951–53), to which he wrote a sequel 30 years later, *Foundation's Edge* (1982); *The Naked Sun* (1957); *The Gods Themselves* (1972). Among his major science books are the *Biographical Encyclopedia of Science and Technology* (1964; rev. 1982) and *Asimov's New Guide to Science* (1984), a recent revision of his widely acclaimed *Intelligent Man's Guide to Science* (1960). Later works include *Foundation and Earth* (1986); *Prelude to Foundation* (1988); and *Forward the Foundation* (1992). A two-volume autobiography, *In Memory Yet Green,* appeared in 1979.

ASMARA, also Asmera, city, N Ethiopia, capital of Eritrea Province, near the Red Sea port of Massawa. Industries include tanning, lumber and flour milling, vegetable processing, and the manufacture of perfumes, glass, cement, bricks, and buttons. A hydroelectric plant and gold and copper mines are nearby. A technical and professional school is located in the city. Asmara succeeded Massawa as capital of the Italian colony of Eritrea in 1900. Pop. (1984) 275,385.

ASMODEUS, in Hebrew demonology, the chief of the demons, occasionally identified with the prince of demons, Beelzebub. He figures largely in later Hebrew tradition, appearing in the Book of Tobit in the Old Testament apocrypha as an evil spirit possessed of great lust. He is represented as having loved Sarah, daughter of Raguel, and as having slain seven men who were successively married to Sarah. Tobias, who intended to marry Sarah, succeeded with the help of the angel Raphael in exorcising the demon. Raphael pursued Asmodeus to Upper Egypt and bound him, enabling Tobias and Sarah to live in peace. In talmudic legends, Asmodeus is associated with Solomon, whom he aided, notably in building the Temple. He is also regarded as the cause of the excesses ascribed to Solomon.

ASMONAEANS *or* **HASMONAEANS.** *See* MACCABEES.

ASOKA (291?–232 BC), third Mauryan king (c. 273–232 BC) of Magadha and the most celebrated ruler of ancient India, known for his benevolent rule and for making Buddhism the official religion of his empire.

The grandson of Chandragupta, founder of the Maurya dynasty, Asoka enlarged the kingdom he inherited until it embraced most of the subcontinent. In the process, he made war on the state of Kalinga, conquering it about 261 BC. When he saw the suffering he had caused, however, he was overcome with remorse. Renouncing warfare and his religion, Brahmanism, he turned to Buddhism, with its doctrine of *ahimsa* ("nonviolence"). Wishing to apply Buddha's principles to all aspects of everyday life, he instituted gentler laws than the rulers before him and went among the Indian peasants, preaching and ministering to their needs. He had rest houses constructed, trees planted, and wells dug, and he opened medical centers. He issued orders forbidding the harsh treatment of animals, regulated their slaughter, and established hospitals for them.

In his efforts to propagate Buddhism, Asoka built shrines and monasteries and inscribed Buddhist teachings on rocks and pillars in many places. He sent missionaries to countries as remote as Greece and Egypt; his own son, a monk, carried Buddhism to Ceylon (now Sri Lanka), where it is still the major religion. Despite Asoka's vigorous exertions in behalf of his faith, he was tolerant of other religions, and India enjoyed marked prosperity during his reign.

For further information on this person, see the section Biographies in the Bibliography in volume 28.

ASP, common name loosely applied to several unrelated poisonous snakes, notably *Vipera aspis,* the European asp or asp viper, and *Naja haje,* the Egyptian cobra. The former is found from central France south to Sicily and east to the Balkans; the latter is found throughout northern Africa and in areas to the south. The asp that the Egyptian queen Cleopatra used to cause her death was probably either the Egyptian cobra or the horned sand viper, *Cerastes cornuta.*

ASPARAGUS, common name for about 50 to 60 species of herbs of the family Liliaceae (*see* LILY), and for their representative genus *Asparagus.* The parent of most varieties cultivated for food is *A. officinalis,* a native of Europe. It bears flowers of one sex on each plant, the sex being identifiable in the first year of growth. Asparagus beds may bear for 50 years. The plant grows best in a fresh, sandy soil. The spears (shoots) are not cut until the second or third year. Once used as a medicine, asparagus spears are rich in vitamin A and ascorbic acid. In the U.S. asparagus crops are grown principally in California, New Jersey, and Washington. France and Italy are important producers in Europe.

Asparagus fern or florist's fern, *A. plumosus,* is not a true fern but has delicate, lacy foliage used in making bouquets, as do the species *A. sprengeri* and *A. asparagoides.* These three plants may be grown indoors.

ASPARTAME. *See* SWEETENER, ARTIFICIAL.

ASPASIA (c. 470–410 BC), Greek adventurer and consort of the Athenian statesman Pericles, born in Miletus, Asia Minor. She was noted for her beauty, genius, and political influence. She married Pericles after he secured a divorce from his first wife; subsequently, their home became a gathering place for the learned and distinguished people of Athens. Aspasia apparently exercised considerable influence on Pericles and has been charged by some historians with responsibility for the Samian revolt and the Peloponnesian War. On one occasion the Athenian comic poet Hermippus charged her with impiety, but she was successfully defended by Pericles. After the death of his two sons by his first marriage, Pericles obtained from the state full rights of citizenship for his son by Aspasia.

ASPEN, city, seat of Pitkin Co., central Colorado, on the Roaring Fork R., in the Rocky Mts., at an elevation of about 2410 m (about 7900 ft); inc. 1881. It is a stylish resort, famous for its winter skiing and its summer cultural events. Founded in 1879 by prospectors and named for trees in the area, Aspen was a booming silver-mining center until the early 1890s, when the demonetization of silver reduced prices for the metal. The modern resort city was developed after World War II by Walter P. Paepcke (1896–1960), a Chicago industrialist, who also founded the Aspen Music Festival and the Aspen Institute for Humanistic Studies here. Pop. (1980) 3678; (1990) 5049.

ASPEN, common name for certain trees of the genus *Populus* (*see* POPLAR), particularly the so-called quaking aspens, several species of which have the petioles, or leafstalks, so compressed that the leaves can move easily from side to side but not up or down. A breeze sets all leaves of one of these trees into motion. The most familiar species are *P. tremuloides,* the American aspen, found in North America; *P. grandidentata,* the large-toothed aspen, found in eastern Canada and the U.S.; and *P. tremula,* the European aspen, found in Europe, western Asia, and northern Africa.

Aspen trees display their autumnal colors in the locale that was named for them, Aspen, Colo.; in the background are the Aspen Mts. Aspens belong to the poplar group. The wood of the large-toothed aspen and the American quaking aspen are used in the manufacture of high-quality paper pulp.

Margaret Durrance–Photo Researchers, Inc.

ASPHALT, black, cementlike material varying in consistency at room temperature from solid to semisolid. It can be poured when heated to the temperature of boiling water. It is present in most crude petroleum, from which it is separated by refining processes. It is used in surfacing roads, in water-retaining structures such as reservoirs and swimming pools, and in roofing materials and floor tiles. It is not to be confused with tar, a black substance derived from coal.

Natural deposits of asphalt occur in pits or lakes as residue from crude petroleum that has seeped up through fissures in the earth. Typical of these deposits are the La Brea tar pits in Los Angeles, in which the remains of prehistoric fauna and flora have been found. A natural asphalt pool is Pitch Lake on the island of Trinidad. This lake and one in the state of Bermudez, Venezuela, provided most of the asphalt used for paving roads in the U.S. before the 20th century, when the refining of crude petroleum began. Deposits of asphalt-impregnated rock, called rock asphalt, are found throughout the world, including many parts of the southern and western U.S. Some of these deposits are used locally to surface roads. A natural asphalt deposit of commercial importance is Gilsonite, also called uintaite, found in the Uinta River Basin in Utah and used in the manufacture of paints and lacquers. Compared with petroleum-based asphalts, however, natural asphalts have only minor importance today.

Natural asphalt was known and used extensively in ancient times. Ancient Babylonians used it as a building material, and it is referred to several times in the Old Testament books of Genesis and Exodus as a caulking material. *See* BITUMEN.

The use of asphalt for street paving in the U.S. began in 1870; by 1903 more than 35 million sq m (about 42 million sq yd) of U.S. streets were paved with asphalt. Today, asphalt derived from petroleum is used to surface 90 percent of the paved roads in the U.S. Of U.S. production of petroleum asphalt, about 75 percent is used for paving, 15 percent for roofing, and 10 percent for the more than 200 other known uses of asphalt.

ASPHODEL, common name applied to flowering plants of the genera *Asphodelus, Asphodeline, Narthecium,* and *Tofieldia,* of the family Liliaceae (*see* LILY). Native mostly to the Mediterranean region, many of the 35 to 40 species are widely cultivated for their yellow, white, or pink flowers. The ancient Greeks planted asphodel over graves.

ASPHYXIA (Gr., "pulselessness," from *a,* "not"; *sphyzein,* "to throb"), unconsciousness or death produced by failure of the blood to become properly oxygenated in the lungs. This failure may be due to inability of air to reach the lungs, as in hanging, suffocation, or chest injuries; it may be due to paralysis of the nerve centers that control lungs, either because of an inadequate supply of oxygen or because of failure in the respiratory system (*see* RESPIRATION). In most cases of asphyxia, artificial respiration, if applied in time, will save the life of the victim.

ASPIDISTRA, genus of perennial herbs of the family Liliaceae (*see* LILY), native to China and Japan. The flowers are inconspicuous and often hidden. The glossy, evergreen foliage and resistance to unfavorable conditions of heat, soil, and light make aspidistra popular for home cultivation in pots and window boxes. A variety with green and white striped leaves reverts to solid green when placed in rich soil.

ASPIRIN, synthetic chemical compound, acetylsalicylic acid. It is made from salicylic acid, found in the bark of the willow tree, which was used by the ancient Greeks and American Indians, among others, to counter fever and pain. Salicylic acid is bitter, however, and irritates the stomach. The German chemist Felix Hoffman synthesized the acetyl derivative of salicylic acid in 1893 in response to the urging of his father, who took salicylic acid for rheumatism. Aspirin is currently the first-choice drug for fever, mild to moderate pain, and inflammation due to arthritis or injury. It is a more effective analgesic (q.v.) than codeine. Aspirin causes insignificant gastrointestinal bleeding that can over time, however, cause iron deficiency; gastric ulcers may also occur with long-term use. Complications can be avoided by using enteric-coated aspirin, which does not dissolve until reaching the intestine. Aspirin should not be given to children who have chicken pox or influenza, because it increases the risk of contracting the rare and frequently fatal Reye's syndrome, a disease of the brain and some abdominal organs.

Aspirin is thought to act by interfering with synthesis of prostaglandins (q.v.), which are implicated in inflammation and fever. Studies of aspirin's anticlotting activities suggest that half an aspirin tablet per day may reduce the risk of heart attack and stroke in some persons.

ASPLUND, Erik Gunnar (1885–1940), Swedish architect, who led the International Style in Sweden. He combined an austere modernism with a lightness and delicacy derived from traditional Scandinavian architecture and from his own love of Greek classicism. His landmark works of the 1920s and '30s, such as the Woodland Crematorium chapel in Stockholm, laid the foundations of a school of Swedish architecture that influenced later styles in Europe and the U.S.

ASQUITH, Herbert Henry (1852–1928), British statesman, prime minister before and during World War I.

Asquith was born at Morely, in the north of England, on Sept. 12, 1852. He practiced law after graduating from the University of Oxford in 1874 and was elected to Parliament as a Liberal in 1886. He attained national prominence as junior defense attorney for the Irish nationalist leader Charles Stewart Parnell, when the latter was under investigation by Parliament in 1888, and in 1892 he became home secretary under Prime Minister William Gladstone. Out of office from 1895 to 1905, he then joined a new Liberal government as chancellor of the Exchequer. In 1908 he succeeded Henry Campbell-Bannerman as prime minister.

Asquith's tenure in office was marked by a series of domestic and international crises. The first began in 1909, when the House of Lords rejected the government budget, causing Asquith to embark on a campaign to abolish the veto power of Britain's nonelective upper house. After a lengthy struggle he succeeded in his aim with the passage of the Parliament Act in 1911. He then set about plans to accomplish another Liberal objective—the enactment of home rule for Ireland. Controversy over this issue divided the country for the next three years. Confronted by threats of armed rebellion by home-rule opponents in Ulster and open encouragement of these threats by British Conservatives, Asquith temporized throughout 1913 and well into 1914, during which time the pressure continued to build. A violent solution was averted only by the outbreak of World War I.

A firm believer in the necessity of supporting France against Germany, Asquith nevertheless adroitly waited to declare war until public indignation was aroused by Germany's violation of Belgian neutrality. As the war dragged on, however, successive military reverses and acute shortages of munitions made his government the object of increasing criticism by Conservatives and Liberals alike. In May 1915, Asquith yielded to demands for a coalition government; in December 1916, the opposition movement forced him to resign in favor of his war secretary, David Lloyd George. Asquith remained in Parliament, but never held office again. He was raised to the peerage in 1925. He died in Sutton Courtenay, Berkshire, England, on Feb. 15, 1928.

ASS, also donkey, common name for a mammal of the genus *Equus,* of the family Equidae, which includes also the horse and the zebra. The domestic ass was probably derived from two wild

Wild donkeys, Equus asinus, *are still numerous in the interior of Australia. This animal was found in the Macdonnell Ranges in the Northern Territory.*

© Eric Crichton–Bruce Coleman, Inc.

species, *E. africanus* and *E. somalicus,* both native to Africa and sometimes classified as constituting the subgenus *Asinus.*

Smaller than the horse, the domestic donkey and wild African asses stand about 1.4 m (about 4.5 ft) high at the shoulder. They have very long ears, a gray coat with white underparts and muzzle, a short, erect mane, and a tail with a tuft of long hair only at the tip.

The ass was domesticated by the Egyptians about 3000 BC; it is more surefooted than the horse, which makes it better on mountain trails. It also lives longer than the horse, generally from 25 to 50 years. The wild ass runs so swiftly that it is difficult to overtake on the open plains.

The Asian wild ass, *E. hemionus,* which lives in the desert regions of Mongolia, is somewhat smaller than the African species and has much smaller ears. The Asian wild ass is usually reddish brown in color. It moves very quickly and is capable of maintaining a pace of about 24 km/hr (about 15 mph) for as long as two hours.

The kiang, *E. kiang,* the largest of the wild asses of Asia, lives on the high plateaus of Tibet. The only other Asian species is the onager, *E. onager,* known also as the Persian wild ass, a smaller, fleet animal with a rich yellow-brown coat. It ranges over the desert from Iran and Syria eastward to India.

The wild ass is hunted for its flesh, considered superior to venison, and for its skin, which is used to make a leather called shagreen. The wild ass is almost extinct in Africa, but in Mongolia some wild herds number as many as a thousand individuals. The mating period is in the early fall, and the female, called a jennet or jenny, bears a single foal in May or June, when the herd breaks up into small family groups. The male ass is called a jack or jackass.

In the U.S. the donkey has been used as a beast of burden and for the breeding of mules, which are hybrids produced by mating mares and jackasses (*see* MULE). Small donkeys, or burros, played a major role as pack animals in opening up the western U.S. Although regarded as stubborn and stupid, the donkey, if well treated, is an intelligent and enduring pack animal.

ASSAD, Hafiz al- (1928–), president of Syria (1971–), born in Qardahah. He was educated in Syrian military colleges and received additional military training in the Soviet Union. He joined the Baath party in 1946 and was made general of the air force in 1964 after the Baathists had come into power. He served as minister of defense from 1966 until 1970, when he seized control of the government, assuming the prime ministership until he was elected president in 1971. Assad cooperated with Egypt in the Yom Kippur War of 1973, but he rejected Egypt's accommodation with Israel in the late 1970s. He intervened in the civil war in Lebanon (in 1976; 1987; 1990), and he supported Iran against Iraq during their 1980–88 war. The target of several coup attempts in the early 1980s, Assad dealt brutally with his political opponents; in 1982 he sent thousands of troops to Hamah to crush an uprising led by the Muslim Brotherhood. Syria had long been the USSR's closest ally in the Middle East, but when Soviet power weakened at the end of the 1980s, Assad moved to improve ties with the West. Assad sent troops to Saudi Arabia to fight against Iraq in the Persian Gulf War (q.v.).

ASSAM, state, NE India, bordered by Bhutan, Burma, and Bangladesh. The most important river in the state is the Brahmaputra, which enters in the NE and flows in a southwesterly direction. The river is navigable from the Bay of Bengal to the city of Dibrugarh. The state has a humid, subtropical climate with extremely heavy rainfall. Assam is subject to floods and earthquakes.

Much of the state is covered with dense tropical forests of bamboo and, at higher elevations, evergreens. Common animals of Assam include the elephant, tiger, leopard, rhinoceros, and bear.

Assam is rural and agricultural. Tea is cultivated in the hilly regions, and the state provides much of the tea grown in India. The valley of the Brahmaputra R. is important for rice, the major food product of Assam. Other agricultural products are jute, sugarcane, cotton, oranges, and potatoes. The cultivation of silkworms is common in many areas. Lumber is valuable to the economy of Assam, and the extraction of oil is gaining in importance. The primary industries of Assam are textile manufacturing, cement production, and oil refining. The capital of the state is Dispur.

Assam was settled at an unknown date by the Ahoms, an Asian people. Rule over Assam was contested until 1826, when the British took control. When India and Pakistan became independent in 1947, Assam was divided between the two countries, most of Assam going to India. The N border of Assam has been insecure since 1959, when the Chinese invaded the region. During the late 1960s instability in the state increased as several tribes demanded greater political influence or independence from Assam. Partly as a result, the new state of Meghalaya and the new Union Territory of Mizoram were formed from Assam in the early 1970s. Area, 78,523 sq km (30,318 sq mi); pop. (1981 est.) 19,902,800.

ASSAULT, in criminal law, any attempt to use illegal force on another person. Verbal threats do not constitute assault. If violence actually occurs, the act is termed battery; criminal assault is a tort (q.v.). A simple assault is a misdemeanor, punishable summarily or upon indictment. Aggravated assaults, such as those committed with a deadly weapon with the intent to kill, to do great bodily harm, or to rape, are considered felonies. Reckless endangerment of human life and malevolence are also considered felonies in many jurisdictions.

ASSAYING, in metallurgy, the process of determining the amount of a specific metal in a mineral, ore, or alloy; it differs from analysis (*see* CHEMICAL ANALYSIS), in which the entire composition is determined. Assaying is usually reserved for ores of gold, silver, and the platinum group metals.

The first operation in making an assay is to take ore samples that must be typical in all respects of the ore being mined. The samples may be selected either by hand or by machine. Each sample is assayed separately. If the ore content of the samples is about the same, the sampling is taken as correct, and the average of the assays constitutes the final assay.

The fire-assay method utilizes heat and suitable fluxes to separate the metal from gangue (worthless material) in the ore. A sample weighing 1 assay ton, that is, 29.166 g for gold ore, is blended with a flux mixture containing varying amounts of litharge (lead monoxide), silica, soda ash, borax, and flour. The blended material is fused at about 1000° C (about 1832° F) for approximately 1 hr after which the entire mass is poured into an iron mold and cooled. The mass settles into two distinct layers: a top layer of slag, which when cooled can be chipped away, and a bottom layer consisting of a lead alloy "button" weighing about 20 to 30 g. This button contains all the gold, silver, and other precious metals originally present in the ore sample. If the initial sample contains volatile impurities, such as antimony or arsenic, the fire-assay method employs a refinement called scorification.

The process of removing the lead from the alloy button, leaving the gold and silver in a pure state, is called cupellation. This step is based on the fact that when an alloy of gold, silver, and lead is heated in the presence of air, lead monoxide or litharge is formed. The alloy button is placed in an open, porous container called a cupel, which absorbs the litharge that forms during the heating. Air is forced past the heated cupel until all the lead is absorbed, and the mass of metal remaining contains only gold and silver. This alloy is commonly known as a doré bead. Just before the last traces of lead are removed, the bead changes color, darkening and then finally brightening, thereby indicating the completion of the operation. The cupel is removed from the furnace and cooled, and the bead is cleaned of any foreign particles.

Next the gold is separated from the silver in the bead by a process called parting, which consists of dissolving the silver in dilute nitric acid. Usually, the gold-silver bead must contain at least three times as much silver as gold in order to ensure satisfactory dissolution of the silver. If the natural ratio is less, more silver must be added. The bead is then flattened and boiled in nitric acid to remove the last trace of silver. The result is a spongy mass of pure gold. This gold is weighed and the proportion of gold in the original ore determined. The difference between the weight of the gold after parting and the weight of the gold-silver bead after cupelling gives the proportion of silver present in the gold ore. K.B.H.

ASSEMBLIES OF GOD, Pentecostal, evangelistic, and missionary Protestant cooperative organization, founded in 1914 in Hot Springs, Ark., by a group of independent ministers. Although forms of worship vary, articles of faith include salvation through a life of holiness; baptism with the Holy Spirit, accompanied by speaking in tongues (ecstatic, inspired speech often unintelligible to listeners); divine healing; and the second coming of Jesus Christ. Each congregation is sovereign in management of local affairs. Regional matters are handled by 55 district councils, and a general council is held every second year. A 13-member executive presbytery maintains offices at Springfield, Mo., home of the international headquarters of the group. According to the most recent statistics, the denomination has more than 9000 churches and about 1,630,000 members in the U.S. Churches and missions are also maintained in more than 90 foreign countries, and the worldwide membership numbers about 6 million.

ASSEMBLY. *See* LEGISLATURE.

ASSER, Tobias Michael Carel (1838–1913), Dutch statesman and jurist, born in Amsterdam. He became professor of law at the Athenaeum in Amsterdam in 1862 and at the University of Amsterdam in 1876. In 1893 he became a member of the council of state. As an authority on international law he represented Holland at The Hague Peace Conference in 1899. In 1911 he was awarded the Nobel Peace Prize jointly with the Austrian pacifist and publicist Alfred Hermann Fried (1864–1921). He wrote *International Arbitration Between the United States and Russia* (1902).

ASSIGNATS, notes issued by the French revolutionary government in 1789 promising to pay various sums to the holders, with confiscated church and crown lands and the estates of the Royalist refugees as security. The first issue amounted to 400 million francs. In 1789 the assignats paid interest at 5 percent. In 1790 the assignats were declared legal tender, and issues thereafter earned no interest. Inflation was inevitable, and by 1796 the total issue was 45.5 billion francs exclusive of forgeries, but their value had depreciated to 30 to 1 of coin. At this value they were converted into 800 million francs' worth of land warrants, or *mandats territoriaux,* which constituted a mortgage on all public lands. The floating of these *mandats* was unsuccessful, and they were finally redeemed by the state at one-seventieth of their face value. By March 1796, 1 franc in specie equaled 300 francs in notes. In 1797 assignats and land warrants stopped being issued, and France returned to metal currency.

ASSIMILATION, the process by which one group of people is absorbed into the culture of another group. The term *assimilation* is generally used with regard to immigrants to a new land, such as the various ethnic groups who have settled in the U.S. New customs and attitudes are acquired through contact and communication. The transfer of customs is not simply a one-way process. Each group of immigrants contributes some of its own cultural traits to its new society. Assimilation usually involves a gradual change and takes place in varying degrees; full assimilation occurs when new members of a society become indistinguishable from older members. *See also* ACCULTURATION.

ASSINIBOINE, river, S central Canada, 1070 km (665 mi) long. The river rises in SE Saskatchewan and flows SE into S Manitoba, where it joins the Red R. of the North, at Winnipeg. Its principal tributaries are the Qu'Appelle and Souris rivers. Located in the wide valley of a former glacial river, the Assiniboine flows through fertile grain- and livestock-producing regions. Formerly called the Stone Indian R., it is named for the Assiniboin, or Stone, Indians, a Siouan-speaking tribe who occupied the valley in the 18th century.